THE NATAL
CAMPAIGN

THE NATAL CAMPAIGN

A SACRIFICE BETRAYED

HUGH RETHMAN

AMBERLEY

First published by Amberley 2017

Amberley Publishing
The Hill, Stroud
Gloucestershire, GL5 4EP

www.amberley-books.com

British Library Cataloguing in Publication Data.
A catalogue record for this book is available from the British Library.

ISBN 978 1 4456 6421 7 (paperback)
ISBN 978 1 4456 6422 4 (ebook)

Typesetting and Origination by Amberley Publishing.
Printed in the UK.

Contents

Acknowledgements

Many years ago I took my young English bride on a tour of the Natal battlefields. In those days there were no luxury guided tours. Instead we would follow a rough track to the vicinity of the battlefield and there, sometimes with the aid of passing people, build a picture in our minds of the stirring events that had occurred at Isandlwana, Rorke's Drift, Spion Kop, Colenso and Wagon Hill. Ann was fascinated and, from that time, shared with me a lasting interest in the history of the peoples of Natal. After going into exile, I decided to write this book and Ann offered her full support, provided she could read and correct the text. By this means she banished the dreadful legalese into which lawyers are so prone to lapse. Her influence is present throughout the book.

It is impossible to name here all the people who have given me assistance and support. Especial thanks are, however, due to the following individuals: the late John McKenzie, Douglas and Di Campbell, Andrew Campbell, Keith Archibald, Denise Carrick, Mike Sparks, Lynne and Graham Hope, Bev Nicholson, Nunez Pottie, Robert and David Lewis, Peta Campbell, Pam Mc Fadden, Norman Leveridge, Mark Coghlan, Curtis & Lane Photography, Stephen Foster for his excellent maps, N3XUS Computing, Sudbury, Suffolk, and Samuel Goba, descendant of one of the prominent founders of the Natal Native Congress, who gave me information that enabled me to track down documents relative to the affairs of black people in Natal during the Boer War.

My thanks are also due to staff of the following archives, museums and libraries:

National Archives, Kew, London.
National Army Museum, Chelsea, London.
Brenthurst Library, Johannesburg.
Ladysmith Siege Museum, Ladysmith.
Talana Museum, Dundee.
African Studies Library, Johannesburg.

Acknowledgements

Killie Campbell Museum, Durban.
Natal Archives, Pietermaritzburg.
The South African Museum of Military History, Johannesburg.
King's College, London.
Natal Carbineers Museum, Pietermaritzburg.
Old Fort Museum, Durban.
Natal Society Library, Pietermaritzburg.
Natal Mounted Rifles Museum, Durban.
The Estcourt Museum, Estcourt.
Sudbury Library.

Introduction

By the end of the nineteenth century the attitude of Britain's subjects towards the empire was changing. Informed opinion envisaged it being transformed into an alliance of independent countries, which might counter any aggressive intent by other powers. Canada, Australia and New Zealand were well on the way to achieving this but elsewhere more complex issues had to be solved before the bonds of empire could be disentangled.

In Southern Africa, Natal and the Cape Colony had obtained a degree of independence, but were under constant threat from the two Boer republics on their northern borders, the Transvaal and the Orange Free State. The Transvaal was particularly aggressive and its leaders made it clear that they – and they alone – would rule Africa from Cape Town to the Zambezi River. They invaded Natal in 1838 and again in 1881, but lacked the military capacity to conquer it. This changed in 1886 when the world's largest gold deposit was discovered in the Transvaal and money began to flood into its treasury. Now able to buy the best modern rifles and artillery, the Boers could again cast covetous eyes on the Cape and Natal colonies and began arming themselves to achieve their dream of conquest.

By the end of September 1899 the republics were ready to invade, and on 11 October 1899 they declared war on the British Empire. With 52,000 mounted men backed by professionally trained artillery with modern guns, they were confident of a speedy victory and had every reason to be so. In both potential theatres of the war, the Boers outnumbered the defenders by more than two to one. In addition, most of the troops opposing them were infantry and in South Africa one mounted man was worth more than three infantrymen, so, in practical terms, the invaders had a six to one advantage.

To add to the British Army's difficulties, the Government had made some serious blunders. The Colonial Office instructed the Governors of Natal and the Cape to exclude the local governments from all matters pertaining to the war, the War Office issued a directive that no information of a military nature was to be given to locally raised forces, and Sir William Butler, Britain's senior official in South Africa, issued a further directive that in the event of war with the Boer republics, no black people were to be employed in any military capacity whatsoever. These decisions, apart from being an insult to Britain's most important allies in the war, deprived the army of its most valuable source of information.

Leo Amery, editor of the seven-volume *Times History of the South African War*, in describing the British Army facing the Boers wrote:

> It was the whole training, composition and organization of the force that were defective, and it was not till the army in South Africa was remodeled by the practical sense of its officers, its composition altered by the wholesale incorporation in it of colonial, South African, and other improvised volunteer forces, and the whole trained anew in the school of experience, that it became a more or less adequate instrument for overcoming the stubborn resistance of the Boers. The conquest of South Africa has been the work of the British Empire and the British officers and men on the spot. It has not been the work of the War Office or the Army system.

As a war correspondent, Amery had first-hand experience of the war but he had to rely on British sources for information. Now, by using rapidly disappearing colonial sources, it has been possible to set out for the first time how the vital changes referred to by Amery were effected and the invaders were driven out of Natal. After a long guerilla war, the Boers sued for peace. It was then that the greatest error of British government was made and it has a thoroughly modern feel. Having driven the Boers out of Natal and the Cape, the war was extended into the Boer republics without there being any plan about what would happen if the army was successful.

Britain signed a peace treaty with the Boers in 1902. Not consulted about the terms of the treaty that gave control of the whole of South Africa to the Boers, who now called themselves Afrikaners, were the two South African colonies and the semi-autonomous black areas of South Africa. In control of the present, the Boers now controlled the past – and they set about obliterating from history the part played by the colonials and the black peoples in this conflict. Sadly, the Boers succeeded in their ploy and for generations the British have been content to acquire information about South Africa from Afrikaners. In the process, much misinformation has been created and the contribution by the colonials and black peoples – and their suffering – has been ignored. By drawing aside the curtain of propaganda imposed by the Apartheid government, much new material has been brought to the attention of the public for the first time, with the aim of changing perceptions.

This book is about people caught up in a war – soldiers and civilians, men and women, black and white, children and the elderly, and the terrible trials they all endured. During the ten years I have spent researching and writing this book, I entered a world where integrity, loyalty, compassion, courage and a sense of duty held sway: Karri Davies declining to have his name put forward for a Victoria Cross; General White refusing to abandon the civilian inhabitants of Ladysmith; General Buller agonising over the fate of each one of his men; women going about their daily lives despite being subjected to constant shellfire; the black people whose loyalty and courage never wavered; Natal civilian stretcher-bearers being shot down in cold blood while treating the wounded. It is a story of the triumph of humanity in such testing times. It is hoped that this book will provide a change in direction in the way this part of British and South African history is approached in future.

Hugh Rethman

1

The Long March and
the Drift to War

As Great Britain and the Boer republics drifted steadily towards war, six young Boer policemen were amusing themselves with some target practice next to the Natal road on the flat, treeless plain of the Eastern Transvaal, South Africa. Watching were 7,000 young Zulu miners and their two colonial guides, Sidney Marwick and Guy Wheelwright. As all trains had been commandeered by the military, the miners, escorted by the policemen, were attempting to walk the 200 miles and more from Johannesburg to their homes in Natal and Zululand.

The marksmanship of the Boers was impressive and one of them, Trooper Bretz, could hit the distant target almost every time he fired. After a while he handed his rifle to Wheelwright so that the Natalian could show what he could do. It was a superb new Mauser, better than any firearm Wheelwright had ever handled. As he raised the rifle and looked down the sights, there was quiet. Gently he squeezed the trigger and for a moment after the shot, dead silence. Then 7,000 faces broke into big smiles. Wheelwright handed the rifle back to the now thoughtful young Boer. Perhaps it was not going to be quite so easy to drive the Natalians into the sea.[1]

In 1895, the Department of Native Affairs of the Natal Colonial Government had opened agencies in Johannesburg and the nearby town of Germiston. Mindful of the fact that many black migrant workers from the colony were illiterate and spoke neither English nor Dutch, making them vulnerable to the wiles of the unscrupulous, these offices were set up to help them. Most of the migrant workers were employed in the gold mines.

Marwick had been appointed head of the agency in Johannesburg and Wheelwright to a similar position in Germiston. Apart from competence in their administrative duties, the agents were expected to have a deep knowledge of the Zulu language and customs. Absolute integrity was presumed. Long hours were worked, and much was achieved. They acted as a conduit through which the workers could maintain contact with their families. Finances were looked after, and money remitted to those in need at home. Claims were successfully pursued on behalf of those who had been cheated, or injured at work. Zulus have a great talent for bestowing nicknames that say much about a person's character. Marwick was given the name *Muhle,* which is the Zulu word for things that are good. He was just twenty years old when he was appointed to the post in Johannesburg in 1895.

In September 1899, Marwick arranged rail tickets for those miners who, because of the impending threat of war, wished to return to Zululand or Natal. However blacks had to have passes to travel in the Transvaal and the State Secretary, F.W. Reitz, refused to issue these passes. Marwick then went over Reitz's head to the Kommandant-General, P.J. Joubert, the commander of the Boer army then preparing to invade Natal. The general agreed to the issue of the passes, subject to their being stamped by the Natal Agent.

On 1 October about a thousand men were able to take advantage of this concession. The next day passenger traffic to Natal was suspended, as all trains were required by the military. Those who had been able to get on the last train were regarded as the lucky ones.

General Joubert had left for the front, so Marwick approached his secretary, Louis de Souza, with a proposal that the remaining miners be given leave to walk to Natal. If the proposal had been rejected, the Transvaal would have had thousands of hostile, unemployed and hungry Zulus prowling around behind their lines – a situation that would have done nothing to assist the war effort. And so it was agreed that Marwick, his staff, and about 5,000 blacks were given permission to travel from Johannesburg to the Natal border, provided they walked in one group. Strict discipline was to be maintained, and they were to be accompanied by six mounted Transvaal policemen, the charge for which would be sixty pounds.

Approval from the Native Affairs Department in Natal was sought and promptly given, the Prime Minister taking the trouble to telegraph his own support for the operation. New Herriot Mine benevolently loaned to them, free of charge, two Cape carts and a four-wheeled trap, vehicles that were to prove invaluable on the long march. In an astonishing feat of organisation, Marwick and Wheelwright were able to assemble the refugees for their march by 6 October and on the 7th, they were on their way. They were to witness the demonstration of Boer and Natalian shooting skills and have many other adventures before completing their long walk home.

The miners walking to Natal were among the last refugees to leave Johannesburg. The exodus had already begun four months earlier when talks between Britain and the Boer republics broke down and war became not a possibility but a virtual certainty. Tens of thousands fled to the British colonies of the Cape and Natal; some because they feared internment, others because they did not relish the prospect of being conscripted to fight for the Boers, and yet others because the imminent war had cost them their livelihood.

Among these refugees were two men determined to resist Boer oppression and expansion, and to assert what they believed to be right, Walter David 'Karri' Davies and Aubrey Woolls Sampson. At the beginning of September 1899, they were in the Natal capital, Pietermaritzburg, organising a regiment to oppose the Boers. Recruits had to be of good character, fine shots and excellent horsemen. The regiment would be called the Imperial Light Horse.

Davies was an Australian. His father Maurice had emigrated with his parents from London to Tasmania in 1840. After seven years, the family moved to Victoria. Maurice had a successful period working on the Victorian goldfields, after which he moved to Adelaide to start a business as a contractor and builders' merchant. He had married and in due course, six sons were born. Walter, their second son, was born in 1867.

In 1875 the family moved to Western Australia where Maurice intended to establish a sawmill. In 1878 he acquired shares in the timber industry near Karridale with access to the port facilities at Barrack Point. The business expanded rapidly. Further mills were opened, bridges were built over rivers and jetties built at different points along the coast to facilitate the export around the world of the timber from the famous karri and jarrah trees. When Maurice Davies arrived in this South West corner of Western Australia, it was almost uninhabited; by his efforts and imagination, he had transformed it into a thriving community. However, his interests extended beyond his timber enterprise. He still worked as a contractor, being involved in such diverse projects as the construction of the Cape Leeuwin Lighthouse and jetties from Freemantle to Eucla near the South Australian border.

His son Walter was educated at Winhames College, Adelaide, and Scotch College, Melbourne. The Davies boys were encouraged to become an integral part of the family business and so they might thoroughly understand the industry, they started as labourers and had to work their way up from there.

While retaining his interest in the timber industry, Walter also studied engineering and was a brilliant student, rapidly making a name for himself and being involved in several major engineering projects around Australia. He was highly articulate and, as a student, such was his promise as a public speaker that he was chosen to meet the well-known orator Lord Rosebery in a public debate in the Melbourne Town Hall. Unfortunately, he broke his collar bone playing cricket on the day before the debate and had to withdraw from the debate. A few years later, Lord Rosebery became Prime Minister of Great Britain.

In 1893 Walter contracted blood poisoning, which totally incapacitated him and, to restore his health, it was suggested that he take a sea cruise. He chose to go to South Africa and, once there, his curiosity ensured he visited the new boom town of Johannesburg and the gold mines of the Rand. He realised, immediately, that the rapid development of the gold mines and the linked construction of new railways and harbours provided a great opportunity for the family firm. He set up business as a timber merchant and in no time, ships were plying from Australia to South Africa laden with karri and jarrah timber for the new mines, railways and harbours. He was given the nickname 'Karri', the tall hardwood an appropriate name for a big man with an intellect and character to match. To distinguish himself from the other Davies's in the Transvaal, he changed his name to Walter Karri Davies.

Coming from Australia, it was a matter of astonishment to him that those people in the Transvaal who contributed 97.5 per cent of the State's revenue (the mining community provided 92.5 per cent and the black peoples 5 per cent) had no say as to how such money should be spent, all power being vested in a minority of the population who contributed a mere 2.5 per cent of the revenue. The dominant minority appeared to have every intention of maintaining the status quo. Inevitably, he was drawn towards the Reform Movement and there he met Aubrey Woolls Sampson, who was to become a lifelong friend. On Woolls Sampson, Karri bestowed the nickname 'Sambo'.

Woolls Sampson, like President Kruger of the Transvaal, had been born in the Cape Colony and like the president, Aubrey also had an iron will. His father was a judge; however, it was from his mother that he inherited his character. She was known in Cape society as a strong, uncompromising personality who was implacable in what she considered to be right.

The Sampson children led an idyllic life at the Cape. Their father leased a small farm just outside Cape Town, close to both the sea and the lofty Devil's Peak. The boys were able to lead a very active life – swimming, exploring and climbing all over the mountain. Their neighbour and landlord was a Dutch farmer and as the two families were frequently in each other's company, the children grew up as fluent in Dutch as they were in English. When their father employed a Zulu groom, Sam, he taught them Zulu, the first of a number of indigenous languages Aubrey was to master. Sam also taught the boys *veldcraft* and in particular how to find a beehive. This entailed following a bee back to the hive, an exercise that required not only an ability to move quickly across country, coupled with great concentration, but also very sharp vision. This was to stand Aubrey in great stead in later years when as a military scout he was able to see things invisible to others.

The boys learned to read and write at home, and Aubrey only went to school when he was eleven. School was not really to his liking, it was adventure he craved – so he decided to run away. Hearing of his plan his mother confronted young Aubrey. 'I hear you are planning to run away,' she said, 'don't do that, just pack your bags and say goodbye'. This took the wind out of his sails and he remained at home, but the adventurous spirit remained.

When he was fifteen, his father, who was to preside over the Circuit Court at the Diamond Fields, decided that Aubrey should accompany him. It was a strange decision as Kimberley at that time was far from being the respectable place it was later to become. Perhaps the judge thought it would toughen his son up. For Aubrey, the life of adventure had begun. He took any work he could get, acting as a messenger and labouring on other men's claims. In Kimberley at the same time, Cecil Rhodes was working in his little mineral water factory, trying to raise sufficient money to study at Oxford to obtain the education he believed necessary to be successful.

Young Aubrey looked at the people about him and absorbed a wide knowledge of human nature in all its diversity. Alcohol was a problem and he, though never a total abstainer, hardly ever drank – and throughout his life he despised drunkenness. He read voraciously and building on his limited formal education, he made a careful study of all those matters with which he came in contact, be they technical matters such as mining, or the languages and customs of black peoples.

He added his mother's maiden name, Woolls, to his surname and thereafter he was Aubrey Woolls Sampson. Not long after he arrived in Kimberley, the Diamond Fields Revolt broke out and though only fifteen, he joined it and impressed all with his courage. This revolt, which had been sparked by maladministration, was settled amicably – enabling Kimberley and the diamond fields to settle down to a more orderly existence.

In 1873 Aubrey went with his father to Barberton in the Eastern Transvaal. The next few years were spent gold prospecting and big game hunting. After the British annexed the Transvaal in 1877, he took part in a campaign that brought an end to the Sikukuni war and he also took part in the Zulu War of 1879. In the Transvaal, a rebellion against the new British rule was being carefully prepared. In December 1880, the rebels proclaimed a republic and the country was plunged into war.

Aubrey joined a commando of South African-born Volunteers fighting on behalf of the British. When its commandant fell ill, Aubrey took his place at the head of the commando, which was one of the units defending Pretoria, the centre of the British administration. And so it came about that when battle was joined with a Boer kommando led by one Hans Botha, a most desperate shootout occurred between the two leaders, each having taken cover behind an anthill with no more than fifty yards between them. Both men were superb marksmen and the slightest exposure by either was instantaneously pierced by a bullet. The duel continued like some medieval contest with the champions of each side fighting to the death. From time to time one thinking perhaps the other had been killed would raise himself a little, only to receive yet another wound. Gradually the two champions, weakened by their many injuries, lapsed into silence behind their respective anthills and the men on both sides fell back, leaving the field to the wounded.

Aubrey had been shot in the arm and shoulder and, most seriously, in the neck, a wound that exposed his jugular vein. Hans Botha had been shot seven times through the body. At this point, a future mining magnate, Harry Struben, appeared on the scene with an ambulance and despite their protests, the two men were taken to hospital, where they were placed in adjacent beds.

Pretoria being besieged, no definite news could be obtained in the outside world – but such were Aubrey's wounds that word went out that he had been killed and obituaries were published. Only his mother refused to believe that he was dead and announced that Aubrey would never allow himself to die while he was needed, and she was right. Miraculously, the thin membrane enclosing his jugular vein held and, slowly but surely, his wound healed. Equally surprising, none of the seven bullets that went through Hans Botha had hit a vital organ and he too survived. In hospital there was much banter between the two men; a lifelong friendship had been formed, which was to survive the troubled times that lay ahead.

As soon as his wounds had sufficiently healed, Aubrey went to the family home in the Cape to recuperate. Once again he could walk along the beach at Kalk Bay, swim in the surf, or climb mountains. With his wounds completely healed, his vibrant health returned; the once scruffy youth had now matured into a confident young man with an optimistic, charismatic personality that ensured his company would be sought and enjoyed by one and all. Women could not help but notice his extraordinary good looks, and it was said that Aubrey, 'had a great way with the ladies and that many were generally inclined to go a great way with him'.

Life was pleasant at the Cape but Aubrey needed a challenge. He joined the Cape Infantry, a Regular unit, and received a commission. In due course he was appointed commander of Fort Donald situated at the juncture of the Cape Colony, Natal and Pondoland, an independent and extensive country wedged between the Cape and Natal. Fort Donald was out in the wilds, the nearest settlement being the little Natal village of Harding, three or four hours' ride away. The Fort wasn't really a fort, but a hill. There were no permanent buildings and the garrison consisted of a few orderlies. However, on a clear day, one can see over the rolling green hills of Pondoland to the sea, fifty or so miles away. The wild and beautiful coast of Pondoland with its romantic tales of treasure-laden ships being wrecked was an irresistible attraction for Aubrey. He didn't find much treasure, but he did acquire considerable knowledge of the people, their rulers, culture and language.

When the Cape Government disbanded the Cape Infantry, Aubrey decided against joining another regiment and instead to go prospecting in the Transvaal. In 1886, when disputes between various tribes threatened to bring chaos to Pondoland, someone remembered Aubrey and he was selected by the Cape Government to be one of a four-member delegation, under Walter Stanford, the Chief Magistrate in Kokstad, tasked with restoring peace to the area. The Pondos under Chief Umqikela had long-running disputes with the Xesibe and Baca peoples. Stanford was able to rely on Aubrey to negotiate with the opposing parties in a situation where one word out of place could have spelt the end of the peace process. The negotiations were a success and war was averted. The official report on the matter stated 'Mr Sampson would appear to have conducted a delicate and difficult matter with firmness and discretion.'

Over the following years, Aubrey travelled in Rhodesia and explored unknown areas north of the Zambezi River in what is now known as Zambia. In 1895 he returned to Johannesburg to find the place in ferment. Relations between the Transvaal Government and the inhabitants of Johannesburg had reached a critical point.

To understand this crisis, the events that followed, and their effect on the people involved, it is necessary to give a brief account of the country's history.

2

The Boer Republics

In 1652 Cromwell ruled England but the Dutch ruled the seas. In the religious wars that wracked Europe during the previous century, the Dutch had emerged as the champions of the Protestant cause and, with Britain preoccupied with internal disputes, became the leading trading nation of Europe. In the East, the Dutch East India Company had acquired a pre-eminent position, which brought much prosperity to Holland. However, the journey by sea around Africa took many months and there were no ports at which the Company could call to effect essential repairs to ships and obtain fresh provisions for passengers and crew. So, in 1652, the Company established a station at the Cape of Good Hope with a small fort and adjacent gardens to be cultivated by its employees.

Though not uninhabited, the land appeared to be only sparsely populated by nomadic herdsmen, the Khoi-khoi, otherwise known as Hottentots who, because of their appearance, were thought to be of Chinese origin. Indeed, many of the early explorers referred to them as Chinese although their language and customs bore no similarity to those of the Orient. The Company encouraged intermarriage, hoping by this means to breed out the locals. This, probably Europe's first attempt at social engineering in Africa, was a complete failure. However, the idea of a halfway house, where ships could call on their way to and from the East, met with instant success. The Company's gardens were unable to keep up with demand. People were allowed to establish privately owned farms and in 1658 slaves were brought from the East Indies to help work the land and do other manual work. A substantial stone castle was built, not to protect the settlement from the locals, but as a defence against jealous European rivals. In 1688 Huguenots fleeing from religious persecution in France were permitted to settle at the Cape – provided they broke off all links with France and adopted the Dutch language and culture. The Huguenots brought many skills to the Cape. They also reinforced hostility towards Roman Catholicism and bolstered the process whereby the local Dutch population would decide the cultural norms and language of the country.

The Khoi-khoi, being few in number and now ravaged by diseases against which they had no resistance, could do little to resist the invaders. They retreated to the fringes of the expanding settlement. Some worked for the Dutch as servants. To get by, they learnt Dutch and in the course of time their language was almost lost, only existing today in some remote areas of Namibia.

Over the next one hundred and fifty years, Cape Town grew steadily in size and importance and, in its immediate hinterland, towns and villages were laid out where a settled and comfortable way of life was established. Beyond this settled area, the mountainous terrain impeded but did not stop further expansion of the colony. Dutch pioneers crossed the mountains and, adopting a semi-nomadic lifestyle, trekked ever northwards and eastwards.

By the end of the eighteenth century, the area of land nominally under the control of the Company was about the size of England. From the beginning the colonists had chafed under the rule of the Company and nowhere was this rule more resented than in the outlying districts. Necessity required that these pioneers be self-reliant, which in turn bred an independence of spirit. Education was often limited to learning to read the Bible, which for many was only book they ever read. Gradually, their cultural ties with Europe became ever more tenuous and what remained was firmly anchored in the religious ideas of the seventeenth century. They called themselves Boers, that is to say 'farmers', though this is not wholly accurate.

While the Boers were struggling to subsist in the dry interior of the Cape, momentous changes were taking place in eighteenth-century Europe. Trade had brought prosperity and a great flowering of scientific discovery accompanied by equally important changes in the way people thought. The Industrial Revolution was beginning. The American colonies had rebelled and acquired independence, while the French had suffered a bloody revolution. The frontier Boers envied the Americans their independence but other changes in the outside world had little effect on the way they lived their lives.

Holland had lost its pre-eminent position as a trading power and the Dutch East India Company was no longer the force it once was. When Napoleon Bonaparte conquered the Low Countries, the Dutch government fled to Britain and requested Britain to take over the defence of the Cape. It was not a situation that appealed to the British – however, they could not let Napoleon control the sea route around the Cape. In 1785 they sent troops to garrison the Cape. In 1803 it was handed back to the Dutch, only for the British to re-occupy it in 1806. Finally in 1815, by the Treaty of Vienna, which brought a formal end to the Napoleonic wars, the Dutch ceded the Cape to Britain. No one in Britain could have realised the burden they had taken on.

The change of governors in Cape Town was only one of the new problems facing the frontier Boers. Towards the end of the eighteenth century they clashed with a new force on the Eastern frontier, the amaXhosa. These people were numerous, strong and warlike. The Xhosa were not going to be easily brushed aside and the Boers on their scattered farms began to feel their very existence threatened. Into this cauldron on the frontier, in 1820 there arrived nearly five thousand British settlers at Algoa Bay, now known as Port Elizabeth.

On the whole, with similar trials and dangers to endure, the new settlers' relationship with the Boers was cordial, but they had come from a very different culture. Many were well educated and regarded themselves as enlightened, modern people. Education was important and schools were established. The rights of all people were to be respected and slavery was regarded with abhorrence. They were not prepared to give up their Anglo-Saxon heritage but were tolerant of the customs of others.

With tact and common sense, the conflicting interests of all three very different cultures might have been reconciled. This was not to be. In 1834, slavery was abolished in the Cape Colony. This the frontier Boers resented, however, the demonisation of them by 'interested and dishonest persons under the name of religion',[1] caused such hurt among the religious Boers that it burned into their very being a bitter and lasting hatred of all things British. This, combined with the refusal of Lord Glenelg, the Colonial Secretary, to have any regard for local opinion convinced many Boers that life in the colony would be intolerable.

In their travail, they turned to their Bibles for inspiration and, in particular, to the Book of Exodus. From 1835 to 1837 a great migration occurred, which became known as the Great Trek. From all over the Cape interior, groups of families and friends came together, loaded their few possessions onto their wagons, and set off northwards to the lands across the Orange River, beyond the furthest reaches of British influence. They called themselves Voortrekkers and numbered somewhere between six and ten thousand. Among the migrants was a twelve-year-old boy, Paul Kruger.

When the Voortrekkers crossed the Cape's northern border at the Orange River, they entered a land of wide, grassy plains teeming with game yet sparsely populated with other humans, truly the Promised Land. They pegged out their farms and formed the republic, which became the Orange Free State. To the north, the nascent state was bounded by the Vaal River.

Latecomers, and perhaps those who hated Britain most, crossed the Vaal in search of their paradise and there they founded four further republics. Life was harder there, with constant wars with the black people they encountered and the little republics also squabbled endlessly among themselves. So quarrelsome were they that in 1857 Paul Kruger, now a kommandant in the Potchefstroom Republic, went so far as to make an unsuccessful raid into the Orange Free State in an attempt to overthrow its government.

In 1860 the Transvaal Republics agreed to unite but, shortly thereafter, war broke out between them. It was not until 1864 that unity was finally achieved, with the formation of the South African Republic, colloquially known as the Transvaal.

The first years of this new republic were not edifying. Many of its citizens were too poor to pay taxes and the wealthier burghers simply refused to pay.

The result was there was no money in the treasury to pay the salaries of the few civil servants, thereby encouraging the development of the corruption that was to become a striking feature of Transvaal officialdom. The State was lapsing into chaos, a situation not improved by a disastrous war against the tribal chief Sikukuni and on-going disputes with the Zulus. In the Transvaal, the idea that the country should seek protection from Britain began to find favour. At the end of 1876 Sir Theophilus Shepstone, as British Agent, travelled to the Transvaal and demanded that the Government introduce certain reforms immediately, lest the whole region be plunged into war.

The reforms were not carried out and on 12 April 1877, Shepstone announced the annexation of the Transvaal by Britain. Shepstone had no authority to do this but, as it was done peacefully and appeared to be supported by the locals, Britain did not repudiate his action. A leading Boer newspaper stated that ninety-six per cent of the country's citizens supported the annexation. Among the four per cent opposing it were Paul Kruger and Piet Joubert, although they was subtle enough to tone down their hostility for the time being.

Annexation brought prosperity to the Transvaal. The State finances were put onto a sound footing, a transformation that was achieved by the British taxpayer paying the country's not inconsiderable debts. The Sikukuni dispute was settled and, in 1879, Britain fought and subdued the Zulus while, at the same time showing she was not invincible. Those factors that had favoured annexation had disappeared, and there had been a change of government in England.

For those who wished to drive the English out of the Transvaal, the time had come to act. On 15 December 1880, a republic was formally proclaimed, and on 20 December, two companies of the 94th Regiment were ambushed at Bronkhorstspruit, resulting in fifty-six British soldiers being killed and 101 wounded. Other British garrisons in the Transvaal were surrounded and besieged until the end of the war. Nourse's Horse, with Aubrey Woolls Sampson, was one of the regiments besieged in Pretoria.

Having neutralised the British units in the Transvaal, the Boers invaded Natal. The small British force sent to stop them suffered three defeats in quick succession at Laing's Nek, Ingogo Heights and Majuba, the mountain passes it had been thought would protect Natal. The British hastily sued for peace and the Transvaal again became an independent republic. Paul Kruger, with majority support in the Transvaal legislature, the *Volksraad*, became president.

In 1873 gold had been discovered in the Eastern Transvaal. To these fields, centred on the town of Barberton, gold prospectors and camp followers came from all over the world, hoping to make or mend their fortunes. Many were pick and shovel men, uncouth, unsophisticated, uneducated and often unscrupulous, who led hard-drinking, irresponsible lives. The pious Boers and their straight-laced president looked on in horror. In 1884 President Kruger visited Europe and at a sumptuous reception, the French president, seeking a compliment, asked Kruger if he had ever seen such a magnificent sight. The old Boer looked at the ladies in their décolleté gowns. 'Not since I was weaned,' he dryly commented. No wonder he looked with some disfavour on the rip roaring mining communities of the Barberton goldfields, where the highlight of the day was the auction of the favours of Cockney Liz and Trixie the Golden Dane. But the State needed money and the mines did provide some revenue. Also, as the goldfields were far away near the border of the Portuguese colony of Mozambique, it might be possible to avoid contamination until such time as the gold petered out and the miners went away.

The Barberton goldfields were not the success they had promised to be. Gold strikes there were a-plenty, but too often the gold-bearing seams ran out before expenses had been recovered and by 1886 people were beginning to drift away to seek their fortunes elsewhere.

Against the trend, an Aussie battler, George Harrison, was on his way to Barberton. Indeed he should never have been in South Africa at all. Flush with money after six months prospecting in the American West, he decided to have a night out in New York. He overdid the party and when he woke up, he was penniless and on a sailing ship bound for Cape Town. Disembarking there, he set out to walk the five hundred miles to the diamond fields at Kimberley, supporting himself by doing odd jobs along the way. In Kimberley all the claims had been bought up by wealthy financiers and there was no room for the small man. He hitched a ride on a wagon going to Pretoria, hoping to find his way from there to the goldfields of the Eastern Transvaal. When he reached the Witwatersrand, a range of hills just south of Pretoria, he was desperately short of cash and it was still a long way from Barberton. Hearing that the widow Oosthuizen was looking for someone to build a house on the farm Langlaagte, 10 miles to the east, he jumped at the opportunity to earn some cash.

On the first Sunday in March 1886, George and a friend were sitting on a kopie looking over the half-finished house, towards the plain beyond. To complete this idyll they needed a drink, so George set off down the hill to get what was required. Near the bottom he tripped over a small boulder and fell headlong. In anger he picked up the rock and smashed it to the ground. Looking at the broken pieces he could hardly believe what he saw. He called his friend over and together they picked up all the pieces of the offending rock and took them to the house where they found a big old bolt and a ploughshare. The pieces of rock were placed on the ploughshare and beaten into a mixture of sand and gravel by the bolt. This was placed in a frying pan still greasy from the breakfast George had cooked that morning. The pan was filled with water and the men began the age-old process of swirling the pan around and around, occasionally pouring off superfluous muck, then adding more water and repeating the process. Eventually all the sand and gravel was gone. The two men stared at the pan. They had never seen anything like this. Not in Ballarat, nor in California, nor in any of the many other diggings they had visited. The world's greatest goldfield had been discovered.

In 1884 at a convention in London, the Transvaal delegation, led by Kruger, with many pious utterances expressing gratitude to Her Majesty's Government and their love of peace in their time, obtained further concessions from the British government. A week later, at a banquet in Amsterdam, the Revd S.J. du Toit, Superintendent of Education, a signatory of the convention and speaking with the full knowledge and consent of his colleagues from the Transvaal delegation said, 'The South African flag shall yet wave from Table Bay to the Zambezi, be that end accomplished by blood or by ink. If blood it is to be, we shall not lack men to spill it.'

This would seem to be a fair summary of the foreign policy pursued by the Kruger Government over the next fifteen years. The flag would, of course, be that of the Transvaal. To execute such an aggressive policy, a vast amount of money was required and Digger George Harrison had just discovered where it could be found.

When news of the find got out, men of all types and conditions came from all over the world to the Witwatersrand. A shanty town, Johannesburg, came into being and rapidly expanded. To the dismay of many, the surface gold soon ran out and Johannesburg might have become yet another nineteenth-century ghost town, a monument to a gold rush that had been and gone. But this gold reef was different. The gold bearing conglomerate ran down and down, deep into the bowels of the earth, further down than man had ever been before. The ore was low grade but, unlike other goldfields, it was consistent – so, once the reef was found, it was possible to calculate the value of the gold that could be extracted.

To establish a mine, substantial capital was required and this could only be raised abroad by financiers in whom investors felt they could place their trust. Furthermore, given the low grade of ore, for a mine to survive, its management had to be very efficient. Mining is a dangerous occupation, particularly when operating at great depths, and the mines therefore required engineers and geologists who were more than competent, they had to be the best. When the colourful financier Barney Barnato wanted a mining engineer, he sought the best in the world. John Hays Hammond had built a reputation in the United States that he was without peer. Barnato sought him out and persuaded him to come to Johannesburg. Hammond's father had won fame as a Texas Ranger in the Mexican War, he took part in the Californian gold rush of 1849, and became the first mayor of San Francisco. Having grown up in a gold mining town, it is not surprising that young John Hays Hammond became a mining engineer. He also had the advantage of growing up in a family that had played a major part in the conversion of a wild mining settlement into one of America's great cities.

When Hays Hammond eventually left South Africa, he was employed by Presidents Teddy Roosevelt, Coolidge and Taft as a presidential advisor. Bob Taft even tried to persuade him to accept nomination as vice-president, an offer Hays Hammond refused as he did not seek political office.

With the mining personnel, there came to Johannesburg all those other people necessary for a settled society, doctors, dentists, architects, builders, and tradesmen of all descriptions. Thus it came about that many highly skilled men from colonial South Africa, Britain, Australia, the United States and indeed the rest of the world came to Johannesburg. In typical colonial fashion it was not long before patches of veld were cleared for rugby, soccer and cricket. Of course there had to be horse racing, which required a one-and-a-half mile track. This was not easy to find as claims were pegged out all over the place. As a result, at the initial meetings, the horses had to run over a zigzag course between the claims, which must have been a nightmare for the stewards and a source of frequent arguments. The town had started as a rough mining camp and it still had some rough edges but, by the middle of the 1890s, it was well on the way to becoming one of the world's more sophisticated cities.

President Kruger and his followers in the Volksraad viewed the developments on the Witwatersrand with extreme distaste. It was bad enough having miners at Barberton but to have all these foreigners so close to the heart of the Republic was indeed dreadful. Perhaps because of its association with the East India Company, or perhaps because Britain was a trading nation, the conservative Boers looked on all forms of trade and commerce as essentially evil and dishonest. Thus on one of his rare visits to the Witwatersrand, Kruger opened his address to the assembled people with the words, 'Burghers, friends, thieves, murderers, newcomers, and others'. But he needed the revenue from the mines.

Kruger's foreign policy had suffered a few reverses. An attempt to overrun Bechuanaland had failed when Britain stepped in to assist the locals and made the country a Protectorate. His plan to extend the Republic northwards to the Zambezi was frustrated when Cecil Rhodes annexed for Britain the country now known as Zimbabwe. In the east, parties of Boers – disregarding protests from Natal and Britain – had moved into northern Zululand and formed a republic, which they called the New Republic. If the Germans had not threatened to annex St Lucia Bay in northern Zululand, Britain would probably have permitted the Boers to overrun the whole of Zululand. Frightened that Germany might cut off the route to the East, Britain promptly annexed what was left of Zululand. Thus are empires often built.

In Europe, Kruger decided to swim with the crocodiles and sought alliances with the Kaiser's Germany and other powers that might be hostile to Britain. However, beyond a willingness to spread anti-British propaganda, no real assistance came from this quarter. Kruger's foreign policy did have one major success. In 1888 the wise and capable President Brand of the Orange Free State died and the Anglophobe F.W. Reitz succeeded to the presidency. From then on, the Orange Free State was more and more under the influence of the Transvaal.

In a strange corollary to the belief that all commerce was by its very nature dishonest, some Boers appeared to believe that in their own commercial dealings, it was right and proper to be dishonest. Paul Kruger was prepared to overlook the taking of bribes by his officials on the grounds that they should be able to set aside something for their old age! Also, although the consumption of alcohol was regarded as sinful, the liquor laws of the Republic virtually encouraged excessive drinking, particularly among the blacks. This Kruger justified on the grounds that it enabled farmers to get higher prices for their grain.

To the inhabitants of Johannesburg, be they colonials or immigrants from Britain, this attitude was repugnant. They had worked hard to establish a mining industry whose technical achievements were truly remarkable. To finance this, they had invested not only their own money but also that of tens of thousands of shareholders from around the world. They had smiled when the Volksraad debated whether it was shooting at God to send exploding rockets into clouds to bring rain, or when Paul Kruger opened a synagogue with the words, 'in the name of our Lord Jesus Christ, Amen'. But they were seriously concerned by the corrupt nature of the State, which was being run for the benefit of a small oligarchy to the detriment of the rest. In addition, it was impossible to effect any change through the ballot box as Kruger constantly manipulated the franchise so as to ensure control would never pass from his faction. In an attempt to redress their grievances, a pressure group, who were labelled Reformists, came into being. It was not a political party and had as its supporters such diverse figures as the republican Hays Hammond and the imperialist Cecil Rhodes.

3

Dissent in the Transvaal

Walter Karrie Davies   John Hays Hammond

Neither the discovery of gold on the Witwatersrand nor the growth of the burgeoning town of Johannesburg prompted the Transvaal Government to make any administrative changes that would take into account the new developments. As there was no local authority, the miners, being practical men, set up a Digger's Committee to attend to such matters as drains, demarcating streets and other tasks that would normally fall within the ambit of a local authority. Out of this committee was to evolve the Reform Committee.

From the start, relations with the Pretoria government were strained, a situation that did not improve with time. The *Uitlanders*, as Paul Kruger contemptuously referred to the more recent arrivals in the country, felt they were being unfairly exploited by a corrupt and incompetent regime. Among their complaints:

1. The ill-treatment of black peoples and the callous disregard of their rights caused constant friction, and did not bode well for the future.
2. Permanent residents not of Boer origin were denied voting rights, a restriction that applied to their children even though they were born in the Republic.

3. Monopolies and concessions granted to the ruling elite and their coterie not only resulted in inefficiencies but also brought much hardship to the general public. Particularly irksome was the dynamite monopoly and the concession granted to the inefficient Netherlands Railway syndicate. The former raised concerns about safety and obliged the mines to use dynamite that was not only expensive but also of poor quality. The railway monopoly greatly hindered the development of a modern transport system, which was so badly needed by the country.

4. Residents with no voting rights were subject to military service.

5. Many of the necessities of life were taxed, causing hardship to the poor.

6. Johannesburg had no local authority to manage its affairs.

7. The police were not properly supervised, and no serious effort was made to control crime.

8. Children from English-speaking families did not have the same rights to education as Boer children. The government spent eight pounds six shillings per child per annum on the education of Boer children while a paltry one shilling and ten pence per child per annum was spent on Uitlander children. In other words, the government spent more than eighty times as much on the education of a Boer child than it did on the education of an Uitlander child, despite the fact that the Uitlanders provided ninety per cent of the state revenue.

9. Little or nothing was done about corruption in the civil service.

10. Delays in the criminal justice system resulted in prisoners having to spend up to 18 months in gaol before being brought to trial. In one group of sixty-three men, thirty-one died before being brought to trial. The deaths were attributed to the absence of vegetables.

As the year 1895 drew to a close the citizens of Johannesburg, having had no success in their attempts to ameliorate their grievances by consultation, were getting desperate. Kruger's attitude was succinctly expressed in a statement by him to an Uitlander delegation, 'Protest! Protest! What is the good of protesting? You have not got the guns, I have.'

He did have the guns. With revenue pouring in from the goldfields, the country was stockpiling arms and ammunition far beyond what would normally be required for its defence. The Government had built a fort overlooking Johannesburg, which seemed to indicate that an attack on the town might be planned. Further, as it made no secret of its intention to throw the British out of Southern Africa, many of Johannesburg's residents, being of British descent, did wonder what was planned for them.

In their everyday dealings with the Boers they found there were many who were practical and intelligent men with whom they could reason and they knew that in the *Volksraad* there was a progressive faction, which opposed Kruger. However, they also knew of Kruger's ability to manipulate the franchise in his favour, and how deftly he used the system of monopolies and State concessions to shore up his support. In this atmosphere, the idea of a coup d'etat was born.

One of the more fanciful schemes was that residents would arm themselves with whatever weapons they had, storm the fort, thereby supplementing their arms, and then march on Pretoria, where Kruger would be deposed and a more progressive Boer administration installed. Free and fair elections would then be held. Some had wanted Britain to annex the country, but there was strong opposition to this led by the republican American, John Hays Hammond, whose views prevailed.

Cecil Rhodes, now Prime Minister of the Cape Colony and resident in Cape Town, arranged for some rifles to be smuggled into Johannesburg so that its citizens might be able to defend themselves. Rhodes also arranged for a force from the British Chartered Company's territory (now known as Zimbabwe) to be stationed on the western border of the Transvaal. This contingent of five hundred mounted men and three field guns, led by a certain Dr Jameson, was to provide assistance should the Reformists request their help. Kruger, fully aware of Jameson's movements, made his preparations and waited. To use his own metaphor, he would wait until the tortoise stuck its head out – and then chop it off.

Aubrey Woolls Sampson could not have chosen a more tumultuous time to arrive back in Johannesburg. He fully sympathised with the motives of the Reformers and the need for the changes they sought. However, he was also aware of the military strength of the Boers and how rapidly their kommando system functioned to meet any threat. Having heard the plans of the proposed coup, he asked to see the arms they had collected and what he saw horrified him. They had scarcely enough rifles for the leading Reformists and a few of their friends. He knew the degree of loyalty the backveld Boers felt for their president. He knew how Kruger had outwitted the British by his apparent complaisance in annexation, and had seen the efficacy of his campaign to regain independence in 1880. To Aubrey, the plans to overthrow Kruger were sheer folly. Passionately he argued for, at the very least, a postponement of any coup. To his relief it was decided that Charles Leonard should immediately go to Cape Town to enlist the aid of Cecil Rhodes in stopping any attempt to invade.

Any satisfaction that might have been felt by the prevention of the coup was dispelled when the horrifying news reached Johannesburg that Jameson, ignoring requests not to invade the Transvaal, had crossed the border on 29 December 1895, and was on his way to Johannesburg. The tortoise had stuck its head out.

Kruger, having successfully divided the opposition, decided to deal with Jameson first, and then give the people of Johannesburg his full attention. In the meantime, he sent an emissary to the Reformers to indicate a willingness on his part to discuss Uitlander grievances. Johannesburg's communications with the outside world were cut, and the Transvaal Police were quietly withdrawn from the town.

At a meeting of many prominent men of Johannesburg on Monday 30 December 1895, the Reform Committee was formed. Karri Davies and Aubrey Woolls Sampson were among those elected. This committee was faced with some serious dilemmas:

Firstly, most were furious with Jameson and would have been quite happy to disown him and leave him to stew in his own juice. As Hays Hammond said: 'Without any consent on their own part the reformers were made partners in an attempt at conquest, instead of reformation.'

Unfortunately *The Star* newspaper had got hold of the news that Jameson had crossed the border and was on the way to Johannesburg. Jameson became an instantly popular hero against whom the committee dare not act. Secondly, law and order had to be established and maintained. It was known that there were criminal gangs operating, the most notorious being the Irish Brigade. Composed of sweepings from the streets of Dublin, their behaviour in Barberton was such that even that permissive town had found them intolerable and had chased them out. They were thought to be in Johannesburg. The committee assigned Andrew Trimble, a former sergeant in the Inniskilling Dragoons, the task of organising a citizen's police force. Most of the men chosen by Trimble were Australians and in due course arms were issued to them.

Thirdly, the Reformers intercepted a telegram from the Kommandant-General in Pretoria to the Heidelberg Kommando ordering them to ride through Johannesburg indiscriminately shooting right and left so that any idea of a revolution could be crushed before it started. A few hours later another telegram was sent by General Joubert cancelling the order. These telegrams reinforced the idea that the government was planning to attack Johannesburg.

To protect the unarmed population, it was decided to fortify the perimeter of the town with as many men as their limited supply of arms permitted. Karri Davies and other Australians were charged with guarding the Robinson Mine on the western fringe of the town. On the afternoon of Tuesday 1 January 1896, they received orders from the committee to have food and drink available for Jameson's men. Next morning trestle tables were laid out with bread, meat and crates of beer, but Jameson never arrived.

The Boers had been tracking Jameson's column from the time it crossed the border but it was not until it was within 14 miles of Johannesburg that the Boer kommandos surrounded and attacked the raiders. The outcome was never in doubt. At 9.15 a.m. on Thursday, 2nd January, 1896, Jameson surrendered, after receiving a guarantee of safe conduct out of the country for every member of his force. They were taken to the Pretoria gaol pending their extradition.

In Johannesburg the sounds of battle had been heard and later news of the surrender reached a shocked populace who, looking for scapegoats, blamed the disaster on the leading Reformers. No mention of the offer of safe conduct leaked out.

With Jameson his hostage, Kruger turned his attention to the subjugation of Johannesburg. He invited the British High Commissioner in Cape Town, Sir Hercules Robinson, to Pretoria to discuss the crisis. Though old and ill, Sir Hercules at once set off on the long train journey to Pretoria and on the morning of 6 January, he had an hour-long discussion with Kruger. Sir Hercules was told that the government would not open negotiations or consider any Uitlander grievances until Johannesburg surrendered its arms. It was pointed out to him that there were eight thousand Burghers under arms who were anxious to finish the matter and they might at any time shoot the raiders and attack Johannesburg. The Reform Committee members were to have twenty-four hours to accept or reject the ultimatum. Kruger, knowing Sir Hercules and the Reformers were unaware of the promise of safe conduct given to Jameson, made no mention of it.

A telegram was promptly sent to the Committee advising them of the terms of the ultimatum and all its members were summoned to a meeting that afternoon. The leaders believed the Committee had no choice but to accept the terms; however, the majority were not convinced and argument continued until late in the afternoon, when another telegram arrived from the British Agent Sir Jacobus de Wet stating he was coming to see them.

They met early the next morning. Sir Jacobus said the lives of Jameson and the other prisoners were in their hands and Kruger had assured him that once the arms were relinquished, Jameson and his men would be handed over to the British government. This was fine as far as Jameson was concerned but what about Johannesburg, the Reform Committee, and Uitlander grievances? Sir Jacobus gave the assurance that not a hair on the head of any man in Johannesburg would be touched and as far as the Committee was concerned: 'Not one among you will lose his liberty for a single hour. John Bull would never allow it.' He added that the Uitlander grievances were being considered.

The conditions of the ultimatum were accepted and it was arranged that a public meeting be held at noon outside the Rand Club. Word of the meeting quickly spread and by noon a sizable crowd had assembled. Sir Jacobus told them that Johannesburg could not defend itself against the Boers, an argument that was not only rejected but which seemed to make the populace aggressive and determined to fight. It was only when they were told that if they did not immediately surrender their arms, Jameson and all his men would be shot, that they abandoned their aggressive stance and agreed to hand in their arms. The process of collecting the arms immediately began and by the next morning, all weapons issued by the Reform Committee had been handed over to the Boers. On Wednesday evening, the Transvaal police emerged from seclusion and took over police duties from Trimble's men as unobtrusively as the change that had occurred eight days previously. During those eight days Johannesburg had been virtually crime-free for the first time in its short history. Karri Davies, Aubrey Woolls Sampson and the others accepted at face value the assurances given by Sir Jacobus de Wet, the Queen's agent in the Transvaal.

On Thursday 9 January a government proclamation stated that the leaders of the revolt would be prosecuted, and that night the arrest of the members of the Reform Committee began. For a while they all thought it a bit of a joke. Bags were packed as if they were going on a picnic but the smiles vanished when they reached Pretoria. A large, ill-tempered mob had gathered at the station to meet them. When the prisoners began their walk to the prison they were set upon. In vain did their small police escort attempt to control the mob; in the end the prisoners had to make a dash for the protection of the gaol, while the escort attempted to hold back their pursuers. Some of the slower prisoners were roughly manhandled, spat on and severely beaten. Along the road from the station to the prison were littered the shattered remnants of the suitcases and parcels of those little luxuries that it was thought would make life in prison tolerable for the few days they might be there.

The prison had been built by the British during their brief occupation of the Transvaal and was designed to hold no more than twenty criminals. It now had to hold more than sixty of Johannesburg's most prominent citizens. Four of them – Lionel Phillips, George Farrar, Frank Rhodes and Hays Hammond, who was suffering from severe dysentery – were put together in a cell ten feet by ten. There were four filthy canvas stretchers for them to sleep on and the only ventilation was a narrow iron grille above the door. The other prisoners were split up into small groups and herded into cells in which there were no beds, and barely enough room for them to lie side by side on a floor covered in excrement, fleas and lice. Many could not bring themselves to lie down, eventually collapsing from exhaustion. The doors of the cells were locked at six o'clock in the evening and not re-opened until six o'clock the next morning. Jameson and five of his officers were in the same gaol but no contact between the two groups was possible.

The prisoners made the best of their miserable surroundings. They were permitted to purchase meals from the Pretoria Club, they cleaned up their cells and were allowed visits from wives and relations. By the end of the month all members of the Reform Committee except the alleged ringleaders, Lionel Phillips, George Farrar, Frank Rhodes, Hays Hammond and Percy Fitzpatrick, were released on bail of £2,000 each.

The raid had left Johannesburg stunned, but not for long. Lord Hawke arrived with an English cricket team and for a time it was cricket and not politics that dominated conversation. Thousands flocked to see the matches and though the visitors took some time to get used to the light, matting wicket, and grassless field, they were able to beat the local side. Boers watching this strange game were puzzled. Obviously the Uitlanders were up to something evil, but they were not quite sure what it was. One who could not be there was the mining magnate Abe Bailey. He was in gaol in Pretoria with the rest of the Reform Committee. A keen cricketer, he was a great patron of cricket and spent considerable time and money on the promotion of all sport in South Africa. Some years later his son was to marry Diana, daughter of Winston Churchill.

January turned to February and it seemed everything was getting back to normal. On Sunday16 February 1896, eight railway trucks loaded with more than sixty tons of dynamite and detonators were shunted into the goods siding at Braamfontein, on the edge of the city. The representative of the concessionary dynamite company refused to accept the consignment, claiming their magazines were full. The trucks were left at the siding to be unloaded at a time more convenient than a hot Sunday afternoon. For three days the trucks stood in the hot sun and just after 3 p.m. on the following Wednesday, a gang of labourers with their mule wagons arrived to unload the dynamite.

A kilometre away in Government Square, the Circuit Court was in session. The accused took the Bible in his right hand and promised to tell the truth, the whole truth, and nothing but the truth. At that moment the building shook, a glass chandelier crashed down on the Bench, while at the same time there was the almighty roar of an explosion as a blast of air shattered the windows. The judge, despite his gown, leapt over the Bench and was first into the street. The accused, still clutching the Bible, was seen running towards the open veld promising never to tell another lie. People rushed into the streets and after the initial panic it was realised that something had happened at Braamfontein.

A great crowd headed in that direction and there, where once the station had stood, was a huge hole – 250 feet long, sixty feet wide and about forty feet deep. Of engine, trucks, wagons, mules and men there was no sign save for a few pieces of twisted metal and charred flesh.

The station had been located in a poor neighbourhood, which had its houses flattened by the blast. A rescue operation began immediately. The hospital was soon overflowing so the Wanderers Club, which a few weeks before had hosted the English cricketers, was turned into a second infirmary. That night the Rand Club held a meeting to form a relief committee and more than £4,000 was immediately subscribed. The next day the Stock Exchange boosted the fund to over £100,000. The concessionaire, The Netherlands Railway Co., donated £10,000, a gift regarded in Johannesburg as conscience money. Subsequently the Government donated a further £25,000 and announced that a Commission of Enquiry would consider the cause of the disaster.

The explosion had shaken the whole of Johannesburg, both physically and mentally. On that fateful Wednesday afternoon, young Jackie Hays Hammond, no doubt keen to become a miner, was digging in the garden when suddenly the earth shook and there followed the great noise of the explosion. The child rushed into the house shouting, 'Mommy, Mommy, I've dug up hell.' Mrs Natalie Hays Hammond thought she had been there for some time already.

The trial of the Reform Committee was set down for hearing at the Market Hall, Pretoria, on 24 April 1896. There were four charges;

(1) Inviting Jameson to invade.
(2) Inciting the people of Johannesburg to assist him.
(3) Distributing arms and ammunition.
(4) Forming and arming a police force.

Kruger appointed the State Attorney of the Orange Free State, a Mr Gregorowski, to preside over the trial. Judge Gregorowski made no attempt to conceal where his sympathies lay and, before the trial, made enquiries as to where he might obtain a black cap for use when passing sentence. About a week before the trial the State Attorney approached Advocate Wessels, who represented the accused, with an offer; if Phillips, Farrar, Frank Rhodes and Hays Hammond pleaded guilty to the first two charges, he would withdraw the other two charges against them, provided the remaining sixty-three pleaded guilty to counts three and four. In which case, counts one and two would be withdrawn against the sixty-three, who would only receive a nominal punishment. Some suspected another trap and many were innocent of all charges, but, as the offer demanded unanimous acceptance, and rejection might prejudice the position of the leaders, it was accepted. The State withdrew charges and the accused pleaded guilty as agreed. For sixty-three the trial appeared a mere formality, but, for the others, Phillips, Farrar, Frank Rhodes and Hays Hammond, the matter was more complex. There was no doubt that there had been a plot to overthrow the regime and this could be treason.

The Transvaal legal system was based on Roman Dutch Law, which had been developed by Dutch jurists during the period between the Renaissance and the imposition of the Napoleonic Code on the Netherlands. The penalties for treason in Roman Dutch Law were, as one would expect from laws developed in those far-off times, brutal. However, the Transvaal legislature, the Volksraad, had in the early days of the republic repudiated these penalties, and laid down that the penalty for conspiring with a foreign power to overthrow the state would be a fine and banishment. Did they perhaps remember that raid by the Transvaal into the Free State in 1859, or anticipate the revolution of 1880? Be that as it may, it was trite law that if there existed a conflict between Roman Dutch law and local law, the latter would prevail. Further, if the law provided differing penalties for an offence, the court should impose the lesser penalty.

Advocate Wessels, one of southern Africa's great jurists, had every reason to believe that the four leaders faced no more than a fine and banishment, though even this might not be imposed in its entirety as they had not conspired with a foreign power, (unless the freebooter Jameson could be described as a foreign power) and no one had been shot or injured as a result of any action by them. He was to be disappointed.

The judge found, without there being any evidence to support the finding, that the Reformers had conspired with Britain to overthrow the government. He also gave to himself the power to decide whether to apply Roman Dutch law or local law and chose the former. He found the four leaders guilty of high treason and proceeded to pass sentence. Lionel Phillips was brought forward. The judge placed a black cap on his head and sentenced him to death. George Farrar and Frank Rhodes followed and were, in turn, also sentenced to death.

When the time came for the seriously ill Hays Hammond to be led forward, the court interpreter, who had shown mounting distress, broke down sobbing and had to be comforted by the condemned man's doctor. There was a disturbance among the public as a woman fell down in a dead faint and the Dutch sergeant in charge of the prisoners said something about a dog biting and guzzling. The judge ignored it all and went on in a monotone, informing the prisoner that he would be taken to a place of execution and there hung by the neck until he was dead. The four men were led out.

While they were being led away, the judge busied himself writing and when he was ready he asked the remaining prisoners to stand up. Smiling benevolently, he carefully looked them over, then, wiping the smile off his face with a deft movement of his hand, he pronounced the sentence. They would each go to gaol for two years and pay a fine of two thousand pounds sterling. In addition, after the expiration of their gaol sentence, they would be banished from the Republic for three years. By no stretch of the imagination could this be called a nominal sentence.

As the judge was about to leave a voice called out, 'Just a minute, Judge!' and a man strode into the well of the court, as the stunned lawyers moved out of his way. Both the lawyers and the judge knew who he was. It was Barney Barnato, the Cockney prize fighter from the East End of London who had gone to Kimberley and made a fortune, which had been considerably increased by wise investment in Johannesburg. Barney prided himself on his lack of interest in politics and regarded himself as a personal friend of Paul Kruger. When his nephew Solly Joel joined the Reformers he was disappointed, but, when Solly was arrested, Barney, always loyal, attended the trial. Now he stood in the well of the court, and told the judge just what he thought of him and his judgment. Transfixed, the judge listened until Advocate Wessels distracted Barney and the judge shuffled out of court. Of course Barnato should have been arrested for contempt of court, but in the old Transvaal one did not readily arrest friends of the president.

As the prisoners were led out, Barney told them not to worry, he would have them out in no time. In the street outside the court, Barney continued his diatribe against Kruger and his judicial lackey, much to the delight of an assembled crowd of Uitlanders. From there he went to the Pretoria Club where a few drinks did nothing to quell his fury. He was still holding forth on the subject, when who should come into the bar but Judge Gregorowski, who should have known better. Barney had abused the judge in court, and now on his own turf he was in no mood to exercise restraint. In response to further invective, Gregorowski shouted out, 'Mr Barnato, you are no gentleman.' 'And you, Mr Gregorowski, are no judge,' replied Barney, who had never pretended to be a gentleman.

In London, news of the sentences was read to a concerned House of Commons. In Washington, the US Congress requested the Secretary of State to intervene on behalf of Hays Hammond and the other condemned men. In Johannesburg, the Reformers, once reviled by the populace for failing to support Jameson, now had the sympathy of the people. The battle for the release of the prisoners had begun.

One cannot leave the trial without mentioning that while awaiting trial, Hays Hammond had been released on bail of twenty thousand pounds sterling so that he might receive medical attention in Cape Town. This bail was provided by Barney Barnato. After the trial, Barnato asked Hammond why he did not skip bail and leave the country, rather than risk being sentenced to death. Hammond replied if he had done so he would have broken his undertaking to present himself for trial, and also the bail money would have been forfeited, a loss he could not inflict on a loyal friend.

The next day Barnato decided to see Kruger, but first he would call on Mrs Hays Hammond. Natalie Hammond and Mrs Phillips had just returned from a visit to Pretoria where they had seen Mrs Kruger in the hope of getting her to intercede on behalf of the condemned men. Mrs Kruger sat in stony silence, knitting, while the women made their tearful pleas for their husband's lives. When they had finished, Mrs Kruger replied coldly, 'If the Raid had succeeded, my husband would have had to get out the white horse he has not ridden for years and join the fighting. Would you have thought of me then, ladies? Would you?'

When Barney arrived at the Hammond home he found Natalie in a distraught state. For once he was lost for words and could only hold her hand in silence. As he rose to leave he gently said, 'Don't fret, my dear. I brought your husband to Africa and I'll stand by him until he's safely out of the country. That's a promise.'

Kruger gave his erstwhile friend a very frosty reception. The president declined to shake his hand or to remove his stovepipe top hat, but sat behind his desk, in his buttoned up frock coat bedecked with the broad sash of the Republic, and glowered at his visitor.

Barney apologised for his behaviour in court and the offence he might have given, but would make no concessions with respect to the sentences. He told the president that unless the death sentences were commuted and the Reform Committee released, he would close down all his companies, thereby putting one hundred and twenty thousand people out of work; the country would lose one of its principal sources of income, and the economy would be ruined. A slight exaggeration but flamboyance always comes with some exaggeration. The next day, the principal South African newspapers carried a Preliminary Notice of the intended sale of all the Barnato properties.

Barnato was not the only one in the Transvaal to take action. The Mercantile Association held an emergency meeting on the day following the sentencing and decided unanimously to close all premises the next day. The Stock Exchange suspended business as a protest against the sentences. Johannesburg was tense but restrained.

It began to look as if another tortoise was in trouble but this was a wily old tortoise, who knew when and how to retreat into his shell. On that Wednesday morning, two days after the passing of the death sentences, it was announced that they had been commuted. However, nothing further was done and a few weeks later one of the little-known prisoners, unable to stand the prison conditions any longer, cut his throat. Ten thousand people attended his funeral and the clergyman officiating described his death as judicial murder.

Shocked into action, the Government announced new sentences. The ringleaders were to undergo fifteen years imprisonment followed by banishment and the others to serve terms varying between three and twelve months. These others could be released if they signed a petition for clemency and gave an undertaking not to interfere in the politics of the country for a period of three years, on pain of banishment. In addition, they were to pay a fine of £2,000 sterling. In consequence of the unhygienic conditions in the prison, many of the prisoners were seriously ill on their release.

Agitation for the release of the ringleaders continued and on 11 June, one hundred mayors from all over South Africa, including the first citizens of every major town, assembled in Pretoria to plead for their release. They were discussing the matter when a messenger arrived with the news that the four had been released after they had each paid a fine of £25,000 sterling. Three had also signed an undertaking that they would not interfere in the internal or external politics of the country, a breach that would result in lifelong banishment. Frank Rhodes did not sign and left the country immediately.

Frank was the elder brother of the empire builder, Cecil Rhodes, but had a very different character. Whereas Cecil was terrified of women, Frank enjoyed their company. Cecil possessed a burning ambition to modernise Africa to the British way of life by education, to which end he acquired enormous wealth. Frank appears to have sought no more than a comfortable living surrounded by friends. Born in 1851, Frank entered the 1st Dragoons in 1873, and by 1889 held the rank of colonel. He seems to have been a competent and loyal officer. To supplement his army pay he acted as a reporter for *The Times* on various occasions. A severe attack of black-water fever resulted in his retirement from the army in 1893. On his recovery, he went to Africa and Cecil appointed Frank as his representative on the board of Consolidated Goldfields in Johannesburg. He was loyal to his younger brother, who had provided him with an income to supplement his army pension. Not unnaturally, many of his friends were Reformers. No doubt the Boers would have preferred to prosecute Cecil but, being unable to do so, Frank was a convenient substitute. When Frank died in 1905, the net value of his estate was a modest £102,139 (modest in comparison with the wealth accrued by his brother, at least). We shall hear more of this amiable, kind man.

With their minds occupied by the trial, few noticed the publication of the report by the Commission into the Braamfontein explosion. It was found that it might have been caused by a box of dynamite falling off a truck onto the rails and no one could be blamed for that.

Not all the prisoners had been released. Walter Karri Davies and Aubrey Woolls Sampson were still in gaol. They refused to pay the fine or to sign the petition. To do so would, in their opinion, amount to an admission that they had been correctly prosecuted and sentenced. As they felt this was not the case, they refused to compromise their personal integrity and accept the terms for their release. In July 1896, they wrote to the Acting British Agent giving reasons for their failure to pay the fine or sign the required undertaking. The reasons given were:

(a) They had been deceived by Sir Hercules Robinson's statement that Jameson and his party might be shot if Kruger's terms were not accepted.
(b) Sir Jacobus de Wet had also deceived them, when he told them that the Reform Committee would be fully protected by the British Government and that not one of the Reform Committee would, 'lose his liberty for a single hour. John Bull would never allow it'.
(c) The Transvaal State Attorney had stated that if they pleaded guilty to the lesser charges (3&4) they would only receive a nominal sentence.[1]

It is true that the trial judge was not bound by the agreement, but the Transvaal Government was bound by the undertaking of its State Attorney. It should have ensured immediate compliance with the agreement and set aside the sentences, while Britain, and perhaps Western Australia, should not have turned a blind eye to the manner in which the men had been tricked into pleading guilty. Joseph Chamberlain, the British Colonial Secretary, subsequently denied that Sir Hercules Robinson and Sir Jacobus de Wet had made the statements attributed to them. This denial may have carried some weight in Britain but, to those most affected, Chamberlain's denial was an obvious lie.

If Karri and Aubrey had heavy hearts when they began their sentences, it was not the prospect of two years in jail that disturbed them as they had no fear of hardship, but the disdainful deceit of the British officials. They knew life in prison would be hard, and it was. The head gaoler, one Du Plessis, never lost an opportunity to insult them or to make their lives as unpleasant as he possibly could. However, the two men were kept apart from the common criminals and some of the staff did treat them decently. One of the clerks, Matthys Human, became a friend, a friendship that was to stand Karri in good stead some years later.

Making the best of their situation, Karri and Aubrey worked out an exercise routine, which they meticulously followed and which ensured they maintained their physical fitness. Using their knowledge of mining they dug an escape tunnel under the prison wall, which could be used in an emergency, though they had no intention of escaping.

Their families, knowing the appalling conditions in the Pretoria gaol, were worried about their welfare. Mrs Sampson wrote from the Cape, begging Aubrey to pay the fine and sign whatever was necessary to get out of prison. Maurice Davies travelled from Australia and once he reached Durban, sent a petition in Dutch to the President, begging that his son might be released. Kruger was unmoved.

Initially the public took little interest in the fate of the two in prison but, after a time people, began to consider the matter more carefully. The Cape Colony sent a delegation to Pretoria to plead for their release. Their friends in the old Reform Committee collected money, which was given to them to pay the fine. The gift was appreciated but instead of being used to pay the fine, it was put into trust. Every week *The Cape Times* published a notice in the following terms, 'Today Messrs. Sampson and Davies complete the ... week of their imprisonment in Pretoria gaol for the crime of not signing a petition.'

Many Boers called for their release and none was more pressing in his entreaties to the president than old Hans Botha, who had been so badly wounded by Aubrey fifteen years before. Karri and Aubrey became a major talking point and the longer they stayed in prison, the more Jameson and his Raid slipped from public consciousness, to be replaced by concern over the way the country was governed. Kruger was embarrassed and did not know what to do. It would be humiliating to release them, yet their presence in prison gave the lie to the carefully nurtured belief that the Uitlanders were a bunch of unprincipled, money grabbing, cowardly scoundrels. At last, in 1897, after Karri and Aubrey had served fourteen months of their sentence, relief came for Kruger in the form of Queen Victoria's Diamond Jubilee. He used the occasion to release them in what he hoped would be regarded as a magnanimous act of clemency. In submitting to imprisonment, they had sought to expose injustice and the absence of integrity in public life. They had succeeded in this objective but their sacrifice brought no improvement in the manner the Transvaal was governed.

Karri Davies and Woolls Sampson are generally recognised as being the first prisoners of conscience in the modern era. The idea of going to prison for one's beliefs was a strategy subsequently used very effectively by the suffragettes in England and M.K. Gandhi in India.

Kruger did effect some changes. Johannesburg was given a Town Council but it was so constituted that 2,000 Boers would have a permanent majority over the rest of the residents, who numbered well over 100,000. It was decreed that the decisions of the Volksraad would take precedence over the law. When Chief Justice Kotze protested that this would destroy the independence of the judiciary, Kruger sacked him, appointing Judge Gregorowski in his place. Powers to expel aliens were widened, the conditions enabling immigrants to obtain citizenship were made even more difficult and press restrictions increased.

A slump in the economy caused President Kruger to appoint an Industrial Commission to inquire into the gold mining industry. Perhaps it would show how the Rand's mining magnates had, by their greed and inefficiency, brought about the current economic depression.

Schalk Burger, a respected member of the government's executive council, was to chair the Commission, which conducted a thorough and detailed investigation into the mining industry. Its report was not quite what President Kruger expected. It stated, 'at present there exist all the indications of an honest administration, and the State, as well as the mining industry, must be congratulated upon the fact that most of the mines are controlled and directed by financial and practical men who devote their time, energy and knowledge to the mining industry.'

The report went on to criticise the application of the Liquor Law and the Gold Law relating to the theft of gold. Ten per cent of the gold extracted was being stolen and nothing was being done about this, the philosophy being that as it was the Boer's country, they owned the gold, so they could not steal their own property. The report also recommended a reduction in railway rates and import tariffs, and an investigation into the dynamite monopoly. It went on to recommend the formation of a joint mining board, to be composed of nominees of the government and mining industry, 'so that the Government should have the benefit of the experience of men whose daily occupation it is to look closely into all the affairs appertaining to the mines'.

For Kruger it was a bitter blow. A Volksraad committee was appointed to study the report and in due course dutifully rejected it.

Meanwhile in the Cape, Sir Alfred Milner had replaced Sir Hercules Robinson as High Commissioner. Though a competent and intelligent administrator, Sir Alfred was unfortunately a self-opinionated, arrogant man, unsuited to the task ahead of him, which required tact and not a little humility. His reaction to the Mining Report was typical. He was surprised by the report; he had not realised any Boers were capable of such breadth of understanding.

Before the Jameson Raid, the Boers had been stealthily arming themselves but after it, preparations began in earnest. By 1899 they had built up their military strength to the point where they should have been able to sweep all before them. The old Boer dream of conquering Natal again began to surface.

Between 31 May and 5 June 1899, a conference was held in Bloemfontein attended by the presidents of the Boer Republics and Sir Alfred Milner. The purpose was to prevent war. Although the war was likely to be fought over their countryside, Natal and the Cape Colony were not invited. A number of Natal politicians, including the former Prime Minister Sir Harry Escombe, requested Milner to consider the views of Colonial Ministers before any final decisions were made. This suggestion was rejected with fury by Milner, who regarded it as an unjustified interference in Imperial affairs. The petitioners he described as 'wobblers and mugwumps'. In London, Lord Wolseley, Commander-in-Chief of the British Army, requested a similar exclusion of the colonial governments from military decisions and information.

Sir Alfred and the British Colonial Secretary, Sir Joseph Chamberlain, appear to have come to the conclusion that there would be no peace in the region until the Kruger regime was removed from power. The major threat to peace was the danger of the Boer Republics attempting to annex the Cape and Natal. The Transvaal had never made any secret of its intention to conquer Natal, and Britain may well have allowed this – but for one important fact. British goods were increasingly being carried around the world in steamships, which needed coal, and Durban was the principal port where ships travelling between Britain and the East via the Cape could fill their bunkers. The British could not let this port fall into the hands of a hostile power.

There was no question of Britain launching a military attack against the Boer Republics. She had made no preparations for any military campaign against them; indeed, she had made no adequate arrangements to defend the Cape Colony or Natal. Outside a small circle of people with relatives in South Africa, the British public did not care one iota what happened there. Their knowledge of the country was slight and probably limited to the fact that gold had been discovered in the Transvaal. Of the strategic importance of the South African colonies they knew nothing, and would never have condoned an unprovoked attack against those distant Republics. For all practical purposes it was the Boer Republics who would decide whether or not there would be war.

Milner believed some sort of suzerainty agreement with the Boers might solve the crisis. Britain would control the foreign relations of the Boer Republics, which in turn would have a wide discretion in their internal affairs. This, Milner believed, would protect British interests and avert war. The Boers, on the other hand, were not going to surrender any part of their independence. Not surprisingly no agreement was reached at the 1899 Bloemfontein Conference.

Over the next few months a campaign in the Uitlander press criticising the treatment of coloured people by the Transvaal Government exacerbated the worsening relationship between the Boers and the other inhabitants of the Transvaal, while Milner continued to seek acceptance of his feudal idea that Britain should have suzerainty over the Transvaal and Free State.

We have seen how in 1884 the Revd S.J. du Toit had spelt out Boer ambitions in Southern Africa and that these ambitions had not died is dramatically illustrated by a memorandum written by the Transvaal State Attorney, Jan Smuts, in September1899. He wrote that if the Boers were victors in the coming war, they would be 'founders of a United South Africa, one of the great empires of the world, an Afrikaner republic stretching from Table Bay to the Zambezi'.

Knowing how the Voortrekkers had behaved towards civilians in their abortive attempt to take over Natal between 1838 and 1842, and being aware of the treatment meted out to the Uitlanders in the Transvaal, the Natalians were not going to consent to the Boers taking over their well-ordered little colony and expressed their support for the Uitlanders' struggle.

When Karri Davies and Aubrey Woolls Sampson were released from prison, Aubrey joined his family in the Cape while Karri went back to his business, journeying to England, Egypt and China seeking new markets for its timber. In June, 1899, he was in Cairo on business when news reached him of the deteriorating situation in South Africa. He returned and, after discussions with Aubrey and others, the idea of forming a Volunteer Mounted Regiment was conceived.

They initially sought permission from the army commander in the Cape, Sir William Butler. An anti-Semite, Sir William believed that the political situation in South Africa was being manipulated by a colossal syndicate of Jewish capitalists in Johannesburg, which he referred to derisively as, 'Jewburg'. This anti-Semitism was not peculiar to Sir William. In the final decade of the nineteenth century there had developed in Britain a philosophy that a coterie of Jewish capitalists sought to dominate the world. As many of the prominent personalities involved in the development of the gold mines in the Transvaal had names which were or could be Jewish, it was but a small step to persuade the gullible that Jewish goldbugs were leading the country into war in order to enhance the power of Jewish financiers. The 'Jew-Jingo' owners of the *Daily Telegraph* were portrayed as 'gold-greedy ghouls thirsting for blood', and the Trade Unions Congress denounced the spending of a hundred million pounds of taxpayer's money to secure the goldfields of South Africa for cosmopolitan Jews, most of whom had no patriotism and no country. Cecil Rhodes was denounced as a mere puppet of the Jewish conspiracy.[2] It was not only in the labour movement that this theory found support. In the military establishment there were some who had more than a little sympathy for anti-Jewish sentiments.

The British Prime Minister, Lord Salisbury, was another who shared the distaste for the threatening war in South Africa. In a memorandum to Lord Landsdowne, Secretary for War, he wrote: 'I see before us the necessity for considerable military effort – and all for a people whom we despise, and for territory which will bring no profit and no power to England.'

When Aubrey Woolls Sampson and Karri Davies saw General Sir William Butler, he refused point blank to sanction the raising of a regiment of Volunteers stating, 'England is not preparing for war, even if the Transvaal is.' However, in Natal, Aubrey and Karri were made welcome.

4

The Colony of Natal

Natal was named by the Portuguese navigator and explorer, Vasco da Gama, who had made landfall near Durban on Christmas day, 1497. Three centuries were to pass before it attracted any lasting interest from European travellers.

Following the success of their settlement at Cape Town, the Dutch wondered whether a similar port of call might be practical on the Natal coast, and in October 1688, the Cape Governor ordered one of their vessels, the *Noord*, to survey the east coast and search for any survivors of shipwrecks. At Port Natal the *Noord* found two survivors from the wreck of a Dutch ship the *Stavenisse,* which had run ashore on the Natal south coast on 16 February 1686. Though pleased to see their countrymen, they had been well treated by the locals who were 'friendly, and there was an abundance of food and fresh water to be had'.[1] On their return to the Cape, their report seems to have impressed the Governor who sent the *Noord* back to Port Natal with instructions to buy the Bay of Natal and adjacent land. The *Noord* was welcomed on its return to Natal and the local chieftain put his mark to an agreement selling the land to the Dutch East India Company.[2] On 11 January 1690, the *Noord* left Port Natal for Cape Town with the Deed of Sale on board. Five days later she ran aground near Algoa Bay. Of her original complement of eighteen only four were able, after much suffering, to survive the shipwreck and the overland journey to the Cape. The Deed of Sale was lost to the sea.[3]

In 1705 there was a shortage of timber at the Cape and the Governor ordered another vessel, the *Postlooper* under Johannes Gerbrantzer, one of the survivors from the *Noord,* to investigate whether Natal might be able to supply timber. On arrival he found that the old chief had died and had been succeeded by his son. The son expressed complete disinterest in any agreement purportedly made by his father, saying he now ruled the district and only his own decisions had any validity. Gerbrantzer was wise enough not to argue with the chief. He reported unfavourably on the harbour and though he found an abundance of timber, its quality was no better than that grown in the Cape.[4] So ended Dutch interest in Natal for almost 150 years.

Over the centuries many ships were wrecked on the eastern seaboard of southern Africa. Most of the survivors attempted to walk to Delagoa Bay (now Maputo) or the Cape. Many died en route, some were murdered and some were absorbed into the local native tribes. To these early reluctant travellers, Natal appeared to be a veritable Garden of Eden with a superabundance of wild birds and animals, and many exotic fruits growing wild on the fringes of the forests where the trees grew tall and straight. The inhabitants near Port Natal were described as being of middle stature, with very good limbs and graceful.

A Captain Rogers who called at Port Natal in the 1690s found they were, 'very just and extraordinarily civil to Strangers'.[5] In their intercourse with each other, they were 'very civil, polite, and talkative, saluting each other, whether young or old, male or female, wherever they meet; asking whence they come and whither they are going, what is their news, and whether they have learned any new dances or song's.[6]

The country was ruled by a number of petty chiefs until early in the nineteenth century when a man of exceptional ability, Dingiswayo, united many of the Zulu clans. To ensure security, he reorganised the country's defences. All young men were obliged to serve in his army, which was divided into regiments and these, in turn, were divided into companies. The companies were named and distinguished by the colour of their shields. Regimental and company commanders were recognisable by their imposing dress.

Unfortunately, in a campaign against a recalcitrant tribe in 1817, Dingiswayo was captured and executed. Shaka, the leader of one of the smaller tribes who paid tribute to Dingiswayo, came forward to claim the vacant throne. Brave, intelligent, ambitious, and ruthless, he was nonetheless capable at times of great kindness and loyalty. Shaka soon consolidated his position as successor to Dingiswayo. He retained the military structure established by his predecessor and tightened discipline. However, the method of fighting was drastically altered. Previously, warriors had thrown long spears at each other. Shaka abolished the long spear and equipped his men with a large shield and a short stabbing spear. In battle his impis, like the Greek and Roman phalanxes, would advance in close formation, using their large shields as protection from missiles. The enemy would then be engaged at close quarters, where the short spear was deadly.

Having secured his position as ruler of Zululand, Shaka turned his attention to the neighbouring peoples. To ensure they would no longer pose any threat to him or the Zulus, they were attacked and those who escaped the slaughter of battle were driven from the land, their kraals and crops destroyed and their cattle expropriated. From the Tugela River in the north to the Mzimvubu River in the south, and from the sea to the

Quathlamba (Drakensberg) mountains in the west, the land was almost emptied of inhabitants. At this time when nations trembled at the mere mention of his name, such was the complexity of his character that he insisted on personally attending to the needs of his venerated and frail old grandmother, even cutting her toenails.

After the Dutch had ceded the Cape to the British in 1815, a group of Cape merchants decided to explore the possibility of trading with the Zulu people. They knew Zululand was ruled by a mighty monarch, Shaka, whose military genius had resulted in vast tracts of land being subjugated by the Zulus. However, as it was not their intention to conquer the Zulus but to trade with them, in 1823 they fitted out a brig, the *Salisbury,* under the command of James Saunders King, who was tasked with finding a suitable site for the establishment of a trading post in Natal. King had been born in Canada in 1795, joined the Royal Navy as a ship's boy in 1805, and left the Navy in 1815 with the rank of midshipman. Assisting King was Lieutenant George Francis Farewell, who had served on a naval vessel conducting a survey of the South East African coast. They first sailed to St Lucia Bay on the Natal North Coast. Here three of a landing party drowned in the surf while, at the same time, the *Salisbury* was blown many miles out to sea. It was five weeks before the winds permitted the *Salisbury* to return to St Lucia to pick up the survivors of the landing party. After visiting Algoa Bay for supplies, the *Salisbury* returned to Natal where King charted the sheltered estuary at Port Natal (now known as Durban Bay) in detail before the party returned to Cape Town in December 1823. King went to England on an unsuccessful mission to obtain a commission, while Farewell concentrated on persuading merchants that Port Natal was a suitable place for a trading site. Like merchants of all times and in all places, they sought customers who were prosperous and content. At the beginning of 1824 it was decided to go ahead with the venture.

To reconnoitre the locality prior to the arrival of the main group, an advance party, under the leadership of a young man, Henry Francis Fynn, was sent ahead. On or about 10 May 1824, they arrived safely at the bay on the sloop *Julia.* This land, which the writer Alan Paton described as 'lovely beyond the singing of it', was found to be almost deserted. The only locals they saw were a few wretched people hiding in the coastal bush, and subsisting on such shellfish as they could scavenge on the shore.

Having established a camp, Fynn, accompanied by an interpreter and a local inhabitant, set out northwards to find Shaka. They had not travelled far before they were overtaken by a Zulu impi many thousands strong, returning from an expedition against the Pondos whose lands lay some 100 miles to the south. At the first hint of the presence of the Zulus his companions bolted, but Fynn stood his ground. Though later to become a pre-eminent authority on the Zulu language, he knew no Zulu and could only repeat the name 'Shaka' when approached. This was enough. The Zulus accepted him as a friend, and placed him in the care of one of Shaka's uncles while instructions were sought from Shaka himself, who was then at his capital, Bulawayo, 125 miles to the north.

Shaka had heard of the English, whose arrival seems to have pleased him for he immediately sent a present of forty cattle and several tusks of ivory as a gift. When later Farewell arrived in Natal, he and Fynn set off directly to visit Shaka, from whom they received a most cordial welcome with dancing, feasting and the interchange of presents. Shaka gave permission for the establishment of the trading station as well as making a grant of land (*see* Appendix 1), which included the coast of the future colony and extended about 60 miles inland.

To Fynn must go much of the credit for the success of the visit and the establishment of the trading station. His personality was such that he won the friendship and trust not only of Shaka but of all Zulus. This bond was strengthened when Fynn, using knowledge gained while working as a loblolly boy at Christ's Hospital, successfully treated wounds suffered by Shaka in an assassination attempt. Shaka appointed him chief of the natives living in Natal. This included those destitute souls living near the coast and several small clans near the mountains. Many were refugees from Zululand, who would have been hunted down and killed by Shaka but for the influence of Fynn. When the escape and flight of these people to Port Natal was reported to the monarch he is reputed to have said, 'They have gone to my friends and not my enemies.' Thus it came about that several thousand Zulus collected at Port Natal and Fynn noted, 'the fate of the natives became identified with our own, and could scarcely be separated.'[7] Many years later it was written of Fynn:

> His intimacy with the Zulu language, his travels on foot amongst the Native people, his warm hearted disposition, his unfailing humanity to those in distress, and in these times they were very numerous and everywhere in hiding, especially in Natal, were such that even in these days a century later, his name is held in honour throughout the length and breadth of the land. In these things he was always first.

Because of his concern for them, those people over whom he was chief came to venerate him almost as a god.[8] Fynn was given the name Mbuyasi and when a son was born to Shaka's nephew Mpande, the baby was named Mbuyazi, presumably in honour of the visitor who had arrived among them.

While Farewell and his party were establishing their little settlement, King had not been idle. In Britain he acquired a two-masted square-rigged vessel, the *Mary*, for use at Port Natal. He sailed via St Helena where he delivered a consignment of goods to a merchant on the island. The merchant's sixteen-year-old nephew, Nathaniel Isaacs, persuaded King to take him to Natal. Isaacs was an intelligent young man with a good command of English and fine powers of observation. They arrived at

Port Natal on 30 September 1825. A strong onshore wind and heavy seas caused the ship to run aground at the harbour entrance. Fortunately, no lives were lost, but the ship was irretrievably damaged. Over the next two years, the foundations of the settlement were laid. Of necessity, dwellings were at first primitive and designed to do no more than to provide protection from wild animals and shelter from the elements. Isaacs found the climate healthy and congenial and delighted in the lush vegetation and the abundance of wild fruits and vegetables.

The little settlement had its vicissitudes. Wild life such as leopards and snakes were a constant threat. When in 1827 medical supplies ran out, a fifteen-year-old boy, John Ross, was given the task of walking 300 miles north to the Portuguese post at Delagoa Bay, to obtain fresh supplies. Shaka provided a bodyguard of warriors and the medicines were duly obtained. In spite of difficulties, the beauty and promise of the land was such that the settlement continued to steadily grow.

Good relations were maintained with Shaka – but at a price. Some were obliged to assist Shaka in his military campaigns. On one such campaign, Isaacs was wounded. All food was withheld from him until he drank a concoction made from some roots and the gall and entrails of a heifer. The smell of the potion was so vile that Isaacs wondered whether death might not be a better alternative to drinking it. Perhaps their greatest trial was being obliged on visits to Shaka to witness the purposeless slaughter of his subjects, a form of entertainment to which Shaka was becoming addicted.

March 1828 saw the launching of the first ocean-going vessel built in Port Natal. Using timbers from the wrecked brig *Mary* and local trees, Hatton, chief officer of the *Mary*, and four crew members had taken two years to build the ship, which was named the *Elizabeth and Susan* in honour of the wife of Farewell and the mother of King. On 30 April 1828, the vessel left for Algoa Bay. On board were Lt and Mrs Farewell, King, Isaacs, Hatton, and two of Shaka's headmen who were to negotiate a friendly alliance with King George. (*See* Appendix 2.)

So anxious was Shaka to form an alliance with the British that he conceived the idea of obliterating the tribes that lay between the southern border of his domain and the Cape Colony. He was persuaded to give his emissaries two months grace before embarking on any such campaign. However, the *Elizabeth and Susan* had no sooner set off on her maiden voyage than his impis attacked the Pondos on his southern border. In support of his army, Shaka came south with his entourage and visited Fynn at his home near the Mzimkulu River. Fynn fortunately was able to persuade Shaka to take his impis back to Zululand. The Zulus retired with ten thousand captured cattle.

The mission of the Zulu chiefs to Algoa Bay was an abject failure. British officials treated them as spies or criminals and subjected them to lengthy interrogation while keeping them under virtual house arrest. They were refused permission to see the Lieutenant Governor at Grahamstown.

After three months, the British decided to send Shaka's men back to Natal on HMS *Helicon*. They refused to board the ship without King, who returned with them to Natal. Farewell, Isaacs and Hatton returned at the same time on the *Elizabeth and Susan*. King was deeply affected by the failure of the mission and, afflicted by severe depression; he fell ill and died on 7 September 1828. He was buried near his home on the Bluff, the promontory that shelters the bay from the ocean. Isaacs left a moving description of his funeral: 'The whole of the vicinity was crowded by natives from the surrounding districts, all lamenting the death of our friend. Their lamentations were sincere, their tears genuine drops of sorrow, that fell involuntarily from their streaming eyes.'

Shaka was infuriated by the treatment that his emissaries had received, and believed that King had been poisoned by the British. With Shaka in such a bad mood the settlers had to walk on eggshells, however, he went no further than directing abuse at them. Indeed such was his unpredictable nature at the time that he made grants of land to Isaacs and Fynn without any regard for the fact that the same land had already been granted to Farewell and King.

Perhaps because he had exercised absolute power for so long, Shaka was becoming ever more brutal and cruel to his subjects. His many military campaigns had exhausted his army, which longed for the day when they could marry and settle down to a more peaceful existence. Dingane, Shaka's half brother, noticed the monarch's waning popularity and, when an opportune moment occurred, on 23 September 1828 he assassinated Shaka and usurped the throne. Dingane appears to have had a genuine desire to rule humanely, and his accession was welcomed by most Zulus. He sent a reassuring message to the settlers at Port Natal.

In December, 1828, the *Elizabeth and Susan* again sailed from Natal to Algoa Bay. On board were Farewell and Isaacs. On arrival at Algoa Bay, the port authorities seized the vessel because she had no register. This was despite the fact that there was no shipping registrar at Port Natal, the vessel had lain in Algoa Bay for three months earlier in the year, and had been given written clearance. The ship was sold and the proceeds divided between the seizing officers and the Crown. It was simple bureaucratic piracy. Deprived of the *Elizabeth and Susan,* Farewell decided to wait until his wife had been delivered of a child she was expecting before returning to Natal by the overland route. In September 1829, Farewell and two companions set off for Natal. Near the Mzimvubu River they met a Zulu clan that had fled south after the accession of Dingane. Their chief, Queto, invited Farewell's party to visit him, and on their arrival at his kraal Queto gave them a warm welcome and a gift of cattle. That night, 6 October 1829, the guy ropes of Farewell's tent were cut and Farewell and his companions were stabbed to death through the canvas. The Pondos subsequently drove Queto back to Zululand, where he was executed by Dingane.

On the whole, relations between Dingane and the settlement at Durban were cordial. Isaacs, who had been to St Helena, returned in 1830 and noticed that all had gone well in his absence. On his visits to the Royal Kraal, he had long talks with Dingane as they watched the sun go down and his host amused himself by displaying his magnificent herd of three thousand snow white Nguni cattle.

A traveller from the Eastern Cape, a Dr Cowie, visited Dingane whom he found to be 'anxious to anticipate their wants, hospitable without ostentation' and displaying, 'a magnanimity and capacity befitting the chief of a great people'. Dingane told Cowie that his conduct would be of an opposite character to that of his predecessor and that his only ambition was 'to make his subjects free and happy'. Cowie noticed their huts were 'clean and commodious, the country was fertile and cultivation was extensively practised'.[9]

Isaacs noted that unlike Shaka, Dingane tended to vacillate in his opinions, and lacked constancy. However, when he spoke his language was fluent, impressive and to the point. He expressed a desire for education both for himself and his people and thought this might be obtained from missionaries. On one of their visits to Dingane, the settlers appeared on horses. Dingane had never seen a horse before and immediately realised that foot soldiers would be no match for mounted men in Natal.

In 1830 Dingane sent two settlers, Cane and Holstead, on a mission of friendship to the Cape with two great tusks of ivory as a gift. The Cape Government refused to see the emissaries, a rejection that bitterly offended Dingane. In just two years, British officials had treated the representatives of two Zulu monarchs with contempt and in so doing, insulted the whole Zulu nation. This behaviour by the British authorities should have spelt the end of the settlement at Port Natal, but this did not happen. Because of the good relationship between the settlers and the Zulus, the latter made no attempt to drive the settlers out of the country.

The next few years were a period of steady growth and stability at Port Natal. New settlers arrived and although trade was still the principal source of revenue, farms were being established. In establishing the settlement, the founders believed they were advancing British commercial interests, while at the same time bringing stability to the region, including the Cape's eastern border, and providing a base to combat the slave trade further north along the East African coast. They also knew that nature abhors a vacuum and if Britain did not act, other European powers would. Repeated requests to Britain to establish an administration at Port Natal were ignored. Among those anxious for the governance of Natal to be placed on a proper footing was a former Attorney General of New South Wales, Saxe Bannister. On 12 May 1829, he sent a detailed submission to the Secretary of State for the Colonies pointing out the advantages of bringing the settlement under the jurisdiction of the Crown and the dangers of not doing so. He met with no more success than other petitioners.

One issue had become a cause of friction between the new Zulu monarch and the settlers. Zulus who had fallen foul of Dingane would flee to Natal, where they were given sanctuary. Dingane, unlike Shaka, felt these emigrants should be returned to Zululand.

In 1834 a former naval commander turned missionary, the Revd Captain Allen Francis Gardiner, arrived in Natal. He left an account of his experiences from which he emerges as an absurd figure – the comic wrestles with the tragic. His safari overland from the Cape was filled with a series of self-induced calamities. One of his happier experiences on this journey was the discovery that the people of Pondoland were remarkably honest and theft appeared to be almost unknown, a characteristic that survived in Pondoland until at least the middle of the twentieth century.

On Gardiner's arrival in Natal, such was the fierce heat of his religious fervour that he immediately set off to convert Dingane, who was much changed from the man Cowie had met a few years before. He had put on weight and much of his time was spent with his numerous wives. Attempts to engage him in religious discussion achieved no more than to demonstrate that in theological argument Gardiner was no match for the wily Zulu monarch. Undeterred, he took it upon himself to negotiate a treaty with Dingane, wherein the latter agreed, 'never to molest any of his subjects now at Natal for past offences', in exchange for which Gardiner agreed, 'never more to receive any deserter from his dominions'.[10] By this means, Gardiner obtained temporary consent to undertake missionary work in Zululand. Back at Port Natal and anxious to comply with his treaty, he arrested two men and two women who had recently fled from Zululand. He handcuffed the fugitives and took them back to Dingane, who promised not to kill them. Dingane kept his promise but denied the prisoners any food. Hearing what had happened, Gardiner, in full naval uniform, returned to Dingane to plead for the lives of the prisoners. Neither the plea nor the uniform impressed the king, who remained unmoved. Gardiner concluded the interview by measuring Dingane for a new pair of boots that he intended to have made for the monarch. In order to recover his handcuffs, which he thought might be needed at some future date, he visited the poor starving prisoners, removed their handcuffs, and recommended a prayer to them. They thanked him, and wished him a happy journey. On the way back he chose the site for his mission station in Zululand. It would be called '*Culoola*', to set free!

Worse was to follow. One of the women had three children and Dingane demanded that they be delivered to him. A relative of the children offered to take their place but Gardiner refused, commenting, 'of course it could not be permitted'. So the children were sent off to suffer the same fate as their parents, while Gardiner wrote a letter to Dingane in which he stated: 'If deserters must be killed, let them be killed at once; but if they are to be starved to death, we are resolved that not another individual shall be sent back.'[11]

Dingane responded with a decree that all traders wishing to trade in Zululand needed a permit from Gardiner, who would be responsible for ensuring compliance with the treaty. Gardiner now attempted to lay out a township for Port Natal. Because there was no executive authority to enforce decisions, nothing was to come of this enterprise except that the township was named d'Urban after a successful Governor at the Cape. Realising the need for a civil authority at the settlement, Gardiner decided to visit England in the hope of obtaining an official position for himself.

He arrived in England in May 1836, and shortly thereafter gave evidence to a Select Committee of the House of Commons on the treatment of aborigines in the British Colonies. His was the only evidence given to the Committee about Natal. He repeatedly stressed that the settlers were in grave danger of being slaughtered by Dingane, though there is no evidence that the Zulu monarch had ever contemplated any such action. Gardiner accused the settlers of irritating Dingane by encouraging Zulu women to go to the Port, and of harbouring deserters from the kingdom. Some of the settlers were 'notoriously living in a very immoral state' and many lived in a disgraceful way without chairs or tables. They persuaded villagers to sell them cattle by pretending it was the King's orders. On one occasion a Hottentot told him he had heard a shot being fired and Gardiner was amazed that the settlers had not cut each other's throats a long time ago.

The Committee questioned him about the settlers' behaviour towards the natives.

Question: 'Did the English residents at Natal instigate the natives of the settlement to annoy their Chief Dingana?'

Answer: 'Not in the least.'

Question: 'Then according to your knowledge the English residents at Natal had conducted themselves with propriety as far as relates to the natives?'

Answer: 'As far as relates to the natives.'[12]

From their report, it appears that the Select Committee regarded the settlers as a band of high principled clergymen who from time to time were tempted to neglect their pastoral duties for a little barter on the side. (*See* Appendix 3.) One wonders what the traders and hunters would have thought of the role assigned to them!

The Preamble of the Cape Punishment Act, which followed the Report of the Select Committee, stated, 'Whereas the inhabitants of the country north of the Cape Colony were uncivilised, and offences against them were frequently committed by British subjects with impunity.'[13]

No matter how reprehensible was the absence of household furniture, however scandalous it was that some settlers lived with women to whom they were not married, or frightening the sound of a gunshot might be to a sensitive soul, or miraculous the fact that the settlers had failed for years to sever each other's jugulars, none of this can be offered as concrete evidence for the Committee's assertion that crimes against natives were frequently committed with impunity. No doubt the Committee and the Commons meant well.

While Gardiner was away, refugees from Zululand continued to seek sanctuary in Natal. The settlers, lacking the physical capacity to prevent the entry of these immigrants, and believing it would be inhumane to send them back to certain death, ignored Gardiner's treaty. In April 1837, two tribes fled from Zululand to Natal causing Dingane to suspend all trade. Fearing they might be attacked, the settlers took steps to defend themselves and, with black immigrants, formed several companies of militia, which they called the Port Natal Volunteers. On 26 May they received a message from Dingane who swore that he never had the slightest intention of attacking or destroying the settlement, and that he would never kill a white man. He said Gardiner had recommended that he should stop the trade and had also suggested he should have nothing to do with white men who were all rascals. The Volunteers were disbanded and trade with Zululand resumed. On his return to Natal, Gardiner received a hostile reception from the settlers and moved to a site on the Tongaat River, 20 miles north of Durban. He visited Dingane, who was so delighted with the boots Gardiner had brought him that he made yet another grant of Natal, this time to the British monarch. Gardiner failed to obtain permission to establish a mission station in Zululand.

In 1837 a group of Voortrekkers under Piet Retief found a pass from the Free State through the Drakensberg and descended into Natal. Retief immediately rode on to Port Natal and in the course of his journey of 200 miles to the sea, did not see one living soul. On arrival he was given a cordial welcome, and told the settlers he would report further after seeing Dingane.

Retief told the monarch how the Voortrekkers had defeated Mzilikase and his Matabele warriors and chased them across the Limpopo River into what is now known as Zimbabwe. Dingane listened to this boast without making any comment. Instead he expressed a willingness to cede land to the Voortrekkers, provided Retief and his principal lieutenants came to his kraal unarmed so that the matter might be finalised. Retief accepted the proposal and in February1838, he and his party went unarmed to Dingane's kraal, where they were killed. At the same time, Zulu impis crossed the Tugela and fell upon the Voortrekkers, who were camped in laagers over an area of about 45 miles by 25 miles near the present town of Weenen. Some groups were able to defend themselves but 281 were killed as well as 531 camp followers.[16]

Under pressure from Zulu refugees, and believing in the friendly intentions of the Boers, some of the English settlers at Port Natal unwisely got together a force consisting of sixteen settlers, thirty Hottentots, and

800 Zulus drawn from those who had fled to Natal following the death of Shaka. This contingent crossed the Tugela into Zululand on 16 April 1838. The next day they were surrounded by Dingane's warriors who quickly overwhelmed them. Only four settlers and about two hundred Zulu immigrants escaped the massacre.[17] One of the survivors, Dick King, known to the Zulus as *uDiki*, was to become a legendary figure in Natal colonial history.

To follow their victory, the Zulus crossed into Natal and arrived at Durban on 24 April. The residents took refuge on an island in the middle of the bay while the Zulus wreaked havoc on the settlement, destroying everything – houses, furniture, clothing, cattle, poultry, dogs, cats. Nothing was spared. Presumably satisfied that they had inflicted sufficient punishment on the settlers, after nine days they re-crossed the Tugela into Zululand.[18]

After the massacres around Weenen, the Boers, led by a Transvaaler Andries Pretorius, regrouped, obtained reinforcements from the Highveld, and comprehensively defeated Dingane's warriors at Blood River on 16 December 1838.

On 27 March 1839 yet another petition to annex Natal was addressed to the British Parliament on behalf of the English settlers. (*See* Appendix 4.) An interesting document, it displays an enlightened and practical approach to the region's problems, the implementation of which would have burdened the British Government with little expense, while at the same time it would have avoided many of the difficulties that were later to arise. However, practical suggestions from colonials were not going to disturb the equanimity of British opinion, which continued to be guided by the Preamble to the Cape Punishment Act. The petition was ignored.

After the defeat of Dingane, the Voortrekkers set up a republic, which they called Natalia, and had as its capital the nascent town of Pietermaritzburg, named after the Voortekker leaders Piet Retief and Gert Maritz. About thirty Boers went down to the coast and laid out a village at Congela, on Durban Bay but some distance from the English settlement.[19]

The Boers and the settlers at Durban were soon on a collision course. The Boers believed they alone would decide who could or could not live in Natal, and who would govern the land. The worsening relationship between the two groups was observed by a young Zulu, Ndongeni. He was of royal Zulu blood, and was born in 1826. While still a toddler, his father was put to death by Dingane, so mother and child fled to Port Natal, where they were given sanctuary by Dick King. He later wrote a memoir in Zulu describing the events of those times. In 1905 it was translated into English. This is what he said about the dispute: 'It became evident that the Boer attitude towards the English living in Durban was one of hostility. They said the country had been given to them by Dingane, and yet the English had been given it some time before by Shaka.'[20]

It is often suggested that the grants made by the Zulu monarchs to the English settlers should be ignored because the kings were illiterate and would not have understood the full implications of the documents. In these matters, intention is everything. When William the Conqueror made grants of land to his barons in 1066, neither he nor they were learned people, and none of them could have anticipated the rights and duties imposed on both the State and the citizen by modern land law, and yet ownership of almost every acre of land in England can be traced back to a bequest made by William. When Shaka made a grant to the English settlers, his clear intention was to grant them the right to live in Natal according to their customs. He also believed he retained certain rights over the land. He did, for example, move his armies across Natal to attack the Pondos, and he appointed Fynn chief of the black people living in Natal, rights that were not disputed by the settlers. No doubt there were other issues that still needed agreement, but this does not detract from his intention to give the English traders the right to live and trade in Natal, which was never challenged by him.

The offer made by Dingane to the Voortrekkers was different. He had no intention of permitting them to live in Natal, and when making the offer, had already made plans to kill Retief and expel the Voortrekkers. Besides, as Ndongeni stated, neither Dingane nor his successor Mpande could give that which had already been granted to someone else.

The British Government believed the Voortrekkers still owed allegiance to the Crown, and this obligation was not altered by their emigration. The Republic of Natalia was not recognised, and their dispute with the settlers was regarded as a quarrel between two groups of British citizens. Nonetheless, Sir George Napier, the Governor at the Cape, decided to send eighty men and some artillery under Major Charters to Fort Victoria at Port Natal to keep an eye on things. They landed without opposition on 4 December.[21] They found there was no such place as Fort Victoria, so Charters commandeered Maynard's Store belonging to a Mr Dunn and a warehouse owned by Mr J. Owen Smith. To comply with orders, a small fort called Fort Victoria was built near the northern entrance to the harbour. On 16 December 1838 the British flag was hoisted amidst scenes of jubilation among the settlers.[22] The following month Charters departed for the Cape, leaving Major Jervis in command.

In July 1838 the fortunes of the Voortrekkers received an unexpected boost. Dingane had quarrelled with his brother Mpande, who arrived in Natal with over fifteen thousand followers. The Boers immediately took him under their protection. Full of confidence, they told Major Jervis he and his troops had to leave. Jervis felt he had no choice but to comply and left with his small force on 24 December 1839.[23] The British had decided to await events.

The Voortrekkers now became much more aggressive towards the English settlers. All new immigrants to Natal would have to submit to the jurisdiction of the Volksraad (the Voortrekker Council) and English settlers wishing to travel were required to obtain a pass. One of the first to fall foul of the new 'pass law' was Henry Ogle. One of the original settlers, he had brokered a peace deal between the Voortrekkers and Dingane in which the Zulu monarch agreed to return the cattle and arms his impis had captured in February 1838. In order that he might help the Boers collect the cattle, Ogle travelled to Pietermaritzburg where he was promptly put in gaol for not having a pass.[24]

Dingane was unable to make immediate payment of the full amount due under the settlement resulting in the Volksraad deciding in January 1840 to invade Zululand and destroy Dingane.[25] A kommando under Andries Pretorius was assembled and set off for Zululand. Just before they left, emissaries arrived from Dingane. Despite being diplomats, they were promptly arrested and subsequently shot.[26] Mpande had meanwhile taken his impis into Zululand by a different route, and had met and routed Dingane's force. Dingane fled to Swaziland, where he was murdered. Having triumphed without firing a single shot, Pretorius annexed to the new republic a substantial slice of north-western Zululand,[27] proclaimed Mpande king of the now reduced Zululand, and appropriated some 22,000 cattle to stock the Voortrekkers' new farms.[28]

While Pretorius was away hunting down Dingane, the Volksraad was busy establishing its administration. On 6 February 1840, they published Port Regulations for Natal. Of particular interest to the English settlers at Port Natal was Regulation 14, which stated, 'That a licence of 20 Rds. per annum be taken out for every boat used for the purpose of landing or shipping goods, and that no such licence is to be granted to any person not being a burgher under this government'.[29]

So all trade was to be controlled by the Boers while the British settlers who, by their labour, courage, and enterprise had created and built up that trade, were to be deprived of their livelihood.

During this period a Dutch ship, the *Brazilia,* called at Durban. Though the visit was to have no immediate effect on South Africa, it did create in Boer minds the idea that they might receive support from European powers, while at the same time it alerted the British to the possibility that Port Natal might prove a valuable asset to Britain's European rivals.

Towards the end of 1840, the Boers suspected that the Baca people, who lived to the south of Natal near the source of the Mmzimvubu River, might have stolen some of their cattle. They attacked the Baca, killing about forty tribesmen and appropriating 3,000 head of cattle.[30] Chief Faku, the ruler of neighbouring Pondoland, was alarmed by this aggressive action by the Boers and requested assistance from Britain. Sir George Napier responded by sending Captain Thomas Charlton Smith with two companies of the 27th Foot (the Inniskillings), some guns, a few Cape Mounted Riflemen and Engineers plus 250 civilian workers to Mgazi in Pondoland.

In August 1841, the Volksraad passed a resolution that all wandering or detribalised blacks were to be expelled and settled south of Natal, in the land between the Mzimkulu and Mzimvubu rivers.[31] The possible domino effect of this action posed a direct threat to the Cape border and this could not be ignored by Britain. In December 1841, Captain Smith was ordered to proceed overland to Port Natal to protect Britain's interests. Camp was struck, and soldiers and civilians, with sixty wagons and six hundred oxen to provide transport and food, set off on the long, tortuous journey to Natal.

Several women went with the party. Among them were the wives of Captain Lonsdale and the Revd Archbell, both of whom had three children. A few days into the journey, Mrs Gilligan was delivered of a son and the next day the wife of the Commissariat Issuer gave birth to a 'beautiful daughter'. It was a difficult journey, and when they reached the Mkomazi River, 30 miles south of Durban, Private Devitt collapsed and died of exhaustion. After a brief rest, the column moved on towards Durban. About 25 miles from Durban they met four heavily armed Englishmen who stated that the Boers had threatened to hang them if they did not fight against the advancing column.[32] The following day they met a larger group of English settlers, also heavily armed, who gave the troops a great welcome. No armed Boers were seen as Captain Smith led his column through Durban to the little fort at the northern entrance to the harbour. The Voortrekker flag was lowered and the Union flag was again raised.[33] For his base camp, Smith chose a site about a mile away from Fort Victoria. Two ships, a ninety ton schooner *Mazeppa* and the *Pilot,* arrived and anchored in the harbour. They brought with them supplies of salt beef, pork and biscuits. Also on board were nine would-be settlers who must have been wondering why they had decided to settle in Natal. The English troops were confined to camp and at night they could hear wagons arriving with Boer reinforcements, some coming from as far away as the Transvaal and the Free State.

The Boers assembled a kommando at a camp about 3 miles south of Durban. An ultimatum was sent to Smith demanding his withdrawal from Voortekker territory and, on 23 May 1842, the Boers stole most of the cattle the troops had brought with them.[34] That night Smith launched an attack on the Boer camp, the line of advance being along the edge of the Bay. A howitzer was to follow a deep channel where it would give support to the attackers. Boer scouts tracked the column and when the infantry encountered mangrove trees near Congela, the Boers opened fire on them from concealed positions. Struggling among the mangrove roots and unable to manhandle their guns, the attacking troops were soon in trouble. To add to their difficulties the boat with the howitzer became stuck on a sand bank and was unable to take part in the action. Smith had no option but to call off the attack and retire to his base camp. The two guns were abandoned.[35] The Boers followed the retreating soldiers and attacked the British camp from three sides. The camp might have been overrun had the Boers not been subjected to unexpected cannon fire from the rear. A settler, George Cato, and some friends, had taken two cannon behind the Boer lines and at the opportune moment opened fire.[36] Thrown into confusion by this new development, the Boers beat a hasty retreat. In the engagement, which terminated just before dawn, the British suffered thirty-four killed, sixty-three wounded and six missing.[37] Heavy losses for so small a force.

The next day Smith set about fortifying the camp by forming a laager with his wagons, building earthworks and digging trenches. Not knowing how to send a request for help to Grahamstown, Smith asked George Cato for advice. Cato offered to take the dispatch himself, but Smith felt Cato's services were needed 'on the spot'. Cato suggested that if he was given two troop horses, he would find someone to carry the dispatch to Grahamstown. Suitable horses were found and Cato decided to entrust the task to the settler Richard (Dick) King. Sixteen-year-old Ndongeni was to accompany King.

On the night of the 25 May 1842 two boats manned by George Cato and his brother Christopher quietly rowed the two men, with their horses swimming behind, across the bay to begin their epic ride. Ahead of them lay 600 miles of uncharted land, much of it ruled by chiefs whose co-operation was essential. They had to cross hundreds of rivers, traverse forests and wide deep valleys, which had over millennia been gouged out of the land by rivers. Even today, these are wild and inaccessible places.

Their first great challenge was to elude the Boers, who had picked up their trail and were in hot pursuit, chasing them as far as the Mkomazi River. Near the Mzimkulu River, they were stopped by some Baca, who thought they were Boers. Knowing their language, King persuaded them that this was not the case and they were allowed to continue. They now had to face the natural hazards of leopards, crocodiles, hippos and the venomous snakes that abounded along the coast and in the river valleys. With the most difficult part of the journey completed, Ndongeni fell ill and King was obliged to leave him at the Mission Hospital at Buntingville.[38]

The day after King's departure, the Boers attacked and captured Fort Victoria, killing two soldiers and taking prisoner sixteen of Smith's men. Among the settlers who had fought alongside the soldiers, Charlie Adams was killed while ten others were captured. In this group was George Cato. The Boers seized and plundered the two ships in the harbour and in the process captured several cannon and a large quantity of stores. Though the ballast was removed from the *Mazeppa* and the Master was taken into custody, they did not remove the rudder and permitted ten of the crew and two ship's boys to remain on board. They failed to notice that Christopher Cato, an experienced seaman, had passed himself off as a member of the crew. The settlement's civilians were incarcerated near the Boer camp. One who attempted to escape was shot dead. The ten civilians who had been captured fighting alongside the British were to receive special treatment.

On 31 May the Boers again attacked the British camp. With better fortifications, the attack, which lasted most of the day, was beaten off. During the day the women and children in the camp were constantly exposed to enemy fire. Subsequently it was arranged under a flag of truce that seven women and eighteen children be transferred to the *Mazeppa*.

Without the stores from the two ships, the lifting of the siege acquired greater urgency. Lest King should fail to reach Grahamstown, it was now vital to arrange an alternative plea for help. On the *Mazeppa* food was surreptitiously saved from the rations supplied by the Boers. Citing laundry needs, extra fresh water was taken on. The women adopted the routine of hanging their washing over the bulwarks. So meticulous were they in their household chores, that they even took out the sails and dried the dew off them. The ship's longboat floated idly astern. An air of peaceful domesticity pervaded the scene. Ever cautious, the Boers had placed an eighteen-pounder cannon about fifty yards away, sighted on the bulwarks of the *Mazeppa*.

On 10 June, the wind changed to the southwest. That day the women washed the blankets and hung them out to dry over the port bulwark. All of a sudden the Boers noticed the sails were going up and the ship was underway. They rushed to the cannon, but before it could be fired, the ship had rounded a corner and was heading down the channel towards the harbour entrance.

Christopher Cato, assisted by Isaac Craig, the ship's carpenter, had threaded the ropes that raised the sails below decks. On command, the anchor was slipped while below decks every available person, man, woman and child hauled frantically on the ropes to raise the sails. Cato stationed himself on the bow while Craig steered.

Though clear of the big cannon, the ship still had to pass on her port side about eighty Boers at the harbour entrance. They were armed with elephant guns and a four-pounder cannon. The cannon fired ball after ball at the ship and there was a continuous roar of fire from the elephant guns but the ship sailed on, out of the harbour and into the open sea. Once out of range of the shore guns, she hove to.

The women, when hanging the blankets out to dry over the port bulwarks, had placed mattresses behind them, which had absorbed the Boers' fire. Having reached the safety of the open sea, the damage to the ship was assessed. When leaving the harbour the longboat had been swamped and sank. The sails were riddled with holes, the rigging torn and the mattresses and other padding filled with bullets. Ballast-free, the ship rolled about, resulting in almost everyone on board suffering appalling bouts of seasickness. Nonetheless, the men and women immediately set to repairing the sails and rigging, while the children picked the bullets out of the mattresses. In five hours, much of the damage had been repaired and it was decided to sail before the wind to Delagoa Bay, where they might meet a British warship.

They had food and water for four days. If the wind changed, they would rapidly die of thirst and starvation. If the wind increased, the ship, without its ballast, would probably founder and all would drown. Luckily, the wind held fair and by the night of 13 June they had reached Delagoa Bay. There were no British ships in port and none arrived over the next few days, so, nothing daunted, they took on food, water and ballast and then set sail for Algoa Bay – 1,000 miles away. When they reached Port Natal, the siege was over.[39]

Dick King had ridden the 600 miles to Grahamstown in just eleven days and, on 24 June 1842, the first warship had arrived at Durban to be followed by another the following day. On 26 June, British troops disembarked and in the skirmish that followed two men were killed. One, Private McCaffrey, when struck in the breast, refused medical attention uttering the immortal last words, 'Sure, never mind me. Attend to the man that's kilt.'[40]

The Boers offered little resistance and soon melted away; the siege had been raised. The conditions at the British camp were appalling. Twenty-six sick and wounded, many with arms and legs missing and suffering from dysentery, lay in a trench four to five feet deep with uncured horse hides providing the only shelter. The stench from the hides and rotting offal was horrible. There was no sanitation. Captain Lonsdale, who had been wounded and whose wife was on the *Mazeppa*, had lain there for twenty-seven days 'without so much as a jacket on'. One woman, who refused to leave her husband when the siege began, told a relieving officer that, because of the incessant fire from the Boers, she had not dared to stand up for nearly a month.

When the siege began Captain Smith ordered that all cattle in the camp be killed and following local practice their meat was salted and dried in the sun. By preserving their meat in this way, its shelf life was considerably extended. When this source of food was exhausted, they were forced to eat their horses. After the loss of the *Mazeppa* and the *Pilot,* daily rations were reduced to 6oz. meat and 4oz. biscuit dust. When relief came all but one of the horses had been killed and eaten. The sole surviving horse was found sitting on his haunches, too weak to get up.[41]

Captain Bell, commander of one of the two relieving ships, left this quaint description of Captain Smith: 'He was very much reduced by the hardships he had endured; his rigging much chafed and out of order, but his interior remained sterling steel.'[42]

Joseph Cato and the carpenter Isaac Craig have never received the recognition that was due to them, a comment that applies equally to the women and children on the *Mazeppa*. Tough, resourceful and loyal are adjectives that apply to pioneer women. These women, two of whom were nursing six-week-old babies, displayed courage, determination, and stamina. The same can be said of the discipline and fortitude of the children.

Those residents who were captured by the Boers while fighting with the British, H. Parkins, D. Toohey, B. Schwikkard, H. Ogle, J. Hogg, J. Douglas, G.C. Cato, F. McCabe, S. Benningfield and F. Armstrong, were kept in stocks at Congela for a week, after which they were sent to Pietermaritzburg, where during the day they were chained two by two and exhibited to the public – objects of abuse and vilification. Their nights were spent chained together with their feet in stocks in a locked room eight feet by nine feet. On 7 June 1842 they sent a petition to the Voortrekker leader Andries Pretorius in which they pointed out that they had committed no crime and continued,

> We humbly submit to you and hope you will take into consideration and kindly ease us of being chained during the day and of the intolerable stench caused by our being obliged to ease ourselves inside the *Tronk* [cell], this with being confined with closed windows which may soon cause a disease fatal to us and spread through the whole town. We sincerely hope you will ease us of the above grievances and we hereby promise you with the help of God to submit patiently to His will and your orders and you will have no cause to repent of your kind indulgence. We are your humble Petitioners.[43]

Nothing was done to relieve their suffering until the British troops landed at Port Natal on 26 June. During the siege, the farms, homes and businesses of the British residents were looted by the Boers. By their own admission, they removed all the cattle and horses and took seventy to eighty wagon loads of goods from Durban to Pietermaritzburg.[44]

A few days after King had left him at the Buntingville Mission, Ndongeni saw the British warships making their way up the coast and he knew uDiki must have succeeded in his mission. He duly recovered from his illness and made his way back to Durban to receive an emotional welcome from King and his friends. After the epic ride, Dick King was given the further name – *Mlamulankunzi*, literally, the separator of fighting bulls, or the peacemaker. In later years Ndongeni was given a farm by the Natal Government to mark the appreciation they felt for his contribution to Dick King's ride.

Three weeks after the relief, the Pietermaritzburg Volksraad, despite vigorous opposition from their women folk, decided to submit to British rule.[45] Col Cloete, commander of the relief force, negotiated a treaty with the Voortrekkers, who immediately began to search for ways of avoiding their obligations under the treaty. They refused to return the horses, cattle and goods they had stolen and troubles were fermenting between them and the blacks. The result was that in 1843, Britain annexed Natal. Though the paramount British official in South Africa remained the Governor in Cape Town, a Lieutenant-Governor was appointed to administer Natal. The first person to hold this post was Martin West, an Anglo-Indian.

Although there was no pressure on them to do so, most of the Boers went back over the Drakensberg to join their compatriots in the Free State and Transvaal. By 1848 there were about sixty Boer families in Natal, and those who stayed were given the same rights as the English settlers and, in addition, were permitted to keep their farms, which were usually about 6,000 acres in extent.

When Britain annexed Natal they made it clear that the colony should become self-supporting as soon as possible. It was expensive to administer a colony, so, in the hope that it might become self-sufficient and able to defend itself, British settlers were encouraged to go to Natal. Various schemes were set up with the principal groups arriving between 1849 and 1852, though further settlers continued to arrive throughout the nineteenth century.

One such scheme was set up by Joseph Charles Byrne, a Dubliner, who, although not known for his honesty, was a persuasive speaker and opportunist. He had never been to Natal, yet he toured Great Britain giving glowing accounts of the land and in the process persuaded 2,500 people to emigrate there. Settlers were promised that each family would receive a twenty-acre farm plus five acres for each child and a half-acre in the local village. Each of these farms would have water, arable land, pasturage and timber and be close to markets.

The voyage, which was supposed to take six weeks, took twice as long in slow, heavily laden ships. At the end of this grim voyage, in which people died and babies were born, the settlers found that their trials, far from being over, were just beginning. Because there was no jetty in Durban, they had to wade ashore. Those who had difficulty, especially the women in their long skirts, had to be carried.

To get their possessions ashore proved most difficult and much was lost or damaged – the most serious catastrophe being the sinking of one of the larger ships, the *Minerva*, on rocks near the anchorage. Although the passengers were saved, much of what they had brought with them was lost. These were not luxury goods but such vital items as tools, cooking utensils and clothing. One woman, having been saved from the sinking *Minerva*, went into labour shortly after getting ashore and gave birth to her second son under a tarpaulin on the beach. The landing place was just over a mile from Durban. One settler left this record of his first sighting of that town.

> I landed with my father in 1850. After landing, we walked a mile or so when we came to a man standing alongside the road with a flour-sack apron on. My mother said, 'Can you tell me, sir, how far is it to the town of Durban?' He replied, 'God bless you, mum, you're in the middle of Durban now.'[46]

Among those Byrne settlers were a young tenant farmer from Scotland, Duncan McKenzie, and his wife Margaret. Like so many others, they had lost nearly all their possessions to the sea at Durban. They had been allocated land at Richmond, approximately 65 miles inland. There was no road to Richmond and the wagon journey there was slow and difficult. One glance at the allocated land was sufficient to convince them that there was no prospect of earning a living from it. The holding was too small, there was no infrastructure and the place was too far from potential markets. They had no choice but to move back to Pinetown, near Durban, where Duncan was able to obtain work as a pick and shovel man on the road being built to Pietermaritzburg. He increased his income by doing piecework and with hard graft it was not long before he was made a superintendent over a section of the road. By the exercise of strict economy, he and Margaret saved every penny they could and, after seven years, they had £300, enough to buy a farm, Lion's Bush, near Fort Nottingham in the Natal Midlands.

This farm, sold to them by a Voortekker returning to the Highveldt, had a wattle and daub thatched cottage but was otherwise undeveloped. To buy the necessary livestock and equipment to make the farm viable, Duncan continued to work on the roads. Children came along at regular intervals, their first son Donald being born in February 1851, followed by two daughters and a second son, Archibald, in 1858. A third son, Duncan, was born at Lion's Bush in August, 1859, followed by two more boys. Not only was Margaret responsible for bringing up the children but in the absence of her husband, much of the day-to-day work on the farm was done by her.

Once he had raised sufficient capital, Duncan left the roads department and went into business transporting goods to the Free State and the Transvaal by ox wagon, the only viable means of transporting goods in those days. Virtually all the exports and imports for the Free State and Transvaal were shipped through Durban, so there was plenty of business. But this was no sinecure and many were the difficulties and dangers. Anyone who has tried to plough a straight furrow with two oxen will understand how difficult it must be to control a team of sixteen pulling a wagon. Great skill and nerve was a prerequisite for all drivers. The oxen had at all times to be fit and strong. Each one had a name and a particular position in the team. The driver had to know the name of each ox, its position and what was required of each animal, while at the same time navigating the wagon across country where there were no roads or bridges. Swollen rivers would require that the oxen should first swim across the river and once on the far bank, they would be inspanned and as many as three spans (forty-eight oxen) might be used to pull the wagon across, all the time care being taken to ensure there was no water damage to the goods. Any mistake could mean potentially catastrophic loss or damage to the goods or wagon. As always, those receiving the goods were in a hurry to receive the consignment so any delay could be expensive. In these tough competitive conditions, McKenzie thrived. The discovery of the Barberton goldfields brought more work and more challenges as heavy machinery had to be transported over very difficult terrain. McKenzie was up to the task and established a reputation as a transport rider without peer. But it was not only the wagon trains that were doing well; the farm, with astute and enlightened management, was also prospering.

The eldest son, Donald, received little formal education. In his younger years he had to help his mother on the farm and by the time he was fifteen, he had joined his father transport riding and trading. The other children were able to have more formal schooling, which of necessity required going to a boarding school. The boys went to the newly established Hilton College near Pietermaritzburg which, apart from teaching academic subjects, placed great emphasis on the importance of integrity in all things. Archibald, after showing considerable promise at school, studied medicine in Edinburgh and on his return to Durban achieved great renown as a surgeon, general practitioner and public benefactor. In the Boer War he served as a major in the Natal Medical Corps and in the Great War as a colonel in the South African Medical Corps.

Duncan junior (references to Duncan McKenzie will from now on refer to the son) was a good rugby player but it was as a horseman that he was really talented. He took part in the various equestrian competitions then popular among the rural settler communities. He was, from his schooldays, an excellent polo player and at country race meetings rode in steeplechases and on the flat. He was able to kick a rugby ball over the posts while mounted! Like other colonial children, he learnt to swim at an early age and was a strong swimmer. In the early days of the colony people had, of necessity, to wash in rivers and there being no bridges, often the only way of crossing a river was to swim.

Duncan left school when he was sixteen and decided to follow his father and elder brother into farming. Like other members of the family, he went transport riding to acquire the necessary capital to enable him to farm. Though railways were beginning to make their presence felt in South Africa, there were still opportunities for the wagon trains. Like his father and brother before him, Duncan soon became known for the speed and reliability of his wagon trains and his ability to transport the heaviest and most difficult loads. Goods were carried not only to Bloemfontein, Johannesburg and Barberton, but as far afield as Rhodesia. For his services, customers were prepared to pay a premium, and after six years transport riding, he was able to go farming on his own account in 1881. He brought to farming the same meticulous attention to detail and striving for excellence that he had employed with his wagon trains. He married a local girl, Katherine Agnes McArthur, in 1883. He bred cattle, sheep and horses as well as selling timber, hay and dairy products. He always sought to improve his stock and did not hesitate to import the best for breeding. Because of its altitude, his farm was ideally suited to the breeding of horses and many of South Africa's best racehorses were bred by him. He never took any interest in politics.

Living in the Natal Midlands, Duncan was invited to join the Volunteer regiment, the Natal Carbineers, and did so as a trooper in 1880. In 1885 he became a lieutenant, in 1887 a captain, and in 1897 he was promoted to major. Of medium build, he had a commanding appearance, which impressed all who met him. It was not only his appearance that drew respect. Characteristically, his soldiering had the same qualities of attention to detail and striving for excellence that marked his farming and transport riding. In addition he had learnt from the latter how to read the lie of the land ahead, an essential skill when no maps were available, and the long hours in the saddle had taught him just what could be expected of men and horses. He was a strict disciplinarian and some of his men gave him the nickname 'Shaka', a reference to the stern discipline that monarch had imposed on his impis. However, they also knew of his absolute fairness, his strict sense of duty and loyalty to them. In return, he received their affection and respect.

In 1899 he and his wife visited Britain where he bought thoroughbred breeding stock and South Devon cattle. While there, he received a telegram stating that war with the Boers was imminent and he was to report for duty as soon as possible. He caught the first available ship home. It was fortunate that he arrived back too late to be incarcerated by the Boers in Ladysmith with the rest of his unit.[47]

Apart from the Byrne Settlers, other groups settled in Natal, one such being thirty-five families from Germany who arrived at Port Natal in 1848 under a scheme to grow cotton. Unfortunately the cotton seed they brought was infected with boll weevil, which resulted in the collapse of the enterprise. Among these settlers was a blacksmith, Georg Friedrich Rethmann, with his wife and child. His wife died shortly after they arrived in Natal and his child a couple of years later. In 1851 he married Barbara Field, a schoolteacher who had come out with a group of English settlers. Like many of the settlers, Georg found it difficult to obtain regular employment and at various times worked as a blacksmith, farmer, labourer, a 'professor' of music, musician, engineer, piano tuner and turner. To provide for a growing family Barbara taught, often having to create the school where she was to teach. Their eldest son John Frederick 'Jack' Rethman was born in 1852. As was the case for most settlers, life was not easy for the family. Lack of funds resulted in Jack having to leave school at an early age and take work as a messenger for a firm in Durban.

When he was sixteen he and a friend took mules loaded with goods into Pondoland, then an independent country south of Natal, intending to barter them for cattle. They were able to exchange the goods but just before they set out for home, the cattle were looted in fighting that had broken out between the clans Mzizi and Madiba (Mandela's people). Though his companion returned to Natal, Jack pursued the spoor of the cattle until he found them in the Xesebe country. There Chief Jojo made the raiders return the cattle and in addition gave the young man a horse as a gift. Using the contacts made, Jack (known as Mxhakaza, the Confounder) went on to build up an extensive trading business in Pondoland, which continued until the Apartheid government expelled whites from the territory a hundred years later. He was one of the pioneer farmers in southern Natal and in 1890 was elected to the Natal Legislative Assembly. He had joined the local Volunteers in 1884 and rose step by step until he was appointed to the command of the Border Mounted Rifles in 1895, with the rank of major.

In 1824, when Lt Farewell established his little trading post, Natal was an unpopulated land approximately half the size of England. Seventy-five years later, it was a well ordered little country the short history of which had been packed with incident.

The assassination of King Shaka and the accession of Dingane brought an influx of black people seeking sanctuary. The Voortrekkers had come and gone and the arrival in mid-century of approximately 5,000 European settlers brought not only more people but with them, the demand for the creation of schools, hospitals, roads, piped water and other infrastructure the modern world takes for granted. Agriculture also changed and now meant more than just living on a farm and shooting any available game. Crops and livestock had to be efficiently produced and marketed.

On the colony's northern frontier, a dispute as to who should succeed Mpande, the Zulu monarch, resulted in a bloody civil war in 1856, in which the half-brothers Cetshwayo and Mbuyazi fought for paramountcy in the kingdom. Cetshwayo emerged victorious, defeating his opponent in a battle fought near the lower Tugela River. The bodies of many of those killed were washed down the river and into the sea from whence they were carried south by the Mozambique current to be deposited on the beaches of Natal.

In 1879 there was the trauma of the Zulu War, which included the famous battles of Isandlwana and Rorke's Drift. Natal had never sought to acquire Zulu territory and lived on good terms with its northern neighbour. In contrast, there was constant friction between the Transvaal and Zululand. When in 1876 the Transvaal attempted to impose taxes on Zulus in disputed territories, the Zulu king Cetshwayo began to prepare for war.

As we have seen, in April 1877 Britain took over the administration of the Transvaal. At the same time, a new Governor arrived at the Cape, Sir Bartle Frere, who was also appointed Commissioner of Native Affairs for the whole of southern Africa. He had had a distinguished career in India and had acquired, in his opinion at any rate, some experience of Africa, having four years previously visited the Sultan of the Island of Zanzibar. Sir Bartle believed that it was his duty to create a federation in South Africa. It seems that he had come to the conclusion that war with Zululand was necessary if the desired federation was to come into being. The prospect of war delighted many British officers anxious to distinguish themselves and thereby gain promotion.[48]

To the people of Natal, this talk of war was alarming. In an attempt to settle the matter peacefully, the Governor, Sir Henry Bulwer, suggested that an enquiry be held into the boundary dispute between the Transvaal and Zululand. The proposal was accepted by the British and the Zulus.

Michael Gallwey, the Natal Attorney General, was appointed chairman of the commission, the other members being John Shepstone, and Lt Col A. Durnford. In Britain, in the Transvaal, and in the Cape it was assumed that the commission would find in favour of the Boers, but they did not take into account the integrity of the commissioners. In their report submitted on 20 June 1878, their main conclusions were in favour of the Zulus. The finding does not appear to have had any influence on Sir Bartle. Nonetheless, he took the precaution of not releasing its findings until war was inevitable.

A few weeks later, two wives of a Zulu chief, Sirayo, fled to Natal with their lovers. The adulterers were pursued by two of Sirayo's sons, Mehlokazulu and Mkumbikazulu, who captured them, and took them back to Zululand where they were executed. This violation of the colony's frontier, coupled with the brutal penalty, did much to quell criticism of Frere's policies and to foster the belief that perhaps the proposed campaign might bring future security.

It was not disclosed to the public that Sirayo was visiting King Cetshwayo at the time of the raid into Natal, neither had prior knowledge of it, and both recognised that the violation of the border was wrong. Initially, the British demanded the return of the culprits but subsequently agreed that a fine of 500 cattle be paid. When Cetshwayo asked for time to collect the cattle from Sirayo's tribe, Frere ignored the request. By the beginning of December 1879, Sir Bartle felt the army was ready to act and on 11 December, served an ultimatum on the Zulus. The terms were insulting and compliance impossible. The inevitable non-compliance provided Sir Bartle with an excuse for the invasion of Zululand. Now that the findings of the Boundaries Commission were irrelevant, Frere released their report.

Despite British attempts to spread alarm among the Natal settlers, their attitude towards the war was often ambivalent, as can be seen from the diary of a volunteer, Fred Symons, who describes how one day during the campaign, while his troop was resting on a hill, an officer came up to him and said,

> 'Well, Symons! Wouldn't you like to see this slope covered with dead Zulus?
> I replied, 'No Sir, I wouldn't!' '
> Why not?' said he.
> 'Because we have no quarrel with the Zulus and I consider this war an unjust one.'
> He turned and walked away without a word.[49]

The Zulu king, Cetshwayo, said after the war:

> This war was forced on me and the Zulus. We never desired to fight against the English. The Boers were the real cause of that war. They were continually worrying the Zulus about their land, and threatening

to invade the country if we did not give them land, and this forced us to get our forces ready to resist, and consequently the land became disturbed, and the Natal people, mistakenly, believed we were preparing against them.[50]

Robert Samuelson, who knew Cetshwayo well, said of him, 'He was a great friend of all white people, except the Boers, who were always filibustering in Zululand. He was kind and liberal to a degree.'[51]

Though eventually victorious, the war proved humiliating for Britain, and certainly did nothing to promote the federation Sir Bartle sought.

While these events were occupying the British, that wily old tortoise Kruger was biding his time in the Transvaal. Let the British secure the Transvaal borders and then perhaps another federation, with another ruler. Another Transvaal personality, General Piet Joubert, less subtle in his choice of language, said in a speech at the end of January, 1879, 'If the Zulus enter Natal and kill every Englishman, woman and child I shall say that the Lord is righteous.'[52]

The Zulu War and other disturbances in neighbouring states had resulted in a flood of further refugees into Natal, which the government accommodated by allocating land to the different clans or tribes while at the same time granting corridors of land to white farmers to separate potential warring factions.

Many Indians had come to Natal under three-year contracts of service, and, liking the country, they stayed on after their contracts had expired. The discovery of gold in the Transvaal provided a big economic boost for Natal as well as drawing more immigrants there from Great Britain and its colonies. Railways were built to the Free State and the Transvaal and, despite the obstructionist attitude of the Kruger regime, it was through Durban that much of their trade passed.

When the first settlers arrived, the entrance to the harbour was little more than four feet deep. By 1854 this had been increased to six-and-a-half feet. This, however, was not sufficient for most ocean-going ships, so goods and passengers had to be transported to the shore in lighters. In the 1860s after a north easterly gale, young boys would run down to the beach to see which ships had been blown ashore and to swim out to any wrecks – wonderful fun for young boys, but not for anyone else. Over the years, works steadily increased the depth of the harbour entrance until by the 1890s it had been increased at high tide to nineteen feet, deep enough to take all but the largest ships. By 1908 the entrance was deep enough to take any ship and Durban was southern Africa's premier harbour, handling more cargo than all the others combined. It had become one of the great ports of the world.

Durban was also the largest town in Natal and in July 1899, its population was 41,259, of whom 19,762 were of European descent, 9,562 were of Indian descent and there were 11,935 blacks, most of whom were Zulus and among whom there were only 601 women. This last remarkable statistic will be referred to again.

The capital, Pietermaritzburg, was about 50 miles inland from Durban and although much smaller than the port, it was a town of substantial size. One hundred miles north of Pietermaritzburg, on the Klip River, and at the junction of the railways from the Transvaal and the Free State, was the little town of Ladysmith. The construction of the railways to the Free State and the Transvaal had brought a mini boom to Ladysmith, which was reinforced by the British establishing an army base near the town. North of Ladysmith, an extensive coalfield had been discovered, which not only created little communities around the mines, but breathed life into the pretty little towns of Dundee and Newcastle nearer the Transvaal border.

Elsewhere in the Natal hinterland, villages had come into being to serve the needs of the local farmers, who all the while were making the land more productive. Sport provided the principal recreation in the colony and almost everyone either played, or took an interest in, rugby, cricket and tennis. As horses played such a key role in their lives, horse racing was popular and equestrian sports such as polo had a substantial following without the elitist connotations found elsewhere.

In 1899 the threat of invasion by the Boer republics hung over the colony, which had built up an efficient and disciplined corps of Volunteers. However, this force was tiny when compared with the superbly armed and equipped kommandos, which now threatened to drive them into the sea. It is not surprising that they welcomed Karri Davies' and Woolls Sampson's decision to form a mounted regiment to assist in the defence of their country.

5

The Opposing Forces

The Imperial Light Horse, on parade in Pietemaritzburg.

The Boer Republics

In the course of their many wars, the Boers had developed a form of conscription, known as the kommando system, which ensured that a formidable army of Volunteers could be rapidly mobilised. All the men between the ages of sixteen and sixty were obliged to join their local kommando and, on a call to arms, had to assemble immediately at a prearranged place with a horse, a rifle and food for eight days. They were unpaid, and had no uniforms so wore whatever took their fancy. Apart from attending occasional shooting competitions, they received no military training – but they had a lifestyle that made them formidable foes. The ability to shoot game was often an essential survival skill, and this made them superb marksmen, able to hit a moving target, gauge distance and adjust their sights appropriately. They were able to conceal themselves from approaching prey, or approach their target without being seen or heard. Because much of their life was spent in the saddle, they were good horsemen who also understood what their horses needed by way of water, food and rest. Their horses were trained not to wander off when dismounted, which avoided the detailing of men to oversee picket lines whenever they went into action. When it was necessary for the men to stay in one place for any length of time, family and friends would visit in their wagons, bringing with them servants and provisions. However, when deployed against an enemy they could move quickly without a burdensome commissariat.

The command structure was simple. The smallest unit was the corporalship of about twenty-five men. Five or six of these units would combine into a field-cornetcy, a similar number of which would constitute the district kommando. A corporal, a field-cornet and a kommandant in the Boer army were roughly the equivalent of a lieutenant, a major and a colonel in the Imperial army. In command of the whole army was the kommandant-general, who was assisted by a number of combat-generals. The men elected their officers and all had a right to be heard in a *krygsraad* or war council. This was democratic but not good for discipline. The problem was aggravated by the individualism of the burghers who, while they could be trusted to exploit opportunities in battle without waiting for orders, would also refuse to obey orders with which they disagreed. There was no legal penalty for refusing to obey.

When the Boer forces mobilised in September 1899, the Transvaal kommandos mustered about 32,000 men and the Free State about 22,000. In addition to these, the uniformed Transvaal Police supplied 300 mounted officers and men and 600 officers and men on foot.

Approximately 2,000 foreign mercenaries, known as the Uitlander Korps, served in the Boer army and formed themselves into appropriately named units, the Legion of France, the Hollander Corps, the American Volunteers, the Irish Brigade, the Russian Scouts, the German Corps, the Italian Corps and the Scandinavian Corps. The Boers did not have a high opinion of their Uitlander Korps.

The diary of a young Boer girl, Freda Schlosberg, includes a description of a visit by these warriors to the family farm.

Members of the Uitlander Korps have been arriving all day, carrying bundles of luggage, rifles and ammunition. The detachment consists of two or three hundred mercenaries – Hollanders, Germans, Frenchmen, Americans, Italians, Hungarians – all rough-looking, common men, evidently from the lowest classes. They are armed not only with the usual rifles and revolvers, but also with swords, daggers, etc., the Italians especially with homemade stilettos. Some of the korps were Uitlanders from the Transvaal; others had come from abroad through Delagoa Bay.

The first thing they did after settling down was to steal some of our fowls, geese and ducks; then they took most of the wood lying in our yard without even asking permission. They are undisciplined and unprincipled, and under no control whatever by their officers. Later in the day they broke into the cattle camp of one of our neighbouring Boers, Mr Erasmus, on the excuse that tents must be pitched there. When Mr Erasmus, who is also acting Field Cornet of the district, remonstrated with them, they answered, 'We are our own masters and do what we please'. In the afternoon some of them went to the river to practice shooting and they nearly shot the old Boer guarding the bridge.

Next morning they went out in groups to the neighbouring farms, stealing poultry, pigs, sheep, and whatever they could lay their hands on. A few who remained in the camp had a terrible quarrel about a stolen rifle. A German was about to shoot an Italian but was stopped by the others. They all behave outrageously and declare repeatedly that they can do whatever they wish. Their presence near our farm is terrifying.[1]

Some modern writers have confused the Uitlander Korps with Imperial Volunteer Regiments such as the Imperial Light Horse and the South African Light Horse, who fought on the other side and whose character and demeanour was very different.

Though almost all the burghers had their own rifles, which they could use if they so chose, the government was willing to sell them the latest new rifles, at cost. If a burgher was too poor to buy a rifle, one was given to him. Most chose to arm themselves with the 1898 Gewehr pattern German Mauser. Having a 0.275 inch calibre, it fired a bullet smaller than the .303 inch British rifles, used smokeless cartridges, had better sights and a longer effective range (about 1500 yards) than any other rifle. To these advantages it added the innovation of having its cartridges inserted into the magazine in clips of five. This gave it a significantly quicker firing rate than other rifles, which required that cartridges be inserted into the magazine one by one. At that time, the Mauser was the best rifle in the world. It is estimated that in September 1899, there were about 43,000 Mausers in South Africa, 38,000 being in the Transvaal and 5,000 in the Free State. As most of the Free State burghers used Mausers it must be assumed that they were supplied from Transvaal stocks. In addition, the Transvaal had approximately 34,000 Martini-Henri and other rifles. This apparent over-supply of rifles appears to have been intended for the arming of rebels in the Cape Colony.

The Republics took care to acquire plentiful supplies of small arms ammunition and it is estimated that by October 1899, they had upwards of seventy million rounds in stock, including at least twenty-five million rounds of Mauser ammunition that the British had, in September, allowed to pass through their blockade at Delagoa Bay.

In their preparations for war, the Republics did not neglect the artillery. German instructors were brought out to train what was to become a disciplined, efficient and uniformed unit, firing the best guns in the world. The Transvaal trained a corps of 800 artillerymen and the Free State 400. Recent gun imports by the Transvaal were:

Four 155 mm. (6 inch) Creusot fortress guns which threw a 94 lb. shell up to 11,000 yards – these were the famous 'Long Toms'.
Four 120 mm (4.7 inch) Krupp howitzers.
Six 75 mm Creusot quick-firing field guns.
Eight 75 mm Krupp quick-firing, high velocity field guns.
Five 75 mm Vickers-Maxim quick firing mountain guns.

At least twenty-two Vickers-Maxim automatic guns (pom-poms) firing a 1 lb shell with a bursting charge.
At least thirty-one Maxim machine guns of .303 or .45 calibre.
Fourteen 75 mm Krupp quick-firing, high velocity field guns.

The Free State had fourteen 75mm Krupp quick-firing, high velocity field guns. Unlike the Transvaal, the Free State used black powder.

Both republics had other guns, which were obsolescent to varying degrees. All in all, they had about sixty or seventy pieces of modern artillery and about thirty older guns. They had not neglected to buy ammunition for the guns at the time of purchase. In addition, a factory was set up to manufacture shells in the Transvaal under the supervision of two members of the Creusot Company.

An effective Intelligence Department was organised and experts were employed to prepare detailed maps of the areas where the war was likely to be fought. As a result, when the Boers went to war they had the benefit of excellent intelligence and good maps.[2]

The Boers were well mounted on locally bred horses. For the best part of 200 years, the Dutch had been importing Arab horses into the Cape. Their progeny developed over the years into a distinct type later known as the *Boereperd*. They were tough, sure-footed, possessed of almost limitless stamina, and were fast over country. They were smaller than English horses and for this reason they were often described as ponies – but they bore no resemblance to the British native pony breeds.

The Boers did have their weaknesses. Their discipline was poor. In Natal they would be fighting in country that was strange to many of them. They could expect hostility from the black population and, because of their belief that everyone should speak Dutch, few could speak Zulu or any of the other African languages. There were some who, having become urbanised, were initially poor marksmen. Past victories over poorly armed tribesmen, as well as their easy victory over the British in the War of 1879/1880, had resulted in over-confidence.

Natal

Though Britain had granted the colony its own government in 1893, any decision by the Colonial Government required the consent of the British Government. This inevitably resulted in the British being not a little arrogant in their dealings with the colonials, as can be seen from Alfred Milner's refusal to permit the Colonial Governments to take any part in negotiations with the Boer Republics.

The Prime Minister of Natal from June 1899 to August 1903 was Lt Col Albert Hime. He had studied engineering at Edinburgh University and on qualifying, joined the Royal Engineers. His ability was soon noticed and shortly before the Zulu War (1879) he was appointed Colonial Engineer to Natal, a position he filled with distinction. When Natal was granted responsible government, he was elected to the Legislature and in 1897, became Minister of Lands and Works, a portfolio he retained when he became Prime Minister. After the outbreak of war and the imposition of martial law, the British abandoned any pretence of regard for colonial opinion. In spite of this, and many other difficulties facing them, the Natal Government was able to keep the machinery of state running efficiently throughout the war.

Natal had, from its earliest days, relied on Volunteers for its defence. With its small tax base, and needing every penny it could get to build up the infrastructure of the colony, there was no question of the Natal Government being able to maintain a regular army, or to spend lavishly on armaments.

In September 1899, the commander of the Natal Volunteers was Col William Royston. William came to Natal with his parents in 1872 and joined the Natal Carbineers as a trumpeter when he was sixteen. His ability as a soldier was soon recognised and by 1881 he was in command of that regiment. In 1889 he was appointed Commandant of Volunteers. An intelligent and reliable man, he was respected by all, one contemporary describing him as a 'fine Christian gentleman'.[3]

His Chief of Staff, Lt Col Hilmar Bru de Wold, never swore on Sundays. Born in Trondheim, he had arrived at Natal as a twenty-year-old in 1862, not on an immigrant ship, but on a Norwegian naval vessel. Following a quarrel with an officer, he decided to desert, and swam ashore when the ship anchored off Durban. He walked down the coast seeking work as a labourer in the sugar fields. At Ifafa he had the good fortune to be offered work by John Bazley, a pioneer sugar farmer. He fell in love with his employer's daughter Sarah and they were married in 1871. By 1882 he was farming on his own account. A short, wiry man, he never lost his seaman's rolling gait or his strong Nordic accent. His choice of words and expressions was quaint and unconsciously humorous even when he was being serious. When reprimanding a delinquent he added a collection of imaginative and colourful swear words, which were delivered with a furtive smile flickering about his face. The result was that the offender, though thoroughly chastened, would have difficulty suppressing his mirth and would bear no ill will for the telling-off. Bru de Wold joined the Volunteers in 1865, saw service in the Zulu War, being mentioned in dispatches, was commissioned in 1880 and in 1894 became commander of the Border Mounted Rifles. He resigned from this post in 1895 when he was appointed District Adjutant for southern Natal.[4]

The colony was fortunate in having these two excellent officers in charge of its Volunteers, one entirely conventional and the other entirely the opposite.

Apart from regular local parades and shooting practice, the Volunteers were required to attend an annual training camp lasting at least ten days. They had to pay for their uniforms, and each mounted volunteer had to provide himself with a horse, saddlery and top boots. They were given rifles and were paid while on duty. When ordered to mobilise on 28 September, the Volunteers numbered just over 2,000 comprising the various corps, described below. All these regiments were armed with the obsolete .303 Martini-Enfield or Martini-Metford rifles, without magazines, giving them a much slower rate of fire than the Boers, with Mausers and British rifles. The Vounteer regiments' officers were elected, resulting in a good relationship between officers and men. Their fighting skills were more than a match for the Boers, and to this they added good discipline and local knowledge.

The Natal Carbineers

The Carbineers had been in existence since 1855 and drew their recruits from Pietermaritzburg, the Natal Midlands and Northern Natal and from the beginning were a mounted regiment. Its commander in 1899 was Lt Col E.M. Greene and its strength 508 (all ranks). The regiment had achieved great renown in the Zulu War of 1879. They formed part of the column that Lord Chelmsford led into Zululand in January of that year. On 20 January the Carbineers camped with the British troops at the foot of Isandlwana Mountain. The following day Chelmsford, with about half his troops, pushed on into Zululand taking with him, as scouts, twenty-seven Carbineers.

The remaining twenty-eight Carbineers, under Lieutenant Frederick Scott, remained at Isandlwana. This troop was detailed to keep a lookout from a small hill a few miles to the north east of the main camp. On the morning of the 22nd they spotted a large force of Zulus approaching and immediately set off back to base. When still about a mile from the main camp they joined Col Durnford of the Natal Native Contingent, who had with him about one hundred men. This group of Durnford's men and Carbineers now came under attack by the Zulus. In an attempt to protect the British right flank they tried to make a stand in a dry water course but, faced by repeated and determined attacks by the Zulus, they were slowly driven back. The Zulus had meanwhile broken through the British defences leaving Durnford's group surrounded. Against overwhelming odds they fought on. A Zulu leader, Mehlokazulu, described their final stand, 'They threw down their guns when their ammunition was done, and then commenced with their pistols and then they formed a line, shoulder to shoulder, back to back, and fought with their knives.'[5]

Overcome by assegai and bullet wounds, they collapsed and died where they stood. Lieutenant Scott was among the eighteen Carbineers who died with Durnford and the Natal Natives. They could have mounted their horses and escaped but instead stayed to help Durnford. For two-and-a-half hours they had fought and by so doing, enabled others to escape.

Elsewhere on the field, five other Carbineers died and five were able to escape. During the flight from Isandlwana, one of the survivors, William Barker, repeatedly risked his life to save others fleeing the battlefield, including giving his horse to an exhausted British officer, Lieutenant Higginson. Barker was recommended for a Victoria Cross but this was refused by the British authorities, although a British regular soldier was given a Victoria Cross for a similar deed.[6]

When Chelmsford's column heard the sound of the battle at Isandlwana, they immediately retraced their steps back to the doomed camp. Four scouts from the local Buffalo Border Guards rode ahead and that evening were the first to arrive at the camp site. That morning they had breakfasted with comrades whose mutilated corpses were now scattered over the campsite. In charge of these scouts was Sergeant-Major Charles George Willson. In 1899 Charlie Willson was a captain and leader of the Dundee troop of the Natal Carbineers.

The Natal Mounted Rifles

This regiment had been formed in 1873 and drew its members from the Durban area. It succeeded other militia groups, which had been raised from time to time to meet crises in the history of the settlement. During the Zulu War, the regiment was required to guard the Natal border and was not involved in any of the major battles of that war.

In September 1899, it was commanded by Major Robert W. Evans and its strength on mobilisation, inclusive of all ranks, was 220. Based in Durban, this was surprisingly few for a fairly large town, however, it should be borne in mind that Durban provided other military units, and not all of its urbanised citizens were horsemen.

Being the entry port for Natal there were a substantial number of Australians around Durban, who, with a similar pioneering background, integrated well with the locals. In later years an old veteran recalled an incident when they were trying to break-in two big thoroughbreds, which had just been commandeered. About ninety per cent of the men present at the camp attempted to ride the horses but none lasted more than a few seconds. Then a new recruit, 'a lean Australian, who looked like a Sunday school teacher, mild face and eyeglasses, said he would like to try. Everybody laughed, as the man looked so unlike the job, but he swung into the saddle, yelled, "let go", and boy could he ride! That horse tried everything, even attempting to get among the seats on the grandstand, but in a very short and exciting time Le Mesurier (for that was his name) had that horse gentled, sweating and obeying his commands. He rested a little, and did the same with the other one. I have seen many good men with horses, but have yet to see one better than him.'[7]

The Border Mounted Rifles

Its members, who were farmers or traders, came from the south of the colony. Like other Natalians, most of them could speak Zulu but, being far from the Boer Republics, few had ever heard Dutch spoken. The regiment came into being in 1884 as part of a rationalisation of the existing volunteer units. Its commanding officer in 1899 was Major John Frederick Rethman, MLA, and its strength on mobilisation 286.

In March 1899, the Governor, Sir Walter Hely-Hutchinson, made his annual visit to the training camps of the Volunteer regiments. Having wined and dined with the officers of the Natal Carbineers whose table was adorned with the glittering trophies of that illustrious regiment, he came to the much simpler mess of the Border Mounted Rifles. Glancing at the table before him he said, 'This is very Spartan, Rethman, and what I like to see.'

'We are rough but ready,' was the reply.

The Regimental Medical Officer Captain H. T.Platt then placed a top boot complete with spur on the table and said, 'This is all the plate we have.'

The Governor suggested the regiment should adopt 'Rough but Ready' as their motto, and the 'Boot and Spur' as their badge.[8] This was done and in later years when the regiment amalgamated with the Natal Mounted Rifles, the motto and badge followed them.

The regiment was divided into four squadrons. No. 1 squadron was led by Captain John Robinson (Galloping Jack) Royston who, later in the Boer War and in the First World War, was to serve with Australian units, ending his military service as a Brigadier General.

The Umvoti Mounted Rifles

Founded in 1864, it was the smallest of the mounted regiments, its strength on mobilisation being only eighty-nine. On this little regiment with its headquarters in Greytown fell the duty of protecting the colony against attack from the north east. It was commanded by Major George Leuchars, an experienced officer with a profound knowledge of the difficult terrain he had to protect.

The Natal Police

Commanded by a Canadian, Col J.G. Dartnell, the Natal Police were usually mounted, and were scattered over the whole of Natal. At the start of the war they numbered 317. John Dartnell was born in Canada in 1838 and joined the British army when he was seventeen. He was posted to India, and served with great distinction in the Mutiny. He retired from the army with the rank of major in 1869, and moved to Natal, where he intended to farm. In 1874 he was persuaded to accept appointment as commander of the newly formed Natal Mounted Police.

The Chief of Police was old friends with the Prime Minister in 1899, Albert Hime. In their portraits they display all the gravitas one would expect from people of their standing in the late Victorian era, however, they had quite a mischievous sense of humour. In 1880 work had begun on the construction of a harbour at Port Shepstone on the mouth of the Mzimkulu River in southern Natal. The then Governor, having embarked on a tour of inspection of southern Natal, decided to visit the harbour works at Port Shepstone. Included in his entourage were Dartnell whose police formed the Governor's guard, and Hime the Colonial Engineer.

The construction of the harbour had been entrusted to William Bazley who was one of those marvellous self-taught Victorian engineers who so often achieved the seemingly impossible. But with this there came a degree of eccentricity. Where the estuary flowed into the sea there was an underwater reef that had to be removed by blasting. Wearing the diving suit provided by nature, Bazley would dive down to the reef, place the dynamite charges, and after the blast he would go down again to clear away the debris. He spent long hours underwater. His only aids in these diving operations were a tube, which brought him oxygen from a primitive hand-operated pump, and a long pole at the end of which was a large gaff hook. The pole he used as a prodder to drive away inquisitive sharks and, from time to time, to wake up the pump operator. When he wasn't diving, Bazley habitually carried sticks of dynamite in his pockets, which he would sometimes use as giant firecrackers, to enliven proceedings. The Governor, a nervous and delicate man, had been very frugal in the arrangements he made for his escort, who were a little peeved by the lack of consideration shown to them. It had been arranged that the Governor would be rowed in a barge from a river crossing, several miles upstream, down to the river mouth where he would inspect the harbour works.

Dartnell and Hime felt that it would not do to have a naked Bazley emerging like Neptune from the sea to welcome the Governor, so they sent a message to Bazley that he should wear a frock coat and top hat. They also added that the Governor was very deaf, which was not true, and that Bazley should take care to speak up. The Governor was told that Bazley was a little eccentric and always carried in his pockets sticks of dynamite and detonators along with his pipe, tobacco and matches. Somehow Bazley achieved the impossible and obtained a frock coat and top hat in Port Shepstone.

With due pomp and ceremony the official party in the barge were rowed down to the harbour, and when His Excellency stepped ashore, he was confronted by a strange figure dressed in a frock coat and top hat carrying a long pole at the end of which was a large hook. Bazley, never shy, closed in on the Governor and leaning forward, began shouting out in minute detail how he was constructing the harbour. Startled, and no doubt anxious about the dynamite, the Governor stepped back but Bazley followed, shouting even louder. This was too much for His Excellency who turned and fled back to the barge.[9] Subsequently, the expenditure on the harbour works at Port Shepstone was approved without query by the Governor.

William Bazley was Bru de Wold's brother-in-law and his son George served as a trooper in the Border Mounted Rifles and as such, was incarcerated with his regiment in Ladysmith during the siege.

Natal Field Artillery
Led by Captain Dan Taylor, they had six obsolete 2.5 inch guns manned by 123 men. They were well trained and could be relied on to hit a target within the limited range of their guns.

The Natal Naval Volunteers
This unit had come into being in 1885. Britain had quarrelled with Russia about Afghanistan, and feared that the Russian navy might attack Durban, so heavy guns were installed to protect the harbour. The Russian fleet remained in the Baltic and the attack did not materialise, but the unit remained, and by adapting the naval guns, they were able to play a significant role in the coming conflict.

The Durban Light Infantry

This regiment, which could trace its origins to the earliest days of the settlement, numbered 416 on mobilisation. Realising the importance of mounted men, they applied to be converted to a mounted unit but the British would not consent to the request.

The Natal Volunteer Medical Corps

A Volunteer medical corps with doctors, nurses and orderlies had been organised and on mobilisation accompanied the Volunteers to the front. They were led by Dr James Hyslop who had trained in Edinburgh, Berlin, Vienna and Munich. This corps provided the Volunteers with medical attention not only better than that provided to the Regular Army, but probably better than that which had ever been provided to any army in the field. Two of the doctors in the corps were Australians, Rupert Hornabrook from Adelaide, and Robert Buntine from Melbourne. They were to achieve great distinction during the war.

The Natal Bridge Guards and Natal Royal Rifles

With a strength of 150 and 61 respectively, these units were absorbed into other units in the first few months of the start of the war.

Scouts

Various scouting units, manned by the peoples of Natal, were formed during the war. They will be dealt with on an ad hoc basis.

The citizens of Natal hoped and prayed that war could be avoided, but if the Boers decided to go ahead with the invasion, they would defend themselves. It would not be for the glory of the Empire, nor to avenge Majuba, nor to show that they were better men than the Boers, nor for any British strategic interest. For them, it would be a struggle for survival. However, excellent as their Volunteers might be, because they were so heavily outnumbered, and because Britain was not prepared to permit them to raise further units, they were going to need some assistance.

Great Britain

By June, 1899, it was obvious to the Natal Government that the Transvaal intended to invade the country and they begged for help, but Britain, doubtless anxious not to get involved in a war, initially hesitated. However, she could not turn a blind eye to the events unfolding in Southern Africa forever. In July two companies of Engineers were sent to South Africa. By 15 August they had 6,000 men in Natal. Following further representations by Natal, the British cabinet agreed on 8 September to double the strength of their Natal contingent by sending reinforcements from the army in India, which was achieved with remarkable efficiency. The result was that when war was declared Britain had approximately 11,000 men in Natal, apart from the 2,000 Colonial Volunteers. On that same day in September, the War Office gave approval for the formation of the Imperial Light Horse, which would add a further 500 men to those preparing to defend the colony.

On 22 September the War Office decided to call up an Army Corps of 42,000 men for service in South Africa, but this Corps had still to be raised, equipped and shipped to South Africa, and it would therefore be a few months before they could provide any protection for the colony.

Although no one doubted the courage of the British, they did seem to have some serious weaknesses. Many colonials, having close relatives in Britain, regarded the British as allies, whereas the British regarded the colonials at best as subordinates whose opinions were not sought, and who should do as they were told without question. It was not long before friction began to surface. Early in September, Major Rethman of the Border Mounted Rifles received from a friend in Johannesburg details of the preparations being made by the Boers to invade Natal and of the armaments, including machine guns, they were importing right under the noses of the British. Feeling the information was important, he immediately travelled to Pietermaritzburg and passed the report on to his Commandant, Col W. Royston.

Royston, realising the gravity of the intelligence, arranged a meeting with the Governor. The Governor requested the newly arrived commander of the British army in Natal, General Penn Symons, to join them. The general scoffed at the information, making caustic comments about the usual colonial exaggerations. The Major, stung to the quick, expressed himself 'very forthrightly', and the Governor had to intervene several times.[10] The information turned out to be correct, and the grave of General Penn Symons is to be found in Dundee, near the site of the first battle of the war.

Apart from this unfortunate attitude to the colonials, the training the British troops received did not teach them the skills they would need in the coming war. Their experience of warfare had been gained in the confined spaces of Europe or against poorly armed tribesmen. Now they had to contend with a mobile, unseen enemy that was equipped with weapons superior to their own. Much of their training was done on the barrack square and on the parade ground, where they learned how to perform various drill movements with clockwork precision. Much of the rest of their time was spent cleaning their uniforms, polishing buttons, scrubbing floors and other menial tasks. Very little effort was made to improve their marksmanship, their shooting being limited to firing 200 rounds at a fixed target annually at a set distance. Parliament declined to provide adequate funds for the improvement of this most essential skill. No attempt was made to teach them how to camouflage themselves, or to impress on them the importance of ensuring they would not be seen by the enemy. They were, in the words of a contemporary, 'indifferent shots, careless of cover, slow to comprehend what was taking place, or to grasp the whereabouts of the enemy, always getting surprised or lost, helpless without their officers. In a word, the British soldier was well disciplined but ill-trained.' Their regimental officers, though capable, also lacked the training that would have enabled them to improve the effectiveness of their units, and what applied to these officers applied even more to their generals. The army had to learn on the battlefield what it should have learned in training.[11]

Serious as it was, lack of proper training was not the only difficulty the British faced. The artillery for example, though well-trained and disciplined, were in danger of being outranged by the Boer guns. Their Intelligence Department had been starved of funds, the budget for the whole Empire being smaller than that of the same department in the Transvaal Republic, with the obvious result that British commanders often lacked the information they needed to make informed decisions. In particular, they were not provided with adequate maps. An excellent geodetic triangulation survey of Natal had been completed by 1892 and in addition there were boundary, mining and railway surveys. Maps could have been obtained from the Natal Department of Works, a course the British were not prepared to follow. The army required maps that had been prepared by their own surveyors. Such maps had not been prepared of the country over which the war was likely to be fought. The excuse given for this omission was that such activity might be dangerous as it might offend Boer farmers.[12] There were some Dutch farmers in Northern Natal but they were in a minority. These Dutch farmers could not have prevented the country being mapped by the British army's survey section, which would have had the full protection of the Natal Police, had this been necessary. Counter-intelligence was virtually non-existent, and the British took little interest in Boer spies who were able to operate unhindered.

Even if they chose to ignore colonial advice, the British should have noticed that apart from a few policemen and the artillery, the entire Boer army was mounted. As mentioned earlier, informed opinion was that one mounted man was worth at least three men on foot. Three-quarters of the British troops in Natal were infantry. If this wasn't bad enough, British numbers were inflated by a substantial number of non-combatants attached to each unit, whereas the numbers given for Boers referred to men with rifles.

The training of the cavalry also left much to be desired. Each day the men would take the horses out of their stables for a couple of hours' exercise, which generally involved schooling to execute various parade ground manoeuvres, after which they were returned to their stables to be fed and groomed. 'Of the things that are vital in war, the limit of a horse's capacity to cover long distances and to carry heavy weights, the minimum of food, water and rest it requires for continuous effort, the precautions by which its strength can be husbanded, they had no inkling.'[13] Their horses also tended to be too large and heavy for the conditions on the South African veld, burdened with largely unnecessary equipment. Here again, the British army officers made no attempt to obtain local advice, and imported many unsuitable horses thereby wasting money and severely restricting and sometimes endangering mounted units.

Duncan McKenzie was one of the best mounted men on either side. He chose as his mount 'Inspector', a part-bred (seven-eighths thoroughbred) entire, who had already covered his book of mares for the 1899 season. At 15.3 hands high, he was a little taller than most of the Volunteers' horses.

Close coupled, he was tough, endowed with both speed and stamina, and had a wonderful temperament. As an entire he would be able to maintain condition and fitness, where a gelding might need extra feeding and rest. Obviously the whole army could not have been mounted on such a horse, however, he was the type the British should have sought, and by so doing they would have avoided such blunders as buying thousands of Argentinian heavy cobs, which were, for all practical purposes, useless in South African conditions.

Almost too late it was realised that it was mounted men who were going to be in demand in South Africa and the War Office gave its consent to the raising of mounted units. The first regiment raised under the new policy was the Imperial Light Horse. The War Office limited its numbers to 500, and required that the regiment be commanded by an Imperial officer. Col Scott-Chisholme of the 5th Lancers was appointed its first commander.

In a few days 3,500 applications to join the regiment had been received at their recruiting office in Pietermaritzburg. Karri Davies and Aubrey Woolls Sampson were now in the fortunate position of being able to choose their men, and they took care to choose the best. As the recruiting took place in Pietermaritzburg, many of the applicants were locals; however, from the start, the regiment attracted men from many different backgrounds and countries. From Australia, Canada, New Zealand, Britain and Ireland they came. Some had worked in Johannesburg and others had only just arrived in South Africa; all were determined to resist Kruger's desire to chase the British out. Despite their diverse origins, they blended well and relations between all ranks was excellent. They were divided into six squadrons, each with eighty-six men including NCOs. They were armed with second-hand single-shot obsolete rifles, which had a Lee-Metford bore and Martini-Henri action. These were supplied from stock by the Natal Government. No bayonets were issued, and they were only to receive modern rifles with magazines after the relief of Ladysmith.

The Imperial Government agreed to pay members of the regiment at the same rate as other Volunteers.[15] It was up to the regiment itself to fund its establishment costs, the principal items being the provision of horses, saddlery and uniforms for the men. It should be remembered that the Natal Volunteers had also to provide their own horses, saddlery and buy their uniforms. Many of the ILH recruits lacked the means to equip themselves. The £4,000 that the Reform Committee had given to Karri Davies and Aubrey Woolls Samson to pay their fines after the Jameson Raid was donated to a fund to meet establishment costs. However, more money was needed. The horses alone would cost about £10,000. So Woolls Sampson approached his friends Percy Fitzpatrick and Lionel Phillips for help and, through them, received an offer from the German mining house Wernher Beit & Co. to pay the balance of the establishment costs of the 500-strong regiment.[16]

The money given by Wernher Beit & Co. was a single donation, given unconditionally. When, after the Relief of Ladysmith, they were asked for another donation to replace horses which had died or been eaten, they replied that in making their original contribution they did not intend to assume the position of sponsors of the British Empire.[17] They did, however, agree to lend money for the purchase of the replacement horses. When, after audit, the British Government repaid this loan of approximately £25,000, Wernher Beit donated the money to a fund formed to assist members of the regiment who had been disabled by their wounds and the widows of those who had been killed.[18]

In Pietermaritzburg, Karri and Sambo were re-united with an old friend, Charlie Mullins. Charles Herbert Mullins was born in Grahamstown in the Eastern Cape in 1869. For generations the Mullins clan of Grahamstown contributed much to the community in which they lived. In particular, their contribution to education in that part of the world has been enormous. However, it was not only in education that they served their community. For example, Charlie's brother was a surgeon and served as such throughout the Boer War with the British forces, and later with the South African Medical Corps in France in 1917/18.

Charlie Mullins, on completing his schooling in Grahamstown, went to Keble College, Oxford, read law, and in due course was called to the Bar by the Inner Temple, and practised as a barrister. In 1894 he moved to Johannesburg, where he practised as an attorney in the firm Bell & Mullins. He was appalled by what would today be described as the human rights abuses of the Kruger government. He joined the Reform movement and became a close friend of Karri and Sambo. He was among those Reformists who were arrested and imprisoned after the Jameson Raid. He paid the fine imposed and, on his release, went to Pietermaritzburg, where he became a partner in the firm Hudson, Hutchinson & Mullins. When war appeared inevitable, Charlie Mullins, though by nature a man of peace, gave Karri and Aubrey his full support and with them is regarded as one of the driving forces behind the formation of the Imperial Light Horse.

Horses for the regiment were bought in Natal, Pondoland, Basutoland (now Lesotho) and, cheekily, in the Transvaal. They cost between £20 and £50 each and were generally of good quality. Some were unschooled but after a few days under Australian Rough Riders, they were ready for duty. The purchase of saddlery virtually exhausted stocks in Pietermaritzburg and some was of poor quality.

In the British Army, it usually took six months to train a mounted man to the stage where he would be fit to take the field. With war imminent, this had to be achieved in weeks. Training began immediately. In the morning there was mounted drill and the grooming of horses. In the afternoon they drilled on foot and practised shooting.

Mounted training was sited at Foxhill on Pietermaritzburg's southern outskirts. The colonel began by requiring the squadrons to advance in parallel lines across the veld. F squadron unexpectedly encountered a donga (a dry water course), and in the process of negotiating it, got themselves hopelessly jumbled up. Scott-Chisholme, not knowing what had caused the problem, saw the squadron disintegrate into a disorganised tangle of men and galloped across to them.

'Who commands this squadron?' he demanded.

'I do, Sir!' answered the Squadron leader while extricating himself from the others.

Chisholme looked at the shambles for a second or two before galloping back to his original position. As he did so he was heard to mutter, 'poor bloody men'.[19]

The attitude of the colonel soon mellowed. The men were capable, intelligent and enthusiastic, perhaps a bit too enthusiastic, and he was even moved to warn a group at work: 'Look here, you men, there is such a thing as being over-keen. If you are not careful half of you will be killed in your first fight.'

When the colonel went to the shooting range to see how the recruits were getting on, he could hardly believe his eyes. Turning to Regimental Sergeant-Major M. Dryden, who had also been in the 5th Lancers, he said, 'Surely this is remarkable shooting,' and received the answer, 'Yes. Sir, we never saw shooting like that in the 5th.'[20] The 5th Lancers were the crack shots of the army in India.

The Chief of Staff designate in Natal, General Sir Archibald Hunter, in evidence given to the War Commission after the war, described his first meeting with the regiment.

> The first time I ever saw them was on the first day I arrived at Pietermaritzburg. It was the first day they had ever been on parade as a regiment; up to that time they had only paraded as squadrons under their squadron leaders; it was the first day that Colonel Chisholme had ever had them under his command. Sir Walter Hely Hutchinson drove up to the ground, as he wanted to see them, and he asked me to go round and look at them. I had not long come from a tour abroad, where I had seen nothing but the picked guards of Sweden, Denmark, Russia, Prussia, and Saxony, and there was nothing I saw on the Continent then, and nothing I have ever seen here, except the Irish Constabulary, that could put a patch on them. You can tell men when you look at them. Every man was a picture of manhood; he was beaming with intelligence. They were a great success, a most undoubted success. They were the finest corps I have ever seen anywhere in my life.[21]

When war was declared on 13 October 1899, the corps were still in Pietermaritzburg but were taken to the front within the next few days. The senior officers under Col Scott-Chisholme were Major Woolls Sampson, Major Karri Davies, Captain Charles Mullins, Major Doveton and Lieutenant Bottomley. Over the next few months there were promotions and other officers came to the fore.

The Imperial Light Horse was the prototype of scores of mounted regiments raised in South Africa during the war, the most prominent in the Natal Campaign being The South African Light Horse, Thornycroft's Mounted Infantry, Bethune's Mounted Infantry, the Imperial Light Infantry, as well as various scouting units and the Natal Volunteer Ambulance Corps. Shortly before hostilities broke out, Col W. Royston heard that a ship carrying members of the British Indian Army back to England on leave would be calling at Durban. He persuaded many of these men to disembark in Durban, with the result that they provided the leavening of British officers that the British authorities required before they would consent to the raising of these Volunteer regiments, which were to make a contribution to the defence of Natal out of all proportion to their numbers.

A serious mistake made by the British was to disregard those thousands of Natalians who, though not members of one of the established regiments, were keen to contribute to the defence of their homeland. Duncan McKenzie has this to say about them,

> If the Colonists had been called out, they would have formed some of the best irregular Cavalry in the world. They were good shots, and would have been well mounted on their own horses. They would have consisted mostly of farmers who understood the Boer ways, and would have been equal in every respect to the Boers themselves. Had this been done, and five or six thousand Colonials been brigaded under their own officers, the Boers would have been driven beyond the Tugela in a very short time, and I feel quite sure there would have been no siege of Ladysmith.[22]

Lord Milner discouraged the recruitment of Volunteers in South Africa, it being his opinion that the arming of such Volunteers would achieve no more than provide additional arms for the enemy.[23] This prejudice might explain why the arms made available to the Volunteers were obsolete and would have been of little interest to the Boers.

It was also unfortunate that the British treated lightly the offer made in June 1899 by Australia, New Zealand and Canada to send mounted troops to South Africa. These countries realised before Britain that the Boer Republics had every intention of going to war and also that it would be mounted men who could best thwart Boer ambitions.

Despite Boer superiority in numbers and equipment, they were going to struggle to drive the *rooinek*s into the sea, and it was not only because thousands of British soldiers would in a few months be on their way to South Africa.

6

Invasion of Northern Natal

On Monday 9 October 1899, the Colonial Secretary in London received a telegram from the State Secretary of the Transvaal Republic, F.W. Reitz. It demanded that troops on the borders of the Republic be instantly withdrawn, that all reinforcements which had arrived within the last year should leave South Africa, and that those upon the sea should be sent back without landing. Failure to make a satisfactory response to the demand within forty-eight hours would be regarded by the Transvaal Government as a declaration of war by Her Majesty's Government.[1]

F.W. Reitz disliked the English with a passion that at times made even Paul Kruger look pro-British. He had been a judge in the Orange Free State and on the death of President Brand in 1887, was elected president. In 1895 he became ill and resigned, the presidency being taken over by Steyn. On his recovery, Reitz went to the Transvaal and was appointed State Secretary. Long before gold was discovered on the Witwatersrand or Cecil Rhodes had made his fortune, and at a time when Britain had recognised the independence of the Transvaal, Reitz was working for the expulsion of people of English descent from Southern Africa. His message was spread by every possible means; in the press, the pulpit, schools and in the Volksraad. One prominent Afrikaner wrote, 'Believe me, the day on which F.W. Reitz sat down to pen his ultimatum to Britain was the proudest and happiest moment of his life, and one which had for long years been looked forward to by him with eager longing and expectation.'[2]

Reitz knew the British could not, and would not, comply with the demand and the following day, the Colonial Office advised him that it was not prepared to comply with the ultimatum. So it was that at 5 p.m. on Wednesday 11 October 1899, the Boer Republics went to war with the British Empire.

As we have seen, the invasion and conquest of Natal had long formed part of the strategy of the Transvaal Government. Revenue from the gold mines had provided the money to purchase the necessary arms, however, the timing of the invasion was governed by a more mundane issue. If thirty to fifty thousand mounted men were to invade Natal, they would take with them thirty to fifty thousand horses, which had to be fed each day. As the Boers carried no feed for their horses, they had to rely on grazing the *veld* and this would only be possible after the first spring rains. They, therefore, had no choice but to wait until the spring of 1899 before launching the invasion. By 27 September it was felt the time to act had arrived, and the Transvaal called out its kommandos.

Trains leaving the Transvaal were packed with refugees fleeing to the British colonies. On 29 September, the railways were taken over by the State and all civilian rail traffic to Natal was stopped. The trains were now packed with kommandos travelling to the Natal border. On the 30th alone, twenty-six military trains left Johannesburg and Pretoria for the Natal frontier.

In response to events in the Transvaal, all the Natal Volunteers were ordered to mobilise on 29 September, ostensibly for ten days' training.

Among the first kommandos leaving Pretoria for the Natal border that day was seventeen-year-old Deneys Reitz, son of the Secretary of State. Heavy traffic on the railway resulted in the train taking three days to reach Sandspruit, 10 miles from the Natal border. Here was mustered the largest body of mounted men ever seen in South Africa and what a confident crowd they were. Writing after the war, Deneys, loyal to his father, describes the British Government as the chief culprit and then continues, 'but the Transvaalers were also spoiling for a fight, and from what I saw in Pretoria during the weeks that preceded the ultimatum, I feel sure that the Boers would in any case have insisted on a rupture.'[3]

Deneys Reitz was not the only observer of events in Pretoria. Teise Ndhlovu came from the Ladysmith district and was fluent in Zulu, Sotho, English and Dutch. For some time prior to 1899, he had worked as special groom to Kommandant General Piet Joubert. As such, Teise would regularly accompany the general and hold his horse when he was visiting. Prior to the ultimatum, they went to Kruger's residence in Pretoria where Joubert found Kruger seated on his veranda. Quietly holding Joubert's horse, Teise listened to the conversation on the veranda and later reported its content.

Kruger urged that they should get everything ready to fight the English, but General Joubert replied that he had better arrange matters peacefully; that he had been in England and knew the power of England. The Boers might succeed for a time but end in being beaten. Mrs Kruger, who it appears, had been listening to the conversation, then came onto the scene and said, 'Kruger, do you agree that we should not fight the English, you had better put on my clothes, stay at home and do my work, and I will put on your clothes and lead the Burgers to fight against the verdomde [damned] English,' this speech altered his mind and he decided to fight.[4]

Teise abandoned his employment with Joubert and made his way to Natal, where he arrived on 8 October 1899. Here he immediately enlisted as a scout. We shall come across him again.

While Teise was on his way to Natal and the kommandos were waiting for the spring rains, young Reitz and his friends were enjoying camping on the *veld* at Sandspruit and looking forward to the expected excitement of the coming weeks. In Pretoria the Attorney General, Jan Smuts, and the State Secretary, Reitz, were frustrated by the delay and deplored the lack of action. But then neither was familiar with conditions in Natal.

Young Freda Schlosberg went with her family to see their local kommando leave for the Front. Before the train steamed off, their Field Cornet, holding the Transvaal flag, made a long speech, which was loudly applauded. She noted, 'Few, very few tears were shed by the women at the station. Why should they weep? The war would not last long and their men would soon return triumphant, after having driven the English into the sea and taken over their farms and homes'.[5]

On 2 October, President Steyn called out the Free State kommandos and a few days later it rained. By the 9th the grass was sprouting and at long last the Secretary of State could sign the ultimatum.

At Sandspruit on 10 October, a great parade was held to honour Paul Kruger's birthday and great was the excitement when General Joubert told them of the ultimatum. Deneys Reitz wrote, 'The great throng stood in its stirrups and shouted itself hoarse, and it was not until long after the Kommandant General and his retinue had fought their way through the crowd that the kommandos began to disperse.'

War was officially declared on 11 October. Each Boer was issued with rations for five days and early on the morning of the 12th moved off, and what a sight it was: 'As far as the eye could see the plain was alive with horsemen, guns, and cattle all steadily going forward to the frontier. The scene was a stirring one, and I shall never forget riding to war with that great host.'[6]

Deneys Reitz had a fairly accurate idea of the troops that opposed them, believing about seven thousand troops were at Dundee 60 miles away, and 40 miles further on at Ladysmith, were a further six or seven thousand. The Boers knew Britain had no troops to withdraw from the Natal frontier, and that with such a disposition, it was highly unlikely that there were any plans to invade the Transvaal. Indeed, Britain had no clear idea as to how its colonies could be defended.

When the probability of war was finally realised, the British military establishment at last began to seriously consider how the colony might be protected. Northern Natal is in the shape of a triangle, at the northern apex of which is the hamlet of Charlestown. To the west are the Drakensberg Mountains and the Free State, and in the east the Buffalo River formed the boundary with the Transvaal. Between Charlestown and Newcastle, the first substantial town in Northern Natal, are three mountain passes, Laing's Nek,

Majuba and Ingogo Heights. General Sir William Penn Symons, who in May had been appointed commander of the army in Natal, rejected these passes as possible defensive positions, as the defenders could easily be cut off and surrounded by the Boers invading from east and west. By 13 September, he had devised a plan. Once the additional troops arrived from India, Natal should be occupied as far as Newcastle, where his troops would have no trouble beating off any attack.

As Britain had doubled the strength of the army in Natal, it was decided that a more senior general should assume command. On 6 September, General Sir George White, VC, formerly Commander-in-Chief in India, was appointed commander in Natal. He had shown himself to be a brave, cautious and able leader and, though sixty-three and a little lame from a riding accident, was thought to be eminently suitable for the task ahead. He was given no clear directives by the War Office.

Sir George hastened to South Africa and arrived in Durban on 7 October 1899. He spent one day in Durban, acquainting himself with the latest developments with respect to the troops from India and making arrangements for their transfer upcountry. The next day he travelled to Pietermaritzburg to meet the Governor, Sir Walter Hely-Hutchinson, and Penn Symons. During the sea voyage to South Africa, the old general had spent many hours trying to work out where the British forces should draw their defensive line. Given that most of his troops were slow-moving infantry, it appeared to Sir George that the border at Charlestown, the three mountain passes, Newcastle and the coalfields extending down to Dundee were all indefensible against the highly mobile Boer forces. At Ladysmith, the railway from the coast divided, with one line going west to the Free State and the other north east to the Transvaal. At this road and rail junction the British army had a camp and had accumulated a considerable quantity of stores. There were also railway workshops at Ladysmith, which could be useful to the military. Initially, Sir George thought the Biggarsberg range of hills between Ladysmith and Dundee might form a suitable defensive line but the absence of a reliable supply of water caused him to abandon this idea. It seemed he would have to make a stand at Ladysmith. At his meeting with the Governor and Penn Symons, his plan was turned on its head.

Before Sir George arrived in Natal, Penn Symons had already taken 4,000 men from Ladysmith to Dundee, thereby splitting the army in two. In addition, the Governor begged Sir George not to abandon Northern Natal. Firstly, because of the importance of its coalfields, access to which was vital to British interests as both naval and mercantile ships relied on the bunkering facilities at Durban for their coal-fired steam engines. Secondly, if Britain appeared weak and unable to maintain order, conflict might break out between various groups of Zulus. The Boers were adept at exploiting tribal rivalries to acquire land for themselves, as had occurred in northern Zululand in 1877 (*see* Chapter 4). He must have known that from the border at Charlestown to the sea lived British subjects of all colours, who looked to Britain for protection and who, in an invasion, would lose everything. We shall see that Sir George White, throughout the time he was in Natal, took into account the interests of the civilian residents when making military decisions. Penn Symons was adamant that with a few more troops in Dundee, he would have no trouble dealing with the Boers. Sir George was not entirely convinced but being new to the country he bowed to pressure and agreed to leave Penn Symons and his troops in Dundee. In addition, he dispatched to Dundee the 1st. Royal Irish Fusiliers who had only just arrived from India. On 11 October, the day the ultimatum expired, General White arrived in Ladysmith.

Two days before, there had occurred the display of Boer and Colonial shooting skills described in Chapter 1. This great humanitarian exercise to rescue 7,000 men from behind enemy lines was conceived and executed by officials of the Natal Government. Neither Lord Milner nor Chamberlain had anything to do with the plan. The official who carried ultimate responsibility for the venture was S.O. Samuelson, the Natal Under-Secretary of Native Affairs and Marwick's immediate superior. Samuelson has been described as Marwick's 'boss'.[7] However valid such terminology might be in some trade union circles, it is completely inappropriate in a society that did not have British class distinctions and prejudices. Marwick and Wheelwright would have had the same regard for Samuelson as they would have had for a competent captain of a sports team of which they were members.

Samuel Olaf Samuelson was an extraordinary man. The son of an early Zululand missionary, he grew up in that country during the reign of King Cetshwayo. In due course he went to school in Cape Town, where apart from other achievements he mastered Latin, Greek, Xhosa, Sesotho, Portuguese, Norwegian, Dutch, Italian and Hebrew. However, it was in his knowledge of Zulu customs and the classical Zulu language that he was pre-eminent, and it is a tragedy that so little of his knowledge was recorded for posterity.[8]

Marwick was born in Richmond, Natal, to a family with Scottish antecedents. As a local, he knew how Zulu society was organised and how disciplined its people were. His achievement during the walk was to get the Zulus themselves to organise and control the 7,000 people walking to Natal. His and Wheelwright's main function was to decide on the route to be followed and to liaise with the Boers along the way.

Much of the culture of the black peoples of Natal has been destroyed over the past 100 years so it might be appropriate to say a little about them as they were a century ago. When Henry Francis Fynn arrived at the *kraal* of King Shaka, he found a people who were content with their own civilisation and culture, which was perfectly adapted to the world in which they lived. Central to their society was the family, or kraal. It was a patriarchal society in which the head of each family was the eldest male. A wife was expected to always treat her husband with respect and to obey his commands. She managed the household, looked after the children and prepared the meals. In return, the husband was expected to treat her courteously at all times and to thank her for her efforts on behalf of the family.

The husband was expected to perform those duties imposed on the family by the king or the local chief, to maintain the fabric of the family buildings and stock enclosures, as well as overseeing the care of the family's livestock. All dealings with the outside world were carried out by him and, with a few exceptions, he owned all family property.

Children were at an early age taught to respect their parents and elders and to carry out their instructions promptly and without demur. From about the age of seven a young boy would begin his training for life in Zulu society. He would start with some simple task such as looking after the calves, and graduate from there to looking after larger animals, then to hunting and finally came his military training. They learned strict codes of behaviour – the elderly were treated with deference, and strangers were always to be greeted and treated courteously. They would be taught songs and many of their tasks would be performed while singing. They heard their history and learned the stories of their national heroes. In this way they were taught how to be brave and loyal citizens.

Girls would help their mothers with household chores and as they got older they would help with the more difficult tasks such as hoeing the fields and cooking. Women lived lives separate from the men, and girls, like boys, were taught their duties to society. Complex rules governed courtship procedures.

Governing family relations was the custom of lobolo. Often described as a dowry paid to buy a wife, it was a lot more complex than that. It ensured that everyone had a place in society and was part of a family. No one starved. If a young Zulu wished to marry, he would first discuss the matter with his family, who would then send messengers bearing gifts to the family of the proposed bride. Negotiations would decide how many lobolo cattle would be paid. Once this had been done, the local chieftain would indicate where the new family might build their home and what land they might cultivate. Communal grazing was available for any cattle the young suitor may acquire. If a husband ill-treated his wife she would, with her children, return to her father and his care. The husband would lose all rights over his children, including the right to receive lobolo when his daughters married. If the wife misbehaved, the husband would not only keep the children but could demand the return of lobolo from his father-in-law. Both the groom's and the bride's families therefore had a strong interest in ensuring the union was successful.

Wealth was measured in cattle and it was some time before the early settlers were able to persuade the Zulus that money had value. It was considered ridiculous that a coin or piece of paper with an image of some unknown stranger should have value. Initially, all trade was by barter. Inevitably there were some tribesmen who, attracted by the perceived advantages of western civilisation, went to Durban and elsewhere to work. Generally they did not regard this as a permanent change of lifestyle and retained their tribal links. They kept their homes in Zululand where the women and children continued to live a traditional rural life. This explains why in 1899 there were 11,935 Zulu men in Durban and only 601 women. (*See* Chapter 4).

The developing goldmines in Johannesburg badly needed labour, but they were faced with two difficulties. Firstly, the Transvaal Government was not prepared to allow additional blacks to settle in the country, though they were prepared to issue a short-term work permit, on the expiry of which the worker would have to leave the country. Secondly, the black people from the rural areas were not seeking permanent employment. The gold mines therefore had no choice but to employ short-term migrant labour. This was not a situation created by them, neither was it in their interests. The recruits came into an environment completely foreign to them. They did not understand Dutch or English, and could not read or write. To impart to them the necessary skills and knowledge to enable them to function properly was a costly process, and no sooner had it been achieved, than the men would leave to be replaced by a batch of fresh recruits. This made their labour expensive. Further, if the mines were to recruit any workers from Zululand or Natal, they had to tempt them with wages that would persuade them to give up, for a time, their rather pleasant lifestyle.

One factor did assist the mines in recruiting labour. A young Zulu had not only to obtain the consent of his father to his marriage, but he had also to rely on his father to provide lobolo. It was the father as kraal head who would decide when the son would marry and have children. In the nineteenth century, a Zulu woman would be considered ready for marriage at twenty-five and a man at thirty or older. Into this established world came the gold mines' need for labour. If a man worked on the gold mines for six months and managed his affairs prudently, he was able to save enough money to buy the lobolo cattle himself. No longer would he be beholden to his father. The long-term effect on their society was profound and not always for the better.

In 1899 the gold mines offered recruits a package that included travelling from their homes and back, full board and lodging, sport and other entertainment at weekends, and a salary of three pounds and six shillings a month. To put this in perspective, in 1922, when the value of the pound had sunk significantly below its 1899 value, the author's father started work in Pondoland just south of the Natal border. He could read, write and speak English, Zulu and Pondo. His employer gave him full board during the week, his annual subscription to the local cricket club, and a monthly salary of one pound and ten shillings; that is less than half the salary a Zulu or Pondo recruit on the mines would have received twenty-three years earlier. In 1900 a young man in rural England, seeking work on a farm, could expect to receive by way of remuneration his board and lodging, boots and clothing, and a sovereign at Christmas.

When Marwick's group settled down for the night, the miners would have sung about their adventures on the mines and their walk home. Marwick, Wheelwright, and the six policemen would have had the privilege of listening to a unique and awesome choral concert, words and harmonies unpremeditated. Once heard so often, such singing is seldom heard today.

Before leaving Johannesburg, Marwick and Wheelwright on behalf of the miners transmitted £9,500 to their families. An additional £10,000 was entrusted by the miners to them for safe-keeping until they reached Natal. The miners had sufficient money to buy food during the journey, and because of the disciplined manner in which they conducted themselves, Boer farmers and traders were only too pleased to sell them food. There were a few minor incidents along the way, which were sorted out by the Zulus themselves.

The delivery of the ultimatum put considerable pressure on the walkers to get through Boer lines before the hostilities began. On 10 October 1899, they were close to Standerton where Marwick was able to get some of the stragglers onto a train going to the Natal border. On the 11th they were advised by the *Landrost* (magistrate) at Standerton that the ultimatum would expire in a few hours and that a state of war was imminent. They pressed on towards the Boer camp at Sandspruit where they found the Boer army had already left. Only the Irish Kommando remained. They were said to be tidying up the camp. Marwick, somewhat naively it must be said, tried to send a telegram from the Sandspruit post office. The postal official pointed out that he was an enemy who should be shot and he was only saved by the intervention of their police guard. Marwick was able to get some further stragglers onto a train and the main group set off hot foot for Volksrust and the border.

At Volksrust they were challenged and again luck was with them. Marwick recognised an officer in the Transvaal Artillery. This man, though Dutch, had previously lived in Natal, where he had been a member of the Umvoti Mounted Rifles. He was able to smooth things over and see them on their way. They followed a detachment of the Transvaal artillery through the mountain passes, but after passing Majuba they were again stopped by a Boer kommando. Once again the artillery officer came to their rescue and persuaded the Kommandant to let them through.

On 14 October, they set off before dawn, passed through the Boer lines, and marched without stopping to Newcastle. Here they received rations from the Magistrate, who, as the district representative of the Natal Government, had authority to give food to the indigent. As they were leaving the town, the vanguard of the Boer kommandos was entering it. They only had time for a brief rest that night before setting off again. They were able to keep ahead of the Boers and during the day, groups would split off to take different routes to their homes.

At about 5 o'clock on the afternoon of Sunday 15 October, Marwick and the remaining marchers, who numbered about 1,000, arrived at Hattingh's Spruit station where they were able to entrain for home. Most of these remaining refugees would have been Pondos, whose homes lay to the south of Natal and would use Natal's transport system to travel to and from Johannesburg.

Marwick arrived in Pietermaritzburg the following day to a hero's welcome and much praise in the local press. The Prime Minister telegraphed his congratulations. To pluck 7,000 people out of enemy territory was indeed a remarkable achievement by the two young Natal officials. However, all those participating in this long walk deserve praise. For nine days and nights, without shelter and in all weathers, this great throng of people had by their orderly and disciplined behaviour succeeded in reaching the safety of Natal. Samuelson and the Natal Government also deserve credit for the part they played. On 5 October 1899, when Marwick advised Samuelson by telegram of his plan to walk with the miners to Natal, telegrams were taking up to four hours to get through. Samuelson had to consider the safety of the walkers for whom he was responsible, and as the proposed walk was to take place in a foreign country, it was necessary to consult the Governor before taking action. The Prime Minister therefore saw the Governor, who raised no objection to the plan. Samuelson telegraphed approval through to Marwick, who received the consent that same day. Samuelson also confirmed the arrangements for the journey and gave Marwick some useful advice, which contributed much to the success of the enterprise. On one point Marwick was unable to comply precisely with his instructions. Only Zulus and other blacks from Natal were supposed to be part of the group. There were some Pondos and Swazis following the same route and in practice it was impossible to exclude them.

As we have seen, the Prime Minister had sent a telegram of support to Marwick before the march. Both the Prime Minister and Samuelson urged Marwick not to incur unnecessary expenditure, an instruction that has been portrayed as meanness. In colonial Natal this was regarded as good governance and with war imminent, money was tight. Another criticism is that neither sent a telegram wishing Marwick 'good luck'. Reliance on luck was never a feature of the Natal administration.[9]

Very few bureaucrats would make such a bold decision as that made by Samuelson in authorising the walk. Certainly there was no one in the Cape who was prepared to do so. The migrant workers from the Cape were left to find their own way home and what happened to them no one will ever know.

The £10,000 entrusted to Marwick and Wheelwright was duly paid to the correct recipients shortly after their arrival in Natal. No one expected anything else.

Marwick was asked by Samuelson to write a full report of the rescue of the migrant workers and when it was completed, a copy was dispatched to the Colonial Office in London, where Chamberlain commented, 'Mr Marwick and others responsible for carrying out the arrangements for the return of the natives deserve great credit for its success.' The expense incurred in the rescue was paid by Natal, not Britain. Among those congratulating Marwick was Joseph Baynes, a member of the Natal Legislative Assembly, who farmed in Marwick's home district of Richmond. In a letter to Marwick he said, 'We have reason to be proud of the stand taken by our Colony in this serious crisis and proud, very proud of our Volunteers but I think there is no act greater than your achievement.'[10]

The first two weeks in October 1899, were very traumatic for the people of Natal. Many found it difficult to believe that they were about to be attacked by the Boer Republics. After all, President Kruger had stated at the June conference with Milner, 'we shall never be the attacking party on another man's land.' Kruger was subtle enough to avoid stating he regarded the whole of Southern Africa as his land.

While Marwick and the miners were on their walk, a former Prime Minister of Natal, Sir Harry Escombe, was touring Northern Natal telling people there was no immediate danger of war. In the end, to avoid Boer patrols, he had to make an undignified escape in a post cart disguised as an old woman.

The Volunteer unit in northern Natal, initially known as the Buffalo Guards, was absorbed by the Natal Carbineers. At the beginning of September 1899, the squadron of the Carbineers based in Dundee, about forty strong, were the only military force guarding Natal north of Ladysmith. The citizens of Dundee, alarmed by reports of Boer kommandos assembling on Natal's borders, decided to form a Town Guard and 150 men enrolled. The proprietor of the Masonic Hotel was elected commandant and to assist him, six lieutenants were also elected. For two weeks they drilled, built fortifications and had rifle practice. Many were crack shots.

On 25 September, the first of General Penn Symons' Imperial troops arrived. Into Dundee came the 18th Hussars, the Royal Dublin Fusiliers, the Leicester Regiment, the King's Royal Rifles (the 60th) and finally, on 16 October, the Royal Inniskillings, who had been sent on from Ladysmith by Sir George White. There were some mounted infantry attached to the Leicesters, the Rifles and the Dublins. With them were three batteries of artillery, and two hospital corps. Completing the military were some Natal Police under Col Dartnell and of course the local Carbineers. All in all, just over 4,000 men, fewer than Reitz expected, but nonetheless a substantial force.

Gerard Bailey, the Anglican Vicar of St James' Church in Dundee, kept a diary describing what happened to the civilians in the town. On 1 October his wife left for Durban, the couple thinking they would be parted for a few weeks. Dundee was soon to receive a flood of refugees. Fleeing before the advancing Boers, many of the residents of Newcastle headed for Dundee. The rain that ensured adequate grazing for the invaders added to the misery of the refugees. The vicar, moved particularly by the plight of the women and children, took as many as he could into his home and a Relief Committee was formed.

Among the refugees were two stonemasons who had walked unmolested through the Boer lines. They had noticed that the Transvaal railway carriages had written on them their intended destinations 'Durban' or 'Pietermaritzburg'. The Boers also had plenty to say for themselves. They told the masons that they were truly sorry for the British soldiers, who were coming to South Africa only to be shot. They said that they were going to walk through Natal, and drive the *rooineks* into the sea. They even offered to employ the stonemasons to build their houses in Durban.

Bailey found Penn Symons to be bright, affable, genial and popular with the townspeople. No doubt they found his self-confidence reassuring. It was not his first visit to Dundee. As a young man in 1879, he was with Chelmsford's column when they discovered the slaughter and destruction at Isandlwana. Penn Symons was shocked and unnerved by the experience and took a few weeks recuperative leave at Talana, the home of Peter and Ann Smith. Ann Smith mothered the young man until, with his confidence restored, he returned to his regiment.

Gerard Bailey's Relief Committee never had a chance to carry out their good works. On Monday 16 October, all women and children were requested to leave Dundee on the train that had just brought the Inniskillings from Ladysmith. The vicar helped his guests carry their few belongings to the station and watched them, packed like sardines, leave on the train. Returning to his empty home he reflected on the plight of the refugees, who did not know where fate was taking them or how long their ordeal would last. Over the following two days further trainloads of refugees left Dundee.

The fate of many of the refugees was to be worse than Gerard could have imagined. Most went to Durban, where local authority facilities and charities were overwhelmed by the thousands of destitute people fleeing from the Transvaal and Northern Natal. Where possible, local families gave them shelter but this was only able to benefit a small proportion of them. Land was set aside where they might set up tents, which cost between £1 10s and £4 10s. Those who were unable to afford the tents made shelters from tins and boxes. Few had money to buy food. Local charities attempted to provide food but the task was beyond their resources. Mr Haggar of the YMCA wrote to the *Natal Mercury* describing some of the problems he faced on a typical day:

Woman with two children, husband's whereabouts unknown; no money, not a change of clothing. Brings me a note from a gentleman who knows her to be respectable. My funds are exhausted, and all the clothing left was an old black skirt – that was better than nothing, and she took it.

Woman with four children; husband supposed to be in Johannesburg; rent and relief stopped; could get work but who is to look after the children? Besides, what can a woman do with four children and only two pounds per month [pay] at most?

Very delicate woman; no shamming about her; has two children; her husband went to Ladysmith with a convoy before the siege; has heard nothing since; all relief stopped, and is in arrears for rent; needs a prolonged course of medical treatment. All I could do was to express sympathy and give her a little clothing for her boy. She had no money;

neither had I, and the poor woman has to live on hope – a very cruel protector.

A poor woman stood at the door of my room, unable to speak because of the lump in her throat. After some minutes, she said, 'I have never asked for help before, and it will be too cruel for me to go and perhaps be told, there is no money. I have come to you because I come from Australia. My husband is dead.'[12]

Although almost all the refugees were British subjects, the British Government showed no interest in their welfare. When word of the appalling conditions under which they were living reached London, the Lord Mayor set up an emergency fund to provide basic necessities. People contributed generously and the money was sent to Lord Milner for distribution in South Africa. The Durban Relief Fund received £11,000 – without which many of the refugees would have died of starvation.

7

Border Patrol

Captain Robert Buntine, an Australian who had settled in Natal, performed the first conspicuous act of gallantry in the war, and went on to perform complex medical operations in the field.

Scout Teise Ndlovu with Lt R. Samuelson; Teise arranged for the photograph to be taken and paid for it.

The Natal Volunteers responded promptly to the order to mobilise. At 6 a.m. on 1 October 1899, those Natal Carbineer squadrons based in Pietermaritzburg paraded in the Market Square, then marched to the station accompanied by a band playing *Soldiers of the Queen*. Along the route they were cheered by a large crowd. They entrained at 8.15 a.m. and arrived at Ladysmith that evening. The Natal Mounted Rifles reached Ladysmith on the morning of the 2 October and the Border Mounted Rifles, many of whose members had a long ride to their nearest railway station, assembled in Ladysmith at 7o'clock that same evening. The Natal Field Artillery and the Natal Naval Volunteers were also sent to Ladysmith. The Estcourt squadron of the Carbineers assembled at Estcourt and from Greytown, the Umvoti Mounted Rifles moved north towards Helpmekaar to patrol the crossings of the Tugela River near the Transvaal border. The Durban Light Infantry, who mustered 430 men, went 10 miles south to the hamlet of Colenso, the site of important road and rail bridges across the Tugela. The Dundee squadron of the Natal Carbineers remained in Dundee.

As the mounted regiments required veterinary surgeons, a Volunteer Veterinary Corps was recruited and most of its 10 members went to Ladysmith. Their senior officer was Major Herbert Watkins-Pitchford, who had been in charge of the Natal Government's veterinary research station at Allerton, Pietermaritzburg. Over the years, their research had many successes in the fight to control animal diseases, which threatened stock all over Africa. During the siege, he kept a diary in the form of a letter to his wife.

Doctors and nurses of the Natal Volunteer Medical Corps accompanied their regiments to Ladysmith. Three doctors went out on patrol with their units – Robert Buntine with the Carbineers, Rupert Hornabrook with the Natal Mounted Rifles, and Dr H.T. Platt with the Border Mounted Rifles. The other doctors manned the tented Volunteer Hospital in Ladysmith. Included in the Corps were eighteen qualified nurses.

Despite the refusal on 28 July 1899 by the then British Commander in Chief in South Africa, Major General Sir William Butler, to authorise the enlistment of armed or unarmed native scouts as this might offend the Boers, the Natal authorities decided in September 1899 to defy the order and to enlist a corps of Native Scouts.

Among the Carbineers in Ladysmith was Robert Samuelson, a practising attorney and brother of S.O. Samuelson, the Natal official whose prompt action and expert advice would play such an important part in the rescue of the 7,000 Zulus who were in danger of being trapped in the Transvaal. Colonel W. Royston knew Robert Samuelson and felt he would be the ideal person to raise and command the Scouts. Apart from his professional career, Robert, like many colonials, was a keen sportsman and in more peaceful times had established a reputation as a promising cricketer.

On 3 October, Robert Samuelson was appointed the Officer Commanding of the Natal Native Scouts and ordered to raise 150 men to cover the Drakensberg from Tintwa Pass in the west, to the Biggarsberg hills to the north of Ladysmith. He was given full discretion with respect to their recruitment and deployment. On receiving the orders, Samuelson, accompanied by the magistrate, immediately rode out to the home of Chief Khumalo, which was some 20 miles north of Ladysmith near a place called Driefontein. The magistrate introduced Samuelson to the chief and then returned to Ladysmith. At that time the chief was over 100 years old but was still in full possession of all his mental faculties. The next day he summoned his people:

> My children this is the day of days; an impudent foe, the Boers, are preparing to fight against her Majesty the Queen, our Sovereign and Mother, who has for so many years spread her wings over us to protect us, and who is minded to continue spreading her wings like an Angel over us till they touch the earth; That Queen requires your services, go and serve her till death.[1]

A chorus of approval was shouted by all present, whereupon the Chief instructed them to get everything ready. Horses, bridles and saddles were collected. As there were not enough saddles to go round, some of the scouts had to ride bareback. Samuelson decided to adopt the Zulu system of scouting. Men were stationed at intervals along the border and gallopers went to and fro between the different scout groups bringing back to Samuelson the information that had been gathered. He kept several scouts with him who would take such information he thought important to Colonel W. Royston in Ladysmith. Much of the activity, including feeding the scouts, was undertaken at night so as to avoid detection by the Boers. Samuelson also sent men, fluent in Sotho and Dutch, across the border, where they would mix with the Boer servants and gain much useful information.

One scout even fell into conversation with some Boers and among other things learnt that if they caught old Chief Khumalo they would gouge his eyes out. Samuelson immediately arranged for a Cape cart to take the Chief to the home of Simeon Khambule, a hero on the British side of the Battles of Isandlwana and Ulundi and now resident in Ladysmith, where he was leader of the scouts working out of Ladysmith. Because of his extreme age the old chief delegated many of his duties to his grandson, Joseph Khumalo, and it was with Joseph that Samuelson arranged much of the day-to-day work of the scouts.[2]

Although war had not yet been declared, the Volunteers went out on patrol as soon as they arrived in Ladysmith. The Carbineers, the Border Mounted Rifles and the Natal Mounted Rifles patrolled the area covering the mountain passes, through which the Free State might launch a surprise attack. It was very hard work. They would rise well before dawn, breakfast, saddle up and be on their way before first light. In the evening they would unsaddle and have something to eat. As soon as it was dark they would strike camp, saddle up and ride to another site about 10 miles away. On arrival, which was generally at about 1 a.m., they would unsaddle and get what sleep they could before repeating the routine the next day. This procedure ensured that they would not be surprised by a night attack, however the many hours in the saddle and sleep deprivation were exhausting.

A Field Day was held during which the various corps in Ladysmith put on a display. The Natal Carbineers gave a display of their horses lying down to order and remaining so despite rifle fire. The colonel in charge complimented the Border Mounted Rifles on the manner in which they were able to get over rough, stony ground. The highlight of the day was a charge by the full complement of the 5th Lancers. It was a magnificent sight as they charged across the plain, lances at the ready and bugles sounding to disappear in clouds of dust. When the dust cleared it was seen that about a dozen horses had come down and the riders were busy picking themselves up. Fortunately only one rider was injured, and he not too seriously.[3]

On 12 October 1899, Mrs Portsmouth, whose family had a farm and shop near Van Reenen's Pass, noticed men and guns coming over the passes into Natal.

On that same day, the Natal Volunteers were told that war had been declared. In contrast to the invading Boers, who stood in their stirrups and cheered themselves hoarse when they heard of the ultimatum, the Volunteers greeted the news with quiet determination. No one stood in their stirrups or cheered. As usual they were ordered out on patrol. The Natal Mounted Rifles patrolled north of Ladysmith in the direction of Dundee, the Border Mounted Rifles watched the border between Mont aux Sources and Tintwa Mountain and the Carbineers from Tintwa to Van Reenen's Pass. It was not long before Major Taunton of the Carbineers reported signs of enemy activity. The Intelligence Section at Headquarters doubted the validity of this information.

The following day the Carbineers again reported Boers descending into Natal and the Border Mounted Rifles reported a strong column of Boers coming into Natal by the Tintwa Pass. That day a rumour was circulated in Ladysmith that the Border Mounted Rifles had been surrounded and all killed. Whether it was for this or some other reason, a column of about 4,000 Imperial troops marched out along the road towards Van Reenen's Pass. Showing a complete lack of sporting spirit the Free Staters declined to show themselves. After marching about 8 miles, and hearing from an orderly with the BMR that the rumour of the destruction of that regiment was false, they returned to Ladysmith.

That night it was cold and poured with rain; nonetheless, the exhausted Border Mounted Riflemen went to sleep in the mud. At about 9.30 p.m. the alarm sounded. Scouts and native spies reported a large body of Boers was approaching. In seven minutes the men were saddled up with packs and ammunition ready and all fallen in. Captain Jack Royston was delegated to investigate and found it was not Boers who were approaching but a large body of civilian refugees. They had come from Harrismith in the Free State, where they had been told by the Boers to get out immediately. They had no choice but to attempt to walk the 50 miles to Ladysmith over a high mountain pass, where it was likely they would encounter snow and blizzards. It was a miracle they survived.

For the next few days the cat and mouse tactics continued. The Volunteers would see a group of Boers approaching, there would be an exchange of fire and the Boers would retreat. After one such skirmish, a group of Hussars and Lancers under a Major Adye came out from Ladysmith. Major Rethman pointed out the position of the Boers. Major Adye surveyed the scene and announced there were no Boers there, and proceeded to lead his men forward. They immediately came under rifle fire and had to retreat back to their original position. Major Rethman asked whether they were about to attack the Boers and was told by Adye that he had merely come out to check the Volunteers' report.[4]

On 17 October, the Carbineers came under heavy fire from a Boer kommando. In response, the regiment's Maxim gun went forward with Lt Gallwey and opened fire. Col Greene, in command, then noticed that the Boers were attempting to outflank him, so he ordered the Maxim group to come back. They returned with the Maxim but without Gallwey who, after receiving a kick from his horse was prevented from withdrawing with the others.

Outnumbered and in danger of being surrounded, Col Greene decided that any attempt to rescue Gallwey would put the whole regiment at risk, and accordingly ordered that they retire. As they did so, one of their horses fell, throwing his rider heavily. Seeing what had happened, Dr Buntine immediately rode back, under fire, to assist the injured trooper who had been stunned. He tried to get the injured man onto his horse but was unable to do so until his orderly, F. Duke, joined him. Together they were able to get the trooper mounted and, with Buntine running alongside the injured man, they arrived back safely to their comrades. Despite their Red Cross badges, Buntine and Duke were under persistent fire from the Boers while attending to the injured man.[5]

Robert Andrew Buntine was born near Melbourne, Victoria, in 1869. He attended Scotch College from 1884 to 1886. He received a Queen's College scholarship and studied medicine at Melbourne University, graduating M.B. in 1891 and B.Sc. in March 1892. Several subjects were passed with honours. He excelled as a sportsman, being the University champion athlete. In 1892 he was appointed resident surgeon at Melbourne Hospital. He married the daughter of Henry Pinson who had moved from Australia to Natal. Perhaps because of this family connection, Robert Buntine moved to Pietermaritzburg in 1893. Afterwards he spent a year in England. When he was offered the post of resident surgeon at Grey's Hospital in Pietermaritzburg, he returned to Natal.

The rescue of the injured trooper by Buntine and Duke was the first conspicuous act of bravery in the war, though it was never officially recognised as such because headquarters had not authorised the action.

The Volunteers' orders were to report on the enemy's movements but not to engage them, so, strictly speaking, the action by the Carbineers exceeded their orders. However, it is difficult to see how this logic can be applied to giving medical attention to an injured soldier. We shall come across Buntine again. His orderly, Duke, died during the siege.

On 18 October, both the Carbineers and the Border Mounted Rifles came into contact with the Boers, and after an exchange of fire, the Boers occupied the railway siding at Besters on the Ladysmith/Harrismith line. In the course of the action Trooper J. Surgeson of the Carbineers lost his horse but was able to hide from the Boers until he was found by a group of Samuelson's scouts, who were on their way to report the movements of the Boers. As a result of their report Samuelson ordered the whole line of Scouts to retire towards Ladysmith where they would receive further orders. They successfully completed their retirement over the next few days. A horse was found for Surgeson who, with Samuelson, rode into Ladysmith to resume duty with the Carbineers.

After they had withdrawn from Besters, the Volunteers received orders to retire to Ladysmith, coupled with advice that as the enemy had penetrated between the Volunteers and Ladysmith, it was no longer practicable to return by the direct road. The order to retire was brought to the BMR by a veteran Carbineer, W. Leathern, owner of the farm where the BMR were temporarily camped. Major Rethman decided to send his commissariat wagons back to Ladysmith via the main road, telling them if they saw Boers, they were to tell them that the regiment would be following an hour later. Immediately they were out of sight, the rest of the regiment, guided by Leathern, set off on a circuitous route back to base. Riding hard with scouts out, they were able to reach Ladysmith at 2.30 a.m. Maj. Rethman immediately went to Col W. Royston to advise him that he had had to sacrifice his wagons, only to find that the wagons had arrived safely in Ladysmith, without having seen any Boers. The men were exhausted, having been in the saddle almost continuously for 24 hours and the horses had had no rest for 36 hours. They fed the horses, put their saddle blankets down on the road and fell asleep instantly. But not for long.

At daylight they were called upon to sort out their lines and get everything straight. The next day they were called out at 4.30 a.m. Headquarters urgently wanted information as to the movements of the Free State kommandos. Though it was pouring with rain and they had had nothing to eat, they nevertheless immediately saddled up and rode out on patrol. They found the Boers near Besters Station and tracked their movements through the day, returning to Ladysmith at 5 p.m. Major Rethman reporting his losses as being one hat.

One of the most severe tests of stamina of man and horse during this period was carried out by C Squadron of the Natal Mounted Rifles, led by Captain L.T. Wales. This troop was out for five days during which it covered about 200 miles over all sorts of country. In one 24-hour period they covered 70 miles.They gained and transmitted to headquarters much valuable information regarding nests of Boers who were awaiting the arrival of the main kommandos. On their return to camp in Ladysmith, the men were so exhausted that some had to be assisted out of their saddles, others, half asleep, simply tumbled out and, refusing food, slept for a day and a night without a move. The horses lay down in the lines for several days, getting up only to eat. In the long history of equestrian warfare this must rank as one of the most remarkable displays of stamina by man and horse.

The outbreak of war did not change the attitude of many in the British army towards the colonials. One junior British artillery officer, more perceptive than most, complained in his diary of the 'criminal ignorance and negligence of our Intelligence Department, who are above acting on news received from Colonial troops who prove a jolly sight better scouters than our regular cavalry'.[6]

One who had begun to get some idea of the capabilities of the colonial Volunteers was General White. On 18 October he selected Captain F.S. Tatham of the Natal Carbineers and 21 NCOs and men of the Natal Mounted Rifles to be his personal bodyguard.

8

Battle of Talana Hill

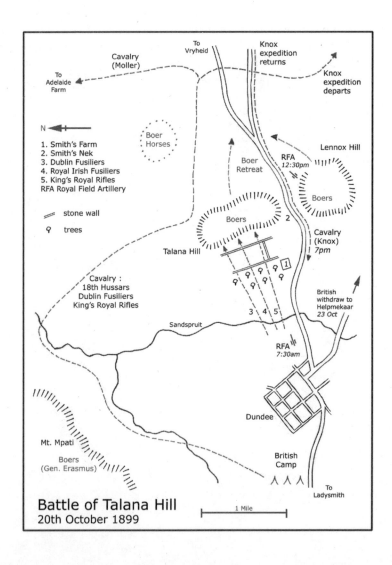

To Vryheid

Knox expedition returns

Cavalry (Moller)

To Adelaide Farm

Knox expedition departs

N

1. Smith's Farm
2. Smith's Nek
3. Dublin Fusiliers
4. Royal Irish Fusiliers
5. King's Royal Rifles
RFA Royal Field Artillery

Boer Horses

Boer Retreat

RFA 12:30pm

Lennox Hill

stone wall

trees

Boers

Boers

2

Talana Hill

Cavalry (Knox) 7pm

Cavalry :
18th Hussars
Dublin Fusiliers
King's Royal Rifles

1

British withdraw to Helpmekaar 23 Oct

Sandspruit

3 4 5

RFA 7:30am

Mt. Mpati

Dundee

Boers (Gen. Erasmus)

British Camp

To Ladysmith

Battle of Talana Hill
20th October 1899

1 Mile

On Sunday 8 October 1899, the Revd Gerard Bailey in Dundee chose as the text for his sermon, Psalm 121. 'I will lift up mine eyes unto the hills, from whence cometh my help.'

Less than two weeks later, the vicar, when visiting the hospital, was told by a wounded officer that it was not help that came from the hills, but Boers.

If one stands in Dundee and looks north towards Newcastle the view is of a broad shallow valley dominated by two hills. On the left is the massive bulk of Mpati. This hill, which in many places would be called a mountain, is about 3 miles from Dundee and rises about 1,500 feet above the valley floor. On the right, about 1½ miles from Dundee, is a longer lower hill generally known as Talana but sometimes as Smith's Hill. Further still to the right (or the east) and connected to Talana by a saddle known as Smith's Nek, is another eminence called Lennox Hill. In the shallow valley between Dundee and Talana is a stream known as the Sandspruit.

In the 1850s Thomas Smith emigrated from Scotland to Australia and, after spending five years on the Australian goldfields, moved to Natal where he purchased a farm he called Dundee after his home town in Scotland. On the farm was Talana Hill and it was on the slopes of this hill that the farmhouse and other buildings were sited. Thomas worked as a building contractor and small-time farmer. In 1864 he persuaded his brother Peter and family to join him. They burnt their own bricks for building, and built up fine herds of South Devon cattle and Merino sheep. Shortly after his arrival in 1864, Peter Smith found coal on the farm. The coal turned out to be of high quality and a small mining community gradually developed. In due course Peter inherited the farm from his brother. In 1882 it was decided to lay out a township to accommodate the growing population. This new town was called, unsurprisingly, Dundee. Its founders were Peter Smith, his son William Craighead Smith, his son-in-law Dugald MacPhail and Charles George Willson.

William Craighead Smith had served with the Buffalo Border Guards in the Anglo-Zulu war and in 1899 was a member of the Dundee squadron of the Natal Carbineers. William's son also served with the Carbineers and was to be killed by shellfire during the siege of Ladysmith. Dugald MacPhail owned a neighbouring farm, served in the Anglo- Zulu war, and was one of the few survivors of the Battle of Isandlwana. In 1940 he enrolled with the police reserve, the oldest reservist and the oldest ex-serviceman in the Empire. He died in 1941 aged 100. In 1899 he was a member of the Dundee Town Guard. Charles George Willson was born in London in 1850 and arrived in Natal with his parents in 1852. In 1873 William Smith persuaded him to open a business in Dundee to serve the growing community. He joined the Buffalo Border Guards and served as a sergeant major in the Anglo-Zulu war. He was the leader of the scouts sent out by Lord Chelmsford to find out what was happening at the Isandlwana base camp, and was the first man to reach that stricken battlefield. In the Carbineers he was appointed Lieutenant in 1888 and Captain in 1895. In 1899 he was the senior officer of the Dundee squadron of the Carbineers.

Charlie Willson was a man of prodigious energy who had a long record of public service. Not only was he one of the founders of Dundee but he was mayor of the town for many years. His drive and initiative was primarily responsible for the construction of the town's waterworks and electricity power station and it was he who persuaded the railways that instead of bypassing Glencoe and Dundee, to route the mainline through Glencoe with a branch to Dundee. He was president of the local Building Society from its foundation to his death; a prominent man in agricultural circles, he was one of the founders of the Natal Wool Company. He played a leading role in the development of coal mining in the district, an industry that was to contribute much to the development of South Africa. A keen sportsman, he was president or vice-president of a number of sports clubs. He and his wife were two of the most popular and respected people in northern Natal, which he had represented in the Legislative Assembly for four years from 1893.

When the British troops arrived at Dundee on 25 September, there was of course a military presence already there, namely, the Natal Carbineers commanded by Captain C.G. Willson. On arrival, Penn Symons, as a matter of courtesy, ought to have sought out the commander of the Carbineers, explained what he was doing in Dundee, and asked for Willson's assistance and advice. With his knowledge of the district and its people, no one was in a better position to advise the general than Charlie Willson, and no one was more in need of such advice than General Sir William Penn Symons. Sadly, Penn Symons appears to have taken little or no interest in the assistance he could have obtained from the local Carbineers or their commander. A possible reason for this attitude might be that both Penn Symons and Sir Archibald Hunter, Chief of Staff in Ladysmith, would have been fully aware of Sir Garnet Wolseley's directive that military information should not be passed on to colonials.

Even before they received the order to mobilise, the Carbineers would have been anxiously watching developments across the nearby Transvaal border. After mobilisation, they and some members of the Town Guard patrolled the district so as to immediately detect the presence of any Boers.

During the initial stages of their invasion of Natal, the Boers advanced very cautiously as General Piet Joubert, the Transvaal Commandant-General, feared the British had laid minefields. It took their army from 12 to 16 October 1899 to cover the thirty unopposed miles from the border to Newcastle. While Joubert was searching for landmines, another peril was threatening the Transvaal. In Pretoria there was considerable concern that Britain was about to invade the Republic with a great fleet of war balloons! Telegraph stations were ordered to immediately report any sightings and many reports of balloons with coloured searchlights were daily reported from every corner of the Transvaal. Freda Schlosberg noted in her diary, 'Several balloons are rumoured to have been seen over Johannesburg, Pretoria and Standerton, and it is said that the government has given orders to shoot at them; so several stars have been shot at.'[1]

When the Boer army had crossed the last mountain pass before Newcastle and had reached the crossing of the Buffalo River, one of their leaders was moved to make a speech. Deneys Reitz recalled, 'General "Maroola", with a quick eye to the occasion, faced round and made a speech telling us that Natal was a heritage filched from our forefathers, which must now be recovered from the usurper. Amid enthusiastic cries we began to ford the stream. It took nearly an hour for all to cross, during this time the cheering and singing of the Volkslied was continuous, and we rode into the smiling land of Natal full of hope and courage.'[2]

Of the reception of the Boers in Newcastle, Deneys wrote, 'such of the inhabitants as sympathised with us waving encouragement, and the rest looking on in sullen resentment, as the long lines of horsemen went by.'[3]

Of course 'the rest' did not include those train loads of refugees who had already fled Newcastle.

At Newcastle General Joubert decided on his tactics for the invasion. One column of about five thousand men under General Lukas Meyer would cross the border at a point east of Dundee. The centre column, with another five thousand men, including young Reitz and commanded by General Erasmus, an older brother of 'Maroola', would continue along the main route south and link up with Meyer at Dundee. A third smaller column under General Kock would move west, link up with the Free State commandos, then the combined force would turn south and cut the railway line between Ladysmith and Dundee, thereby isolating the latter.

By the evening of 19 October, the Boer kommandos were closing in on Dundee. General Kock had succeeded in cutting the rail and telegraph link with Ladysmith at Elandslaagte, though the telegraph link through Greytown remained open. General Erasmus had reached the northern slopes of Mpati and in the east, Lukus Meyer had crossed the Buffalo River and was well on his way to Talana. It was from the two hills, Mpati and Talana, that the Boers planned to launch their attack on Dundee.

The British camp lay in the valley to the west of Dundee, and not only was it overlooked by both Mpati and Talana, it was also within the range of artillery placed on either. Penn Symons, for some inexplicable reason, had decided not to occupy either of the hills. He paid no regard to the reports by scouts warning of the approach of the Boers, and when on the morning of 19 October the manager of the Navigation Colliery, which is on the northern slope of Mpati, rode in and reported the Boers were bringing up guns with the intention of shelling Dundee, the General retorted that this was 'ridiculous'.[4] Initially he made no attempt to guard Smith's Nek, a natural doorway from the Transvaal to Natal. However, on the evening of 19 October, a picket of mounted infantry drawn from the Dublin Fusiliers was sent there.

At 3.30 a.m. on 20 October, the now dismounted Fusiliers on Smith's Nek were fired on by scouts from Lucas Meyer's kommando. Lt Grimshaw, in charge of the picket, wisely decided to retire. The gunfire had stampeded their horses but shielded by mist and the dark they were able to withdraw on foot.

A sergeant was sent back to the camp with the news and, in response, two companies of the Dublin Fusiliers were sent out to support their comrades. The picket was able to find their horses and, with their reinforcements, they dug in along the Sandspruit at the bottom of Talana Hill.

Apart from this minor incident, it was just the start of another day in the British camp, and what better way to welcome the cold dawn than to have a cup of good hot tea. As the officers looked at the dawn breaking over Talana they could, through the swirling mist, see little black dots moving about on the top of the hill. Could it be? No, impossible. Better check through the field glasses. It was. The Boers, in some numbers, had occupied Talana. No one paid much attention to Mpati, which was still shrouded in mist.

The Revd Bailey had heard the rifleshots just after 3 a.m., got up and he too had had a cup of tea. At 5 a.m. he and a friend went down to the market place, where they met some members of the Town Guard, who were going home after a night patrolling the town. They told Bailey that the picket at Smith's Nek had been fired on. The parson had a look at Talana through his field glasses. He could see people moving around but concluded they must be British troops investigating the attack on the picket.[5] He did not entertain this illusion for long. Suddenly a big gun boomed, followed by a rushing sound as a shell came over the town, pitching somewhere to the north west. The spectators concluded that the British had placed a gun on Talana and were shelling a target near Mpati. The next landed just past the British camp. The third landed in the camp and thereafter shell after shell crashed into the camp. The townsmen hurriedly sought shelter though for the time being they were safe as the Boers concentrated all their fire on the army.

The first shell to hit the British camp landed a few feet from the tent of General Penn Symons and would surely have killed him had it exploded. But like most of the other shells sent over by the Boers that day, it failed to explode as the percussion caps were incorrectly set, resulting in the shells burrowing into the soft, wet ground rather than exploding. If the arrival of the Boer shells surprised the general, they certainly did not fluster or intimidate him. Within a few minutes, his artillery had attempted to return the Boer fire and the general had formed his plan of action.

The infantry, backed by the artillery, would make a frontal assault on Talana, thereby dislodging the Boers from the hill, while the cavalry would go round to the back of the hill, and, cutting off the Boer retreat, deliver the coup de grace. The Dublin Fusiliers would assault on the left and the King's Royal Rifles on the right. The Royal Irish Fusiliers would provide support for the other two regiments. The 1st Leicester Regiment, supported by 67th Field Battery, were ordered out to protect the western approaches to the town. Brigadier-General Yule, Penn Symons' second in command, suggested that to support the main thrust, a flank attack be made on the northern shoulder of Talana. Such an attack would not only assist the main thrust but would have been sheltered from flanking fire from Lennox Hill. Penn Symons rejected this proposal by Yule out of hand.

Penn Symons did not forget the Natal Carbineers. They were given the task of guarding the base camp, something that could have been done quite effectively by some of the less able members of the Town Guard.

The first salvo of shells from the Royal Artillery fell well short of the target on Talana. They quickly moved forward to within 3,000 yards of the target, only to find that they were still outranged. Finally at 2,300 yards they were able to reach the target and silence the Boer guns on Talana and Lennox Hill. Not long afterwards the Boers removed their guns from the battlefield.

Meanwhile the infantry, cheered on by the civilians, marched through the town, and successfully made their way across the open ground to the Sandspruit. Though rifle fire was directed at them, they were, because of the extreme range, able to make the safety of the banks of the stream without any serious casualties. The Boers now knew precisely where to expect the attack.

British officers surveying the scene saw that from the stream stretched 800 to 1000 metres of open grassland before the farm and its buildings were reached. Here there was a band of trees roughly parallel to the stream and the summit of the hill. Beyond the trees was another stretch of open grassland above which was a stone wall, again approximately parallel to the trees and the summit. Beyond the stone wall, the slope of the hill to the top became progressively more precipitous though just how steep, rocky and awkward the final climb would be, was not readily apparent from afar.

Down in the bed of the stream, Penn Symons sorted out his infantry regiments into the proposed attack formations and at 7.30 a.m. they broke cover and charged in open order towards the trees. A withering fire from the Boers greeted this move and men began to fall. On reaching the trees it was found that they provided but little cover, compelling the men to go to ground. Fortunately, there was another stone wall running along the upper edge of the wood and this provided some shelter. At right angles to these two walls was yet another, which ran straight up the hill. This third wall was to provide, later that morning, valuable shelter from flanking fire coming from Lennox Hill.

At about 9 a.m. Penn Symons, apparently concerned that the attack might have stalled, sent two staff officers to Yule, the commander in the wood, instructing him to proceed with the assault. Yule replied that he would do so as soon as possible.[6] Apparently not satisfied with this response, the general decided to go to the wood himself. His horse was brought to him and accompanied by Col Dartnell and Majors Hattersley and Murray they galloped under heavy fire across the open grassland towards the wood.

At the edge of the wood was a fence and seeing it the general kicked on and soared over the fence and into the wood. Once there he dismounted, and ignoring enemy fire, walked through the wood urging the men forward in readiness for the final assault. As they approached the further edge, Major Hattersley was wounded and shortly afterwards the general, seeing a gap in the low wall, stepped across to look at the position. A moment later he turned to Murray and said, 'I am severely, mortally, wounded in the stomach.'

Murray helped him back across the wall and to his horse. Riding back through the wood the general gave no sign of being injured, until, having passed out of sight of his men, he collapsed.

Brigadier General Yule, now in overall command, ordered the assault on the summit to proceed. Using the wall going straight up the hill to give some protection from flanking fire, the attackers extricated themselves from the wood and, under heavy fire, gained the upper stone wall. Here they were pinned down for almost two hours during which time they were constantly under fire, not only from the Boers on the summit but also from snipers on Lennox Hill. Meanwhile, the Royal Artillery had continued their bombardment of the Boers occupying the summits of Talana and Lennox Hill.

At midday there was a lull in the artillery fire, which was taken as the signal for the final rush to the summit. It must have seemed an almost impossible task to climb that precipitous slope. Nothing daunted, the attackers jumped over the wall, to be met by a barrage of rifle fire. Despite heavy losses, they scrambled ever upwards over the rocks and through thorn bushes. As they reached the crest, their own artillery re-opened fire on the summit and, before the blunder could be corrected, more losses were inflicted and they had to retreat down the rocks. However, as soon as the artillery fire stopped, they climbed back and the Boers were driven from the summit. In the attack 41 officers and men had been killed and 203 wounded.

Now that the British were in possession of the top of the hill, the Boers retreated not only down the reverse slope of Talana but also from Lennox Hill. As soon as this was realised, two artillery batteries under Col Pickwoad immediately pushed up the hill and unlimbered on Smith's Nek. Though it was drizzling, the gunners had a fine view of the retreating Boers and could have wrought havoc amongst them. Instead they held their fire.

The mounted troops who were to deliver the coup de grace consisted of three squadrons of the 18th Hussars, and some mounted infantry from the Dublin Fusiliers and the King's Royal Rifles. Commanded by Colonel B.D. Moller, they left the camp at about 7 a.m. with orders to work round the north of Talana and there take up a concealed position and await an opportunity to strike at the enemy. It seems these rather vague orders were considered adequate and the details were left to the discretion of Col Moller. As they rode up the Sandspruit valley between Talana and the mist covered Mpati, they were spotted by the Boers on Talana who sent some machine gun fire in their direction but because of the long range, no damage was suffered. They continued north until well past Talana then turned right, crossed the stream, and took up an excellent concealed position on the right rear of the Boers on Talana.

A golden opportunity to influence the day's proceedings now presented itself. They had discovered the Boer 'ponies'. Majors Knox and Marling of the 18th Hussars begged for permission to fire on them with a machine gun to drive them away and leave the Boers stranded on the hill. However, Col

Moller would have none of it and forbade any interference with the ponies. Instead they were ordered to take two squadrons to the rear of Lennox Hill to discover what the Boers were doing. The two squadrons made their way in gathering mist towards the back of Lennox Hill. They met several parties of Boers, some of whom they charged and struck with their swords. Whether it was because the swords were blunt or the homespun jackets of the Boers were very tough is not known, but what is known is that the swords failed to cut through the Boers' coats. Nevertheless thirty or forty prisoners with rather bruised shoulders were taken prisoner by these cavalrymen as they galloped to and fro in the mist.

By midday this escapade had taken them to a point some distance behind the Boer lines and to the east of Smith's Nek. Col Moller now arrived with the rest of the mounted men. He ordered Knox and Marling to take the two squadrons to the south to reconnoitre the land in that direction. Knox handed over the prisoners to Moller, and he and his squadrons departed on their venture of discovery. In the course of the afternoon Knox and Marling were at various times in contact with large groups of Boers but were able to extricate themselves from danger and arrived back in Dundee at 7 p.m.

The remainder of the mounted force, including the Hussars' Maxim detachment, were ordered by Moller to take up positions across the anticipated Boer line of retreat. About 200 men armed with rifles and one machine gun planned to stop nearly 4,000 Boers. Moller realised what he was up against and hastily tried to get his men away. The prisoners were abandoned and when the Maxim gun became bogged down in the Sandspruit, it and its crew were also abandoned. Subsequently, four of the crew were killed and the fifth was wounded and taken prisoner. Instead of returning the way he had come, Moller drifted steadily northwards past the back of Mpati. There the mist was beginning to clear and Denys Reitz with some of his friends were admiring the view northwards from the back of that hill when they were astonished to see a troop of English horsemen, pursued by Boers, riding in a northerly direction up the valley. They quickly saddled up and set off down the steep hill to join the turkey shoot.

Moller appears to have become completely disorientated because every move he made took him further from his base and deeper into Boer territory. Finally, with his men exhausted and night approaching he decided to make a stand at a farm whose buildings and stone walls might provide some protection. The Boers quickly surrounded the farm and though the defenders fought bravely, they were running out of ammunition. When the Boers brought their artillery to bear on the farm, Moller felt he had no alternative but to surrender. He had lost eight men killed and had eighteen wounded. Nine officers and 200 men were captured. Moller had made his stand at Adelaide Farm about 8 miles from Dundee.

From the moment Moller set out that morning he was doomed. Coming from the northern hemisphere his sense of direction would have sent him all the wrong signals and, because of the iron in the hills, compass readings would have been inaccurate. If he had been accompanied by some Natal Carbineers these difficulties might have been overcome but nothing could have saved his command from his failure to seek good advice.

In Dundee Gerard Bailey had watched the progress of the battle. By the time the infantry had reached the wood at Smith's farm, 'the rifle firing was continuous and incessant. To us at a distance it sounded like bubbling boiling water; no rests, no pauses, no intervals. The Maxims augmented the din, and the artillery pounded away.'

Soon the wounded began to arrive, carried in by the bearers the army had brought with them from India. These men from Major Donegan's 18th Field Hospital, showed great courage on this day and continued to do so throughout the Natal Campaign. A warehouse in the town was converted into a temporary hospital and the vicar noted how among all the horrors of war, 'everything was done so quietly and orderly.' He was amazed at the fortitude and cheerfulness of the wounded. He asked one young lad with a bandaged head about his wound and received the reply, 'I've got one in my head, and one in my chest, there's nothing like being greedy.'[7]

Looking through his field glasses, the vicar noticed how crowded together the men were. Later he saw some of the infantry leave the shelter of the stone wall and climb to the crest of the hill, only to return to the wall. He adds, 'They probably found that they were too near to the shells.' He was probably twice as far from the hilltop as the artillery who failed to recognise their own troops. Once the crest had been gained, the vicar saw twelve guns unlimber on Smith's Nek. He knew that behind the hills lay many miles of open country. The foe was at their mercy and should surely have been compelled to surrender. And yet nothing happened. G.B. Fyfe, a refugee from Newcastle, later told the vicar of a conversation he had had with an army officer on that day. Fyfe had followed the artillery up onto Smith's Nek and was looking at the retreating Boers when an officer asked him, 'Are those the enemy?' 'They most certainly are,' was the reply. The officer then said he had no orders to fire.[8]

The courage and sacrifice of the infantry had placed the British in a position where they could have annihilated a substantial portion of the invading army and possibly brought the war to a speedy end. Instead, they turned imminent victory into defeat, which was achieved by the failure of the artillery to press home the advantage gained, and the purposeless galloping around of the mounted men.

Responsibility for the failure by the artillery rests with General Yule, and it was not the only example of erratic behaviour by Yule that day. In the weeks leading up to the battle, as second-in-command he would have been aware of the great danger being created by Penn Symons' over-confidence and no doubt he was becoming increasingly nervous about the situation. When Penn Symons announced his plan of attack early in the morning, Yule had made the eminently sensible suggestion of an attack on the Boer's right flank at Talana. This proposal was, as we have seen, peremptorily rejected. Yule nonetheless loyally led the assault from the Sandspruit up into the wood at Smith's farm. Once in the wood, he found there was inadequate shelter and that the men were crowded far too closely together. Any further advance would require the troops to cross open veld in which they would be exposed to fire not only from the crest of the hill, where concealed Boers were waiting for them, but also to flanking fire from Lennox Hill. He seems to have been reluctant to submit his men to the certain slaughter the proposed attack would bring. When Penn Symons ordered an immediate attack, his reply that he would attack when ready, came as close to defiance as one could reasonably go without actually refusing to obey orders.

The arrival of Penn Symons in the wood, his suffering a mortal wound, and the assumption of overall command, seems to have changed Yule. He casually ordered the assault up the hill to commence immediately. He made no attempt to get the men into a more open order. There was no attempt at a flanking attack, or to co-ordinate the actions of the cavalry, artillery and the infantry. He simply let the battle run according to Penn Symons' plan. When the Boers had completed their retirement, he withdrew the British regiments from the hill.

The capture of mounted men under Moller, and the purposeless galloping around of the squadrons under Majors Knox and Marling, should be attributed to the arrogance of Penn Symons. Captain Willson and his Carbineers should have been with the British cavalry commanders, who ought to have regularly consulted them on all matters. After the withdrawal from the battlefield, Yule's inertia continued.

Lt Crum, a mounted member of the King's Royal Rifles, was severely wounded shortly after the Boers began their retreat. He was found by a Dr Hardy, who applied a dressing to his wound and arranged for Crum and other wounded to be taken to the farm at Talana where a field hospital had been set up. After a long and painful night, dawn at last came and with it the hope that ambulance carts would come and collect them. Crum recorded his experiences at Talana on the day after the battle.

> There were about sixty Boers and a few English ... Many of the wounded Boers came in and looked at us. They shook their heads when they saw Masters, who seemed to be very near dying. Some came and talked to me. All were kind and sympathetic. Our shrapnel seemed to have done terrible work among them, and we all agreed that modern warfare was not 'goot'. We had taken the hill; but no guard was left there; and those slightly wounded, with their rifles, ponies, and wagons were allowed to go off as they pleased! They kept leaving in large numbers with rifles, ponies and wagons, and all seemed agreed that they did not intend to fight any more ... Time dragged on and we seem to have been forgotten. The thought of being dressed and the feeling that something ought to be done for my arm made me fret.

About 12 o'clock some of the Dundee Town Guard came up and found us. I told them how we stood and one of them rode back to get an ambulance. It was great relief when these good fellows came and gave us drinks. The Boers had nearly all cleared. About 1 o'clock the ambulance turned up and at last we got away.[9]

For Charlie Willson and the Carbineers it had been a very disappointing and frustrating couple of days. They were well-trained, experienced, knew the country intimately, and had volunteered so they might contribute to the defence of their town and country. The Carbineers knew the Boers had gone on an orgy of destruction, looting and pillaging after crossing the border. The farms, businesses and homes being destroyed or appropriated by the invaders belonged to them and their friends, and had been created over many years by hard work. Now, when they were most needed, they were required to look after the tents and baggage of the newly arrived British troops.

It was not only the British commanders who had failed so miserably at Dundee. The Boers too had their problems. They had permitted their force to be split in two, with one half under General Erasmus sitting in the mists on top of Mpati, able to contribute nothing more to the battle than listen to the sound of firing. They had failed to ensure their retreat was safe from artillery attack and to take adequate precautions to guard their mounts, without which they would have been helpless. Finally, because they were unfamiliar with conditions in Natal, the *Staatsartillerie* had failed to take into account the fact that the soils in Natal were softer than the hard ground of the Transvaal Highveld, with the result that in spite of being able to outrange the British artillery, they were ineffective.

On 21 October the British moved their camp southwards, hoping thereby to be beyond the range of the Boer guns believed to be on Mpati. However, at 4 p.m. Boer shells arrived in the new camp, causing casualties. In the pouring rain that night it was moved 2 miles further south. On the following day came the cheering news of a British victory at Elandslaagte, a hamlet and rail siding a few miles north of Ladysmith. This lifted spirits and the British contingent marched out along the Glencoe road to intercept Boers fleeing from Elandslaagte. The hopes turned out to be illusory as the Boers were moving towards Ladysmith rather than fleeing. The column had no choice but to march back to their camp. General Yule now wished to move his men to the top of Talana and hold out there until relief came. It was with some difficulty that Col Dartnell and others persuaded him that he had no alternative but to retire to Ladysmith by the more circuitous southerly route along the Helpmekaar road. Only a few senior officers knew of this plan. From about this time, contemporary writers make frequent references to General Yule being ill – though the nature of his illness is never stated.

Major Marling has left an account of the British camp on the evening of 22 October,

There was the most awful confusion: regiments without their commanding officers, and commanding officers without their regiments. No one knew where the General was, and all the Staff but two had been knocked over. The Headquarters telegraph clerk came and asked me where the General was, as he had been hunting for him with a most important message for an hour. It was to this effect: 'From GOC Ladysmith. I cannot reinforce you without sacrificing Ladysmith and the Colony behind. You must try and fall back on Ladysmith. I will do what I may to help when nearer. Cheery under the circumstances, I couldn't find General Yule so gave it to old Pickwoad in the RA, the next senior officer, who nearly fell off his horse when he read it. It had been drizzling since 5 p.m., and now rained in a steady downpour ... We got no orders at all, and none of us had any idea what we were to do in the morning.[10]

It had been decided to leave Dundee that night. The troops were told to leave the candles burning in their tents but were not told what they were to do or where they were going, with the result that when the men fell in and were marched through Dundee, few would have guessed they were leaving for good. That was only realised when they had covered some considerable distance out of town. The Town Guard had been ordered out to Talana to guard the eastern approaches to the town. No one mentioned the proposed flight from Dundee to them.

On the night of 22 October Gerard Bailey accepted an invitation from Father Murray to sleep in the Roman Catholic Church, as it was felt that in the event of the Boers shelling the town it would be safer there than in the Anglican vicarage, which was in the centre of town. The sisters of the convent had left them blankets and pillows so the Anglican and Roman priests made up their beds behind the altar. Before he fell asleep, Gerard Bailey thought of the psalmist, 'I will lay me down in peace and take my rest; for it is Thou, Lord, only, that makes me dwell in safety.'

He awoke at about 11 p.m. He looked out of a window and saw infantry quietly marching along at a steady pace. The cavalry had apparently already passed. After the infantry came the supply wagons, which somehow created a traffic jam that an officer was trying to sort out. Overcome with tiredness, he fell asleep before the last wagon had passed.

Monday 23 October was Gerard's birthday. He awoke to find the British troops had left Dundee. Where they had gone, no one knew. Some civilians had set off, some on foot, others by horse, for Greytown – or along the railway to Ladysmith. At about 10 o'clock he went to the local grocer to find he, too, was about to leave. Gerard bought all the groceries he could carry. He saw the erstwhile proprietor of the Masonic Hotel and Commandant of the Town Guard driving away in a cart. He had left no orders for his men for whom he appeared to have no concern. To make matters worse he failed to destroy the list of Town Guard Members, a document which the Boers were to find most interesting. Serious as this misdemeanour was, it was nothing like as bad as that perpetrated by the British. They had left two of their code books in Dundee.

The Town Guard had helped with the wounded on the day of the battle and on the days which followed they were employed on guard duties by the British. Notwithstanding the subsequent poor conduct of their commandant, the vicar had no doubt that they had been treated very badly and the manner in which the British army had sneaked away, abandoning the Guard, created much resentment in Natal at that time.

At about 11 a.m. the magistrate released seventeen Boer prisoners, having extracted from them a promise not to take up arms against the British. At about 1 p.m. the Boers rode into town. Gerard Bailey watched them riding in. They came in cautiously as if expecting a trap and seemed puzzled by the absence of any troops. Once they had satisfied themselves that they were safe they rode round town enquiring 'Where's Charlie? Where's Willson?'[11] Of all the Queen's horses and all the Queen's men who had defended Dundee, the one who concerned the Boers most was Captain C.G. Willson of the Natal Carbineers.

9

Battle of Elandslaagte

With an establishment of four officers and eighty-six other ranks, A Squadron of the Imperial Light Horse was the first in the regiment to be armed and equipped. Shortly after war was declared, they entrained for Estcourt, a small town about two-thirds of the way between Pietermaritzburg and Ladysmith. Under Major D.E. Doveton, their duty was to scout the area from Weenen to Oliviershoek Pass, the most westerly pass over the Drakensberg into Natal. As the distance between these two places is about 80 miles as the crow flies, and the countryside is very hilly, it was quite a formidable task. Fortunately, they would patrol in conjunction with the Estcourt squadron of the Natal Carbineers, who knew the country well, and they could rely on the support of local civilians.

The remaining five squadrons were armed and equipped by 16 October and immediately entrained for Ladysmith. Col Scott-Chisholme was in command, and had as his senior officers Majors Aubrey Woolls Sampson and Walter Karri Davies. With a Boer attack on Ladysmith expected at any time, they knew it would not be long before they would be in action, and that they would be singled out for special treatment. The colonel had received a letter from the Krugersdorp Kommando requesting details of their distinguishing pennant so that they could be easily recognised.[1] They also knew that the commandant of the Johannesburg Kommando, Ben Viljoen, was responsible for an order that anyone who had ever lived in Johannesburg and was now fighting against the Boers, should, on capture, be immediately shot.[2]

While General Joubert's central and eastern columns were held up at Dundee, his western column under General Kock was making good progress towards Ladysmith. Aware their very existence caused such great offence to the Boers, the local civilian population fled before the invaders and joined the refugee trail to Ladysmith. Among those able to get away just in time was farmer James Grey and his family, which included his father-in-law Peter Smith, the owner of the farm near Dundee on which the battle of Talana was to be fought.

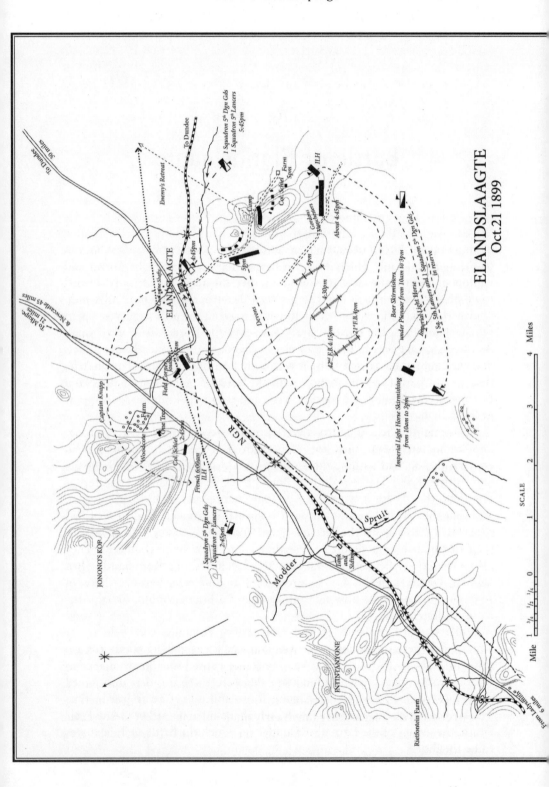

ELANDSLAAGTE
Oct.21 1899

On 19 October, Kock's forward scouts reached Elandslaagte, a railway station about 12 miles north of Ladysmith. As they approached, the Boers saw a train at the station, apparently about to leave for Dundee. No doubt sensing the possibility of acquiring some loot, the Boers raced to the station, however, an alert stationmaster had seen them coming and was able to get the train away, just in time. The Boers galloped after the train in a vain attempt to stop it and in an exchange of fire one Boer was wounded and one of their horses killed. This infuriated them, so they immediately arrested the stationmaster and his staff. Not long afterwards a second train loaded with supplies for the army at Dundee steamed into the station and was promptly captured.

The telegraph wires to Ladysmith were cut and black mineworkers from the nearby coalmine commandeered to pull up the railway line. The Boers now set about examining the contents of the goods trucks standing in the station. They were amazed at some of the paraphernalia, such as sporting equipment, which the British carried about with them on a military campaign. However, speculation about the lifestyle of the British ceased when liquor was found. Soon jovial but drunken Boers were staggering about the platform of the Elandslaagte railway station. It was at this point that Colonel Adolf Schiel, commander of the German Kommando in the Boer Army, arrived.

Col Schiel had served in the Prussian Army, probably as a sergeant, before coming to the Transvaal in 1878. He had become a friend of Paul Kruger and had done much work developing the German-trained Transvaal Artillery (*Staatsartillerie*) into the disciplined and effective force it was in 1899. Karri Davies and Aubrey Woolls Sampson were well known to him as he was Superintendent of Prisons when they were incarcerated in Pretoria. Schiel possessed in full measure the Germanic passion for order and discipline and was often frustrated by the ways of the Boers and complained about 'the disorder and complete lack of discipline amongst the burgher kommandos'. He found the Boers viewed with 'distrust, even aversion, any military innovation, and would meet any representations in this regard with a supercilious smile'.[3]

For their part, the Boer military leaders often found him exasperating and resented his lack of respect for their African experience. On one occasion, an irritated General Piet Joubert dismissed a suggestion from Schiel with the comment, 'Schiel you always bother me with your European military ideas.'

Schiel had brought with him into Natal 150 members of the German *Uitlander Korps*, no doubt the pick of that corps, and probably the best of the foreign units fighting for the Boer Republics. His adjutant was the German aristocrat Count Zeppelin. Attached to General Kock's western column, the Korps crossed the Biggarsburg range early on the morning of 19 October, and later that morning stopped at a farm that seemed a suitable campsite. On the approach of the Boers, the owner and his family fled, leaving a manager in charge. From this man, potatoes and a fat beast were requisitioned and a fine barbeque was in prospect. However, this was not the only reason for Schiel calling a halt.

Field Cornet Potgieter had been scouting ahead and Schiel felt they should not proceed further until Potgieter's report had been received and considered. Also he was not happy with the manner in which the advance was proceeding and wanted to discuss the matter with General Kock. In a book published after the war Schiel wrote,

> Our advance was again unplanned and to put it mildly, quite careless. General Kock did not keep his units together and every Field Cornet went his own way which means he advanced without concerning himself with keeping in touch with other detachments. It seemed inevitable that this unplanned riding would sooner or later have disastrous results. Nobody seemed to be concerned that we found ourselves in enemy country and that we could be attacked at any moment.[4]

Schiel sent a message to the general expressing his concerns and requesting a meeting. To his surprise, Kock agreed with the colonel's comments and said he would see him that afternoon.

The smell of the roasting meat must have filled the men with eager anticipation of the feast to come but, just as the food was ready, a message arrived from Field Cornet Potgieter saying that he had captured two heavily laden trains and two of his men had been wounded; he urgently needed reinforcement as otherwise he could not hold the trains. Schiel ordered 100 men to saddle up immediately and, after sending a message advising Kock of the position, the barbeque was abandoned and they set off for Elandslaagte about 17 miles from Ladysmith.

The sight of drunken Boers staggering around Elandslaagte station would have done nothing to strengthen the colonel's confidence, however, the position had to be defended so he took his unit out to a small hill from which he could cover both the road and the railway line from Ladysmith. From the train they took oats for their horses and a case of whisky for themselves. As darkness fell, it began to rain in torrents. Cold, wet and hungry, the Germans kept vigil through the night.

Late that evening Schiel went to the Hotel at Elandslaagte to check the condition of the wounded men. He found the hotel full to bursting with a party in full swing. Kommandant Ben Viljoen had arrived with his Johannesburg Kommando. It wasn't only Boers who were present; their prisoners and local residents had also been invited. A Boer, in a wet raincoat with his carbine slung over his back, sat at the piano and played popular songs that were sung lustily by the men gathered around him. Schiel considered himself fortunate to obtain a cup of tea laced with a liberal shot of rum, which gave him some warmth as he went back in the rain to his unit. It is said that the proceedings at the hotel that night closed with everyone singing the Transvaal anthem, *Die Volkslied,* and *God Save the Queen.*

Early the following morning, General Kock arrived with the rest of his detachment plus two 75mm field guns and a Maxim. Despite the joviality of the previous evening, the Boers arrested the general manager of the Elandslaagte Colliery, David Harris, along with his management staff, and took them to the local hotel for trial. The presiding officer was General Kock's son, who conducted proceedings while having a breakfast of grilled goat ribs. At the conclusion of the trial, Harris and his fellow employees were released on parole. The Boers permitted him to remove 100 bags of rice from the train, as this was part of the rations to be given to Indian workers at the mine. One of the trucks contained some fine furniture, which Harris had imported as a gift for his new bride. The furniture remained on the train.

When Schiel arrived that morning he was disgusted to find broken boxes of liquor, food, musical instruments, regimental records, private luggage and all manner of other goods littered all over the muddy station platform. Fearing a drunken orgy, he ordered that all liquor be destroyed. A Hollander, Captain de Witt-Hammer, was entrusted with this task. The order was only partially obeyed.

Acting on his own initiative, Schiel decided to patrol in the direction of Ladysmith. After they had ridden for about an hour, Count Zeppelin, whose troop provided the vanguard of the patrol, reported a strong enemy force approaching from Ladysmith. On receiving the report, Schiel immediately returned to Elandslaagte.

At the station he found the trains being looted by Indian mineworkers, many of whom were lying about dead drunk. Presumably they had found the leftovers in the smashed liquor bottles. Elsewhere, Boers were preparing for the coming battle, building sangars and getting the artillery into place. Other burghers visited the nearby coal mine. Apart from ransacking the offices and breaking open empty safes, they found 200 pounds of dynamite as well as 3,000 rounds of ammunition, which had been intended for use by the local rifle club.

Schiel met General Kock at the station and was surprised by Kock's lack of interest in the chaos and looting. Instead Kock pointed out a line of hills, about a mile south of the railway, and said that it was there he would meet the enemy attack. Schiel then drew Kock's attention to the fact that their task was to cut the track and establish contact with the Free Staters, not to provoke a battle in which they would be outnumbered. He suggested they retreat to the Biggarsberg, where they could easily hold off a British attack.

The general was unmoved and replied, 'I am a general myself – I take instructions from no one. This is not only where I shall await the enemy, this is where I shall defeat him. This will not be the first time I have done that.

You come with me to the hill and take up your position.'[5] Schiel saluted and withdrew to collect his unit.

On getting back to his men, Schiel found that Zeppelin had returned with a report that the enemy had withdrawn to Ladysmith, the immediate danger had passed. He now called a meeting of his officers and it was decided to make one final effort to persuade Kock to change his mind and burn the trains, break up the railway track, and return to the protective cover of the mountains. Schiel added that if the general was not prepared to change his mind, he would place pickets along the Ladysmith road that coming night.

A messenger took the suggestion to Kock and half-an-hour later returned and reported; 'The General says he did not come to guard mountains, but to fight, and directs you to place pickets on the road to Ladysmith at night as suggested by you, but with the break of dawn you shall fall back on the position already allocated to you.'[6]

Before dawn the next day, forward pickets reported the approach of an enemy detachment with artillery. Schiel ordered the pickets not to fire but to fall back. In the dark, Schiel's unit, which now included about a hundred Free Staters, saddled up and readied themselves for the return to the main Boer position, as directed by Kock.

When the telegraph line was cut at Elandslaagte on 19 October, General White sent the Natal Carbineers to scout along the Newcastle road as far as the Modderspruit, approximately half-way between Ladysmith and Elandslaagte. No contact was made with the enemy. The following day the Carbineers, accompanied by the 5th Hussars, were again sent out scouting in the same direction. This time contact was made and four prisoners were taken.[7] It would seem that these prisoners were part of the patrol that Schiel had sent out under Count Zeppelin.

On arrival in Ladysmith, they were interrogated and, from information gathered, General White was able to get some idea of the force camped at Elandslaagte. He decided to attack before further reinforcements arrived.

The next day, Saturday 21 October, Major General Sir John French was ordered to clear Elandslaagte, repair the railway line, and restore telegraph contact with Dundee. Chief Staff Officer under General French was Major Douglas Haig. They were accompanied by five squadrons of the Imperial Light Horse, with some Natal Mounted Rifles. The Natal Field Artillery, with their six obsolete 2.5 inch muzzle-loading guns, were to go by road. Infantry, consisting of half a battalion of the Manchester Regiment, were to travel by train. They were to be accompanied by the Royal Engineers' Railway and Telegraph sections.

The mounted men set off at 4 a.m. and by dawn they had reached a vantage point about 1½ miles from the railway station. The rain had stopped and before him, French saw a broad valley along which ran the road and railway line to Dundee and Newcastle. The railway was on his right and was fenced on both sides with barbed wire. To the right of the station could be seen a line of hills that rose a couple of hundred feet above the valley floor and which were at right angles to the railway. On his left was the towering peak of Jonono's Kop, at the foot of which were some smaller hills. Though the day promised to be fair, patches of mist still hung about the higher ground. Concealed in these hills were Schiel and his men, watching.

E Squadron of the Imperial Light Horse under Captain Knapp was sent ahead to see if it was possible to outflank the Boers. Possibly a fortuitous patch of mist concealed their departure, as Schiel was unaware that they had left the main group.

Without waiting for the infantry to arrive by train, French decided to test the enemy defences. The artillery unlimbered and fired a salvo at the station. Schiel, having been associated with the Transvaal's *Staatsartillerie* and its professional members with their modern guns, was rather scornful of their effort. However, it was not too bad. One shell struck a shed, another killed a mule, another hit an inadequately marked empty ambulance wagon, thereby disturbing a pharmacist's morning toilet without injuring him, while yet another hit the truck in which Mine Manager Harris' furniture was stored. The furniture was blown to smithereens. Apart from the damage to the ambulance, the Boers were unscathed. They now sent their reply. Firing from a position well beyond the range of the little Natal guns and near the hills to the right of the station, the Boer artillery almost immediately disabled the Volunteers' ammunition wagon and would have caused far more damage had their shells been properly primed.

It was now apparent to French that the main Boer force was located on the hills to the right of the railway. Realising his guns were outranged, he withdrew to a position beyond the range of the Boer guns. The arrival of the train with the Manchesters and Engineers enabled him to telegraph Ladysmith with a request for reinforcements.

While withdrawing, Karri Davies noticed the squadron of the ILH under Knapp was continuing down the valley getting further and further away from the main column with every passing minute. He realised that Knapp did not know of the order to retire and his squadron was heading straight for the Boers' main camp where they would be annihilated. A sergeant and a trooper were sent to warn Knapp to fall back on the main column. Karri watched the two through his field glasses as they galloped down the valley. Suddenly a number of shots were heard, the trooper fell from his horse, the sergeant stopped, dismounted, helped the wounded man back into the saddle, and led the horse back towards his own lines.

Watching the incident, Schiel recognised that the two men were from the Imperial Light Horse and, being impressed by the heroic action of the sergeant, was pleased when his own men shouted, 'Don't shoot that man – let him go.'[8]

Through his glasses Karri saw Knapp's squadron beginning to disappear behind Elandslaagte station and Boers moving in the same direction, apparently with the intention of cutting them off. When the sergeant returned and reported their failure to get through, Karri, without showing any regard for his own personal safety, immediately charged down the hill and galloped down the wide valley in full view of the enemy. Heavy fire was opened on him. To those watching, it seemed that there was only a chance in a million that he would get through but by a miracle, neither horse nor rider was hit. Once through the danger zone, Karri was able to locate Knapp and, by taking a wide detour, lead the squadron back to the main column.[9]

Though they played no further part in the day's proceedings, the Natal Artillery had caused sufficient chaos at the station to enable Harris and other mine employees to make off across the veld to British lines. Although his wife would probably be infuriated by the loss of her furniture, Harris must have been very relieved that he had got away. He was chairman of the local Rifle Association and once the Boers linked him to the 3,000 rounds of ammunition found at the mine, he would have been in big trouble. The railway employees who had been locked up in the station escaped through the ticket office window, taking their guard with them as a prisoner. These two groups of escapees were able to provide French with valuable information regarding the disposition of the Boer forces.

In Ladysmith, White responded immediately to French's request. By road he sent two squadrons of the 5th Lancers, a squadron of the 5th Dragoon Guards, three squadrons of the Natal Mounted Rifles and the 21st and 42nd Batteries of the Royal Field Artillery with 18 guns between them. By train came seven companies of the Devonshire Regiment, five companies of the Gordon Highlanders and members of the Natal Volunteer Medical Corps. Stretcher bearers who had accompanied the British regiments from India must also have come on the train, as they later helped with the wounded. As a precaution against an attack by the Free Staters from the west, the Border Mounted Rifles and Carbineers were ordered to guard the western approaches to Ladysmith. General White and his guard of twenty-two men from the Natal Mounted Rifles joined the mounted men en route to Elandslaagte.

Earlier, French had asked Col Scott-Chisholme what the ILH would like to do. The colonel replied that they would like to take the hill on the Boer's left flank. French gave him permission to do just that. The ILH therefore, with one squadron of the 5th Lancers in reserve, rode south to engage the left flank of the Boers, who had positioned themselves some way forward of the Boer's main position. Before they went into action, Scott-Chisholme called a meeting of his officers, at which he told them that the Boers were a disorganised bunch of simple farmers from whom they had little to fear.[10] By mid-morning the Light Horse had made contact with the Boer kommando, and began to drive them back.

During the day two Carbineer messengers arrived from Dundee with news of the battle at Talana and the mortal wound suffered by General Penn Symons. Sensing that the coming day might see him taking part in an historic event, General Kock donned a black frock coat and top hat. Later that morning an alert observer would have noticed banks of cumulus clouds building up over the mountains, a sure sign of an impending storm.

The withdrawal by French after the early morning abortive attack lifted the spirits of General Kock. Seeing Schiel had complied with orders and placed his men on the chosen hill, Kock strode over to Schiel with a friendly greeting and said, 'Do you see now our position is not as bad as you tried to make it.' By noon Kock had changed his mind and ordered Schiel with one hundred of his men to go back to a position to the northwest of the Elandslaagte station, where they were joined by some men from a Free State kommando.

It took some time for the train from Ladysmith to arrive with the re-enforcements, however, by 3 p.m., the British forces were all present. On the left, facing Schiel, were the Dragoons and a squadron of Lancers supported by the 42nd Battery, with Natal Mounted Rifles in reserve. In the centre were the infantry, positioned from left to right, the Devons, the Gordons and the Manchesters, who were to attack the Boer's main position on the hills lying to the right of the station. With them were two batteries of the Royal Artillery. On the right, the Imperial Light Horse continued to drive back the kommando that was guarding the Boer left flank.

When General White arrived, French offered to hand over command to him; however, White insisted that French should direct the coming battle. To defeat a force of approximately 850 Boers with two guns and one Maxim, French now had under his command 1,630 infantry, 1,314 mounted men and eighteen modern guns. Although it would only be a couple of hours before darkness descended, he decided to attack at once. All the while those banks of cloud over the mountains were becoming larger and blacker.

Col Ian Hamilton, who was to lead the infantry attack, began by getting his troops into open order, an almost unknown practice in the British army of that time. The veld the British had to traverse appeared, from a distance, to be flat but there were a number of low ridges and hollows that would provide some cover for the advancing men, nonetheless, for much of the advance they would be exposed to enemy fire.

The British opened their attack with a barrage from their artillery directed at the Boers' guns in an attempt to put them out of action, an objective they were never quite able to achieve. The Boers' guns replied and the artillery duel continued for some time before fire from the Boers died down. The British artillery now switched to shrapnel and raked the hills occupied by the Boers. At about 4.30 p.m. the Devons began the infantry advance towards the Boer centre while the Manchesters and Gordons worked round to the right so as to attack the Boer left flank.

Hamilton had spread the firing line of the infantry over approximately 1,000 yards with successive lines of reserves each set back a further 400 yards. This gave them a depth of almost a mile. The Boers' artillery sent shell after shell into the advancing infantry but this was completely ineffectual against the widely dispersed men. After the Devons had advanced to within

1,000 yards of the Boers, intense rifle fire forced them to take cover and await the development of the attack on the Boer left flank.

By 5 p.m. the Manchesters and Gordons had linked up with the Imperial Light Horse and were ready to attack the Boers' left. Between them and the crest of the hill occupied by the Boers lay about 800 yards of veld exposed to fire from virtually the entire Boer front. The dismounted ILH took up a position on the right of the infantry. In front of them the ground was covered by boulders and rose steadily, becoming steeper near the crest.

The storm, which had been building up for hours, now broke and the men of both sides felt its fury. Lightning lit the sky, the crash of thunder added to the cacophony of artillery and rifle fire, while torrential rain soaked everyone and everything, and the ground underfoot turned to slippery mud.

As the rain-soaked infantry and the Light Horse rose to advance, they were met by a hail of bullets. Nonetheless, by advancing in rushes, the tide of attackers moved steadily up the hill. A barbed wire fence temporarily slowed the advance and men fell. The wire was cut and the forward surge continued.

Col Ian Hamilton, disregarding the storm and enemy fire, rode back and forth on the battlefield exhorting and encouraging all to maintain the momentum of the advance. One who did not need encouragement was Col Scott-Chisholme of the Imperial Light Horse. Appointing Major Woolls Sampson to lead on the left and Major Karri Davies on the right, Chisholme placed himself in the centre of the regiment. Instructing his men to follow, he held aloft a walking stick to which was attached a little red flag, and set off up the rocky slope towards the hidden enemy. Though the artillery continued to rake the summit with shrapnel, rifle fire from the crest never slackened for a second. Fierce as it was, it failed to check the inexorable advance of the ILH. Hamilton left this description of the gallant colonel leading his regiment up that slope, 'To see that little red rag going on and on and on without a falter was the bravest sight I have ever seen in my life.'[11]

Hamilton also saw Major Woolls Sampson at the head of his men. Exposed to enemy fire and seemingly oblivious to danger, he was twirling the stick he always carried, while at the same time, pouring out a torrent of curses at his men for not taking cover between rushes forward. In one such advance, one man failed to rise and told Woolls Sampson he was so paralysed with fear that he could not move. The Major went on but had not gone far before a bullet found its mark and Sambo was down. His thigh had been shattered by a soft-nosed bullet. As he lay there unable to move, he saw a trooper with blood flowing from a wound to his face leading the charge, shouting curses and yelling defiance at the enemy. It was that same individual who, a few moments before, had been paralysed with fear.[12]

On the right, Karri Davies and his men were not so much going up the hill as going round the end of the hill towards the rear of the Boer position. Though the approach to the summit was not as precipitous as that scaled by the Dublins and Irish Fusiliers at Dundee, it was sufficiently steep to compel the defenders to look over the edge. Not wishing to be silhouetted against the sky, their fire slackened. A piper with the Gordon Highlanders played out the call to charge. Far away on the left, the call was repeated by the bugles of the Devons, who, with the Manchesters and Gordons, fixed bayonets and charged towards the crest. The Imperial Light Horse, not having bayonets and relying solely on their single shot rifles, went with the infantry and stormed over the crest in the expectation that victory was only moments away.

With the British steadily advancing up the hills occupied by his kommandos, General Kock sent an order to Schiel to bring his men back immediately. As soon as they received the order, the Germans and Free Staters set off at a gallop to join Kock. At the railway they had to stop to cut their way through the barbed wire fences. This gave their horses a breather and the men an opportunity to drink a toast to their 'Most Gracious Kaiser'.

Having established where their loyalties lay, the kommando galloped on. While crossing a flooded stream, Schiel's horse sank up to its saddle in the mud, and though he jumped off, it was unable to extricate itself. His men quickly came to his assistance, pulled the horse out, and on they rode. Schiel noticed groups of Boers leaving the battlefield and could not resist saying to one of his lieutenants, 'If only we had a gun, instead of firing at the British I would let those bastards have it.'[13]

As they made their way towards the left of the Boer line, they came under artillery fire. Graf Zeppelin died instantly when hit by shrapnel. On reaching the place where they had been that morning, they dismounted and began to climb the hill. As they neared the top, Schiel was horrified to find Scottish infantry were in the process of outflanking them. They raced onto the summit and with no more than one hundred yards separating them, the two sides poured a murderous fire into each other. Then in Schiel's words,

A new disaster struck. A detachment of Imperial Light Horse appeared on the flank of the enemy ... Next to me knelt a certain Ludwig von Borries; I admired the calmness with which he fired. Every one of his shots found its mark. He jumped up to advance a few paces, then he fell back right at my feet with a bullet through his forehead. Field Cornet Potgieter knelt two paces to my half right. He used a big rock for cover. I saw him lift his rifle to take aim then suddenly his head jerked to the right and he too sank to the ground ['we never saw shooting like that in the 5th']. Left and right my poor boys lay on the ground but no help was in sight.

In pressing forward I called to Captain Weiss to send an orderly to the General to tell him that we had been overtaken and to advise him that if he could make no further change in his front we would endeavour to delay the enemy to cover the retreat.

My rifle became so hot that I could scarcely hold it. All of a sudden I felt a jab just below the heel of one foot as if someone had prodded me with a red hot poker and I was convinced that I had been struck by a bullet. My magazine was again empty; I took a fresh clip of cartridges from my bandolier and fired another three shots towards the enemy who was already so close that we could discern the whites of their eyes.

The air was thick with bullets. I intended taking a pace forward, but felt all of a sudden as if I had been dispossessed of my left leg; I fell and blacked out.[14]

Along the whole length of their line the Boers were being pushed back and were making their way down the reverse slope of the hill. Their guns were captured and it seemed that the British hold on the hills was secure.

In the course of the advance a high number of officers had been killed or wounded with the result that when the summit was reached not only were Devons, Manchesters, Gordon Highlanders and Imperial Light Horse all mixed inexorably together but the chain of command had become very blurred, many of the men being uncertain to whom they should look for orders.

Some time after 5 p.m. Hamilton noticed a white flag in the Boer camp. In spite of the fact that Boers could be seen riding away from the battlefield, he ordered the trumpeter to sound 'cease fire'. This was done.

Down in the Boer camp Dr Coster, who had been State Attorney at the time of the trial of the Reformers in 1896, tore down the white flag saying, '*Liever sterven*' (Rather Die!). At the same time General Kock and a party of about fifty Boers who were concealed just over the reverse slope of the hill launched a vigorous counter-attack, storming back onto the summit and firing at point blank range into the British.

One of the first hit was Col Scott-Chisholme. He was shot in the ankle while bandaging a wounded trooper. Clifford (Dick) Turpin from Grahamstown and C. Lamb attempted to carry him to cover but he was struck by two further bullets, which killed him. His last words were, 'My Boys are doing well. My Boys are First.'[15]

For a time it looked as if the counter-attack might succeed. Bewildered by the call to 'cease fire' and the vicious enemy attack that followed, the British infantry began to retire down the hill. The Boers re-captured their guns and immediately brought them back into action. Their success was short-lived. Led by Ian Hamilton and officers from the Imperial Light Horse, order was restored among the British troops who rapidly turned the tables on the Boers who raced down the reverse slope to their horses and flight.

In turning the potential disaster into the final successful rout of the enemy, three officers of the Light Horse played a particularly important role, Captain Charles Mullins, Lieutenant Robert Johnstone and Lieutenant A.E. Brabant. Seeing the predicament in which some of the Regulars found themselves, they instantly rushed to their aid, assumed leadership, rallied them and reformed their lines. For their courage and leadership at a critical moment of the action, all three were recommended for the Victoria Cross.[16]

Throughout the advance General French had been among the men, rallying and urging them forward. General White too did not limit his role to that of a mere spectator. He rode in amongst the troops encouraging them. Twice both he and his bodyguard narrowly escaped death when shells failed to explode.

We left Karri Davies and his squadron rounding the hill on the Boers' left flank. Here lay a farm with several outbuildings. As the Light Horse approached, heavy fire emanating from the farmhouse was opened on them. Realising that the Boers holding the farm constituted a threat to the British flank and rear, Karri ordered it to be taken.

Through a curtain of Mauser bullets they rushed towards the farmhouse and as they did so the man next to Karri fell, shot in the leg. Lying in that exposed position he would almost certainly have been killed. The big man didn't hesitate. He picked up the wounded trooper and carrying him made for the nearest shelter, one of the farm's outbuildings.

On reaching it, Karri put his shoulder to the door and pushed into the darkened room. As he was putting the wounded man on the ground, something made him look round. A yard away stood a big Boer with a Mauser pointing straight at his head.

'Drop your gun or I'll blow your brains out,' shouted Karri. From across the room another voice cried, 'Don't shoot! It's Karri Davies.'

The Boer lowered his rifle and a big smile spread over his face as he saw the cane Karri was pointing at him. It was the only weapon Karri ever carried. Looking across the room Karri saw a wounded Boer whom he recognised at once. It was Matthys Human, the clerk at the Pretoria gaol who had befriended Karri and Sambo. For a few moments the bedlam of war was forgotten to be replaced by smiles, friendly greetings and handshakes as introductions were made all round.[17] By this time the ILH had surrounded and taken the farmhouse. Twenty-three prisoners were captured, among whom was General Kock.

During the day the farmhouse and its outbuildings had been used by the Boers not only as a fortified strongpoint, but also as a temporary shelter for their wounded. Given the extraordinary way General Kock dressed that day, it is not surprising that when he launched his final counterattack he was one of the first to fall, seriously wounded. A Dutch lawyer named Tindell saw the general fall and carried him to the nearest shelter, which was the farmhouse now under attack from the ILH, who were about 100 yards away. Seeing what was happening and realising Tindell's courage, the ILH held their fire until the two had passed into the safety of the house.[18]

When firing between the two sides finally ceased, the general was carried back to the Boer campsite where a tarpaulin shelter was made for him. A mattress was found (probably in one of the station houses) and he was made as comfortable as possible. Throughout the night, the British cared for the old general as if he was one of their own. A nephew of General Kock asked if he could remain with the general and this request was granted. In describing the treatment of General Kock, Ian Hamilton wrote, 'a deadly poison was injected by the black mamba snake called Propaganda into the body politic of South Africa.'[19] The metaphor was to apply to far more than the treatment of the old Boer general.

Having captured the Boer position, the British did not direct artillery or rifle fire at the fleeing enemy. It was now the turn of the British cavalry to show what they could do and deliver the coup de grace by cutting off the Boer retreat.

The cavalry assigned this task were commanded by a Major Gore and consisted of a squadron of the 5th Lancers and a squadron of the 5th Dragoon Guards, each having about one hundred men. During the afternoon they were positioned near the station and to the north of the railway line where the shafts and slag heaps of a coal mine concealed them from the enemy, whose anticipated line of retreat was about 2 miles away from their position. They were not on the green swards of the Curragh or Windsor Great Park but on the rough South African veld. Visibility was poor, the grass was long by British standards and concealed rocks and holes, which, like the ubiquitous anthills, could bring down horse and rider. It was raining, making the ground wet and slippery. Barbed wire fences and flooded streams would add to their difficulties. At Dundee the day before, Majors Knox and Marling had, in far better conditions, achieved no more with their cavalry than the bruising and the capturing of some prisoners. At 5.30 p.m. Major Gore gave the order to advance. Because of the conditions, Gore decided to abandon the usual knee to knee formation and gave the order to proceed in extended files.

Many are the gory tales that have been written about what happened next. Propagandists have had a field day. Their reports of helpless unarmed men and women being skewered by brutal Lancers, egged on by bloodthirsty officers, were readily accepted by those who were either disposed to think ill of Britain, or whose lifeblood was the waging of the British class war. Tales even came from the cavalry itself; some rather crude boasting from the ranks and some hearsay of reputed statements by officers in which irony was probably misunderstood.

These lurid stories have one thing in common, they are all suspect – and a cursory examination of each will show fundamental flaws. Many of the 'eyewitnesses' can easily be proved to have been many miles away at the time of the action, while others describe acts it would be impossible to execute. These tales were met with some scepticism by the Natal Volunteers.

With General Kock at Elandslaagte was the Johannesburg Kommando. Many of its members had been conscripted into the Boer army and were very reluctant to fight against the British. As a refusal to join the kommando would have meant imprisonment or possibly being shot, an opportunity to be taken as a prisoner of war was an attractive option. In the first few months of the war, there were many 'soft' captures of prisoners who chose to surrender in this way.

As the heat of the battle intensified on that momentous day, many men quietly slipped away from the battlefield. Among the early leavers was General Ben Viljoen of the Johannesburg Kommando. With the collapse of the Boer resistance, more Boers joined those fleeing. Instead of retreating in an orderly fashion with scouts out, the Boers gathered in a hollow where they could not see the approaching cavalry, whose appearance came as a complete surprise. The Boers' reaction was to scatter, galloping off as hard as they could in different directions. Viljoen was among those who escaped in this manner by the simple process of outdistancing his pursuers, who could not keep up on their unwieldy horses.

However, there were some in the kommando who chose not to ride away but instead to surrender. Sadly, before it was realised that they were surrendering, some were attacked and wounded with lances, swords and pistols.

Major Gore, in a rather vague report, gives no figures for the number of enemy dead or wounded, only admitting to taking thirty or forty prisoners. Neither does he mention any falls or casualties suffered by the Lancers or Dragoons. It would have been quite a simple matter to count the dead and wounded. After more than a hundred years and the spread of much misinformation, it is impossible to say how many Boers were wounded by the Lancers or how many, if any, were killed. The attempt by the cavalry to cut off the retreat of the enemy had been a dismal failure and the engagement had shown quite conclusively that lance and sword were now obsolete weapons of war.

For the Boers, the incident was a godsend. Instead of having to explain the folly of engaging in the battle and why they had run away at a crucial stage of the engagement, they were able to harangue the listener with tales of atrocities committed against them by the English. In recent times another variation has appeared on this theme. The Lancers and Dragoons swept on leaving dozens of Boers and some of their African retainers spiked and slashed on the ground.[20]

No authority has been given for this statement. The men who were attacked by the cavalry came almost exclusively from the Johannesburg Kommando, who would not have taken retainers on campaign. Any retainers at Elandslaagte would have stayed with Kock's wagons at the Boer camp, instead of wandering about the veld in the pouring rain several miles away. Further, there is no reason why the British cavalry should have attacked unarmed civilians in this manner. Such unfounded statements fuel racial resentment.

As darkness fell, the ceasefire sounded and the violence of the storm was replaced by steady drizzle. On the battlefield at Elandslaagte lay the dead and wounded of both sides.

That day the total Boer casualties were forty-five killed and 110 wounded. On those hills where General Kock made his stand, the defenders had been subjected to two hours of intensive artillery fire in which almost 500 shells had landed on the confined space where they had stood. The infantry had fired 61,000 rifle bullets at them and more than 1,500 men attacked them with bayonets. It was a miracle their losses were so small. With the exception of General Ben Viljoen, every Boer leader on the field that day was either killed or wounded. There is no room in these statistics for the propaganda of the slaughter of Boers and their retainers by the cavalry.

The British casualties were fifty killed and 213 wounded. These figures include the losses of the Imperial Light Horse who suffered fourteen killed and thirty-four wounded. Their commanding officer had been killed and their second-in-command had been seriously wounded and lay somewhere on the battlefield. Karri, with only a few weeks training behind him, now found himself in command of a regiment described by an officer of the Gordons, who had seen them in action that day, as 'the finest regiment in the world'. From the battlefield could be heard the piteous cries and groans of the wounded and dying from both sides. Volunteers were sent out to assist in finding and bringing in the wounded.

It is said that General White had sent only one doctor to Elandslaagte. This might be true if one only counts doctors attached to British regiments; however, Dr Rupert Hornabrook went to Elandslaagte with the Natal Mounted Rifles and Surgeon-Major W.T.F. Davies and Sergeant Dr C. Ligertwood accompanied the Imperial Light Horse. In addition there were doctors serving as troopers in the ranks of the ILH, orderlies from the Natal Volunteer Medical Corps, and the Indian stretcher bearers who carried the wounded on stretchers (called *dhoolies*) fitted with a shelter to protect the patient from sun or rain. Throughout the day and throughout the night, ignoring the vagaries of the weather and danger to themselves, these men, with the Boer doctors, worked to ease the suffering. No distinction was made between friend and foe. Makeshift first aid posts were established at the railway station and the farmhouse. Some urgent and delicate operations, including a tracheotomy, were carried out in the field by lamplight in the pouring rain.

And all the while that mamba was gliding over the field spreading his poison. Included among the tales was one that General Kock had his money, rings, and watch stolen from him. He was stripped of all his clothes except for his trousers; and thus, wounded as he was, had to lie out in the cold all night half naked.

While these cruelties were supposedly being inflicted on Kock, lying on the battlefield was that doughty old opponent of Britain and the Uitlanders, Col Schiel. When he regained consciousness the tide of battle had passed over him. Looking around he saw a trooper approaching and realised he was a member of the Imperial Light Horse. He called out to the trooper: 'Hello! You are one of the ILH. Ylease give my regards to Woolls Sampson and Karri Davies.'[21] Then as an afterthought he gave his rifle to the trooper to keep as a memento. The trooper, M. Greathead, was later killed in the battle of Wagon Hill. Schiel gave this description of the battlefield that night.

How dreadful was the sight that met my eyes. All around me my brave lads were lying on the ground; only a few had made it. Scottish soldiers and our own lay intermingled. To my left lay the dead body of Herr von Borries, a pace in front of me Field Cornet Potgieter on his back: his pale face with a black beard and his large wide-open eyes presented a dreadful aspect. His eyes were turned towards me as if he was on the point of speaking to me. Three paces behind me sat Potgieter's youngest brother with a bullet through both shoulders. Close by, two paces to my right, lay an Afrikaner. Groaning, he turned towards me, saw me and said, 'Is the Kommandant not dead?'

Notwithstanding my pain I could not help but smile at this naïve question. The poor fellow had a bullet through the chest and a shattered arm. A little further on lay Schmidt, a former Prussian Artillery NCO, obviously dead.

A Light Horse who was collecting rifles approached me. 'Great Scot!' he said, 'it is Colonel Schiel!' He was an acquaintance from Johannesburg. 'Who won?' I asked, as we shook hands.

'We,' he said hesitatingly, 'We won, but a large number of your chaps got away!' Thank heavens for that, I thought to myself.

I wanted to say something, but darkness again overcame me and I fell over. The friendly Light Horse took his field flask and held it to my lips. That worked wonders; his cognac sent the blood coursing through my veins again, but I could feel the blood still running from my wound.

Another Light Horse turned up. 'Have you any arms?' 'Yes two,' I said, 'but only one leg!' 'No,' he said, 'that's not what I mean.' Now I understood. I thought he had enquired as to whether I had been shot through the arms. My rifle was gone, my revolver as well. When he saw that I still had my binoculars he took them away. I must say I would rather have given them to his friendlier comrade who later came back, after it had started to rain heavily, to give me his raincoat for protection and as a souvenir.

As darkness fell, some other Light Horse came along to carry me to the First Aid Post. I requested them, however, to attend rather to those of my men who were more seriously wounded. I must admit that it was not only compassion for the other wounded which prompted me to turn down the friendly offer of help, but rather the hope that during the night Weiss or von Albedyll would come with their men to look for me.

My brother Max told me later that he had heard that I had been killed. Some men had seen me fall down on my side and had reported this fact to him. He spent the whole night walking around and towards midnight had come upon a few Gordon Highlanders. He asked one of them if he had seen me, giving him as detailed a description of me as he could. 'He is dead,' said the Gordon, 'I blew his brains out!' [It was not only cavalrymen who indulged in imaginative boasting!]

The rain began to fall heavily; the night was bitterly cold. Fortunately I still had a little cognac in my flask. I crept up to poor

Potgieter who could not lie still for agony of his wound. The poor fellow moaned pitifully; only a few paces away lay the corpse of his brother. A few paces further on lay a Gordon, also with a bullet in his leg. We shared the brandy. He still had some tobacco and some dry matches, so we smoked a pipe of peace together. The raincoat which the friendly Light Horse had given me I passed on to Potgieter. Soon after the Gordon was carried away. A few paces from me lay one of our lads. He must have been close to death for his breath rattled, almost like a snoring man, and continued until midnight when all of a sudden it stopped.

The English soldiers, particularly the Light Horse, helped our wounded wherever they could, and when darkness fell many had already been taken to the First Aid Post. I asked one of them to give Potgieter a little water. They gave us all they had.

A Sergeant, a musician or piper, sat himself next to me and offered me his help. When he saw I had not yet been bandaged and that my riding breeches were soaked in blood, he took his knife out of his pocket and without hesitation cut my left trouser leg from top to bottom through breeches, underpants and riding boots, to dress the wound. I was grateful for his well-meant assistance, but wished, however, he had not cut my clothes in this manner because, notwithstanding my severe pain, I had remained warm. Now, however, the cold rain struck my naked leg and I began to shiver until my teeth chattered. The sergeant stayed with me for a long while and told me about his little daughter who was, as he said, his one and only joy. I thought of my little girls whom I had not seen for a whole year. When this good fellow saw how I shivered from the cold he went away to fetch help to carry me away; his own raincoat he had already given away long ago. Later on he visited me in hospital in Ladysmith and told me that he had gone to fetch two Gordons but was unable to find me again in the dark.[22]

Aubrey Woolls Sampson was one of the last wounded brought in. He was found by a group of Light Horsemen led by Karri Davies. To carry Sambo they constructed a rough litter out of three rifles and in that way, they were able to convey him over the rocky ground to the first aid post at the station. It must have been an agonising journey for him. One of those who helped carry him left this account,

> He was cheerful when I first saw him and was merely solicitous on behalf of other wounded men in his more immediate neighbourhood and anxious that a Gordon Highlander, who had been killed in close proximity, should have decent carriage to his own lines.
>
> Major Sampson bore his wounds with great fortitude and during the six hours it took us to carry him to the station he uttered no word of complaint though undoubtedly suffering the acutest of agony.[23]

Early the next morning General Kock, Col Schiel, Woolls Sampson and other wounded from both sides were taken by hospital train to Ladysmith.

Late that night an officer with the telegraph section went to the Elandslaagte Hotel and noted with a hint of disapproval that Boer prisoners, who were having their wounds dressed, appeared to be having a good time. They were eating and drinking with their opponents as if nothing had occurred. Among those present were Douglas Haig and Karri Davies. The officer was invited to take a seat and despite the unusual circumstances he had a 'jolly time' and was disappointed when at 4.30 a.m. his orderly arrived with a message that the horses were ready for the trip back to Ladysmith.[24]

Perhaps Col Schiel should have the last word on the battle; 'How easy it would have been for the English to surround us completely. If they had done this instead of launching a frontal attack they could have achieved victory due to their artillery superiority without losing hardly a man.'[25]

10

Fall-out from Elandslaagte

In Pietermaritzburg on the morning of Sunday 22 October 1899, an excited 24-year-old nurse, Kate Driver, was up early. She was going to Ladysmith.

Kate's grandparents had come to South Africa with the 1820 settlers, and she had grown up in Queenstown in the Eastern Cape. After she left school, the family moved to Pietermaritzburg and Kate trained as a nurse at Grey's hospital, which was already acquiring a reputation for excellence. On completion of her training she stayed on in Pietermaritzburg, working as a private nurse.

At Grey's she had worked under the guidance of an outstanding doctor, Dr O.J. Currie, who had spent some years in India working on the prevention of malaria, after which he came to Natal where, amongst other things, he contributed much to the fight against the spread of that debilitating disease. When in 1899 war appeared inevitable, Dr Currie joined the Natal Carbineers as a Surgeon Captain and asked Kate if she would be willing to go as his surgical nurse if war came. She readily agreed.

This decision was made with some sadness. In the Eastern Cape there were many Dutch families and there had been little or no animosity between them and the English but, if there was to be war, she felt it was her duty to assist where she could. Mixed with the sadness, she felt a 'wild gaiety and energy' at the prospect of adventure.

Kate's uncle, Clement Webb, was an officer in the Imperial Light Horse and while the regiment was undergoing their initial training in Pietermaritzburg, he would most certainly have spent some time with his sister and niece, and when they met they would have had tea or a meal together. Also in the regiment was a young trooper, Guthrie Smith, who came from King Williams Town in the Eastern Cape. The Webb and Guthrie Smith families had many friends in common and no doubt the trooper attended one or more of these social meetings of family and friends.

Kate's mother did not like the idea of her daughter following the ILH to Ladysmith and, unknown to Kate, wrote to the Principal Medical Officer of the Volunteers saying her daughter was not strong enough to endure the hardships she would have to suffer on the campaign. Kate was very upset when she was not included among the nurses who received instructions to travel to Ladysmith. Noticing how distraught she was, her mother confessed to what she had done and promptly wrote to the Medical Officer withdrawing her earlier letter. Kate's services would have been in demand at the Military Hospital being created in Pietermaritzburg, however, she was determined to go to Ladysmith.

And so it came about that at 9.a.m. on the day after the battle at Elandslaagte, Kate Driver, after saying goodbye to her tearful and anxious mother, caught the train to Ladysmith. She has left a description of that journey.

We had not gone far on our journey before we learnt that a train previous to ours had been fired upon. People up the line were in a great state of excitement. Boers had been sighted in groups about the *veld*. At every station there were men in khaki. Some of them, noticing my red cross arm badge, saluted, and suddenly I remembered I too was wearing a uniform. I smiled and returned the greetings of those who passed near my window, and then I found myself watching a very tall young man with red hair, carrying a cup of tea with great concentration so as not to spill it. He stopped as he reached my compartment and took his eyes off the tea.

'This is yours, Nurse. We may not be able to get tea at every station.' I thanked him warmly.

'I saw your red cross. My sister is a nurse too. She is coming from Australia to nurse in this war.'

'A long way to come!' I said.

'Some girls now-a-days will come a long way for this job,' he replied.

At the next station I saw some men of the Imperial Light Horse, an irregular regiment formed in Johannesburg and destined to become quite famous. I had many friends and relations in it. I already felt a pride in it, a kind of belonging. I scanned their faces eagerly in case there should be some I knew. My heart was beating faster for the joy and pride of being part of all this.

During our slow progress of the next few hours, trains crammed with soldiers came champing past us – our slower wheels, their quicker wheels all pounding out the forceful rhythm of war.

The war was in khaki and I was in the surge of it all now, and I did not know what I felt, save excitement and a kind of proud thankfulness that I too could help.

At about five o'clock our train stopped just outside Ladysmith. By now it was raining heavily.[1]

For a long time Kate waited patiently on the train but in the end decided to walk through the rain to the station, where she found the platform and yard were packed with rows and rows of dhoolies with moans of agony coming from under the covers. She began to realise what war meant and to struggle with a paralysing fear that beneath the green covers she might see a face she knew.

At the station she was directed to the town hall, which had been converted into the military hospital, while the adjacent public library held the operating theatres. Next to these buildings was a collection of marquees which formed the headquarters of the Natal Volunteer Hospital. Although the Volunteers had suffered no casualties on the previous day, she found the staff up to their eyes in work. 'Night nurses as well as day nurses were on duty to cope with all the operations, and men were being brought in as fast as possible.'[2]

Kate was welcomed by the matron, an old friend from Grey's, who took her to the nurses' marquee so she could take off her wet clothes, while the matron fetched her some tea. In a few minutes all thoughts of tea or dry clothes disappeared when it was realised that the nurse's tent was needed for patients and Nurse Driver began work. 'As fast as beds were put up and made, men were brought in, some waiting in great pain, while the more urgent cases were taken to the operating theatre.'[3] It was midnight before she and the other nurses were able to have something to eat.

It had been arranged that Kate and another nurse should stay in a private house in the town. They were given directions and the two young women set out into the night to find the house where they had been billeted.

As we made our way through the dark muddy square, suddenly there was a flash of steel and we were challenged by a big Indian doing sentry duty. After a little discussion we showed him our Red Cross badges. This time there was a flash of white teeth as he smiled and let us pass.

Their hosts were not pleased at being woken in the middle of the night but as soon as they realised the girls were volunteer nurses, they were welcomed. Weary beyond words, Kate was at last able to go to bed and steal a few hours sleep. She had travelled a long way that day.

Among the first batch of wounded to arrive in Ladysmith was General Kock. His condition was desperate and this, combined with his age and status, made it desirable that he should have the best possible care. The medical authorities should not have had any worries on this point. As soon as it became known that General Kock had been seriously wounded, the correspondent of the *London Times* made available his bed and blankets to the old general, so that he might be as comfortable as possible. The person who chose to sleep on the floor so that a wounded Boer general might be comfortable was Colonel Frank Rhodes.[4]

It had been an exhausting couple of days for all the medical personnel at Ladysmith. Surgeon Captain Rupert Hornabrook had ridden out with the Natal Mounted Rifles when they were ordered to join French's force at Elandslaagte. Rupert Hornabrook had followed a similar route to Natal as Dr O.J. Currie – after he had qualified as a doctor, Rupert went to India where he took part in the campaign to eradicate malaria and other tropical diseases and from there he moved to South Africa to help prevent the spread of disease among mineworkers. When war threatened, he moved to Natal and became the medical officer of the Natal Mounted Rifles.

Although the Natal Mounted Rifles were in reserve throughout the battle, as soon as the British troops began to suffer casualties in the afternoon, Rupert, with the other Natal Medical Volunteers, immediately went to the assistance of the wounded. We have seen that as afternoon turned to evening, the number of casualties on both sides increased and, as darkness fell, the overburdened medical staff not only had to attend to the wounded in temporary first aid posts but also had to go out into the rain to give emergency treatment to those who had yet to be brought in from the battlefield. It was not until the early hours of the next morning that the young doctor was able to saddle up his horse for the ride back to Ladysmith.

After he had ridden a couple of miles he spotted a group of twenty-five armed Boers. He rode up to the Boers and told them they were surrounded and should surrender immediately! Three of the Boers were directed by him to collect their comrades' rifles. They complied with his directions and were led back to Elandslaagte where the prisoners and their arms were handed over to the British Regulars.[5] It was a very brave action by the young Aussie to approach these strangers and demand that they surrender. However, their behaviour indicates that it might have been a 'soft' capture and that this group of 'Boers' were actually seeking to be taken. (*See* Chapter 9.)

The arrival of the Boer prisoners in Ladysmith caused quite a stir as they were marched through the town on their way to the train that would take them to the coast and a PoW camp on the island of St Helena.

Living close to the Transvaal and Free State borders, the Zulus working in Ladysmith were fully aware of the manner in which the Boers behaved towards other black peoples. In addition, they had seen and heard what happened to those refugee mineworkers from the Reef, who had thought themselves fortunate to catch a train home from Johannesburg. Once on the train, these refugees were required to hand over all their money to Transvaal officials. As a general rule no receipts were issued, neither were records kept of the money so confiscated. Many who failed to hand over the money or attempted to hide it were beaten with a sjambok. The mineworkers usually kept their money in a knot tied in one of their garments. If the Boers found the money, the refugee not only lost it but often his garment as well. One refugee, S. Msimang, stitched five sovereigns into both his shirt collar and the shoulder padding. The sovereigns in his shirt collar were discovered and expropriated. With only half his savings purloined, he was fortunate. When the Boer prisoners arrived in Ladysmith, the Zulus took the opportunity to deride and taunt them.

The battle at Elandslaagte had convinced General White that his force would not be strong enough to hold that position once the main Boer army arrived. He therefore decided to withdraw all units to Ladysmith immediately.

When the worn and weary Imperial Light Horse reached Ladysmith, they dismounted alongside the lines of the Gordon Highlanders, where the men were lining up to receive their daily beer ration. They had missed this little luxury the previous day and no doubt were looking forward to their pint. There then occurred a spontaneous act, splendid in its simplicity and immense in its significance. As each man received his measure of beer, he carried it across to a comrade in the ILH – a generous tribute from those in the ranks of a famous old regiment to their colonial brothers-in-arms.[6]

On that same Sunday, General French sent for the new de facto commander of the Imperial Light Horse, Major Karri Davies. French told Karri that he knew not only of his brave ride, which had rescued Captain Knapp and E squadron, but also how, later in the day, he had in the face of terrific fire and at point blank range, picked up a wounded man and carried him to safety. Because of his great courage in saving these lives, the general told Karri it was his intention to recommend he be awarded the Victoria Cross. Karri's reply must have astonished General French. He thanked him for offering to put his name forward, but asked him not to do so. He said that on signing up he had given an undertaking to General Penn Symons that he would serve throughout the war without pay, promotion or decoration, and that the only reward he sought was to serve Queen and Country.[7]

The circumstances under which he gave the undertaking are not recorded; however, Penn Symons, alone among British senior officers, was unimpressed by the ILH while they were in Pietermaritzburg. We also know of his low opinion of colonials and no doubt he possessed in full measure the disdain which some of the military caste felt for those involved in trade. It is not difficult to imagine the type of comment that would have goaded Karri into making the undertaking. To some his reaction might appear to be overly pedantic. After all, Penn Symons was dying and no one else would know about the undertaking he had given. The award would have been the first Victoria Cross to an Australian and his countrymen would no doubt have been immensely proud of such an honour, as would the Imperial Light Horse. However, Karri knew he had given the undertaking and for him, his word was his bond.

Captain Knapp, in his report on the battle, described how his squadron had been saved by Major Karri Davies whose prompt and heroic action had saved them from annihilation. The report was submitted to his commanding officer, who happened to be Karri, with the result that this part of the report went no further.

Subsequently it was recommended that four members of the Imperial Light Horse be awarded the Victoria Cross. They were Major Aubrey Woolls Sampson, Captain Charles Herbert Mullins, Captain Robert Johnstone, and Lieutenant A.E. Brabant.

In due course a reply was received from the War Office in London stating that while Colonel Woolls Sampson evidently led his men with much gallantry, Lord Wolseley does not feel that his conduct was sufficiently exceptional to call for the bestowal of the great favour of the Victoria Cross. With respect to the other three, the War Office apparently felt all three deserved the award but were only prepared to award two to the regiment. The responsibility of deciding on whom these much-prized decorations should be conferred fell on the ILH Adjutant, Captain Barnes. Barnes consulted with the regiment and it was decided that the award should go to Mullins and Johnstone, though all felt that Brabant had also deserved it.

Robert Johnstone was a well-known international rugby player, having played many games for Ireland. Shortly before the war he toured South Africa with the 1896 British Lions rugby team. With war clouds gathering he stayed on and subsequently joined the ILH. After the war he returned to his home in Ireland. Lt Brabant, the son of a general, was born in the Cape Colony. Less than a fortnight after Elandslaagte, this talented and unassuming young officer was to die of wounds suffered in an engagement on 3 November. He was killed before the decision of the War Office was received in Ladysmith.

Robert Johnstone wasn't the only Irish international rugby player at Elandslaagte. Dr Tommy Crean was also a member of the 1896 British Lions team. A big, brawny man with a perpetual smile on his face, he loved the rough and tumble of rugby. After the game he would challenge his team mates to a fight, individually or the whole lot together. He survived the tour and settled down to practise medicine in Johannesburg. Despite his sometimes unusual behaviour, or perhaps because of it, he soon acquired a substantial practice. On one occasion a patient barged into a room where Tommy, dressed only in a short shirt, was shaving. Tommy glared at the man, 'Is it no manners that ye have intruding on the privacy of a gentleman? And your face is a cruel one; it needs hitting. Will ye fight with me?' The patient was out of the house in a flash running down the street with Tommy after him. On reaching his home the man rushed inside and bolted the door, leaving Tommy on the mat, demanding that he 'come out and fight'. A crowd soon collected and in due course a policeman arrived. Tommy, unabashed, offered to fight the policeman for his trousers. The law melted away, and Tommy was able to borrow a jacket to walk home.[8]

Tommy gave the Uitlanders unqualified support in their struggle against the Kruger regime, and was one of the first to join the ILH at Pietermaritzburg. Because the regiment already had its full complement of doctors, he with other medical men chose to serve as troopers. Tommy was among those wounded at Elandslaagte.

In addition to the VCs awarded Mullins and Johstone, Captain Meikeljohn and Sergeant Major W. Robertson, both of the 2nd Gordon Highlanders, were awarded Victoria Crosses for their gallantry at Elandslaagte.

Also arriving in Ladysmith on Sunday 22 October 1899, was Captain C.G. Willson with the Dundee squadron of the Natal Carbineers. They were accompanied by four Boer prisoners they had captured in the course of their ride from Dundee. On arrival, Charlie Willson was promptly arrested and relieved of his duties.[9] Quite what Charlie had done to deserve such treatment was not known. One rumour was that he had failed to obey orders, another that he was charged with cowardice. Bearing in mind that the Carbineers in Dundee were not billeted in the British camp and the chaos that existed in Dundee at the time, one does wonder what the orders were that he failed to obey. Similarly it is hard to imagine what act of cowardice could have been attributed to him while his squadron was guarding the British camp during the battle of Talana.

Not surprisingly there was some dissatisfaction among the Carbineers regarding the treatment Charlie had received. He had, after all, brought his squadron to Ladysmith without losing any men, while at the same time taking prisoners.

There were officers among the Carbineers who could have taken over leadership of the Dundee squadron, however the military did not follow this route. Instead, to replace Charlie, Lieutenant Archibald Wales of the Natal Mounted Rifles was moved across to the Carbineers and promoted Captain.

11

Retreat of Dundee Column
to Ladysmith

General White had never liked the idea of sending a substantial number of his troops to northern Natal and now the situation he feared most had come to pass, his army was split in two. During the battle at Elandslaagte he received news of the inconclusive engagement at Dundee and the serious wound suffered by General Penn Symons. The next day he received a telegram from the Dundee column to say they were falling back on Helpmekaar, a village about 25 miles due south of Dundee. White replied with an order that they retire to Ladysmith immediately.

The upshot was that the Dundee column under Col Yule would go south along the Helpmekaar road for about 15 miles to the hamlet of Beith and there turn right and follow the track to Ladysmith, which lay about 45 miles to the west. The column would be vulnerable during the entire march and particularly so while crossing some hills near Beith, an area known as Van Tonder's Pass.

It was decided to send a squadron of Volunteers out along the Beith road to make contact with Yule. The squadron chosen to perform this duty was the Dundee Troop of the Natal Carbineers. They had arrived from Dundee on the afternoon of 22 October and no doubt both they and their horses were exhausted. Added to this their new senior officer, Captain Wales, came from the coast and was not familiar with Northern Natal. And yet on the day after their arrival in Ladysmith, they were the ones selected to embark on the long ride to find Yule. This arrangement did have the advantage that they would be out of Ladysmith until such time as Yule's column arrived, thereby enabling the arrest of Captain Willson to be kept under wraps for the time being.

On Monday 23 October 1899, Martial Law was extended over the whole of Natal. Free State Boers re-occupied Elandslaagte station and the kommandos under General Erasmus entered Dundee.

Lieutenant Hugh Brooking of the ILH was ordered to take twelve men out to Elandslaagte to collect the bodies of the colonel and other regimental dead. With them were burial parties from the Gordons, Devons and

Manchesters. They all set off on a train bedecked with white flags but after they had travelled about 5 miles the Boers opened fire, compelling them to turn back. They had just begun the return journey when alongside the train came a troop of Hussars, 'riding a finish'. They had been racing the enemy from Dundee and their horses were exhausted. Two of the horses were 'cooked', so these two and their riders were taken onto the train. The rest rode alongside while the train steamed at walking place back to Ladysmith.[1]

Lt Brooking reported to headquarters and was told to try again. He was given a letter of introduction from a Boer prisoner. This time they were stopped, not by enemy fire, but by stones across the railway line. Boers rode up and an *indaba* (conference) was held. The Boers told them the rails had been ripped up and a bridge burnt, so they had no choice but to walk the rest of the way under escort. Arriving after dark, they were invited to spend the night at the station master's house. Under the watchful eye of a sentry, they spent an uncomfortable night attempting to sleep in station chairs.

The next morning they found that all the bodies had been buried, so the Gordons, Manchesters and Devons immediately returned to Ladysmith, leaving with the ILH a chaplain, Major Grant of the Royal Engineers. They exhumed the body of Colonel Scott-Chisholme and the chaplain read the burial service over the other graves. The Boers asked if they would exhume the body of Dr Coster, as his wife wished to bury him elsewhere. So they set to and exhumed his body and handed it over to the Boers.

During the day sounds of battle were heard, which was frustrating; they had no choice but to continue with the task in hand until it was completed.

The Boers lent them two wagons, one to carry the body of the colonel, the other for the burial party. They set off in the evening, Brooking recording that they, 'Had a quiet night on the road back, but the Dutch Doctor driving our fellows was in such a desperate hurry to get through, most of our fellows got out and walked. Collared a real good Dutch pony but it was collared again from me the same night.'[2]

During the flight from Dundee, Yule was so incapacitated by his curious illness that the task of leading the column fell on Col Dartnell of the Natal Police. Although a Canadian, as a former British Army officer Dartnell was given more credence than would normally be given to a colonial officer. To this advantage he added knowledge of Northern Natal. When dawn came on 23 October, the column was 12 miles from Dundee. By midday they had passed Beith and were resting in the hills of Van Tonder's Pass. It was here that they were met by Captain Wales and his troop of Carbineers. That night they marched through the hills into the comparative safety of the Sundays River valley.

Concerned that the Free State kommandos might cut off the retreat of the Dundee column, General White decided a show of force against them might persuade them to remain in the hills to the north of Ladysmith.

On the 23rd he ordered five men from his bodyguard to scout along the Newcastle road to find out the position and strength of these kommandos. In charge of the party was Corporal C.J. Landsberg, the other members being Troopers L.V. Ash, A.C. Brandon, G.J. L. Golding and A.W. Evans, the son of the officer commanding the Natal Mounted Rifles. They rode out along the Newcastle road until they reached a dry water course that led up to the hills thought to be occupied by the Boers. Concealed from anyone on the hills, they were able to ride a considerable way before Landsberg decided it was time to dismount.

Leaving their horses in the care of the other three members of the squad, Landsberg and Golding crept forward through the tall grass and rocks until they were within 500 yards of Boers. Here they were able to note the disposition of the enemy and watch them as they went about their daily routine. Eventually they perceived a movement among the enemy, which threatened to cut them off, so they decided to break cover and run for it. As they rose from their sheltered position, they were spotted by the sentries, forcing them to race a zigzag course down the hill, over rocks and through long grass, as they could hear hundreds of Mauser bullets whistling past them. Their luck held and they reached the shelter of the riverbed unscathed. The rest of the squad were anxiously waiting with their horses and, as the fugitives arrived, they were given their horses and everyone galloped off. Everyone, that is, except Trooper Golding. As he was about to mount, his horse shied and breaking loose, it galloped after the others. Exhausted by his hard run Golding could only stagger along the riverbed as Boer bullets threw up spouts of sand around his feet. He was about to give up when he heard his name called. This produced just enough adrenalin to enable him to make it round the next bend. There he found a dismounted Trooper Evans holding the runaway horse. Evans said, 'Jump up smartly, it's too hot in this quarter, let's get out of it.' Muttering his thanks, Golding scrambled into the saddle and together they raced back to the rest of the squad and safety.

Golding subsequently learned that while the squad was under fire, Evans saw the loose horse, caught it and turned back to find out what had happened to the rider. By this time the Boers were pouring heavy fire into the watercourse, forcing Evans to dismount and continue his search for Golding on foot. Evans was the youngest trooper in the Natal Mounted Rifles and his action was much applauded by all in Ladysmith. He received the DCM for so courageously returning to save his fellow trooper.[3]

With the information gained from this sortie, and from the Natal Native Scouts, General White now knew where to launch a diversionary attack. At 1.30 a.m. on Tuesday 24 October, 5,300 men were roused from their slumbers and an hour later they had assembled and set off along the Newcastle road. It was a mixed group of Volunteers and Regulars. The Imperial Light Horse, the Natal Mounted Rifles, the Natal Carbineers, the Border Mounted Rifles, the 5th Lancers and the 19th Hussars constituted the mounted contingent. The infantry were represented by the Devons, Gloucesters, Liverpools and the

Kings Royal Rifles. In support were two batteries of field artillery and one mountain battery.

The rains of the past few weeks had abated, leaving the promise of a glorious morning. After they had travelled about 8 miles, the expected rifle fire was received from the Tintwanyoni hills on their left. Herbert Watkins-Pitchford, the veterinary surgeon serving with the Carbineers, noted that the first shot in the engagement was fired at eleven minutes past seven.

Reaction to the enemy fire was prompt. The Hussars, the Lancers and some squadrons of the ILH immediately went forward along the Newcastle road, thereby securing the right flank of the British force. The artillery rapidly silenced the Boer guns, which had begun firing on the column. The infantry, with a detachment of the Imperial Light Horse, crossed the railway and took up a position about 800 to 1,000 yards from the Boers and the two sides began an exchange of rifle fire that lasted about four hours. The Volunteers were delegated the task of protecting the British left. At 10 a.m. it was noticed that Boers on a hill to the west of Tintwanyoni were attempting to circumvent the British left. The Volunteers were ordered forward.

With the Border Mounted Rifles and the Natal Mounted Rifles in the van, the Volunteers pushed up a valley and occupied a *kopie* to the west of the British infantry. Robert Samuelson, who was acting as galloper between Col Royston and the regimental commanders, watched the Volunteers move up to a ridge and bring their machine guns into action, 'a hail of projectiles, great and small, were hurled at them, but they went on as coolly as if they were at an ordinary parade, and returned the compliment.'[4]

Fighting in rocky, broken country, the Volunteers were not only able to check the Boer attempt to outflank the British but also to drive them back. At 11 a.m. an unfortunate incident occurred. The Gloucesters broke cover and advanced towards the enemy, apparently with the intention of driving the Boers off the secure position they occupied on the hills. They were immediately subjected to heavy fire. Their commander Colonel Wilford and six men were killed and forty were wounded before they were able to crawl back to cover.[5] The ILH who joined them in this escapade were fortunate not to suffer any casualties.

At noon General White received a heliograph message that the Dundee column had reached the Waschbank River, 18 miles away. As the diversionary attack had succeeded in its objective, General White decided it was no longer necessary to continue the engagement and gave the order to retire to Ladysmith. The artillery successfully covered the retreat of the infantry off the hills and during the retirement along the Newcastle road, the Volunteers formed a defensive shield at the rear of the column. All were back in town by 3.30 p.m.

In the engagement the Border Mounted Rifles had two men killed (Troopers S. Brown from Harding and P. Nilsen from Port Shepstone) and nine were wounded; the Carbineers lost two men (Sgt A.E. Colville and

Trooper W. Cleaver) and had nine wounded; the Natal Mounted Rifles had three men wounded.

In his dispatch of 2 December 1899, General White mentioned the gallant manner in which Major Sangmeister (BMR) and Major Taunton (Carbineers) seized a kopie and by speedily bringing a Maxim gun into action, cleared out the enemy. Surgeon Captains R. Buntine and H.T. Platt were mentioned in the same dispatch for the courage displayed when, under heavy fire, they tended the wounded.[6]

The effect of the smaller high-speed Mauser bullet was dramatically illustrated by the wound suffered by one NMR trooper. During the fighting he felt a sharp pain and cried out, 'I'm hit.' 'Nonsense, man, it's only your horse,' said a comrade. Accepting the assurance, he went on fighting. That night he suffered a great deal from what he called 'spasms'. The next morning it was found that he had been shot through the body. He collapsed and was taken to hospital.[7]

The following day Major Herbert Watkins-Pitchford and Surgeon Major James Hyslop were ordered to take a detail of ten men with a mule-wagon to recover the bodies of those who had been killed on the previous day. As they neared the scene of the battle, they could see clumps of Boers scouring the hills.

Uncertain of the reception they might receive from the Free State Boers, Hyslop and Watkins-Pitchford took off their tunics bedecked with Major's badges, and put on trooper's coats. With each holding a Red Cross flag they rode over to the Boers. Their flags were respected, the Boer general having left a message that they were to be given 'every assistance'. They signalled to their wagon to come up, which it presently did. They had no trouble finding the bodies as vultures were already circling in the air above each corpse. When they had collected the Volunteer dead, the Boers told them there were nine more bodies on the hill that had been occupied by the Gloucesters. As no Imperial people were to be seen, it was decided to take up their picks and shovels and bury these unfortunate men.

On the way up the hill the officers and men somehow separated with the result that when they found the bodies, the burial party consisted of the two officers and Father Ford, a Roman Catholic priest. The bodies lay where they had fallen. Their boots had been taken and their pockets rifled but otherwise they were undisturbed. They collected the bodies together and, after Father Ford had said prayers over them, the three set about digging a grave. Before they had finished a squad from the Gloucesters arrived who took the bodies into their care.

On the way back they called at the now-vacated farm of the local member of the Natal Legislative Assembly, Mr Pepworth. The Boers had been through the place but had not taken anything of value. The detail loaded some of the more valuable items in the house onto the wagon for safe-keeping in Ladysmith. On arrival, the bodies were unloaded for burial and Pepworth's belongings were left in the custody of the police.[8]

Also in Dundee on Wednesday 25 October 1899, the Reverend Gerard Bailey and Father Murray, the Roman Catholic chaplain to the Dublin Fusiliers, attended to the burial at Smith's farm of thirty-five men who had been killed during the battle the previous Friday. They were finally laid to rest near the Smith family graveyard, which is in the wood and a little higher than the farmhouse. (The farmhouse, graveyard and much else beside now form part of the excellent Talana Museum.)

The funerals were to have taken place at 6 p.m. on Saturday 21 October. However, as Gerard was about to set off to walk to Talana, Boer artillery opened fire on the British camp and in the Vicar's words 'it was soon clear that they had more powerful guns than we had.' Having created havoc in the British camp, the Boer gunners decided to deliver 'a dose all round'. Gerard was walking along the path from the vicarage to the church,

> ...when I heard the Boer gun again and this time very distinctly, and in a moment I realised that a shell was about to strike near me. Before I had time for another thought I found myself full length on the ground. 'Thank goodness I am lying down,' was the flash thought which came to me. There was a heavy thud and a shower of mud played on and about me. The shell had missed striking the house by a few feet, and had landed half way between the house and the church. Fortunately the ground was very soft, as there had been a good deal of rain, and so the shell buried itself and the force of the explosion was confined.

He hurried on down to the drift to cross the Sandspruit, which he found was in flood. There was no sign of a burial party at Smith's farm so he decided the funerals must of necessity be postponed. The following days were so packed with incident that it was not until the 25th that an opportunity arose to attend to the burials at Talana.

On Sunday the 22nd the Vicar and Father Murray conducted the funerals of eight men in the grounds of the hospital and in the afternoon four more were buried in the churchyard of St James' church. In the course of the day Gerard and Father Murray struck up a friendship that resulted in their being continually in each other's company from then on. Unlike the Boer Republics, where there existed strong anti-Catholic sentiment, in Natal there was no hostility between Catholics and Protestants and the fact that the two men became friends would not have surprised anyone. Natalians did, however, find it bewildering that some Irish Catholics, in America and elsewhere, should support the Boer attempt to subjugate their country.

The following day, Monday 23 October, the Boers entered Dundee and that evening General Penn Symons died. The next day Gerard conducted the burial of the general in the churchyard of St James. Only a handful of people were present.

Dundee had a peacetime population of approximately 1,000. This had swelled with the arrival of refugees but had shrunk again as the Boers approached. In the days that followed the battle at Talana, many of the residents fled, some to Greytown, others towards Weenen and Estcourt. Every wheeled vehicle was pressed into service. Those who didn't have a vehicle, rode, while those who didn't have a horse, walked. When it was discovered that the army had sneaked off, many citizens chased after them and walked with the column to Ladysmith. It seems all those who attempted to get away succeeded. They, like the British column, could have been intercepted and captured if the Boers had not been otherwise engaged. Deneys Reitz was among the triumphant Boers who rode into Dundee on 23 October 1899:

> Soon 1,500 men were whooping through the streets, and behaving in a very undisciplined manner. Officers tried to stem the rush, but we were not to be denied, and we plundered shops and dwelling-houses, and did considerable damage before the Kommandants and Field-Cornets were able to restore some semblance of order. It was not what we got out of it, for we knew we could carry little or nothing away with us, but the joy of ransacking other people's property is hard to resist, and we gave way to impulse.[9]

Reitz was ordered to remain in the Dundee area when the rest of his kommando moved south. At Glencoe station he saw the wife of General Kock searching for her husband, the memory of her tear-stained face impressing on the young man the first hint of what women suffer in time of war.

Not all the residents of Dundee had joined the exodus. When the Boers rode in, some 250 still remained in the town as well as the sick, wounded and medical personnel of the military camp. The majority of those who remained were men, and many were the differing reasons they had for staying on. Some such as the doctors, nurses and medical orderlies, stayed because they felt they had a duty to continue to do the best they could for those in their care, others had been so overwhelmed by the swift turn of events that they did not know what to do and so did nothing, while others, such as the magistrate, felt they should not desert their posts. There were even some who believed that they had nothing to fear from the Boers.

General Joubert had issued a widely-publicised proclamation addressed to the inhabitants of the Cape Colony and Natal:

> The Government and people of this Republic have been forced into war by evil disposed capitalists and war-like British ministers; and they must now stand up and fight in the true interest of the whole of the South African people irrespective of place or origin. It is not the intention of officers and burghers to molest or injure any individual or private property of those who are friendly disposed towards, and desist from all hostilities against us. If it should happen, which is not desired, that any inhabitant is harmed by circumstances or by casualties, the officers and war council will be prepared to lend a willing ear to all complaints or objections reasonably

brought before them. No persons will be allowed to commit a culpable act without coming under severe punishment. We will, however, carry on this war, forced upon us, according to civilised and humane usages and under the guidance of an all-directing God in heaven.

'All very nice,' commented the Rev Gerard Bailey, who was soon to learn how the Boers interpreted, 'the guidance of an all-directing God in heaven'; an interpretation to which the people of Dundee had perforce to submit. Gerard wrote:

I was in the streets of Dundee constantly during the first week so I had ample opportunities of witnessing the work of destruction. Out of all the stores, including Arab stores, only two escaped, the rest were wrecked.

The owners or their representatives, of stores and offices were many of them in town, but the work of destruction was so rapid and violent that it was of little use protesting. One of our townsmen who kept a restaurant told me that his was one of the first places the invaders came to. They helped themselves wholesale to the liquor, and then turned their attention to the cigars. He began dealing them out one by one, but they demanded boxes and ignoring him altogether seized his whole stock. They then went into another room, here they smashed up a new cinematograph, wrenched the action out of a piano, and demolished several musical instruments. I myself went through the rooms with the proprietor and saw how they served him.

I visited a bookseller's store where I had left my camera. Books, stationery, pictures, ornaments, etc. all lay on the floor. The camera may have been buried beneath the debris. The Boers as they came in trampled everything underfoot. The safe I found forced open. This was the case pretty well in every office. I do not suppose the burglars were rewarded for their pains. You can be sure all moneys were removed. A Dutch photographer came to me, anxious to get plates, chemicals, etc. I told him there was a studio in town. He came back to tell me everything had been destroyed, even the printing papers torn open and exposed. A watchmaker, who had remained in town, and was helping at the hospital, lost everything. He found watch glasses, main-springs etc. strewn about and crushed and spoilt in the most reckless manner, likewise all his valuable tools gone, and everything in the shape of silver and electroplate. But the same fate awaited every store and office. The only two that resisted the looters were Messrs Oldacre's and Handley's and these only to a limited extent, as later on they were taken over by the Transvaal authorities and then looting was done in a more genteel manner. [The Natal Magistrate had persuaded Oldacre and Handley not to leave so as to provide some continuity of normal civilian life.] The Boer in his looting had his own particular fancies. Macintoshes were eagerly snapped up, sardines never passed over, and Dutch Bibles taken as godsends. I found one Boer gloating over a heavy well bound one. 'Hullo, got a Bible?' I said. His eyes beamed with satisfaction. If he survives the war, he will read it every night to his vrou and kinders [wife and children] and tell them how the Lord gave him the Bible when the burghers took Dundee, and smote the English hip and thigh. I said to one Boer, 'I think we shall have to start a new set of commandments. The eighth seems a bit out of date just now.'[10]

At that time in rural Natal, the only way many clergyman could visit parts of their parish was to ride. Indeed it was not until the second half of the twentieth century that a good seat ceased to be a necessary accomplishment for a priest in some parishes. The Baileys had three horses. One was his wife's much-loved pony, which had taken first prize at the Weenen show. The other two horses were used by the vicar to get around, visiting mission stations, and so on. The Boers lost no time appropriating the three horses, all their tack and Gerard's saddle. They knew his wife had a saddle, a much prized wedding present, however it had been hidden by Gerard and they were never able to find it. Gerard consoled himself with the thought that the Boers generally treated their horses well.

While the Boers were thus occupied in Dundee, the British column, nominally under Yule, was struggling on towards Ladysmith. After the engagement at Tintwanyoni, a report was received from Native Scouts that the Free Staters were preparing to cut off the Dundee column. Colonel Royston persuaded General White to permit him to take all the Natal Volunteers to meet the column, and hurry them to Ladysmith. He found them about 15 miles out on the Helpmekaar road, about to set up camp in an extremely vulnerable position. With difficulty he persuaded them to break camp and resume their march.

The correspondent of the *London Daily Mail*, George W. Steevens, gave this account of the meeting of the two groups.

'Come to meet us!' cried the staff officer with amazement in his voice; 'what on earth for?' It was on October 25th, about five miles out along the Helpmekaar road, which runs east from Ladysmith. The staff officer could not make out what in the world it meant. He had pushed on from the Dundee column, but it was a childish superstition to imagine that the Dundee column could possibly need assistance. They had only marched thirty odd miles on Monday and Tuesday; starting at four in the morning, they would by two o'clock or so have covered the seventeen miles that would take them into camp, fifteen miles outside Ladysmith. They were coming to help Ladysmith, if you like; but the idea of Ladysmith helping them!

Eight miles or so along the road I came upon the Border Mounted Rifles, saddles off, and lolling on the grass. All farmers and transport riders from the northern frontier, lean, bearded, sun-dried, framed of steel and whipcord, sitting their horses like the riders of the Elgin marbles, swift and cunning as Boers, and far braver, they are the heaven-sent type of irregular troopers. It was they who had ridden out and made connection with the returning column an hour before.[11]

Except that the BMR came from the southern border, Steevens' description rings true.

It had been a glorious morning on 24 October when General White's troops marched out to engage the Free Staters on the Tintwanyoni hills but by the night of the 25th, the rains had returned. As the rain poured down the men, horses, guns, cattle, wagons, and mules turned the track into a quagmire. Horses, sometimes up to their hocks in mud, struggled to drag the guns along. By the time they reached Ladysmith the next morning, men, animals and equipment were all caked in mud. But they had reached base, when they could so easily have been in a prison in Pretoria.

12

The Situation in Ladysmith

A section of the Ladysmith Town Guard; 176 men enrolled and despite their civilian clothes and obsolete rifles would, in all probability, have been more than a match for the Boers.

As gold prospectors flock to remote corners of the globe at the first hint of a gold strike, so journalists, war artists and photographers came to Ladysmith. The town had acquired celebrity status, with all the minutiae of its daily life being reported to the world. Neither this status, nor the war, had been sought by its residents.

The town had a fine setting and a healthy climate. No newly established town is beautiful. It takes time for trees to grow and an infrastructure to be created, however, from its founding, the townspeople had striven hard to create their little bit of paradise. They were proud of their town hall and adjacent library. The Roman Catholic Convent and small government school provided an excellent and inexpensive education. Various denominations had built churches that were well supported and there was cricket, rugby, hockey, and tennis. It even had a racecourse. As in other country towns of the period, its businessmen, craftsmen and professional men offered a range of services that today would be difficult to find in a town ten or twenty times its size.

The residents soon found out what happened when 12,000 soldiers, with 8,000 retainers, arrive in a little town. The newcomers also brought with them approximately 10,000 horses, 2,500 cattle, several hundred mules, hundreds of sheep, innumerable wagons and carts and all the other impedimenta of an army. Not surprisingly, grass and other vegetation rapidly disappeared and, when the rains came, the bare soil turned to mud, churned up into a soup by thousands of animal and human feet. When the sun came out the mud turned to fine dust, which permeated everything. The smell of horse manure and cow dung was everywhere. Trench latrines were dug for the troops and the town was soon infested with swarms of flies.

When the press arrived, this badly bruised little town was not at its best. Obviously in coming to Ladysmith they hoped to improve their personal fortunes and, when submitting their reports, they took into account the views of their employers and the characteristics of their potential readership. For example, British reporters thought it important their readers should know that the houses in Ladysmith had corrugated iron roofs, while the correspondent of the *Melbourne Argus*, Donald Macdonald, did not think this worth a mention. Most journalists made a genuine attempt to give an accurate report on the war. Unfortunately, there were some whose primary concern was to promote a cause in their homeland and, if the facts did not suit their purposes, adjustments had to be made.

H.W. Nevinson was employed by the *Daily Chronicle*, a London newspaper that was a staunch opponent of the ruling Conservative Party. If it could be shown that it was wrong to resist the Boers, or that the war was improperly conducted, the British Government would be embarrassed and its standing with the electorate damaged. Nevinson empathised with his employers but was unable to send them regular reports while in Ladysmith. He did, however, make up for this deficiency by publishing, in 1900, a book about his experiences in South Africa. This book was one of the first to be published on the war and was to be influential in creating sympathy for the Boers and in demonising the peoples of Natal and their allies.

Henry Woodd Nevinson, though a socialist, came from a privileged English background and had attended an English public school, Shrewsbury, and Christ Church, Oxford. In many ways he resembled Sir Alfred Milner for he never doubted his own superiority, had already formed his opinions about South Africa before leaving England, and would never consult colonials, or seek their opinion on anything.

He arrived in Cape Town before hostilities began and immediately set off overland, through the Boer Republics, to the British base at Ladysmith.

Though he was to stay in hotels that provided full board, he hired two manservants. While passing through the Republics, he took the trouble to acquire some knowledge of the character of the Boers. He noted that the Boer 'like the English poorer classes has large quantities of relations and one of them is always dying'.[1] He observed with satisfaction the neatness of their homes and their attempts to beautify them with little gardens. He found them hospitable and noticed they had little libraries of English books, Greek coins, and other evidence of culture. However, their broad-brimmed hats were often stained and dirty. His observation was that in South Africa corrugated iron was practically the sole building material and there were 'few architectural features to boast of'. Thus informed, he was able to tell his readers that the Boers were 'armed and mounted peasants'.[2] Given that many of their farms comprised at least 6,000 acres of good farmland, they were quite unusual peasants, and one does wonder what the Boers thought of this patronage.

Shortly after his arrival in Ladysmith he travelled to the top of Van Reneen's Pass, which crossed the mountains into the Free State. There in the crisp clear mountain air he saw spread before him a vast panoramic view of the colony.

Where Churchill saw 'smooth slopes of the richest verdure, broken only at intervals by lofty bluffs crowned with forests', and 'wide tracts of fertile soil watered by abundant rains', and Deneys Reitz saw a 'smiling land', Henry Nevinson saw something different.

> ...a parched, brown land like the desert beyond the Dead Sea, dusty bits of plain broken up by line upon line of bare red mountains. It seemed a poor country to make a fuss about, yet as South Africa goes, it is rich and even fertile in its way. Indeed on the reddest granite mountain one never fails to find multitudes of flowering plants and pasturage for thinnish sheep.[3]

The readers of the *Daily Chronicle* knew nothing about Natal and when reading this description they would not have challenged its veracity. They must have thought their government either evil or stupid to even consider going to war over it.

On 21 October Nevinson and other correspondents rode to Elandslaagte to witness the anticipated battle. In the darkness and 'blinding rain' after the battle, they walked around the field. He subsequently wrote:

> I was two hours on the ground moving about. The wounded lay very thick, groaning and appealing for help. In coming down I nearly trod on the up-turned white face of an old white-bearded man. He was lying quite silent with a kind of dignity. We asked who he was. He said, 'I am Kock, father of the commandant.' But the old man was wrong. He himself had been in command.[4]

When writing this, he had no doubt already heard the propaganda that the seriously wounded General Kock was stripped of most of his clothes, and then left out all night in the cold rain. We know that when the general fell, he was carried by his men to the shelter of the farmhouse as described in Chapter 9. After the ceasefire, he was brought to the first aid post near the Boer camp.[5] It is not even remotely possible the Boer doctors, medical orderlies and other non-combatants would have carried him out into the rain and abandoned him there. Another question arises from Nevinson's statement. If these reporters did find the old general on the battlefield, why did they not do something to help him? They could have covered him up, or carried him to a first aid station, or fetched stretcher bearers, or reported his presence to the doctors or the military. Instead they returned to Ladysmith, supper and a comfortable bed. What a pity he did not go out with one of Karri's search parties. That would really have given him something to write about. He might even have had a drink and a bite to eat with Karri Davies, Douglas Haig and the Boers.

South Africa is a complex society, and one can understand how a person new to a country can fail to pick up subtle nuances and, as a result, come to an incorrect conclusion. Nevinson has, however, gone much further than this. In the two passages quoted above he deliberately misinformed his readers. He knew Natal was not a desert and even he must have realised that this land, from its golden beaches along the warm Indian Ocean to its high mountains, is one of nature's glories. His tale about General Kock is so improbable that it must be rejected as pure invention designed to create sympathy for the Boers and hostility towards their opponents. This lack of integrity requires that a reader should be sceptical about everything he wrote. However, he should not be ignored, not only because of the influence he has had on many modern British historians, but also because he possessed to a remarkable degree those characteristics that over the years have bedevilled relations between the British and colonials everywhere.

On arrival in Natal, Nevinson was presented with another difficulty that had to be accommodated if the desired perception was to be created. People were already living in the country. The existence of the British settlers and their descendants was a direct threat to his and his employers' policy to use the war to embarrass the British Government. In an apparent attempt to discredit the locals, Nevinson tells us that a loaf of bread, 'costs a shilling. Everything costs a shilling here, unless it costs half-a-crown; and Natal grows fat on war. A shilling for a bit of bread! What is the good of Christianity?'[6]

The price of bread in Natal was always high because wheat was one of the few crops that did not flourish in the colony, resulting in wheat having to be brought half-way around the world before it could be milled in Ladysmith. This situation was exacerbated by the declaration of war. The high price of imported wheaten products was the subject of much debate in the colony and is a complex subject beyond the scope of this work. For the people living in Natal, bread was a luxury and for most, maize products were their staple food. Farmers would begin their day with a plate of unrefined yellow mealie (maize) meal porridge and many, including the writer's grandparents, would include it in all their meals. To suggest that 'Natal grows fat on war', because a hawker was attempting to sell bread at the railway station in Ladysmith, is as ludicrous as to suggest that Britain grew fat on war in 1940 because avocado pears were expensive in London. This clumsy attempt to defame the colonials is reprehensible, but the manner in which Nevinson, with his crude Darwinism, describes the Zulus and other blacks is even more repugnant. The blacks soon had his measure.

While Nevinson was attempting to put the world to rights by abusing the peoples of Natal, the residents of Ladysmith had other matters to occupy their minds. George Tatham, a lawyer and land surveyor, had been for many years a member of the Natal Carbineers. In 1899 he was a captain and senior officer in the Ladysmith squadron of the regiment, and had been selected to command General White's personal bodyguard. A number of letters written by his wife Frances have survived. These letters, while concerned principally with family matters, provide valuable insights into the feelings, fears and fortunes of those women who chose to stay in the town, no matter how dangerous life became. On 10 October she wrote to her sister Polly in England:

> The Boers are such cruel brutes. Just fancy, in one truckload of women and children there were six births and one death. [A woman who died in childbirth.] The Boers would not allow the poor refugee creatures even a drink of water at any of the Transvaal stations.
>
> Maggie and her two daughters and two grand daughters are still in Harrismith. They did not manage to get away before the commandeering began and so Artie Smith, Jessie's husband, has been commandeered. He refused to fight against the English, so they have taken his four horses, saddles and bridles and fined him £60. He now has to do work in the town but is exempt from fighting.
>
> Oh dear Polly, it is all so sad to see people wandering about homeless who had nice homes and were doing well before all this began. The Boers take possession of everything they can lay their hands on and destroy what they don't want. Poor old Sarah, it is hard for her. She has had to scatter all her things and leave her farm to the mercy of these rebels. Their crops will be destroyed. She had to get rid of poultry, pigs and everything. It will be like starting again. My Willie is in the same case. I had six destitute refugees here in my laundry for some time, but had to put them on the Relief Committee when Sarah came, as we had no room for them. You will think this a very selfish letter, all about ourselves, and our anxieties, but one can think of little

else. I am determined to leave this Colony, if I am spared, after this war is over. I have arranged that if Maritzburg is in danger, the girls are to be sent to Ada who can easily get on board a steamer and be off. We have made our wills and done all that is necessary. Our children are doing so well. Dolly had taken two certificates for Music during the last term, and Georgie a class 1st Prize and an Oxford Certificate.

...All the young men here are anxious to go to the front. We have completed our Ambulance classes, and are now competent to stop a bleeding wound and dress it, put on bandages properly, turn, lift and wash a patient. When the worst comes I am going to turn four large rooms into hospital wards and our class will nurse Volunteers. The Regulars will be provided for. I must close now. With much love to you and hoping to hear from you. And with warm love to Richard and the girls and boys.[7]

The Tatham family had some choices open to them; others were less fortunate and had to accept what fate sent their way.

William Watson was born in Yorkshire and came to Natal as a seventeen-year-old in 1851. In 1854 he moved to Ladysmith and established a successful business selling goods sent out from Yorkshire by his father. He married, but sadly his wife died in 1879, leaving him with five young children. On his being appointed Town Constable and Foreman in 1882, he closed his business. In his younger days he had found time to serve as a sergeant major in the Natal Frontier Guards. His eldest daughter, Annie, married a dentist from Edinburgh and the young couple went to live in Paarl, near Cape Town. Tragically, after three children had been born, the young dentist suffered a stroke that left him paralysed. Unable to manage on her own, Annie, with three young daughters and a paralysed husband, moved back to her father's home in Ladysmith.

In 1899 William Watson was retired and, apart from his family, his pride and joy was his garden with its orchard and copse of trees, which he had carefully nurtured over more than thirty years. This doughty old Yorkshireman kept a diary laced with irony during the period 30 October 1899 to 2 March 1900. As one would expect, he had very decided opinions and little respect for the political correctness of the time. He believed the war had come about as a result of the British premier Gladstone's feeble response to the Transvaal's attempt to subjugate Natal in 1881 and the machinations of 'old Barabbus at Pretoria with his selective biblical quotations'. Though he believed the Boers were 'by no means Sybarites', they were accustomed to a degree of comfort and because 'a few volleys from their deadly rifles exterminated a tribe, or laid a regiment low', they had become overconfident.[8]

Though their future appeared bleak, the people of Ladysmith put on a brave face and did their best to appear to be living a normal life. Women continued to chat to each other and sometimes even drank tea together. Some brave souls rode out on their bicycles to view military emplacements and even rode out of town to watch the fighting at Tintwanyoni.

The losses at Elandslaagte had compelled the Imperial Light Horse to make some changes. Aubrey Woolls Sampson was promoted to lieutenant colonel and in theory commanded the regiment. But he was in a very poor state. His femur had been so badly shattered that the doctors believed amputation of the limb was absolutely necessary. This he would not allow, and the doctors had no choice but to accept his decision. To achieve any mobility he would have to undergo an operation, which could not be done in Ladysmith. It was to be many months before he could get about. Command in the field therefore passed to the next ranking officer, Major Karri Davies. To replace Chisholme and Woolls Sampson, Major Doveton came over from Estcourt, leaving Lt Herbert Bottomley in charge of A squadron in Estcourt. Bottomley proved to be a very capable officer and it was not long before he had been promoted to major.

Meanwhile the Natal Volunteers continued their patrols in the hills near Ladysmith, which enabled them to keep headquarters advised of Boer troop movements. In the east of the colony, Major Leuchars of the Umvoti Mounted Rifles withdrew from Pomeroy and fell back on Tugela Ferry. The Boers occupied Pomeroy, where they went on another spree of looting and destruction of civilian property.

With the Dundee column now reunited with the rest of his force, General White set about formulating a plan to drive the Boers back into their republics. He was one of the first to realise the strength of the Boer artillery and, on 24 October, he sent a telegram to the British naval base at Simon's Town in the Cape urgently requesting some long range naval guns.[9] He has never been given full credit for his enterprise in taking this step, which despite being greeted without any enthusiasm by some senior officers on his staff, was to prove vital for the defence of the town. White had decided to stand firm in Ladysmith and plans were laid. But first he hoped to inflict a stunning defeat on the Boers, which would send them scuttling back across the border.

The plan devised by the British to inflict this defeat bore all the hallmarks of contemporary military thinking. An attack would be launched against the Transvaal burghers who had been assembling in some numbers in the hills to the north east of the town. Once the enemy had been dislodged from their positions, they would be driven west into the hills to the north of Ladysmith, where another British column would hold the Free Staters in check and be ready to deliver the knockout blow against any fleeing Transvaalers. Monday 30 October was chosen as the date for the attack. It was all to go horribly wrong.

On 28 October, HMS *Powerful* had arrived in Durban carrying guns destined for Ladysmith. There were two quick-firing 4.7 inch guns, three long 12-pounders (weight 12 cwt), one 12-pounder (8 cwt) naval field gun and four Maxims. Captain Percy Scott RN had, on receipt of White's telegram, designed, constructed, and tested wheels and platforms for these guns. By the next day, the guns had been transferred from the ship onto a train and were on their way to Ladysmith. A naval brigade commanded by Captain H. Lambton RN comprising eighteen officers and 267 men accompanied the guns. Travelling as fast as it could, by dawn on 30 October the train had reached Estcourt, and by 8.30 a.m., it was at Colenso. They could hear the sound of almost continuous firing, including the roar of big cannon. As the rail track was still intact, they pressed on.

At 10 p.m. on the previous night, a column, commanded by Lt Col Carleton, comprising the Royal Irish Fusiliers, the Gloucesters and a mountain battery, marched out of Ladysmith intending to take up a position on Nicholson's Nek, about 7 miles north of the town. They were to be guided by Major Adye, whom we met in Chapter 7. The major had no doubt about his ability to guide the column. The plan required that they hold the Free Staters in check while the attack was being launched against the Transvaal kommandos by the rest of the Ladysmith garrison. It was a dark moonless night and the track they had to follow was rough and not always easy to see. The success of the manoeuvre depended on absolute silence being maintained throughout the march, something the column had no hope of achieving as they stumbled along in the inky blackness.

While the British were preparing their attack, a significant change occurred in the Boer camp. Sick and exhausted, General Lucas Meyer surrendered the command of his 4,000 burghers to Louis Botha, an ambitious and capable man anxious to display his powers of leadership. He was born in Greytown, Natal. As a young child he had moved with his family to the Vryheid district, which the Boers had expropriated from Zululand and became part of the Transvaal. His success as a general in Natal is attributed by some authors to his knowledge of the country, which he is said to have acquired as a youth while hunting buck over land that would become the various battlefields. This is not so. As will be seen, nearly all the farms over which the war in Natal was fought were owned by people with Anglo Saxon or Scottish names. Given that Louis Botha grew up in a society dedicated to driving these farmers into the sea, it is highly unlikely they would have invited him to hunt buck on their farms. It was in the Transvaal that Botha learnt the capabilities of the long-range rifle and the importance of concealment.

The Boers had for some days been gathering on Long Hill and Pepworth's Hill to the north east of Ladysmith, and at Lombard's Kop and Bulwana in the east. It was against the Boers at Long Hill and Pepworth's Hill that the main British attack would fall. A brigade, under the command of Col Grimwood, consisting of five battalions of infantry with supporting artillery, was to dislodge the Boers from Long Hill. A second brigade under Col Ian Hamilton, consisting of four infantry battalions, artillery and some regular cavalry was to attack Pepworth Hill once Long Hill had been cleared. The Border Mounted Rifles and the Natal Mounted

Rifles were to protect the British right by covering Lombard's Kop and Bulwana. This whole force moved off from camp at midnight on Monday 30 October, and most were in position before dawn. Two of the infantry battalions and the artillery had wandered off course and contact with the cavalry had been lost.

At first light Grimwood launched his attack against Long Hill only to discover the Boers weren't there. Possibly forewarned by spies, they had withdrawn from the hill and established themselves across the Modderspruit in the rough bushy country on the eastern bank of that stream. From concealed positions, they opened withering fire on Grimwood's infantry as they attempted to cross the open ground leading to Long Hill, obliging them to go to ground behind whatever shelter they could find. To add to their misery, Boer guns on Pepworth Hill, which included a Creuzot Long Tom, opened fire on them.

Hamilton had no choice but to abandon any thoughts of capturing Pepworth Hill and concentrate instead on assisting Grimwood. His infantry went forward to reinforce Grimwood's left and the artillery attempted to put the Boer guns out of action. Initially they were outranged but by courageously going forward under fire, they brought the enemy guns within range and succeeded in scoring some hits; however, the fire from the Boer guns was only temporally stilled and the artillery had to disperse to avoid being annihilated.

Having neutralised the attack by the infantry, the Boers – in an apparent attempt to effect a breakthrough into Ladysmith – launched several attacks against the British right flank, but the line held. Instead, the Border Mounted Rifles and the Natal Mounted Rifles, by making frequent dashes to secure advantageous positions, began to drive the Boers back.

While all this activity was taking place, the Boers' Long Tom on Pepworth found time to send four of its 96-pound shells towards Ladysmith. These shells were apparently aimed at the railway station where a train had just arrived with the guns from HMS *Powerful* and Lambton's men. The Boers had yet to find the range with the result that the shells flew harmlessly overhead. Army personnel helped the sailors detrain the guns and, after a quick breakfast, three 12-pounders were lashed to ox wagons and under the command of Lieutenant Michael Hodges they set off for the battlefield. Leading them was a young local boy on a bicycle who was to show the way.[10]

On reaching Limit Hill they came under fire from the Boer artillery. Hodges unlimbered his guns and was about to fire when orders came through that they should withdraw. Shellfire had already wounded three of his men, knocked a wheel off one of the guns and the oxen had bolted. Nothing daunted, the sailors rounded up the oxen, found a spare wheel and were able to get back to the safety of their new base at Gordon Hill. Here Hodges unlimbered and opened fire on Long Tom at a range of 6,000 yards and with only his third shell, he silenced it for the day.[11] Unfortunately, Long Tom was back in action the next day.

At midday Colonel Knox, commander of the small reserve in Ladysmith, sent a message to White advising that the Free State kommandos appeared to be gathering to launch an attack on the town from the west. With Grimwood's infantry in disarray, White felt he had no alternative but to call off the attack and order an immediate return to base. The artillery came forward to cover the retirement of the infantry, thereby considerably reducing their casualties. Once the infantry had reached safety, the artillery batteries successfully covered each other in alternate retirements. Once the guns were safely back in Ladysmith, the Natal Volunteers retired, being among the last to leave the battlefield.

During the day General White had heard gunfire coming from the north, so he knew that Carleton's column must have engaged the enemy. He would have realised that as a result of the failure to defeat the Transvaal kommandos, Carleton was in danger of being surrounded and there was nothing he could do to help.

After Carleton and his column had travelled about 5 miles along the track to Nicholson's Nek, he noticed a large hill on his left and decided it should be occupied. In the pitch dark, the men climbed up in single file. As the leading men reached the top, someone dislodged a rock which, as it tumbled down the hill, dislodged other rocks, some shots went off and for a few seconds there was pandemonium. Some said a Boer picket had been disturbed and, panic stricken, they had run down the hill adding to the tumult. All of this was too much for the column's 200 mules, which bolted into the night, taking with them the guns of the Mountain Battery, the water kegs, almost all the reserve ammunition and the two heliographs that provided the only means of communication with headquarters.

The men climbed to the top of the hill to await the dawn, which was to bring them no joy. As the dawn light spread over the hill it was obvious to all that they were surrounded. They fought courageously, though there was never any doubt what the outcome would be. With ammunition running out, they surrendered. Forty-four men were killed, 150 wounded, and 843 taken prisoner. About seventy men escaped back to Ladysmith with news of the defeat. Two men from the Mountain Battery were found by some of Chief Khumalo's men from Driefontein. They were taken to Joseph Khumalo, who was acting chief in his grandfather's absence. Joseph was able to care for them and hide them from the Boers until, in March 1900, he was able to bring them safely back to Ladysmith.[12] General White was devastated by the day's events and accepted full responsibility for the disaster, saying that it was he, and he alone, who was to blame.

The Imperial Light Horse, with Karri Davies in command, had gone out with Hamilton but had a quiet day, acting in support throughout. Lt Brooking recorded in his diary with bitter irony the feelings of many in the regiment:

When at last we got back to camp we heard that the Glosters & Royal Irish Fusiliers were all taken prisoners. Then was the day called 'Black

Monday' and nobody seemed a bit pleased with the day's fight, until we were told that we had achieved our object and made a Reconnaissance in Force. No doubt the Glosters and RIF were delighted at the idea of having such a nice long rest in Pretoria.[13]

On a day when little went right for the British, Sir George White was able to state in his dispatch,

The services, which Colonel Royston and the forces under his command have rendered to the State and the Colony, have been of the very highest value. In him I have found a bold and successful leader, and an advisor whose experience of the Colony and of the enemy has been of great value to me. Employed on arduous duty from the commencement of the campaign, in touch with the enemy, I have found him prompt and ready for any emergency; he and his force reflect the greatest credit on the colony of Natal.[14]

During the engagement, Lt W.J. Clapham of the Natal Mounted Rifles died instantly when he was shot through the heart, and Lt D. Brown, Cpl P. Lloyd and Trooper A.F. Sander were wounded. Sgt E.F. Gibbens and Cpl A. Stuart of the Border Mounted Rifles were wounded.

It had been a bad day for Britain but it was not without positive aspects. The big naval guns had arrived in Ladysmith, providing cannons that could challenge the Boers' Long Toms. In spite of the fact that they were outranged, the regular artillery had also done well and, with help from the Navy, there was every reason to suppose the dominance of the Boer artillery was at an end. The amazing efficiency and speed with which the naval guns had been adapted for use on land and transported to the battlefield showed what Britain could do if pushed into a corner. Perhaps the most important consequence of the humiliation was that British public opinion began to swing against the Boers. This was the first time Britain had sent its mightiest cannons into battle with a young colonial boy on a bicycle showing the way.

(For a map of the siege of Ladysmith, see page 11 of the plate section.)

13

Investment of Ladysmith

Although the medical staff in Ladysmith did everything they could to save him, General Kock died of his wounds on 31 October 1899. General White gave permission to his widow to remove his body for burial in the Transvaal. His nephew, who had been with him since Elandslaagte, was permitted to leave with the bereaved widow. While in Ladysmith, she went out of her way to thank General White for the courtesy and kindness which both she and her late husband had received from the British. The body of the old Boer general was taken to Pretoria, where he was given a state funeral.

While Mrs Kock was engaged in the sad task of collecting her husband's body, the troops in Ladysmith were frantically building fortifications on the defensive perimeter approved by General White. Over the years he has been much censured for his decision to stand firm in Ladysmith.

It is said that because the town lay in a valley surrounded by hills, it was indefensible. In 1902 Sir George said in his evidence in London to the Commission on the War in South Africa, 'I defended it for 118 days against the headquarters and united armies of the South African Republics' – which was a succinct and complete answer to this criticism.

In London Lord Wolseley believed that White should have withdrawn even further south, to Mooi River or even Pietermaritzburg. It has been said that Wolseley 'was almost as familiar with Natal and Zulu countryside as the Boer'. This is probably correct – neither party knew much about Natal.

In deciding to remain north of the Tugela, General White took into account another factor. The flow of rivers in Natal is determined by the level of the subterranean water table. During the dry season, from May to September, this level gradually falls, as does the flow in rivers. When the rains come in spring, the water table does not rise immediately and, generally, it is only in January that the flow of rivers begins to rise substantially. Sir George was quite correct when he told the London Commission that 'in November, 1899 the Tugela could have been crossed on foot almost anywhere. Against an enemy with more than double my numbers, and three times my mobility, I could not hope to maintain such a line with my small force.' Added to this, the topography of Natal is such that that the major rivers the Boers would have crossed on their way to the coast had high hills on their northern bank and gently sloping hills on their southern bank, thereby providing a natural fortress against any relieving army trying to fight its way from the coast into the interior.

Sir George has also been criticised for failing to blow up the railway lines leading to the Boer Republics. Minor damage would merely have been an irritation to the Boers; more serious damage would have destroyed an asset whose value to the colony was exceeded only by the harbour at Durban. In the course of their advance from Charleston on Natal's northern border to Ladysmith, the Boers' invasion ran parallel to their own borders, which were never far away. They did not rely on the railway and even during the investment of the town, they relied principally on ox-wagons and horses for transport. Beyond Ladysmith, every yard they travelled would take them further and further away from their republics and, if they were to successfully subjugate Natal, the railway was vital. By retaining control of the junction at Ladysmith, White ensured any further advance into Natal by the Boers would be temporary.

Finally, Sir George is criticised for permitting non-combatants to remain in Ladysmith until it was too late to get rid of these 'useless mouths'. Many of the civilians in the town were employed by the army and no doubt they remained because the army still needed their services. Some of the residents, like the Watson family, had no choice but to stay in the town, either because they were physically incapable of leaving or because they had nowhere else to go. Others chose to remain because they wished to contribute to the defence of their homes and businesses. For example, the nursing home created by Fanny Tatham in her house provided a much-needed contribution to the care of the sick and wounded. Almost all the men joined the Town Guard and, with a little training, they could have become one of the key units defending it. Before the war there were not many blacks resident in the town. There were some employers who provided temporary accommodation for their employees, however, most Zulus chose to live at their kraals in the country and to ride or walk into town to work or attend to their affairs. Once the Boers invaded Natal, blacks such as Samuelson's Scouts sought shelter in the town. Indian nationals employed by the Natal coal mines were herded into Ladysmith by the Boers. Colonial refugees from Northern Natal congregated in Ladysmith and having nowhere else to go, stayed in the town. Finally we should not forget the war correspondents, their manservants and horses, all of whom would require feeding.

Short of shooting all these people, or arresting them and sending them under guard to Durban, it was impossible for General White to get rid of them, however inconvenient their presence might be. But General Sir George White never even considered such a course. He believed it was his duty to do everything in his power to protect the civilians who were in Ladysmith and although he made mistakes, his consideration for these unfortunate people adds a dimension to his character often ignored by his detractors. It was not only the residents of Ladysmith for whom General White felt responsible. Throughout Northern Natal there were Zulus who had come to Natal for protection and who, as a result of the Boer advance, faced a very uncertain future. If Ladysmith was to be abandoned, not only would more colonials have had their farms, businesses and homes looted and destroyed but thousands of Zulus would have been forced to submit to Boer government and face the possibility of having their land confiscated.

Though his decision to stand firm at Ladysmith was undoubtedly, in my opinion, correct, General White did make mistakes with regard to the disposition of his forces. It was a mistake to send the Durban Light Infantry to Colenso, where their lack of numbers and mobility rendered them almost useless. They should have been brought to Ladysmith where they could have made a substantial contribution to the defence of the town. The Natal Field Artillery, with their obsolete muzzle-loading guns, should have been sent back to Durban and equipped with modern guns or, if this was not permitted, discharged.

Different considerations applied to the mounted Volunteers. They were highly mobile, knew the country and were able to detect and track Boers while remaining concealed. They owned their horses, which were suited to the conditions in which they were to operate. Though equipped with obsolete rifles, such was their marksmanship that they were the opponents most feared by the Boers. In addition, they spoke Zulu and their relationship with the black people was good. To keep these units in Ladysmith was to fail to make full use of their potential.

On 27 October, the Natal Governor, Sir Walter Hely Hutchinson, wrote to the Colonial Secretary advising him that should the Boers raid Pietermaritzburg or Durban, the populace would hold the Volunteers responsible. The Volunteers were fully aware of the reliance placed on them by the people of Natal. Once it appeared inevitable that Ladysmith would be besieged, officers in the Volunteer regiments were concerned that while they were shut up in the town, the invading Boers would have a free hand to loot and destroy throughout the country. Major Rethman of the Border Mounted Rifles drafted a letter to General White requesting permission for the mounted Volunteer regiments to leave Ladysmith before the Boers closed the door. He knew that as a major in a Volunteer regiment he had no right to make any such suggestion to a senior British officer, so he wrote the letter in his capacity as an elected member of the Natal Legislative Assembly. He discussed the letter with some of his officers and it was decided to send it to the local army headquarters. The result was predictable. Headquarters refused to consider the suggestion and he was given a terrific dressing down.

Having failed to persuade them to permit the Mounted Volunteers to leave Ladysmith, the major requested permission for his regiment to cultivate a kitchen garden. This was also refused on the ground that it was alarmist. Frustrated by the lack of co-operation they received, Major Rethman and

Captain Sparks from the Natal Mounted Rifles went to see a Dutch farmer whose land lay within the defended perimeter chosen by General White. They persuaded the farmer to plant as much of his land as possible with maize. Over the next few weeks, the farmer and his labourers were seen ploughing, preparing and planting their fields, apparently oblivious to the war being waged around them. Even when the Boers sent some shells in their direction, they were not distracted from their work. The maize turned out to be a godsend during the later stages of the siege, providing fresh corn for those besieged. In addition, the cobs and maize stalks provided much needed food for the Volunteers' horses. The Dutch farmer did well out of his maize that season.[1]

The officer in command of the infantry regiments in Ladysmith, Colonel Ian Hamilton, later noted in his diary, 'The cavalry ought, beyond doubt, to have been cleared out of here as soon as it was clear we were going to be invested.'[2]

When Kate Driver reported for duty on the day after her arrival in Ladysmith, she was told that she had been assigned night duty. The Volunteer Hospital had five marquees, each being a separate ward. Four nurses would be on duty at any one time. In Kate's ward were several Gordon Highlanders, one of whom had been shot in the head while climbing through a fence at Elandslaagte. During her first night on duty this man became delirious and began singing, 'Yes please Sirs! Yes please Sirs!' to the tune of *Three Blind Mice*. When she came on duty the following evening she found that he, with two other delirious men with bad head wounds, had been placed in a separate marquee. She was made responsible for this ward as well as her original one. She would often sit outside between her two tents and listen:

> For nearly two weeks this poor shattered piper of the Gordon Highlanders screamed and moaned and sang his scrap of song more and more out of tune. Morphia seemed to have little effect upon him. Most of the men in most of the tents were kept awake, and some were badly affected by the noise. Then, quite suddenly, the noise stopped and he was dead.[3]

During her first ten days in Ladysmith, the post did much to relieve the stress Kate and her colleagues felt. It brought little luxuries for the nurses as Natal friends had sent boxes of good things for the hospital. Kate had the comfort of being able to send letters describing her experiences to her mother. She told her about 'my dear Gordon Highlander' and about her friends from Pietermaritzburg,

> Nurse Otto nursed one of the officers, Lieutenant Campbell, until he died. She tells me how heart-rending it was. Poor Nurse Early lost one of her boys this morning and was terribly cut up, a friend of her friends. Every two or three minutes I can hear some young fellow

with fever calling out in his delirium, and on the other side, Nurse Thompson has a man with a very badly broken leg, he keeps calling out too.[4]

Very early on the morning of 31 October the Boer artillery began their bombardment of the town. This was the first time Kate had heard the sound of oncoming shells and seen them explode. Possibly because she had yet to realise the danger, she felt no fear, only excitement. When the night nurses went off duty in the morning, they went up Convent Hill to see from whence the shells came. They were shown around by the soldiers and allowed to look through a telescope and field glasses at the various gun emplacements, including the newly arrived naval guns. Their curiosity aroused, they walked to Gordon's Hill to have a closer look at the new arrivals. Here the gunnery officer permitted them to look through his glasses at the great gun the Boers had placed on Bulwana Hill, after which they were introduced to Captain Lambton, commander of the naval squadron. Dressed in full uniform including a cocked hat, he made a big impression on the girls. Presumably he was on his way to introduce himself to General White.

On arriving back at base, Kate received a message that she was wanted by Dr Currie. At the operating theatre a Zulu had just been brought in. He had been looking after some mules, when a shell hit his thigh causing a horrendous wound. Before anything could be done for him, he died. Sixty years later Kate could still picture 'the ghastly wound and the face that showed the shocked and sudden crumpling up of life'.[5] He was the first civilian to be killed in Ladysmith.

Also on this day, 31 October, Kommandant General Joubert demonstrated why he was known as 'Slim Piet' (Sly or Cunning Pete). A Boer ambulance wagon was sent into Ladysmith with wounded British prisoners, the Boers stating that they wished to exchange these men for wounded Boers, and a twenty-four hour truce was suggested to enable women and children to leave. The British not only agreed to the request but permitted the wagon to enter Ladysmith accompanied by their escort of twenty men, all with Red Cross badges prominently displayed. No attempt was made to blindfold any of this group who were permitted to wander around Ladysmith without any restriction and unaccompanied. They were permitted to talk to unwounded Boer prisoners and known Boer sympathisers. They drank at public bars and one of their number asked to have Frank Rhodes, Dr Jameson and Sir John Willoughby pointed out to him. This behaviour did not appear to have raised any suspicions among the British military. The local residents noticed among the escort several well-known Boers who were neither doctors nor in any other way qualified to attend to wounded men. Of those recognised, Mattey was a well-known member of the Boer Artillery corps.[6] They were allowed to take an inordinately long time collecting the wounded exchange prisoners and no doubt were able to obtain all the information they wanted about Ladysmith's defences. For the Boers it was a great intelligence coup. It was no coincidence that in the days that followed, the Boer artillery were able to shell with pinpoint accuracy the camp of the Imperial Light Horse, important military stores and places known to be frequented by officers. The ILH were obliged to hastily move their camp to a more sheltered position and dye their tents with mud, while the stores had to be moved and some imperial officers had their social life severely disturbed.

Meanwhile, two men who had been at the head of the Jameson Raid, Jameson and Willoughby, had arrived in Ladysmith on 28 October. What they hoped to achieve in the town is a mystery. Jameson was ill, and because his Raid had provided Kruger with an excuse to build up Boer armaments, he was not popular in Natal. In Ladysmith he presented a picture of abject misery and loneliness. Sir John Willoughby was an Englishman who had served in the Royal Horse Guards. He was the senior officer under Jameson during the Raid and was sentenced to ten months imprisonment in England. He was of no consequence in Natal, though he was regarded as important by the Boers and latterly by conspiracy theorists. Willoughby left South Africa in 1900.

Among the prisoners exchanged was Major C.S. Kincaid of the Irish Fusiliers who reported that the prisoners had all been well treated. Whether the depositing of sick and wounded men in a town, with the intention of either killing them with shellfire or starving them to death is good treatment, is moot! The major obviously thought so, but then he probably expected the siege to be raised within a few weeks. While in captivity he had the opportunity of observing the Irish Brigade and discovered that almost all were Americans and those who were not Americans were English. There was not an Irishman among them.

In the days following Black Monday, the Natal Volunteers, the ILH and the British cavalry continued to patrol the countryside around Ladysmith. In a few desultory exchanges of fire they were able to harass the enemy but, as they were always outnumbered and the Boers were able to call on artillery support, they were unable to halt the inexorable drift towards complete encirclement of the town.

Captain George Tatham, during one of his brief periods off duty, was asked by his wife to leave an order for a few weeks' supplies at Sparks Bros. When delivering the order, George told the shopkeeper to double the quantity of all items requested.[7] Events were to show whether he was an alarmist or a realist.

Old William Watson noted in his diary that General Buller, who had boasted that he would be in Pretoria in a month, had landed in Cape Town. He wryly commented that now Buller was in the country, 'he will have the satisfaction of knowing that a very considerable body of our troops, horse, foot and artillery are already in Pretoria, as prisoners of war.'[8]

All over Natal the families and friends of the Volunteers were, of course, very concerned about their loved ones. Just before the siege closed in,

Lieutenant George Archibald of the Border Mounted Rifles received from his sweetheart and future wife Rosie, a letter expressing some of the concerns they felt.

Mother heard that there are 20 000 refugees in Durban; is it not sad, so many homeless people, whatever will become of them all? When Sir Redvers Buller does come, do you think there will be any chance of you all coming home, or will they still keep you away? It is exactly a month since that day you came to tell us you had to go to the front, that Friday so long ago. Are you in more danger from those horrid Boers? Of course no one would like to go to shoot a man, even though he be a Boer, for the sake of shooting, but why have they come down and attacked us? Natal is not quarrelling with them. We cannot pity them when it is through them, all you brave Volunteers have to be taken away. I wish you were all at home, the Boers too, if only they could have a good beating first ... [the horses] Sultan and Chick will not understand such hard times, is there grass enough for them?[9]

During the last days of October the Boers were seen placing their big Creusot Long Tom gun on Bulwana, a massive hill about 4 miles south east of Ladysmith. Once the gun was in place, men could be seen building fortifications to protect it. It was apparent to all that from this hill the Boer artillery would command much of the town. It therefore came as a surprise to many that the military took no steps to prevent the gun being placed on the hill or to stop the building of the fortifications. Some even thought the British should have included Bulwana within their defensive perimeter. The 1902 London Commission questioned General White's Chief of Staff, Sir Archibald Hunter, about these matters. In his evidence, Sir Archibald admitted, 'I do not know the country well, except from maps. I only passed up once from Pietermaritzburg, and down again in the dark.' Perhaps relying on the fact that he had spent more than four months in Ladysmith, the Commission asked him about the defences of the town:

Chairman: 'And there had been no preparations for defence in Ladysmith?'

Hunter: 'None whatever, and the conditions of the life of the garrison there were such with the local farmers, and so on, that you dare not go off the roads. The cavalry officers were supposed to do reconnaissance every year, and to send sketch maps to show what work in this respect they had been doing. But there were simple sketches of the line of the track: they dare not go off it.

'Every farmer was a Boer or a Dutchman with Boer sympathies; and there was not a single man (Briton) who had been on top of Bulwana, except one and he is dead now, Captain Valentin of the Somersetshire Light Infantry. He had been asked by one of these young farmers to go out for a day's shooting, and in the course of the day he crossed over the top of Bulwana Hill and down the other side, and he was the only man who had ever been on top. Nobody knew whether there was water on the other side or whether there was not.'

Chairman: (incredulously) 'Do you mean that before the war, in our own colony, a British officer could not sketch the country? I mean that in our own colony in the neighbourhood of Ladysmith, that is to say within a girdle of ground that would be naturally occupied in any system of defence for the town, covering stores and so on, there was not a single officer except this Captain Valentin who had been on the main feature or any of the features that dominated a position that had to be held?'

Hunter: 'Not one.'

Chairman: 'Because the farmers would have offered violence?'

Hunter: 'No, they would have summoned them before the magistrate for trespass, and the magistrate would have given a decision against them, and they would have been bound by the magistrate's order.'

Chairman: 'Did it ever happen?'

Hunter: 'It was threatened.'[10]

General Hunter can be forgiven for being unfamiliar with the local terrain and his ignorance of the law of trespass, as applied in Natal. However, he did look at maps and those maps, inadequate as they might have been, did mention the names of farmers. On one contemporary map of the environs of Ladysmith appear the following names of farmers: Farquhar, Pepworth, Bell, Tatham, Nicholson, Hobbs, Walker, Kirk O'Tulloch and Smith. On the same map appear only three names of Boer farmers: Bester, Potgieter and De Waal. This map does not pretend to give a comprehensive list of the farmers but clearly most of them were of British descent. The proportion of British to Dutch near the borders of the Boer Republics was about five to one, a difference that dramatically increased south of Ladysmith.

One name not mentioned on that particular map is W.W. Willis, a former mayor of Ladysmith and in 1899 the owner of the farm on which Bulwana Hill was situated. He was in Ladysmith throughout the siege and begged the military to attack the Boers on Bulwana, and was able and willing to give the British any information they might want. All his offers of help were spurned.

With the confidence of ignorance, Hunter went on to tell the Commission about the attitude of the Zulus at the start of the War:

On the one side was this big force of savages waiting to see what we were going to do, and of course the Boers would have sent their agents among them, and have pointed out that we had run before we had been hit, which would have had a very disastrous effect – it might even have led to the massacre of every white man, woman and child they could get at, and the whole of the eastern part of the colony, in Natal, at the foot of their mountains would have been absolutely at their mercy, and also it would have had a very exhilarating effect to say the least, upon the Boers themselves.[11]

Curiously, those colonials in Natal who spent much of their daily lives in the company of Zulus seem to have been blithely unaware of the terrible fate hanging over their heads. The Commissioners questioned Hunter about this issue.

Sir George Taubman-Goldie: 'Just going back to the argument used about the 70,000 Zulus sitting on the fence in case we withdrew from the northern apex of Natal: as a matter of fact, nothing did happen when we were driven out of the northern apex by the Boers?'

Hunter: 'No. But then of course we were driven out as a result of a fight. It was not as if we had turned tail before we were hit, and the result of the fight was an acknowledged British success.'

Taubman-Goldie: 'And the 70,000 Zulus were aware of that fact?'

Hunter: 'Yes they were, and they saw us always holding out. And I think it is an acknowledged thing throughout the whole of South Africa that the fall of Ladysmith was to be accepted as the promised sign. They are very biblical in their ways of thinking, and so on, and the Cape Colony, and the Zulus and everyone else, who were watching to see who was going to be master, were practically asked whether they would accept the fall of Ladysmith as a sign. Therefore if Ladysmith had fallen, I believe all the Dutch in the Cape Colony would have risen, the Zulus and everyone else. They would have plumped then for the Boers as their future masters.'[12]

This is nonsense. When speaking about matters with which he was familiar, General Hunter had said such appreciative things about the Imperial Light Horse, we should perhaps try to understand how he came to give this extraordinary evidence.

From the earliest days of the British trading settlement, a substantial and influential group of intellectuals in England, who had never been near Natal, believed that a terrible mutual animosity existed between the English settlers and the Zulus. In addition, Boer propaganda carefully nurtured the belief that Natal was a country occupied by Dutch farmers. In spite of the inherent contradictions, Hunter appears to have accepted the veracity of these propositions in their entirety. One can understand how Hunter possessed these opinions on arrival in Natal, but how did they survive his four-month stay in Ladysmith? The answer to this question lies in the customs and traditions of the British army.

The Regular units tended to look down on Volunteers and perhaps for this reason, Volunteer officers were not welcomed into the officers' mess of the regiments in the Regular army. The result was contact between the two groups was generally restricted to the giving and receiving of orders. The informal contact and discourse that would have come as a result of eating and drinking with the Volunteers would have been of inestimable value to the British army officers and would have prevented many of their blunders. Though Hunter and his colleagues appear to have stuck religiously to the prevailing custom while in Ladysmith, there was, on his way to South Africa, a British officer who was prepared to break the mould.

Meanwhile, during these busy days before the siege began, an enquiry was held into the health of Brigadier General Yule and it was decided he was no longer fit for duty and should immediately be shipped back to England. An enquiry was also held into the conduct of Captain C.G. Willson of the Natal Carbineers, and it was decided that he should be court-marshalled. I have been unable to trace any record of the court martial either in London or in Natal.

Realising that Ladysmith might be besieged for some time, Herbert Watkins-Pitchford felt he should make a quick journey to Pietermaritzburg to ensure that matters at the Veterinary Research Station would be properly managed while he was away. To this end on 1 November he went down to the Ladysmith station.

Two long trains were standing full to overflowing with women and children, the men struggling with the luggage which blocked the way everywhere. So I sent my bag back and rode back to camp again.

It was midnight before they got the last women away in trucks. The next afternoon I saw Leumann at the station for a few minutes looking absolutely thin and pinched. He was taking down a trainload of men wounded at Tinta Inyoni and the poor chaps were brought from the hospital in dhoolies or square hammocks with green coverings slung on a long bamboo and carried by four dhoolie bearers. Some of the poor fellows were badly hit and groaned loudly as they were lifted into the carriage, but it was imperative to empty the hospitals as it was expected that they would be overflowing again shortly. So Leumann went off after a few minutes' chat, and a special train carrying General French and Major Haig followed immediately. This train was the last to get through and only just managed to run the blockade, being heavily fired upon. We heard that night that the wires were down, and natives reported the line cut and held by large bodies of Boers just above Colenso.[13]

During the journey of that last train, the Boer fire was so intense that the two future Field Marshals, John French and Douglas Haig, were obliged to lie on the floor and even there they were far from safe, one bullet hitting a suitcase Haig had with him.

The following day it was decided General Brocklehurst should make a reconnaissance in force to the south west of the town to ascertain the number of the enemy in that locality as well as the number and calibre of their guns. Brocklehurst took with him the British cavalry, the Imperial Light Horse and a brigade of artillery. The action that followed has been described as 'hopeless in its inception and bad in its execution'.[14]

Outside the defended perimeter to the west of Ladysmith lay a broad plain, called Long Valley, beyond which were a number of hills on which the Boers had placed guns. Due west was Rifleman's Ridge and south of it another eminence, Lancers' Hill. To the south east of them were three flat topped hills, Mounted Infantry Hill, Middle Hill and End Hill.

On arrival in Long Valley the 18th Hussars were ordered to guard the right flank while the19th Hussars attacked Rifleman's Ridge. A mounted infantry company occupied the appropriately named Mounted Infantry Hill to protect the left rear. The 5th Dragoon Guards with the 21st Battery moved south down Long Valley. When Karri approached the new cavalry commander, General Brocklehurst, for orders, he was told, 'I've heard your men are very fine fellows Major, do what you like.'[15]

It was less than two months since Karri and the rest of the ILH began their training, which was received from British instructors following traditional British principles. At Elandslaagte the ILH had shown their ability and courage and they had witnessed the gallant manner in which Colonel Scott-Chisholme led the regiment. No one mentioned that the brave colonel, by setting off up the rocky slope towards a hidden enemy, with walking stick and flag held aloft, was setting an appalling example. It was the virtues of stealth and surprise that should have been emphasised.

When General French asked Col Scott-Chisholme at Elandslaagte what he would like to do, the colonel replied that they would like to take the hill on the Boer left flank. Having received carte blanche from General Brocklehurst, Karri, following Scott-Chisholme's example, looked for a target that could be attacked. The artillery had been shelling Lancer's Hill and the Boer gun there had been silenced, causing Karri to believe, wrongly, that the enemy were vacating it. He decided to attack the hill. He sent two squadrons to Middle Hill to protect his left flank, then turning towards the remaining two squadrons said, 'Load your guns. You see that kopie, that's the Boer laager, we're going to take it. Right squadron go on, Left in support.'[16]

To reach the hill they had to cross one-and-a-half miles of flat, open country. After they had covered about half-a-mile, they were met by surprisingly heavy rifle fire. Fortunately, a donga (dry watercourse) offered them some shelter where the horses could be left while they went forward on foot. They were able to get within 800 yards of the enemy before the fire became so intense that they had to shelter in another donga. Major Doveton led a charge towards the hill but half the men failed to follow him, and he and his group were forced to go to ground hiding behind anthills and whatever other cover they might find. During their advance, Captain Knapp was killed instantly when he was hit in the head. To add to their problems, the ILH attack on Middle Hill had been checked and the Boers on this hill were bringing raking fire to bear on Karri's squadrons. In the attempt to take Middle Hill Lieutenant Brabant was mortally wounded. Unable to advance or retreat and with substantial numbers of Boers arriving from the east, Karri called for reinforcements.

In fighting that lasted several hours, the dismounted 5th Dragoons, with artillery support, were able to cover the retreat of the ILH from Lancer's Hill. The Natal Volunteers were called out and secured the left by clearing the Boers off Middle Hill and End Hill.

In driving the Boers off those hills, two Carbineers, Major Taunton and Sergeant Mapstone, were killed and four men were wounded. Corporal Silburn of the Natal Mounted Rifles was wounded. No Border Mounted Riflemen were killed but the adjutant, Captain Arnott, and three troopers, G.L. Edmunds, A.G. Goldstone and F.J. Thomas, were wounded. Captain Arnott was shot through both legs while leading his men on the left flank. He had fallen in an exposed position and seeing him, Major Evans of the NMR, with a complete disregard for his own safety, bandaged the wounds and after making him as comfortable as possible, sent for an ambulance. The rifle fire became so intense that Arnott struggled back to cover, crawling from stone to stone until he joined his men. Noticing more ammunition was needed and seeing Surgeon Lieutenant Platt and Lieutenant J.R. (Galloping Jack) Royston approaching, Arnott shouted 'Go back and fetch more ammunition.' Royston hurried the ammunition mules forward and went along the lines serving it out, while Platt, under heavy fire, stayed with the wounded man until the stretcher bearers arrived.[17]

Major Rethman and Lieutenant Andreason had a narrow escape when a shell burst within a couple of yards of them. Such was the severity of the explosion that onlookers thought they must have been killed; however, both were unscathed. Over the next few months there were many instances where individuals narrowly missed being killed but surely none can surpass the experience of Trooper G.L. Edmunds. A Mauser bullet hit him in the centre of his chest, passing through his lungs and back. As he fell, a second bullet hit him a little lower down, passing through his lower abdomen and coming out in the thigh without breaking a bone. For several days the doctors thought he had no hope of surviving and his bed was allotted to another wounded man. However, he gradually gained strength until an attack of pleurisy in the wounded lung again brought him to death's door. Again he rallied and was almost convalescent when, in a violent thunderstorm, lightning struck his tent. At the time he was holding the tent-pole and should have been killed instantly but survived, suffering a severe electric shock.[18]

Once the ILH had been extricated from their dangerous position, General Brocklehurst, noting the steady build-up of Boer forces, decided to call off the engagement and return to base. The withdrawal was completed without further incident.

The engagement of 3 November did confirm that the encirclement of Ladysmith was complete, and some information was gained about the number and calibre of the enemy guns. The Imperial Light Horse had seven killed, including two of its best officers, and ten men, including Trooper Guthrie Smith were badly wounded. When Karri was asked by one of his officers for an explanation of his headlong interpretation of his orders, he replied, 'Well Jimmy, as the Regiment was formed to fight the Boers, I went for them.' General Brocklehurst was the party principally to blame for the fiasco as he should never have granted carte blanche to an inexperienced officer and he should have explained to Karri and his officers what their objectives were and what was required of them. But Karri did recognise that he too was at fault and wrote to General White stating that because of his lack of experience and training, a more experienced officer should be appointed to lead the regiment. In due course the following order was promulgated: 'At the request of Major Karri Davies and the officers of the ILH, Major A.H.M. Edwards, 5th Dragoon Guards, is appointed to the command of the ILH during the absence of Lieutenant-Colonel Woolls Sampson, and is granted the local rank of Lieutenant-Colonel while so employed.'[19]

The choice of Lt Col Edwards to lead the regiment was a happy one. He got on well with the regiment and they with him. About Karri he wrote, 'He promised me that he would give me every assistance and support. This I have no hesitation in saying he always did. As I got to know him I found him to be a straight-forward, warm-hearted, generous man. A most extraordinary character.'

While Gen Brocklehurst was carrying out his reconnaissance in force, the Boer artillery made use of some of the information they had gained during the prisoner exchange. A shell hit the Royal Hotel at lunchtime causing extensive destruction in the dining room. Although many British officers and members of the press corps were present, no one was hurt. Another shell burst in the backyard of Dr Rouillard's house, an event that might have been of no great significance had the army not stored their ammunition on either side of that yard. Unaware of these dramas, William Watson noted in his diary, 'Water works destroyed, reservoir dry. I have the pleasure of carrying water in buckets from the river, which is half a mile distant. It is hard work for an ancient Briton like me.'

14

The Defence of the Natal Midlands

Once Ladysmith was invested, the Boers had to decide whether to attempt to take the town by storm or to continue their drive south towards Durban and the sea. At a meeting of their war council on 9 November 1899, a compromise solution was reached. It was decided that a portion of their army should maintain the siege while the balance should continue southwards.

The main road to the south and the sea crossed the Tugela River near the village of Colenso, about 18 miles from Ladysmith. The Durban Light Infantry, the Natal Field Battery and the 2nd Battalion Royal Dublin Fusiliers with its one hundred mounted infantry had been sent to Colenso to guard the road and rail bridges across the Tugela. When on patrol, the mounted Infantry were assisted by the Estcourt squadron of the Natal Carbineers under Captain Mackay. The whole force was under the command of Col Cooper of the Dublin Fusiliers.

On 1 November, the mounted infantry and the Carbineers exchanged fire with a strong force of Boers scouting towards Colenso. After losing several men, killed or wounded, the Boers retired. One man from the mounted infantry was killed in the engagement. On that same day, the Durban Light Infantry at Colenso were shelled by the Boers. Col Cooper, fearing his small force might be overwhelmed, decided to withdraw to Chieveley, about 5 miles south of Colenso.

The following day at Nottingham Road, Major Duncan McKenzie, who had just arrived back from England, boarded the train to Ladysmith. At Chieveley the train was stopped pending the arrival of a train from Ladysmith. After a considerable delay the train from Ladysmith came through bearing the marks of the gauntlet shell and rifle fire it had run through. It was, of course, the last train from Ladysmith and was carrying General French and Major Douglas Haig on the first leg of their journey to the Cape front.

Uncertain what course he should follow in the rapidly changing circumstances, Col Cooper decided to seek the opinions of the other officers, and invited the newly arrived Duncan McKenzie to join the discussion. When Col Cooper asked for his opinion, McKenzie replied, 'Well, Sir, if your information is correct, and there are 6,000 Boers advancing on Colenso, the wisest thing you can do is fall back on Estcourt, for the river is not full, and they can easily cross higher up and so cut off your force from Estcourt, and so hem you in against the Tugela River.'[1]

After further discussion, Col Cooper decided to heed McKenzie's advice and fall back on Estcourt. During the night the infantry entrained for Estcourt, the last train leaving at 3 a.m. The Natal Field Battery marched by road, setting off at 9 p.m. Though Captain Mackay was an excellent officer, McKenzie decided to assume command of the Carbineer squadron.

When the last batch of infantry had left, McKenzie moved the mounted men back a mile or two and after following his usual practice of sending out patrols to the right and left, they waited for dawn. When daylight came, there was no sign of the enemy, and it seemed the Boers had yet to cross the Tugela. Nonetheless the Carbineers remained in position until the evening, when they retired to Estcourt.[2]

The senior officer in Estcourt was a Colonel Long who instituted the practice of sending an armoured train to Colenso from time to time, presumably to scout or to show the flag. The engine pulled a number of open trucks, the sides of which were reinforced with steel plates; firing holes had been cut into them. With no sign of activity from the Boers, the train was able to make a number of these excursions without being attacked.

Initially the British took no steps to call up the rifle associations, which existed in most country districts. However a British visitor, the Hon. T.K. Murray, saw the value of tapping into this resource of mounted men who could shoot straight, and he obtained permission to recruit a unit that would be known as Murray's Horse. By 2 November, Murray had eighty men at Mooi River, a small village approximately half-way between Ladysmith and Pietermaritzburg. Within the next few days the strength of the unit had increased to 150 men.[3]

All the while ships were bringing further men and supplies, which were rushed to the Natal front. One of the first of the new arrivals was a young Winston Churchill, who arrived in Estcourt on 6 November. He had gained some military experience in India and the Sudan before abandoning the army in favour of a career in politics. After defeat in his first attempt to be elected to Parliament, he had persuaded the *London Morning Post* to appoint him as a special correspondent to cover the war in South Africa. His employers paid him a salary that made him the highest paid correspondent in South Africa – and it is easy to see why. His grandfather was a Duke, his father a prominent Victorian politician and his mother an American heiress, connections which should ensure that he would obtain access to the best stories. In addition, he was already well-known to the English public, had a great command of English and his writing was always entertaining. For Churchill the appointment not only gave him financial security, but also gave him a wonderful opportunity to promote his political career. Sometimes his descriptions of events are woefully inaccurate and one must always be careful to sort the wheat from the chaff.

The little coaster that had brought Churchill from East London, in the Cape Colony, to Durban, arrived at midnight on 4 November 1899. He caught the 7 a.m. train to Pietermaritzburg. In those few hours, he had visited the hospital ship *Sumatra*, where he found several friends. One who had been badly wounded at Elandslaagte told the budding member of parliament, 'I never felt safe with those politicians.'[4]

Churchill found Pietermaritzburg to be a 'sleepy, dead-alive place', which might account for the nickname 'Sleepy Hollow' so often applied to this town. In spite of their rather laid-back approach to life, Churchill could not be effusive enough in his praise of its inhabitants and wrote, 'I wish it were within the power of my poor pen to bring home to the people of England how excellently the colonists of Natal have deserved of the State.'[5]

They knew that if war should come, on them would fall the first fury of the storm. Nevertheless, they courageously supported and acclaimed the action of the Ministry. Now at last there is war. It means a good deal to all of us, but more than to any it comes home to the Natalian. He is invaded; his cattle have been seized by the Boer; his towns are shelled or captured; the most powerful force on which he relies for protection is isolated in Ladysmith; his capital is being loopholed and entrenched; Newcastle has been abandoned, Colenso has fallen, Estcourt is threatened; the possibility that the whole province will be overrun stares him in the face. From the beginning he asked for protection. From the beginning he was promised complete protection, but scarcely a word of complaint is heard. The townsfolk are calm and orderly, the press dignified and sober. The men capable of bearing arms have responded nobly. Boys of sixteen march with men of fifty to war – to no easy light war. All the Volunteers are in the field bearing their full share of the fighting like men.[6]

And with an eye to history:

Viewed in quieter days, the patient, trustful attitude of this colony of Natal will impress the historian. The devotion of its people to their Sovereign and to their motherland should endear them to all good Englishmen, and win them sympathy and respect.[7]

Although he spent only one day in Pietermaritzburg, Winston set about acquiring as much local knowledge as possible, and even found time to visit the wounded in hospital and to speak to some of the men. 'I talked with a wounded Gordon Highlander – one of those who had dashed across the famous causeway of Dargai and breasted the still more glorious slope of Elandslaagte. "We had the Imperial Horse with us," he said, "They're the best I've ever seen."'

The unsolicited praise heaped on the ILH by those of all ranks and classes on first meeting them, is interesting. No doubt they were, in every way, a fine body of men, but the reaction hints strongly that there had existed in the minds of many people in Britain negative preconceptions about the character of the Johannesburg Uitlanders. Churchill refers to one such misconception when, speaking of the part played by the ILH at Elandslaagte; he states, 'After this who will call the Outlanders cowards?'[8]

Soon after his arrival in Estcourt, Churchill let it be known that he would pay £200 to anyone who would guide him into Ladysmith. A nineteen-year-old trooper in the Carbineers, Park Gray, heard of the offer, which seemed to him to promise almost unbelievable riches. His family farmed in the foothills of the Drakensberg and being thoroughly conversant with the locality, he was confident that he could guide this generous benefactor through Boer lines and into Ladysmith. So he went to see Churchill in his quarters near the station. He was surprised at how young, pink and white Churchill looked; however, he also noticed how carefully Churchill was weighing him up. Park Gray thought it would take three days to complete the mission and after some discussion he went to see Major McKenzie to ask for three days leave. At the time the mounted men in Estcourt were very busy and Park Gray was recognised as the best shot in the Regiment. So when McKenzie heard that he required the leave to escort a war correspondent, the request was indignantly refused, McKenzie stating that he was not prepared to lose one of his best men for some 'bloody war correspondent'.[9]

Unfortunately when Park Gray told Churchill that leave had been refused, he quoted McKenzie a little too fully. Churchill never forgave this lack of deference to the grandson of a Duke.

With his plans for the visit to Ladysmith frustrated, Churchill accepted an offer of a ride to Colenso on the armoured train. At Colenso they found the village looted and deserted, the bridge intact, a section of the railway line ripped up and telegraph wires cut. The inspection complete, the train steamed back to Estcourt without incident. On the return journey Churchill fell into conversation with a trooper from Durban who was a builder by trade and was serving with the Durban Light Infantry. Before the war he had employed nine men, whom he had had to discharge when called up. Although he did not know how he would be able to re-establish his business after the war, he bore no resentment for being required to defend his country, believing it was no more than his duty.

On 9 November most of the troops in Estcourt made a reconnaissance towards Colenso, without the train. Churchill, as expected, was not going to be left out.

Galloping over the beautiful grassy hills to the north of the town, I soon reached a spot whence the column could be seen. First of all came a cyclist – a Natal Volunteer pedalling leisurely along with his rifle slung across his back – then two more, then about twenty. Next after an interval of a quarter of a mile, rode the cavalry – the squadron of the Imperial Light Horse, sixty Natal Carbineers, a company of Mounted Infantry, and about forty of the Natal Mounted Police. This is the total cavalry force in Natal, all the rest is bottled up in Ladysmith, and scarcely three hundred horsemen are available for the defence of the colony against a hostile army entirely composed of mounted men. Small were their numbers, but the quality was good. The Imperial Light Horse have shown their courage, and have only to display their discipline to equal advantage, to be considered first class soldiers. The Natal Carbineers are excellent volunteer cavalry: the police an alert and reliable troop.[10]

After the mounted men came the infantry – on this occasion, the Dublin Fusiliers and the newly arrived Border Regiment.

When the force had 'passed in review' Churchill with two companions set off for a high, flat-topped hill to the north west, which promised a view of the country towards Ladysmith. It took them an hour to climb and from the top they could see the roofs of the houses of Colenso set out in neat squares and oblongs. Beyond the village, hills obscured Ladysmith, but the long black outline of Bulwana Hill was visible. From time to time, a white flash could be seen on that hill. Long Tom was at work. The owner of the farm, a tall red-bearded man, joined them. Absorbed by the distant drama, their conversation was suddenly interrupted.

Over the crest of the hill to the rear, two horsemen trotted swiftly into view. A hundred yards to the left, three or four more were dismounting among the rocks. Three other figures appeared on the other side. We were surrounded – but by the Natal Carbineers. 'Got you, I think,' said the sergeant, who now arrived, 'Will you kindly tell us about who you are?' We introduced ourselves as President Kruger and General Joubert, and presented the farmer as Mr Schreiner, who had come to a secret conference, and having produced our passes, satisfied the patrol that we were not eligible for capture. The sergeant looked disappointed. 'It took us half an hour to stalk you, but if you had only been Dutchmen we'd have fixed you up properly.' Indeed the whole manoeuvre had been neatly and cleverly executed, and showed the smartness and efficiency of these irregular forces in all matters of scouting and reconnaissance. The patrol was then appeased by being photographed 'for the London papers', and we hastened to accept the farmer's invitation to lunch. 'Only plain fare,' said he, 'but perhaps you are used to roughing it.'

The farm stood in a sheltered angle of the hill at no great distance from its summit ... 'We have always known,' said the farmer, 'that it must end in war, and I cannot say I am sorry it has come at last. But it falls heavily on us. I am the only man for twenty miles who has not left his farm. Of course we are defenceless here. Any day the

Dutchmen may come. They wouldn't kill us, but they would burn or plunder everything, and it's all I've got in the world. Fifteen years have I worked at this place, and I said to myself we may as well stay and face it out, whatever happens.' Indeed it was an anxious time for such a man.[11]

Over the years General Joubert has been much criticised for failing to press on into southern Natal immediately after Ladysmith had been invested. Ten days were to pass before the Boers crossed the Tugela and began their drive south, by which time reinforcements had arrived to strengthen the British force. Whether an earlier start would have enabled the Boers to advance further into Natal is by no means certain.

Joubert, as we know, was opposed to the war with Britain. In an article written by him published in German journals before the declaration of war, he expressed the opinion that the Boers' foreign friends would not intervene, and that the Boers would not succeed in driving the British into the sea. He conceded that

…in Natal and the south we have to deal with unfamiliar conditions. In contrast, on the high plains of the Transvaal and the Orange Free State we shall be at home, and the British will meet opposition from us and from Nature every step of the way, and at all times be prepared for action on two or three fronts. In this way will be developed a guerrilla warfare of a most inconceivably bloody character, such as the British will be unable to endure for more than a few months.[12]

In anticipation of this guerrilla war, lines of depots had been constructed and communications systems set up between them. It seems Joubert's heart was not in the Natal Campaign and besides, he had other difficulties.

As the Boers on kommando would come and go as they pleased, no one knew how many men would be available for any particular operation. The Free State had annexed Northern Natal and with Boers pegging out farms for themselves, an administration had to be set up. His generals had let him down badly by failing to obey their instructions. In Dundee, Generals Meyer and Erasmus had failed to co-ordinate their actions, with the result that the British column at Dundee had been able to escape. At Elandslaagte, General Kock had failed to wait for the main Boer force to arrive before provoking a battle, with the result that the kommandos had been badly mauled. Joubert was infuriated by reports that blacks had been ill-treated by his kommandos, something he believed threatened the very existence of the Boer people and thought such conduct deserved the death penalty. His edict against looting and the harassment of civilians was almost everywhere ignored.

His dislike of the foreign contingents fighting on behalf of the Boers had intensified. Commandant Ben Viljoen, whom it will be remembered was in command during the retreat from Elandslaagte, felt the full force of a tongue lashing from Joubert. 'As for those Germans and Hollanders with you,' he told him, 'they may go back to Johannesburg. I won't have them here anymore.'[13] Although this outburst was perhaps unfair on the Germans, who had fought bravely at Elandslaagte, Joubert had clearly lost patience with the various Boer Uitlander Korps, who had shown more interest in looting than fighting.

A man known only as Jim, son of Antoni, who lived near Port Elizabeth, made a statement to the Natal Police at the end of November, 1899. He describes an incident that provides an interesting insight into some of the problems the Boers faced and how they dealt with them. Jim was probably a Fingo, people who had been granted land near Port Elizabeth after one of the wars with the Xhosa. The statement appears to be genuine as many of the facts stated were subsequently found to be correct and would not have been known in Natal at the time.

1. About eight months ago I left home and went to Port Elizabeth from where I left, accompanying a labour Agent, to Johannesburg.
2. I was employed at Rooipoort Mines until about three months ago when we were informed by the Manager that war had broken out and that we had better go home.
3. I left Rooipoort Station by rail and on arriving at Elandsfontein [not to be confused with Elandslaagte in Natal] station with twenty-one others also from Port Elizabeth, we were arrested and taken to Pretoria Gaol. After being in gaol for three days we were taken out and divided amongst the Boers as servants, and I so happened to be made General Joubert's servant.
4. We left Pretoria by rail as far as Volksrust when we left the train and proceeded by ox wagon to Newcastle. The kommando remained there a few days, during which time they burnt a few of the big stores down, as they said they were going to destroy all Englishmen's property and drive them into the sea.
5. After leaving Newcastle we went to Dundee, and just before reaching it we captured, I think, about 174 English soldiers, who were at the time going towards the Buffalo River, they were surrounded and captured by the Boers.
6. We then moved towards Dundee and about two or three days after they had captured the 174 soldiers, they caught four more, dressed in khaki, one of whom was tied to a tree by a lot of the Burghers, among whom I knew four, as follows:- Joseph Foree of Pretoria, De Lang, son-in-law to General Joubert, John Joubert, and Joseph Joubert.
7. After tying this man to the tree, they went about 100 yards away and shot him, this was done by Joseph Foree who was to fire first.
8. The man who was shot like this, was not dressed like the others. He had brown leggings with straps round them; he was about five feet

in height; middle aged; moustache, but no beard. He had two small yellow things on his shoulders; on his hat, which is like the hats the soldiers wear, was a puggaree on which was a little piece of red.

9. The Boers say they shot him because he was the oldest of the four and an old scoundrel. The other three were dressed in putties and black boots and had long knives.

10. We then left for Ladysmith and on our way we met some men that took part in the Elandslaagte fight who were running away at the time and the General made them go back again.

11. After we reached Ladysmith a few days the English blew off the mouth of the big gun that was placed on the big hill by Ladysmith and a few days afterwards blew it all to pieces; then Joubert said it is no use staying there we will move on to Estcourt, which we did and we crossed the Tugela, and there they had a fight with a train and took a lot of English prisoners, I saw three English killed and three Dutch and a lot of English were killed falling under the trucks. The Boers then moved to Ulundi, and then to Mooi River, from where I ran away.

(Sd.) Jim

Witness to Interpretation (Sd) A.R. Brandon, Tr. NP.[14]

Three of the prisoners appear to have been captured with Col Moller near Dundee, in which case they would have been sent to a PoW camp. The identity of the man executed is not known. His description does not fit that of a member of the British forces, or the Volunteers. The Irish Brigade fighting with the Boers had adopted a red flag as their banner, which raises the possibility that he belonged to that unit. Members of the Irish Brigade had attempted to persuade Dublin Fusiliers captured with Moller to join the Boers, an act which would have resulted in those Fusiliers being executed as traitors had they subsequently fallen into British hands.

By 14 November General Joubert was finally ready to begin his incursion into Southern Natal. With Louis Botha and his kommando leading, Joubert and his army of three to six thousand Boers crossed the Tugela. It had been decided the main force should by-pass Chieveley, Frere and Escourt on the west, while a smaller force of six hundred men under David Joubert, nephew of the Kommandant-General, was to advance via Weenen in the east. The two columns would then meet in a pincer movement near Mooi River, and thereby cut Estcourt off from the south.

Scouts from the Volunteers quickly picked up the movements of the enemy, and the news was conveyed to Col Long, who, unimpressed, decided that on the following day, 15 November, the armoured train, under the command of a Captain Haldane, should, as usual, carry out its reconnaissance to Colenso.[15]

Haldane was far from delighted by the prospect of a ride in the armoured train that almost everyone, with the notable exception of Col Long, regarded as a dangerous and useless contraption, which could not do the job half as well as a single mounted scout. Haldane was to be accompanied by a company of ninety Dublin Fusiliers, eighty men from the Durban Light Infantry and an obsolete 7-pounder gun with ten Naval gunners.[16] Haldane invited three newspaper correspondents, Winston Churchill, Leo Amery and John Atkins, to join the venture. Churchill, despite having reservations, accepted the invitation. Atkins declined, stating he was being paid to cover the war, not to become a prisoner of war, while Leo Amery gave as his excuse for not going, the possibility of rain – a strange excuse for an Englishman.

At 5.30 a.m. the train steamed out of Estcourt bound for Colenso with 180 men and a number of civilians aboard. The foremost truck had the naval gun placed on it, next came an armoured truck filled with Fusiliers, then the locomotive, followed by two further trucks with the balance of the Fusiliers and the DLI, and finally a flatbed truck on which were a telegrapher with his equipment and a group of platelayers. In the still morning air, the sound of the train would have been heard many miles away. At Frere they met a small patrol of Natal Police who told them there were no Boers for the next mile or two.

Haldane, against his better judgment, but urged on by Churchill, decided to press on to Chieveley more than 10 miles away. On arriving at Chieveley, Boers were seen riding southwards. Haldane instructed the driver to return to Escourt at once. The order of the trucks on the train was, of course, now reversed. The platelayers and telegraphist were in front followed by trucks filled with infantry, the locomotive, more infantry, and at the rear the sailors, and the 7-pounder gun. It seemed the return journey might be uneventful until, about 2 miles from Frere, Boers could be seen on a hill 600 yards away. The infantry loaded their rifles and the gun was readied to fire. Suddenly on the crest ahead appeared two large field guns and a rapid-firing Maxim. The engine driver slammed on full speed and as the train gathered pace, it rounded a bend and crashed straight into a pile of rocks placed across the line.

The leading truck with its passengers was thrown high into the air and overturned against the embankment. The second truck containing the Durban Light Infantry ploughed on for about 20 yards before falling on its side and spilling out its passengers on the leeward side. The next truck was derailed and was leaning over precariously. Miraculously, the locomotive and the rest of the train remained on the rails. In Churchill's words, 'We were not left long in the comparative peace and safety of a railway accident.'[17] The Boers opened fire on the wrecked train, however, the infantry were not slow in responding and to some extent checked the enemy fire. Relying on the shelter of the train, Churchill jumped off the truck at the back and ran forward to see what had happened up front. The line was blocked by the derailed truck. To clear the line the Durban Light Infantry under Captain Wylie pushed and heaved at the obstructing truck while the engine, acting as a battering ram, made repeated attempts to knock it out of the way. It took more than an hour to clear the line during which time a shell smashed the coupling between the locomotive tender and the truck behind, thereby isolating the trucks at the rear. The wounded were placed on the locomotive which, with its wooden fitments ablaze and the platelayers clinging on where they could, steamed away towards Estcourt.[18]

Throughout the engagement the entire train had been subjected to heavy shell and rifle fire. Everyone behaved with great courage. Churchill was indefatigable in giving encouragement to those struggling to clear the line. The sailors were able to fire three shots at the Boers before a shell struck the old muzzle-loader and put it out of action. Those Dublin Fusiliers trapped in the armoured truck at the rear maintained an effective fire through the firing holes, thereby helping the DLI in their struggle to free the locomotive. When the locomotive steamed away, Churchill decided to lead the infantry to safety and set off to find them. He didn't find them. Instead the Boers found Churchill wandering about, alone on the veld, and took him prisoner. Over the years Churchill was to make a number of contradictory statements about his capture. Five days after becoming a Boer prisoner, he was able to send a dispatch to the *Morning Post,* which brought him fame and propelled him into Parliament.

The departure of the engine left those Fusiliers trapped in the rear trucks no choice but to surrender. Louis Botha, who had initiated the attack, was delighted and cabled Pretoria, 'Our guns were ready and quickly punctured the armoured trucks. The engine broke loose and returned badly damaged. Loss of the enemy 4 dead, 14 wounded and 58 taken prisoner, also a mountain gun ... Our loss 4 slightly wounded.'[19]

It is at this point that accounts of the armoured train incident end. However, it was not the end of the affair. Louis Botha stated the British losses to be seventy-six and we know 180 men plus some civilians went out on the train that morning. If one allows for ten wounded on the locomotive, at least ninety-four men appear to be missing from the final tally.

Captain Wylie, in command of the Durban Light Infantry, suffered multiple wounds and was one of those who escaped on the locomotive. After the locomotive had left, the infantry not trapped in the train broke up into small groups, and set off on foot for Estcourt. Not surprisingly, the Boers followed.

When the sound of gunfire was heard in Estcourt, Major Duncan McKenzie was ordered to go to the relief of the armoured train with his squadron of the Carbineers (forty-five men) and a squadron of the Imperial Light Horse (eighty men). Being a local regiment consisting primarily of farmers, the Carbineers knew the country well. They also knew that despite a failure by the Boers to expel the English settlers from Natal in 1842, the Boers still coveted Natal and had equipped their kommandos with the latest weaponry. Anxious lest the Boers make another attempt to drive them into the sea, the local Volunteers adapted their training and strategy to meet the danger posed by mounted men who were good marksmen, armed with modern, long-range rifles. Although an Imperial regiment paid by Britain, the ILH had been recruited in Pietermaritzburg, and were quick to learn the methods employed by the Natal Volunteers.

After riding a few miles the Volunteers met the engine with the wounded and McKenzie was told what had happened. It had begun to rain steadily, nevertheless the two squadrons as quickly as possible pressed forward along the line of the railway. Near the rail siding of Ennersdale, they passed a group of infantry trying to make their way back to Estcourt and further groups were passed as they hurried on. Finally they sighted the Boers pursuing the hindmost infantry. The Boers checked at the first indication of the presence of the Volunteers and retired in a north-easterly direction until stopped by a wire fence. While they were cutting the fence, the Carbineers opened fire from concealed positions at a distance of about 800 yards, killing several Boers who were later found dead on the field. (Remember Jim's affidavit, above.) Once through the fence, the Boers took up a position on a kopie. In an exchange of fire that followed, they appeared to suffer several casualties. Noting the fire against them was increasing, McKenzie ordered the Carbineers to retire while at the same time an orderly was sent to the ILH with instructions to follow suit. They retired along the railway line in extended order, with the Carbineers on the left, and the ILH on the right. Being locals and intimately knowing the lie of the land, they were able to conceal their movements from the enemy who, disconcerted by their inability to see their enemy or gauge their strength, gave up the chase after a few miles. Watching the Boers dismounted in the open, McKenzie estimated that they numbered three to five thousand.[20]

McKenzie's small force of just over one hundred men had held in check a Boer force of at least 3,000 men and, in doing so, had enabled half the men who had set out on the train that morning to get safely back to base. McKenzie had kept his men hidden from the Boers who never knew how many men opposed them or precisely where they were located. Because the Carbineers were good shots, they were able to wait and then strike hard as soon as the Boers were vulnerable, after which they would melt back into the veld. The Carbineers suffered no casualties and the only casualty of the ILH was one wounded man. Duncan McKenzie had given his first demonstration of how to defeat the invaders.

A new commander of the mounted troops had arrived in Estcourt, Lt Col C.G.Martyr. He was described by Lt Malcolm Riall of the West Yorks as a 'bloodthirsty soldier with two rows of medal ribbons'. Martyr had served in the Egyptian Expedition of 1882, the Sudan Expedition of 1884-5, Sudan 1888–91, the Expedition to Dongola of 1896, and Uganda in 1896[21] – experience unlikely to be of value in Natal.

Each morning McKenzie would send patrols out towards Beacon Hill in the west and towards Weenen in the east, with instructions to obtain information from the Zulus about the enemy's activities, while being careful not to show themselves. One morning Col Martyr arrived at the Carbineers' camp and asked McKenzie what dispositions had been made. McKenzie told him about the patrols, whereupon Martyr told him not to do this as they would probably be captured. McKenzie replied that it was better to have a patrol captured than to have the whole unit surrounded before the approach of the enemy was known. Unconvinced, Martyr ordered that the patrols cease. McKenzie did not quibble but surreptitiously sent out the same patrols.[22]

On 13 November the famous West Yorkshire Regiment, commanded by Col Walter Kitchener, had arrived in Estcourt. Walter Kitchener was six years younger than his celebrated brother Herbert, the future Field Marshal Lord Kitchener. The differences between the two brothers were almost as marked as those between Frank and Cecil Rhodes. Lord Kitchener was excessively reserved, even by Victorian standards, and was terrified of showing any emotion, preferring to be misunderstood rather than display his feelings. When doing good, he did so by stealth. Disappointed in love as a young man, he concentrated his energy on the promotion of his career in the army. His brother was far more approachable and was prepared to laugh, even when the joke was on him. Not long after Walter Kitchener arrived, McKenzie went to see him and found the Colonel looking very serious. The infantry had been firing at a farmer's goats. McKenzie said he hoped the troops had killed them all. Kitchener looked horrified and asked, 'Why?' 'Well Sir,' replied Duncan, 'If they cannot kill goats, they cannot kill Boers.' Walter laughed.[23]

On 17 November, David Joubert's kommando entered Weenen and set about destroying everything in the village. As was the case in Dundee, while the Boers were destroying the property of civilians, the British were given a few more days to organise themselves.

General Hildyard displaced Col Long as senior British officer in Estcourt on 16 November when he arrived with the 2nd Battalion Royal West Surrey Regiment and the 2nd Battalion East Surrey Rifles. They were followed the next day by Bethune's Mounted Infantry and the 7th Field Battery. The 2nd Royal Irish Fusiliers arrived in Mooi River, 20 miles south of Estcourt, on the 16 November, to be followed two days later by General Barton with the 1st Royal Welsh Fusiliers and Thornycroft's Mounted Infantry.

It will be recalled that during General White's brief stay in Pietermaritzburg in early October, Colonels Thornycroft and Bethune had been given permission to recruit men for their Volunteer regiments. Thorneycroft, who personally paid the establishment costs of his regiment, recruited in Pietermaritzburg, while Bethune recruited in Durban. Recruits had to be good horsemen and able to shoot straight. There was no time available to teach other elementary skills. It says much about the quality of the officers and men of these regiments that they were considered fit to be on active service so soon after they had been recruited. Being Volunteers, they were armed with rifles without magazines, and did not carry bayonets. They were not 'Uitlander' regiments but were all drawn from men in Natal at the time. Local rifle associations were a fertile source of good recruits, as were the Australians who came to Natal with the thousands of horses being imported into Durban by the British. Alfred Ernest Henry Carrick was typical of these recruits. As a young man, he served as a trooper in the Australian Light Horse in the Middle East in 1885. On his return to Australia he worked for his uncle, who owned Warwick Farm Race Course and stables, 'Hurstville', Sydney. In 1899 he arrived in Durban as one of forty horse handlers on a ship with 700 horses. With no wharves available, they had to swim the horses ashore. This task completed, Alf Carrick and his friends joined the Volunteer regiments.[24]

On Sunday 19 October McKenzie was told that Boers had been seen at Wallace's Farm, which lay to the east of Highlands rail siding between Estcourt and Mooi River. Taking about fifty Carbineers he found the Boers, part of David Joubert's kommando, encamped on the other side of a deep valley. A few desultory shots were exchanged between the two groups but being at very long range, no damage was done. At about 4 p.m. a troop of Thornycroft's Mounted Infantry under a subaltern arrived and took up a position next to the Carbineers. After a while the subaltern asked if they might charge across at the Boers. 'Certainly not,' replied McKenzie. Some others of Thorneycroft's regiment closed on the enemy and lost a few men. Later the subaltern asked McKenzie if he and his men might retire to the camp at Mooi River. Once again the Major refused, telling the young officer that they could not leave until the Carbineers left, which would be after dark, so as to leave the Boers uncertain as to whether or not the position was still occupied.[25]

On the way back to camp the Carbineers met Col Martyr who, with a Carbineer as a guide, had come out to meet them. Martyr told them they had to go back to the position they had occupied. McKenzie told him this was out of the question as his men had had no food all day, and Martyr then agreed to permit them to continue back to camp. At Mooi River the garrison was strengthened by the arrival on 19 November of the 14th Battery of the Royal Field Artillery and, on the following day, they were further reinforced by the arrival of the 2nd Devonshire Regiment.

Early on Monday 20 November, General Hildyard moved his infantry south to Willow Grange and then marched out along the road to Mooi River hoping to find the Boers. Having failed to find them by midday, the infantry marched back to Willow Grange. Col Martyr's mounted force, who had been waiting, with saddles on, since 3 a.m., now rode down the same road towards Mooi River. The Carbineers were scouting in front when they saw a small Boer patrol advancing from the east where the engagement had occurred on the previous day. As a nearby plantation offered an excellent opportunity to trap the patrol, the Carbineers took care to keep out of sight; but the rest of the force made no effort to conceal themselves and were seen by the Boers, who immediately cleared off. Near Highlands Station, McKenzie noticed mounted men lining the hills to the north of Mooi River and reported this to Col Martyr, who said they were trees. McKenzie disputed this and said he was quite sure they were Boers from Weenen attempting to join the main Boer column coming from Colenso via Ntabanhlope. However, Martyr insisted they were trees. When the mounted men arrived at Highlands Station, they found other British troops looking through field glasses at those same Boers –who were still clearly visible. The Carbineers stood about for some time, then received an order to unsaddle. They had no sooner done this, when they received an order to saddle up, and ride back to Willow Grange, where they were ordered to retire on Estcourt without delay. McKenzie immediately went to Col Kitchener, who was in overall command, and implored him not to move until after dark. After some persuasion, Kitchener agreed to this and arranged for the Carbineers to do outpost duty and form the rear guard during the retirement. The whole column arrived in Estcourt without the Boers having realised that they had left Willow Grange. That day the two Boer columns converged. The pincers had closed and Estcourt was now cut off from Mooi River.

The next day Duncan McKenzie received a message that General Hildyard wished to see him. He hurried up to the general's headquarters at the Old Fort in Estcourt. Hildyard welcomed Duncan and said, 'I understand you know a good deal about the country and the Boers.' He got out his maps. After some discussion Duncan asked if the general wished to re-open rail contact with Mooi River. The general replied in the affirmative and asked Duncan how it could be done. McKenzie thought it could be done by a night attack. He told the general that there was a stone wall several miles long that ran right up to the top of a hill, Brynbella, where the Boers had placed guns, which dominated the surrounding countryside. If the infantry followed this wall it would guide them right onto Brynbella and the Boer guns, which could be captured or destroyed. McKenzie emphasised the importance of silence and, in particular, that there should be no shooting, as it would give the whole show away. McKenzie, General Hildyard, Col Kitchener and other officers who might take part then rode to the hill above Estcourt where McKenzie pointed out the stone wall and all other features that might be important; he also gave as his opinion that the guns could be taken without any casualties being sustained, however, the infantry would be in real danger if caught retreating from Brynbella the next morning. Artillery cover would then be essential. General Hildyard decided to launch the attack that night and requested that the Carbineers do the scouting. McKenzie arranged that an old friend, Frick Chapman, should act as guide for the infantry.

The troops marched out from Estcourt to Willow Grange, with McKenzie and the Carbineers scouting ahead, and taking care to keep under cover of the hills. The East Surreys and the West Yorks were to carry out the night attack with a regiment on either side of the wall. The rest of Hildyard's force, the West Surreys, the Durban Light Infantry and the Border Regiment, were to keep under the cover of Beacon Hill, from the top of which a Naval 12-pounder and the 7th Battery were to cover any retreat in the morning.

Heavy rain and hail during the afternoon, followed by dense mist, created miserable conditions for the infantry. Col Kitchener was nervous about the coming engagement and was particularly concerned about the slouch hats worn by the colonials, which he thought might cause confusion as they looked similar to Boer headgear.

Before even reaching the wall along which they were to approach the enemy, the East Surreys and West Yorks mistook each other for the enemy, and in the resulting shooting match and bayonet charge they suffered several casualties. These casualties would have been much higher, but for the prompt intervention of Captain Mackay of the Carbineers. McKenzie could not resist pointing out to Kitchener that no one in this fracas wore a slouch hat, and that the goats had been shot despite being hatless.

It had been decided that the Carbineers would not take part in the coming engagement but instead should return to Estcourt. Before he left, McKenzie reminded Kitchener of the necessity of having artillery to cover any possible retreat off Brynbella. Kitchener wrote out an order for the 7th Battery, which he asked McKenzie to deliver. McKenzie found the battery and explained to the officer in charge precisely where Kitchener wanted them positioned early the next morning. The officer replied that he was 'damned if he would take his guns up there'.

A little further on, the Navy were struggling in the wet and cold to get their gun onto Beacon Hill. Their two teams of oxen were in a hopeless muddle and it seemed unlikely that the sailors would succeed in getting it into position before dawn. McKenzie and the Carbineers dismounted, took off their jackets and strode over to the beasts, which were quickly formed up in their correct positions and, on command, began the ascent of the hill. With McKenzie in charge, some Carbineers drove the oxen while others pushed the gun. The old transport riding skills were still there, and the big naval gun was soon in position on top of the hill. A heavy mist had concealed these movements from the Boers, but suddenly the mist lifted and exposed some infantry on the side of Beacon Hill. Though it was getting dark the Boers sent some harmless long-range rifle fire in their direction. An appalling blunder was now made.

The naval gun fired several shots at the Boers on Brynbella to which the Boer guns replied. The Boers now knew where the British were and where their naval gun was positioned and the approximate range. But worst of all, they knew the British knew where their guns were sited. As Duncan McKenzie and the Carbineers rode back in the dark to Estcourt, Duncan had some doubts as to the prospect of success on the following day.[26]

Early the next morning the camp in Estcourt heard that everything had gone off successfully although only two or three prisoners had been taken.

The Boers had apparently retreated along the high ground, which lay to their rear. Later heavy firing was heard, and ambulances began to stream into Escourt with dead and wounded.

Col Kitchener had assembled his men with bayonets fixed and sent them up Brynbella on both sides of the stone wall as planned. They reached the top unperceived and as they topped the crest the Boer sentry challenged them. The reply was a volley of rifle fire, strictly against orders, and a ringing cheer from the West Yorks, also against orders. The infantrymen rushed on over the dead sentry to the Boer lager. There they found some blankets, saddlery and thirty or forty ponies. No Boers and no guns. The Boers had fallen back about 1,500 yards during the night, taking their artillery with them. A small contingent had been left on the eastern end of the hill, however as soon as the British appeared they fled back to their main force.

It was now about 3.30 a.m. and as soon as it became lighter Kitchener placed his firing line of the West Yorks among the boulders along the highest part of the crest. The rest he withdrew behind the wall. For a couple of hours harmless fire was exchanged between the two sides while the Boers concentrated on creeping up on both sides of the hill. The Boer attack on the British troops clinging to the end of Brynbella now intensified. Two field guns and a pom-pom were moved so as to bring converging fire on the narrow position occupied by the West Yorks. The artillery support that Kitchener expected did not materialise because the Boer guns were beyond the range of the naval gun, which could only search the northern slopes of Brynbella, and the 7th Battery was lying idle at the foot of Beacon Hill, its commanding officer claiming he had no orders. Presumably orders carried to him by a colonial officer did not count.

Kitchener now decided to retreat off Brynbella. Half his men were to go north towards Beacon Hill, and there join the rest of the infantry, while the others were to retreat north east towards a small plantation in the Willow Grange Valley. General Hildyard arrived on the scene, and supporting the decision that the British should withdraw, ordered the West Surreys and the Border Regiment to advance across the valley until their left converged with Kitchener's men. With some protection from the rocky terrain, and the wall which had been followed the previous night, they were able to assist the withdrawal of those retiring on Beacon Hill.

On the left flank mounted units, commanded by Col Martyr, were ordered to assist the infantry retiring on Willow Grange. They dismounted, and with the Imperial Light Horse leading, climbed to the crest of Brynbella where they found only one company of the West Yorks still on the crest. Holding the line under heavy fire, the ILH waited until the West Yorks had completed their retirement and taken the wounded to safety, before they began their move down the hill. The artillery should have covered their retreat, but again they were not there. The result was that the ILH had no option but to run down the hill as fast as they could, while the Boers on the summit directed heavy fire at them. Perhaps because they were excited, the Boer fire was wild and only one Light Horsemen was killed and two wounded before safety was reached.[27] To add insult to injury, the Boers brought back into action on the eastern edge of Brynbella those very guns, the capture of which was the raison d'être of the whole sortie.

At the end of a frustrating day, the British retired to Estcourt. They had suffered sixteen killed, over sixty wounded and eight were taken prisoner. Among those killed was the civilian guide, Frick Chapman, who had successfully guided the West Yorks to the top of Brynbella.

Next day, Friday 24 November, Duncan McKenzie and some Carbineers rode out to Willow Grange to keep an eye on enemy movements and to recover the body of Duncan's old friend, Chapman. Col Kitchener asked Duncan if he would also try to recover his Regiment's mess tins, which had been left behind. They recovered Chapman's body and the mess tins. The Carbineers were also able to observe and report on the movements of the Boers. In the east, a large group of Boers was retiring towards Weenen. In the west, a smaller group rode towards Ntabanhlope and Colenso. The Boer advance into southern Natal had petered out.

In the campaign the Boers had lobbed a number of shells into Mooi River, thereby inflicting a severe attack of inertia on General Barton. This enabled small groups of Boers to penetrate as far as Nottingham Road. Everywhere the looting and destruction continued but things were becoming a little more difficult. Murray's Horse, with informal groups of farmers who had banded together to protect their farms, were causing problems for the Boers who did not know where this enemy was, the numbers involved, or when and where they might strike. Also the Tugela River might be rising, which could result in them being cut off in this hostile country – and all the while their scouts told them that more and more British troops and guns were continuing to arrive.

After the engagement at Willow Grange, the Boers held a meeting to decide on their future strategy. Louis Botha was all for pressing on to Pietermaritzburg and the sea. The majority, which included Kommandant General Joubert, thought it would be wiser to retreat back across the Tugela, where they would find it easier to defend the territory they had conquered. The day before this meeting, Joubert had been injured in a fall from his horse and received internal injuries that were to result in his death. However, his decision to retreat across the Tugela was sound and his injury does not appear to have influenced his judgment. In pain, Joubert had to return to the Transvaal and Louis Botha became the Boer commander in Natal.

At 5 a.m. on the morning of 25 November, all the mounted troops in Estcourt, with the exception of the Carbineers, were ordered to move out in the direction of the Ntabanhlope Road. Four hours later, the Carbineers received an order to join the rest of the mounted column. They responded promptly and had gone but a little way before they came across them. McKenzie reported to Col Martyr, who ordered the Carbineers to scout the high hills in front of them, where it was thought the enemy might be found. McKenzie asked for artillery support, which Martyr refused. Surprised and disappointed by the refusal, McKenzie was nonetheless flattered by the thought that this brigade of mounted troops should be waiting on him and his forty Carbineers, unable to move on until they had done the scouting.

Deprived of artillery cover, McKenzie ordered six Carbineers to gallop forward and climb the first hill, while he with his men dismounted and covered the advance with their rifles. When the scouts reached the top of the hill and waved everything clear, another troop would gallop up the hill in support and once they were in position, McKenzie followed with the remainder. Once at the top, McKenzie would scout around, and if everything was clear, he would report to base, before repeating the procedure on the next hill. Following this procedure and always being careful not to show themselves, the Carbineers located the Boers who were retiring towards Colenso on the Ntabanhlope road. A galloper was sent back to Martyr advising him that the Boers, unaware of the presence of the Carbineers, were riding into a position where they could easily be trapped. The galloper returned with an order that the Cabineers were to return to the main column at once as the Boer column was too strong. McKenzie had no choice but to obey. En route he was disappointed to see many of Martyr's men on the skyline where they would have been visible to the Boers. On joining the column he reported to Col Martyr, suggesting that they should take up a position on a certain hill that had to be passed by the Boers and where they could be easily ambushed. This group was about 500-strong and though they had come into Natal lightly equipped, they were now burdened with a long train of looted livestock and wagons filled with looted goods. The livestock contained substantial numbers of valuable pedigree breeding stock acquired by the farmers over many years. Martyr refused to consider the proposal, stating the orders were to retire to Estcourt while shepherding the Boers back to Colenso. This refusal even to consider an operation that would not only have inflicted serious losses on the Boers but would also have compelled them to abandon vast quantities of loot, infuriated McKenzie, who blurted out, 'I feel ashamed to disgrace the uniform I wear.' He then turned away and Col Martyr rode on to join the other troops retiring to Estcourt. Not long afterwards McKenzie received a dispatch from Col Martyr ordering him to accompany him on a visit to General Hildyard that evening. This probably meant trouble.

When they arrived in camp McKenzie found the order had been countermanded, and McKenzie was instead requested to write a report stating what he had seen that day.[28] When McKenzie attended Brigade Headquarters next morning there was no sign of Col Martyr, who was never again seen by the Natal Volunteers. The Carbineers were ordered to scout the land to the east in the direction of Weenen. McKenzie took his regiment to the highest ridge of a line of hills between the Estcourt/Weenen and the Weenen/Colenso roads. From this high ground he had a wide view of the country and could see young Joubert's camp next to the Weenen road, not more than a mile from him. The road that Joubert had to travel to reach Colenso had to pass through a narrow defile near the Blaaukrantz River, an ideal place for an ambush. McKenzie at once reported what he had seen but there was no response. That night, both Boer columns with all their looted wagons, goods, and cattle reached Colenso unmolested. This wagon train of stolen goods stretched from Mooi River all the way to Weenen, a distance of more than 30 miles.

Not only did the Boers plunder everything that could be taken away, they also destroyed possessions they could not move or did not want. Safes were blown open with dynamite, lamps and furniture were destroyed, doors and windows smashed with crow bars, papers, photographs and other documents were torn into pieces, orchards chopped down and vital rainwater tanks punctured. Livestock that could not be driven away was slaughtered. Fifty young turkeys were among the dead poultry found rotting on one farm. On another, 300 head of cattle and sheep were poisoned with arsenic. Businesses, farms and homes all suffered in this orgy of destruction. A German who was riding with Botha's invasion force described the raid as a *Lumpen Kreuzug* (Tramps Crusade). It wasn't Britain, or Milner, or Rhodes, or Chamberlain they punished, but civilians who had never done any harm to them, or posed any threat to their republics.

After Colonel Martyr left, Duncan McKenzie was told that a Lord Dundonald was the new commander of the Cavalry Brigade. Duncan had never heard of him. Colonel Douglas Mackinnon Bailie Hamilton Cochrane, the twelfth Earl of Dundonald, had inherited a title but not much money. His forbears had won fame and fortune at sea during the wars of the eighteenth century, a fortune that had been much reduced during the industrial revolution. His grandfather developed many improvements to the machines being used by the new industries, but refused to patent any of his inventions – believing a man's knowledge should be shared free of charge with all mankind. The result was that others profited from his work and when the future twelfth Earl joined the Life Guards, he had difficulty maintaining the lifestyle expected of an officer in that elite regiment. He had had the misfortune to contract malaria while campaigning in the Sudan; that debilitating disease seriously affected his health and caused him to suffer bouts of fever for the rest of his life.

Possibly because of his health, he was not among those originally selected to go to South Africa. However, as a soldier he believed that he should, in time of war, serve his country, so he paid his fare to Cape Town, where he went to see the newly appointed Commander-in-Chief in South Africa, General Sir Redvers Buller. General Buller knew Dundonald and asked him to take on the command of the Mounted Brigade in Natal. Lord Dundonald would have under his command:

The Royal Dragoons
The 13th Hussars

Thorneycroft's Mounted Infantry
Bethune's Mounted Infantry
A squadron of the Natal Carbineers (which included some men from
the BMR and NMR)
A squadron of the Imperial Light Horse
A Naval Brigade with two 4.7inch guns and fourteen 12 cwt guns.

In all, this amounted to about 1,800men. It was an unexpected but wise
choice for the vital post. Dundonald realised how vulnerable the British
Army had become and, in particular, that the standard of shooting was
very poor. On taking command of the 2nd Life Guards in 1895, he set
about improving matters. At that time, if a regiment wished to use in target
practice more than the allotted number of rounds per annum, the officers of
the regiment had to pay – out of their own pockets – for extra ammunition,
the hire of the range and the men's rail fares. Dundonald could not afford
this, so he organised a shooting club and wrote to all old officers of the
regiment, asking them to subscribe to the fund. This helped but only to a
limited extent and, of course, it was only his regiment that benefited. Later
he was to write, 'During the South African War, I used to talk with first-
class rifle shots such as men in the Border Mounted Rifles, who when they
fired, killed, and the consensus was that to keep up first-class marksmanship
a man required much practice and would have to expend 400 to 500
cartridges a year.'[29]

Marksmanship was not his only concern. He believed the non-commissioned
ranks should receive more information as to what was required of them. To
this end, he drafted and had printed a map to be distributed to all ranks,
entitled *To Find the Way*. This map gave instructions how to move over
a trackless country by day by compass or at night by by the stars. He also
had prepared, printed and posted in every barrackroom large placards
giving information on such subjects as Field Engineering, Reconnaissance,
Map-reading, Outpost Duty, etc., which he believed every cavalry soldier
should know.

He was concerned about the divide that existed between Regular units
and Volunteer regiments. When the colonel of a Volunteer regiment
wrote to Dundonald asking if he would 'allow the officers the use of the
Officers' Mess of the 2nd Life Guards; to mix with your officers on terms
of equality would be something they would never forget', Dundonald
had no hesitation in issuing an invitation to them. The Volunteers came
and everyone liked them. It was the first time Volunteer officers were
made honorary members of an Officers' Mess of a Household Cavalry
Regiment.[30] Not only was he willing to dine with Volunteers, he was
willing to listen to them and to have regard for their opinions. These
concepts were revolutionary ideas in the British Army of that time. To
these attributes, he added loyalty both to those in authority over him and
those under his command.

On arrival in Natal, he went to Mooi River and from there he was ordered to take those of his command at Mooi River to join General Hildyard at Estcourt. He arrived at Estcourt just as Hildyard and his column were about to set off for Frere in pursuit of the retreating Boers. Dundonald has left a description of what they found on arrival:

The Boers had destroyed the iron railway bridge at Frere and a very complete destructive effort they had made; the Natal railwaymen with us said that they would soon erect a temporary bridge of wood, which they did in a very short time. Frere had been occupied by the Boers in their advance in Natal. Every man one met, including even the Kaffirs, said that the Boers had loudly expressed their intention to drive the British into the sea. We were all of us furious to see the cruel havoc they had made in the houses of this small town; it looked as if it had been devastated by savages. The first house we entered was Bartle Cottage; it belonged to two maiden ladies, The whole place was a wreck, little mementoes of home scattered on the ground, photographs torn up; the beds were ripped up, and one walked knee-deep in the fluff from them. All the other houses were treated in the same way but none were destroyed by fire, showing that the Boers had set a limit to their work of destruction. I heard that the better class of Boer did not approve of this work.[31]

On his sea voyage to South Africa on board the *Carisbrooke Castle*, Dundonald had met an ambitious young officer of the 16th Lancers, Captain Hubert Gough. Gough wrote to Dundonald telling him that he was with a squadron guarding a railway, work he did not like. Dundonald invited him to Frere and appointed him to his staff as Intelligence Officer.

On arrival in Natal, Gough joined the Mounted Brigade and this is how he described his first reconnaissance with a Natal Volunteer unit.

I found them a friendly, practical body, prepared to fight when required, but not at all inclined to gallop thoughtlessly into danger. My military experience of this war began at once. At dawn the next morning we set forth on a reconnaissance to the east of the railway. Riding with these Natal farmers we covered about thirty miles out and back in a day, and returned to Nottingham Road that same evening. We did not encounter any Boers, but in that long ride they taught me more about conducting a reconnaissance than I had learnt in over ten years service in the Cavalry! They moved by bounds – like a wild animal carefully approaching his prey, which has now become the classic method of advance for scouts.[32]

While the main Boer invasion south from the Tugela had followed the main road and rail route from Ladysmith to Pietermaritzburg, a smaller force of three hundred to four hundred Boers was making its way south on a more easterly route closer to the Zululand border via Helpmekaar, Pomeroy, and

Tugela Ferry. From there they were to press on to Greytown, Pietermaritzburg and the coast. To bar their drive south were about seventy men of the Umvoti Mounted Rifles, who had dug themselves in along the southern bank of the Tugela River.

On 18 November, General Sir Francis Clery, temporarily in overall command in Natal, instructed Major Leuchars of the Umvoti Mounted Rifles to destroy the punts at Tugela Ferry and Keat's Drift and thereafter withdraw to Greytown. Leuchars started his withdrawal, leaving a detachment at the river crossing to destroy the punt and the road on receipt of instructions. The following day, General Clery amended his orders to Leuchars stating he should watch the road between Tugela Ferry and Mooi River, while at the same time he was to use his discretion as to the destruction of the punts and further retirement. Leuchars wired back to say he would delay the destruction until the last moment. On 23 November, the Boers attacked the detachment Leuchars had left at Tugela Ferry. Assisted by a full river, they were able to hold their own until Major Leuchars arrived with the rest of his small force. After an exchange of fire lasting several hours, the Boers withdrew and made no further attempt to pursue their invasion of Natal along this route.[33] As the Boer threat to Southern Natal had been contained, Murray's Horse was disbanded.

15

'What are we fighting for?' –
Inside Ladysmith

After his capture, Churchill and his fellow prisoners were marched to the railhead near Elandslaagte. As they neared Ladysmith they could see the smoke of Boer artillery fire from Bulwana. The Boers were happy to converse with their prisoners. Churchill recounted their conversation.

'That goes on always,' said a Boer. 'Can any soldiers bear that long? Oh, you will find all the English army at Pretoria. Indeed, if it were not for sea-sickness we would take England. Besides, do you think the European Powers will allow you to bully us?'
I said, 'Why bully if you are so strong?'
'Well, why should you come and invade our country?'
'Your country? I thought this was Natal.'
'So it is but Natal is ours. You stole it from us. Now we take it back again. That's all.'
A hum of approval ran round the grinning circle. An old Boer came up. He did not understand what induced the soldiers to go in an armoured train. Frankland (an English prisoner) replied, 'Ordered to. Don't you have to obey your orders?'
The old man shook his head in bewilderment, then he observed, 'I fight to kill: I do not fight to be killed. If the Field Cornet was to order me to go in an armoured train, I would say to him Field Cornet, go to hell.'
'Ah, you are not soldiers.'
'But we catch soldiers and kill soldiers and make soldiers run away.'
There was a general chorus of 'Yaw, yaw, yaw', and grunts of amusement.
'You English,' said a well-dressed man, 'die for your country: We Afrikanders live for ours.'
I said, 'Surely you don't think you will win this war?'
'Oh yes; we will win all right this time, just the same as before.'

'But it is not the same as before. Gladstone is dead, they are determined at home. If necessary they will send three hundred thousand men and spend a hundred millions.'

'We are not afraid; no matter how many penny soldiers you send,' an English Boer added, 'Let them all come.'

After about ten hours marching, the prisoners reached the camp site where they were to spend the night. An exhausted Churchill complained that during the march the prisoners had received 'no food except for toasted ox, a disgusting form of nourishment' – barbeques had yet to become fashionable among the British aristocracy. The Field Cornet gave them some tea and bully beef and invited the British officers and Churchill to share his tent. Refreshed by food far more to his liking, Churchill was ready for further argument. The Boers crowded into the small tent.

'Will you tell us why there is this war?

I said that it was because they wanted to beat us out of South Africa and we did not like the idea.

Oh no, that is not the reason. Now that the war had begun they would drive the British into the sea; but if we had been content with what we had they would not have interfered with us – except to get a port and have their full independence recognised.'

'I will tell you what is the real cause of this war. It's all those damned capitalists. They want to steal our country, and they have bought Chamberlain, and now these three, Rhodes, Beit, and Chamberlain, think they will have the Rand to divide between them afterwards.'

'Don't you know that the gold mines are the property of the shareholders, many of whom are foreigners – Frenchmen and Germans and others? After the war, whatever government rules, they will still belong to these people.'

'What are we fighting for then?'

'Because you hate us bitterly, and have armed yourselves in order to attack us and we naturally chose to fight when we are not occupied elsewhere.' Agree with thine adversary whilst thou art in the way with him.

'Don't you think it is wicked to try to steal our country?'

'We only protect ourselves and our own interests. We didn't want your country.'

'No, but the damned capitalists do.'

'If you had tried to keep on friendly terms with us there would have been no war. But you want to drive us out of South Africa. Think of a great Afrikander Republic – all South Africa speaking Dutch – A United States under your President and your Flag, sovereign and international '

Their eyes glittered. 'That's what we want,' said one. 'Yaw, Yaw,' said the others, 'and that's what we are going to have.'

'Well, that's the reason of the war.'

'No, no. You know it's those damned capitalists and Jews who have caused the war.'

And the argument recommenced its orbit.[1]

Winston had let the cat out of the bag. There runs a deep vein of anti-Semitism through Boer attitudes of the period and, as many of the men who arranged finance for the goldmines were Jews, the Boers lost no time in exploiting this prejudice in their campaign against the Uitlanders. Johannesburg was given the disparaging nickname of 'Jewburg'. Modern apologists for the Boers leave out the anti-Semitic component of their philosophy and have even gone so far as to substitute 'Judasburg' as the nickname for Johannesburg. I have on innumerable occasions heard Afrikaners refer to 'Jewburg', but never once to 'Judasburg'.

Churchill was to receive further illumination of Boer attitudes, when a Boer told him, 'Is it right that a dirty Kaffir should walk on the pavement – without a pass too? That's what they do in your British Colonies.'[2]

Churchill was taken to the Model School in Pretoria, which had been converted into a PoW camp for British officers. On the night of 12 December 1899, Churchill escaped and, after some exciting adventures, reached Delagoa Bay in Portuguese territory. He caught a ship to Durban, arriving there on 23 December and within a day or two was at Frere, where the British had set up their headquarters. On his return to Natal, the relieving force was no nearer Ladysmith than when he was captured and Ladysmith was just as firmly besieged.

Early in the morning of Friday 3 November 1899, Kate Driver was making her patients' beds and clearing up before going off duty when there was a tremendous explosion. 'The ground I stood on seemed to heave, the trees swayed violently. Then in the comparative quiet that followed came the sound of shouts and of running feet and of shell fragments rattling on the pavements and on the tents.'

A Boer shell had hit the town hall hospital. Fortunately there were no serious injuries, however, the psychological damage was considerable. Kate recorded her feelings.

The possibility that a shell should come right into the Hospital, flying the Hospital flag, had never for an instant come to my mind. In a flash, in a burst of noise, the red cross that had seemed to me an infallible symbol of protection for the sick and wounded everywhere, lost its power. The ruthlessness of war overwhelmed me.[3]

And her anguish was to continue. News came through that Guthrie Smith had been badly wounded. Being a member of the ILH, his care was not the responsibility of the Natal Volunteers, however, it was arranged that he would be nursed by Kate in the Volunteer Hospital under the supervision of Dr Currie. When Guthrie Smith was brought into the hospital that evening, the seriousness of the wound was immediately apparent. He had been shot through the liver and there seemed to be little hope of his survival.

When she came off duty the following morning she was unable to sleep, so Kate and some of the other nurses went shopping. They were surprised to find the army had commandeered the leading shops and Kate was able to obtain a large raincoat, which was to prove very valuable in the months ahead. That night Kate noticed that Guthrie Smith had begun to show signs of improvement. When Dr Currie confirmed this improvement, her hopes began to rise.

Meanwhile the Town Council had decided to urge Sir George White to ask General Joubert to permit civilians and the wounded to leave for the south. The request was sent to Joubert, who turned it down. He did, however, suggest an alternative; that a camp for non-combatants and a hospital be set up in no man's land at a place known as Intombi, which lay about 4 miles to the south of Ladysmith. The site lay near the railway so patients, medical personnel and supplies could be brought by rail or by wagon from Ladysmith. The move was to begin at noon on Sunday 5 November from which time there was to be a twenty-four-hour ceasefire. General White accepted the offer.

When Kate came off duty that Sunday morning, she was immediately plunged into the task of arranging the transfer of the patients to Intombi. She was able to obtain mattresses for Guthrie Smith and another seriously ill patient. The nurses were to travel on the train with the wounded and they did their best to make the men as comfortable as possible in the cramped coaches. Before boarding the train, Kate noticed a nurse had brought a cooler of water with her. A civilian seeing Kate eyeing the cooler, told her there would be no water at the place where they were going. Kate looked up and down the platform until her eyes lighted on a fire bucket. The civilian read her thoughts, ran down the platform, grabbed the fire bucket, and after filling it with clean water brought it back to the train. This bucket of water and that in the cooler was the only water the nurses and their patients had for the whole of that day and the following night.

The British military were responsible for setting up the camp and conveying patients, medical staff, civilians and goods to Intombi. One tented camp was to be the hospital and about 400 yards away another was to be set up for civilians. It was well into the afternoon before the nurses and their patients set off for the new hospital. It did not take long for the train to cover the few miles to the selected site. In dismay the nurses looked at the bare veld on which the camp was being set up. Two bell tents and a marquee constituted their new home and hospital. It was placed in a hollow, which would fill with water when it rained. There was no platform so the nurses had to jump from the train. Being young and fit, they did this easily, though they did struggle manhandling their bags and parcels off the train. Having alighted, they were confronted by a barbed wire fence. By helping each other they were able to scramble through and make their way over to their tents.

The military brought over all the hospital equipment, medicines, bedding and so on in a completely haphazard manner, resulting in chaotic conditions, which became worse once darkness descended. Somehow, the nurses had to turn the muddle to some sort of order. Captain Murray, Chaplain to the Gordons, found them candles, which provided the only light as they set to work. Kate later wrote that if she lived to be a hundred she would never forget those first few days at Intombi. She had been without sleep for almost three days and nights.

It began to rain. The wind got up with a roar. The patient's mattresses were right up against each other, and to get to a man one had to step onto his bed. At one corner of the tent the wind was blowing the rain in. As I stooped to try and fasten it down I seemed to lose myself for a moment. The dread of falling on the poor wounded boy whose bed I knelt on made me give a little scream. In a second, Nurse Otto had helped me onto an empty mattress. She thought I had fainted, but in a few moments I was myself again.

There was a brief pause. We had a quick meal. By now it was said all the men had been brought into the tents, but we saw a number of our patients had not arrived. 'Oh, they'll have been taken to the Military Hospital tents,' said the soldiers who had been helping the d'hoolie-bearers to bring in the men. 'They'll be quite all right, you needn't worry.'

We did worry. Nurse Ruiter decided to go and investigate. Off she went in the darkness towards the barbed wire and the standing train. About twenty minutes later I heard some shouts from that direction and we guessed Nurse Ruiter had found some patients and was having difficulty in getting them brought to the hospital tents in the pitch darkness. I was too busy, however, to know what was happening, and shortly afterwards was sent off duty for the first half of what remained of the night.

In the nurses' tent the mattresses were packed like sardines. No sooner did I put my head on the pillow than I had a violent attack of toothache. Nurse Otto again came to my rescue. Climbing through the tent ropes she went and fetched me a cup of stout. In ordinary life I detest stout. I drank it now as much for the kind thoughtfulness as for the hope it would cure my toothache. However, in a few moments I was asleep, and when after a couple of hours we were called up, I felt somewhat refreshed.

As day came on I was told the whole story of what had happened when Nurse Ruiter went off to search for the missing patients. As she neared the train she heard someone calling. In the van were my two most seriously injured patients waiting to be taken out. She shouted at some d'hoolie bearers at the other end of the train, and the sick men were lifted out. Guiding them as well as she could in the pitch dark, she led them towards our tents.

'As we got near the marquee,' she said, 'one of the stretcher poles broke and the patient fell out. We could see nothing but when we called two men came running to our help, bringing a lantern.'

'Who was the patient?' I asked, my heart standing still. 'Guthrie Smith,' she said sadly, pointing to the far corner of the marquee. I hurried to him. He lay quietly in great pain. I stood and looked down at him. Only the day before the doctor had said he thought now there was very good hope of recovery.

He opened his eyes and recognised me. 'Oh my little nursie, I'm a gonner,' he said.

There was not much to do just then as many of my patients were sleeping. I sat on the ground next to him. I could see too that he was 'a gonner'. I tried to persuade him otherwise. We had mutual friends in the Cape. I talked of these, and I tried to get knowledge of his relations.

'In case I kick the bucket?' he said looking at me. I could not tell him 'yes'. He pointed to his tunic that lay near him. 'In that little purse in the top pocket – it's all in there,' he said. 'In another pocket are my badges. I wanted you to have those.' Then we talked of other things for a few minutes until I was called away.

When the light came it was clear for all to see what a desolate place we had come to. It was time to wash the patients. Where was there any water? I hunted round for my fire bucket in case I should find water, but neither water nor bucket could I find, and in those few moments of frustration the image of that red bucket with the black letters FIRE painted on it became indelibly associated for me with the inhospitable veld on which we had been dumped.[4]

Kate's mood did not improve when she found that although it was 10 a.m., the patients had not yet received any food. She saw Dr Currie, who went to see the Military Hospital authorities and arrangements were made for the food to be sent over to the Volunteers hospital. She nearly quarrelled with one of the Military nurses but checked herself. Finally she took Dr Currie round to see all the men and then at last she could make her way to bed.

When I got to our nurses' tent, the other night nurses asked me where I had been and what I was doing and why on earth did I not come to bed? I tried to explain, standing in the hot tent taking off my apron.

Suddenly the feeling of anger and pity that had filled me during the last busy hours overwhelmed me and I burst into tears. They comforted me and I went off to sleep.

After a long day's rest we got up to find that a new marquee of enormous size had been put up, and all the men comfortably arranged in it, each of the four nurses having a quarter of it as her responsibility. We were, however, disappointed to find we did not have our own patients in our own quarter. I talked with the matron and she kindly moved Guthrie Smith into my corner of the ward as an extra patient. He was very bad indeed and had a special day nurse. Nurse Otto and I had been trained in the same hospital in Maritzburg where one of the unwritten rules was; the patients who are the most ill must be the only ones petted or spoiled.

One of her worst cases was also in my quarter of the ward but several beds lower down than Guthrie Smith unfortunately. Neither of these two patients slept well, and I hardly seemed to get to the one before the other poor man wanted me.

Webber, Nurse Otto's patient, said, 'I believe, Nurse, if you would let me put my head on your lap, I'd go to sleep.' Perching beside him, I lifted his head on to my lap and before long he was sleeping calmly. Nurse Thompson attended to my patient for me. After some time the boy woke and did not take long to fall deeply asleep on his own pillow again.

By the next night Guthrie Smith had been moved into another tent alone, and with him sat Nurse Mary watching over him. She said he had been calling for me during the day, but now when I spoke to him he did not recognise me. Up to now he had been so glad to see me when I came on duty at night. He was near the end and soon became unconscious. Of all my patients he was the only one I had nursed from the beginning. I felt stunned and sick at heart at losing him. His was the first death that occurred in our camp, and it was indeed a pitiful case, for having begun to recover from his severe wound in the liver, he died from peritonitis as a result of the fall.

I looked for the badges he had wanted me to have but they were gone. After crosses were put up to all the first casualties, I asked our orderly to photograph the cemetery so that his name could be seen.[5]

Oh, Kate. To set up the hospital and civilian camp in the time permitted was an impossible task and the British should have made it clear to Joubert and his staff that their demands were inhumane. Their task was not made easier by a requirement that at all times medical units should carry medical supplies that might be needed in any part of the Empire. A unit in a tropical jungle would therefore have medicines available to treat frostbite. The result was that the British army carried around with it vast quantities of medical supplies that were not always relevant to the campaign they were fighting. At Intombi they drafted civilian orderlies to work in the camp who were not suited to the tasks they had to perform. Some consultation with the locals would have helped. Another difficulty lay in the personality of the Principal Medical Officer, Colonel R. Exham, who believed a doctor's primary duty was to comply with regulations. These set out the minimum quantities of drugs and medicines a medical unit should hold. Once the supply of a medicine had dropped to this minimum level, Dr Exham would refuse to permit its further use as that might result in a breach of the regulations. How many died as a result of this policy cannot be accurately assessed but it certainly caused much suffering and distress that could have been avoided. He was also pompous and unable to get along with either the British or Volunteer doctors.

Initially, at Intombi, there were 300 beds divided between two British military hospitals and the one hospital for the Volunteers. To man these three hospitals there were thirty doctors, 120 trained medical personnel – which included the nurses and fifty-six Indian bearers whom the army had brought from India. Dr Currie was in charge at the Volunteer hospital. The civilian refugee camp fell under the authority of Mr Bennett, the resident Magistrate of Ladysmith.

In the town, hospitals were still necessary, so the Town Hall and the Convent continued to fly the Red Cross flag, and residents made their houses available as nursing homes for recuperating soldiers. As time wore on and conditions at Intombi deteriorated, more and more of the wounded and sick chose to remain in Ladysmith. Unfortunately, the records of civilians at Intombi were destroyed in a fire, however, it does seem that most were refugees and not many were residents of the town.

At the start of the siege, the principal stores announced they would not increase their prices while the siege lasted. They complied with this undertaking, however, the Army commandeered their stock in any case. Among the items taken by the army were 1,700 slaughter cattle, 14,000 tins of condensed milk and many hundreds of thousand pounds of mealies (maize). The town's weekly market was discontinued, so, for the time being, the local auctioneers decided to provide twice-weekly sales, where people could sell produce and surplus food.

As soon as the ceasefire expired on 6 November, the Boers recommenced their artillery bombardment of the town. The Roman Catholic Convent was on a hill near the centre of the town and had been converted into a hospital. A big Red Cross had been hoisted on the highest part of the ground. Ignoring the flag, the Boers directed their fire at the convent, scoring several hits. Luckily there was no loss of life as the terrified nuns had crammed themselves into a cellar with a few wounded officers. To avert a potential tragedy, it was decided that the sixteen sisters and nurses should go at once to Intombi camp. They gathered together their few possessions, and with some of their patients in dhoolies, they set off for the camp where they thought they would only remain a few days. They were about to experience 'holy poverty' beyond anything they had ever imagined.

Although not young and dressed in voluminous habits, they somehow clambered off the train and through the barbed wire fence and made their way to the site allocated to them. Here they found three tents. The Reverend Mother, Marie des Anges wrote:

> One was needed for Rev Father Saby, one for our four secular nurses, and the third to shelter our provisions, and be used as a kitchen and sleeping room for two of our sisters. The difficult question was where to lodge the other ten Sisters. Fortunately an old pupil brought her father, who was an engineer, to see us and he very kindly sacrificed a kind of hut which he had made with branches of trees. It was also he who improvised for us a kind of stove with a few stones. That 'tent', we used as a Chapel, a Refectory and a Community Room during the day, and as a dormitory at night for two of the Sisters. Towards evening two of our doctors came to ask if we were in need of anything. The most essential thing was a tent for the other six Sisters without shelter.[6]

The doctor was able to arrange a tent for the exhausted sisters, who at long last were able to get some rest, though the tent only had room for three small mattresses. The Reverend Mother was grateful that they were a little isolated from the main crowd, but even this one consolation was taken away the following day when two hundred men were lodged next to them. These men had been taken prisoner by the Boers and were, because of their wounds or for other reasons, no longer considered a threat to their captors. Then, as today, the sending of prisoners of war into a situation of great peril would be regarded as a war crime. To the sisters, it meant a loss of their peace and quiet; however, there were compensations.

> All night we could hear them and sometimes they held concerts. However, we had not much to complain of regarding them. They were always ready to help us. Amongst them were several Catholics who increased the number of those who attended Mass.[7]

There were also problems in Ladysmith. Henry Nevinson's two manservants wanted to leave, and if this was not bad enough, he was arrested by the 5th Lancers when he failed to produce a pass. To prevent spies operating in the town, on 29 October the army had issued a directive that everyone in the town should carry a pass. Nevinson made such a fuss when required to produce a pass that he ended up being escorted to the General Staff by the Colonel himself, three privates armed with rifles and a mounted orderly with a lance. He was eventually able to persuade the army to let him go, but not before Zulus and Indians had had some fun pouring derision on him in a manner they normally reserved for the Boers.[8]

Once the town was besieged, the most urgent task facing the military was to strengthen its fourteen-mile defensive perimeter. Each unit was allocated a section of the perimeter, which it had to defend. The Natal Volunteers, with some help from the Ladysmith Town Guard, were to protect the town from an attack on a front of about 2 miles, across the flat plain in the Klip River valley between Ladysmith and Bulwana Mountain. The Volunteers lost no time constructing trenches and sangars, which were constantly improved – making this one of the best defended sections on the whole perimeter. At night selected Volunteers would quietly sneak up to the Boer lines and watch and listen, before silently going back to their own lines before dawn.

On the Volunteers' right was a flat topped hill known as Caesar's Camp, joined at its western end to Wagon Hill. It is about two-and-a-half miles from the eastern end of Caesar's camp to the western extremity of Wagon Hill. The Manchesters were responsible for the defence of Caesar's Camp and Wagon Hill. The ILH were to provide back up for them.

On 7 November, Col Edwards of the ILH went to Caesar's Camp to look at the defences and noted that Wagon Hill had not been occupied, although the ground beyond it was 'dead' and might well have been used by the enemy as a place of assembly prior to an attack. He realised the danger it presented and took it upon himself to occupy the far end of Wagon Hill with a detachment of the ILH. From that time until the end of the siege it was never left unoccupied.

On 9 November, artillery fire from the Boers began at 5 a.m., followed by probing attacks on various positions on the perimeter. None of these attacks were persisted with for any length of time. Finally their guns began to rake the Manchesters' position on Caesar's Camp, and Boers were seen attempting to cross the valley in front of them. They were, however, beaten back by the Manchesters who, with their flanks protected, were able to concentrate their fire on the attackers. At noon the naval guns slowly fired twenty-one rounds at regular intervals. Not surprisingly, the Boers were puzzled by this turn of events and their fire died down. It was a twenty-one gun salute to commemorate the Prince of Wales' birthday! In due course the Boers resumed their fire on them, which continued until sunset. Lieutenant Fisher of the Manchesters in his report told of some curious manoeuvres by the enemy.

> One contingent, apparently some foreign legion, showing traces of elementary discipline and evidently not numbering in its' ranks many Boers of the old school, advanced boldly across ground that afforded them little cover, and there began to 'front form' in fairly good order. They were well within range of Lee Enfield rifles, and a few well-directed volleys sent them to right-about in anything but

good order. Soon after, a second column advanced with even more bravado, headed by a standard bearer, who carried a red flag. These were said to be Irishmen, who, having elected to serve a republic, and being debarred from fighting under the green banner of their own country, yet not quite ready to acknowledge the supremacy of another race, may have flaunted the emblem of liberty by way of compromise. More probably, however, they were a mixed lot owning no common country, but willing or unwilling to serve under any colours with equal impartiality. After two or three shrapnels bursting in front of them to a vibrato accompaniment of rifle fire, many were seen to fall, but whether badly hit or not, nobody on our side could say. At any rate, these adventurous auxiliaries are likely to learn discretion from the wily Boer after such an experience.[9]

As night approached, the rifle fire between the two sides died down. The British had lost four killed and twenty-seven wounded, mostly by shells, in twelve hours of intermittent fighting. An Irish American, who had deserted from the Boers, arrived in Ladysmith a few days later and claimed the Irish brigade had lost heavily, one shell alone killing ten of his erstwhile colleagues. This story, it is said, should only be swallowed with more than a pinch of salt.

At Intombi, the nuns never lost faith, despite their miserable lot.

When it rained heavily it was impossible to light a fire. We had to go to bed without supper. At other times the strong winds tore the ropes of the tents. Rain filled the trenches which overflowed and inundated the interior, soaked our beds and forced us to climb on the boxes to avoid sinking in the liquid mud. Oh! The miserable nights, when it thundered unexpectedly and awakened us with a start. We had to get up to see that our luggage was safe. Many a time we could not help laughing at our good Mother Assistant trying to sleep under an open umbrella while the storm was raging. The next morning our goods had to be put out to dry. After a heavy rain undesirable visitors swarmed in, mosquitoes, scorpions, frogs, snakes and the rest. Imagine three mattresses for six people, no sheets, no pillows. Each one wrapped herself in her blanket and went to sleep, all the feet tending to the central part of the tent and the heads to the circumference of the circles. When everybody was lying down it was impossible to move without disturbing the whole colony.

They were only able to celebrate Holy Mass when the weather was fine.

What a lesson to us to see Our Divine Master come down in such poor habitation on an Altar made of wooden boxes, covered with sheets, and a quilt as Altar Cloth. The tent was too low to allow us to stand, the seats were most primitive, trunks of trees, wooden boxes and big stones. We were not quite out of danger in the neutral camps. More than once stray bullets hit people in their tents or within the enclosure.[11]

When the Boers' supply of chlorodyne ran out a few days later, General White supplied the medicine without query or condition.

Except on Sundays, when they limited their martial actions to preparing for the next day's fighting, the Boers continued to send a steady stream of shells into Ladysmith. As a defence against the bombardment, the ILH came up with the idea of burrowing into the banks of the Klip River to create bomb shelters. At first they cut mere niches into the bank where a group of men could huddle during a bombardment. When it was found that it was relatively easy to tunnel into the banks, the mining engineers in the regiment created a labyrinth of interconnecting tunnels with substantial caves, which could house a whole regiment and their ammunition. The excavations were deep enough to ensure safety even in the event of a direct hit, and were so constructed that they didn't even require supporting timbers.

Seeing how successful the ILH had been, many of the residents began to dig out shelters for their families in the river bank. These shelters, though by no means as smart as those created by the ILH, were nonetheless quite adequate. In these early days of the siege, the men could be seen with picks and shovels constructing caves for their families, while their wives would be looking after the children, ensuring that, no matter how pleasant it might be to play in the sand by the river, they took shelter when a bombardment threatened. Lines were placed in the river in the hope of catching eels, more for something to do than to supplement the diet, as the eels tasted of mud and slime laced with needle-sharp bones.

A Mr Brockbank, realising the difficulties under which William Watson's family laboured, excavated a shelter in the river bank for them. At daybreak William, his daughter accompanied by her children, and with his disabled son-in-law on a stretcher, would go down to the river and return home to sleep at nightfall.

When white smoke was spotted spouting from the barrel of Long Tom on Bulwana it would take twenty-three seconds before the shell arrived in Ladysmith. To warn all of the approach of one of these shells, the army erected a platform on which was stationed an orderly, who waved a flag to warn of the approach of a shell, before he himself retreated to the shelter at the base of the platform. To carry out this duty the military chose two reliable men from the auxiliary units that had accompanied the soldiers from India.

In spite of these precautions, shellfire still provided a constant threat – but such is human nature that many learned to live with it, and were prepared to take chances rather than let the Boer artillery dominate their lives. On 12 November, 1899, Mrs Moor gave birth to a baby on the family farm, which was in the centre of defensive works. They had tried living in a dugout by the river, but Mrs Moor did not like the damp atmosphere so she, with her husband and other children, moved back to their farm for the birth of the first siege baby.

In those early days of the siege George Steevens, correspondent of the *Daily Mail*, amused himself by observing the ILH,

> They were a curious regiment. They appeared to consider that it rested with themselves when they rose in the morning, and remonstrated loudly with the non-commissioned officers when, as rarely befell, they were ordered on fatigue. They grumbled about everything, especially their food, being accustomed to eat twenty-four hours' rations at a meal.
>
> They considered no Imperial Officer knew anything. No Imperial troops could do anything. They considered that they alone won Elandslaagte, and alone averted disaster at Lombard's Kop.
>
> As for talk ... never was there such a corps to talk...
>
> Withal, they were an honest, sober and well-behaved lot of men. They were conspicuously clean in camp, as they were consistently brave in action. And when a few Regular Officers and Sergeants were imported among them, their discipline improved every hour.[12]

On 14 November, General Brocklehurst took out a mounted patrol, comprising the ILH and the Natal Volunteers, into the area to the west of the town lying between the British and Boer lines. One of their objectives was to clear the area of snipers, and to destroy places such as farm buildings and deserted native kraals that might provide cover for them. It should be mentioned here that modern accounts of the war often leave out the word 'deserted' when describing native kraals being destroyed by the British army in such circumstances. This gives a completely different impression of the purpose of such sorties. The British army had faults enough, but a desire to inflict unnecessary suffering on native peoples was not one of them. As the patrol was coming in, the Boer artillery opened fire and though shells exploded next to and among them, no one was hit. Staff who were watching saw a shell burst between Dr Hornabrook and Dr Platt. The smoke momentarily hid them from view and the watchers thought they must have been killed. Yet when the smoke cleared, they were quietly riding on. Trooper Schram of the NMR said to a comrade as he rode into camp, 'You missed nothing. It was a wasted day. Let us go and have a sleep.' He went to his tent, and as he slept a shell almost severed his head, killing him instantly. He was the first soldier killed by a shell pitched at random into the town.

As previously mentioned, one of the first things the Boers did on investing the town was to cut off the water supply, leaving the town dependant on the Klip River. The spring rains – and overgrazing of the river valley – resulted in the water carrying a lot of mud. In addition, dead animals were being washed into, or perhaps placed in, the river, further polluting the water. Mr Binnie, a civil engineer employed by the Natal Government, and Chief Engineer C.C. Sheen of the Navy, created between them three condensers capable of producing daily 12,000 gallons of potable water, for as long as supplies of coal lasted. At Intombi, purified water was obtained by sinking barrels into the sand of the river. This supply was supplemented early in December by the discovery of a spring within carrying distance. Indian inhabitants were permitted to cultivate kitchen gardens and, by their horticultural diligence, they raised a substantial crop of seasonable vegetables, which they sold at great profit to themselves and to the benefit of the general health of the troops.

Colonel Ward was in charge of the food stocks in the town and at the beginning of the siege, it was calculated that the food should last for approximately two-and-a-half months. The initial daily ration per person was:

Bread one and a quarter pounds, or, one pound of biscuits,
Coffee, one ounce, or Tea, half an ounce.
Sugar, three ounces.
Pepper, one and a third ounces.
Potatoes, half a pound, or, Compressed vegetables, one ounce

Whatever food was available, the flies in Ladysmith would have ensured eating was never very pleasant. As has been mentioned, the vast quantities of horse and cattle manure in the town, plus the trench latrines used by the troops, resulted in a plague of flies. To ease the situation a mixture of Cooper's dip powder and water was spread out. This killed countless millions of flies and special fatigues were employed to sweep them up and carry them away in wheelbarrows.

Throughout the siege, both civilians and the military relied on black runners to carry letters and other documents to the outside world, and to bring letters and even newspapers into Ladysmith. Generally, fifteen pounds was charged for this service, which of course would be doubled if there was a return trip. The work was dangerous but obviously profitable. Apart from physical fitness, it required knowledge of the country to be traversed, the habits of the Boers, and careful planning.

The Boers employed great ingenuity in their endeavours to trap these runners. Their paths were carefully watched, and bell wires set. One would be placed close to the ground and the next at about head height, so that the runner, in keeping a sharp lookout for one was almost certain to strike the other. This would set off a bell, which would bring the Boer guards swarming down from their camp. The runners matched cunning with cunning, and were equal to every emergency. When they were put through the outer line of pickets they flitted away silently like shadows into the night to a nearby Zulu kraal. Here the documents would be passed on to one of the women who would surreptitiously take them to an agreed place where another girl would collect them and carry them on to the next agreed spot, and so on until they were finally handed over to General Buller's staff. The plan was expensive, since so many had to be paid for their labour; but it was effective. It also required great courage and audacity from all concerned.[13] Henry Nevinson had difficulty obtaining runners to carry his dispatches. On 16 November he was able to obtain a runner and celebrated with another insulting racist comment.[14]

When war was declared, a new cricket season was just starting. In Ladysmith, rugby posts would have been taken down, and the cricket pitch prepared for the new season. The field bore little resemblance to the luxurious greensward that were the norm in England. Because of the warmer climate and cold dry winters, the fine grasses that grew in England could not survive in South Africa without constant irrigation. The pitch, therefore, was plain earth rolled flat and smooth. Soil from ant hills provided the best finish. In the first years of its existence, the energies of a club would be devoted to obtaining funds to buy a coir mat to cover the pitch from batting-crease to batting-crease. This would provide a true wicket with a regular bounce, which always took some spin. Fast bowlers found that their best deliveries bounced high and batsmen found they acquired a lot of bruises. A big advantage of such a wicket was that it could be used day after day with minimal repairs. With the number of grazing animals in the town it is unlikely that it was ever necessary to cut the veld grass that constituted the outfield. Equipment, such as bats, balls, pads, and gloves, would have been in short supply, and many a batsmen would have faced the chin music with no more protection than a pad on his leading leg.

As always in Natal, rain was a problem, but when the sun shone, out came the cricketers. The townspeople played against the military, and the regiments played each other. The Boers watched these strange rituals and from time to time directed shells at the field. On one occasion, warning was given that a shell was on its way, and the players scurried from the field to find shelter. The batsman, his mind still wrapped up in the game, dallied, and as batsmen so often do, played a phantom shot at an imaginary ball. Only it wasn't an imaginary ball that landed in front of him but a shell. He was knocked down but suffered no injury. One wonders whether the incident affected the batsman's concentration for the remainder of his innings.

Karri Davies was active in the organisation of all sport during the siege and, in particular, organised successful athletic competitions. There were some excellent athletes among the besieged and competition was fierce. One of Karri's fellow officers in the ILH, Lt Brooking, said they had to compete in an aloe field. But it wasn't quite as bad as that.

In spite of the heat, some soccer matches were organised. In a game between the Gordon Highlanders and the Imperial Light Horse, a shell landed on the field. In the dust, smoke and confusion caused by the explosion, the Gordons scored a goal, much to the indignation of the ILH whose belief in the integrity of the Scots was severely dented. One Boer artilleryman, when asked how effective the shelling of Ladysmith had been, commented, 'What is the use of shelling them? They just go on playing cricket.'

On 23 November, the Boers sent 230 Indians, who had been living in the Transvaal, into Ladysmith. Realising, at last, that these non-combatants were being sent to Ladysmith to consume the garrison's supplies, General White hardened his heart and refused to accept them, telling the Boers that they should be handed over to the British forces south of the Tugela. The Boers, who must have been surprised by the unexpected resolution shown by the British, had no choice but to take the Indians as directed to the south. As if in spite, that day a splinter from a shell killed a dhoolie bearer near the Town Hall. He appears to have been the first dhoolie bearer killed, although from the beginning of the invasion of Natal, they were prominently exposed on the battlefields when collecting the wounded.

That evening an attempt was made to destroy the only locomotive the Boers had on the Harrismith line. An old engine was selected and once it had built up a full head of steam, it was sent, driverless, along the line to Harrismith and the Free State. The Boers had anticipated the ploy, and had destroyed a section of the line just before their terminus. When the engine hit the damaged line, it fell on its side and lay hissing and steaming on the veld like some wounded monster. Fearing it might be filled with explosives, the Boers did not approach until the next morning, when their artillery fired some shells into it. Later the Boers were seen cautiously approaching the still steaming and hissing locomotive, and poking and prodding it with their rifles.

On 24 November, slaughter cattle belonging to the military and herded by unmounted Zulus guarded by a British Mounted Infantry unit were permitted to stray beyond the town's defences. Quick to grasp the opportunity presented to them, the Boers fired shells onto the town side of the cattle causing them to hasten towards their lines. Not surprisingly, the unarmed herdsmen abandoned the cattle and sought shelter. Belatedly the Mounted Infantry attempted to recover the herd, but it was too late and 228 cattle were lost to the Boers. It was a humiliating incident for the British. An attempt was made to blame the herdsmen. The real blame rested with those who had placed the mounted infantry in charge, when they knew these troops had no experience of herding cattle or knowledge of the Zulu language. After this incident, a detail of Natal Volunteers or the Imperial Light Horse went out with the cattle.

Three days later the Boers attempted to repeat their success and capture some horses that were grazing on the veld towards Bulwana. Henry Pearse of the *Daily News* described what happened next.

But they have to do now with the Natal Carbineers, many of whom, like themselves, are veld farmers, familiar with every trick of rounding up horses and oxen. In vain do the gunners of 'Puffing Billy' (a Boer cannon) throw percussion shells to drive the herd towards their lines. In vain is shrapnel timed to burst in a shower where Carbineers sweep round like Indian scouts to herd the startled horses back. The Volunteers do their work neatly, coolly, quickly, to the chagrin of Boers who wait in kloofs beyond Klip River for a chance of carrying off some valuable horses. In their disappointment the Bulwaan battery tries to get some consolation by shelling the camp of the Carbineers.[15]

On 30 November, 1899, another Boer shell hit the Town Hall hospital, killing one patient and wounding ten others. In contravention of international usage, the Boers had persistently shelled this building and to protests they replied that all patients should be moved to Intombi. After this incident, patients at the Town Hall hospital were moved to another site in town, however, the Boers should have been told in no uncertain terms that it was not up to them to decide where British field hospitals and dressing stations were to be sited and that failure to respect the Red Cross flag would have dire consequences. This was not done and as a result the Red Cross flag was not respected.

During these last days of November, the people in Ladysmith saw long wagon trains travelling to the railhead at Elandslaagte loaded with vast quantities of loot the Boers had plundered in southern Natal. On 28 November, Donald Macdonald counted 160 loaded wagons on their way to Elandslaagte. Great herds of cattle were also seen being driven from the south, along the roads leading to van Reenen's Pass.

The arrival of some post from Pietermaritzburg resulted in Henry Nevinson discovering, much to his chagrin, that local newspapers did not publish English football results.

On 1 December an early bombardment resulted in four men being killed before breakfast. Two Gordons were ripped to pieces while standing in their lines and a driver with the artillery died when a shell took off both his legs. At the other end of town, nineteen-year-old Trooper Crickmore of the Natal Mounted Rifles was hit by a shell as he rode past the Town Hall. His horse was reduced to pulp and a piece of one lung was torn away leaving part of the shell protruding under his left arm. He should have died instantly but lived for several hours. He saw many of his friends and cheerfully told them that in spite of all he would pull through and then, at the height of his good spirits, his head fell forward and he was dead.

It had been noticed that for some days the Boers had been carrying out works on a hill (now known as Gun Hill) due west of Lombard's Kop. On 2 December a six inch Long Tom opened fire from this hill at various targets near the Convent. Also on this day heliograph contact was re-established with Weenen.

The long hours spent on patrol by the mounted men were exhausting and when Lt Douglas Campbell of the ILH led his squadron back into camp on the afternoon of 6 December, he was looking forward to a few hours of undisturbed sleep. He had just dozed off when a shell came through his tent and burrowed into the ground by his feet without exploding. He stalked out of the tent cursing the Boers and saying it was criminal that they should be able to disturb a man's sleep. His was one of many lucky escapes since the start of the siege, nonetheless, from to the beginning of November to 6 December, shellfire had killed thirteen men in Ladysmith and injured another 148. Whether these figures include civilians is not clear.

A concert was held in the ILH camp on the evening of 7 December. The proceedings were in full swing, when at 9 p.m. the ILH, the Carbineers and the Border Mounted Rifles were ordered to assemble immediately at Devonshire Post on the eastern edge of the town. They were requested to wear soft soled shoes. The Volunteers had already acquired a reputation for the speed at which they could assemble, so it came as no surprise when they were assembled and ready to march at 10.15 p.m.

The force consisted of 500 Natal Volunteers under Col W. Royston, 100 men of the ILH under Col Edwards, a detachment of Engineers under Captain Fowke and some guides under Major Henderson. General Hunter was the senior officer present. They marched for a couple of miles along the Helpmekaar Road and then turned left and made their way through scrub to the foot of Gun Hill, which was about a mile from the road. Silence was maintained.

On reaching the foot of Gun Hill, the 100 Imperial Light Horsemen and 100 Natal Carbineers under Major Addison, accompanied by the engineers, were instructed to destroy the guns on the summit. The Border Mounted Rifles, under Major Rethman, were detailed to protect the left flank of the assault party, while the balance of the Carbineers, under Col Royston, would protect the right. Slowly and steadily the assault force began the 250-foot ascent of the steep, boulder-strewn slope. It seems they passed the first picket without at first being noticed. When the sentry realised something was amiss he shouted several times in an ever more anxious voice, 'Wie kom daar?' (Who comes there?); then, 'So waar as God, hier is hulle.' (As true as God, here they are). A shot rang out, followed by some ragged firing from the crest of the hill. The attackers pressed ever upwards, clambering over the boulders and into the dead ground near the summit where the enemy's fire went over their heads. Someone shouted, 'Fix bayonets,' and another voice ordered, 'Give them cold steel.' In a few seconds they were over the crest, just in time to see the defenders disappearing down the other side of the hill. The ILH and the Carbineers moved across the top of the hill and took up defensive positions on the crest while the engineers prepared charges to destroy the Long Tom and a howitzer. Then followed the explosion of the charges, which wrecked the guns. General Hunter now called for three cheers for The Queen. The order to retire was given and they were able to get back to base before dawn and without further incident. Seven men were wounded in the action, the most seriously wounded being Trooper R.G. Nicol, who had been shot through the spine. Ambulance Sergeant Dr Charles E. Ligertwood dressed his wounds and stayed with him and the non-walking wounded. Sergeant Ligertwood was a well-known medical practitioner in Johannesburg. In the First World War, he became a combatant Lieutenant Colonel and commanded the ILH in the German South West Africa campaign.

The troops brought back with them a Maxim gun found on the summit as well as other trophies, the principal one being the breech block of the Long Tom. Karri Davies was solely responsible for the removal of the breech block, which, although regarded as his property, was for many years placed on the table at any dinner or function given by the ILH. Karri subsequently presented it to General Smuts with a view to it being placed in the War Museum in Pretoria. It is now in the Siege Museum, Ladysmith.

Col Royston had been pressing for many weeks for such an attack to be made and in the Volunteers' camp, he was credited with conceiving and planning it. With the exception of the three cheers, the sortie carries all the hallmarks of a Colonial operation. Some British historians believe General Hunter conceived, planned and organised the raid. Given his apparent dislike of night-time operations and his complete ignorance of local conditions and people, as evidenced by his statements to the Boer War Commission, it is difficult to imagine that he was the driving force behind this raid. Other British historians give the credit to Lt Col Sir Henry Rawlinson, while yet others believe Col W.G. Knox was the instigator of the sortie. That night Col Knox did take out three companies of the Liverpools, a company of mounted infantry and the 19th Hussars in what was thought to be a diversionary action. The cavalry burnt down Pepworth's Farm where the Boers had established a commissariat, but committed the elementary error of failing to get back to Ladysmith before dawn broke. They were subjected to vigorous shell and rifle fire, which resulted in them losing three killed and fifteen wounded.

At daylight on the following day, Surgeon-Major Davies of the ILH returned to Gun Hill with an ambulance to bring in the wounded. Dr Davies and Sergeant Ligertwood were arrested and taken to General Schalk Burger. Burger was in no mood to let the doctors go and made various false charges against them, all of which Davies refuted. Finally, he accused Davies of having been a member of the Reform Committee who was sent to gaol, and was only released on giving an undertaking not to fight against the Transvaal again. Davies admitted being a member of the Reform Committee and being sent to gaol, but said his undertaking was not to interfere in Transvaal politics for three years. At this point a *Landrost* (magistrate), who was present, felt he should intervene and told Burger that the Doctor was correct. The Landrost told Davies and Ligertwood that they could go back to Ladysmith and take back with them the wounded men, the ambulance and their horses. Davies did not think Trooper Nicol would survive the journey so it was decided to leave him in the Boer hospital. Nicol died the next day. His body was sent under a white flag to Ladysmith, together with sixteen pounds cash, which he had with him, and his watch. Everything possible had been done to save him.

Anxious to emulate the Volunteers, the Regulars went out on a sortie on the night of 10 December, intending to destroy a howitzer that the Boers had placed on Surprise Hill. They did not bother to wear soft shoes. Initially, luck was with them. The Boers had not put out their forward pickets, resulting in the British reaching the brow of the hill before they were challenged. After a sharp exchange of rifle fire the Boers were driven off the summit and an explosive charge was placed on the gun. Nothing happened. Another charge was prepared and placed in position. This time there was a suitable explosion followed by the traditional cheering. The troops hurried down the hill at the foot of which a line of Boers was waiting for them. With bayonets fixed they charged the Boers and by sheer weight of numbers they were able to break through and make their way back to Ladysmith. The British lost fourteen killed and fifty wounded. The howitzer and some ammunition had been destroyed.

As the Volunteers did not carry bayonets the call to 'Fix bayonets' near the summit of Gun Hill had been a bluff. Many attributed this ruse to Karri Davies and so the story might have remained but for the intervention of Karri himself. In 1904 a dinner was given in Johannesburg for Field-Marshal Lord Roberts by the officers of the Imperial Light Horse. When the Field-Marshal was returning thanks he turned to Karri Davies and pointing to the breech-block which was on the table, congratulated him on his timely bluff in calling to his men to 'Fix bayonets.' Karri at once corrected him; 'It was not me Sir, it was Colonel Edwards.' Today Edwards is generally given credit for the bluff and Karri credit for the reference to cold steel.

A letter was found at Gun Hill, which a Burgher had been writing to his wife. A translation gives some idea of the feelings of one young Boer.

It is one month and seven days since we were besieged Ladysmith, and don't know what will happen further. The English we see every day walking about the town, and we bombard the town every day with our cannon. They have erected plenty of breastworks outside the town. It is very dangerous to take the town. Near the town they have two naval guns from which we receive very heavy fire, which we cannot stand. I think there will be much blood spilt before they surrender, as Mr Englishman fights hard and well, and our burghers are a bit frightened.

After perusal by Headquarters, Karri posted it to the addressee with a covering letter:

Dear Madam,
Enclosed please find a letter addressed to you which we found in a tent on Lombard's Kop on the morning of 8 December when we captured some guns from the Boers. Duty necessitated my handing it to the military authorities whom I asked to return it to me to enable me to forward it to you. I regret the unavoidable delay, but hope it will reach you safely. Trusting your husband will return to you safely after the war.
I remain, dear Madam, W. Karri Davies, Major, ILH

On 6 December, a baby boy, Harry Buller Siege Willis, was born in Ladysmith. Had he been born a fortnight later his parents might have named him differently.

16

Battle of Colenso

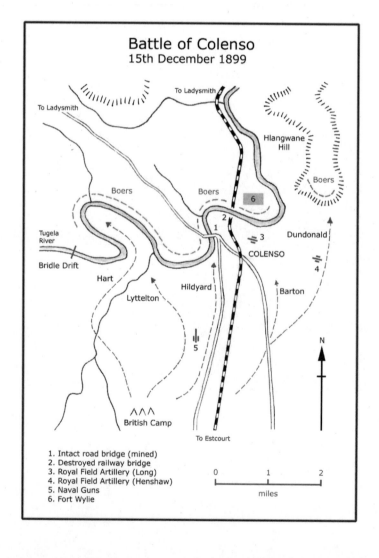

Battle of Colenso
15th December 1899

To Ladysmith

To Ladysmith

Hlangwane
Hill

Boers

Boers

Boers

6

Tugela
River

2

1

Dundonald

3

COLENSO

Bridle Drift

4

Hart

Hildyard

Barton

Lyttelton

5

N

^ ^ ^
British Camp

To Estcourt

1. Intact road bridge (mined)
2. Destroyed railway bridge
3. Royal Field Artillery (Long)
4. Royal Field Artillery (Henshaw)
5. Naval Guns
6. Fort Wylie

0   1   2

miles

Lt Douglas Campbell, who rose from the dead after being shot through the head at Wagon Hill. (See p 250.)

Major Gen Fitzroy 'No-Bobs' Hart, Commanding Officer of the Irish Brigade.

In those early months of the war when disaster followed disaster, one thought consoled the British – General Sir Redvers Buller VC was on his way to take command of the army.

On 8 August 1899, the anti-Semitic, pro-Boer Commander in Chief in South Africa, Sir William Butler, resigned. General Buller, who for the past few years had held the powerful position of Adjutant-General at the War Office, was regarded by most people as the obvious choice as a successor to Butler, and it came as no surprise when he was appointed. On 14 October, Buller boarded the S.S. *Dunottar Castle* bound for Cape Town.

Redvers Buller was the second of seven sons of a wealthy landowning family at Downes in Devon. He went to Harrow, but had to leave after an incident in which some doors were painted red, and completed his schooling at Eton. His holidays were spent on the family estate where young Redvers would undertake any work that might be required of him, whether it was in the smithy, carpentry shop or stables. The family had always taken a keen interest in the welfare of the tenants and workers at Downes, and Redvers inherited this characteristic.

On leaving school he decided to join the army and in 1858 became an Ensign in the 60th Rifles. His family paid for his commission. His fellow subalterns tended to regard him as a country bumpkin but were nonetheless a little in awe of him, not only because he had grown into a phenomenally strong man with flashes of bad temper, but also because he was forthright and constant in his opinions.

His bouts of ill temper would pass rapidly and those who knew him soon discovered that he was by nature a very kind-hearted man. His upbringing at Downes led him to identify with his men and there was no barrier of class distinction between them. The rank and file adored him. He served in many of the smaller wars in which Britain was engaged in Victorian times and showed himself to be a man of great courage, being awarded the Victoria Cross in the Zulu War. He always worked hard and it was not surprising that he was noticed by General Wolseley, who made Buller his Intelligence Officer in the Ashanti War of 1873. He was loyal to Wolseley and as the latter rose in power, Buller also climbed the army ladder. When his elder brother died, he inherited the family estate and could have retired to a comfortable life as a country squire; instead, he decided to continue with his army career. In 1886 he was sent to Ireland to deal with a group of nationalists known as the Moonlighters who were stealing cattle and collecting arms. He was reasonably successful in checking the Moonlighters but was appalled by the manner in which many landlords treated their tenants. In his report to the Chief Secretary for Ireland he said, 'For 120 years British bayonets have backed up landlords in extracting excessive rents, and have supported them in grossly neglecting their tenants.' Such statements might have spelt the end of his career but as Wolesley's star rose, Buller continued his upward climb. Queen Victoria liked his bluff manner and with his patron Sir Garnet

Wolesley now Commander-in-Chief, the goodwill surrounding him when he left for South Africa was almost tangible.

One of the few people not moved by this adulation was Redvers Buller himself. He had never held an independent command and doubted whether he was suited to do so. He saw himself as an able administrator who could carry out other men's ideas but, as he confessed to his wife, 'I never credited myself with much ability on the inventive side.' Early in his career he found that war, despite its excitement, was 'wicked and brutal,' a feeling that would only have grown stronger with the passing of time. The years working long hours at an office desk in Whitehall had resulted in his putting on weight and losing much of his former physical vigour, while the duty of having to attend an endless round of functions resulted in his acquiring a taste for fine champagne. He never sought the posting to South Africa, did not want to fight the Boers and fervently hoped the war would soon be over, so that he could return home.

To have fulfilled the expectations that rested on him would have required an imaginative military genius of almost supernatural power and foresight. Like his army, Buller was to follow the tried and tested solutions to problems that in other places and at other times had been successful. However, if the Boers were to be defeated a new way of fighting was required and the British habit of not listening to other opinions ensured that the lessons were to be learned the hard way.

When the bad days came, his detractors were quick to draw attention to his love of champagne and other small luxuries, but the men he commanded knew that General Buller would not touch his food until every man in the ranks had been fed. Indeed, one of his biggest weaknesses was the large commissariat he required to accompany his army. He insisted that everything that might possibly be required to ensure the well-being of the troops was available. Also, in the same manner that the once-gauche West Country subaltern had awed his peers by his sheer persistence, so the older Buller was able to infuse into his army that same determination to fight on and never to give in.

Buller was given no specific instructions as to how the campaign in South Africa was to be conducted. It was, however, decided that he would go to the northern Cape and from there advance through the Free State via Bloemfontein, then on to Pretoria to accept the surrender of the Boer forces. During the voyage to Cape Town he received a report that the Boers had been defeated in three battles and Penn Symons had been killed. On 31 October 1899, he arrived in Cape Town, where he received news of the capture of the British soldiers at Nicholson's Nek. Over the next few days he received nothing but bad news from all fronts.

He spent three weeks in Cape Town. During this period he decided to split the Army Corps, which had followed him out from England. One half would join Lord Methuen in the northern Cape and relieve Kimberley, while the other half would accompany him to Natal where the first priority would be the relief of Ladysmith. With only a scratch staff, he displayed his great powers of organization – sending troops off to their appropriate fronts and arranging all their transport and supplies. He also authorised the raising of the South African Light Horse and several other groups of Colonial troops. He embarked for Durban on 22 November, and on arrival he sent General Clery to Frere to organise the troops already there, while he himself remained in Pietermaritzburg organising various supplies. He had conceived the idea of a large field hospital, erected as close as possible to the front line to enable wounded troops to receive early treatment. He now set about organising such a hospital. He also arranged the creation of a Field Canteen, where little luxuries not normally included in army rations could be purchased. The profits from the Canteen went to the next-of-kin of those killed in action.

While Buller was in Pietermaritzburg, the mounted troops under Lord Dundonald were on constant patrol monitoring the Boer movements. In the early hours of 28 November, Dundonald led a force of mounted men on a reconnaissance in the direction of Colenso. With him were the Natal Carbineers, a squadron of the Imperial Light Horse, Bethune's Mounted Infantry, Thornycroft's Mounted Infantry, a company of Regular Mounted Infantry, some Natal Police and a battery of Field Artillery. At dawn, Boer scouts were seen ahead, but they disappeared without a shot being fired. When they reached the crest from which they could see the land sloping down to Colenso and the Tugela River, McKenzie pointed out to Dundonald the trenches the Boers were digging on Robinson's farm across the river from Colenso. To obtain a better view of the Boer defences, McKenzie advised that they could advance to the next patch of shelter, since the Boers would be reluctant to use their big guns as this would give away their positions. Dundonald then ordered the column to advance and as they did so, McKenzie glanced round and noticed the whole mounted brigade was in close order. As he was only a volunteer and a major, he should perhaps have kept quiet, but felt it was his duty to say something as the men made a most tempting target for the enemy's guns, so he said, 'I think you have not noticed, Sir, that the men are not in extended order.' Dundonald at once told McKenzie to give the order to extend, which was promptly done. The Boer's guns now opened fire but because the troops were now in extended order, no damage was done. The British Artillery unlimbered and attempted to return the fire but were outranged. Meanwhile the Natal Police, who had formed the advance guard of the column, had reached a position with little cover. McKenzie, noticing this, asked that they should be given leave to retire, as it served no purpose to have the Police in this forward position. Dundonald agreed, and McKenzie rode forward to the Police with the order to retire. When they arrived back at the guns they found the other mounted men had already retired. McKenzie told the officer in command of the guns to follow him. This was the same officer, Major Henshaw, who had been so uncooperative at Willow Grange, but this time he followed McKenzie, who led them through a little valley that hid them from the enemy's view until they were out of effective range. The column returned to Frere having obtained useful information about the Boer's defences. The only damage suffered was an injury to a horse's hoof.

General Buller arrived at Frere on Wednesday 6 December 1899, and immediately set off with his staff, including Dundonald, to inspect the position at Colenso. Dundonald had brought along Duncan McKenzie, whom he introduced to Buller. On reaching the high ground a few miles south of Colenso, General Buller was able to look over the gently sloping veld to the village, beyond which could be seen the Tugela River. North of the river was Fort Wylie and a line of hills, which provided an even more formidable natural fortress. McKenzie pointed out where the Boers had dug their trenches and also drew attention to a hill, Hlangwane, which lay to the east of Colenso and which appeared to be situated to the north of the river, whereas in fact it lay south of it. From Hlangwane it would be possible to bring flanking fire to bear on the main Boer position as well as providing protection for troops crossing the river. Buller thanked McKenzie for his help and the party returned to Frere to consider how to break through the Boer line.[1]

It was during this period that one of the most significant conversations of the campaign took place. For centuries European armies had placed great store on intimidating their opponents with a show of force. Having recently come from Britain and being fully aware of Britain's heroic past, Dundonald asked McKenzie whether the Boers would fight 'when they saw Her Majesty's troops'. McKenzie replied that the Boers, far from being overawed, would fight. From that time Dundonald abandoned the old idea of intimidating the enemy and followed the Volunteers' creed of keeping his position, strength and intentions hidden from the enemy.[2]

While Buller and his staff were preparing an attack on the Boer positions along the Tugela, the newly recruited mounted regiments – Thornycroft's Mounted Infantry, the South African Light Horse, and Bethune's Mounted Infantry – were able to get some essential training. Initially Dundonald was disappointed with these regiments commenting, 'What a formidable force they would have been if they could have shot as well as the Border Mounted Rifles, but a novice with any tool – more especially a rifle or a revolver – cannot use it with efficiency until after much practice.' It was soon Dundonald's turn to be amazed at how quickly they learned and he soon noted the 'astonishing progress in the direction of efficiency'.

Meanwhile, Duncan McKenzie, with the assistance of some of his Zulu-speaking officers, built up a small Native Intelligence Corps to assist Dundonald's Brigade. This Corps was able to furnish a great deal of information for the Natal army, many were to show great courage in the face of the enemy and several were to lose their lives. On 14 December, Dundonald had under his command approximately 1,150 mounted men, all but the 13th Hussars being Volunteers.

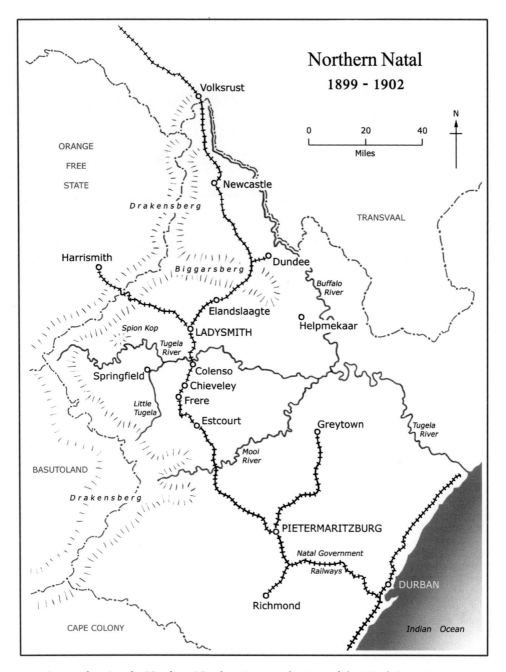

A map showing the Northern Natal territory at the time of the Natal Campaign.

Above left: Cockney Liz, the belle of Barberton.

Above right: President Paul Kruger and his wife Sannie.

Barney Barnato, the Cockney prizefighter, flamboyant financier and friend of Paul Kruger.

NATAL MOUNTED POLICE.

Trooper, Review Order.

NATAL CARBINIERS.

Officer, Review Order.

TYPES OF NATAL FORCES.

OFFICERS.

DURBAN LIGHT INFANTRY.   NATAL POLICE.   IMPERIAL LIGHT HORSE.

Review Order.   Service Kit.

TROOPER, NATAL CARBINIERS.

Service Kit.

The different kits worn by the troopers and officers of the Natal Mounted Police, the Natal Carbineers, the Durban Light Infantry, the Natal Police and the Imperial Light Horse.

Left: Charles Herbert Mullins VC.

Below: One of the stocks used in 1842 to exhibit Natal residents objecting to the invading Dutch Voortrekkers taking over their settlement at Port Natal.

Bottom: **Field Day in Ladysmith**: A Carbineer demonstrates how the regiment's horses had been schooled to lie down on command and remain lying down despite rifle fire.

LIEUT. COLONEL St JOHN GORE,
COMM^G. 5TH DRAGOON GUARDS, LADYSMITH.

Major (later Lt Col.) St J. C. Gore, Cavalry Commander, Battle of Elandslaagte.

Officers of the Imperial Light Horse.

On Patrol: With invasion imminent, the Natal Carbineers leave Ladysmith for the frontier.

This rare picture shows the organisers of the Driefontein Scouts, who played an important role in assisting the British. *Back*: S. Gule, R. Mdaweni, L. Kumalo, A. Msimang, P. Malinga, S. Silgee; *Middle*: E. Msimang, A. Mtimkulu, Chief Johannes Kumalo, Rev'd L. Msimang, Rev'd J. Msimang; *Front*: S. Kambule and Asst. Chief Khumalo.

Staff Officers of the Natal Volunteers in Ladysmith, pictured with Colonel W. Royston in the centre and Colonel Bru de Wold on the right.

The First Shell
Ladysmith, November 1899

Captain Clive Dixon of the 16th Lancers, A.D.C. to Gen. Sir George White VC, drew cartoons between 2 November 1899 and 28 February 1900, published in book form in March 1900. These are his comments:

Above: 'The shells from "Long Tom" that fell in Ladysmith during the first week or so of the siege were treated with considerable respect by all ranks.'

Below: 'With the Naval guns that arrived so opportunely on October 30th, 1899, were two 6.3-inch Howitzers of somewhat antique pattern. These, however, proved themselves invaluable, and were much sought after by the Officers commanding the three sections into which our defences were divided.'

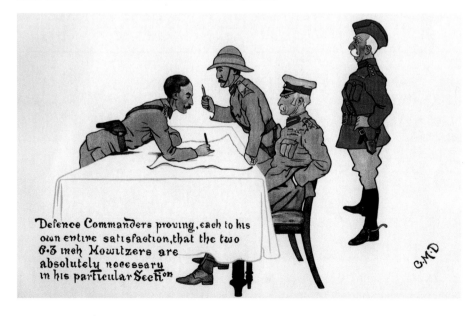

Defence Commanders proving, each to his own entire satisfaction, that the two 6·3 inch Howitzers are absolutely necessary in his particular Section

Above: 'The farm of Mr. Bester, who professed strong pro-Boer sympathies, to put it mildly, lay in the valley between our defences and the Boer lines of investment. As it seemed a pity that the Boers should fatten on the poultry and live stock, a party of Major Altham's Guides raided the farm early one morning, and made a clean sweep of everything.'

Below: 'With apologies to a body of loyal men who were ready to take their share in the defence of their town.'

Above left: Colonel Adolf Schiel, Commander of the German Kommando.

Above right: Surgeon Captain T.J. Crean VC.

After his escape from Pretoria, Winston Churchill is pictured standing next to the wrecked armoured train.

Above left: Lord Dundonald, Commander of Buller's Mounted Brigade.

Above Right: Kate Driver, nurse.

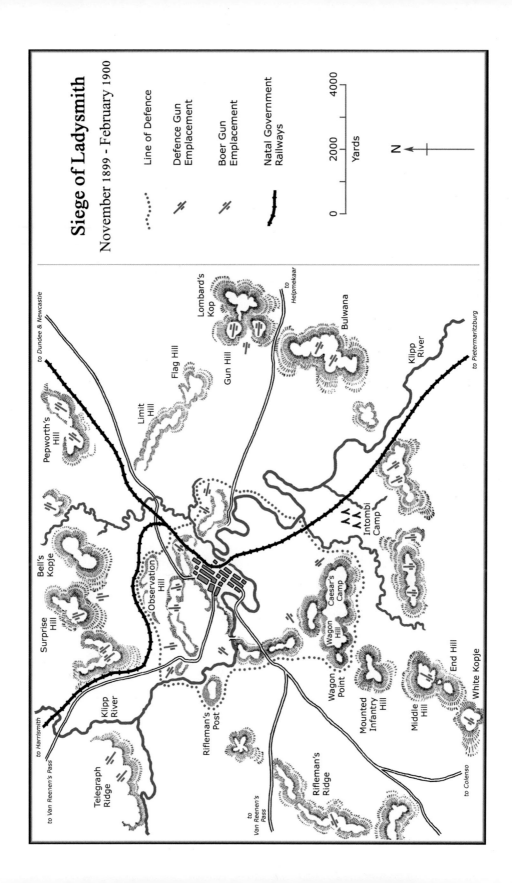

Siege of Ladysmith
November 1899 - February 1900

Line of Defence

Defence Gun Emplacement

Boer Gun Emplacement

Natal Government Railways

0   2000   4000

Yards

N

to Dundee & Newcastle

to Harrismith

to Van Reenen's Pass

Pepworth's Hill

Surprise Hill

Bell's Kopje

Telegraph Ridge

Klipp River

Observation Hill

Limit Hill

Flag Hill

Lombard's Kop

Gun Hill

Bulwana

to Helpmekaar

Klipp River

to Pietermaritzburg

Rifleman's Post

Rifleman's Ridge

to Van Reenen's Pass

Caesar's Camp

Wagon Hill

Wagon Point

Mounted Infantry Hill

Middle Hill

End Hill

White Kopje

Intombi Camp

to Colenso

A converted naval gun on the quayside in Durban.

A naval 4.7-inch gun at Ladysmith waiting for the word to fire.

A lucky escape: On 18 December Saddler Sergeant Lyle was sitting on a box reading. In front of him lay his rifle and behind him, three companions were standing and chatting. A shell hit the rifle, smashing it to smithereens, went through the box on which Lyle was sitting and then into the tent where clothing and bedding was shredded. None of the men were injured. The photograph shows the men in the positions they were in when the shell struck.

Above left: Tpr Herman Albrecht, ILH, posthumously awarded the Victoria Cross for gallantry at Wagon Hill.

Above right: The Imperial Light Horse dugout in the bank of the Klip River.

The Border Mounted Rifles receiving rations. The tedium of siege life has begun.

The Imperial Light Horse first aid post in Ladysmith.

Top: Buller's Army travelling along the rough track from Frere to Springfield.

Above left: A Natal family returns to their home after the Boer retreat from the Natal Midlands.

Above right: An artist's sketch of the ambush of a Boer Kommando by the Natal Carbineers and the Imperial Light Horse near Acton Homes on 18 January 1900. Note the rifles do not have magazines.

Below right: **Spion Kop**: British and Colonial dead lying in a shallow trench on the day after the battle.

The gun of the 7th Battery clearing the road to Ladysmith.

After the initial phase of looting in Newcastle the Boer authorities dumped what remained of the residents' possessions in the Town Hall for everyone to take what they liked.

Brigadier General Sir Duncan McKenzie. This portrait was created after Sir Duncan had defeated the German forces occupying southern German South West Africa in 1915.

One of the big difficulties faced by Buller and his staff was that they did not have any reliable maps. The Tugela had for a long time been considered by the British as a possible line of defence and the area should have been properly surveyed and mapped before the war. Even after the ultimatum had been sent, such an important survey should have been made. The owner of the land across the river from Colenso, Robinson, would, if approached, have given the army every possible assistance. As was the case around Ladysmith, the army spurned what could have been a very valuable source of information. Without the maps, Buller relied on his own observation and by 12 December, had come to the conclusion it would be too costly to relieve Ladysmith by means of an attack on the enemy positions at Colenso. With his army now 18,000-strong, he decided instead to use his numerical advantage over the Boers and to attempt to bypass the Boer right flank by a rapid night march to Potgieter's Drift, some 18 miles upstream from Colenso. He heliographed General White in Ladysmith to say that he would start his advance to Potgieter's Drift on the 12th and hoped to be in Ladysmith five days later.

On the evening of 12 December, Major-General Barton's 6th brigade were ordered to take up a position in front of Colenso and act as a distraction, while the rest of the army began its preparations for the move to Potgieters Drift.

The following day General Buller changed his mind. He would instead attack the Boers at Colenso, something which a mere twenty-four hours before he had thought would be too costly. It is, of course, impossible to state precisely what brought about the change in plan, though receipt of the news of the defeat and death of General Wauchope at Maggersfontein and the reverse suffered a few days before by General Gatacre at Stormberg must have weighed heavily with him. In abandoning his sensible plan, he displayed his own lack of self-confidence and his indecisiveness. He heliographed White to say the plan had changed and he was now coming through via Colenso and Onderbroek Spruit. (The literal translation is Underpants Stream.) Buller omitted this time to say when he would arrive in Ladysmith.

On the afternoon of 14 December 1899, Sir Redvers Buller advised his senior officers that he intended to attack Colenso on the following day. At about midnight they received their orders. On the left, a brigade under General Fitzroy Hart was to advance down to the river, which would be crossed at a place known as Bridle Drift, and then move along the northern bank attacking the Boer right flank. They were to be supported by two artillery batteries. In the centre, Hildyard's Brigade, supported by two artillery batteries and six naval guns, were to advance down past the village, cross the still intact road bridge before driving the Boers off the kopies that they occupied. It should be mentioned that the Boers had destroyed the rail bridge, which lay about half-a-mile downstream from the road bridge. On the right, Lord Dundonald and his Mounted Brigade, with the support of one artillery battery, were to occupy Hlangwane Hill and from there direct flanking fire at the Boers. Generals Lyttelton's and Barton's brigades were to remain in reserve to render support where required. Placed between Hildyard and Barton were some naval 4.7- and 12-pounder guns, which were available to support either advance. Buller stationed himself near these guns. The Natal Naval Volunteers under Lieutenants Anderson and Chiazarri with forty-seven men were part of the naval brigade that took part in the action. Officers were instructed not to carry swords to prevent identification by the enemy.

The Boers too had made plans for the coming battle. They had mined the road bridge with explosives but did not detonate the charges. There was a reason for this. It was the route they believed the British would follow. Louis Botha's plan was to permit the British to cross the river unchallenged, and only when they were in the open on the northern bank, would his concealed riflemen and artillery open fire and the bridge be blown up. Trapped in the open against the river, the British force would be annihilated. Because possession of Hlangwane Hill would present an opportunity for the British to outflank his forces, Botha was concerned that every effort should be made to ensure the retention of the hill. However, the individualistic Boers did not like the idea of fighting on Hlangwane as they could easily be trapped on the wrong side of the river. On 13 December, they deserted the position and nothing Botha could say would persuade them to go back across the river. Botha telegraphed Joubert in Pretoria who replied that Hlangwane must be re-occupied at all costs. Still Botha's kommandos refused to move. Finally, Botha resorted to the biblical method of selection, lots were drawn. The 800-strong Wakkerstroom Kommando was selected and at 3 a.m. on 15 December they crossed the river and took up their positions on Hlangwane.

On the 15th the British troops had their breakfast at 3 a.m. and fell in at 3.30 a.m. General Hart, who had the nickname 'No-Bobs' because he never ducked while under fire, began the day by subjecting his command to half-an-hour of parade ground drill. This preliminary over, he and his men joined the rest of the British force just before dawn as they marched towards the Tugela River. Hart rode at the head of his brigade who followed in tight columns of four. First came the Dublin Fusiliers, then the Inniskillings, the Connaught Rangers and the Border Regiment. Hart insisted that the men remain in close order. At 5.30 they heard the big naval guns firing at the Boers. The Boers made no reply. Hart continued to the river where a Zulu, apparently under the impression that he was seeking a punt to cross the river, advised him to follow the river as it turned northwards to form a loop before turning south. Though the Boers would have removed the punt, Hart seems to have been persuaded that the crossing was at the northern end of the tongue of land formed by the loop and led his men into the salient. The Boers were unable to resist the bait any longer, they opened close-range rifle fire from three sides on the Irishmen. Hart's response was to bring even more men into the salient while, sword in hand, he urged them ever forward. Some men made it into the water where most were either shot in the water or drowned. Despite the Boers having hidden barbed wire in the water, a few men made it to the other side, only to find they had no support and had no choice but to attempt the hazardous return crossing. Hart appeared to have become completely irrational and men were beginning to disobey his commands even though he threatened to shoot them.

Scorning cover and waving his sword around No-Bobs must have provided a tempting target and few would have been willing to be in his vicinity. One Colonial ignored the exceptional danger of being near Hart, who had this to say about him, 'Mr Norgate, a civilian gentleman, not called upon by his engagement to risk his life, kept near me under that heavy fire, in case he could be of any use to me; very gallant, patriotic conduct that I hope will be recognised well.' An hour or so later Norgate was injured while carrying a wounded man from the field.

Buller, from his vantage point had seen the trap into which Hart had led his men and before 7 a.m. sent a messenger down with an order for immediate retirement. He then rode down to the salient and personally confirmed his order, before riding over to General Lyttelton, who was acting as reserve for Hart's Brigade, telling him, 'Hart has got into a devil of a mess down there, get him out of it as best you can.' There was nothing Lyttleton could do other than cover Hart's retreat, which was conducted in piecemeal fashion throughout the day.

In the centre the British had fared no better. Col Long's orders were to move forward and cover Hildyard's advance. It was not indicated precisely how far he should advance, or that he should not get ahead of the attacking infantry, or indeed that he should not bring his guns within rifle range without adequate cover. Perhaps General Buller thought these were matters for common sense. Col Long had other ideas. He was going to smash up the Boers. Before 6 a.m. twelve 15-pounder horse-drawn field guns had formed up in drill formation and with Col Long and his officers riding abreast trotted forward down the long slope towards Colenso. Six 12-pounder naval guns followed but because they were drawn by oxen they were slower and were soon some distance behind the field guns. On and on went the guns. When their scouts reached the river, the guns unlimbered and prepared to 'smash up the Boers'. Estimates as to precisely how far they were from the Boers vary between 500 and 1,000 yards. They were certainly well within the range of the Boer riflemen.

The Boers had watched, with some amazement, the steady approach of the artillery. They held their fire until the British guns unlimbered before opening withering rifle and artillery fire on the unfortunate gunners. Showing tremendous courage, the British artillery stuck to their guns, though the slaughter of men and horses was terrible. Because the Boers had cunningly disguised their positions and used smokeless powder, the British artillery could not discover precisely where they should direct their fire. Nonetheless they kept firing for almost an hour until a shortage of ammunition and men to serve the guns forced them to abandon them and seek shelter with the dead and wounded in a donga a few hundred yards further back. Col Long was one of the first men wounded and was carried to shelter in the donga.

The naval guns, which had set off early that morning with Col Long, were some way behind when the firing started. They were, however, within range of the Boer artillery whose shellfire killed some of their oxen. In the resulting general chaos, the rest of the oxen stampeded. With difficulty the sailors unlimbered their guns, manhandled them into position and began a bombardment of the Boers. A gun was spotted near Fort Wylie, so they concentrated their fire on it and were delighted to see it topple over. However the Boer gunfire, instead of abating, intensified. In response the sailors set to work pulling the guns back into a safer position in another donga. The heavily laden ammunition wagons proved a difficult proposition and required that every available man lend a hand in hauling them to shelter. General Buller, who happened to be nearby, saw what was happening. He dismounted, and putting his shoulder to the wheel heaved and shoved with the sailors until the wagons had reached safety.

During this process, a spare ammunition wagon had been left behind. A local farmer, a Mr Pringle, ignoring the enemy fire, rounded up a few oxen, inspanned them to the wagon and single-handedly brought it to safety. Pringle owned the wagon and following Boer looting, it would have been very difficult to replace.

Buller had been so preoccupied with the calamity on the left, that it was only after receiving a report from one of Long's staff officers that he rode to see what could be done for the artillery. He seems to have instantly formed the opinion the engagement should be broken off. The naval guns were in a position to withdraw but what could be done about the twelve deserted field guns?

Hildyard had explicit instructions to move out with his infantry at 4 a.m. to attack the Boers at the bridge and form a bridgehead where the army could cross the river and begin the advance to Ladysmith. He and Long had failed to co-ordinate their movements and when Buller arrived at about 7 a.m. Hildyard's infantry had yet to begin their attack. Buller ordered them to advance to the left of the abandoned guns so as to provide covering fire for an attempt to extricate the guns. The infantry now advanced in exemplary fashion with a widely extended line. They passed the deserted guns and occupied the ruined houses and sheds in Colenso. Here they were able to counter Boer fire but were unable to advance any further.

Buller instructed a Captain Schofield to try to get the guns away. Schofield called for volunteers. Two officers were among the original volunteers, a Capt Congreve and Lt Freddie Roberts, only son of Field Marshal Lord Roberts. Buller had been at considerable pains to protect the overenthusiastic young Roberts and had placed him on General Clery's staff but could do nothing to save him now. When Schofield and his volunteers with two teams of horses galloped out to retrieve the guns they were met by fire as fierce as any which had been directed at the British that day. Captain Reed and two teams from the 7th Battery also joined the rescue operation. Two of the twelve guns were recovered before ever-increasing Boer fire made further sorties impossible. The slaughter of men and horses during the attempt to was appalling. One of those killed was Freddie Roberts, who rode towards the guns laughing and waving a whip in the air. When he fell Captain Congreve, who was also badly wounded, and Major Babtie of the Medical Corps, at great risk to themselves, crawled out to the unconscious Roberts and brought him to the sheltering donga. He died the next day without regaining consciousness.

By 11 a.m. Buller could stand the slaughter no longer and decided on a general withdrawal and to abandon the ten field guns. He sent a message to Hildyard to withdraw from Colenso, then rode over to the naval guns and told them to withdraw. Finally he rode across to Dundonald with instructions that he too should disengage all his men.

From the time McKenzie had drawn his attention to Hlangwane, Dundonald had felt that here lay the key to success of an attack against the Boers on the Colenso front. As we have seen, Louis Botha and General Joubert were very anxious to prevent the British from gaining control of this hill and had risked 800 men from one of their best kommandos to defend it. Dundonald had been obliged to withdraw from his brigade Bethunes Mounted Infantry for baggage and other duties, and if account is taken of the men required to look after the horses, he had no more than 600 men with rifles to carry out the attack. Not only was he outnumbered but the majority of his men were green recruits. The Boers were ensconced on a boulder-strewn hill, which made an ideal defensive position that could not easily be carried by a frontal assault. While at Frere and at a time when Buller had yet to finalise his plans, Dundonald had met a Major Elliot of the Royal Engineers who was the railway staff officer at the nearby station. Elliot asked if he might accompany a reconnaissance, which gave Dundonald an opportunity to point out to him Hlangwane and the neighbouring hills of Monte Christo and Cingolo. Elliot was impressed by the opportunity this configuration of the land offered, and drew a map of the area, while Dundonald wrote out a report on the subject. The map and report were then presented to General Buller who, apart from showing annoyance, appeared to show no interest in the suggested plan of attack. The failure of Buller to consider this option was to prove an appalling blunder, which carried a heavy price tag.

The Mounted Brigade had moved out towards Hlangwane at 4 a.m. on 15 December. The Native Intelligence Unit recruited by McKenzie reported that the Boers had occupied the hill during the night. Dundonald decided that Duncan McKenzie should remain with him, resulting in Captain MacKay taking over command of the Carbineers. Dundonald placed his portion of the Royal Artillery's 7th Battery, commanded by

Major Henshaw, on a small hill south of Hlangwane, where it was hoped it would be able to assist the Mounted Brigade on Hlangwane and if required Hildyard's advance.

Thornycroft's Mounted Infantry and a composite regiment (comprising the Carbineers, the ILH, the Natal Police some Mounted Infantry from the King's Royal Rifles and the Dublin Fusiliers), were to attack the south eastern slopes of the hill, while the South African Light Horse simultaneously attacked the southern slopes. The 13th Hussars were placed in support on the small hill with the 7th battery.

Thornycroft's MI and the Composite Regiment in their attack from the south east had only advanced about half-a-mile before they were checked by heavy fire from Boers among boulders on the hill. At 7.40 a.m. Thornycroft sent a message to say the Boers held very strong positions and not only had the advance been held up, but his right might also be threatened. Dundonald and McKenzie went to see for themselves what was happening. They found that Thornycroft's MI, the Composite Regiment and the SA Light Horse had all been checked by heavy rifle fire. Though they could hold the Boers, it was impossible to advance further without re-enforcements. McKenzie noticed the recurring problem caused by the British being unable to see things readily apparent to locals. He could see the Boer positions on Hlangwani but found they were invisible to Dundonald.[3] It takes time to learn how to notice things on the veld. This phenomenon can be seen on modern safaris when tourists generally fail to see animals until they are pointed out by a guide.

Dundonald's orders clearly stated that the 6th Brigade under General Barton should, if necessary, support the Mounted Brigade as they moved towards Hlangwane. With all his men committed, Dundonald asked General Barton for a battalion of infantry to go round to the northern side of Hlangwane and thereby threaten the Boer's retreat. Using as an excuse the fact that he did not have specific orders to do this, Barton turned down the request. Added to this the artillery with Dundonald fired 530 rounds, which were concentrated almost exclusively on assisting Long and Hildyard. Thus was lost the one opportunity the British had of compensating for the losses they suffered elsewhere on the field.

Concerned about the Carbineers, McKenzie persuaded Dundonald to let him return to his regiment and he immediately set off to locate them. He had not gone far when he discovered the Hussars had retired and had formed up behind a ridge and were sitting on their horses. The Carbineers, the ILH and a few other details were still out, so McKenzie sent a request to Dundonald asking that the Hussars cover the retreat of the Volunteers. Dundonald agreed and sent an order to that effect to the Major in command of the Hussars. 'Damn the Carbineers,' was the curt response of that officer, who ignored the order.[4]

With no help coming from that quarter, McKenzie and two companions set off to find the Carbineers, their guide being the sound of firing. They found the Carbineer horses in a donga with three men in charge of them. When asked where the Carbineers were, they pointed out the direction in which their comrades had gone. McKenzie and his companions had not gone far before they met and had a brief chat with a wounded friend, Captain Otto from Greytown, who had enlisted with Thornycroft's MI and was now being carried from the field. A little further on McKenzie was hailed by Captain Bottomley of the ILH who said, 'Hullo, Mac, where are you going?' to which McKenzie replied, 'I am looking for the Carbineers. Can you tell me where they are?' 'They are all right. I sent an orderly to tell them to retire. You had better not go on, or you won't get back,' responded Bottomley.

McKenzie now found himself alone, his companions having evidently gone towards a donga on his right. To get to the donga McKenzie had to cross some clear ground, which he was able to do with only a few shots being sent his way. In the donga he found footprints but no men and received no response to calls for the Carbineers. He decided to return to the spot where the Regiment's horses had been. He was about to experience an exciting few minutes.

Immediately I started I came under a very hot fire, and am not ashamed to say I ran as hard as I could. The heat was so great I soon got pumped and lay behind a thorn tree for a short time before going off again at full tilt. I had another rest behind an ant-heap, and then got clean out. Just as I neared the horses I saw the Carbineers coming out of the donga with their horses: they told me Capt Mackay was badly wounded in the face and Troopers Warren, Grey, Jenner and Adie had been killed, and some others were wounded, besides several missing, but these men gradually came in, and whenever we saw anyone on foot a mounted man galloped out with a horse and picked him up, and we were fortunate in picking up all our missing and wounded, and accounting for all our men before moving. Captain Briscoe of the Medical Corps got them into camp in a very short time.

The Boers did not follow up, otherwise we should have had to 'get' pretty quickly, as all the other troops had moved off, and the Estcourt squadron of the Carbineers were the only mounted men left.[5]

Captain Mackay was shot through the cheeks, just below the eyes, and was given little chance of survival. However, he made a remarkable recovery and was back with his regiment by 21 February 1900. When Mackay was hit, nineteen-year-old Trooper Frederick Charles Farmer of Weenen braved fierce rifle fire to bring him back to safety. For this Farmer was awarded the Distinguished Conduct Medal.

In the course of their withdrawal the Carbineers passed the ridge where Long's guns were standing deserted. They met an artillery man who told them what had happened. McKenzie sought out Dundonald but found that he had already left, though he did find his CSO, Major Graham. McKenzie told

Graham of a plan to save the guns, which he was confident the Carbineers would be only too willing to undertake.

The plan was to follow the donga as far as it provided good cover and then send forward about a dozen men, in extended order, who would crawl towards the guns trailing long ropes that they would secure to the guns before crawling back. In the donga other men would haul the guns off their elevated position into a little valley where there was sufficient cover to take off the ropes and hitch them to mules or horses to gallop away with them. Artillery, with infantry lying down in extended order, would have provided covering fire at very little risk. Graham replied that he could do nothing as both Buller and Dundonald had left the field. Presumably they could not be disturbed. McKenzie's plan had nothing of the dash and glamour of earlier schemes to rescue the guns, but it would have ensured that, with little loss, the guns did not fall into the hands of the Boers, who were later able to cross the Tugela without opposition and collect them.

Mc Kenzie recorded the feelings of his men after the engagement, 'we felt very down on our luck, for we realised what a terrible hash our commanders had made of everything.'[6]

The day was marked by the great courage and sacrifice of the Irish Regiments under General Hart and the equal heroism of the Royal Artillery. The British suffered 1,139 casualties −145 killed, 755 wounded and 239 missing, most of whom were captured. Almost half these casualties were suffered by the Irish regiments under Hart and most of the others were suffered by the artillery. Of the 175 artillery horses, 111 were killed and of the remaining sixty-four, only thirty-eight were unwounded. Seven Victoria Crosses were awarded, the recipients being Captain Congreve, Corporal Nurse, Major Baptie, Captain Reed, Private Ravenhill, Captain Schofield and posthumously Lt F. Roberts. Initially there was some opposition to Captain Schofield receiving the award because Buller had told him to try to rescue the guns, which was regarded as less meritorious than volunteering to do so!

Unknown to Buller and his staff an important figure in the history of the British Empire was on his way to Colenso. On 16 October 1899, in Durban, a meeting of wealthy Indian merchants and professional men decided to offer unconditionally to the Natal Government a volunteer unit drawn from the Indian community in Natal. Mohandas K. Ghandi wrote to the government about the offer stating that although the men did not know how to handle arms, there were other duties they could perform on the battlefield. The members of the government were deeply impressed by the offer, as was the former premier Sir Harry Escombe. Early in December, Sir Redvers Buller asked the Natal Government to assist in raising an Indian Ambulance Corps. A corps of 600 bearers and twenty-five leaders was rapidly assembled and at 3 p.m. on 14 December, they arrived safely at Estcourt. The following day they travelled by train to Chieveley station where they were given their Red Cross badges, and ordered to march to the Field Hospital nearly 6 miles away. During the day they could hear the sound of the battle being waged at Colenso. On arrival at the field hospital they were asked to carry wounded officers and men from the field hospital to the base hospital at the station.

Without having anything to eat, they set about the task and with three men to a stretcher they carried nearly fifty men to the hospital. It was nearly midnight before they were able to have their evening meal. The following day they carried patients from the hospital to the Red Cross train. After a couple of uncomfortable days at Chieveley, they entrained for Estcourt where on 19 December, they received orders to temporarily disband. They were thanked for their services and told that they would probably be called on again.[7]

Although Boer figures of their losses at Colenso are unreliable, they were probably about ten killed and twenty wounded. During the engagement the Boers received assistance from the Uitlander Korps. One Boer left a description of one of these men.

> I notices [sic] in the laager, an American, the most vicious looking human being I have ever seen. He glitters with knives, bayonets and revolvers; belts and ammunition were wound round him hither and thither in coils. His many weapons flashed the morning and afternoon sun all over the camp. To look at him was terrifying. I was pleased to think he was on our side. Yet I was told that during the fighting at Colenso this glittering Hector hid in an antbear hole for three days.[8]

An antbear, otherwise known as a pangolin, is about the size of a large dog.

The events of the day came as a great shock to Buller who seemed to lose his nerve completely. Though Hart and Long badly let him down he had, in fact, been quite fortunate. Long, by his reckless advance, had tempted the Boers into firing on them prematurely, and thereby destroyed Louis Botha's plan to entice the British force across the river via the still intact road bridge. Despite the foolhardy manner in which Hart had carried out his attack, he did engage a substantial portion of the Boer army, who could not have easily been moved elsewhere. Hildyard's Brigade, having finally been stirred into action, could more than hold their own. With his substantial reserves, Buller could have surrounded Hlangwane and pounded it into submission with his artillery. The Boers on the other side of the river, if there were any, could have done little to help their compatriots, and any intervention by their artillery would have put the lives of the Boer defenders at risk. In March 1900, General Botha's headquarters published a letter in the Boer press:

> An important point, and where the main attack was expected was the Langweni Hill, on the southern bank of the Tugela, which was occupied by only some 800 Boers, who were selected from the best shots.

Had the British made themselves masters of this position, they would have commanded all the Boer positions on the flank. A couple of cannon there would mean a flight to us, and victory to the British. As they were unacquainted with this position, we watched it with the greatest anxiety.

Having by his loss of nerve turned the engagement into a disaster, Buller now compounded his misfortunes by sending a series of unfortunate cables on his return to Chieveley. To the War Office he reported that he had suffered a serious reverse, followed an hour later by another telegram where he stated. 'I am not strong enough to relieve Ladysmith ... I do not think either a gun or a Boer was seen by us all day ... I consider I ought to let Ladysmith go and to occupy a good position for the defence of south Natal and so let time help us.'

He heliographed White in Ladysmith advising him that he had suffered a reverse and said it would take at least one month for him to gather a force together to cross the Tugela. He asked White how many days he could hold on and continued: 'After which I suggest your firing away as much ammunition as you can, and making best terms you can. I can remain here if you have an alternative suggestion, but unaided I cannot break in.' He went on to suggest that White should burn his cipher, decipher and code books, and all deciphered messages.

White, no doubt wondering if Buller had taken leave of his senses, sent a very firm response. 'I can make food last for much longer than a month, and will not think of making terms unless I am forced to ... the loss of 12,000 men here would be a heavy blow to England. We must not yet think of it.' London reacted promptly and immediately telegraphed Buller.

> The prosecution of the campaign in Natal is being carried on under quite unexpected difficulties, and in the opinion of Her Majesty's Government it will require your presence and whole attention.
>
> It has been decided by her Majesty's Government under these circumstances to appoint Field-Marshal Lord Roberts as Commander-in-Chief, South Africa, his Chief of Staff being Lord Kitchener.

What a tactful way to demote Buller, who accepted the situation with good grace. On the same day that Roberts received the appointment, he received the news of the death of his only son.

Whatever London might have thought of Buller, the rank and file of his army never lost faith in him for an instant. They had witnessed his courage and complete lack of concern for his own safety, and knew that at all times his prime concern was the welfare of his men. At camp in Chieveley and Frere, Buller gradually recovered his self-confidence and began to plan his next move.

The week of 10 to 17 December 1899, in which the British had suffered defeats at Stormberg and Maggersfontein in the Cape as well as the disaster at Colenso, became known as 'Black Week'. Bad as it might have been for the British, it was not an auspicious week for the Boers either. Britain decided to start recruiting Volunteers and changing their original policy, asked the Australian Colonies, New Zealand and Canada to supply mounted troops. The Colonies responded generously, and the Boers soon found themselves facing an enemy very different from the British army they thought could be driven into the sea in a few weeks.

Black people also observed the events unfolding. Their reaction was not quite what General Hunter imagined it might have been. Prior to the war, Walter Stanford had been Chief Magistrate in East Griqualand, which abutted the southern border of Natal. When Buller arrived in Cape Town it was arranged that all military questions touching the predominately black Transkeian Territories be channelled through Stanford, who effectively became a member of Buller's staff. These territories, which included East Griqualand, stretched about 250 miles down the east coast and extended about 150 miles inland to the Lesotho border. They were strategically important because they lay between the Boer forces occupying the north eastern Cape and Natal. After the disasters of 'Black Week', Walter Stanford received this letter from a man who had been a member of his staff at Mount Fletcher.

But, oh, it has grieved me very much to hear of the way brave English soldiers losing so many of their valuable lives which need not be lost. May I give some advice in my poor little opinion of what ought to be done. I am only a native but I know something or two about the Boers; and you are, in your position, able to consult with all the Heads of Departments, and might pass on what I say. I have a tearing fury in my heart and feel throttled in my eager wish to see this plan carried fully out against the Boers. I wish I were a bird with wings to fly just now to you and go to the English chiefs and urge them to what I think the best plan. The Boers are strongly entrenched in their schanzes and defended behind loopholes – good: let them starve and stew there and let the English army just watch them to keep them from any advance. And there is the Stormberg commando of the Boers in a strong position in a country they know well. Let General Gatacre watch them there: no more. Then march another army along to Bloemfontein; in full sight of the Boers; they will say, 'What is it? To get behind us? or to get to Bloemfontein?' Then they must leave, not to be enclosed or to defend the home at its centre and Gatacre will be free to march on and join his forces to the other and then the Boers in Natal will begin to shake, and one morning their camps will be empty, for all men love their wives and their children, and the oxen and the sheep, and wish not an enemy to reap their fields, and they will go to support the Free State, or to fight for their own centre at Pretoria. Why do the English try to drive straight on against the Boers where they are now in their mountain fastnesses?

The wild cat is in the hole and the bull dogs get their nose torn to pieces and their eyes scratched out, and their paws mauled and get weak losing blood, and out of breath. Watch the wild cat in the hole and dig in behind him.

That is the plan I would like to see carried out; and the Boers would have to melt away from the borders of our colonies, when they saw us doing to them in their own country what they are doing down here; and the English would win, for round Colesberg or about there, is open country on to Bloemfontein and the English swordsmen and the Lancers would have full play and work the lyddite.

I very much wish I could see the English chiefs and tell them what is in my heart and my throat is dry and tight and my mind feels a warrior's fury to see all the Boers smashed up, for they do not treat us well and we have peace and equal justice under English rule.[9]

As Buller had moved to Natal, Stanford sent the letter to headquarters in Cape Town. The two weeks following the battle at Colenso were a period of inaction as both sides attempted to digest the lessons learned. Buller awaited the arrival of re-enforcements, in the form of General Sir Charles Warren and his 5th Division. At Chieveley and Frere, Christmas was a time for festivities and sports. Among these scenes of jollity one important event appears to have passed unnoticed.

Mabizala's and Silwane's men from the Weenen district had presented themselves fully armed at Buller's headquarters and asked to join the column at Chieveley as they wished to take part in the defence of Natal. Buller's predecessor as Commander-in-Chief in South Africa, Sir William Butler, had issued an order that in the event of hostilities against the Boers, no native peoples should be permitted to bear arms against them. Buller felt bound by this order and refused to permit them to join his force. They were told to take their rifles home and come back when they would be given work as labourers. The Zulus explained that they had not come to seek work as labourers but to fight. They were then told that if they carried rifles the Boers would fire on them, which produced the riposte that that was just what they wanted! The men had no choice but to return to Weenen. Until this time, Natal Zulus and the Colonials had fought together when threatened so this action by the British army would have caused considerable resentment. Once back at Weenen, the Zulus went to see the local Natal Magistrate, Maynard Matthews, who reported to the Governor and complained bitterly at having thrust on him the unpleasant task of attempting to explain to these men why they were not permitted to join the fighting ranks.[10] Maynard Matthews would have understood the insult that had been directed at them and he also knew when the war was over, and all the British soldiers were back in England, he and his fellows would have to live with the resentment that had been created.

17

Boer Attack on Ladysmith Defences

After the night sorties against the Boer gun positions around Ladysmith, it was felt that the Boers might attempt a reprisal. At the start of the siege, the Town Guard had been disbanded – but with more manpower needed, General White embodied the Town Guard and two Rifle Associations into one unit, which provided a further 200 men who were required to defend the Klip River bank facing Bulwana. Despite their unmilitary appearance they were in all likelihood a very effective fighting force, and recognised as such by the Boers who made no attempt to attack this section of the line.

On 11 December 1899, a colonial woman was killed while washing clothes in the river. She was the first woman killed by shell fire, though some had died in childbirth.

When early on the morning of 15 December, the people in Ladysmith heard Buller's naval guns begin their bombardment, their hearts must have leapt with joy, salvation was at hand! Full of optimism, they listened all morning to the artillery and even when the firing died down, their spirits remained high. Buller had crushed the Boers and relief was on its way. However, strain as they might they could see no sign of the relief column. Perhaps it might arrive on the morrow.

At dawn the next day, the Boers subjected the town to one of the heaviest bombardments so far. This increase was attributed to the Boer's celebration of their defeat of the Zulus on 16 December 1838. However, it is more likely they were simply trying to hurry along the capitulation of the garrison. Two British soldiers were killed. One, while exercising his horse, was struck in the back by a shell that mutilated him terribly. The Boers scored another hit on the town hall and several houses were badly damaged. Henry Pearse, correspondent for the *London Daily News* gave this description of the bombardment of Ladysmith.

They have tried their hardest, though not successfully to make every house in the place untenable between sunrise and sunset, doing infinitely more damage to private property than to military defences; and they have thrown shells about some parts of the long open town with a persistence that would seem petty in its spitefulness if we could be sure that the shots strike near what they are aimed at. So long as the Boers do not violate any laws of civilised warfare nobody has the right to blame them for trying the methods that may seem most likely to bring about the fall of Ladysmith. They have, however, simply wrecked a few houses, disfigured pretty gardens, mutilated public buildings, destroyed private property, and disabled by death or wounds a small percentage of our troops, without producing the smallest effect on the material defences, or weakening the garrison's powers of endurance in any appreciable degree. Such a bombardment day after day for seven weeks would doubtless get on the nerves if we allowed ourselves to think about it too much; but happily the civilians, men and women, who resolved to 'stick it out' here rather than accept from their country's enemies the questionable benefits of a comparatively peaceful existence under the white flag at Intombi Spruit, have shown a fortitude and cheerfulness that wins respect from every soldier. Shelters are provided for them and their children, but they do not always take advantage of these, even when a bugle or whistle from the look-out post warns them a shell is coming. Ladies still go their daily round of shopping just as they did in the early days of bombardment, indeed more regularly, and with a cool disregard of danger that brave men might envy.[1]

The women did, of course, have as an example the courage of those pioneer settler women who were so brave and suffered so much after the first invasion of Natal by the Boers in 1838.

On Sunday 17 December, the Boers, showing respect for the Sabbath, did not shell the town. Newspaper correspondents were invited to the intelligence office, where they were informed that General Buller had suffered a reverse having 'failed to make good his footing'. They were requested when writing their reports not to dwell on the fever and sickness in the town. That day notices were displayed in prominent places so that the cryptic message given to the correspondents should be known to all. For more than six weeks the discomforts of the siege had been endured in the sure expectation that relief was on its way, and now hope itself seemed to be destroyed. Sickness was becoming an even greater enemy than the Boers. More than fifty members of the Imperial Light Horse had been invalided, the Carbineers had 106 men on the sick list, and ninety-six men of the 19th Hussars were down with enteric – another word for typhoid. The doctors found that if they told a patient that he had typhoid it was regarded as a death sentence. On the other hand, patients tended to believe they might recover from enteric. Thus, by calling it another name, typhoid was banished from Ladysmith.

Monday 18 December 1899, was a sad day for the Natal Volunteers. The Carbineers had just returned from outpost duty and were attending to their horses when a shell from Bulwana hit one of the horses and exploded. As the smoke cleared four men lay dead or dying and another eight badly wounded.

Eleven horses were dead or so badly injured that they had to be destroyed. One was plunging wildly among the tents with one leg shot away. Troopers Billy Buxton and R.M.M. Miller from Pietermaritzburg lay dead together, one with his legs missing. A few paces away lay two troopers from Dundee. Sixteen-year-old T. Elliott had both his legs cut off at the thigh, and lying there, he begged the orderly to pour cold water over his legs as they felt so hot. In a few minutes his life had ebbed away. Being so young, comrades had always tried to shield him from danger, keeping him in camp on one pretext or another when they went out to fight. Partly over him lay the body of Craig Smith. A couple of years older than Elliot, Craig was the grandson of Peter Smith, on whose farm the Battle of Talana had been fought. He was beginning to show real promise as a rugby player. The fathers of both boys were in Ladysmith. Craig's father was serving with the Carbineers, while Elliot's father had been sent to Intombi. Among the wounded was Trooper A. Nicholson, one of whose legs was hanging on by a piece of tendon. When the Carbineers' veterinary surgeon, Major Watkins-Pritchard, arrived at the scene one man was putting five human legs in a sack.

There were some lucky escapes among the Carbineers. Trooper H.A. Craig, also from Dundee, had three holes through his breeches but did not receive a scratch. Saddler Sergeant Lyle was sitting on a box outside his tent talking to some friends when the shell exploded. A piece of it passed through the box on which he was sitting, smashed four rifles strapped to a pole, and then went through Sergeant Major Mitchell's kit and blankets tearing his things to pieces. None of the group was injured.

A couple of hundred yards from the Carbineer's camp and across the river, an engineer had just come off duty and was lying down to rest when he was struck and killed by the base of the shell that had caused such carnage in the Carbineer's camp. A shell killed three Zulus and a colonial who were digging a trench. Another pitched among the Manchesters, killing one man and seriously wounding another and, at the other end of town, a Zulu woman was blown to pieces by another shell.

The Boers continued to shell the residential section of the town and again there were some lucky escapes. Col Hamilton and Major Ludlow were resting in the bedroom of a requisitioned house, when a shell came through the roof and though a large splinter of the shell hit the Major's bed, neither was injured. In another house a civilian named Marchant was sleeping in his room when,

> ... a shell came through the window, passed between his feet, carried on to the end of the bed and burst beneath the floor. There was not a foot of that room which was not shot torn: the floor was mostly sticking to the ceiling, yet its occupant, unhurt, climbed out of the window, bringing the sash with him, as the door was blocked with debris.[2]

To avoid enemy fire, funerals were held after dark. It was not necessary to wait for graves to be dug as there were always seven or eight already prepared. As darkness descended that evening, it was the turn of the Carbineers to make their way up the hill to the cemetery. Accompanying them were details from the Natal Mounted Rifles and the Border Mounted Rifles. Trooper Elliot's father was forbidden to leave Intombi to attend his son's funeral, as this might be considered a breach of the agreement with the Boers that residents were not permitted to leave the camp. There was no gun carriage, no band playing, no coffin, and no last volley. Each of the deceased was brought to the graveside on a field stretcher, wrapped in a brown blanket that was both shroud and coffin. By the faint light of a darkened lamp the funeral service was read, the dignified simplicity contributing to the poignancy of the burial.

Many of the Volunteers were saddened to see among the dead horses in the Carbineers camp a grey thoroughbred, Auld Robin Gray. For years he had been a great favourite of racegoers around the Colony.

On 22 December, a shell from Bulwana fell in the camp of the Gloucesters while the men were eating breakfast. Six men were killed and nine wounded, three of them seriously.

Two very capable men, Colonel Ward and his second-in-command, Colonel Stoneman, had been placed in charge of supplies in the town. They not only carried out a comprehensive survey of the stores the army had accumulated in Ladysmith but also of other food that was available. Though the leading shops maintained prices at pre-siege levels, the army requisitioned all stock they thought they might need, leaving little choice for civilians. At the auctions, prices were often too high for the locals, the principal buyers being mess-presidents of regiments. It was not long before most of the residents had used all their supplies and had to submit to army rations.

The reverse suffered by General Buller created new problems for Ward and Stoneman. Initially it was thought the siege was bound to be raised within two months, but now rations had to be reduced to cater for a longer period, and the careful accounting by Ward and Stoneman now paid off. Rations were reduced and would have to be constantly reviewed. Blacks, Indians and whites were given different rations. This was not because the authorities sought to favour one group above the others, but because they had to take into account cultural differences and the type of food to which the people were accustomed. In their basic rations, whites received fresh meat, biscuits and maize meal. Blacks received twenty-five per cent more meat than the whites and almost three times as much maize meal, but no biscuits. Indians received the same amount of maize meal as the blacks and some rice. The Indians did not receive any meat because they did not eat beef or horseflesh, the only meat available in Ladysmith where there were few, if any, sheep, thin or otherwise. The Indians seem to have had the worst deal and the blacks the best. The Regular troops probably had not acquired the taste for maize meal and this might account for them being given the not-very-appetising army biscuits. Zulu runners carrying messages through the Boer lines would probably have taken with them ukota, a meal ground from roasted maize with added salt and honey (or sugar). This mixture had great sustaining qualities, was easily carried and could be eaten dry or mixed with water.

As Christmas approached, Australian journalist Donald Macdonald reflected on how the horrors of war, flies and disease which had 'converted this town by the Klip River from a jewel set in the midst of the veldt into a den of horrors'. When fellow Australian Dr Robert Buntine called on Donald for a chat it was inevitable that their conversation should turn to home: 'How would you like to be taking a header off the springboard at St Kilda now?' 'Or riding out to Keilor on a bicycle,' suggested Donald, 'for a quiet tea at Hassed's in the evening?' 'Or sitting in the Melbourne pavilion, watching Bruce and Trumble bat?'[3] That was all part of the world outside. Perhaps the Season of Goodwill might connect them to the rest of the world and lift the air of despondency that was beginning to hang over the town.

In no man's land to the south of Caesar's Camp was a farm owned by the Bester family, who were known supporters of the Boers. The young men had joined the Kommandos investing Ladysmith and their parents were notorious spies. The British were very tardy in taking any action against them and even after they had arrested father Bester, his wife was permitted for some time to cycle into Ladysmith where she could obtain much useful information for the Boer artillery. From time to time the Boers were seen making night time visits to the farm.

At the camp of the Imperial Light Horse it was thought that, 'the military situation clearly required that the nocturnal comings and goings of the enemy in and about the homestead should be investigated, and a night raid was planned accordingly.' Details were carefully worked out. Just before daylight, the party stole out with the utmost caution and quietness. The advance guard, on reaching their objective, hurriedly but thoroughly searched the farmyard and buildings for enemy scouts and patrols, and satisfied that all was in order went about 250 yards ahead, opened out fanwise, and took cover.

So far the raid had proved disappointing, not a single prisoner, not a sign of the enemy, but as dawn broke the main body followed up, armed to the teeth – with grain bags and kerries. They dashed in with élan, and surrenders were instant and numerous, though the captured turkeys, geese, fowls, and pigs raised a pandemonium that threatened to stir the whole of the investing army into reprisals. With prisoners well guarded and shepherded with loving care, the main body withdrew to Wagon Hill, their retirement being skilfully covered by what had earlier been the advance guard.

About a dozen geese and some pigs, too mobile to be caught, were driven in military formation, before the raiding party. As they passed the officer in command of the hill, the NCO in charge reported 'All present and correct, Sir!' and the geese and pigs were duly 'taken on strength'.

Looting was frowned upon. It was thought that the High Command would not enquire too closely into the raid, but nevertheless, some sea lawyer, of cautionary habit, suggested that a fat turkey be sent to headquarters. It was not returned, nor was enquiry made regarding its next-of-kin, religion, or place of birth.

The ILH not only sent the gift to the High Command but also distributed their largesse among other regiments, gifts which were appreciated, the ILH acquiring the nickname 'The Friendlies.'[4]

For a week or so before Christmas, Karri Davies had been touring the town and buying up every toy he could find. He and Col John Dartnell were anxious to provide a treat for the children, whose life during the siege must have been pretty wretched. They came up with the idea of holding a Christmas tree party. Frank Rhodes and Major Doveton were roped in to assist with the organisation. The Walton and Tatham Hall was made available for the occasion and four trees were set up in it. A eucalyptus tree represented Australia, an acacia thorn tree South Africa, a fir tree Canada and another fir Great Britain. Regimental Sergeant Major Bill Perrin of the ILH was appointed Father Christmas. The women of Ladysmith decorated the trees and the hall, and wrapped the presents. Some in the ILH did wonder about the choice of Bill Perrin as Father Christmas, as the RSM was a robust martinet with Olympian aloofness and natural ferocity.

General White instructed Col Ward to issue full rations on Christmas Day and if possible to supply regiments with such little luxuries as raisins, something approaching Christmas fare. An auction was held in the town where some fruit, butter, eggs, poultry and other little luxuries were sold. The goods barely covered one long table but did enable the regimental cooks to acquire further ingredients with which to introduce some variety.

On Christmas Eve someone borrowed a harmonium from the Dutch church and played songs that made many Englishmen miserable with recollections of Christmas in England. The Natal Mounted Rifles amused everyone with a burlesque of a cavalry band.

> The drums, swung across the withers of the gaudiest horse in camp, were a pair of empty carbolic oil drums. The cymbals were the ends of a kerosene tin, the triangles the work of a local blacksmith, and the only instruments that by any stretch of the imagination could be called musical were the tin whistles.

Their uniform was made from gauze and tinsel, the most magnificent being that of the drum major. His baton was surmounted by a boy's spinning top. All those who heard them play were surprised that the music produced by such makeshift instruments was quite good.

Early on Christmas Day the Boers sent some shells into Ladysmith, which failed to explode on landing. On examination it was found that they had scratched on them, 'With the Complements of the Season,' and were filled with something not unlike plum pudding that had been partially cooked by the heat generated by the flight of the shells. Having wasted a few shells playing this practical joke, the Boers concentrated their fire for the rest of the day on the residential part of the town. A Mrs Kennedy was fortunate to suffer only minor injuries when a shell struck her home and burst in the room in which she was standing. The windows were blown out and the furniture reduced to a heap of wood. Fortunately, her children were away at the time.

All the churches were filled to capacity that morning, and despite the difficulties, the cooks were able to produce Christmas dinners that created an illusion of a celebratory feast. The Volunteer Regiments challenged the Regulars to various sporting contests and mule races were organised, care always being taken to remain out of sight of the Boer gunners. The mules gave a fine display of their legendary stubbornness and appeared to delight in destroying their jockeys' reputations as horsemen.

That evening nearly two hundred and fifty excited children emerged from the caves by the river and made their way to the Walton and Tatham Hall. Here they met Father Christmas who had enormous whiskers and wore a coat of white swansdown designed to keep out the Arctic chill. It had been 103 degrees Fahrenheit in Ladysmith that day. Bill Perrin radiated a bland benevolence and had become an unbelievably genial, rollicking, and realistic Father Christmas. To avoid confusion, presents were numbered to correspond with the child's ticket. As they followed Santa round the room, presents were plucked from the trees and given to the children amidst much laughter. Karri and Nurse Yeatman officiated at Australia, Frank Rhodes and Ada Craw at Great Britain, John Dartnell and Olive Barker at South Africa, and Bella Craw with Major Doveton at Canada. Mrs Kennedy, showing no effects from her narrow escape in the morning, was there with her children. Sir George White and his staff attended and joined in the fun. The general seemed delighted by the innocent joy of the children. He had not realised there were so many in the town. Some noted with sadness how thin and pale their happy little faces looked.

Karri Davies, always seeking a solution to any problem, developed a dye from permanganate of potash which turned the coats of grey horses into a shade of brown, an excellent camouflage on the veld. Noticing that his breeches had faded to a very light shade, he decided to darken them with the new product. However the dye did not react in the same way with the fabric which turned bright pink and when hung out to dry, it ran to create pink stripes.

Henry Pearse of the *Daily News* noted how Karri's 'long imprisonment with his brother officer Sampson in Pretoria, far from embittering him against humanity in general, has only made him more sympathetic with the trials and sufferings of others; just as heavy fines and a death sentence seemed to bring out the most lovable characteristics of Colonel Rhodes ... In days to come we may look back to our Christmas under siege in Ladysmith, and think that after all we had not a very bad time.'[5]

After the presents had been distributed, the trees were taken out, the floor was swept, and a dance held. As was the custom in the Colony, the older children participated in the dancing for the first part of the evening. The party broke up at 11 o'clock.

At Intombi the medical staff were struggling to treat the rapidly increasing number of people falling ill with enteric and dysentery. Many of the wounded, having recovered from their wounds went down with one of the infectious fevers. Orderlies were becoming ill and by the middle of December, the nurses were beginning to break down. Of the Volunteer nurses, Nurse Ruiter was in bed with a bad sore throat, Nurse Mary had enteric and appeared to be hallucinating, and shortly before Christmas, Nurse Early's temperature was 105 degrees and she was also sent to bed with enteric. At night, Kate Driver was the only nurse on duty in a fever ward with fifty patients and was near to breaking point.

The heat had become nearly unbearable and the storms were many. The whole camp reeked of dysentery and enteric, for our water supply was always erratic, and disinfectants were very scarce. The flies were black on the canvas of the tents. Over our heads from daylight till dark the continual roar of the big guns was exhausting to all.

Day after day our hopes were raised by rumours of General Buller's coming 'within three days' till the very sound of his name irritated one.

A day or two before Christmas there came a welcome diversion. An African carrier staggered exhausted into the Camp and dropped from his shoulders two heavy sacks, out of which rolled – oh wonderful sight – tins of condensed milk!

'*Pelindaba*!' he gasped, straightening himself up and wiping his forehead with his arm. I understood enough Xhosa to know what he meant. Pelindaba, the end of the story. Many of the tins were dented and dirty, and the man was obviously at the end of his tether. We made him sit down and someone got him a mug of soup, and bit by bit he told his story. He and two other Africans had been sent from a nearby town to try and get through the Boer lines and deliver three sacks of tins of condensed milk for the sick and wounded in Intombi. As they approached the encircling Boers and were seen, they were sniped at so hotly that one of them dropped his sack and fled. The others kept going in spurts until they were very near to the Camp. There was a burst of rifle fire and the second carrier suddenly panicked and careered back down the hill they had just climbed, his sack rolling after him. The third, this staunch man, lay waiting behind rocks. At last darkness came and the firing died down. He crawled down and retrieved the sack of his deserting fellow-carrier, and laboriously lugged the two sacks into camp at last. We were full of admiration for his courage and persistence and commended him warmly.

The milk was put into use immediately, the issue being one tin for twenty-five men for twenty-four hours. It was added to the biscuit pulp.

Sir George White had remembered us nurses, and on Christmas day had sent each of us a parcel of good things. Among these gifts were some bottles of Port Wine, some bottles of lime juice, some currants, some cornflour and a tin of tongue. The matron, without asking if we approved, put all the things into a common fund for use throughout the hospital, most of the Port wine, for instance, being used for the orderlies' Christmas dinner. At the time we merely thought she should have asked us first, as each parcel had a nurse's name on it. Later when our sick nurses were in great need of such things, we wished we had all taken our parcels! Nurse Otto, however, had had the sense to ask for her Port wine. 'It may come in useful,' she said. That bottle of Port wine was long to be remembered by me.[6]

On New Year's Day Kate began to ache all over and had difficulty getting through her round of patients. After going off duty and eating what passed for breakfast, she and Nurse Otto made their way to their to their tent. Too tired to change, Kate lay on the hard, dirty ground. Nurse Otto produced her port and the two girls had a drink, which revived their spirits, but when Kate tried to get up the world was spinning round and the tent was going up and down. When Kate tried to tell Nurse Otto how ill she felt, she found Otto appeared to be suffering from the same malady. Suddenly Kate realised they were quite drunk, which the girls found hugely amusing and laughed themselves to sleep. When Kate awoke she could hear people singing the familiar hymn, 'Hark the herald angels sing'. Listening to the hymn she thought of her mother and wondered what had happened to her brother who had enlisted with the Volunteers. She thought of 'the wives and sisters and sweethearts of men dying because of war, and of all the sad eyes of dying men'. The full force of their deplorable circumstances overwhelmed Kate and she climbed onto her bed choking with great sobs. Nurse Otto was also sobbing. They heard a pause in the service and then the start of the sermon. Another pause and the girls fell asleep. When they awoke the service was over. The Volunteer Chaplain had fainted while delivering his sermon.

When it was time for Kate to go on duty she felt giddy and weak. Otto called the Matron who took Kate's temperature and instructed her not to go on duty. A little later Dr Currie came to see her and told her that it had been arranged that Nurse Ruiter would be doing her night duty. Nurse Kate Driver had joined the sick list.

After Christmas the Boers continued their bombardment of Ladysmith, further damaging houses and other buildings and from time to time killing or seriously wounding their inhabitants. It seemed the bombardments were becoming more intense after the New Year and scouts reported that the Boers were planning an attack on the town.

On 30 December, heavy rains caused the Klip River to come down in flood. At about 1 a.m. the horse guard for the ILH reported the water was rising rapidly and had almost reached the horses. The horses were led out in batches and by the time the last horse was led out, the water was rising so rapidly that it was up to their bellies. All the horses were saved but only just in time, as the river continued to rise before subsiding almost as quickly as it had risen.

To the south of Ladysmith, and within the British perimeter, was a high ridge running from west to east. Rising about 600 feet above the Klip River plain, the ridge was about 3 miles long and consisted of three conjoined hills. At the western extremity was a boulder-strewn rise known as Wagon Point.

A dip known as Howitzer Nek linked it to Wagon Hill, also boulder strewn but with a much larger area. Finally, another dip led to Caesar's Camp, much the largest area on the ridge, being several hundred yards wide and about 2 miles long and possessing less natural cover. These hills were a key element in the defence of the town, with a commanding view of the country to the south. Were they to fall into the hands of the Boers, their proximity to the town would have provided the enemy with a position from which they could have wreaked havoc, making further resistance almost impossible.

The defence of Wagon Point, Howitzer Nek and the western portion of Wagon Hill was entrusted to the Imperial Light Horse. To their left on Wagon Hill were some companies of the 1st 60th King's Royal Rifles. The Rifles, who had lost much of their kit at Dundee, were suffering from exposure and many were sick. One of their officers was of the opinion that they were not fit for active service.

Caesar's Camp, to the east of Wagon Hill, was defended by the Manchester Regiment, assisted by the 42nd Battery of the Royal Field Artillery. Three companies of the Gordons stationed at the north eastern foot of Caesar's Camp at a place known as Fly Kraal were to act as reserves. Forty Natal Police and twenty Carbineers were stationed among the boulders and thorn trees on the flat land lying to the east of Caesar's Camp.

Because the terrain at Wagon Point and Wagon Hill provided some natural cover between boulders, it was decided to rely principally on this, rather than digging trenches or constructing complex forts for protection. At Caesar's Camp the Manchesters had to construct more complex fortifications. Because the plateau at Caesar's Camp sloped slightly downwards from north to south, Colonel Ian Hamilton, who commanded this section of the line, had sangars and a fort built along the northern edge. This meant that any attackers coming over the southern edge of the hill would be exposed against the skyline.

On the evening of 5 January 1900, the British and Colonial units took up their allotted positions along the ridge. That night C and D Squadrons of the ILH were on duty. Sickness had reduced them to a combined strength of 70 men, each squadron having approximately thirty-five members. C Squadron was led by Captain Mathias and was stationed on Wagon Hill. D Squadron was positioned on Wagon Point and was under the temporary command of Captain Richardson, on loan from the 11th Hussars.

On both hills advance posts were created. These were manned by a Corporal with three to five men, and were placed over the southern crest facing the Boers. On Wagon Point the three advance posts were manned by D Squadron while the rest of the squadron, who were to provide support, were positioned in a sangar near the northern crest. The defences on Wagon Hill were similar. C Squadron manned three advanced posts while the balance of the squadron remained in reserve at a sangar again near the northern crest. On their left the Rifles had three further advance posts with the balance of their men in a redoubt near the north eastern corner of the hill.

On the night of 5 January 1900, 'townguard' was the password for the British forces. Like the Volunteers, the Boers probably sent men forward to the British lines to listen to the conversations of the enemy sentries. If they did so they would have heard the word 'townguard' used frequently.

At nightfall Captain Richardson carried out a personal reconnaissance in the direction of Middle Hill where the Harrismith Kommando had their camp. Although he passed through the lines of that Kommando on both his outward and return journeys he did not see any Boers. Whether the Boers saw him is unknown, however in passing through the British lines he would have used the word 'townguard'.

Headquarters had decided to place a Naval 4.7 inch gun and a Hotchkiss in position on the extreme western end of Wagon Point, and this night was chosen for the task. At about 11.30 p.m. the naval gun arrived with an escort of Gordon Highlanders, a Navy gun crew of ten, and about thirty sappers who were to build the gun emplacement on Wagon Point. The Hotchkiss, manned by the Natal Naval Volunteers, was placed on Howitzer Nek. The sappers and sailors set about building the emplacement for the gun. When hostilities were threatened, the gun was taken back to a wagon at the foot of the hill.

At 2.30 a.m. Corporal Dunn at one of the ILH advance posts on Wagon Hill reported that Boers could be heard approaching. The report was received by Lieutenant Patrick Normand who immediately sent a message to Captain Mathias advising that an attack was expected, and without waiting for further instructions he at once put the rest of the squadron on alert and sent the off-duty men forward to support the picket. At 3.15 a.m. a voice called from below, 'Don't fire, we are the Ladysmith Town Guard!' Unconvinced by the ruse, the advanced posts fired a volley in the direction of the call, which seemed to check the advancing Boers, but it was not long before they heard the voice of a Boer kommandant urging his men on. The outposts soon came under heavy rifle fire, the Boers pressing home the attack with all the men and means at their disposal. The advance posts tenaciously held their original positions, firing in the dark at the flashes from the attacker's rifles, which grew ever closer. After half-an-hour, with the majority of those at the advanced posts either killed or wounded, they were ordered to retire to the sangar higher up the hill.

On Wagon Point Captain Richardson heard the firing and decided to get in touch with C Squadron. As he crossed the dip to Wagon Hill he heard voices and realised the Boers had established a footing between the two hills. To warn the others he shouted out 'The Boers are here' and was promptly knocked down by bullet which shattered his right elbow joint. In the darkness he was able to make his way back to his squadron for medical attention.[7]

In order to move silently, most of the Boers had climbed the steep boulder-strewn hills barefoot. The Harrismith Kommando from the Free State was at the forefront of the attack.

Meanwhile Captain Mathias with the remainder of C Squadron and the Naval Volunteers were able to bring the Hotchkiss into action. This checked the Boers, who were trying to break through the defence line via Howitzer Nek. Though the defence line was thin, and was steadily driven back, it remained intact and they were able to withdraw with the Hotchkiss in good order to the comparative safety of their sangar.

Both sides had at one time become so mixed up that Mathias found himself among the Boers. Able to speak Dutch fluently, he played the part of a fire-eater until darkness afforded him an opportunity to slip ahead of the attack and rejoin the remnants of his squadron in the sangar. During his stay among the Boers he heard some of the more enterprising Boers urging, '*Kom kerels, laat ons die plek dadelik bestorm.*' ('Come chaps, let us storm the place at once.') While the more cautious said: "*Nee! Die kannone sal ons koppe afskiet, ons moet liewer wag vir meer manskappe,*' (No! the cannons will blow our heads off, it would be better to wait for more men.')[8]

Lt Normand was holding Wagon Hill with determination, but was concerned about his left flank. He sent for reinforcements and received a Sergeant and thirty men of the Gordons. He extended them to his left but when he went to check on the position, he found only the Sergeant. A further request for additional reinforcements obtained another Sergeant and three men from the King's Royal Rifles. Out-flanked and hard pressed in front, Normand decided to retire his small force. Captain Mathias joined them and together they retired to the sangar where they were united with the rest of C Squadron. Troopers F. Rogers and T.C. Chadwick were killed while attempting to recover a box of much needed ammunition from their original forward post. During the withdrawal, Troopers Gorton and Shed were hit. On Wagon Point D Squadron were holding the attack but were subjected to flanking fire, which caused several casualties. Lt Adams was killed, and with Captain Richardson out of action, Lieutenant Tom Yockney took command.[9]

From the start the ILH knew from the flashes of rifle fire around them that they were hopelessly outnumbered and that their single loading rifles placed them at a grave disadvantage in close range fighting. Yet for two nightmare hours, these two depleted squadrons had held at bay six or seven hundred of the Boers' best men.

As dawn broke Normand took four or five men to occupy a rocky outcrop to the east of C Squadron's sangar. While disposing his men he saw, to his great relief, Col Edwards arriving with reinforcements.

At 4.30 a.m. Col Edwards had been awoken by the arrival of General Hunter's ADC with orders that the remainder of the regiment proceed immediately to Wagon Hill, which was under attack. In accordance with their usual practice E and F Squadrons were already 'standing to' ready to start for Wagon Hill to relieve the squadrons on night duty. Edwards left orders for B squadron to follow as soon as possible and then set off with E and F squadrons.[10] On arrival at the foot of Wagon Hill, Edwards dismounted and, after leaving instructions that the other squadrons should follow him, began the climb up the hill towards the sound of gunfire, which led him to the redoubt of the Rifles. Shortly afterwards E Squadron, commanded by Capt

Codrington, arrived. Realising that Lieutenant Normand needed assistance on Howitzer Nek, Edwards led them to the rocky outcrop occupied by Normand, who was delighted to see them. When Normand attempted to point out the Boers, he was immediately hit in the right arm. Codrington's E Squadron moved into the rocks that had previously occupied by Normand's men and opened fire on the Boers. The weight of their fire forced the Boers to leave the top of the hill and take cover under its southern slope. From this position they returned the fire of E Squadron, the distance between the two groups being about eighty yards.

F Squadron, commanded by Captain Fowler, arrived hard on the heels of E Squadron and was ordered into the gap between E on the rocky outcrop and C Squadron in their sangar overlooking Howitzer Nek.

Not long afterwards, B Squadron, commanded by Major Doveton, arrived and was ordered to occupy another rocky outcrop running north to south and therefore at right angles to the British line. The southern edge of this outcrop was only about twenty-five yards from the Boer line. So close were they that it was possible to add variety to their fighting by lobbing stones onto the rocks over the crest. Major Doveton, who did not realise how close the enemy were, exposed his arm as he raised his field glasses, and had his arm and shoulder instantly shattered by a Boer sharpshooter. Lieutenant Ned Kirk took his place as commander of B Squadron.[11]

All capable members of the ILH, numbering about 200, were now in the front line defending Wagon Point and Wagon Hill. Included in their number were some who, because of illness, were excused duty but came along in any case, and even the cooks abandoned their pots and pans and joined the fray. One of these off-duty men who joined their comrades in the line was a renowned horseman, Jack Plunkett from Roma in Queensland. He did not have time to find his khaki jacket and went out in a blue jersey. He and a companion had a long duel with three Boers in a situation where the slightest exposure brought an instant response. With patience and care each was able to get his man while the third Boer was killed by flanking fire. The sailors and engineers whose orders that night were merely to attend to the emplacement of the 4.7 inch gun enthusiastically took up positions in the defence line.

The struggle that began before dawn was to continue without break till dusk. Men from both sides lay hidden among the rocks and it was only by moving from the cover of one rock to another that either side could hope to drive the other from the hills. It was in the use of this cover and in the accuracy of snap-shooting that success or failure lay. An advance from one rock to another four feet away became a major gain. With the men on both sides moving in this way, continual concentration was vital and even then luck played a big part. A rock which had previously concealed a deadly rifle would become innocuous, while another which had been harmless all morning would suddenly spout death. Even apparent shelter did not ensure safety, as the marksmen would fire at a nearby sloping rock and rely on the ricochet to hit the concealed enemy.

The tiniest mistake could be fatal. Captain Codrington of E Squadron, while attempting to adjust his line, was shot through the liver. Corporal W. Weir, at great risk to himself, dragged the Captain to safety. He was subsequently awarded the DCM for his action. Lieutenant Douglas Campbell now took over the command of E Squadron.

Col Edwards had, since his arrival on the hill, been in the forefront of the firing line, as he felt this would enable him to observe the enemy's every move and to counteract them promptly. This inevitably resulted in a degree of exposure to enemy fire and a bullet hit him through his neck and shoulder. Shortly afterwards another bullet struck him in the buttock. He was pulled back to cover where, despite his wounds, he continued to direct operations. From his new 'headquarters' the Colonel saw a company of Gordons pass along towards Howitzer Nek but otherwise saw no attempt to strengthen the line.

At about 10 a.m., a Captain Bowen and six men of the 60th King's Royal Rifles came clambering up the hill. Colonel Edwards asked where they were going and what their orders were. 'Rush the open ground in front and clear the enemy off the edge of the hill, Sir,' was the reply. One officer and six men were expected to clear from an immensely strong natural position a formidable enemy present in overwhelming numbers. The Colonel told him it was impossible to carry out such an order, but Bowen insisted that he must try. E Squadron were ordered to provide covering fire. Bowen and his men broke cover and rushed forward. They only went a few yards before all seven were down.

To provide the covering fire, Douglas Campbell and his men had to momentarily expose themselves to the enemy. As they rose to fire, Campbell and several of the men were hit. Campbell, lying there quite motionless with a wound at the back of his skull, was covered over and left for dead. Meanwhile Lieutenant Clem Webb of F Squadron crawled forward to see if anything could be done for Bowen and his men. He found they were all dead.[12] Clem Webb was an uncle of Kate Driver.

All day the ILH Medical Officer, Major Billy Davies, oblivious to danger, had been tirelessly tending the wounded. A small man, it was said of him that he 'was five foot nothing but all solid guts'. He had worked his way back to Colonel Edwards and after he had examined him, ordered that the he be taken back to Ladysmith. Command of the regiment now devolved on Major Karri Davies.

Karri ordered the squadrons on Wagon Hill to hold their positions while he checked the situation at Wagon Point. He was wearing the breeches that had been dyed with permanganate of potash. As he darted from rock to rock, a Boer saw flashes of a pink object moving among the rocks. The inevitable duly happened, the Boer scored a bull's eye. Karri had been hit through the buttocks and was furious. Initially he refused to leave the field, but the wounds were bleeding profusely and he began to feel giddy. He had no choice but to submit to the indignity of being carried down the hill on a stretcher. At the dressing station he told the bearers to, 'hurry up and stop this bleeding, I want to get back!' and to some soldiers standing about at a loose end, 'Go on and give them hell! One of the stretcher bearers could not resist commenting, 'The Major has tough luck, only one bullet but four wounds!'[13]

It was about 10.30 a.m. and with Colonel Edwards, Major Doveton and Major Karri Davies all wounded, command of the regiment now devolved on Captain C.H. Fowler, who was to remain in command until the action closed at about 7 p.m. On taking over, Fowler also decided on a personal survey of the whole position. He found a critical situation existed along the whole length of his weakly manned front. Some twenty-five per cent of his small force had been killed or wounded. In places, as little as nine yards separated the two sides between whom was a space void of cover watched so vigilantly that almost any movement was impossible. Cramped behind their rocks the men lay on their bellies all day with the sun burning down on them. The rocks were too hot to touch and they were tortured by thirst.

There were other tragic attempts by small groups of men to storm the Boer lines. On one occasion Captain Fowler had crawled back for water and came across Lieutenant Tod of the Rifles who, with twelve men, was getting ready for one of those futile charges. Tod knew he had no chance of success but was determined to go, so all Fowler could do was to advise him of the positions of the ILH and the Boers. Fowler watched them start and saw Tod drop dead before he had gone half a dozen paces. Many of his men suffered the same fate.[14] Two other officers in the Rifles, Major Macworth and Lieutenant Raikes, led similar futile charges and both were killed. Some survivors were able to crawl back and reinforce the ILH line.

A typical example of the manner in which this small force was able to hold at bay the much more numerous enemy was provided by a Trooper of F Squadron, Ogilvie Norton, a young Natal farmer. He was able to wriggle unobserved into a position behind some boulders, which protected him from the south and east while giving him a view towards the west over an area not yet occupied. He anticipated that if the enemy were to advance they would cross that ground, so sitting behind his rocks he carefully watched for any sign of movement and patiently waited and waited. Eventually, three Boers crept stealthily into his field of fire without being aware of his presence. Three successive shots accounted for all three, without them or anyone else knowing from whence the shots had come.[15]

Both sides utilised their artillery. However, apart from the efforts of the sailors to carry out infantry duties, the gunners were able to contribute little to the outcome of the battle on this part of the battlefield because of the nature of the land and because the two sides were so closely engaged. Colonel Ian Hamilton attempted to organise a movement to outflank the Boer left. This came to nothing though it did frustrate an attempt by the Boers to outflank the British right. Throughout much of the day, Frank Rhodes was seen attending to the wounded.[16]

At 3.30 p.m. a violent storm broke and torrential rain provided a curtain that hid each side from the other. The Boers, believing this provided an opportunity to launch an attack, charged towards the ILH sangar on Wagon

Hill. However, the line held and as the rain slackened many Boers were caught in the open and provided easy targets for the Light Horsemen. Perhaps to create a diversion, fifty Free State Burghers threw themselves into a reckless rush towards the main sangar on Wagon Point. Such was the impetus of the attackers that they swept aside a detachment of the Gordons and in seconds were at the low stone walls of the sangar. Though some of the more recent arrivals in the sangar fled down the hill, bitter hand-to-hand fighting now ensued. Lieutenant Digby-Jones of the Royal Engineers shot the foremost Boer at point blank range. Trooper Albrecht, ILH, shot a Veld Kornet and another Burgher who was about to shoot Digby-Jones. Albrecht was then shot by a Burgher, who was shot by Digby-Jones, who in turn was shot by another Boer. One sapper had his rifle wrested from him by a Boer, who he promptly felled with a blow from a shovel. For a minute or two the desperate hand-to-hand struggle raged but the steadfast defenders fought on, countering every move by their attackers. Unable to overcome the defence, the Boer attack faltered and they retired to the shelter of the rocks near the crest.[17]

C Squadron in their sangar on Wagon Hill had watched the whole dramatic encounter. Because of the intermingling of the enemy with the defenders, it was impossible for them to fire but when the retreat began, they inflicted severe losses on the retreating Boers. The Boer attack on Wagon Point and Wagon Hill had been broken and in Ian Hamilton's opinion, they were waiting for darkness when they would withdraw.

After the failure of this final attack on the ILH line, Kommandant de Villiers told a clergyman, J.D. Kestell, that as he had lost at least a third of his men, killed or wounded, they would withdraw as soon as it became dark.

Over on Caesar's Camp the Manchesters had taken up their positions on the night of 5 January, and must have hoped for another peaceful night. At about 3.30 a.m. they heard the sound of firing coming from the direction of Wagon Hill but as there was almost constant firing at some point on the defence perimeter, they paid little attention to it. Unknown to them, the Boers, having stripped off their shoes, were quietly climbing the southern and eastern slopes of the hill. They reached the crest well before dawn and made their way along the southern and eastern crests, apparently with the intention of attacking the picket at the extreme north east of the hill and thereafter rolling up all the other pickets on the northern crest. They attacked the pickets but met stern resistance. The Manchesters fought back heroically and though their first picket appeared to have been overrun, the Boers could get no further.

The fighting on Caesar's Camp that day was spread over a wide area, and was between fairly small groups of men who each had a different perspective as to what was happening. It would be impossible to give an account of what each unit did and how it affected the eventual outcome. A general summary of the day's proceedings is that the Boers attacked and were driven off Caesar's Camp but clung to the southern and eastern edge until nightfall, when they retired.

At about 4.15 a.m. Colonel W. Royston of the Natal Volunteers received a telephone call advising him that the enemy were making an attack on Caesar's Camp. He immediately dispatched eighty men of the Natal Mounted Rifles, under Major Evans, to assist the Natal Police, who were under attack in the broken country below the eastern end of Caesar's Camp. Although outnumbered, the Police detachment under Sergeant Woon, who had been wounded, held out until the NMR reinforcements arrived. Thus reinforced, the defenders were able to stop any further advance by the Boers on this section.

With arrangements to secure the left flank completed, Col Royston, accompanied by the balance of the Natal Mounted Rifles and the Border Mountain Rifles under Lieutenant Colonel Rethman (promoted in spite of his forthright manner and tendency to express his opinions) rode out to Caesar's Camp. Arriving at about 5 a.m., they could see Boers swarming over the south eastern slope right up to the crest, and it appeared they were intent on working their way round to the rear of the Manchesters. A party of Gordons could be seen among the rocks near the extreme north eastern corner of the hill. Two squadrons of the Border Mounted Rifles under Col Rethman were ordered to support the Gordons, while a third squadron under Captain Jack Royston was ordered to push forward on the eastern slopes. Rethman's men were able to rendezvous with the Gordons under Captain Carnegie, but came under a hot fire as soon as they attempted to advance. The BMR detected a suspicious movement on their right front and a shot was sent in its direction, whereupon a man wearing a uniform similar to theirs, jumped up and shouted, 'Don't shoot, you bloody fools. We are the Town Guard.' For the second time that night the Boers used the British code 'townguard'. The Volunteers dropped their guard for a second or two and a number of Boers showed themselves about fifty yards away shouting 'Hands up you Bastards, we've got you now,' while at the same time a volley was fired killing Troopers Fox, James Gold, Jim Lawson and Percy Hulley, all of the Border Mounted Rifles.

The 53rd Battery had been brought forward into a position where they had a clear view of the enemy, and opened fire on the Boers with devastating effect. The Manchesters, the Gordons, the Rifles and the BMR advanced, while the artillery, by lengthening their fire, followed the retreating Boers until they were driven off the crest.

Once they had retired over the crest, the Boers were able to find cover among the boulders and rocks that covered the area, thereby checking any further advance. On the left, Major Jack Royston was able to drive the Boers back until they too were able to take shelter in the rocky terrain. An exchange of rifle and artillery fire was to continue between the two sides until darkness came, when the Boers retreated back to their lines.

It was a particularly hot day and Trooper Martin of the BMR was detailed to fetch some water for the regiment. Taking as many water bottles as he could carry he made his way to the water point on the sheltered side of

Caesar's Camp. There he found a number of officers, one of whom, a major dressed in the uniform of the Gordon Highlanders, said, 'Hey Ginger, where are you from?' Martin told him and after he had explained that the Gordons were fighting alongside the BMR, he was asked to guide the officers to the front line. Martin loaded himself with the water bottles and following a route sheltered from enemy fire took the officers to a spot where he was able to point out the positions occupied by the Boers. One officer immediately contradicted Martin by looking in the direction indicated and announcing, 'no Boas thar', which in his opinion finalised the matter.[18]

For most of the day the only surgeons on Caesar's Camp were Dr Hornabrook and Dr Wood of the Manchesters, both of whom were to be wounded before the day was over. At one point Dr Hornabrook attended to a Natal Volunteer, a King's Royal Rifleman and a Manchester private, all lying within a few yards of each other. When he went a little over the side of the hill to treat a Gordon Highlander, the wounded man said, 'Don't come here, sir, they'll knock you over.' Hornabrook nonetheless went to treat the man, and received some shots through his clothes and another in his side just above the hip. In spite of his own wound, he continued to treat the wounded until Major Hyslop, his commanding officer, ordered him back to camp.[19] Robert Buntine had by now joined the medical team on Caesar's Camp and like the others, did not hesitate to treat the wounded while under fire. He was able to save one man's life by performing an emergency tracheotomy during the battle.[20]

On Wagon Point, Col Ian Hamilton received orders to clear the enemy off Wagon Hill, for which task the Devonshire Regiment were being sent to assist him. Lieutenant Colonel C.W. Park of the Devonshire Regiment was about to have what he described later in a letter to his wife as 'the most terrible experience of my life'. At 4.p.m. Park had received orders to proceed at once with all available men to Wagon Hill. There were three companies in their camp and in a few minutes Park had them fallen in and marching. He had with him five officers and 184 men and arrived on the hill at about 5 p.m. In his letter Park gives a vivid account of the events that followed.

> I reported to Colonel Hamilton and asked what he wanted me to do, and he said, 'Well Park, there are about fifty Boers holding a small ridge of rocks just in front of the line we are holding here, and only one hundred yards off; they have been there all day and are picked shots, and we cannot get them out. We have our men on three sides of them, but they are all under cover of the rocks and pick off our men, if they show even their heads. If you turn them out we will give you anything in the world. The only way is to rush them with the bayonet; can you do it?' Of course, I could only answer that we would try. We settled details, and I then formed up the companies in column, close behind one another, as there wasn't room to form line in the little hollow in which we were. We fixed bayonets and charged magazines, and I explained to each company exactly what we had to do, and when all was ready Colonel Hamilton

said, 'Go on, and God Bless you,' and away we went, the men cheering and shouting for all they were worth. The first few yards we were under cover, but when we reached the top of the crest line we were met by the most awful storm of bullets. I have never heard such a hot fire in my life, and can only compare it to the crackling of a dry gorse branch when thrown into a fire. We then saw for the first time what we had to do. The little ridge of rocks which the Boers held was in front of us and between us and it was 130 yards of open flat grass without the smallest cover or shelter of any kind. The men behaved most splendidly; every man went as straight and hard as he could for the enemy's ridge, and there wasn't any sign of checking or wavering, though, as I ran, I could see men falling like ninepins; and then at last, to my intense relief, when we were within about fifteen yards of them, I saw Boers suddenly jump up, turn tail, and fly down the hill for their lives, and the position was ours.

After a minute or two, when we had got settled down in the position and I had time to look around, I realised that not only had we lost heavily in the charge, but that we were still exposed to a heavy cross-fire from both flanks, from which we suffered severely. Just then Lafone remarked that he wished someone would tell the Imperial Light Horse fellows, who were holding a little ridge behind us, to fire at the Boers on our left front, and without a word, Masterson jumped up and ran back across the open through the hail of bullets to give the Imperial Light Horse the message, and though he was badly hit by at least three bullets in both thighs, he managed to reach them and give them the message, before he collapsed. It was a splendidly brave thing to do, and I have strongly recommended him for the VC.

Very soon after that I was watching Lafone, who had got a rifle and was sniping at Boers, when I suddenly saw a little hole come in his head just above his right ear, and he just sank down as he sat. I crawled over and found him quite dead, poor old fellow, and a little further on I found poor Field, also lying dead. Walker [of the Somersets] had been shot dead during the charge, and about fifty-two men were either killed or wounded, and I was the only officer left. It was about 5.30 or 5.45, and there was nothing for it but to hang on where we were till dark. The rain and hail had poured down all the time and I had no coat of any sort, and I lay behind a rock fairly blue with cold. The time passed somehow, and never was darkness more longed for, and when at last it came the Boers gave us a final burst of firing for about a minute, which did no harm, and then bolted down the hill finally beaten, and their attack had failed.[21]

The Reverend J.D. Kestell afterwards wrote a description of the Boer withdrawal:

We had been on the hill for sixteen hours under a most severe fire and now we retired; but we were not driven off by the Devons with levelled bayonets as I have read in the English book. We were not driven off the hill. We held it as long as it was light and when twilight fell Kommandant de Villiers considered it useless to remain there. He stopped there till the last man had gone then fired some shots, not however at the Devons advancing with fixed bayonets, but in the air, in order to make the English think we were still in our positions.[22]

Kestell, who came from Devon, was pastor of the Dutch Reformed Church at Harrismith and acting as chaplain to the Free State Kommandos, had been on the field throughout the day tending to the wounded irrespective of their nationality. He dressed the wounds of several ILH men and by stopping the flow of blood, prevented their bleeding to death. Among those saved by him was Sergeant O'Flaherty, ILH, a noted classical scholar and a talented writer and journalist.

As far as the exigencies of the situation allowed, the dead and wounded were taken from the battlefield that night, though many could not be moved until the next morning. On the following day, a truce was declared to enable both sides to collect their dead and wounded. The wounded were collected and given what emergency treatment was possible before being taken to hospital. Many had died of exposure during the night and many were to die during the following few days. Most of the Boers helped with the wounded regardless of which side they were on. But there was also evidence of other behaviour. An Imperial Light Horseman was found with a belt around his neck, having apparently been strangled. Elsewhere a Gordon Highlander was found without any gunshot or stab wounds, having been beaten or kicked to death.[23]

For the burial parties it was a most gruesome experience. Many of those killed by shells were so badly mangled that it was impossible to move their bodies and they were buried where they were killed. For the others, the place chosen for their burial was a grass-covered spot on the northern slope of Caesar's Camp.

The dead in each corps were laid out shoulder-to-shoulder, side-by-side in neat lines next to the long, shallow graves that were being dug. They were lying on their backs, their young faces looking up into the sky where high above the vultures were circling. Friends and comrades walked down the lines making their last farewells to companions. Some stopped and cut off a button or other small item that could act as a memento of the dead man. When the graves were ready, the bodies were wrapped in blankets and placed in the graves. The various units formed up. Sir George White stood bareheaded with the Chaplain at the graveside. The gravediggers stood by with their shovels. The Chaplain began, 'I am the resurrection and the life, saith the Lord'. Then he stopped. He had noticed movement under one of the blankets.

The body was immediately taken out of the grave. It was Lieutenant Douglas Campbell, who was in the process of regaining consciousness. It will be recalled that not long after he had assumed command of E Squadron of the ILH, he had fallen while attempting to provide covering fire for one of the disastrous British charges on Wagon Hill. As he was about to fire, a bullet had hit him in the nostril and come out at the back of his skull. The high speed Mauser bullet would have cauterised the wound as it passed through his head. He was knocked out but miraculously, no vital organ was damaged.

This was not the first time Campbell had narrowly missed being killed. He had been wounded at Elandslaagte, and, on another occasion, an afternoon nap had been disturbed by a shell landing in his tent without exploding; and now he had survived a bullet through the head. He was later to joke that it would take more than a bullet through the head to kill a Scot. Though he could trace his lineage back to Scotland, his family had emigrated to Australia where they had prospered. By the middle of the nineteenth century his grandfather, Robert Campbell, was able to return to Britain and buy the Oxfordshire estate, Buscot Park. No doubt Douglas had come to Africa seeking adventure, which he had certainly found. He was taken with the other wounded to Intombi Hospital.

British and Colonial units suffered 424 casualties of whom 175 were killed and 249 wounded. Five men were awarded the Victoria Cross:

Lieutenant R. Digby-Jones, Royal Engineers (posthumous);
Lieutenant J. Masterson 1st Btn. Devonshire Regiment;
Private J. Pitts, 1st Btn. Manchester Regiment;
Private R. Scott, 1st Btn. Manchester Regiment;
Trooper H Albrecht, Imperial Light Horse (posthumous).

After being orphaned, Herman Albrecht had been adopted by a colonial farming family in the North Eastern Cape. He grew up to be a tall, shy young man who excelled at cricket and swimming and was a fine horseman. At seventeen he was driving a post cart and supplementing this income by breaking in difficult horses. Like many other youths in that area he felt the glamour of Johannesburg calling, so off he went to the big city. A year or so later, with war threatening, he and his friends from Johannesburg travelled to Natal and joined the Imperial Light Horse, which was then being formed in Pietermaritzburg. He was one of those indomitable spirits in the ILH who had repulsed the Boer attack on Wagon Point, and had played an important part in rallying other auxiliary units who showed signs of disintegrating during that attack.

In recognition of the gallantry they displayed throughout the day, four officers of the ILH received the DSO:

Surgeon-Major W.T.F. Davies,
Captain C.H. Fowler,
Lieutenant P.H. Normand, and
Lieutenant G.M. Mathias.

The Imperial Light Horse suffered sixty casualties, of whom twenty-nine were killed or died of wounds, and thirty-one were wounded. Lieutenants W.F. Adams and J.E. Pakeman died on the battlefield and Major Doveton was later to die of his wounds. Trooper "Dicky" Gorton, ILH, a provincial rugby player from Pietermaritzburg, was one of the first men wounded. As he lay on the battlefield he was to receive a further twelve wounds. When being carried away on a stretcher he was able to give a cheery smile and a mute wave to his comrades. He died four days later.

Colonel Edwards, Major Karri Davies and Lieutenant Normand recovered quickly from their wounds. Captain Codrington lay for some time between life and death but he eventually recovered and was able to return to active life, which included commanding the 1st Motor Machine Gun Brigade in the First World War. Douglas Campbell, now a Captain, made an incredibly rapid recovery and was back in mess six weeks later.

The Boers did not keep records of the number of Burghers killed and such information as they released on the subject always tried to play down their losses. They probably had in excess of 100 killed and 200 wounded. Their memorial on Caesar's Camp covers the remains of 310 Burghers who were re-buried there.

On 8 January, General Buller heliographed General White congratulating him on the gallant defence of Ladysmith and giving special praise to the Devons. Shortly afterwards a similar heliograph was received from the Queen in which she also expressed the nation's gratitude for the part played by the Devons. Neither message mentioned the Imperial Light Horse. In an attempt to correct the omission, Col Hamilton wrote an official letter to the commander of the regiment.

> I write this line to let you and your brave fellows know that in my dispatch it will be made clear that the Imperial Light Horse were second to none. No one realises more clearly than I do that they were the backbone of the defence during that long day's fighting. Please make this quite clear to the men. To have been associated with them I shall always feel to be the highest privilege and honour.[24]

18

Maladministration of Dundee

On the day following the battle at Wagon Hill, Sir George White sent a heliograph to General Buller. 'Troops here much played out, and a very large proportion of my officers have, up to date, been killed or wounded, or are sick. I would rather not call upon them to move out from Ladysmith to co-operate with you; but I am confident the enemy have been severely hit.' A few days later some of the men attempted to play a game of cricket, but abandoned it after ten minutes because they all felt too weak to continue. The reduced rations were debilitating for everyone and from now on, there was little to relieve the monotony of the long, hungry days as they waited for the arrival of the relief column.

For the Imperial Light Horse there was one pleasant surprise. On 11 January, Dr Davies brought Aubrey Woolls Sampson back from Intombi. He was driven into the ILH camp in an ambulance wagon and received a great reception from the men. His wound had healed but the damage to his femur ensured that he was still unable to walk. He set up his quarters in the ILH dugout, where he received a constant stream of well-wishers. Col Ian Hamilton was one of his frequent visitors as the dugout lay between his bivouac on Caesar's Camp and Sir George White's Headquarters:

> I always found time to look in upon Woolls Sampson. Usually there were two or three others present, and if, as was sometimes the case, they had come there with the idea of heartening and cheering Woolls Sampson they found themselves walking away with the boot on the other foot: they, not he, were to get the pick-me-up; The hale and hearty were to drink freely from the wounded hero's inexhaustible cellar of that wine of victory, The Will to Win.[1]

The tonic he provided was desperately needed by the despondent, ailing garrison. The hospital at Intombi had been established to cater for 300 patients. At the end of November there were, in addition to the wounded, fifteen cases of enteric and seventy-two cases of dysentery. At the end of

December there were 441 cases of enteric and 361 cases of dysentery plus, of course, the wounded. Most of the patients were compelled to lie on the bare earth and if this was not bad enough, the shortage of food, particularly of such items as fresh vegetables, made recovery difficult for all but the strongest constitutions. During the last week of November, five people died of disease. By the end of December the weekly death rate had increased to twenty-three and was continuing to accelerate.

Journalist Henry Nevinson also had some difficulties. The empty shops could no longer sell him the luxuries to which he was accustomed; the blacks continued to be reluctant to carry his dispatches and the persistent rain was washing away his description of Natal as a desert. However, his hostility towards Colonials continued unabated. Without any evidence to support his opinions, he sent out a stream of vulgar abuse directed at the locals. The Town Guard in their civilian clothes and obsolete rifles were an easy target for his sarcasm, 'Tonight the civilians of the Town Guard went on picket by the river, and bore their trials boldly, though one of them got a crick in the neck.'[2] What a nasty unfounded suggestion of cowardice this is. He must have been getting desperate for derogatory copy about colonials, when just before Christmas, a woman made a complaint to Col Stoneman about alleged theft at Intombi Camp. Nevinson plunged in, 'the sick are robbed or murdered by a mob of cowardly Colonials of the rougher class, who had not enough courage to stay in the town, and now turn their native talent for swindling to the plunder of brave men who are suffering on their behalf.'[3] On 27 December, he continued,

> The 18th Hussar officers at Christmas gave up a lot of little luxuries, such as cakes and things, which count high in a siege, and sent them down to their sick at Intombi. Not a crumb of it all did the sick receive. Everything disappeared en route – stolen by officials, or sold to greedy Colonials for whom the sick had fought.[4]

We know from Kate Driver's diary that Christmas treats at Intombi hospital were pooled and divided among all the patients and staff. Nevinson made such a big fuss about the issue that General White sent Colonel Stoneman to Intombi to investigate what was happening.

Colonel Stoneman saw no evidence of the robbery and murder of patients though he did find a general want of organisation both in the distribution of food and in the care of patients. Colonel Exham, who as the Principal Medical Officer was responsible for these shortcomings, pointed out that it would cost money to provide a bed for each patient and that he could not use all the medicines, as the regulations required that each medical facility should always have stocks of certain supplies. Stoneman was not impressed by these arguments, being of the opinion that the people of England would be happy to spend a few thousand pounds to provide a little comfort for the sick, wounded and dying. He ordered that further beds and bedding be sent to Intombi immediately. In addition, he put in place a proper plan for the distribution of food and medicines.

Given the very mixed collection of people who had been press-ganged into working at Intombi, there might have been some petty thieving, however, it would seem to have been of very minor importance. Kate Driver found the service provided by her orderlies on arriving at Intombi to be poor. The men had been recruited and trained in Pietermaritzburg as stretcher-bearers and resented having to work in the hospital. She set about teaching them their new tasks.

They watched while I sponged one man. He was a malaria patient. 'I'm sweatin' heavy sister,' he said. The man in the next bed turned his eyes towards us and said huskily, 'You don't say "sweatin" to the sister. You say perspoirin.' The laughter helped, and by now the boys had got some idea of what was required of them. I never once after that night had to ask either of them a second time to do anything, much as they hated fever work. They were splendid, these two Volunteers of the Pietermaritzburg Ambulance Corps.[5]

It seems Colonel Exham wasn't happy with Colonel Stoneman's response to the conditions at Intombi, so he asked his friend Henry Nevinson to visit the Camp and give a fair account of what he found. Nevinson applied to Sir George White for permission to visit Intombi. The application was refused, it being stated that the agreement with General Joubert provided that only medical and commissariat officers should visit the camp. It was subsequently found that Exham was diverting supplies, such as bottles of brandy and sago, from the hospitals to his friends among the journalists and others he considered had influence. These items would be indented for use in the hospital and then passed on to Exham's friends. In this manner, the hospital records gave the impression that the stolen supplies had been consumed in the hospital. Blaming the colonials would provide an additional excuse if anything went wrong.

Among the sick sent to Intombi at this time was Lt Robert Samuelson, who had organised the Native Scouts during the early stages of the war. Robert was laid low by dysentery on 5 January 1900, and though he resisted the idea of being treated at Intombi, he eventually had no choice but to submit to transfer to the camp. After long weary days in the hospital on rations, which were constantly being reduced, he was able to get on his feet, toddle about and think of returning to Ladysmith. It was then that enteric struck. He had no pain but as he lay in bed he felt he was quietly fading away. He joined the category of patients who were not expected to survive. The chief nurse occasionally came to talk to him and one day she asked him what he thought were the ingredients of the gruel he was fed. 'Bad arrowroot' was Robert's guess. The nurse smiled and said, 'It was made of violet powder and starch.'[6]

At this low point in his life Robert was visited by a friend from the civilian camp across the railway line. This friend knew of some unsieved Amabele (millet) meal at the civilian camp, which Robert was welcome to try. Some of this meal was secretly boiled up for him. He ate it in small quantities and in two days he began to feel life returning. He sent a message through to his old friend Lieutenant Ben Sparks of the Carbineers to try to obtain some more of this meal. Sparks was able to obtain a little of it. In a few days Robert began to feel much better and in due course felt strong enough to return to Ladysmith. He set off to find Dr Sam Campbell, one of the doctors with the Natal Volunteers. Let Robert describe what happened next.

> I came across a monster in human form, and this was one of the Doctors in the camp. I hope he is still alive and will read this particular book, and shed tears of shame and remorse. The first person I met was a European male dressed in his ordinary clothes, and to him I said, 'Will you please tell me where Dr Campbell is?' The answer was 'Why did you not salute me?' I replied, 'I asked a civil question and expect a civil answer.' He said, 'Do you know who I am? I am Colonel So and So, Doctor So and So,' here he reeled off his titles and I felt inclined to ask him the next question by applying my Bootmaker to his Tailor.

However Robert was too weak to do anything more than turn his back on him and walk towards some tents. This rude and pompous person could only have been Col Exham who, as Principal Medical Officer, was the only doctor in Ladysmith to hold the rank of Colonel. At the tents Robert found Dr Sam Campbell, 'thin and worn, but as manly, kind and considerate as ever. He examined me and to my delight declared that I was fit enough to return to Ladysmith, giving me a certificate to that effect. He cut up some meat he had into thin slices, gave it to me to chew, and then gave me a kind handshake and a cheery "goodbye," and the next day I returned to Siege Town.'[7]

Col Exham was permitted to continue in his post as Principal Medical Officer. This failure by the Military Authorities to take prompt action against him was to cost Britain dearly later in the war, when as PMO in Bloemfontein his maladministration resulted in even more deaths from disease than in Ladysmith.

Throughout this period Robert Samuelson's scouts had been providing valuable information both for the besieged garrison in Ladysmith and the relieving column. One of these scouts, Mdaweni, was sent by Samuelson with a dispatch for General Buller. On his return he was seen near Spion Kop by the Boers, who set off after him. Seeing this he put his horse into a fast trot and made for a church. Before the war he had preached there, and on arrival he told the bell ringer to ring up for church, while he entered the pulpit. Being a Sunday the local people hastened to church, as did the Boers, who came inside and sat there for a short while, and then left. It seems they had decided that the preacher was late for the service and this had caused him to hurry along.[8]

One of the scouts active during the siege was Teise Ndlovu. It will be recalled that he gave that interesting account of the part played by Mrs Kruger in encouraging her husband to go war. Riding a small black Basotho pony and armed with an assegai carried in a leather sheath strapped over his shoulders, Teise would ride up to the Boer lines and relieve them of some of their cattle, which he would drive back to Ladysmith and hand to the military. He was given £5 for each batch he brought in. He was able to carry out six of these daring raids. From time to time, he was sent on errands to deliver messages to people in Boer-occupied country. On one occasion he was spotted by Boer scouts and only escaped arrest by plunging into a pool and hiding among the reeds. On another he was captured by the Boers, tied up and given into the care of their Sotho servants, preparatory to his being shot the next day. That night the Sotho guards told Teise that they were not going to see their countryman shot so they loosened his bonds and so enabled him to escape.[9]

On the night the Volunteers made their successful attack on the Boer guns at Gun Hill, Teise and a companion, who was to act as a guide, set out on a mission to damage the railway line near Waschbank Station and thereafter establish a line of communication between Ladysmith and Pietermaritzburg with the help of Zulu leaders. Teise took with him letters written in Zulu by Robert Samuelson, which were addressed to the various Chiefs along the proposed route. While passing through the Boer lines around Ladysmith they heard Boer horses snorting and coming their way. Teise's companion bolted. The more experienced Teise lay quietly and let the Boers pass before moving on. On his return, he gave an account of what happened.

> I heard the firing on Gun Hill, but did not see my companion again. I gave up going to Waschbank and arranging with the Chiefs communications, as I did not know the country, and instead I kept near to a Boer kommando that was moving towards Weenen, and then eventually called at the Kraal of Chief Bande, near Mhlumayo Hill, who asked me how the Authorities were faring in Ladysmith, expressing a desire to send provisions if it could be arranged. He gave me this man [indicating a tall Zulu who accompanied him], who is his uncle, to come and see what can be done.

Chief Bande's uncle was taken to the military authorities who thanked him for his efforts and asked him to thank Chief Bande for his thoughtfulness. However, they thought it would be impossible to carry out the project safely. Initially this uncle of the Chief attempted to get home alone but, after narrowly avoiding capture, he returned to Ladysmith the next day. It was decided that Teise should accompany the visitor on his return journey, a task that was completed successfully. Teise was back on duty in Ladysmith a few days later.[10]

When the British marched out of Dundee they had left behind 195 wounded, who were cared for in two field hospitals and in the buildings of the Swedish Lutheran Mission. In charge of the hospitals was Major F.A.B. Daly, who was assisted by a local physician, Dr Galbraith. The orderlies came from the Irish regiments and were a cheerful, hardworking bunch. A number of local residents worked as volunteer orderlies; prominent among them was T.H. Brokensha, a Justice of the Peace. Shortly after the British army had left, the field hospitals moved to a piece of vacant land adjacent to the Swedish Mission, a sensible move that benefited both the staff and the patients. With local people helping in the hospital, it became a focal point for many of the residents.

There were about 250 residents still in Dundee when the army left, including were eight women and thirty-two children. Some stayed to protect their businesses or property, while others, such as W.H. Tatham, believed they had nothing to fear from the Boers. Many were surprised by the speed of the Boer advance and being uncertain what they should do, did nothing. All were soon to discover what it was like to live under Boer rule.

To administer the town the Boers appointed a *Vrederechter* (Administrator) who set up his headquarters in the Town Board offices. The Transvaal flag was run up outside the building and it was announced that Dundee was now part of the Transvaal. The *Vrederechter* had wide executive and judicial powers. It was not long before Proclamations and Notices began to flow from this functionary's office. Residents were required to register with him; a permit was required to buy goods from the two shops still open; no one was allowed on the streets after 7 p.m. or to travel more than 3 miles from Dundee; looting was prohibited, though this prohibition apparently did not apply to the Boers. He had the discretion to decide to whom a proclamation applied, and how it should be interpreted and enforced.

During their first phase of looting, the Boers concentrated on the various businesses but after a week or two they turned their attention to the houses. Vicar Gerard Bailey described the despoliation of the town.

> Every house they could get into was looted. They made no distinctions. The Convent House of the Roman Catholic Sisters, and the residences of the Presbyterian and Wesleyan ministers suffered with the rest. The work of destruction and robbery was carried on in several ways. There were those who entered the houses and out of pure wickedness smashed and broke up everything they thought fit, even going so far as to wrench mantelpieces from their place and break them up. There were others who came with wagons and carted away furniture wholesale; others who occupied houses, and on leaving carried off all they could, especially linen and clothes. At the end of January what was left in unoccupied houses was removed and placed in a large hall, the new Masonic Hall. Why this was done, I do not know, but this is certain, that the furniture was so roughly handled and so thrown about that much of it was entirely spoiled.
>
> After this, when new officials or would-be residents arrived, they were taken to the hall and allowed to pick out the furniture they wished for the houses allotted to them. I am sorry to say that the nurses of the Boer

ambulances were as big a thieves as any. Of this I have plenty of proof. The Boers, especially the women, appeared to look upon the town as legitimate spoil. A friend of mine happened upon some deliberate thieving. The woman defended herself by stating that she had a right to take what she liked as all now belonged to the government. 'Well, then,' said my friend, 'I might come to your house and take away what I like.' Few things disgusted one more than the way in which Boer women and their families were allowed to occupy houses and settle in town. The best residences were seized upon with avidity, and if one house did not suit they turned to another. I noticed one family that changed houses three times. As one may suppose the Boer families who were equal to this sort of thing were by no means of the best class.[11]

Gerard Bailey and Father Murray took it in turns to guard the Vicarage and on a number of occasions were able to face down would-be looters. Gerard said of his companion, 'Father Murray behaved like a brick, and guarded the place as if it were his own. He is a big, burly, and formidable person to encounter.'

The Standard and Digger's News, an English language propaganda sheet produced by the Boers, in their issue of 21 November 1899, had this to say about the looting: 'In Dundee town itself all has been done that human ingenuity could devise to generally wreck up the premises. Plenty of evidence that the Boers were on a little venture. I watched one loading up two trolley loads of pianos. But this was purely excess of emotion; and the exuberance of delicious joy.'[12]

The exercise of this exuberance of delicious joy changed with the passing of time, but the effects were the same. Gerard Bailey kept a cow, which provided the Vicarage with milk until a Boer decided he wanted the cow. He went to the *Vrederechter* who gave him a permit to remove it. Fortunately, some of the residents still had cows and Mr A.J. Oldacre was able to offer Gerard and Father Murray some milk. Arthur Oldacre was a shopkeeper, and when the Boers first entered Dundee, his was one of the two shops that were permitted to remain open. No reason was given for this privilege, though the fact that he also owned a shop across the border in Vryheid might account for the dispensation granted to his business. In any event, the privilege did not last for long. His shop, with all its stock, was expropriated by the Transvaal Government.

It was not only over property that the *Vrederechter* had such wide powers. There was no Habeas Corpus Act or other inconvenient legislation to limit his powers over the person. As they were now living in the Transvaal, any criticism by a resident of the authorities could be regarded as treason and result in the offender being shot. They might be imprisoned indefinitely without charge and new crimes were created on the spur of the moment. They could be sent anywhere at a moment's notice, and be used as forced labour.

On 2 November, Gerard, while walking to the hospital, was surprised to see wounded men being loaded onto a train. It transpired that 87 of the men with minor wounds and an officer were being sent to Pretoria. Shortly afterwards he received another surprise. A man was walking around town ringing a bell and displaying a notice in Dutch and English stating,

> Notice is hereby given that all (male) inhabitants residing within a radius of three miles of the office of the Resident Justice of the Peace at Dundee must be present at the railway station at Dundee to leave for Pretoria at 2.30 p.m. tomorrow the 3rd inst.[13]

After reading the notice Gerard continued to the hospital, and discovered that apart from those residents going to Pretoria the next day, all the remaining patients who could possibly be moved, and most medical staff, were to be transported to the Boer camp at Elandslaagte. They would then be passed through the lines into Ladysmith.

Realising that if he was to leave the next day, all his and the church's property would be stolen or destroyed, Gerard and Father Murray worked through the night hiding as much as they could. The more valuable items were hidden under the floorboards in the church and other things were buried in the garden.

The next morning they went to see the *Vrederechter* to ask for permission to stay in Dundee to help with the badly wounded. Initially their request was refused, but they insisted, stating that they were entitled to remain with the seriously wounded, many of whom were dying. Finally it was agreed that they might remain pending further orders. At 5 p.m. the next batch of wounded from the field hospitals left for Elandslaagte. Major Daly with a few of his medical staff stayed to take care of those who could not be moved. Among the civilians who assembled at the station at 2.30 p.m. for the transportation to Pretoria, was W.H. Tatham who must have wondered why he had ever thought the residents had nothing to fear from the Boers. After waiting about eight hours on the station they finally set off for Pretoria.[14] There were 143 residents in this group and they had no idea what awaited them at the end of the line.

The two priests continued with their pastoral duties. Some of the wounded died and funeral services were conducted. They wrote letters for some of the illiterate Boers. Like many men of that era, their knowledge of housekeeping was limited. Gerard decided to try his hand at cooking and found a recipe, which was much praised. The main ingredients were diced beef and condensed milk. He carefully cooked the meal according to the instructions and in due course the new delicacy arrived at their supper table. Gerard said 'the concoction was not satisfactory,' and Father Murray said, 'Gerard was a very poor chef,' or more colourful words to that effect. Gerard had perforce to do his own washing and ironing. He coped very well with his shirts but his clerical dog collar hung like a limp rag about his neck. The collar was vital to him as the Boers always had great respect for the clergy and without it he would lose all protection. Afterwards he found some starch, which worked wonders, and when he visited the hospital wearing his newly starched collar, a wounded officer said he was the best dressed man he had seen there. Gerard was not to know that the starch he used for washing clothes was about to be employed down the road in Ladysmith to fill hungry stomachs.

There were still three officers and about thirty men being treated at the hospital. On most days the two priests would call at the hospital to see the wounded and would stay on for lunch. Major Daly had secured a small flock of sheep, which were looked after by one of the army orderlies and grazed on the open veld. Mysteriously, no matter how many sheep were eaten their numbers never declined. Commandeering was catching!

The deportation of 143 residents did not bring an end to the Boer attacks on the civilians of the town. Two weeks later T.H. Brokensha was arrested and charged with being a dangerous character, that he knew where there were arms, and was ready to head a rebellion. Major Daly went to see the *Vrederechter*, who after receiving a guarantee for Brokensha's future behaviour, released the prisoner. Brokensha was told he was no longer a Justice of the Peace. A couple of days later one of the orderlies was found guilty of being 'out of bounds' and sentenced to the unusual penalty of twenty-one days in bed.[15]

On 24 November, Arthur Oldacre and six other men were placed under arrest and incarcerated in Oldacre's home where the Boers kept them under guard. No one knew why they were arrested, though subsequent speculation was that this was done to ensure that they did not attend meetings scheduled for the following week, at which it was hoped to persuade the Natal Dutch to join the Boer cause. After the meetings they were released without explanation.

On 11 December, word was sent around that all residents were to present themselves at the *Vrederechter's* office at 3 p.m., where they were informed that they would be leaving for Pretoria at 6 a.m. on the following day. Early the next morning Gerard Bailey was at the station to see about twenty men leave under armed guard for Pretoria. That afternoon he went as usual to the hospital only to find it surrounded by armed guards. Nothing daunted, he slipped through the fence but on his way out he was arrested and marched off to the *Vrederechter's* office, much to the amusement of his friends at the hospital. Gerard explained to the official that he knew nothing of the new regulations and was released with an apology.

On 15 December, the sound of cannon fire from the southwest began early and was distinct and continuous. It was apparent that a major battle was taking place. The next day Arthur Oldacre arrived with a telegram with details of the Battle of Colenso: 'British 2,000 killed, 150 prisoners, ten guns captured and a lot of ammunition'. Father Murray and Oldacre were inconsolable. Gerard did not believe the report but as the day drifted on, more reports came in and it was apparent that Britain had suffered a severe loss.

Some of the residents were able to obtain permission to travel to Pretoria and from there to Delagoa Bay in Mozambique. Others were less fortunate. One group of ten residents was arrested for no known reason and locked in gaol where they remained throughout a December heat wave. On 19 December, they were marched out of the gaol to the station to continue their captivity in Pretoria. On Christmas Eve, Father Murray and four civilians voluntarily left Dundee. The next day the remaining patients and staff at the hospital received a Christmas present in the form of a directive that all inmates should hold themselves in readiness for removal to Pretoria. The women and children asked if they could accompany the wounded but received a non-committal reply. On 30 December, a hospital train arrived and took patients, staff (including civilian orderlies) off to Pretoria. Dr Galbraith, being a local doctor, remained, as did one patient who had had a leg shortened and had difficulty walking. A week later Arthur Oldacre left voluntarily, intending to go to Pretoria and from there to Delagoa Day. In two weeks he was in Durban. He must have been a very persuasive man to have received consent for this journey, as he was in possession of much useful information as to the state of affairs in Northern Natal. On 25 January 1900, the Boers made their last arrest and deportation when two residents who had not left their houses for many weeks were sent off to Pretoria. Apart from the women and children, the town had been almost emptied of its original inhabitants. Vicar Gerard Bailey stayed on. The few remaining residents hardly constituted a congregation, however, at the end of November about seventy Cape Coloured people arrived from Newcastle. They were the wives and families of the wagon drivers who were employed by the British army. Gerard found them to be a decent crowd and as some were Anglicans, his tiny congregation received a boost.

During the last two months of 1899, the Boers had been trying to persuade the local Dutch farmers to join their cause. Farms were visited and the farmers were told that northern Natal had been annexed by the Transvaal and unless they took up arms for the Republican cause, they would be rebels to the Republic and dealt with as such, possibly shot. At the meetings in Dundee, the local Dutch were told that if any Dutch farmer was low enough not to join the war between the Republics and Britain, any burgher would be justified in molesting that man in any way. In spite of the threats many of the more prominent farmers remained loyal to the Natal Government and they were made to pay for the stand they took. Most of the smaller farmers yielded to pressure and agreed to serve, generally as non-combatants. L.J. de Jager of Waschbank was told he would be a Kommandant if he could raise 1,000 men. Given the limited number of Boers in the area, this was impossible so he ended up being Native Commissioner for the Dundee District, and looted cattle were sent to him.

In Newcastle, those residents who remained when the British retreated received similar treatment to the inhabitants of Dundee. Many of the farmers fled before the Boers and had their farms looted and smashed up, but those who remained on their farms were left in peace for a time.

In an attempt to clean up the damage made by the looters in Dundee, a large gang of Zulus was commandeered by the Boers. They were housed and fed in the gaol and appeared to be a cheerful crowd who were happy to talk to Gerard Bailey. They felt the English who had run away from Johannesburg, Newcastle and Dundee were great fools. When Gerard asked them what pay they received, they became uneasy and admitted that they received no pay and did not like this treatment. These people belonged to the tribe under Chief Sandanezwe.

The Boers had been courting this chief for some time and had given him a house in Dundee and the green light to attack an old enemy, Chief Dumisa of the Amangwe, who lived in the Dundee district. Chief Sandanezwe approached Chief Bande of Weenen with a proposition that they should combine with the Boers, and launch an attack against Dumisa. This was the classic Boer tactic of siding with one of the parties to a dispute and then picking up the spoils after the fight. As long ago as 1841, the Boers attacked the amaBaca in order to win favour with the Pondo chief Faku. On that occasion they alarmed Faku, who sought British aid. We have seen how in 1884, despite protests from Natal and Zululand, Britain permitted the Boers to use this tactic to annex northern Zululand. Chief Bande was not one to fall for such a ruse and declined to assist Sandanezwe. Instead he reported the matter to the British and sent a warning to Chief Dumisa. Chief Dumisa had already realised the danger facing his tribe and had sent his young men and cattle away before the Boers arrived. Though the Boers threatened to kill him, he would not be intimidated and survived the war.

Chief Mabizela, whose armed followers had tried to persuade General Buller to let them join the fight against the invading Boers, received a message from the Boers requiring him to come to them to explain why his men had attempted to join the British. Mabizela knew it would be fatal for him to attend on the Boers personally so he sent a message to the Boers saying his men only went to Chieveley seeking work as porters. Not quite the truth but understandable.

On 8 January 1900, the Governor of Natal sent a telegram to the Colonial Secretary, 'Prime Minister informs me Chief Nsungulu, head of the Ntombela tribe near the Natal border at Mahlabatini, saying that he wishes to tender allegiance to British Government. I have caused Nsungulu to be informed that as Governor of Natal I have no power to accept offer of allegiance but that I will communicate it to Her Majesty's Government. Saunders reports Nsungulu is a powerful chief.'[17] (Saunders was a magistrate employed by the Natal Government.) Britain made no response to Chief Nsungulu's offer of allegiance, an ill omen for the future.

19

The Army Moves West

The arrival of Winston Churchill at Delagoa Bay.

In the weeks following the Battle of Colenso, General Buller's self-confidence began to return. The arrival in Natal shortly after Christmas of General Sir Charles Warren and the 5th Division almost doubled the infantry and artillery under his command and would have strengthened the idea that it might be possible to outflank the Boer line stretched along the northern bank of the Tugela. Disappointingly, there was only one mounted regiment in the Division, the 13th Hussars, and Sir Charles Warren was not a person Buller would have chosen as a senior commander.

Charles Warren was the son of an Indian army general and his choice of the army as a career followed the conventions of the time. Few would have guessed that he was to become one of the most eccentric figures in the British Army. At Sandhurst and Woolwich he displayed unusual talent as a mathematician, which resulted in him having no trouble obtaining a commission in the Royal Engineers. One of his first assignments was to do a trigometrical survey of the Rock of Gibraltar, which he did to a scale of 50 feet to an inch and in addition produced two monstrous models of Gibraltar, each being over 30 feet in length. In 1876 he was sent to South Africa to survey the boundary between the Orange Free State and Griqualand West and subsequently his engineering skills were used in one of the wars on the Eastern Cape Frontier, after which he was posted to Bechuanaland (now Botswana). When the Boers provoked rebellion in that country, he led an expedition whose mere presence re-asserted British authority. The scope of his career was widening and he was steadily rising in the army lists, though he had never been involved in any actual fighting. On his return to England he stood for Parliament as an Independent Liberal, although as an officer on half-pay this was against army practice. Sir Garnet Wolseley, who was then Adjutant-General, urged him to withdraw from the election, but Warren refused on the grounds that he could not let the electors down. The electors, however, had no qualms about letting him down and voted for his opponent. With his army career apparently over, he now devoted his talents to archaeology, forming a Lodge of Masonic Research and was elected Master. He hardly had time to settle into this post when out of the blue he was appointed to serve on the staff of the army in Egypt. His name had been put forward by Wolseley who, it would seem, admired eccentricity. After only a month in Egypt, where his principal concern was to prevent the servants poisoning the officers, he was offered and accepted the post of Chief Commissioner of the Metropolitan Police in London. For a number of years the London Police had been the subject of scandals over corruption, illegal arrests and inefficiency. During the three years he spent as Chief Commissioner, Warren was to mire them in a series of controversies that were to cause past failures to pale into insignificance. A number of incidents created ill feeling between him and the Home Secretary, a situation that reached its nadir late in 1887, when Socialists attempted to hold a protest meeting in Trafalgar Square.

Warren forbade the approach to the square of any organised procession and to enforce his decision called out 4,000 constables, 300 Grenadiers, and 300 Life Guards. This force clashed violently with a large crowd of protesters. When the Grenadiers were about to execute a bayonet charge, a bloodbath was only averted by the officers and sergeants rushing in front of their men and ordering them to put up their arms. More than 150 people were injured and taken to hospital. Warren had issued orders in doggerel:

The Commissioner has observed there are signs of wear
On the Landseer lions in Trafalgar Square.

Unauthorised persons are not to climb,
On the Landseer lions at any time.

Whatever the Home Secretary might have thought of Warren's ability as a
poet, he was shocked by his militancy, and when a further dispute occurred
regarding the investigation into the 'Jack the Ripper' murders, the Home
Secretary reproved him in public, resulting in Warren's resignation. Within a
few weeks, he was appointed to the command of the garrison in Singapore
and given the temporary rank of major general.

In Singapore he was responsible for constructing the fortifications for
the island. He founded the Straits Philosophical Society, and in his capacity
as District Grand Master of the Eastern Archipelago he founded several
Masonic Lodges. He soon quarrelled with the Governor of Singapore and
supplied the War Office with lengthy accounts of these disputes. Back in
London, Redvers Buller was moved to write to him,

> We are inundated with long correspondence regarding squabbles between
> you and your Governor ... all I want to say is, for heaven's sake leave
> us alone, do not write and send everything here. If you have to fight the
> Governor, fight him. Though I pray you fight as little as possible, surely
> the sun is hot enough in Singapore, trust us, let him send home what he
> likes. You may be assured you will have your say in due time.

Warren spent five years in Singapore during which period his appointment as a
major general was confirmed. On his return to England, he was unemployed for
a year, and, after a period in command of the troops in the Thames District, he
retired. When hostilities broke out in South Africa he wrote to Wolseley asking
if he could be of any service and was pleased and delighted when he received
command of the 5th Division, which was shortly to leave for South Africa. He
was now a lieutenant general and had, as we have seen, little experience of
warfare and such knowledge as he possessed was likely to be out of date. He
was generally disliked by the officers who had to work with him and was well
known for his bad temper, lack of tact, and intolerance of criticism. While on
the ship to Durban he studied maps of Natal and played war games with his
staff officers and on arrival he was confident that he knew the answer to Britain's
military problems. When he met Buller at Frere he suggested that the line of
advance should be via Hlangwane Hill to the east of Colenso. 'What do you
know about it?' was Buller's response. Warren confessed that he had based his
theory on his own general knowledge and war games! Frustrated in his attempt
to dictate general strategy, Warren clung to two ideas. Firstly, that no military
manoeuvre should be attempted without plenty of practice, and secondly, that
it was the duty of the British soldier to show he was 'a better man' than the
Boer. On arrival at Frere his men began practising bayonet charges.

Once he had recovered from the shock of the reverse at Colenso, Buller
began to consider the other options open to him and decided that he would

attempt to circumvent the Boer's right flank. This involved a march of between 15 and 20 miles westwards towards a hamlet, Springfield, now known as Winterton. Here there was a bridge over the Little Tugela, a tributary of the Tugela River approximately 8 miles to the north. From Springfield his force could strike northwards to the Tugela where a number of fords provided potential crossing points. Once the flank had been turned, the numerical superiority of the British artillery would ensure that his force could roll up the Boer line while advancing eastwards across open country to Ladysmith. Reliable maps of the area were not available to him so it was necessary that those in command should be both flexible and pragmatic. Speed was essential as any delay would enable the Boers to fortify their line.

Though there were only two regular cavalry regiments in his force, the 13th Hussars and the 1st Royal Dragoons, Buller nonetheless had under his command some very useful colonial mounted Volunteers. There were squadrons of the Natal Carbineers, the Imperial Light Horse, and the Natal Police, who together were known as the Composite Regiment; Thornycroft's Mounted Infantry and Bethune's Mounted Infantry, both of which had been raised in Natal; and there had recently arrived four squadrons of the South African Light Horse, which had been raised in the Eastern Cape. All in all, Buller had approximately 2,500 mounted men who were brigaded under Lord Dundonald.

The Volunteers had not been idle during the weeks following the Colenso debacle. They were constantly out on patrol gathering information and taking part in several skirmishes with the enemy. Near Chieveley on 20 December, a picket of the 13th Hussars, sheltering from the unaccustomed heat, were surprised by a party of Boers who killed two of them. Lieutenant Silburn of the Carbineers offered to set a trap for the marauding Boers. A detachment was taken out to the area where the previous attack occurred, and while some of the men lounged about in a position that could be seen by the enemy, the others concealed themselves. The Boers duly fell for the trap and in the brief skirmish which followed, the Boers lost four men. The high ground where these incidents occurred was given the name Hussar Hill.[1]

In a situation where urgent messages could only be delivered by horsemen, the Volunteers' knowledge of the country was invaluable to the British. On one occasion a message had to be taken to a District Surgeon living in the foothills of the Drakensberg, behind the Boer lines. Corporal H. Norton and three troopers of the ILH were assigned the task of delivering the message. They passed through the Boer lines and headed north through this exquisitely beautiful and sparsely inhabited part of Natal. En route they came across a native kraal where they were met by an old man with some women and wide-eyed children a respectful distance behind him. Uncertain of the extent to which the kraalhead might have been influenced by the Boers, Norton decided they should test his allegiance by posing as Boers.

They had been living in the open for some days, had had no opportunity to shave or wash for a week, their uniforms were decidedly the worse for wear, slouch hats were the slouchiest, and to all outward seeming they were typical

Boers. Norton, a fine Zulu linguist, said to the kraalhead:'We have been sent by President Paul Kruger to tell you, that all this land now belongs to the Boers, and all you Zulus are therefore Paul Kruger's men!'

The old man shook his head and said, 'No, No, No! Nkosi, that is not so!'

'What!' shouted Norton, working himself up into a well simulated rage. 'If you dare to answer me like that, I will put a bullet through you!' making great play with his rifle bolt and slipping a cartridge into the breach.

The old Zulu, quite unperturbed, took out his snuff box, snuffed deliberately, and in a dignified manner said, 'No! No! Nkosi you are wrong. You see I am a very old man. I was born a Queen's man, and I will die a Queen's man,' and bearing his chest, he added, 'Shoot.'[2]

There was no doubt where this man's sympathies lay and the patrol was so delighted by him that they gave him everything they could as gifts. He, not to be outdone in courtesy, provided them with a feast of chickens, sweet potatoes and milk, before seeing them on their way. The message was duly given to the District Surgeon, and the reply brought safely back to base.

Among the personalities who arrived in Natal that Christmas of 1899, was Winston Churchill. He had escaped from the prisoner-of-war camp in Pretoria, and after an adventurous journey to Delagoa Bay, was able to obtain a passage on a coaster travelling to Durban. Here he made some fine speeches; he told his audiences of the high esteem in which he held the people of Natal. He then travelled to Pietermaritzburg, where he was the guest of Sir Walter Hely-Hutchinson, the Governor. He visited the wounded in hospital and met the Prime Minister before setting off for the front. At Frere he persuaded General Buller to grant him a commission in the South African Light Horse. It was agreed that he would receive no pay and might continue his career as a journalist. Though he had no specific military duties, his position as an army officer did enable him to get close to the action and thereby bring a sense of immediacy to his reports. He liked to create the impression that he was present at the scenes he described.

Buller had hoped to begin moving his army to Springfield on 6 January, but it rained constantly and it was not until the 10th that the British column was finally able to begin the march. Buller had, in his preparations for the move, made two blunders. In his concern for the well being of the troops, the column took far too much baggage. Churchill, though often reluctant to criticise the Army, was moved to write,

> The vast amount of baggage this army takes with it on the march hampers its movements and utterly precludes all possibility of surprising the enemy. The consequence is that roads are crowded, drifts are blocked, marching troops are delayed, and all rapidity of movement is out of the question. Meanwhile, the enemy completes the fortification of his positions, and the cost of capturing them rises. It is a poor economy to let a brave soldier live well for three days at the price of killing him on the fourth.[3]

The second mistake by Buller was to place Sir Charles Warren in charge of the flanking movement. Warren now had command not only of his 5th

Division with its two brigades of infantry and supporting artillery, but also the 2nd Division under Major-General Clery with another two brigades of infantry and artillery, and almost the entire Mounted Division under Lord Dundonald. We shall never know precisely what caused Buller to commit this folly though it probably stemmed from his own lack of experience as overall commander. For his part, Warren had no doubts about his abilities and what should be done. He was, however, concerned that his troops lacked practice fighting the Boers and felt no attack should be launched until they had such experience. He never explained how this objective was to be obtained.

Buller kept under his direct command the 10th Brigade under Major-General Coke. This brigade consisted of three regiments of Regular infantry and one Volunteer regiment, the Imperial Light Infantry, which had only recently been raised in Pietermaritzburg. Commanded by a regular officer, Lieutenant-Colonel W.F. Nash, the ILI consisted of colonials who had received a few weeks training before being sent to the front. Like the other Volunteers, they were not issued with bayonets and were armed with obsolete single shot rifles. General Barton's brigade was delegated the task of defending the Colenso section of the front.

Buller's concern that his troops should have the best possible medical care ensured that the field hospital and medical staff should accompany the soldiers. With most of his stretcher-bearers locked up in Ladysmith, the Natal Volunteer Ambulance Corps was formed with Lieutenant H.S.N. Wright in command. It was recruited in Durban and Pietermaritzburg from those who had lost their livelihood in consequence of the war, or simply wished to help with the war effort. They were expected to work under fire. They were in no way connected to the corps of stretcher-bearers raised by M. Gandhi, which operated exclusively behind the lines.

When the NVAC was leaving for Springfield, they attracted the attention Lt Dr E. Blake Knox:

> They were dressed in ordinary clothes, but the Government had given them a fair amount of equipment, each man having received a couple of blankets, a waterproof sheet, a haversack, a pair of boots. They carried all their belongings with them, and truly it was a curious sight to see them marching past, four deep, not keeping step nor any kind of military formation, some of them encumbered with small portmanteaus, hand-bags, and various kinds of parcels, their white mackintosh sheets rolled around their shoulders, their haversacks bulging and hung around with bundles of various little odds and ends, including small pots and kettles. These were the men who were to make for themselves a reputation second to none in the Natal Army.[4]

The march to Springfield turned out to be a wretched affair. The recent torrential rains brought every river and stream into flood. The track across the veld was soon turned into a quagmire. For those in front, it was a case of slipping and sliding along, but further back things were much worse as the mud became deeper and deeper. Wagons were mired up to their axles and on occasions could not be moved by four teams of oxen. With sixteen oxen to a team this churned up the track even further. The British had brought along a number of steam traction engines, which were most useful. It was found that one of these machines could free wagons that 48 oxen were unable to move, a hint of the mechanised warfare of the future.

On 10 January, Dundonald's orders were to accompany the infantry until they reached their overnight stop. Thereafter they were to press on to Springfield, which should, if possible, be occupied and held overnight, pending the arrival of the main body of Warren's column the following day. The Regular cavalry and Thorneycroft's MI did not ride with Dundonald, being required to accompany the infantry brigades. This left Dundonald with about 1,000 mounted men and an artillery battery of six guns under his command. After they had ridden 2 or 3 miles, Dundonald sought, and was given permission by General Clery, to press on to Springfield without delay.

Dundonald found the bridge across the Little Tugela unguarded and intact. Being in the habit of consulting with his Colonial officers, he was able to acquire information that would not have been available to his colleagues. He wrote:

> Up to 8 January very little rain had fallen in this part of Natal, and the Tugela and other rivers were running very low, and were very easily fordable at the drifts ... On the night of the 8th, however, and during the whole of the 9th, heavy rain fell, with the result that the rivers at once came down in flood and by the morning of the 10th, few, or perhaps none of the drifts over the Tugela were fordable. Today, however (the 10th), the rain had ceased, and as the floods in the Natal rivers fall almost as quickly as they rise, the chances were that with no more rain in the next 24 hours, the drifts would be passable. It appeared to me that with the river still running high the Boers would not dare to occupy in force the southern heights at Mount Alice, and that if I were quick I could seize this important position without much opposition.[5]

About 8 miles north of Springfield lay Spearman's Hill, the western summit of which was called Mount Alice. Beyond Spearman's lay the Tugela. Dundonald decided to use his discretion and take the opportunity offered of capturing this high ground. Leaving 350 men and two guns to guard the bridge at Springfield, the rest of the force set out for Spearman's. With Bethune's Mounted Infantry scouting ahead, they quickly covered the ground and by nightfall had not only established a camp on top of Mount Alice, but also managed to manhandle their four guns onto the summit. Dundonald was particularly impressed by the speed and efficiency with which Bethune's men scouted ahead. Many of these men were Australians who had come over to Natal at their own expense. No Boers were seen, but recently constructed fortifications were found indicating that they had occupied and intended to hold Mount Alice. As suspected, the Boers had withdrawn from the position when the rising river threatened to cut them off from the bulk of their forces.

When the Volunteers awoke the next morning they could see the Tugela River winding along the valley below them. On the far river bank was a large ferry, used in peacetime to ferry men and cattle across the river, and beyond the river bank, Boer pickets could be seen, presumably guarding the ferry and watching the movements of Dundonald's force. Lieutenant Carlisle with Corporals Cox and Barkley and Troopers Howell, Godden and Collingwood of the SA Light Horse volunteered to attempt to bring the ferry across to the southern bank. A detachment of the same regiment was sent down to the scrub near the river bank to provide them with some cover, while Carlisle's men, keeping well out of sight, made their way to the river bank. Here they stripped off and made a dash for the river. They had swum half-way across before the enemy realised what was happening. Though heavy rifle fire was opened on the swimmers they were able to drag the barge in good order over to the southern bank. No casualties occurred though one man suffered cramp in the cold water and would have drowned had he not been rescued by a comrade. The barge was at a crossing of the river known as Potgieter's Drift and was later to play a significant role in ferrying troops across the river. In twenty-four hours the Volunteers with Dundonald had secured the bridge at Springfield, occupied Mount Alice and secured a means of crossing the Tugela at Potgieter's Drift. Lt Carlisle, who was a mining engineer from Johannesburg, was recommended for a DSO, an award that was refused, much to the chagrin of Dundonald, who not only witnessed the heroism that morning but also appreciated the importance of the achievement.[6]

The rest of that day and the night which followed passed without incident. On 12 January, General Buller arrived with a brigade of infantry. The summit at Mount Alice was 1,000 feet above the valley floor giving Buller a fine view of the hills on the northern bank of the Tugela. About 6 miles to the east could be seen the heights of Vaalkrantz, directly in front were the lower hills of Brakfontein and 5 miles to the west the massive bulk of Spion Kop and Twin Peaks. Boers could be seen busily entrenching themselves along the Brakfontein Hills. On 13 January the naval guns arrived and replaced the guns from Dundonald's brigade on Mount Alice. Over the next two days the transfer of the troops from Frere to Spearman's was almost completed. In addition a large accumulation of stores had been built up at Springfield.

On 16 January, Dundonald attended a meeting at Mount Alice of senior officers, at which Sir Redvers Buller gave a broad outline of his plans. Sir Redvers felt that it would be well nigh impossible to break through the Boer lines on the Brakfontein hills in front of Mount Alice and therefore it was his intention that only General Lyttleton's brigade should cross the Tugela at Potgieter's Drift and occupy the kopies lying to the north of the river in front of Mount Alice. Warren, with his two divisions, was to march west, cross the river about 5 miles upstream at Trichardt's Drift, and then execute a flanking movement, refusing his right and throwing his left forward. Clearly Buller intended that Warren's force should skirt round the west of Spion Kop. With the exception of Bethune's MI, who were to assist Lyttleton's brigade, the rest of Dundonald's mounted brigade, numbering about 1,500, fell within Warren's command.

When Dundonald arrived at Trichardt's Drift on 17 January, Lieutenant Tom Bridges, formerly of the Royal Artillery and now with the ILH, offered to swim the river to discover what opposition they could expect from the Boers. With a small patrol, Bridges crossed the river and on approaching a farm on the north bank a couple of Boers fired on them before making off. Otherwise the coast appeared to be clear. While the Engineers were constructing a pontoon and bridge to enable the infantry and transport wagons to cross Trichardt's Drift, Dundonald decided his mounted men should cross the Tugela at another drift about half a mile lower downstream. Probably because their colonial horses were small compared with the big English chargers, the Carbineers were placed at the rear of the column making its way to the new crossing. Duncan McKenzie thought how splendid the cavalry looked marching in columns of four down to the river, but was very surprised to see them stop when they reached the river and counter-march back up the hill. Duncan rode down to find out what was happening and was told by Dundonald that the river was too full to cross. Duncan wanted to have a closer look at the river so he and Dundonald rode back to the drift. The river was fairly full and running swiftly. The drift was formed by a natural weir, downstream of which was deep water. Duncan rode into the drift, and though the water came up to his saddle flaps, he had no difficulty getting across and coming back again. He told Dundonald that despite their smaller horses, the Carbineers would have no difficulty crossing but he was not so sure about the English horses, which were not familiar with flowing water. Having seen how easily McKenzie had crossed the river, Dundonald changed his mind. The 1st Royal Dragoons were to lead the way. They were advised 'to keep their horses' heads facing upstream while the riders should look straight ahead.' Under no circumstances should the rider look downstream as the horse would feel the rider's movement and instinctively move in that direction, causing it to shift into the deeper water, lose its footing and be swept downstream. The Dragoons could not control their horses properly on the drift and were swept into the deep water. Most were able to get onto a shallow bank from which they were later rescued. Others were less fortunate. Troopers David Sclanders and Fred Woods of the Carbineers plunged in and rescued several men, one of whom, Captain Tremayne, was pulled from the water unconscious. Despite the efforts of Sclanders and Wood, one of the Dragoons drowned. Realising that more men might drown, McKenzie suggested that a line of Carbineers be placed across the drift and that the mounted men cross just above them. Dundonald acquiesced, and a human chain was formed along the downstream edge of the drift. Duncan chose big men who were strong swimmers and once they were in place the rest of the column crossed without any further incident.[7] Sclanders was afterwards presented with the Royal Humane Society's silver medal.

That night the mounted brigade bivouacked on the northern bank of the river. Early the following morning they set out to put into effect Sir Redvers Buller's plan to outflank the Boers. They travelled west along the northern bank of the Tugela. In his autobiography Dundonald wrote:

My idea was to try and get to the west of the Boer right flank before it was entrenched, and secure and hold a position commanding the Acton-Ladysmith road. All was going well and I continued my advance, feeling sure that the infantry would be following. About halfway to Acton Homes there is a stream called Venter's Spruit; here I left Thorneycroft's Mounted Infantry on a good defensive position on the kopies at this important point. At Venter's Spruit kopies I arranged for sketches to be prepared of the Tabanyama (Rangeworthy Hills) to the north, as they appeared from Venter's Spruit. It was most important to hold the Venter's Spruit line of kopies, as the infantry could deploy to the west behind them unmolested, in order to take up their position for the wheel. Shortly after leaving Thorneycroft's regiment to hold the Venter's Spruit kopies, I was astounded by receiving the following message from Sir Charles Warren:

'To OC Mounted Troops or next senior.

The GOC as far as he can see finds that there are no Cavalry whatever round the camp, and nothing to prevent the oxen being swept away. You are to send 500 men at once to be placed round the camp.

Sgd. A. H. Morris AAG Col 18/1/00'

There was nothing to do except obey the order I had received, so as the nearest approach to 500 men was the Royal Dragoons, with great regret I sent this splendid regiment back to Sir Charles Warren, hoping that Colonel Burn-Murdoch might argue matters out with him and soon return – but this order paralysed the Mounted Brigade at the very moment it wanted strengthening. Had not Sir Charles the River Tugela behind him, and natives to keep his oxen from straying? He also had his divisional cavalry. The situation seemed quite inexplicable and augured ill for the success of Buller's plans.[8]

Despite the drastic reduction in their numbers, Dundonald decided his column should not retreat but instead hold its position on the Acton Homes Road. When camp was formed, the Carbineers were put on outpost duty. That afternoon Duncan McKenzie saw a large body of Boers riding out from behind Spion Kop in the direction of Acton Homes. A British officer, Major Graham, who was nominally in command of the Carbineers, happened to be at the outpost when the Boers were spotted. McKenzie pointed out the enemy to him saying at the same time, 'I can trap these men if you will let me,' and he replied, 'Do what you like, McKenzie.' Duncan did just that. He gave the order to mount, and in seconds the men were in their saddles and off at a full gallop.[9]

Being aware that if he took the direct route, the Boers on Spion Kop, or the kommando itself, might see them, Duncan decided to make a wide detour and keep out of sight, as they made their way to two kopies where it was intended to ambush the Boers. This meant that they had to travel twice as far as the Boers to reach the desired position in time, resulting in them having to ride hard the whole way. Captain Herbert Bottomley and the Imperial Light Horse had noticed the sudden burst of activity by the Carbineers and anxious not to miss any excitement they mounted their horses and galloped after them. Ever since the incident of the armoured train the ILH had worked closely with the Carbineers, who were delighted to have their help. They had to ride nearly 5 miles and in the course of the gallop four ILH troopers and one or two Carbineers had their horses brought down by holes in the veld. As they neared the kopies, McKenzie slowed down as he was uncertain whether or not the Boers were already there. Trooper Gray of the Carbineers was ordered to gallop on as fast as he could to the nek between the kopies and if the Boers were close, to gallop back. If they were not yet there, he was to remain in position and wave on the Carbineers. Gray galloped to the kopies, dismounted and crept up to the crest of the nek between the two kopies where he had a view of the land ahead. He then drew back from the skyline and waved. McKenzie sent a message back to Dundonald for support, instructed the ILH to occupy the ground on the left, while the Carbineers made for the kopie on the right. All were ordered to hold their fire until McKenzie blew his whistle. They galloped over to the kopies, dismounted and leaving their linked horses under cover, climbed up into the rocks, keeping themselves well hidden.

They had only beaten the Boer kommando to the kopies by a few minutes. From his concealed position McKenzie saw the kommando riding along in the typical irregular Boer fashion with men riding four or five abreast in clumps of about forty or fifty riders. Obviously they were not expecting any opposition, had no proper scouts out, and talked and rode as they felt inclined. There were 320 Boers in the kommando riding against the Carbineers and ILH who together totalled no more than eighty men. McKenzie was almost ready to give the order to fire, when one of the ILH men could stand the tension no longer and fired. McKenzie had no choice but to blow his whistle as a general order to fire. Everyone fired as fast as they could with their single shot rifles. Boer saddles quickly emptied, as riders were either shot or jumped off to seek cover. The Boers at the rear of the kommando turned tail and galloped away. Some of them found cover behind a bank and attempted to return the fire while their commander, Kommandant Mentz, rallied a few men and took up a position on a small stony kopie some 800 yards away. For about an hour the firing continued as the Volunteers steadily eliminated pockets of resistance and Boers surrendered. At one point some Boers raised a white flag causing McKenzie to order a cease fire. When he stood up to tell them to come in a bullet came whistling past his head. A Boer prisoner was then brought forward to tell the Boers to put down their arms and come in. The reply was another bullet, which narrowly missed the prisoner. This apparent abuse of the white flag created some anger, however, it was subsequently discovered that the fire came from the men with Kommandant Mentz from whose position the white flag would not have been visible.

As the engagement drew to a close, the 60th King's Royal Rifles arrived in response to McKenzie's request for support. Instead of joining the Carbineers they attempted a flank attack on the fleeing Boers and lost two men killed. In the engagement one Carbineer and two Imperial Light Horseman were wounded. The 60th KRR suffered two killed and a couple of men wounded. The Boer losses were fourteen killed, about forty wounded and nearly forty taken prisoner. The Boer leader Kommandant Mentz was among those killed. It is said he died holding a letter from his wife. Duncan McKenzie, though pleased with the outcome of the engagement, was saddened by the casualties brought about by war, and described the shooting of the enemy as a 'horrible affair'.[10]

That night six Carbineers escorted the Boer prisoners back to base. It seems word had got out that Boer prisoners had been taken and when they arrived at the camp the next morning they were met by a crowd of Zulus dressed in full war paint, singing a song about the downfall of the Boers, and shouting jeering insults at them. For a moment or two it looked as if a general melee might break out. One Carbineer commented, 'It was a lesson to the Boers because they always ill-treat the natives and flog them.'[11]

Dundonald rode out to Acton Homes as soon as he heard of the engagement. He was delighted by the success of the two Volunteer squadrons and fully appreciated the opportunity they had created. He sent a message to General Warren asking for some guns that could knock out any guns the Boers might bring up to block the advance. He also asked that the Royal Dragoons be returned to his command. That night Dundonald and his three squadrons bivouacked on the two kopies they had secured, which provided an excellent defensive position. He naively imagined Warren would be making haste to reinforce the successful turning of the Boer flank with infantry and artillery. The next morning Dundonald received an urgent message that Sir Charles Warren wished to see him. He found Sir Charles at Venter's Spruit, actively supervising the crossing of the stream by the wagons. With pointed rudeness Warren continued supervising the wagons when approached by Dundonald who repeated his request to Warren for some guns and reinforcements only to receive the retort, 'Our objective is not Ladysmith; our objective is to effect junction with Sir R. Buller's force.'[12] This statement must have been very puzzling to Dundonald. Buller had told them at the meeting on the 16th that he could not break through the Brakfontein Hills. If the objective was to effect a junction with Buller, the obvious thing would have been to turn around and go back to Mount Alice where Buller had set up his headquarters. They were certainly not going to find him on Thabanyama or Spion Kop, which seemed to be the direction in which Warren's force appeared to be heading. Dundonald attempted to get clarification of his orders and left this account of what happened next.

He said he wanted the cavalry close to him; I replied I was trying to carry out Sir Redvers Buller's orders in the only way possible. 'I want you close to me,' he repeated, – then followed a shout at the driver of a transport wagon. I repeated to him the role Buller said on 16 January his mounted men had to play. His eyes remained glued on the drift – then another shout at a wagon driver. I also spoke of the importance of the outflanking movement of the Boer right by the cavalry, and asked him for all the mounted men possible and some guns. Sir Charles Warren was obdurate and insisted on keeping the Royal Dragoons, and also requested that Thorneycroft's Mounted Infantry be sent to him.

I did not understand then that Sir Charles Warren had any idea of abandoning the deployment outwards toward Acton Homes, preparatory to a great wheeling movement to the east, for the very place where I found him was at Venter's Spruit, seated on the ground watching the wagons fording the stream in order to proceed in the Acton Homes direction. Any difficulty in fording Venter's Spruit might have been in my opinion, soon overcome, and in the meanwhile artillery, and infantry marching light, could have made a flank march via our position on the Acton Homes–Ladysmith road, and commenced operations on the enemy's right flank.

When I left Sir Charles Warren I was completely puzzled. One thing was, however, clear, Sir Redvers Buller's plans for a great turning movement were not being rapidly carried out, and every hour's delay meant increased opposition.

After my conversation with Sir Charles Warren, Major Denny, Transport Officer, Mounted Brigade, told me that when he arrived at Venter's Spruit, Sir Charles said, 'Whose wagons are those?' 'Mounted Brigade, sir.' 'Can't pass,' said Sir Charles. 'If I let them go, Lord Dundonald will try and go on to Ladysmith.' But Major Denny was an old hand; he bided his time and slipped across the stream, or I do not know what we would have done without food for men and horses.[13]

With his force weakened by the loss of two regiments (Royal Dragoons and Thorneycroft's) Dundonald spent the night at Acton Homes. The next morning (20 January) Dundonald received a message in triplicate from Sir Charles Warren directing him to come nearer the main force. He had no choice but to withdraw from a position that he felt sure he could hold against attack.

Dundonald was not the only one puzzled by Warren's orders. A substantial portion of the Infantry had crossed Venter's Spruit, which was the road to Acton Homes, not Spion Kop. No explanation was given to them for this apparent change of plan.[14]

Of the engagement at Acton Homes Buller had this to say, 'Dundonald's movement was a decided success, and should have been supported by artillery, while Warren's infantry should have attacked the salient which Dundonald's success had left exposed. On that night I debated with myself whether or not I should relieve Warren of his command.'[15] He failed to do so.

20

Battle of Spion Kop

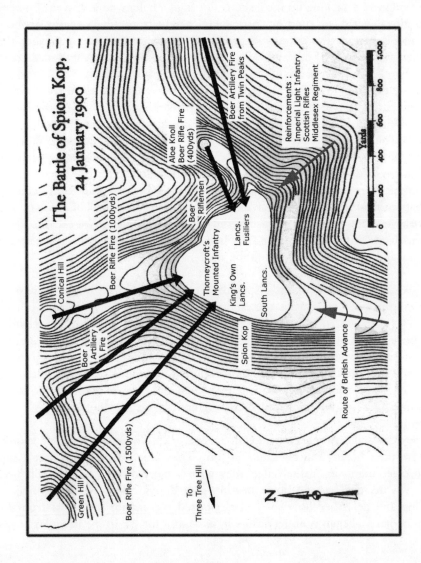

The Battle of Spion Kop, 24 January 1900

Conical Hill

Boer Rifle Fire (1000yds)

Boer Artillery Fire

Green Hill

Boer Rifle Fire (1500yds)

Boer Riflemen

Aloe Knoll Boer Rifle Fire (400yds)

Boer Artillery Fire from Twin Peaks

Reinforcements :
Imperial Light Infantry
Scottish Rifles
Middlesex Regiment

Thorneycroft's Mounted Infantry

Lancs. Fusiliers

King's Own Lancs.

South Lancs.

Spion Kop

Route of British Advance

To Three Tree Hill

N

Yards

0   200   400   600   800   1,000

The order to retire from his position at Acton Homes was the last order that Lord Dundonald was to receive from General Warren. Probably irked by what he perceived as insubordination by his cavalry commander, Warren declined to communicate with him for the rest of the campaign.

After instructing the Composite Regiment to make a demonstration in the direction of Ladysmith, Dundonald set off with the remainder of his force towards Trichardt's Drift. As they rode along he pondered the meaning of his orders. Where was 'nearer' to Warren, and precisely what was he to do when he arrived there? A line of low hills kept the movement of his force hidden from the enemy, while the sound of rifle fire and artillery indicated that an attack was in progress. On their left was the massive Thabanyama plateau at the western end of which was a steep-sided buttress jutting out southwards that Dundonald named Bastion Hill. As they passed it he could see infantry attacking up the eastern slopes of Thabanyama. It was apparent to him that this promontory provided a height from which enemy artillery could dominate the infantry attack currently in progress. To prevent the Boers making use of this natural fortress he decided to occupy it immediately.

Two squadrons of the South African Light Horse were given the task of taking the summit of Bastion Hill while the two remaining squadrons of that regiment and three machine guns were to provide covering fire. As the SALH was Winston Churchill's regiment, he was present and attached himself to the squadrons delegated the task of providing cover for the attackers. Winston watched the first two squadrons gallop across an exposed grassy plain to gain cover, dismount and begin their climb up the precipitous slope. On the summit Boers were seen moving about, however because of the hill's convex shape, the attackers would have disappeared from the sight of those on the crest once they reached the base of the hill. It was now time for the other two squadrons to play their part. They had to cross an exposed area of about a thousand yards before reaching the shelter of a wood. Churchill:

> We moved off at a walk, spreading into a wide open order, as wise colonial cavalry always do. And it was fortunate that our formation was dispersed, for no sooner had we moved into the open than there was a flash of a gun far away among the hills to the westward. It came swiftly, passed overhead with a sound like rending thin sheets of iron, and burst with a rather dull explosion in the ground a hundred yards behind the squadrons, throwing up smoke and clods of earth. We broke into a gallop, and moved in a curving course towards the wood.[1]

They crossed a number of dongas. In one, the colonel decided they should leave their horses and continue on foot. They reached the wood safely but on emerging at its further edge, they were subjected to long-range rifle fire. It was decided to take up a position in a donga about 100 yards ahead. Churchill described how the SALH effected this manoeuvre. 'The troopers immediately began running across in twos and threes. In the irregular corps all appearances are sacrificed to the main object of getting where you want to be without being hurt. No one was hurt.'[2]

Once they were in position they opened fire on the Boers and in the long-range musketry fight which ensued no casualties were suffered. Churchill commented, 'The colonial troopers, as wary as the Dutch, showed very little to shoot at, so that, though there were plenty of bullets, there was no bloodshed. Regular infantry would probably have lost thirty or forty men.'[3]

Meanwhile the three machine guns had been brought up and, faced with this additional hazard, the Boers disappeared from view. The two squadrons tasked with taking the summit had climbed up the face of Bastion Hill with astonishing speed and on breasting the crest found that the Boers had retreated to a line about a thousand yards further back on the Thabanyama plateau. With no cover or artillery support, it was impossible to advance further. Despite Boer shellfire, which killed one of their officers, Major Childe, the colonials consolidated their position. The attack had taken the Boers by surprise and the speed of its execution had left them no time in which to reinforce the southern crest. With the promontory secured, Churchill was able to watch the battle taking place at the eastern end of Thabanyama. Things did not seem to be going quite as well there as they had on Bastion Hill. That night the South African Light Horse was replaced on Bastion Hill by men from Hildyard's Brigade.

On 17 January, General Warren's force had arrived at Trichardt's Drift. It was now time for his troops to practise fighting the Boers. He maintained that no one would play a cricket, football or golf match without practising so why should the same principle not apply to war? Over the next three days his troops did not see any Boers but were subjected to some long-range rifle fire, which Warren believed provided his force with sufficient knowledge of the enemy for the real fighting to begin. It does not seem to have occurred to him that it was the generals who were ignorant of Boer fighting methods, not the men.

On the evening of the 19th Warren held a meeting with his principal officers and told them of his intentions. It was a strange meeting. Lord Dundonald, the one senior officer who knew something of the lie of the land over which they proposed to advance, was not invited. Warren said there were two possible routes along which they might advance, one via Acton Homes and the other along a road that ran between the heights of Thabanyama and Spion Kop, serving the farms Fair View and Rosalie. The route via Acton Homes he rejected as being too long. His officers, who knew nothing of the success of Dundonald's force the previous day or of the configuration of the land ahead, agreed. The attack would therefore proceed along the Fair View/Rosalie Road. It was a rather rough track so Warren intended to make 'special arrangements' to have it cleared. Once this was done the men would be issued with three or four days' rations with which they were to fight their way across the plain behind Spion Kop to Ladysmith.[4] No one asked why, if the men were to carry their rations, it had been necessary to spend days hauling the wagons across the Tugela and Venter's Spruit. Neither did anyone query the fact that no attempt had been made to reconnoitre the land ahead. By 'special arrangements' Warren meant the clearing of the Boers off Thabanyama, and the operation was to begin the next day.

As he was believed to be a master strategist, General Clery, who was almost crippled by varicose veins, was placed in command of the attack on Thabanyama. A number of spurs jutted out southwards from the plateau. Near its western end was Bastion Hill and at its eastern end opposite Trichardt's Drift was a spur crowned by a small eminence, which was given the name Three Tree Hill. Gazing up at the hills, Warren and Clery decided their first move should be to capture Three Tree Hill, which would be achieved by an advance up the western slopes of the spur close to the Fair View/Rosalie Road. General Woodgate with his Lancashire regiments was detailed to lead this attack, while General 'No-Bobs' Hart with his brigade would take up a position to their right and act as a reserve.

At 3 a.m. on 20 January 1900, the Lancastrians moved off. Woodgate, with two of his regiments, led the attack on Three Tree Hill, while his two other regiments were assigned the task of taking the adjoining spur on their left. They soon discovered that the Boers did not occupy either position, and by 6 a.m. Woodgate and his men were firmly ensconced on Three Tree Hill. Orders were given to entrench, pending the arrival of the artillery. With his varicose veins aching, Clery climbed the hill with Warren and, joining Woodgate, they took stock of their position. Ahead of them lay about 2,000 yards of open ground that rose gently to the northern edge of the plateau where Boer entrenchments could clearly be seen. The terrain offered little or no cover. Louis Botha, in forming his defence line, had followed the same principles as Ian Hamilton at Caesar's Camp. Trenches and sangars were constructed at the rear of the position to be defended so that after climbing the hill the attackers would have to advance under fire across open ground. The principal differences between the situations at Caesar's Camp and Thabanyama were that there was some cover on the top of Caesar's Camp and the distance the attackers had to traverse on Thabanyama was three or four times further.

Clery decided to launch his attack across Thabanyama from the spur immediately to the west of Three Tree Hill. Woodgate's two companies of Lancastrians on that spur were reinforced and were also joined by Hart's Brigade, it having been decided that General Hart should lead this new attack. At 7 a.m. the batteries on Three Tree Hill opened fire on the Boer trenches and at 10 a.m. the bombardment increased in intensity when two further batteries came into action. The Boers, secure behind their thick stone walls and deep trenches, held their fire. At 11 a.m. Hart began his advance, and immediately came under fire. At first, some rocky outcrops provided a little cover but when that petered out, men began to fall. The Boers, invisible to the attackers and spread over a wide front, were firing into the exposed and crowded ranks of the infantry. By 3 p.m. the remnants of Hart's leading battalions had reached the very end of what little cover there was and still had to cross 600 yards of exposed ground before reaching the Boer trenches. General 'No Bobs' decided it was time to rush the enemy line and gave the order to fix bayonets. No doubt with sword in hand he intended to lead this attack. However, before he had time to wreak further damage, General Clery decided to intervene, and stopped the advance.

Lt Blake Knox of the Medical Corps, watching the action from a distance, saw specks moving out across the battlefield. His glasses showed these were stretcher-bearers, the majority of whom were civilians of the Natal Volunteer Ambulance Corps:

> Throughout the day these stretcher-bearers ... excited the utmost admiration and praise. They went forward, solidly and unflinchingly, to the very firing line, and could be seen bending over the fallen, tending and removing the wounded with devotion so faithful and a coolness so superb, amidst a hail of bullets and shells, that unfortunately many paid dearly for their self-sacrifice. The Boers fired on them without the least hesitation; either because they could not or would not see the Red Cross brassard worn on their left arm.[5]

Blake Knox was later to moderate this criticism of the Boers by pointing out that the Red Cross armbands worn by the stretcher-bearers were probably too small to be seen. The range of rifle fire had increased considerably in the fifty years since the Crimean War, when wearing the Red Cross by medics was introduced by Florence Nightingale.

It was thought that perhaps the Boers could not see the Red Cross brassards so the practice was introduced that the four bearers for each stretcher should be accompanied by a fifth man carrying a Red Cross flag. The Boers continued to shoot down the stretcher bearers. A diarist serving with the 2nd West Yorkshire Regiment having witnessed three out of four stretcher bearers being deliberately shot down expressed the opinion that 'the devil never hated holy water with half the intensity the Boers hated the civilian stretcher bearers.'[6]

This unplanned and seemingly purposeless attack had cost 308 British casualties, of whom eighteen were killed and 290 wounded. General Warren agreed with Clery's decision and suggested that any further advance should be made that night or perhaps the next day.

On the following day, Sunday 21 January, Col Kitchener of Hildyard's column was given permission to launch an attack against the western section of Thabanyama near Bastion Hill. With no artillery available, the Boer line was subjected to some hours of continuous rifle and Maxim fire, before the advance began. By making use of a donga they were able to make some progress towards the enemy position, but when they made a premature attempt to advance beyond their cover, four out of five officers were immediately hit. When word came through that two batteries were at last on their way, Kitchener felt confident that he could now overrun the weak defences along this western section of the Boer line, and thereby turn the whole line. An order now came through from Clery requiring that the attack be abandoned immediately. Warren had decided that before proceeding further, he would demoralise the Boers with three or four days of continuous artillery fire.

After the ambush at Acton Homes on 18 January, the Boers increased their mounted patrols in the area and from time to time they came into contact with Volunteer units. Churchill contrasted the Colonials with the Regulars, noting that a dismounted squadron of the South African Light Horse held an advanced kopie all day under heavy fire and never lost a man. Two hundred yards back was another kopie held by two companies of regular infantry who lost more than 20 men killed or wounded.[7] Churchill does not mention precisely where this engagement took place and indeed it might be apocryphal. It does however show his opinion of the relative capabilities of the Regulars and the Colonial Volunteers.

The lack of any real progress alarmed Buller, who early on the morning of Monday 22 January visited Warren to express his dissatisfaction with the course of events. Buller wanted immediate action and suggested a whole-hearted attack on the Boer right, but Warren was not going to change his mind on this issue and insisted that the advance should be along the Fair View/Rosalie road. When told that this route could only be followed after Spion Kop had been taken, Buller incautiously said, 'Of course you must take Spion Kop.'[8] The capture of this hill, which had never before even been considered, was now taken for granted. The discussion over, Buller rode over to Bastion Hill, and that afternoon sent a note to Warren suggesting a night attack on the Boer right flank.

Alarmed by Buller's suggestion, Warren called Generals Clery, Hildyard and the newly arrived Talbot Coke to a conference and asked their advice. Clery strongly opposed the idea of moving to Bastion Hill to launch the attack, and pointed out that success could result in their having to take the whole Boer position, which was, of course, what many had thought was the object of the campaign. Clery was supported by Hildyard while Talbot Coke, who had recently broken a leg and was still lame, expressed no opinion at all. By a process of elimination it was thus decided to attack Spion Kop.

It has been written that this hill is 'the highest peak in the Drakensburg Range, and it was from the 460 metre summit of Spion Kop, or "Scouts Hill" that the Voortrekkers had first looked down on the rolling plains of Natal'.[9] This hill is not actually part of the Drakensberg Range and though it is one of the bigger hills in the Tugela Valley, it is not an outstanding feature of the topography of Natal and the view from it is limited to a section of that valley only. The names of these hills are interesting.

Before the arrival of the Voortrekkers and even before the arrival of the British settlers, these hills over which the British and Boer armies were fighting already had names. Thabanyama translates to 'black hill.' The hill runs from east to west so for much of the day its southern slopes would be shaded. There are black hills and mountains all over the world so named because of the play of light and shadow. Spion Kop bore the name 'Ntwananyama', child of the black (hill). This would suggest that guns on the parent hill would be able control activity on the child. The British preferred the Boer name. Even then they did not get it right. The Afrikaans/Dutch word for a lookout, or scout, is *'Spioen'*. The name of the hill should therefore be Spioen Kop. '*Spio*n' is part of a cow's udder.

The next day, 22 January, Warren spent rearranging his command. Clery was placed in command of all troops to the west of Three Tree Hill, while Talbot Coke was given command of the 5th Division and tasked with taking Spion Kop. All that day the artillery continued their bombardment of the Boer trenches. At 4 a.m. on the following day Warren and Talbot Coke rode out to have a good look at Spion Kop.

Later that morning, Warren was again visited by Buller who, alarmed by the delay, gave him the choice of either proceeding with the attack that night or retiring across the river. He criticised the appointment of Talbot Coke to lead the assault and suggested that General Woodgate should lead it, 'as his two sound legs were better adapted for mountain climbing'. At 55, and not in the best of health, Major-General Woodgate would now lead the column up Spion Kop. No one had any idea what the column was to do once it had taken the summit, Buller's sole comment on this subject being that, 'It has got to stay there.'[10]

Warren and Coke spent the rest of the day making preparations for the coming night attack. General Woodgate selected from his own brigade the Lancashire Fusiliers, six companies of the Royal Lancasters, and two companies of South Lancashires, plus a company of Engineers, and 180 men from Thorneycroft's Mounted Infantry, who were to proceed dismounted. A mountain battery was to accompany them, black watercarriers were to take water to the summit, and arrangements were made for a dressing station at the top of Spion Kop and a hospital at its base. A spur or ridge ran down from the summit in a south-westerly direction and it was proposed the column should follow this ridge to the top. Apart from those in command, no one knew of the proposed attack.

When Lieutenant Tom Bridges of the Imperial Light Horse discovered that the British generals had no idea of the configuration of the land beyond that which could be seen from their positions at Mount Alice and Trichardt's Drift, he volunteered to go through the Boer lines to sketch and map the unknown land beyond the visible crests. The offer was accepted. As an assistant, Tom Bridges chose Stanley London, then a trooper in the ILH. This young Natal farmer had enlisted in Pietermaritzburg and was a fluent Zulu linguist familiar with the country they were about to traverse. As dusk was falling on 23 January they made their way through the Boer lines. As they went about their work they heard the sound of a battle raging on Spion Kop. That evening, with their work completed, they were making their way back to the British lines when they saw the enemy trekking away as fast as they could from the battlefield. Delighted, they pressed on until, several hours later, they came upon the British, also retreating. The two armies appeared to be running away from each other. On their reaching the British lines, Tom Bridges was promptly arrested and charged with being 'absent without leave'. The Court found him guilty and he was reduced 35 places in seniority on the Royal Artillery list.[11]

A couple of hours after Bridges and London had left to map and sketch the land to the north of Thabanyama and Spion Kop, 1,700 troops assembled near White's Farm in a gully below Three Tree Hill. Here they received orders to climb the southern slope of Spion Kop and eject the Boers from the summit. Most of the remaining eighteen thousand members of Buller's force were required to do little more than watch events unfold. Woodgate decided that Lt Col Alec Thorneycroft and his dismounted men should lead the assault. At 6 feet 2 inches tall, Thorneycroft was a great bull of a man, full of energy and possessed of great courage. He had reconnoitred a possible route up the hill and this, coupled with the fact that he was fit, were the probable reasons for choosing him to lead the column to the summit. However, like the other British officers, he had no idea what they would find there.

Warren's decision to send a mounted regiment up Spion Kop is, even by his standards, truly astonishing. Buller's army was desperately short of mounted men, and they should not have been called on to carry out a task more suited to infantry. It appears that Sir Charles had never understood the purpose and function of mounted troops. Further, Thorneycroft's MI with their obsolete rifles without bayonets would be at a considerable disadvantage when engaged in the anticipated close range combat. At the field hospital the medical staff hoped the morrow would be a quiet day.

At 11 p.m. Woodgate's assault column set off and though they originally marched in fours, they were soon in single file, with Thorneycroft in front followed by his own men, then by the Lancashire contingents. Orders were passed forward that there was to be no shooting and on contact with the enemy, only bayonets were to be used. Presumably Thorneycroft's colonials, who were leading the climb up the hill, were to use their rifles as clubs! For four hours they climbed. General Woodgate struggled on the climb and had to be helped by his batman up the rockier parts of the ridge. Eventually the track broadened and those in front were able to spread out and lie down while the Lancastrians came up and joined them. With dawn about to break, a heavy mist descended on the hill, limiting vision to a couple of yards. Cautiously they rose and moved forward when out of the mist came the repeated cry '*Wie is daar?*' (Who is there?) followed by some rifle shots. On hearing the sentry's challenge the colonials had dropped to the ground and the rifle fire flew harmlessly over their heads. Thorneycroft now gave the order to charge, causing the Boer sentries to flee into the mist but not before at least one of their number had been bayoneted by a Lancastrian. After the arduous climb Woodgate's men were at last on the summit – they had captured Spion Kop.

Three cheers rang out to tell Warren of their success.[12] Of course this also told the Boers where they were and what had happened. Louis Botha was quick to respond.

Stumbling around in the mist, the engineers chose an area where the ground sloped gently away to the north and there taped a position 300 to 400 yards long, where trenches should be sited. Shaped like a boomerang with its apex facing north, the trenches were intended to provide a clear view of any enemy counterattack. The men started to dig but their spades were too fragile for the task and after they had gone down 18 inches, they struck a solid bed of rock on which even their picks could make little impression. Hurriedly, they attempted to construct stone sangars. Sandbags would have been a big help and were available at White's farm, but had been overlooked and left behind during the excitement at the start of the ascent.

A partial and temporary break in the mist revealed the trenches were not in the right place. North of their trench the ground sloped downwards for about 200 yards, but then fell so steeply that the Boers would be able to climb the hill unseen and remain hidden just over the crest. The British tried to bring their line forward to the northern crest, but were driven back to their original position by increasing fire. In the thick mist no one was quite sure of the location of the Boers firing on them, though General Woodgate remained confident that everything was under control. Prevented by the mist from using flags to signal, he sent a staff officer down the hill at 7.15 a.m. with a letter for Warren: 'I pushed on a bit quicker than I perhaps should otherwise have done, lest it should lift before we got here. We have entrenched a position, and are, I hope secure; but fog too thick to see, so I retain Thorneycroft's men and Royal Engineers for a bit longer. Thorneycroft's men attacked in fine style.'

On the way down, the officer passed the headquarters of General Talbot Coke whose men were entrenched on the hillside to cover any possible reverse. At the foot of the hill he was able to borrow a horse and rode over to Warren's headquarters at Three Tree Hill, arriving at 9 o'clock. He delivered the letter, told Warren a small spring had been found on top of the hill, and asked that a naval gun and some sandbags be sent up to Woodgate.[13] Warren signalled to Coke to ask if support was needed on the summit, and was told that because of the mist it had not been possible to establish contact with Woodgate. Nonetheless, Warren decided to reinforce the summit with a further infantry battalion. Two companies each of the Imperial Light Infantry and the Middlesex Regiment were ordered to proceed at once to the summit. They were not to follow the westerly route chosen by Thorneycroft the previous evening but instead to climb up the south-eastern face of Spion Kop. Perhaps because many of their members came from Natal, and despite the facts they had only a few weeks training and were armed with the obsolete rifles without bayonets, the ILI were to lead the way.

The tops of the hills were still shrouded in mist and it was not until 9.50 a.m. that Warren received a signal from Spion Kop. The message stated, 'Colonel Crofton to GOC Force. Reinforce at once or all lost. General Dead'.[14]

On the summit the mist had suddenly cleared at 8.30 a.m. revealing nearly 1,700 men crowded into a confined space on the summit. On the right (or east) were the Lancashire Fusiliers, in the centre at the apex of the main trench were Thorneycroft's MI, to their left six companies of the Royal Lancaster Regiment and on the extreme left two companies of the South Lancashire regiment. They soon realised the grim reality that the Boers were facing them on three sides. From the left (or west) they received long range rifle fire from Conical Hill (1,000 yards) and Green Hill (1,500 yards). In the centre the Boers had climbed to the northern crest and from concealed positions opened close-range rifle fire on the British 'trench' while at the same time working their way forward towards the British line. About 400 yards to the east was a small hill called Aloe Knoll, the existence of which had been unknown to the British a few minutes before but which now had, concealed among its rocks, Boers who were pouring rifle fire into the exposed right of the trench. So unexpected and effective was this fire that it was found afterwards that seventy per cent of Lancashire Fusiliers who were killed had been shot in the right side.

Botha only had five guns and a couple of pom-poms available to him, but they were superbly placed. In the west two guns were brought up from Acton Homes to the northern slopes of Thabanyama and opened fire on Spion Kop; to the north another gun and a pom-pom near Coventry's farm began to shell the summit; while in the east on Twin Peaks two guns and a pom-pom joined the bombardment. Boer signallers on Aloe Knoll were able to give precise directions to their guns. The British guns, by contrast, were completely ineffectual as they had no idea where the enemy were.

The Boer guns soon forced the British signallers to seek shelter on the south-eastern spur, where the only signal station visible to them was Buller's headquarters on Spearman's Hill, from which signals could be relayed to Warren's headquarters at Three Tree Hill. General Woodgate, uncertain what he should do, had dictated a message asking for reinforcements. The message, the wording of which might have been altered in transmission, stated, 'Am exposed to terrible cross-fire, especially near first dressing station. Can barely hold our own. Water badly needed. Help us. Woodgate'.

In an attempt to find out where the fire into his right flank originated, General Woodgate broke cover for an instant and fell mortally wounded. His Brigade-Major, Captain Vertue, made his way over to Colonel Crofton of the Royal Lancaster Regiment to tell him Woodgate was dead and that as senior colonel, he was now in command. Vertue delivered the message and immediately afterwards he, too, was shot dead.

At Warren's headquarters, Crofton's message was met with some surprise. They clung to the belief that all was well, and felt that Crofton must have lost his head. A message was sent back up the hill saying help was on its way and concluding, 'You must hold on to the last. No surrender.'

Warren had always wanted General Talbot Coke to lead the assault and now rode over to Coke and told him to take command on the summit. Taking with him the Dorset Regiment, carrying sandbags, Coke, aided by a walking stick, set off at 11 o'clock for his new command. Before he left, Warren told him there should be no surrender. Warren did not tell Buller that he had appointed Coke to succeed the mortally wounded Woodgate.

Buller had also received the alarming messages from Spion Kop and from his position it was clear a great struggle was taking place on top of the hill. He sent a heliograph to Warren: 'Unless you put some really good hard fighting man in command on the top you will lose the hill. I suggest Thorneycroft.'

Warren promptly sent a message to Crofton that Thorneycroft was in command on the summit. He did not inform Coke of this change, and what is more, when Coke sent messages back to base that clearly showed he thought he was in command, Warren made no attempt to advise him of the true position. While the generals were playing this clumsy game of musical chairs, the desperate fight continued on the hill.

Reading of these events today it is astonishing that any living creature could have survived the terrible onslaught of bullets and shells on Spion Kop. And yet in the shallow trenches, among the rocks and their dead and wounded comrades, the men fought on. The Boers, who were also suffering casualties, clawed their way over the crest and were beginning to drive back the British line. At about 11 o'clock Thorneycroft led a charge of about forty of his men and the Lancashire Fusiliers to clear the Boers off the crest but the enemy fire was so intense they were forced to go to ground. Thorneycroft fell – but in a day when there was little good news, it turned out he had only twisted his ankle. It was at this stage that he received the news that he had been promoted to the local rank of Brigadier-General and was in command on the summit. The bearer of this message was killed while delivering it. For the time being, all Thorneycroft's energies were devoted to holding the Boers at bay and he was unable to take any action under the new powers that had been thrust on him.

The men had arrived on Spion Kop in cold mist but now they were lying in the scorching sun. The spring, which the staff officer told Warren existed on the hill, turned out to be nothing more than a pool of fetid water. All who were tempted to drink from it became ill and some died from its effects. Water bottles were soon exhausted and a raging thirst was added to the miseries being suffered.

On the right, the Lancashire Fusiliers had suffered more than most. Almost all their officers had been killed or seriously wounded and as they lay on the ground too terrified even to lift their heads to shoot, someone raised a white flag. The Boers rose to accept the surrender. When Thorneycroft discovered what was happening, this great giant of a man stood up, and limping over to the Boer leader said, 'I'm commandant here. Take your men back to hell, sir. There's no surrender.'[15]

He then turned his back on the Boers and limped back to his trench. Nonplussed, the Boers went back to their positions and when everyone had settled down the fighting resumed. Before Thorneycroft's intervention the Boers had taken into captivity about 150 of the Fusiliers.

Shortly after this incident, the first reinforcements arrived – the Imperial Light Infantry. Thorneycroft ordered them to take up a position on the right to compensate for the losses of the Lancashire Fusiliers. Into this maelstrom of flying metal and death, where survival seemed but a remote possibility, these untried Volunteer colonials, with only rudimentary training and obsolete rifles, were now thrust. They did not flinch but fought their way to the shallow trench and then on into the forward firing-line. Casualties were inevitable, but their resolution did not waver for a second and the right flank held. Next up were the Middlesex Regiment, who took up positions among the Light Infantry. One private of this Regular regiment was about to peer over a rock when he was pulled back by a Natal Colonial of the ILI, who told him never to put his head over the top but to fire round the rock.[16] Many of the Middlesex man's comrades were killed that day trying to fire over the sheltering rocks. This private listened to the advice and survived.

When the mist cleared from the summit of Spion Kop that morning, General Lyttleton on Spearman's Hill watched the battle unfolding. Early in the morning his troops had made a diversionary demonstration against the Brakfontein Hills. When messages arrived from the summit requesting reinforcements, Lyttleton decided on supplying more direct assistance to those embattled units. The Scottish Rifles crossed the Tugela, and began making their way up Spion Kop. At the same time, a battalion of the 60th Rifles crossed the river to attack Twin Peaks lying to the east of Spion Kop. Through telescopes, Boers could be seen on Aloe Knoll and they presented an obvious target for the artillery. Lyttelton ordered his eight 12-pounder naval guns and two howitzers to open fire on Aloe Knoll and the eastern slopes of Spion Kop. Two 4.7 inch guns from Mount Alice joined in the bombardment. At last the artillery was making an effective attack on the Boers. Unfortunately, they had hardly begun the bombardment when a message came through from Warren, 'We occupy the whole summit and I fear you are shelling us seriously. Can you not turn your guns on the enemy's guns?'[17]

The assault force only occupied the western half of the summit and Warren had no reason to believe anything to the contrary. Throughout the whole day he was convinced that the entire summit was occupied and nothing would shake this conviction. Lyttleton had no choice but to obey, and ordered the artillery to cease fire. Buller on Mount Alice could see that Warren was mistaken but instead of correcting the error and ordering the guns to resume firing, he remained silent. Lyttelton's artillery may have stopped firing, but the 60th Rifles continued to make their way towards Twin Peaks.

Subjected to continuous, intense fire, on Spion Kop the men had no time to contemplate overall strategy. In the process of dodging from one rock to another, regiments had become muddled up. To prevent the Boers concentrating their fire on officers, badges of rank had been removed – which added to the confusion. In the centre, Thorneycroft and his colonials were fully occupied trying to stem the tide of Boers trying to get a toehold on the summit. To their left, Crofton was engaged in a similar struggle. On the right, the remnants of the Fusiliers with the ILI and the Middlesex Regiment were all the while under heavy fire from Aloe Knoll and also had to deal with a Boer attempt to get around the British right flank. It was impossible for the leaders on the summit to communicate meaningfully in such conditions, and the fight began to separate into sections.

We have seen that Coke, who was painfully making his way up Spion Kop, thought he was in command, as did Thorneycroft. The arrival of the Middlesex Regiment under Colonel Hill added another name to the list of those who thought they were in command. Colonel Hill, senior to both Crofton and Thorneycroft, thought that in the absence of Coke he must now be the commander on the summit.

At midday Colonel Nash of the Imperial Light Infantry received an order to reinforce the summit with every available man. By 2 p.m. he was on the summit with the remaining companies of the ILI and the balance of the Middlesex Regiment. As their comrades had done earlier in the day, these further companies of the ILI rushed fearlessly across open ground to the firing trench, where they immediately went into action. Enemy fire continued all afternoon without a break and when darkness fell they were still in position. Other reinforcements arrived, which crowded the summit still further without alleviating the problems.

At 4 o'clock Coke finally arrived somewhere near the summit. He did not go into the main firing line, being content with a statement that the men were holding their own. Neither did he attempt to contact Thorneycroft whom he regarded as 'a junior brevet Lieutenant-Colonel in command of a small unit'. Coke was considerably shaken by the scenes he found near the summit.

He consulted with his staff and Colonel Hill, and at 6 o'clock he sent a message to Warren asking for orders while at the same time hinting that a withdrawal was necessary. He received no reply.

Thorneycroft meanwhile had seen Colonel Crofton, who confirmed his appointment as brigadier-general. He had no doubt he was in command and sent a dispatch to Warren:

The enemy are now (6.30 p.m.) firing heavily from both flanks (rifle, shell and Nordenfelt), while a heavy rifle-fire is being kept up on the front. It is all I can do to hold my own. If my casualties go on at the present rate I shall barely hold out the night. A large number of stretcher-bearers should be sent up, and also all the water possible. The situation is critical.[18]

At about 7 o'clock, darkness fell. The firing died down and the exhausted, thirsty men lay in their trench and waited. Nothing happened.

It will be recalled that Lyttelton had sent a battalion of the 60th Rifles to attack Twin Peaks, which lay to the east of Spion Kop. The battalion divided in two, each half being assigned one of the hills. The hillsides were, in places, almost perpendicular and it took them some time to make the ascent. When Lyttelton told Buller what he had done, Buller was furious that the battalion had gone out without support and ordered that they return immediately. The commanders of the two half battalions pretended not to have received this order and continued up the hills. At 4.45 p.m. they reached the summit of the eastern peak and after a bayonet charge, the defenders fled. At 5 p.m. the second peak was taken in similar fashion. The Boers had succeeded in getting their guns away just in time. For the remainder of the afternoon, the 60th Rifles were able to take some of the pressure off the troops on Spion Kop. When the orders to withdraw were repeated at 8 o'clock they withdrew in good order. It appears that when the assault on Twin Peaks was made, Buller had already decided Spion Kop was not worth the price which had to be paid, and was anxious to break off the action as soon as possible.

At about 8 p.m., Thorneycroft conferred with Crofton and Colonel Cooke of the Scottish Rifles. No orders had been received from Warren and efforts to contact Coke and Col Hill had proved fruitless; both might be dead. Crofton and Cooke felt they should withdraw. Thorneycroft agreed and at 8.15 p.m. the evacuation of Spion Kop began. Not all those on the field that night agreed with that decision, and attempts were made to stop the withdrawal, but Thorneycroft was not one to change his mind and in the end they all came down the hill.

While the British were withdrawing down one side of the hill, the Boers were withdrawing down the other. The Boers had also sustained heavy losses and after the capture of Twin Peaks by Lyttelton they felt any further attempt by them to regain Spion Kop would be doomed to failure.

Thorneycroft has been criticised for withdrawing without orders. He certainly tried to get orders and the failure of the lines of communication can hardly be laid at his door. Of the 180 men in his regiment, which he led up the hill, thirty-nine had been killed and over sixty wounded. Our diarist in the Army Medical Corps, Lt Blake Knox, saw the conditions on top of Spion Kop and left this description of what the troops had endured.

> It is doubtful whether, in the records of civilized warfare, troops have ever before been exposed to similar conditions. Without sleep the night before, without water, without cover, with a limited supply of food, under a blazing hot African sun, the British and Colonial infantry, unable to move forward, still held their ground. No other troops in the world would have done so. The sufferings of the wounded under these circumstances were too horrible to be described, many of them being shot over and over again, as they attempted to crawl away, and even the torpor of death did not protect their poor lifeless frames.[19]

In the dark, various groups of men joined the procession going down the hill. At about 9 o'clock Colonel Nash received a message to move off the hill. The Imperial Light Infantry formed up and began the march back. They had gone about 200 yards when an officer appeared and wanted to know where they were going. Nash explained he had been ordered to take the regiment off the hill. The other officer then said, 'I am Colonel Hill of the Middlesex, not a man or a regiment is to leave the hill.' The officers of the ILI then told their men that a mistake had been made and the column 'about turned' and marched back to the position they had just vacated. Pickets were put out and they settled down among the dead and wounded.[20]

Unknown to them, the other troops – including Colonel Hill and his regiment – were making their way down the hill. No one told Colonel Nash what was happening so the ILI remained in position. At 2 a.m. someone must have realised they were still on the summit and the following order was issued, 'Officer commanding Imperial Light Infantry. Withdraw at once. 2 a.m. W. J. Bonus, Brigade-Major.' A staff-officer took the message up to Nash and sometime between 3 a.m. and 4 a.m. the regiment assembled again and finally left the summit. Prior to the ILI leaving, no Boers had ventured back on to Spion Kop.[21]

The Imperial Light Infantry casualties were originally stated as being thirty-one killed (including two officers), 113 wounded (including three officers), and nineteen men missing. Subsequently it was found that the missing men had been either killed or wounded.[22]

Colonial Volunteers were the first troops on the summit, and the last to leave. The behaviour of Col Hill and some of the other British officers during the engagement betrayed the extraordinary attitude many of them had towards Volunteers, an attitude they extended to the Regular officers serving with the Volunteers. Although they were fighting in close proximity to each other against a common enemy, these officers showed little or no interest in co-operating with the Volunteer units. Communication might have been difficult during the height of the battle, but there was no excuse for what happened after darkness fell. It must surely have been a simple matter for the officers to have met to decide on a coherent plan, instead of the absurd process of the Regulars wrangling over seniority while doing their best to exclude the Volunteer regiments from the decision-making process.

Lt Blake Knox had had a very busy day. From about midday, stretcher parties began to arrive at the bottom of the hill. He set up a dressing station near a stream sheltered from Boer fire by a bank and close to the path that ran to and from the plateau on top of Spion Kop. A large Red Cross flag was placed above the site. From the time the dressing station was set up, all wounded coming off the hill were checked by Blake Knox. Some had had their wounds attended to at the dressing station further up the hill and all that was necessary was to ensure the bandages were still in place and the bleeding had stopped. Comrades had bandaged the wounds of others, while some had dressed their own wounds, often using their clothing as bandages. Many had died on the way down and others were appallingly mutilated. He noticed how cheerful the wounded were and the absence of any grumbling. Though it was but little comfort, he was pleased that they had gallons of beef tea and brandy to offer the patients before they moved on to the field hospital. One patient stood out in his memory. An old grey-bearded colonial in Thorneycroft's MI staggered in, with the help of his rifle. He was a mass of wounds – one ear was pierced by a bullet; his chin, neck and chest also shot through by others; his back and legs torn by shell fire. 'He came in saying that he had just dropped in to have a finger off. It was so shattered he could not pull a trigger, and it got in the way of the next finger which he could use.'[23] The medics did of course refuse to let him return to the firing line. It was exhausting work constantly bending down and treating the stretcher cases and as darkness came and the night wore on, Blake Knox and his staff had to struggle against creeping tiredness, many falling asleep. The light they received from their two lanterns was inadequate and made their work more difficult. In spite of the difficult conditions in which he was working, the doctor noticed how others were coping.

> The kindness of the stretcher-bearers, many of whom belonged to the Natal Volunteer Ambulance Corps, was splendid. Many a poor man shot in the morning in the front-trenches, who could not be reached, and who had lain, as was often the case in the blazing sun all day without food and water, and then in the cold of the night without his coat, and shivering, was rolled up in the stretcher-bearers' coats, and his wound bound with the bearer's only towel or only handkerchief, which was lost to its owner when the case was passed on.[24]

A soldier of the Lancaster Regiment:

> Them stretcher-bearers worked 'ard too – they may be civilians, and mayn't look over and above smart, but we of the King's Own won't fergit all as they did for our men in a 'urry....Carrying men down a place as steep as a 'ouse and under 'eavy fire too. Body-snatchers, some calls em, and thinks they's being funny. But I says a man wot does that don't know is friends; and wot's more, 'e ought ter be shot. They chaps of the Volunteer Stretcher Bearers worked like 'eroes, and no mistake abahtt it.[25]

Before dawn the next day, Blake Knox arranged for the remaining patients at his dressing station to be sent on to the field hospital and, gathering together as many stretcher bearers as he could muster, set off for the summit. On the plateau all was now silent; in the trenches the dead and wounded lay intermingled. The stretcher bearers immediately set to, placing the dead on one side and doing what they could for the wounded. They had just started work when, suddenly, the silence was broken. 'Hands up,' said a voice in a Dutch accent. They were surrounded by Boers.

Being the only unwounded officer present Blake Knox advanced to parley. He told them he was a doctor. They laughed and pointed at his sleeve. His Red Cross brassard was no longer there. More Boers arrived, including one wearing a brassard. Blake Knox discovered he had an Edinburgh qualification and was able to convince this man of his bona fides. Louis Botha arrived shortly afterwards and, once further proof was produced, he ordered Blake Knox's release on parole, while at the same time offering him some coffee. While this was being prepared, Botha complained of British barbarity. In particular, he referred to the ill-treatment of the prisoners taken at Acton Homes, that ambulances taken from the Boers were sent to Cape Town and that Boer prisoners were tied to guns and dragged along the road. On being asked if he had proof, Botha answered, 'No, but they were common reports in his lines'. Botha was assured that Blake Knox himself had attended to the Acton Homes prisoners and they had not been ill-treated. Perhaps the doctor did not know about the unkind things the Zulus had said to the Boers on that occasion. At 10 a.m., the Boers granted permission for the removal of the wounded and within an hour they were on their way to the field hospital, which lay in a bush covered area on the northern bank of the Tugela below Spion Kop.

On the day following the battle, Dundonald went to see Thorneycroft's regiment as it marched away to bivouac:

> It was a sad sight, half of the horses were led horses with empty saddles, their riders lying dead on Spion Kop, or mangled in hospital. As to Colonel Thorneycroft's behaviour on Spion Kop, there was but one opinion, that he was the life and soul of the defence, performing acts of great gallantry.[26]

On that morning of 25 January, Buller was at last stirred into action. Warren was relieved of the command of all but his 5th Division. Perhaps because the element of surprise had been lost, Buller abandoned the idea of outflanking the Boer right. His troops with their massive baggage train had to return to their positions south of the Tugela. Over the next few days men, animals, guns and wagons were very efficiently moved back across Trichardt's Drift. Perhaps practice does help.

When the last of the wounded left the plateau on 25 January, a party of four army chaplains and 25 men of the Natal Volunteer Ambulance Corps climbed to the summit to bury the dead. Although they took advantage of the excavations of what had once been trenches and now became graves, it took them, because of the hard rocky ground, three days to bury the dead in shallow graves.

In this failed attempt to capture Spion Kop, the British suffered 885 casualties of which 322 were killed and 563 wounded. In addition the Boers took 173 prisoners. The Boer losses were about one quarter of those suffered by the British.

Early in January, M.K. Gandhi's Indian Ambulance Corps was again mobilised and on 7 January they travelled by train to Estcourt. Here they received training on lifting a wounded man onto a stretcher and carrying the laden stretcher. They also took part in several route marches. On 24 January at 2 p.m., when the battle of Spion Kop was at its height, they received orders to be ready to entrain for Frere at 6 p.m. The next day they marched from Frere to Spearman's Farm, about 25 miles away. After a night's rest they were told that there were many wounded in a temporary field hospital at the foot of Spion Kop. These men had to be brought back to the field hospital at Spearman's and this would involve crossing a pontoon bridge, which might be subjected to Boer fire. All the leaders and men in the unit expressed their willingness to take this risk. By that evening they had brought all the wounded across the Tugela to the field hospital, without being subjected to hostile fire. Despite the distance involved, because the journey over the rough, dusty track in an ambulance or wagon would have caused much suffering to the wounded, it was decided the stretcher bearers should now carry the wounded from Spearman's to Frere. Gandhi's men spent approximately three weeks on this humanitarian task[27] and thereby relieved the wounded of much pain and possibly saved some lives.[28]

At Intombi, Kate Driver recovered from her bout of illness and though far from well, returned to work. The matron had enteric, six out of the ten nurses were ill and the remaining four 'not quite so ill anymore'. Many of their Natal orderlies were ill and although they received some excellent help from refugee civil servants from Dundee, the other orderlies with whom she now had to work were not up to standard. She, like everyone else at Ladysmith, was excited when in the last week of January Buller's guns could be heard roaring among the hills to the south.

> Oh, the joy of Buller's approach! From my uncle Clem in Ladysmith I received a bright hopeful letter, and – unbelievable luxury – a cake! It was not large, but many of us had bits of it. No one dreamed of asking what it was made of. It soon came to an end. So did that lovely boom of guns. And the reaction was terrible. Our hopes had been so high.
>
> Into one of my wards they brought a boy of eighteen, wounded in the spine so that he could never get better. His great eyes were seldom off me; and those eyes reminded me of my brother of eighteen who had joined up a few months ago. I kept imagining, as I tried to comfort this boy, that my brother was in a similar state, for a rumour was about that Thorneycroft's men, among whom was my brother, all, except eighty, were killed or wounded. I was in this suspense for days, and then to my great joy, a helio message was handed to me. It was from a friend and it said, 'Your brother and I en route for Ladysmith in the Imperial Light Infantry.'[29]

Owen Driver had enlisted with Thorneycroft's Mounted Infantry but was later rejected because 'his riding was not up to standard'. He then enlisted with the Imperial Light Infantry.

On 24 January 2000, the centenary of this famous battle, a number of people gathered at Spion Kop. One group climbed up the hill following the route taken by the British, while others followed the path taken by the Boers. They met at the summit, where a memorial service was held. Someone looked up and then others. High in the atmosphere above them was a bright circle of light. When the service was over and they had driven down the hill, the circle of light remained visible over Spion Kop.[30] There is, of course, a scientific explanation for the phenomenon – something about light being reflected off frozen particles of moisture. And the coincidence? Well, that's another matter altogether.

21

Battle of Vaalkrantz;
Distress of the Besieged

After the frustration of his plan to turn the Boer's right flank, Buller decided to launch his next attack a few miles further downstream. The Brakfontein Hills ran east from Spion Kop, terminating in a hill known as Vaalkrantz. Below Vaalkrantz a road ran through to Ladysmith and it was along this road that Buller now intended to fight his way through to the beleaguered town. On the other or eastern side of the road, was Green Hill – behind which lay a larger hill, called Doorn Kop.

South of the river, Swartz Kop provided Buller with an excellent site for his artillery. From this hill his guns would be able to dominate Vaalkrantz, Green Hill and Doorn Kop. The whole operation was to be conducted by the Regulars and those ideas had failed so spectacularly at Spion Kop would be tried again in this new attempt to effect a breakthrough.

To the west, Woodgate's brigade, now under the command of Major-General Wynne, crossed the Tugela via the pontoon near Potgieter's Drift and occupied, without opposition, the Maconochie Hills. It was from these hills that General Lyttelton had launched his diversionary attack on the enemy's left during the battle for Spion Kop. General Wynne was to make the same diversionary attack – only on this occasion it was intended to be seen as an assault on the Boers' right. Lyttelton's brigade would now attack the Boer centre and drive them off Vaalkrantz. On the right, General 'No Bobs' Hart's infantry would march north along the road in the valley while, yet further to the right, General Hildyard would secure Green Hill. The Regular cavalry under General Burn Murdoch would follow Hart through the hills, and then move on towards Ladysmith.

Roughly midway between Wynne's brigade on Maconochie Hills and Vaalkrantz, a new pontoon was constructed across the Tugela. Lyttelton's brigade took up a position near this pontoon while remaining on the south side of the river. Its construction and the stationing of Lyttelton's men nearby was intended to deceive the Boers into thinking the main attack would be against Brakfontein.

At 6 a.m. on Monday 5 February, the military squaredance began. The guns on Mount Alice blazed away at the assumed position of the Boer trenches on the Brakfontein Hills, while Wynne's infantry began a steady advance towards those hills. Some long-range fire failed to check the advance, though they suffered a few casualties – one man killed and thirty wounded.

At the same time, Buller's guns on Swartz Kop laid down a heavy barrage on what appeared to be Boer fortifications on the top of Vaalkrantz. It later transpired that the fortifications seen on top of the hill were dummies, the Boer riflemen having taken up concealed positions just below the summit. Meanwhile, Lyttelton's men abandoned all pretence they would support the attack on Brakfontein and marched back to Vaalkrantz.

It was now the turn of the sappers to come forward and show their skill and courage by constructing a bridge across the Tugela over which the main attack could be launched. Under persistent sniper fire from those hidden positions on Vaalkrantz, they constructed a 70-yard pontoon bridge in just fifty minutes. With the bridge in place the main attack could now begin.

Creeping self-doubt again afflicted Buller. Perhaps the attack should not start until the troops involved in the diversionary attack had returned to their strong position on the Maconochie Hills? Wynne was ordered to retire, a manoeuvre he was able to do in parade ground good order, making the guns that supported him available to assist the main attack. It was 2 p.m. but still Buller hesitated and suggested to Lyttelton it was too late to begin the attack and perhaps the whole enterprise should be called off. Lyttelton, whose men had been standing by for hours while the Boers reinforced their defences, promised Buller that if he left at once they would be on the top of Vaalkrantz by 4 o'clock. Buller reluctantly agreed and Lyttelton immediately set off. Hildyard's and Hart's brigades were about to follow when they were checked by Buller, who ordered them to remain south of the river. The result was the Boers retained control of Green Hill, nobody could travel along the road to Ladysmith, and Lyttlelton's brigade was climbing up a precipitous hill in a situation where success would achieve nothing. With great determination, the infantrymen battled up the eastern end of Vaalkrantz and at precisely 4 o'clock, a young officer was seen on the crest waving his helmet before falling mortally wounded. For a few precious moments he had been king of the castle.

Though ordered to retire, Lyttelton decided to remain on the hill that night. However, Boer fire from the north, from Green Hill and Doorn Kop in the east, forced them onto the western side of Vaalkrantz, where they dug in. That night the Boers re-positioned their guns and brought up reinforcements.

Buller was up early the next morning. The tried and tested tactics of the British Victorian army were not working. The speed with which the Boers re-deployed their forces, their reluctance to show themselves and their deadly long-range rifle fire were factors that had never been encountered before. He was in a terrible quandary. Should he continue with the attack or should he order a retirement? The re-deployment of the Boer forces had made the whole operation hopeless and yet he was committed to an attack that could cost two to three thousand lives. He again told Lyttelton to retire and then changed his mind and asked him to stay on the hill during the day while he 'watched developments'. In an attempt to obtain an answer to his problem, he sent a telegram to Lord Roberts asking what he should do. The answer was not what Buller wanted. Roberts said he must attack even if it meant suffering the anticipated casualties. If the men were told 'the honour of the Empire was in their hands,' Roberts had no doubt they would succeed. Buller could not bring himself to sacrifice his men in this manner. During the day the artillery on both sides indulged in an ineffectual duel and that afternoon Buller ordered Hildyard to relieve Lyttelton. Once off the hill, Lyttelton and his Brigade Major went to report to Buller who they found having dinner. Buller asked how they had fared, to which Lyttelton, who was not in the best of moods, replied, 'Very bad, shot at day and night from nearly all sides'. Buller ordered two large glasses of his excellent champagne for his guests who were at least partially mollified.

Dawn the following day brought no solution to Buller's dilemma. The Boers were still in their commanding positions in the hills and he was still uncertain whether to attack or withdraw. He called a meeting of his generals. They met in Clery's tent that afternoon. Lyttelton, Wynne and Clery were for retirement; Hart was, as usual, keen to attack. Warren, who had originally opposed the Vaalkrantz operation, was in favour of continuing the action. The reason he gave for this change of mind was that he had 'taken the pulse of 20,000 men'. When asked if he favoured any other line of attack, he said, 'Hlangwane', and other generals murmured their assent. Buller now had the decision he wanted. It had been democratically decided that they would withdraw so he was now able to give the order to withdraw from Vaalkrantz and return to Chieveley. The whole operation had cost the British thirty men killed and 350 wounded. The Boers lost thirty men killed and about fifty wounded. Though the action would appear to have achieved nothing, this was not so. There had been persistent intelligence that the Boers intended to launch another attack on Ladysmith on 5 February. When Buller's army began its move towards Vaalkrantz, the Boers had been compelled to draw men from Ladysmith to reinforce the long Tugela line. As a result, the attack against the town was abandoned and no further attempt was to be made to overcome its enfeebled defences.

Dundonald's brigade, now consisting solely of Volunteers, played no part in the action at Vaalkrantz. They were required to cover the rear of the column as it retreated to Chieveley. Buller sent a heliograph to General White telling of the change in plan and suggested he 'keep it dark'. In Ladysmith they had heard the sounds of battle from the direction of Vaalkrantz followed by yet another anti-climax as the sound of the guns died down with no sign of the relieving force.

On 24 January, the last of the garrison's maize went through the mill. From now on, not only was the supply of food limited, but its quality and nutritional value steadily declined. The serving out of the rations was strictly supervised. Europeans, blacks and Indians all lined up together and each applicant was required to present himself at a barrier, and after producing his ration permit, pass down a gangway guarded on either side by barbed wire before reaching four depots where each in turn received a little packet of meat, biscuit or bread, sugar, and tea/coffee. The barbed wire entanglements indicated 'that the military authorities looked forward as a possibility to the day when they might have to guard against the rush of starving people inside the town, as well as the rush of an enemy from the outside.'[1]

Mule and horsemeat had become the norm. Many of the horses had already died from starvation and those that had to be slaughtered were generally in the process of dying. Leaving aside the repugnance many felt towards eating horseflesh, the meat would, in any normal circumstances, have been considered unfit for consumption. Two classes of horses were given a slightly privileged position when it came to the selection of those to be slaughtered. The artillery horses were needed for the guns and the Volunteers were permitted a little more latitude regarding the feeding of their mounts. This was said to be because the Volunteers rode their own horses and had in many cases strong personal ties with their mounts. The Regular cavalry, on the other hand, rode army issue horses and would not have had the same rapport with them.

From 1 February the men were given a choice of a full pound of horseflesh as their daily ration or half a pound of tinned beef. Some, finding the thought of eating horse repulsive, initially chose the beef. This option was not only less filling but was also less nutritious and in the end, hunger drove many into eating horsemeat.

On 4 February Henry Pearse of the *Daily News* had brought home to him how desperate the situation was becoming,

> I found sitting on a doorstep, apparently too weak to move, a young fellow of the Imperial Light Horse – scarcely more than a boy – his stalwart form shrunken by illness. He was toying with a spray of wild jasmine, as if its perfume brought back vague memories of home. I learned that he had been wounded at Elandslaagte and again on Wagon Hill. Then came Intombi and malaria. He had only been discharged from hospital that morning. His appetite was not quite equal to the horseflesh test, so he had gone without food. I took him to my room and gave him such things as a scanty store could furnish, with the last dram of whisky for a stimulant.[2]

It should be mentioned that the native peoples of eastern South Africa have a strong aversion to eating horsemeat, and many groups will not touch pork. Most would have spurned the offer of the former.

Horseflesh was also the principal ingredient of an extract given the name Chevril, a reference to the unobtainable beef extract Bovril. Originally intended for use in the hospitals, it proved nutritious and orders were issued that a pint of soup made from Chevril should be issued daily to each man. The bread was made from mealie meal, starch to hold it together, and some unknown substance. The army biscuits, though rock hard, could be eaten if soaked in water and then lightly toasted. There were no vegetables except for wild spinach, which grew in neglected gardens until its value was discovered. Thereafter it became as rare as other vegetables. To combat scurvy, all were required to take a daily dose of vinegar. Tea was dished out at the rate of one-sixth of an ounce per family per day. The coffee was a mixture of coffee and mealie meal. Unfortunately the two ingredients did not mix well, the coffee settling on the bottom of the mug while the mealie meal floated on the surface.

Not surprisingly, relations between the residents and the new arrivals became strained. Mrs Haden, who provided accommodation for a number of war correspondents, was driven to near collapse by certain of her guests who, believing they were entitled to live like kings, demanded that at each meal varied and appetising dishes should be set before them. (Henry Pearse and Frank Rhodes were not among the correspondents living at the Haden house.) Residents of the town who had a surplus of some foods sold it by auction rather than hand it over to the military and received a little extra money as a result. This brought forth from Mrs Haden's royalty howls of righteous indignation about greedy colonials depriving sick children and dying soldiers of the nourishment they needed to survive.

Old William Watson was one of these 'profiteers'. Just before Christmas he sold a dozen eggs for ten shillings. With this money he was able to buy some sugar to sweeten the food of his three grandchildren. Like many families in Ladysmith he kept a few hens, which provided them with eggs and meat. By February, theft had reduced the number of his laying hens to two. William now received a circular requiring that all eggs be sent to the town office so as to ensure they were distributed to the sick in hospital. Failure to comply would result in the fowls being seized. William, who believed that the military had already surreptitiously seized most of his fowls by night, sent his daughter Annie to Col Stoneman with a plea that they be granted permission to keep their eggs for her three young children and desperately ill, bed-ridden husband. The colonel declined to exempt them from the order. Interspersed among other matters in his diary, William described some of the meals the family ate. Back in December they had for dinner a plate of boiled dried beans with a little salt and pepper. There was of course no butter or gravy but they did have a glass of clean water. The following day they had a plate of porridge with sugar, a cup of black coffee, and a slice of dry bread – all they could get that day. On Boxing Day they had a piece of dry bread and a cup of black coffee. William wrote, 'We don't go in for luxuries.'[3] And things were only going to get worse.

Over the years most of the residents had carefully cultivated orchards. That summer soldiers stripped the trees bare of fruit even before it had ripened. William Watson hoped it gave them internal convulsions and judging from the number of dysentery cases, his hope was probably fulfilled. In the last month of the siege, fuel supplies ran out and the military commandeered the timber in his precious copse. He had carefully tended those trees for

36 years. The copse had become a bird sanctuary and he believed it was the 'sweetest spot for fifty miles round Ladysmith'. A Scottish friend told him, 'eh mon, ye'll be peed for ye're trees.' 'Damm the peement,' was the response. As the Commissariat cut down the trees they permitted them to fall anyhow onto the orchard, thereby completing the destruction of the old man's work. William eloquently recorded his feelings:

> It was my hobby and now it is a wreck. As Byron wrote,
> 'Such is the aspect of this shore
> Tis Greece, but living Greece no more.'
> I am like Marius amidst the ruins of Carthage. And Buller will be made a lord, and others will get medals and crosses, stars and garters, for their glorious achievements, although they have achieved nothing.[4]

The dozen eggs William Watson sent to auction was not the only item submitted that could have been used to feed the sick. Some residents sent in their spare tins of jam. One person sent in a jar of stewed peaches. There were also some carrots, marrows and tomatoes, which had been produced despite the efforts of thieves to strip the gardens of everything edible. All were sold at a price well above the normal peacetime rate but, when added together, they were but a trifle. The real money was raised by other things. La Union cigars, common cigars, Old Gold cigarettes, plug tobacco, Boer tobacco, Three Castle cigarettes, brandy, whisky, port, rum and so on. Were these things really to be given to dying soldiers and sick children crying for food? Or was it that some people were disgruntled at having to pay more for their privileged lifestyle while children and sick soldiers were starving?

Alone among the journalists Donald Macdonald followed up one of these cases of alleged colonial profiteering. One woman was rumoured to have hidden away a large stock of so-called luxuries when the army was seizing supplies. When the siege began to bite, she could be seen leaving her home with an old basket over her arm. She would visit families with little children and, unobserved, pass on to mothers little gifts of essential foods for the youngsters.[5]

It was necessary to maintain discipline in the town and one of the easiest ways for the army to do this was to make an example of one of the locals. H.C. Foss, a miller, and his manager William Gradwell were arrested and charged with speaking disrespectfully about British generals. Gradwell was seriously ill and a night in the lockup was more than his constitution could bear, and he died. Foss was tried and sentenced to a year in prison, which one hopes was commuted after the Relief. In colonial society, people were not accustomed to leaving all decision making and responsibility to their 'betters'. Foss, who, after all, was a civilian, would have felt he was entitled to hold and express opinions on all matters affecting his life. Given the manner in which the war had been conducted up to that time, it is difficult to imagine anything Foss could have said which would not have reflected a degree of disrespect for some of the actions of senior British officers.

This cultural difference was noticed by Donald Macdonald. With other newspaper correspondents, he had been waiting near an artillery battery hoping to get some copy, when a colonial galloped in from a forward outpost. Upon being asked what was going on he replied,

'We are retreating.'

'You should know better, sir, than to make such a remark as that within hearing of the soldiers,' flamed out an indignant English correspondent, whose white military moustache and tall soldierly figure always led to his being mistaken for a general at least.

'I know much better than that,' retorted the Afrikander (colonial), 'but you asked me a question, and I have answered it as far as my ability to gauge the situation goes. If you doubt the truth of what I say, go up to the firing line and have a look for yourself.'[6]

In times of adversity, human nature always tries to find solace in humour. 11 February was the one hundred and first day of the siege. The Boers flashed a curt message to Caesar's Camp, '101 and not out yet'. The Manchesters replied 'Ladysmith still batting'.[7]

The Manchesters, in their exposed position on Caesar's Camp, had little more than their sense of humour to provide consolation. If it wasn't raining the sun beat down on their pale skins, adding sunburn to their other miseries. Their clothes, which should have protected them from rain and sun, were not only covered in red clay, but were now collapsing into holes and splits. Their boots had worn out, and most had been discarded, forcing the men to walk barefoot among the rocks and thorns – very hard on those who had all their lives worn shoes or boots. Even in the Carbineers' camp, the sorry state of their clothes was causing concern. An order was issued that they should change their shirts. A sergeant saw an officer and explained that the men didn't have any other shirts. 'I can't help that,' retorted the officer, 'the order is that they change shirts. Let them change with each other.'

It will be recalled that in the early days of the siege Major Rethman of the BMR and Captain Sparks of the NMR persuaded a Dutch farmer to plant mealies (maize), and that the farmer worked day and night planting the crop. With the good rains a fine crop was produced for which the military were happy to pay a high price. Closer to Bulwana and within the range of Boer riflemen, ten acres of the mealies remained untouched. One night some Volunteers slipped quietly into the field and collected bags of fresh green cobs. The following night a larger group went out and stripped the rest of the mealie cobs from the plants. The next night the Volunteers went out yet again, and quietly cut down all the stalks, which they brought back to Ladysmith to provide a wonderful treat for their horses. When morning came the Boers on Bulwana were astonished to see ten acres of bare ground where only a few hours before had stood a fine stand of green maize.

In another attempt to supplement the feed for the horses still in work, a corps of Indian grass-cutters was organised. They went out by day and night, cutting the grass often found near or beyond the defended perimeter. Although frequently subjected to enemy fire and suffering casualties, they continued to bring in feed for the starving animals.

One piece of colonial initiative nearly had an unfortunate ending. Aleck Macpherson, a skilled hunter, noticed some wild duck on a patch of water midway between the Boer and British lines. He crept out one day and was able to bring back three ducks. The next day he went out to the same spot and no sooner had he fired his first shot, than Mauser bullets came whistling past him, compelling him to run home as fast as he could, with Boer fire chasing him the whole way.

Towards the end of the siege it became apparent that there existed a hidden source for the supply of cigars. The provost-sergeant decided to search the stores. At one Indian store the sergeant ordered his corporal to slit the canvas ceiling and put his head through. Ten bags of rice and two bales of tobacco were found and were promptly commandeered. For those unfortunate Indians existing on their meagre rations of rice, this was probably a lifesaver. The same cannot be said for the tobacco; however, it was enjoyed by Donald Macdonald and his friends. 'It was a happy lot of men who sat round, while Mr Arty Spring, a Natal farmer, and an expert in Boer tobacco, chopped up the leaf – chaffed it would be a better word – damped and sweated it, mixed in a little saltpetre, and then— well, it was good to smoke it, better even to be able to give one's friends a pipe.'[8]

As the siege wore on, more and more use was made of the Tathams' home to treat convalescent patients, until it was virtually a fully-fledged hospital staffed by women from the town, supervised by one of the Volunteer nurses and doctors from the Natal Volunteer Medical Corps. One of the patients they cared for was Major Bru de Wold, Chief of Staff to the Natal Volunteers. On 18 January the major had been hit by a piece of shrapnel that struck him just under the eye and came out at the back of the neck.

Bella Craw, one of the young women in Ladysmith, was one of the carers who looked after him from the time he was brought in. Whether it was the Nordic curses of the injured and frustrated major, or a desire to prove to future generations that there is nothing new under the sun, Bella was inspired to kick over the traces. She confessed,

I did an awful thing today which I am afraid I will many a time regret, and that is to have my arm tattooed '1899 Ladysmith Pro Patria 1900'.

No one knows of it yet. I hardly know how to break it to Mama and the boys for I know they will say I am very foolish, as a good many have already told me, Dr Buntine and Dr Currie, Bert and others. However, it can't be helped now, it is done.[9]

Bru de Wold received excellent care and made a remarkable recovery from the wound, which could so easily have been fatal. He was back in harness by the end of the siege.

Major Doveton of the ILH had suffered a serious shoulder wound at Wagon Hill and was taken to Intombi with the other wounded. With his condition deteriorating, he was moved to Fanny Tatham's nursing home on 30 January. By 7 February doctors felt it was impossible to save his arm and amputation was necessary. A heliograph was sent to Mrs Doveton in Pietermaritzburg telling her about the proposed amputation. Someone, said to be anonymous, arranged that she should pass through the Boer lines and come into Ladysmith to nurse her husband. On 12 February Karri Davies accompanied by Dr Rogers went out to the Boer lines in an ambulance and collected her. That day the arm was amputated. Karri had rigged up a tent so she could be near her husband's ward and be as close to him as possible. The amputation proved to be more than he could bear and on the 13th his condition deteriorated. Bella Craw wrote, 'Major Doveton very bad tonight. They are afraid he will not live through the night. Poor Mrs Doveton came in just now to change and put her dressing gown on. She walks and looks in a dream. We are all feeling so miserable and sorry for her, and so helpless and unable to comfort her.'

The next day Bella wrote, 'Poor Major Doveton passed a dreadful night, but passed quietly away at half past ten this morning. The funeral was large and left here at 7.30 tonight.'[10] Karri was able to find a trap and horse to drive Mrs Doveton to the funeral.

The generals and all the important people attended. Doveton had been a mine manager in Johannesburg before the war and was loved by all who knew him. Perhaps because he was a professional engineer, Henry Nevinson had been prepared to converse with him, and even Nevinson could think no ill of the deceased. After the funeral Mrs Doveton spent the night with the Lines family, Mr Lines being the secretary and treasurer of the Town Guard. The next day Karri took her back to the Boer lines for her sad journey to Pietermaritzburg.

The Boers were much praised for allowing Mrs Doveton to visit her dying husband, which is of course as it should be. It would, however, be pleasant to hear one word of appreciation from the Boer side of the kindness shown by Sir George White in permitting Mrs Kock to nurse her dying husband after the battle of Elandslaagte.

It was not only the soldiers who were sick and dying in Ladysmith. The Coventry family, whose farm lay on the northern slopes of Spion Kop, had moved into Ladysmith when the Boers invaded Natal. Mrs Coventry was heavily pregnant and the baby was born in a cellar during one of the first bombardments. Never quite able to overcome its poor start in life, the infant died on 21 February. She was one of many babies to die during the siege. That disease respected neither age nor gender is illustrated by the deaths of two young women – Mary Carbutt on 5 January and her sister Evelyn on 17 February. On 27 January Commandant Willie Royston, who had seemed to have an iron constitution, began to show the first signs of illness.

Despite the efforts of Colonel Stoneman, conditions at Intombi Hospital continued to deteriorate. The death rate was creeping up to twenty a day and new patients to the hospital would pass lines of bodies waiting to be buried, while gravediggers struggled to keep up with the task. Doctors, nurses and orderlies were all being struck down with one or other of the infectious diseases. The rise in patient numbers far outstripped the capacity to expand the hospital's facilities. The supply of beds, which consisted of three planks suspended a few inches above the ground, had again failed to meet demand and many patients had to lie on cut grass put over the bare earth. Many of the orderlies were now drawn from men whom the Boers had sent into Ladysmith during the early days of the siege. On the outbreak of hostilities the Transvaal authorities emptied their prisons by sending the inmates to Natal as refugees. In this manner they were able to get rid of their undesirables, and to pass on to the besieged garrison the duty of feeding them. We have seen it took some time for the British to counter this ploy.

Out in the rural tribal areas of Natal, the people were aware of what was happening in Ladysmith. Without being asked and acting spontaneously, various tribes sent donations to the Department of Native Affairs early in 1900. By modern standards, many of the donations might appear to be small. Often these people had yet to embrace a western-style money economy, and the money donated probably represented all they had. Like the donation of their beer ration by the Gordon Highlanders to the Imperial Light Horse, the monetary value of the gifts was as nothing when compared with the concern, kindness and support displayed. These are the donations that were made.

Donor	Amount	Intended recipients
Ndaleni Community per P.M. Majosi	£3. 0. 0	Sick and Wounded
Ndwedwe:-Chiefs Mbozane, Goba, Sotobe, Cshani, Mbango, Rodoba, Mdiya, and Deliweyo	£36.13	Volunteers in Ladysmith
Chief Ndungwe, Ifafa	£7. 0. 0	Soldiers fighting in Natal
Pinetown Mission	£8. 0. 0	Sick and wounded
Chief Henuhemu	£10. 0. 0	Soldiers who defended Ladysmith
Chief Mzingelwa	£5. 0. 0	Any relief made necessary by present war

Christian communities at Inanda, Cato Ridge, Umzumbe, Verulam, and Mapumulo	£15. 0. 0	Relief of sufferers
Church of Scotland Mission PMB	£9.05.06	Sick and Wounded
Chief Laduma	£8. 0. 0	Sick and wounded
Chief Ncitshuise, Ifafa	£7.15. 3	For Artillery who fought at Colenso, Token of appreciation of bravery attempting to retake lost guns
Mpolweni Mission	£3.17. 4	Sick and wounded
J.H. Khumalo, Lions River	£3.18. 0	Sick and Wounded
Chief Gayede	£6. 0. 0	Sick and Wounded
Chief Mdungazwe ka Makongolo	£8. 9.10	Sick and wounded
Christian natives at New Hanover	£3. 5. 0	Any native requiring relief
Chief Xegwana, Estcourt	£1. 10. 0	Sick and Wounded
Amangwane tribe, Estcourt	£140. 0. 0	Sick and Wounded Soldiers

In addition to the gift of £140, Chief Ncwadi of the amaNgwane, accompanied by his brother Nyanda and other senior members of his tribe whose lands lay near the source of the Tugela and the Free State border, called on Samuel Samuelson of the Native Affairs Department in Pietermaritzburg and handed to him a bag of money that had been collected from his people. For a time during the incursion of the Boers towards southern Natal, they had been cut off from the rest of the colony. When handing over the gift the Chief said,

In this bag you will find a small token of the gratitude of myself and my people for the protection afforded us by the Government and the Army of Her Majesty the Queen. We were told to stay at home and we have done so. The Queen's soldiers have fought, have been wounded and have died for us whilst we remained unscathed in our homes. Many of them are wounded and sick. This small gift from me and my people may furnish some needful comforts for them and for this purpose I have brought it. We have just paid our hut tax and dog tax, we have had anxiety and much expense to provide for ourselves and families, my people have not been able to work and earn money as they might have done. If it were not for these things your table would be red with Amangwane money for the use of the sick and wounded soldiers of Her Majesty the Queen.[11]

The contents of the bag were emptied onto the table, and found to contain £219. 6. 0. The total sum given by the amaNgwane people was therefore £359.06. In today's money that is more than a hundred thousand pounds. This was not a token donation and it says a great deal about the feelings of the black people – a concrete and quantifiable expression of sentiment ignored by some commentators.

In May 1900 many educated black people (the Amakolwa) who had abandoned their traditional way of life formed an association to represent their interests. George Hulett, a successful Natal sugar farmer and Member of the Legislative Assembly, played a leading part in the formation of this association, which was called the Natal Native Congress and was subsequently to develop into the African National Congress. Chief Isaac Mkhize was elected president, Mr H.H.C. Matiwane secretary and Chief Majozi from Ndaleni treasurer. They hoped when the war was over any peace terms would ensure:

(1) They would not be denied education.
(2) A degree of direct representation in the Legislature
(3) They would have freedom to trade.
(4) They would be entitled to acquire land.

In Natal they already enjoyed the rights referred to in (1), (3) and (4). The representation issue was more complex. All prospective voters in Natal had to show they had abandoned any previous domicile and now lived according to the laws of the colony. For a member of the Amakolwa to be registered as a voter he had to show that he was no longer subject to the jurisdiction of a Zulu chief and was living according to the laws of Natal. Because they would constitute a minority of the electorate, few bothered to register. Their attitude on this issue was replicated by many white voters in Natal throughout the twentieth century. Being a small minority and knowing the Zulu leaders would be reluctant to surrender their traditional powers, the Amakolwa did not seek universal franchise. Instead they decided to act as a pressure group like the Farmers' Association.

Their resolutions are interesting. They expressed their gratitude to Joseph Chamberlain for the firm stand he took against the Transvaal; they expressed their admiration for the services rendered by Sir Alfred Milner; and they expressed their thanks to the Natal Government for sending troops to frustrate the Boers 'design to conquer the whole of Natal. Also passed was a resolution proposed by Chief Goba, 'That this meeting places on record its sincere sympathy with the relatives and friends of those who have fallen in the cause of freedom during the present war.'[12]

One delegate expressed concern that the Natal Government tended to place the interests of blacks living according to traditional Zulu custom above the interests of the educated Amakolwa. And yet, two of the most senior positions in the Congress were filled by Chiefs who would, in all probability, have opposed any reduction in their power. To add a further complication, Chief Majozi of Ndaleni, near Richmond, had been elected to the chieftainship by his people, possibly the first democratically elected black leader in sub-Saharan Africa.[13]

The Natal Government noted the formation of the Native Congress. The Secretary of Native Affairs, Mr Moor, was uncertain whether the Congress would garner much support among the blacks without the support of the chiefs. However, in his report to the Governor he stated, 'they cannot permanently be kept in a state of tutelage.'[14]

22

Boer Line Breached; Siege Raised

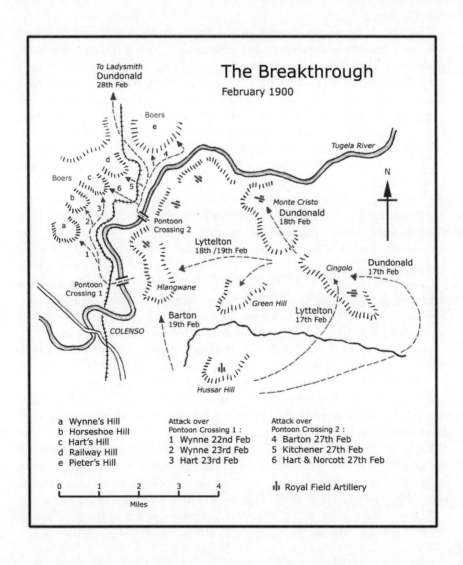

The Breakthrough
February 1900

To Ladysmith
Dundonald
28th Feb

Boers
e

Tugela River

N

Boers
d

c
6 5

Boers
b
3
a
2

1

Monte Cristo
Dundonald
18th Feb

Pontoon
Crossing 2

Lyttelton
18th /19th Feb

Cingolo

Dundonald
17th Feb

Pontoon
Crossing 1

Hlangwane

Green Hill

Lyttelton
17th Feb

Barton
19th Feb

COLENSO

Hussar Hill

a Wynne's Hill
b Horseshoe Hill
c Hart's Hill
d Railway Hill
e Pieter's Hill

Attack over
Pontoon Crossing 1 :
1 Wynne 22nd Feb
2 Wynne 23rd Feb
3 Hart 23rd Feb

Attack over
Pontoon Crossing 2 :
4 Barton 27th Feb
5 Kitchener 27th Feb
6 Hart & Norcott 27th Feb

0   1   2   3   4
Miles

Royal Field Artillery

315

After the British withdrew from Vaalkrantz, Buller sent his Regular cavalry west to Springfield. This was to protect his left, and in the hope that this would bluff the Boers into believing that the next attack by the relieving force could be expected somewhere near Spion Kop. The Boers were not fooled by this manoeuvre and hastened to reinforce their defensive line along the hills lying to the east of Colenso.

After passing Colenso, the Tugela River sweeps around to the left and flows in a northerly direction for about 6 miles before swinging to the right to resume its flow eastwards. Like other stretches of the upper Tugela, a series of hills lies to the north of this stretch of the river. The railway crosses the river near Colenso, and then travels north along its bank for about 6 miles before turning away from the river and passing through a gap in the hills to make its way across the plain that leads to Ladysmith. It was along this route that Buller intended to relieve the siege.

The hills to the north of the river had been cleverly fortified by the Boers who took care to ensure that their trenches and other fortifications were virtually invisible to any would-be attackers. This, however, was only their second line of defence. East of Colenso lies Hlangwane, the hill whose strategic importance had been so sadly neglected by the British commanders during the battle on 15 December. Moving east from Hlangwane is Green Hill (the third hill so named by the British army) and then Cingolo. North of Cingolo is a long section of high ground called Monte Cristo, which runs north for about 4 miles to the Tugela. It is near the northern tip of Monte Cristo that the river resumes its easterly course, while the railway turns away from the river and goes through the hills and across the plain to Ladysmith. The Boers realised that guns placed by the British on Hlangwane, Green Hill, Cingolo and Monte Cristo would provide considerable assistance to any attempt to establish a bridgehead across the river anywhere from Colenso to Monte Cristo. To nullify this threat the Boers occupied Hlangwane, Green Hill, Cingolo and Monte Cristo in some force, and constructed a bridge a couple of miles downstream of Colenso to supply their men on these hills. The land to the east of Monte Cristo and Cingolo was considered too broken for the British to be able to mount an attack from that direction.

On 11 February, Lord Dundonald received orders to occupy Hussar Hill, which lies about 3 miles south of Hlangwane. It will be recalled that on 20 December 1899, the Boers had ambushed a detachment of Hussars on this hill and that when they returned for a second helping a few days later, they themselves were ambushed by the Carbineers. From that time, this high ground was known as Hussar Hill.

Early on the morning of 12 February, the Volunteers went out with Dundonald to Hussar Hill, which they found occupied by the Boers. After a brief skirmish the Boers retired, enabling General Buller to make a detailed telescopic reconnaissance of the Boer positions he proposed to attack.

The reconnaissance completed, the Volunteers were ordered to retire. When this began, the Boers attempted to attack the retreating colonials. The

Volunteers withdrew in alternate sections, one section maintaining a hot fire on the Boers from a concealed position while the other withdrew, then the roles would be reversed. In this way the manoeuvre was completed without any casualties. Following the withdrawal, the Boers resumed occupation of Hussar Hill. The next day Buller issued the following order:

> It is intended to seize Hussar Hill to-morrow, and the spurs to the east of it north of Moord Kraal, and to occupy this position with artillery. Lord Dundonald's Brigade will cover the movement. It will strike its camp and bivouac on a site which will be pointed out to it.[1]

So on Wednesday 14 February, the Volunteers again set out to take Hussar Hill and yet again the Boers defended the hill. However, the South African Light Horse, by advancing quickly, had secured a commanding ridge and bringing up four Colt machine guns, compelled the enemy to retire, leaving two wounded. The infantry occupied the hill and the Naval and other guns were soon on the summit.

While the SALH were engaged at Hussar Hill, McKenzie, who was scouting on the right, took the Carbineers northwards into the inhospitable terrain east of Cingolo and Monte Cristo. They had to traverse boulder-strewn land covered with thick bush and in these dangerous places they really were bearding the lion in his den. They found and climbed a steep path to the summit of Monte Cristo. The path was covered in hoof marks indicating it was being used by the Boers. On the top they received a heliograph message to say the reconnaissance had been completed and they should return to base, which was done without incident.[2] The information gathered in the course of this foray was to prove an inestimable advantage in the coming advance.

General Sir Charles Warren had been out of the limelight for some time when, on 15 February, he joined his infantry on top of Hussar Hill. Enemy shellfire appeared to be causing the men to be a little edgy, so Sir Charles decided something had to be done to give them confidence. He ordered his bath to be brought up to the top of the hill and that it be filled with hot water. This was done and despite the continuing shellfire, he stripped off and climbed into the bath and began soaping himself. The troops at 'a respectful distance' watched in silence. As luck would have it, at this moment General Buller and his staff rode up with the division's orders for the following day. Warren got out of the bath, wrapped himself in a towel and, still dripping wet, was given his instructions. Buller and his staff then rode off. Of this meeting Warren said, 'I felt like an eastern potentate receiving homage.' What Buller thought is not recorded. Warren thought the escapade had been a great success, 'I felt that I had done what I could for the day to amuse the men.'[3] When they were subjected to shellfire on the following day, Warren commented, 'The men must get used to it. There should be no grousing now that I have had my bath in the midst of it, with the Commander-in-Chief's Staff all closing round.'[4]

On 15 February, there was a general advance towards Cingolo and Monte Cristo supported by the artillery on Hussar Hill. By nightfall General Lyttelton's division was about 2 miles from Cingolo with Dundonald's Volunteers covering the left and right flanks. In the course of the advance they passed a farm looted by the Boers. Lt Blake Knox noted, 'The place was a perfect wreck, all the furniture broken, and the floor littered with torn books, letters and photographs belonging to some recent loyal Natalian; amongst the debris lay the family Bible, torn and desecrated.'[5]

Far away to the west in the northern Cape, the siege of Kimberley was raised.

The next day the heat was intense and Buller decided his troops could not be expected to advance against the enemy in such conditions. Captain William Birdwood (later Sir William Birdwood of Anzac fame) who had been made Chief Staff Officer to Lord Dundonald, approached McKenzie and asked if he would put in writing his ideas on the best way to relieve Ladysmith. If McKenzie would do this, Birdwood would see to it that the document was placed before General Buller. Unfortunately McKenzie had to go out on patrol and was unable to write the memorandum there and then, but Birdwood was fully aware of McKenzie's opinions[6] as no doubt was Dundonald.

On the 16th Dundonald received his orders for the following day:

> You will divide your command, half will be on the right and, advancing in the rear of the Infantry, will endeavour, as soon as opportunity offers, to gain ground to the right and outflank any detachment of the enemy that may appear on the Nek. The other half, less one strong troop, will operate on our left up the Gomba Valley (between Green Hill and Cingolo), taking such opportunities as may offer.[7]

Dundonald recorded his response to these orders:

> During the night of 16/17 February, I heard that the enemy was still in occupation of Cingolo; I made up my mind to use some discretion with regard to the orders I had received, and therefore sent one regiment to the left of the infantry, keeping two regiments (some 650 men) for work on the right flank. I also used further discretion with regard to these orders, and instead of advancing behind the right of the infantry, waiting for an opportunity to occur, in the early hours of the morning I took the two regiments which were with me, by a circuitous route to the southern end of Cingolo. My idea was to assist the operations in the most effective manner possible, viz., by ascending the hill, getting behind the enemy, and clearing him off it.[8]

In embarking on this enterprise, Dundonald was disobeying the order to remain behind the infantry. Failure would not only have been calamitous for his own career but might also have severely prejudiced the British advance. The regiments Dundonald took with him were the Composite Regiment (comprising the Carbineers and the ILH) and the South African Light Horse. Winston Churchill was there and wrote this description of the sortie.

By daybreak all were moving, and as the Irregular Cavalry forded the Blue Krantz stream on their enveloping march, we heard the boom of the first gun. The usual leisurely bombardment had begun, and I counted only thirty shells in the first ten minutes, which was not very hard work for the gunners considering nearly seventy guns were in action. But the artillery never hurry themselves, and indeed I do not remember to have heard in this war a really good cannonade, such as we had at Omdurman, except for a few minutes at Vaal Krantz.

The Cavalry marched ten miles eastward through most broken and difficult country, all rock, high grass, and dense thickets, which made it imperative to move in single file, and the sound of the general action grew fainter and fainter. Gradually we began to turn again towards it. The slope of the ground rose against us. The scrub became more dense. To ride further was impossible. We dismounted and led our horses, who scrambled and blundered painfully among the trees and boulders. So scattered was our formation that I did not care to imagine what would have happened had the enemy put in an appearance. But our safety lay in these same natural difficulties. The Boers doubtless reflected, 'No one will ever try to go through such ground as that' – besides which war cannot be made without running risks. The soldier must chance his life.

The general must not be afraid to brave disaster. But how tolerant the arm-chair critics should be of men who try daring coups and fail! You must put your head in the lion's mouth if the performance is to be a success ...

At length we reached the foot of the hill and halted to reconnoitre the slopes as far as was possible. After half an hour, since nothing could be seen, the advance was resumed up the side of a precipice and through a jungle so thick we had to cut our road. It was eleven o'clock before we reached the summit of the ridge and emerged on a more or less open plateau, diversified with patches of wood and heaps of great boulders. Two squadrons had re-formed on the top and deployed to cover the others. The troopers of the remaining seven squadrons were making their way up four to the minute. Suddenly there was a rifle shot.[9]

The Boers had discovered that they were not the only ones on the summit. They thought the British would launch their attack up the western slope of Cingolo and, as expected, Lyttelton's 2nd Division did just that. All morning the Boers behind their fortifications fought back repeated attacks by Lyttelton's infantry. But now with their fortifications providing no cover from the attack from the east, and not relishing the prospect of being sandwiched between the two forces, the Boers abandoned their positions and fled towards Monte Cristo. A running fight ensued in which a Carbineer, Trooper Goldstein, was killed. The terrain with its cover of bushes, boulders, and high grass made pursuit difficult. Added to this, the Volunteers were obliged to work on the eastern side of the crest to avoid being shot by Lyttelton's infantry advancing from the west. With the Composite Regiment near the crest, and the South African Light Horse on their right to prevent any attempt at a flanking movement, the Boers were steadily driven back towards Monte Cristo. When Buller called a halt to the action that evening, the Boers had been cleared off Cingolo, and though they still occupied Monte Cristo and part of the Nek between it and Cingolo, it had been a good day for his army. That night the gunners of the 64th Battery, assisted by the Devons, dragged their guns and ammunition onto the newly captured high ground and worked through the night placing the guns in suitable positions and erecting cover.[10] Before the dawn of the new day, they were ready for action and for once it was the Boers who were not quite sure what was going on.

Losses on both sides had been small. The Carbineers had lost one man killed, several Boers had been killed and a number of their horses captured. But for the danger posed by the friendly fire of Lyttelton's infantry, the Volunteers would, in all probability, have killed or captured all the Boers on Cingolo. When the Volunteers reached the summit Dundonald attempted to advise Lyttelton that his men were now on the summit, but it was some time before they could get the heliograph to work. Of course, he could have told Lyttelton of his plans the previous evening and would by so doing have prevented the friendly fire hampering the Volunteers.[11] However, Dundonald would have remembered what had happened at Acton Homes and his decision to keep the plan to himself seems to have been the correct one.

From his account of the sortie, Churchill betrays not a little anxiety and well might he have been anxious. It is very easy to get lost in the dense bush found in the valleys of many Natal rivers. One is constantly confronted by a dense wall of bush. On peering through the vegetation, one might see what appears to be open grassland ahead, but on getting through the undergrowth it turns out to be nothing more than a patch of grass surrounded by yet more dense bush. In the unfenced land of those days, this process could have gone on for days. What Churchill did not know was that McKenzie had visited the area on 14 February and, with his customary care, had scouted the route Dundonald's men were to follow.

In disregarding his orders and leading his men away from the battlefield for 10 miles over difficult terrain, Dundonald displayed the extraordinary confidence he had in McKenzie. The venture could only have originated from McKenzie, and in its execution, he and the Carbineers had again demonstrated how the invading Boers could be defeated without incurring heavy losses.

At dawn on Sunday 18 February, the attack on the Boer positions resumed. With Dundonald's Volunteers on the right and Hildyard's infantry on the left, they steadily pushed the Boers towards the northern extremity of Monte

Cristo and the Tugela. The Boers on Green Hill, realising their position was enfiladed by guns on Hussar Hill and Cingolo, offered only token resistance to the infantry before fleeing across the Tugela. By the evening of the 18th, only Hlangwane of the Boer's fortress hills across the Tugela was still in their hands. Buller was able to report that from the time he commenced the action on the 15th to the evening of the 18th, he had lost one officer and thirteen men killed, 155 wounded and two missing.[12]

The next day the British infantry advanced towards Hlangwane from both the southwest and the northeast. The sight of this formidable host bearing down on them was too much for the defenders, who chose to hasten back across the Tugela while the opportunity was available to them. At the same time, the Boers evacuated Colenso. There were now no Boers south of the Tugela.

It had all seemed so easy, so easy in fact that Buller was convinced that only a rearguard remained between him and Ladysmith. Perhaps the Boers had realised their folly in invading Natal and had begun their long retreat back to their Republics, in which case there would be no point in risking further lives! The fleeing Boers were permitted to cross the river almost unscathed.

In the lull that followed the engagement south of the river, doctor Lt Blake Knox went for a stroll round Colenso:

> The village had been shamefully looted and polluted. What had once been a peaceful and picturesque little hamlet was now a mass of foetid ruins. In anticipation of our occupation, the enemy had dragged their dead horses into the interior of the houses, and they lay in rooms among broken furniture and debris. The corrugated zinc roofs had been torn from the buildings, all available woodwork had been removed for fuel, windows and doors were wantonly smashed.[13]

This wanton destruction of civilian property in Natal goes far beyond looting and theft. It shows an extraordinary hatred of victims whom they did not know and who posed no threat whatsoever to them.

Buller spent the following days preparing for the final advance to Ladysmith. Though he had the opportunity to construct bridges at various places on the Tugela, he decided that one bridge would suffice and it should be constructed about a mile west of Hlangwane. This pontoon bridge led into a valley surrounded at a distance by steep hills, a natural amphitheatre. The Boers could not have picked a better site for their opponents to begin their campaign north of the Tugela. Unobserved, they could sit in their hidden trenches and watch every move by the British. On 21 February, eleven battalions and forty guns crossed the river and moved onto this natural stage. The following day four more battalions joined them. Some British officers were appalled at Buller's choice of the site for the crossing, and even more appalled by the massing of troops on a crowded plain where they could be subjected to enemy fire from three sides. Warren, whose troops had taken no part in the fighting over the past few days, thought Buller's idea 'a masterly tactical stroke'. Another who was pleased by the turn of events was General 'No-Bobs' Hart. He and his Irish regiments had been cooling their heels at Chieveley but now they were back at Colenso, and the fearless old general would soon have an opportunity to show the Boers a thing or two. So confident was Buller of the weakness of the force confronting him that he moved his headquarters across the river.

The Volunteers spent several days on Monte Cristo guarding the right flank while the Boers were being shepherded across the river. Then they too were ordered to cross on the pontoon bridge and bivouac on the northern bank of the Tugela. Dundonald had always impressed on McKenzie that he should tell him when he thought a forward move should not be made. On this occasion McKenzie told Dundonald that he thought the move was premature, as they would be hemmed in behind the infantry. Dundonald understood the validity of McKenzie's argument but felt that they had no choice but to obey orders.[14] So they crossed on the pontoon and, finding the best cover they could, spent three uncomfortable days being shelled and shot at, before being ordered back to their old position on Monte Cristo.

As the Boers showed no signs of going away, Buller decided it was time to implement his plan to advance along the railway line to Ladysmith. Looking north along the intended route was the small stream, Onderbroek Spruit, beyond which were two hills lying to the left of the railway line. General Wynne, with the Lancashire Regiments who had suffered so terribly at Spion Kop, was ordered to take these hills. On the 22nd they moved against the first hill and despite being subjected to heavy rifle fire were able to take it. Buller's headquarters was badly damaged by shellfire but Buller, as usual, impressed all by his quiet courage. On the 21st and 22nd Buller's force suffered over 500 casualties.

It had been a busy time for Lt Blake Knox. On the 22nd his dressing station came under heavy fire and several Natal stretcher bearers were wounded. He decided to move the station to a safer place under a railway culvert. To convert the culvert into a dressing station required a little labour.

> I accordingly got a number of Natal stretcher bearers to accompany me, and with borrowed shovels and picks, constructed a fairly smooth path from the railway embankment down to the culvert and removed the barbed wire fences on both sides of the line. Although all the time under brisk rifle fire the men set to their task cheerfully and energetically. Never can I look back on these men, who went by the name of 'body snatchers' without thinking how much we all owe to them.[15]

The following morning, General Wynne attacked the second hill in the line and was successful in driving the Boers off it. The capture of these two hills turned out to be a Pyrrhic victory as they were enfiladed on three sides by the Boers and taking them provided little advantage.

At midday General Hart was ordered to take the next hill in the range, Hart's Hill (sometimes called Inniskilling Hill). In addition to the Irish regiments, Hart had with him the colonials of the Imperial Light Infantry. At 12.30 p.m. they moved off along the railway line and for part of the way, they were sheltered from Boer fire by the river bank and the hills recently taken by Wynne – but once they left this cover, they came under fire from the Boers. Two particularly dangerous areas were the railway bridges over Onderbroek Spruit and another stream, Langerwachte Spruit, which lay beyond Wynne's Hill. The Royal Engineers had very courageously begun to place sandbags on the ironwork along the sides of the bridges. Until this was done the men were obliged to run the gauntlet one at a time. Sixty men, including several stretcher-bearers, were to fall crossing these bridges. It was not only soldiers who had to face this peril. A black driver was knocked off an ammunition wagon and with his head covered in blood was taken to a dressing station grinning, laughing, chattering and abusing Dutchmen. A Mauser bullet was extracted from a wound just above the ear. The wound was dressed and bandaged, and before anyone could stop him he had made off back to his wagon.[16]

It was 5 o'clock before the infantry reached the base of Hart's Hill. During the day the artillery had subjected the summit to a tremendous cannonade without eliciting any response from the Boers, leaving their opponents uncertain where they were, or how strongly the hill was defended. Neither of these difficulties nor the lateness of the hour intimidated General 'No-Bobs' Hart. He ordered the attack to proceed at once. With the Inniskillings in the lead, his men clambered up the hill into a wall of fire. With men falling regularly they reached the trenches on the crest about 300 feet above the Tugela – only to find it was a false crest and the Boers had retreated to other trenches higher up. Fully exposed to enemy fire, the infantry attempted to continue the advance but before they reached the enemy, the attack had petered out. There were no longer enough men left standing to carry it through. Sensing that they were gaining the ascendancy, the Boer fire increased and from the rapidity of their fire many thought they must have loaders with spare rifles to hand up from the trenches. In the gathering darkness the survivors were driven back down the hill. In the assault 450 men had been killed or wounded, half of the casualties coming from the Inniskilling Fusiliers.

Apart from the Inniskillings, no other regiment suffered greater losses that day than the Imperial Light Infantry. With their obsolete rifles and without the protection of bayonets they had lost nineteen men killed and 105 wounded. A further eight were missing, presumed killed. Major Hay, their commanding officer, was badly wounded. Throughout the engagement the men of this regiment behaved with great courage. Mentioned in dispatches were Private R. Hunter who, under heavy fire, twice built sangars around wounded comrades; and Private G. Reed who, under heavy fire, carried in a wounded Connaught Ranger to a place of safety, and remained with him after the other men retired.[17]

At about midnight General Hart called at Doctor Blake Knox's dressing station with a request that stretcher parties be sent out to attend to a number of wounded men lying unattended on the hill. Although extremely busy, the doctor called for volunteers. A dozen stretcher squads manned by the Natal Volunteer Ambulance Corps plus some Regulars came forward and went with the doctor onto the hill. In the dark they succeeded in carrying back a good many of the more severe cases. Blake Knox thought all was going well,

> ... until an unfortunate incident occurred. I had to delay over one case which was lying out some distance from the lower crest of the hill. This patient I thought was unconscious, though he was in reality dead. I had handed my dark lantern, with its shutter closed, to one of my party, to enable me to determine by nearer examination whether there was any sign of life in the motionless form, which was still warm. The man holding the lantern, either by accident or thinking to help me, released the shutter, when a broad beam of light flashed out, and this was immediately followed by a volley from the enemy's trenches in our direction. The holder of the lantern was shot dead, and two more stretcher-bearers were wounded. Had not the bullets gone for the most part high, and the lantern extinguished by its fall, more casualties might have occurred. As it was, we had all to lie close behind what scanty cover we could crawl to for over an hour, and make our way back as quietly as we could, for it was impossible to recover any more wounded, the enemy being thenceforward on the alert. On our way down towards the Langerwachte Spruit, we heard some groaning, and, proceeding in the direction of the sound, one of the party stumbled over a stretcher on the ground. On that stretcher lay an unconscious man. His head was partially bandaged, and beside the stretcher lay the two bearers. One of these had been shot dead, and the other was lying in a pool of blood groaning. He had been struck by a bullet through the thigh, the bone being badly broken, which rendered him helpless. We removed both cases, and the poor fellow, who was conscious, told me that he and a comrade had been shot down while dressing the unconscious man's head.[18]

During the night the Irish built sangars all along their line on Hart's Hill. When dawn broke, they discovered the Boers had dug fresh trenches that, in places, were less than 300 yards away. On the open ground between the two combatants lay many of the wounded, dead and dying of the previous day's carnage. There was some desultory firing between the two groups before a further unfortunate incident occurred.

The Boers, near whom most of the wounded lay, came out with a Red Cross flag and firing on that section of the line ceased. After collecting their own wounded, they gave their opponents some water, while taking away their rifles, and then began despoiling the dead and wounded. They pulled the boots off them, and began undressing them as they rifled pockets and searched for valuables. This was too much for the Irish who fired on the Boers. The Boers believed that this was a breach of the Geneva Convention, though the convention was intended to cover people rendering medical assistance, not pillage and robbery. The first shots sent the Boers scuttling back to their trenches, and general firing broke out. The Boers' passions were so inflamed by the Irish troops reaction to their robbery of the dead and wounded, that any slight movement by the wounded resulted in heavy fire being directed at them.[19]

All through the day the rifle and artillery fire between the two sides continued while at the same time the exhausted troops at Hart's Hill were replaced by fresh regiments from Warren's division. General 'No-Bobs' was keen to have another go at taking the hill but no such order came through from Buller who was, as usual, distressed by the casualties that had been suffered – the old uncertainty was still there. His plan required that after securing Hart's Hill, the next hill down the line, Railway Hill, should be captured. He did not believe General Hart was the ideal leader for such an operation and, as the 5th Division should lead this attack, he sent for Warren.

Warren found Buller and his staff pinned down by shellfire. After finding a safe spot for himself, Warren was seen by Buller to be shaking with laughter. Buller sent a message to enquire why he was laughing, to which he received the reply, 'Come over and see'. Under fire Buller crawled over to him and was told, 'look at your Staff' and Warren pointed out that as each shell came over, the senior staff members did not move, but the others would duck, the most junior members lowering their heads the most. This produced the effect of a wave passing through the group. Buller was neither pleased nor amused. He gave Warren his orders and crawled back to his staff and told them to try and keep their heads steady. Warren reflected, 'A good laugh does one's inside so much good.'[20]

Warren went over to Hart and it was arranged that General 'No-Bobs' himself should lead the attack on Railway Hill, while Colonel Cooper of the Dublin Fusiliers should lead the new attack on Hart's Hill. However, as it was now 4 o'clock, it was decided the attack should be postponed until the following day, Sunday 25 February. Through the night the British clung to their positions on the hills, while above them the Boers remained in their hidden trenches.

Whatever his subordinates may have decided, Buller was not prepared to authorise this proposed attack on the Sabbath. Many of the wounded had lain on those hillsides for two days and two nights without food, water, shelter or medical attention. As a result, many, whose wounds would not normally have been fatal, had died. It was imperative that a ceasefire be arranged for the removal of the wounded from the battlefield and the burying of the dead. The Boers were persuaded to permit the removal of seriously wounded soldiers, but insisted that those men who were not badly wounded should become their prisoners of war. Rather surprisingly, the British agreed to these harsh terms. By noon all the wounded had been taken off the battlefield and the dead buried.

That Sunday those close to Buller had noticed a change in him. Energy and a sense of purpose had returned. Colonel a'Court on his staff noted, 'He had suddenly become the old War Office Buller, and dictated so rapidly that I could scarcely keep pace with him, but as he went on I saw that he had a complete grasp of the operation'.

The next day, the Boers saw the British artillery and army baggage going back across the river and men could be seen gathering on the northern bank of the Tugela near the pontoon bridge. Louis Botha advised Pretoria that because of the heavy losses they had suffered, the British appeared to be retiring. The long cherished dream of chasing the rooineks out of Natal and into the sea had once again begun to look achievable.

And still there were no orders from Buller to attack. Instead he rode out along the heights from Hlangwane to Monte Cristo making sure the artillery was in place; seventy-six guns over a distance of about 4½ miles. The infantry, presently entrenched across the Tugela, were instructed to hold their positions while the remainder were marched back across the pontoon bridge to take up positions on the southern bank.

That night the bridge was dismantled and reassembled at a new site about 4 miles downstream, opposite Hart's Hill, and Buller gave his commanders their orders. Barton's brigade would attack Pieter's Hill, Kitchener's would assault Railway Hill, and Hart's, assisted by Norcott's brigade, would assault Hart's Hill. Lord Dundonald's Mounted Brigade were to be deployed to the right of the main attack to provide flank protection and covering fire.[21] When General Lyttelton heard the details of Buller's orders he commented that the ideas behind it 'appeared so sound that I doubted if they were his own'. Perhaps they weren't, in which case Buller should be given credit for listening to sound advice – a rare virtue among British commanders.

When dawn came on Tuesday 27 February 1900, the Boers in their trenches on the hills above the northern bank of the Tugela looked south expecting to see the British Army in full retreat. Instead they saw a new bridge snaking across the river, while at the same time the Royal Artillery opened a terrific barrage on the Boer positions along the whole 4½ miles of the front, making it well-nigh impossible for the Boers to rapidly re-deploy men to threatened areas.

Barton's brigade, consisting of the Scots, Irish and Dublin Fusiliers, were first across the new bridge and on reaching the northern bank, hurried along eastwards in singlefile, using the river bank to hide their movement from the enemy. At Pieter's Hill they left the shelter of the river bank and climbed the precipitous 500 feet up onto the plateau where the Irish Fusiliers were able to rush and capture the nearest kopies. On their right, the Scots were checked by heavy fire from the defenders and were forced to take shelter in a donga. For a while the brigade's forward movement was checked, however, they had gained a footing on the plateau and were able to direct rifle fire not only at the Boers confronting them, but also those attempting to hold Railway Hill.

Kitchener and his brigade of Lancastrians and Yorkshiremen were next into the fray, charging up Railway Hill. The Boers offered little resistance as the infantrymen stormed into their trenches, bayoneting several of the occupants and taking over fifty prisoners. So intent were they on fleeing down the reverse slope of the hill that they did not bother to shoot the British soldier who stood on the highest point of the hill waving his helmet.

It was now the turn of Hart and Norcott to attack Hart's Hill. Suffering under heavy artillery fire, the sight of reinforcements arriving to back-up the Irish already on the hill was too much for the Boers who 'ran like hunted rats from their trenches'.

As evening approached Barton brought three companies of his Irishmen round from the left of Pieter's Hill to clear a kopie on the right, where the Boers had stubbornly resisted the Scots throughout the day. A charge by the Irish Fusiliers drove the last of the Boers off the hill, but at a heavy price. They lost a third of their number and every one of their officers was either killed or wounded.

The enemy had been cleared off all three hills and Buller had at last broken through the Boers' defensive line along the Tugela. The British losses during the two weeks of this extended battle for 'Tugela Heights' were twenty-six officers and 347 men killed and ninety-nine officers and 1,710 men wounded. The Red Cross calculated that the Boers suffered eighty-one killed and 343 wounded.

Dundonald's men had spent the day on the rough rocky ground on the southern bank of the Tugela where, with the assistance of a machine gun, they kept up a continuous fire on the Boers on Pieter's Hill. The covering fire enabled Barton's force to deploy along the river and advance for a considerable distance up the hill without serious molestation.

Winston Churchill was with the mounted brigade on that day, although both he and the South African Light Horse had been away from the Tugela Front for some days, having been ordered to drive off some Boers who were threatening lines of communication near Frere. This they did and they were able rejoin the Brigade on 26 February. It must have been very frustrating for young Winston to be away from the centre of things at such a crucial time. On the evening of the 26th, he told his commanding officer Col Byng that he 'wanted to get the DSO, as it would look so nice on the robes of the Chancellor of the Exchequer'. Byng replied, that he 'must first get into Parliament, if he could get any constituency to have him!'[22]

For a time General Buller toyed with the idea of sending his cavalry in pursuit of the Boers but fortunately abandoned this idea, which could very easily have resulted in the destruction of his entire Regular cavalry. Instead he decided to concentrate on the relief of Ladysmith. Late on the night of 27 February, Dundonald received the orders for the following day. These were: 'To cross the pontoon tomorrow morning and reconnoitre the enemy'.[23]

At dawn on that momentous day, 28 February 1900, Dundonald's brigade saddled up, crossed the river and rode down the valley between Pieter's

Hill and Railway Hill, following the railway towards Ladysmith. Forward patrols from Thorneycroft's MI reported the enemy were ensconced in rocky ground near Pieter's Station. Despite coming under heavy fire, the brigade, assisted by their machine guns, drove the Boers from this position, with Thorneycroft's regiment suffering a few casualties. The brigade now fanned out with the SALH on the right moving towards the Klip River and the Carbineers under McKenzie on the left. Though subjected to occasional sniping from the Boer rearguard, the Carbineers scouted towards Ladysmith until they came to a road that led to a bridge over the Klip River. A Boer kommando was seen approaching along the road, clearly making for the bridge. McKenzie decided to ambush them and with the Carbineers concealed behind a ridge, he was about to spring the trap when a distant Maxim gun opened fire on the Boers, who wheeled around and rode off. McKenzie was furious and when Major Gough arrived a short while later, McKenzie wanted to know 'what fool had fired the Maxims?' Gough blamed a Captain Hill and Dundonald.[24]

Gough returned to brigade headquarters while the Carbineers continued to scout towards Ladysmith, keeping well to the left of the railway line, while the other regiments worked down towards the right. They passed through a looted farm, owned by one Woodhouse, and pressed on towards Caesar's Camp. Coming over a rise they could see below them Intombi Camp and a few miles further across the plain, Ladysmith. They could have ridden straight into Ladysmith, which the men were keen to do, but McKenzie called a halt, so that he could ensure that such action would not prejudice any other unit. In due course Major Gough arrived with the Imperial Light Horse following some distance behind. Greeting him McKenzie said, 'Now, Gough, there is Ladysmith, let us ride in.'[25]

Gough asked for an orderly to take a note back to Dundonald. While Gough was writing out the note, McKenzie instructed the sergeant major to ensure the ILH did not sneak past them. With the message on its way to Dundonald, the Carbineers moved down the stony path off the hill and when they reached the level ground McKenzie had to check his men to prevent them embarking on a wild gallop into the town. It was at this stage that a message came from Captain Bottomley of the ILH asking if they might ride into Ladysmith with the Carbineers. The Imperial Light Horse had throughout the campaign fought alongside Carbineers, shared its vicissitudes, and rendered help without being asked. Without hesitating, McKenzie agreed to the request. So the two regiments lined up in half sections making a column of fours with Duncan McKenzie and Capt D.W. Mackay leading the Carbineers, while Herbert Bottomley with Lt Bridges led the ILH.[26] Hubert Gough was there but not leading the column. The scene was set for a dignified entry into Ladysmith.

They crossed the defended perimeter at an outpost manned by the Border Mounted Rifles. Captain Vause was in charge that day and it was appropriate that the Natal Volunteers should be the first to welcome them.

Their approach had, of course, been seen in Ladysmith. Carbineer Veterinary Surgeon Herbert Watkins-Pitchford in a letter to his wife described the arrival of the relief column:

> Someone came running down the road shouting as he passed, 'Saddle up at once. Buller's in sight!' Then came the bustle and excitement which you can imagine better than I can describe. The General had seen a body of horsemen advancing over the hills several miles from Ladysmith and as such a sight was a very unusual one for the enemy to present, he had them watched carefully, since it seemed extraordinary that, if they were our people, Long Tom did not open fire on them as they were well within his range.
>
> As they came nearer, however, it could be seen from their formation that they were not the enemy, so the General wired down to Royston, 'British cavalry in sight. Turn your men out to meet them.' The Volunteers' horses had fortunately been kept to last, only a few hundreds of our horses and pack ponies having been slaughtered, so that we were able to turn out in some strength – nearly 3 squadrons – while the other cavalry regiments were almost, if not quite, dismounted. Rapidly forming up we galloped across the flats towards the river and down its steep banks into the water, splashing and being splashed until we were drenched. Then a scramble pell mell up the steep and slippery drift on the other side to gain the flat where we had so often fooled Long Tom and his mates in early days, and across the flat stretches, and among the thorn trees as hard as we could gallop. To add to our pleasure, our large 4.7 gun which we had supposed long dead from want of ammunition, opened fire with a crash and sent his shells whistling and roaring over our heads towards the old enemy on Bulwana which had pounded us so unmercifully during the four previous months. This provoked no answer from the well known spot, and we subsequently learnt that the absence of firing was in consequence of the Boer gunners attempting to remove the gun. This in fact I saw, as soon as I could get a glass to bear on the emplacement.
>
> Well, across the plain we pelted as hard as we could gallop drawing nearer and nearer each moment to the dark mass of horsemen rapidly advancing toward us. At the end it was like a hostile cavalry charge rather than the meeting of two friendly bodies of men. As we drew within shouting range we yelled and howled like packs of wild dogs. Caps and helmets were waved, guns frantically brandished, horses plunged and bucked with fright, and in a moment the two columns were merged into a struggling mass of horsemen, besieged and deliverers mixed inextricably in one disorderly mass of cheering, laughing, gesticulating, hand-shaking, back-slapping, men. All showed wear and tear. Tattered and lean and brown, the one side with privation and exposure and long anxiety, and the other with hard fighting and

desperate derring-do. Verney (Veterinary Lieutenant F.A. Verney) was the first man to clasp my hand. He was belted and accoutred like a buccaneer, carrying a long repeating-rifle in a carbine bucket, although he had a star of a lieutenant upon his shoulder. He was very thin, and very vociferous, and seemed unfeignedly glad to see me safe. So back we crowded towards Ladysmith, a noisy shouting rabble, to find the banks of the river on the other side thronged with all the inhabitants of the town who could get down in time. As we plunged and slid down the steep drift to the river the scene was beyond description, the slipping, splashing horses and the excited shouting people on the banks above, mad with delight. It was a picture, my dear, I would not have missed for anything. One's heart was in one's throat all the time to see so much unalloyed human joy. Never this side of heaven can I hope to see such a scene of happiness, and it was all impromptu.[27]

Of course several of the horses came down in the melee but in the excitement no one worried about any bruises that might be suffered in a tumble from a horse.

In a letter published in the London *Daily Telegraph* on 27 February 1950, Wing Commander W.L. Shaw, who in 1900 was a 20-year-old trooper with the Carbineers, wrote that when they were half way across the river, 'Major McKenzie touched his famous bay stallion Inspector with his spur. With one leap he was up the riverbank and into Ladysmith, the first of the relieving force into the town.'[28] For the citizens and Volunteers it was doubly exciting. For four months they had endured this terrible siege, and after so many disappointments, it was their own who had ended their ordeal.

Donald Macdonald had just settled down to a dinner of horseflesh when he heard shouting and above the tumult the cry, 'Buller's cavalry are in sight.' Abandoning their horseflesh he and his companions ran outside and joined the stream of excited people making their way to the nearest river crossing. They could see horsemen coming towards them and all knew it must be the relief column. It seemed the whole town had come down to the river. 'All the colours and all the nations of earth seemed blended together in a confused throng, all its tongues raised in one exultant din. It was worth having lived and suffered through the siege for that supreme hour.'[29] Macdonald noticed that many of the sick and wounded from the hospitals had abandoned their beds so that they might also welcome the column:

There were soldiers with white and shrunken faces; men wounded in the legs, who shuffled slowly down the road. One poor young infantry officer had stopped at a deep street channel – he had not the strength to step over it. I lifted him to the other side, but it was no trouble, he was as light as a child. Two other officers drove down in a pony trap, the ghastliness of their faces impressed one, even in that time of wild excitement. They were, in plain and painful truth, living skeletons.[30]

The relief column was mobbed as it made its way to the centre of town. McKenzie said they 'were pulled about so much that it was difficult to talk to anyone.'[31] People clung to bridles and stirrups as they tried to shake hands or just touch the riders as they came by. Old General White, tired, emaciated, sick and a little bent, rode down to meet them. He had borne a heavy responsibility alone, had been much criticised, but never for a second did he give up, or fail to do what he believed to be right. Now with a fellowship born of their shared suffering, the people crowded round him so he could go no further. He straightened up and attempted to address the crowd. That perceptive witness Donald Macdonald was there.

> Beginning almost inaudibly (he) thanked them for the loyal way they had, civilian and soldier alike, co-operated with him in defence of the town. Then he struck the keynote that went straight to the hearts of all his people, and roused them to an indescribable enthusiasm 'Thank God we kept the flag flying.' Such words, spoken with an intensity of solemn feeling, were a match to the mine of human emotion, and what a roar rose in the night air, while the Zulus, knowing not that something fit to be immortal had been said, but inflamed by the infectious joy of the multitude, sprang into the air again, and shouted the war-cry that some few had heard many years ago when Cetewayo's impis swept down upon them. 'It cut me to the heart,' the General went on, 'to reduce your rations as I did.' Then his voice faltered and failed him, and it seemed for a moment he would break down altogether. The sympathetic crowd filled in the break, helped him over the crisis with another roar of delight long drawn out, and with the promptness of a soldier he pulled himself together, and mastered his deep feeling. A smile came over his face, and he saved the situation with a laughing. 'I promise you, though, that I'll never do it again.' The people laughed and cheered.[32]

Overcome with emotion the general turned his horse away and made his way back to his quarters, and they loved him even more, while those who had so fiercely criticised him felt ashamed. Spontaneously the crowd in their many different voices sang *God Save the Queen*, before drifting away.

Hubert Gough lost no time in making himself known to General White and joined the 'celebratory' dinner held at Sir George White's residence. And what a meal it was. They had two bottles of champagne that had been carefully husbanded, a tin or two of sardines, plus a piece of horse or mule meat, and an army biscuit for each diner.[33] Not fine dining but what a wonderful opportunity for Hubert Gough to advance his career. Duncan McKenzie and Herbert Bottomley were not invited to the dinner.

Whatever was happening at headquarters, it was a great night for the local regiments. The Imperial Light Horse were delighted to be reunited with A Squadron. Apart from the Carbineers, McKenzie had with him seven members of the Border Mounted Rifles as well as a few troopers from the Natal Mounted Rifles and the Natal Mounted Police. Everyone had news to exchange and must have talked well into the night before the weary relievers lay down in their greatcoats and, having given away their rations, went supperless to sleep.

As we have seen, Dundonald with the bulk of the mounted brigade had been left in the rear by the Carbineers and ILH. At about 3 p.m. he received a note from Gough that the hill in front appeared to be unoccupied. He replied, 'Take your regiment onto the hill and I will support'. The whole brigade then moved forward. A second message from Gough was received to which Dundonald replied 'Push on towards Ladysmith, I am supporting'.[34] Dundonald and the brigade continued to move forward in support until they were about 6 miles from Ladysmith. Dundonald now decided that as evening was approaching and their flanks had not been properly scouted, Thorneycroft should take the brigade back to a previously selected position, while he and some of his staff should join the forward regiments. He took with him Major Birdwood, Lieutenant Clowes, Lieutenant W.S. Churchill and some orderlies. This group then set off post haste after the Carbineers and ILH.

They reached Ladysmith some time after the others and made their way to General White's headquarters. The celebratory dinner was already in progress and they were invited to join the other officers. Churchill was a mere lieutenant in a Volunteer regiment so his invitation is surprising. He was 'placed next to Hamilton, who won the fight at Elandslaagte and beat the Boers at Wagon Hill, and next but one to Hunter, whom everyone said was the finest man in the world'.[35]

Churchill appears to have taken the opportunity to promote his personal career as a politician, rather than sticking to reportage. This is how he described his entry into Ladysmith.

> Presently we arranged ourselves in military order, Natal Carabineers and Imperial Light Horse riding two and two abreast so that there might be no question about precedence and with Gough, the youngest regimental commander in the army, and one of the best, at the head of the column, we forded the Klip River and rode into town.[36]

He is misleading his readers into believing that he was with the relief column when it entered Ladysmith, something that would go down well with electors in England. In South Africa it caused a great deal of ill feeling. Many thought Dundonald had claimed to be first into Ladysmith. Dundonald was appalled when he discovered the misinformation being put about. In a letter to Duncan McKenzie he wrote:

> In the same paper it says that I had said I was 'first in Ladysmith' – I said, 'the Mounted Brigade was first'. I did not arrive until 20 minutes

after you all had got into town, having naturally the Brigade to attend to, and send back to its bivouac and the Command to give over, when the road was clear, before I could follow. This is all very trifling but it annoyed me as you know what I think of your gallant Squadron and of you my friend.'[37]

Hubert Gough's brother John was among the besieged in Ladysmith but because of the celebrations at headquarters on the evening of the relief, the brothers arranged to meet at the Klip River bridge at 6 a.m. the next morning. Hubert was there with McKenzie's and Bottomley's squadrons and noticed without recognising an officer with a carefully trimmed naval beard approaching on a grey horse. 'Hello, Hubert,' said the horseman. Hubert recognised his brother's voice at once, and grabbed his hand and shook it violently. Still sitting on the horse, John looked down at his dapper and trim brother. 'Hubert,' he said, 'How fat you have got.'[38]

Shortly afterwards the two squadrons rode back to the brigade bivouac near Nelthorpe station where they were ordered to cover the left flank and front of Buller's army as it advanced towards Ladysmith. After all the torments of the siege, those in Ladysmith were anxious that the retreating Boers should be attacked in some way. Early that morning Karri Davies took the ILH onto Bulwana hoping to prevent the removal of Long Tom. Unfortunately the Boers had already removed the big gun. Back in town the Natal Volunteer regiments with about 2500 infantry and artillery set out towards Elandslaagte. The artillery were able to fire a few shots at the retreating Boers, before the enterprise was abandoned. They were all too weak to continue. The infantry could not march any distance, the mounted men had used all their own and their horses' energy the previous day, and the artillery horses collapsed in their traces, too weak to draw the cannons. They were however able to forage for food in the deserted Boer camps where much food and other supplies had been abandoned. On the other side of Ladysmith, near Bester's farm, a small party of Natal Police lost one man killed and one wounded in a brush with the enemy.

Throughout the British Empire there was much excitement and celebrating on that first day of March 1900; newspaper correspondents and the curious flocked to Ladysmith. Lt Blake Knox visited Intombi Hospital.

There were about 800 patients; the features and limbs of one and all showed unmistakably what the ravages of disease and starvation will produce. Thin, gaunt, haggard men, living skeletons met my eyes everywhere, some in beds, others seated, others crawling rather than walking; listless claw fingered beings in ragged hospital clothes, whose only signs of life seemed centred in their large round glistening eyes, set off by pinched, cadaverous, bearded faces. Such was Intombi. The medical staff themselves were almost as bad: one of them, whom I had known as a stout, well groomed man about town, had now a pale emaciated face, his tattered khaki hanging in folds about a wasted frame; he appeared rather a subject for medical aid than one fit to administer it. He pointed out what seemed to me to be a small forest of short white sticks, glistening in the morning sun, between the hospital and Bulwana. I asked him what it was. 'It's the graves of 1,600 men,' he said. Victims of enteric, dysentery, and wounds. I shuddered.[39]

When on the evening of the 28th the nurses at Intombi realised Ladysmith had been relieved, they were so overcome with joyous emotion that they were unable to speak and carried out their duties as if in a dumb show. The next morning Kate Driver heard a Natal Carbineer asking for her. She looked out of her tent:

It was young Willy Tanner (in the First World War he served with great distinction in France becoming a Brigadier General), a friend I had known in Maritzburg for some time. He told me of my people, and gave me much news I was hungry to have. He said my young brother had been doing great things. 'It was he who volunteered to run down Spion Kop with the message to General Warren for reinforcements, and who had led those reinforcements back up to the top,' he told me. 'Your brother had said when volunteering, that he was less afraid to run down with the messages than to stand there and be shot! He has, however acquired two bullet holes in the flap of his trousers. He is very proud of these two bullet holes.

'But now,' said Willie Tanner, diving into his pack, 'would you like some rice? And would you like some onions and some stale ginger bread? We came through a deserted farm house and I found these.'

I began to clear a tray of dressings so that he could give these treasures to me. Then suddenly I looked at him. 'Ginger bread from a deserted farmhouse. I'm so hungry that I could eat it all this very moment, but somehow specially the ginger bread gives my heart a kind of stab. Being a farmer's daughter, I can so vividly imagine how life went on there before the people had to leave their home.'

'Well,' he answered quietly, 'that is how war goes, doesn't it? But I know how you feel. We have strict orders to commandeer all food and all livestock. A few days ago we came to a dilapidated old farmhouse where there was an old Boer woman alone. She saw us coming and by the time we reached her, she was sitting by her door with her arms round a goose. She gave a great cry as we came up to her and buried her head in his feathers. We stood still. When she looked up again the tears were streaming down her face, and she said, "Then yes – if you must take my things – take everything, take everything! But leave me my man-goose! Do not kill him! Do not take him from me! Do not hurt my man-goose!"

'There are times when one has to disobey orders,' he said. He took my hand, 'Goodbye, I must go now. I am glad you are free at last.'[40]

On 3 March, Buller's army made their formal entry into Ladysmith. This long procession met with a reception more subdued than that which had greeted McKenzie's and Bottomley's squadrons a few days earlier. The proceedings were enlivened when a squad of Gordons on passing General White, stopped, broke ranks and cheered the general.

None of the Volunteer regiments participated in the march past as they were out on patrol. Buller visited Intombi and was appalled by the condition of the patients. He arranged for the immediate transfer of the unpopular Col Exham RAMC to the Cape. Exham's mate, Henry Nevinson, returned to England to write his book, while General Sir Charles Warren was appointed Military Governor of the Cape north of the Orange River, a sparsely populated and arid area.

Though many had tried to rush Buller into taking precipitous action against the Boers, he resolutely refused to move until his army was ready.

In the Boer paper the *Standard and Digger News* of 1 March 1900, Gerard Bailey in Dundee was able to read of the 'Glorious Boer Victory' and that, 'Ladysmith is not likely to be relieved.'[41]

23

Relief of Mafeking and Boer Treatment of Prisoners

Sir Redvers Buller has been much criticised for his failure to pursue the Boers while they were withdrawing from the Tugela and Ladysmith. However, it should be borne in mind that not only were the defenders of Ladysmith too weak to take part in any military action but a considerable number were seriously ill, and almost all needed urgent medical attention. This was a priority for Buller and to make and execute the arrangements for it would take time and effort. In addition, the relieving force had been on the move for more than two-and-a-half months so the men needed rest.

It was not only the men whom Buller had to take into account. To drive the Boers out of Natal, a substantial portion of this force had to be mounted and this meant the men required horses. All the 10,000 horses that had been in Ladysmith before the siege had either died, been eaten, or were otherwise no longer fit for service, therefore had to be replaced. In addition the wastage of horses among his own mounted brigades, the artillery and transport corps had to be made good. Once they arrived, the new horses had to be trained and allocated to units to suit each animal, another time-consuming task.

Further, the army, which for so long had been split into 'relievers' and 'defenders', had to be reorganised into one unit. Among those affected were the Carbineers, whose members were to leave Dundonald's brigade and return their own regiments. When they paraded before Dundonald for the last time he addressed them as follows:

Major McKenzie, officers and men of the Natal Carbineers, as you are leaving me today to rejoin your Regiment, I take this opportunity of saying goodbye to you and how sorry I am at losing you from my command. You belong to a regiment whose reputation stands high and you have done much to cover it with honour. For the time I have commanded you, you have had much hard and dangerous work, but

I have never feared that however difficult the task set to you to perform, and however dangerous the task, it would be well accomplished, and I may say that were I intending to join any regiment and were it open to me to choose, I would prefer to join the Natal Carbineers. I wish you all goodbye.[1]

Dundonald had previously commanded the 2nd Life Guards, one of Britain's most prestigious regiments. It was a wonderful and well-deserved compliment.

Not everyone had a high opinion of the part played by Dundonald's men in the Relief of Ladysmith. Frederick Tucker was a private in the Rifle Brigade and kept a diary. As part of the relieving force he had taken part in the fighting on Hart's Hill on 27 February 1900. On the 28th they buried their dead. In his diary he writes:

We had buried our dead so we made ready for the advance which we expected to make, but after waiting for some hours we found to our disappointment that this was not to be. We were reinforced by a strange regiment we had not seen before. In fact we did not even know that they belonged to the Natal Field Force. I suppose that, while we had been fighting every day and having a rough time, they had been living in comfort at the base or Line of Communication, on soft bread and fresh meat. Even the cavalry came across the Tugela and condescended to approve of the way we had twisted the Boers out from Pieter's Hill, but our men didn't want their approval and some of our fellows gave them to understand as much. 'There was plenty of work for you fellows,' I heard one our men remark to one of the colonial mounted men.

'Yes,' he replied, 'but our horses wanted rest.' I don't know how they got done up for we had not seen them do anything to warrant tiring them. After the guns had crossed the river, the cavalry rode forward to find out if the enemy had gone. They had scarcely gone any distance before they came scampering back as if the devil had them. A few Boers from their rear guard had fired on them and sent them all back to us for protection. However, after being reinforced, they went out again and this time they found nothing. That night they galloped into Ladysmith, and must have snatched all the honours from the papers at home, while we remained on Pieter's Hill for another night in the rain, enjoying the horrid stench of dead horses.[2]

The Rifle Brigade's response to the unsolicited praise from the colonials does seem a little ungracious. The strange regiment Tucker and his comrades saw was almost certainly Thorneycroft's Mounted Infantry. Early on the morning of the 28th it was they who were scouting ahead of the column, made contact with the Boers, and then galloped back with information of the Boer position. It is such a pity that when Thorneycroft's men were on Spion Kop and were anxious for friends to come up and join them, Tucker and his mates were busy elsewhere. They spent that momentous day sunning themselves on Mount Alice.

Once it was established that the Boers had retreated behind the Biggarsberg, the Natal Volunteers went to Highlands, near Mooi River. A camp had been set up to rest their horses, while the men were able to take it in turns to go on a few weeks leave.

Before he left, General White went to see the Native Scouts who were to be disbanded. Robert Samuelson was present and noted the words of the general.

Simeon Kambule and all you scouts, you have done most useful and important service for Her Majesty the Queen, for which I thank you, on her behalf and on behalf of the Army. I will ever be mindful of your loyalty and services, and when I am over the seas I will look back to you with great pride. I have no doubt you will receive all the rewards that fall due to faithful soldiers of the Queen.

Colonel William Royston also spoke to the Scouts saying how proud he was of them, that they and their people had proved to be loyal and true at Isandlwana, and had again displayed these qualities. He went on to say that if he was spared to live, he would persuade the government to form them into a nucleus of a Native Corps.[3]

Reports and dispatches often contain phrases such as 'our information is' without giving the source of the information. In many instances this would have been gathered by these scouts, who deserved every word of the praise they received from White and Royston.

On 4 March, the Imperial Light Horse, with the exception of Bottomley's squadron, left Ladysmith for three weeks rest and change at Hilton, a village on the hills above Pietermaritzburg. Before they left, Aubrey Woolls Sampson had a long interview with General Buller, who eulogised the regiment, and said that he would do all within reason to help. It was agreed that its strength be increased to 600 men. Because of the wastage caused by casualties and sickness, the regiment now needed 300 new recruits to bring it up to strength. Such was the reputation of the ILH that they were to have no trouble signing up good quality recruits, many of whom had been with the Colonial Scouts, a unit which had been raised in Natal and was in the process of being disbanded. Because of the courage they had displayed at Wagon Hill, the regiment was to be equipped with modern Lee Enfield rifles. (The other Volunteer regiments were, for the time being, to continue using single shot rifles and it was only much later in the war that these were replaced by rifles equipped with magazines). The Imperial authorities also agreed to provide them with 400 fresh remounts.[4]

Karri Davies travelled ahead to arrange the camp at Hilton and to buy supplies of fruit and other necessary foods, which had been missing from their diet for so long. Those who had not seen Karri since he left for the front in October noted that although he showed the effects of the siege he was 'in fairly good form'. Aubrey Woolls Sampson was still seriously disabled by his wound, and it would be some time before he would have the operation to join his sciatic nerve. Enteric had reduced Charlie Mullins to a living skeleton hardly able to put one foot in front of the other. Most of the others were still very weak. It was hoped that with better medical care and nutritious food, the health of the whole regiment would soon improve.

The Army Ordinance Department provided uniforms and equipment for the new recruits. On 20 March the regiment received a telegram enquiring when they would be able to take the field, to which they replied, 'about the first week in April'. Because the army had to re-equip a large number of troops at the time, it was unable to carry out all its obligations towards the ILH immediately. Anxious to get into the field again, they applied for and received a loan from Wernher, Beit & Co., as set out in Chapter 5. This enabled them to purchase horses and be ready by the first week of April. There was some talk that they might be transferred to the Cape to take part in the Relief of Mafeking.

Karri had taken a couple of weeks recuperative leave, and being anxious to keep up with developments, sent a telegram to the adjutant, 'Please wire what are your movements?' To which the adjutant replied, 'Thanks once daily after breakfast!'[5] The adjutant was later to become a distinguished general.

Buller was anxious to keep the ILH with his column and on 3 April, they were back in Ladysmith. After a separation of nearly six months they were reunited with A Squadron under Captain Bottomley, whose experienced men would prove a useful leavening for the inexperienced new recruits. Buller's desire to keep the ILH was to be frustrated. On 8 April, they received orders to proceed at once to the Cape. They travelled by sea from Durban to Cape Town and then by train to Kimberley, where a column was being assembled to relieve Mafeking. Aubrey Woolls Sampson remained behind to have his hip operation, while Charlie Mullins, now a major, had recovered sufficiently to accompany the regiment.

Command of the Relief Column was entrusted to Colonel Brian Mahon; Colonel Edwards still commanded the ILH, the second in command being Karri Davies. The column consisted of:

Four guns of M Battery RHA and two Pom Poms,
The Imperial Light Horse,
The Kimberley Mounted Corps,
A detachment of the Cape Police and
some Volunteer infantry.

In all about 1,200 men, almost all of whom were colonials. They were accompanied by sixty mule wagons carrying supplies and baggage. The country they were to traverse was flat semi-desert. For the Natalians, this must have been a strange and inhospitable land, added to which the native peoples had a language and customs very different from those of the Zulu.

On 4 May 1900, they set off for Mafeking, approximately 250 miles north of Kimberley. One mounted regiment would form the advance guard, while the other provided flank and rear guards. The two regiments swapped duties each day. On 10 May, they entered the little town of Vryburg approximately half-way to Mafeking. The town had been vacated by the enemy and they were greeted with enthusiasm by local loyalists. The column was able to wash, and eat a prepared meal before setting off again that evening. The sick, and enemy prisoners captured along the way, were left in Vryburg.

On 11 and 12 May, the column continued its advance, though the enemy was reported to be shadowing them. On the 13th a substantial enemy force attacked the ILH in an area where bush provided cover. Firing took place at close range and though they were outnumbered, the ILH held their ground. However, accurate shelling by the artillery forced the Boers to withdraw. In the engagement the ILH lost six men killed and thirteen wounded. Charlie Mullins was among those wounded and so severe were his injuries that it was thought unlikely he would survive. The wounded were left at Wright's Farm, which would provide more comfort than the ambulance with the column.[6]

Early the next day the column continued its march, hoping to find water at the Maritzani River about 6 miles away. The deep sand they were now traversing made the going tough for all, and especially for the transport wagons. When they arrived at the river, it was dry except for a few fetid pools. Long, deep trenches were dug into the sandy riverbed. Potable water seeped into the trenches, which was then pumped into canvas troughs. Watering the men and animals by this method took from 8 a.m. to 3.30 p.m., when the column resumed its march. At 8.15 p.m. they stopped for a rest, only to resume the advance at 2.30 a.m.

Just before dawn, fires were seen ahead of them. Patrols were sent out to reconnoitre and soon came back with the news that it was Colonel Plumer's column, which had come down from Rhodesia to join them. Early that morning the two brigades met at Jan M'sibi, 18 miles west of Mafeking. The rest of the day was spent readying themselves for the final push to relieve the town. Col Mahon, being senior to Plumer, assumed command of their combined forces and Col Edwards took his place as commander of the Kimberley column. Included in Plumer's brigade were a battery of four 12-pounder guns of the Canadian Artillery and D Squadron of the 3rd Queensland Contingent led by Captain Kellie.

By 7 a.m. the next day the reinforced relief column was on the move again. Colonel Edwards and his brigade were on the left and Colonel Plumer's brigade on the right. By noon they were 6 miles down the road at Sanie's Post where a halt was called to water the horses and give the men an opportunity to have something to eat. At 1 p.m. Edwards saw a column of mounted men moving across their intended line of advance. Higher ground between the two forces appeared to offer a good tactical advantage, so Edwards sought and obtained permission to take it. Taking one ILH squadron with him and collecting two more along the way, they galloped hard and were able to gain possession of the high ground, just before the arrival of the enemy. The ILH dismounted and in the skirmish that followed, the Boers were driven back across the valley. The Boers had launched a simultaneous attack on Plumer's force, and in the fierce fighting that followed, they had no more success there than they had achieved against the ILH. Finding themselves being steadily driven back, the Boers hurriedly withdrew and in the course of this retirement were badly mauled by the artillery. In the engagement Edwards' command lost two men killed and eight wounded.[7]

Without resting, the column resumed its advance until a rest was ordered at 5.30 p.m. As it was not known whether any Boer disposition lay between them and Mafeking, Karri Davies, with six men, went ahead to scout the route into town. They saw no sign of the enemy and rode into the besieged town unmolested. Two of his men, Corporals Warby and Duirs, were with Bottomley when Ladysmith was relieved, a remarkable double. Karri immediately returned to base and reported that the road was clear, whereupon Col Mahon decided to ride into Mafeking at once.

At 3.30 a.m. on Wednesday 17 May 1900, the Relief Column arrived in Mafeking – warmly welcomed by Colonel Baden-Powell. The Imperial Light Horse, who had had no rest since 6 a.m. the previous day, made their way to a patch of cold bare earth, known as the Market Square, dismounted, loosened girths, lay down in their cloaks by their horses' heads, and fell asleep.[8]

News of the relief was flashed around the world; Britain, with much of her Empire, went mad with delight.

That morning the Boers launched a surprise attack on the place where the Relief Column had bivouacked the previous evening, and found no one there. Believing their force was not strong enough to engage the combined forces of the Relief Column and the Mafeking garrison, the Boers rode away to the east to join the kommandos defending their Republics.

The Imperial Light Horse had learnt much since that day they had charged up the hill at Elandslaagte behind Col Scott-Chisholme waving his little red flag. From the Natal Volunteers, they had learnt the value of concealing from the enemy one's position and intentions and, if these elements were combined with speed and decisive action, as at Acton Homes, success could come at little cost.

Far away in Dundee, Gerard Bailey was having his own small struggle with the invaders. The town was again full of Boers, now engaged in fortifying positions on the Biggarsburg. No longer did he hear boasts of 'driving the rooineks into the sea'. Instead, they told him they are ready to give back this part of Natal if they could have a guarantee of independence,

The Boers are styled Federalists. It is the Federal cause, we are the Imperialists. It is always 'Great Federal Victory' – 'Federal Forces' – 'Rout of the Imperialists' and if there is any interchange of courtesies between our generals and their leaders, such is styled, 'The Comity of Nations.' There is no small beer about the Boer newspapers.[9]

The house next-door to the vicarage was owned by a church warden, W.H. Tatham who, it will be recalled, believed the townsfolk had nothing to fear from the Boers but, in spite of this, was carted off to Pretoria. Possibly because he was a church warden and neighbour of the vicar, Gerard Bailey kept a careful watch over the house and at the beginning of March, it was one of the few premises in Dundee still intact. Gerard now noticed policemen removing furniture from the house. He immediately complained in writing to the *Vrederechter*, however, the removals continued. In due course he received a reply to his complaint, the *Vrederechter* stating, 'that in future nothing shall be removed from the premises mentioned by you'. By then the house had been cleaned out, and there was nothing left that could be taken.

Although one could almost stock a library with books about the fate of Boers, both civilian and military, who fell into British hands during the war, little has been written about prisoners taken by them. An exception is the capture, imprisonment, and escape of Winston Churchill, which is one of the best-known episodes of the war. However, Churchill was the grandson of a Duke, and the treatment accorded to him cannot be compared with that given to other prisoners.

During the initial stages of the war, captured British officers were accommodated in the premises of the State Model School in Pretoria. They were allowed considerable freedom and, if they had the means, were able to supplement their rations and in other ways make their lives quite comfortable. After the escape of Winston Churchill, security was tightened; and although there was still plenty to complain about, and on several occasions prisoners were assaulted, some attempt was made to comply with internationally accepted standards. On 16 March 1900, they were moved to Waterval, about 6 miles from Pretoria. Here the officers were housed in a galvanised shed, 24 feet by 15 feet, with earthen floors. Twenty-seven beds were crowded into this room. Lunch was the only meal provided by the Transvaal authorities, who thereby compelled the officers to buy their breakfast and supper. Other necessities such as blankets could also be bought at exorbitantly high prices. Outside, a wired-off enclosure provided space for exercise.[10]

For the 'other ranks' life was very different. They were detained at Waterval from the beginning and were housed in old corrugated iron sheds that were full of holes so when it rained, the roofs leaked profusely. Added to this, the earthen floors of the sheds were below the level of the road outside, resulting in rainwater flowing through them. There were no beds, so the men had to lie on the bare earth. Each man was given a blanket but no waterproof sheets were issued. The roads between the shelters were in an indescribably filthy condition, rotten animal and vegetable refuse, and even human excrement, lay over them. The latrines consisted of trenches, 7 to 8 feet deep, situated about 50 yards from the sleeping quarters. Heavy rain filled the trenches, causing the contents to float all over the camp. It was the rainy season and the men had to live and sleep with this polluted water around them.

By February, the prisoner's clothes were in tatters. Some were without trousers, others without coats or boots. Each man was supposed to receive a pound of meat each week, bread, tea or coffee without milk or sugar and, from time to time, mealiemeal porridge. But often they received nothing at all. Their meat ration was less than a third of the officers' and in addition, their food was often of poor quality. The bread was usually sour or stale before it reached them, and other items included in their rations were either reduced or taken off the menu altogether – all this in a city where there was no shortage of food. Not surprisingly, several men collapsed from weakness, and typhoid and dysentery rapidly spread. Drinking and washing water was kept in separate tanks because the latter was unfit for consumption. Yet the same buckets were used indiscriminately to cart both classes of water, thereby introducing another potent system for the spread of disease. During the months they were incarcerated in Pretoria, fifty-six previously healthy men died.[11] Given the conditions under which they lived, it is surprising any survived.

The Transvaal Government established two hospitals for the treatment of sick or wounded prisoners, one at the Pretoria Racecourse and the other near the prison camps at Waterval. The Chief Medical Officer for Military Prisoners was a Dr Veale.

In the middle of December 1899, a conscripted Uitlander, Dr Haylett, was instructed to take charge of the Racecourse Hospital, which at that time had about sixty patients. The building was adequate and the patients did have beds with straw mattresses, though there were no sheets and few pillows. There were virtually no medicines or cleaning equipment, and despite numerous requisitions for these necessities, they only dribbled through in totally inadequate quantities, compelling Haylett to rely on decoctions of herbs found nearby. In the first week of January 1900, Haylett was transferred to the hospital at Waterval. A few days later he submitted a report to Dr Veale, condemning the sanitary arrangements, the water supply, the building and its equipment, all in the strongest possible terms. In the hospital there were more than sixty patients but only twenty-one beds, eleven mattresses and forty-nine blankets. The food supply was not only inadequate but irregular.[12] Despite receiving no response, Haylett continued to make written complaints to Veale who either would not or could not do anything to alleviate the situation. By the beginning of February, he had begun to wonder whether he had been sent to Waterval to kill or cure the patients, and decided to resign. In his letter of resignation he stated that he wished to serve with the Burghers in the field. No doubt he felt that there his medical skills would at least be used to save lives.

When Veale was finally called to account for his failure to respond to Haylett's reports and requests, he denied having received any letters at all from Dr Haylett. It appears Veale was not prepared to read letters written in English, because Dutch was the official language in the Transvaal. Haylett's requests and reports being in English were therefore set aside unread.[13] Veale, an Englishman and Cambridge graduate, would appear to have come out of the same mould as Ladysmith's infamous Dr Exham.

A German, Dr Rudolf von Gernet, succeeded Haylett and on 20 February, they went on an inspection tour of the camps. Dr von Gernet was appalled by what he saw, and on his return to Pretoria, immediately demanded a meeting with the committee in charge of Prisoners of War. As a German he did, of course, carry more clout than the Englishman, Haylett. On hearing Von Gernet's complaint, the committee called for Dr Veale and after questioning him decided he should have nothing more to do with the hospital at Waterval, except that he should administer the supply of medicines. When Von Gernet reported a week later that the supply of medicines was still unsatisfactory, the committee authorised him to obtain medicines wherever he liked. From this time onwards, conditions at the Waterval hospital dramatically improved.[14] In carrying out improvements Dr von Gernet was assisted by Mr J. Leigh Wood, manager of the Natal Bank, Pretoria; the Revd Goodwin, a Wesleyan minister; and a businessman, Sammy Marks, who was adept at obtaining funds from donors. Wood subsequently gave evidence about the conditions at the hospitals.

In the middle of January, I first heard of the condition of the Racecourse hospital, especially as regards the insufficiency of milk. In conjunction with some friends I remedied this as soon as possible. In the middle of February I started a fund to buy medical comforts and food for the sick prisoners at the Racecourse. At this time I had an opportunity of visiting this hospital. Iron bedcots with mattresses were provided, but there were no pillows, sheets and very few blankets. The floor of the rooms in which patients, mostly suffering from enteric and dysentery, was in an indescribably filthy condition. There were no bedpans or commodes. The resident doctor (Dr Santos) informed me that he had applied repeatedly for scrubbing brushes, soap, soda etc., but without avail. I provided these articles out of my own fund. After this date the Racecourse hospital was greatly improved. In fact, from this date until the British occupation, the complete equipment for some 100 beds, and practically the whole supply of food and ordinary invalid comforts was provided by my fund.

About eight weeks ago (April 1900) I had the opportunity of seeing the British prisoners, other than soldiers, who were also confined at the Racecourse, but apart from the soldiers. There were fifty-eight of them, and they were sleeping without bedding of any description, on the bare ground, and were in rags. Many of them had been there for several months.

As regards the Waterval hospital, at the beginning of February 1900, I heard of the terrible state of affairs existing at Waterval. I went to Dr Veale, and three times intimated to him, that if he wanted money to improve the lot of the sick at Waterval hospital, I would guarantee to find it. He did not accept my offers. I endeavoured then to effect my object through the Boer Authorities – the Under Secretary of State, and the Burgomaster – and through them to the Commission. These efforts had no results. As matters seemed to be going from bad to worse, we took the matter into our own hands, and on 20 February, sent out the first consignment of articles for the sick. On 24 February, Dr von Gernet was appointed resident medical officer at Waterval, and henceforth we continued to supply him with all he asked. We fitted out about 200 beds.[15]

On 18 April 1900, Leigh Wood reported that Dr von Gernet was broken down and seriously ill from overwork. Those who helped Leigh Wood, and by their donations to his fund, saved many lives, were of course Uitlanders who had, with various excuses, obtained permission to remain in the Transvaal.

Soon after the arrival of the first British Prisoners of War in Pretoria on 23 October 1899, the Wesleyan minister, the Revd Goodwin, visited them at the Racecourse camp and, when they moved to the Waterval camp, he sought permission to visit once a week. He was not the only clergyman seeking permission to visit his congregation. A Baptist minister, a Congregational Church minister, and Father de Lacy, a well-known Catholic priest who had been in the Transvaal for more than thirty years, were among those wishing to minister to the prisoners. The Boers, despite their professed Christianity, decided that there would be only one visit by one clergyman per week and that the visit would take place on a Saturday. The result was the inmates could only see their pastor on one day each month. Funerals were conducted by a sergeant. Many who died were denied last rites. Father de Lacy was expelled from the Transvaal on 9 April 1900. No reason was ever given for his expulsion – however, he had always spoken out fearlessly against the ill-treatment of prisoners and other abuses by the government.

One clergyman who was not disturbed by the restrictions on visits to the prisoners was the Anglican priest, the Rev J. Godfrey. He was so scandalised by Churchill's escape, that he decided to distance himself from the prisoners and wrote to the incarcerated British officers,

After what has recently occurred, viz., the escape of Mr Churchill from confinement, I exceedingly regret that, in consideration of my duty to the Government, I must discontinue such regular ministrations, as I desire to maintain the honour due to my position. Of course I shall always be glad to minister to you in any emergency, with the special permission of the authorities, who will, with their usual kindness, duly inform me.[16]

The senior British officers imprisoned in Pretoria, Colonels Hunt, Bullock, Carleton and Moller might have committed some military blunders in Natal but now they showed a better side of their character. Not only did they complain vigorously about the treatment of their men, but also took notice of and criticised the treatment meted out to the colonials.

One such complaint followed the death of a colonial, Lieutenant Tarbutt of the South African Light Horse. He had been captured in Natal and then taken to the Transvaal, where he was held in gaol with common criminals. Here he contracted typhoid and the prison authorities denied him any medical treatment whatsoever until he was at death's door. Only then did they send him to hospital. By this time the disease was so advanced that little could be done to help him and he died shortly afterwards.[17] Another to die in similar circumstances was a doctor, described as 'a native of India,' who died after catching fever at the Racecourse hospital, also having been denied medical attention until it was too late.

In a formal complaint addressed to the Transvaal State Secretary, Lt Col Hunt and his fellow colonels pointed out that the colonials were not in any way subjects of the Transvaal Government and continued, 'The distinction therefore made between these prisoners and those belonging to the Imperial Regular forces, seems at variance with recognized International custom, while their treatment does not seem to be that accorded to prisoners of war.'[18]

Another complaint signed by Col Hunt and eighty officers and civilians stated:

The treatment to which the non-commissioned officers and men at Waterval are subjected, has contributed to the very serious mortality prevalent amongst them. For weeks no soap was issued, so that it was impossible for them to maintain that ordinary cleanliness which is so necessary for health. Many of them are understood to be without boots. The scale of diet is extremely low, and the sanitary conditions generally are very defective, even though some attempts have lately been made to improve them.

We are never officially informed of the serious illness or death of any of our men. We have a right to demand that this should be done, and that in all cases of serious illness, a man should be attended by a minister of his own religious faith. The provision made for religious services for men are entirely inadequate, and unworthy of a Government professing Christianity.

We have previously written on the subject of the prisoners of war detained in the civil gaol, and the danger they incur thereby. For many of the deaths which have occurred, both at Waterval and Pretoria, the gravest responsibility rests directly on your officials, whose duty it should be to see to the reasonable comfort, healthy surroundings, and proper medical care of our men. For all this, the Government of the South African Republic is ultimately responsible.[19]

In reply to the criticism that many men had been kept in gaol without being charged with any offence, the secretary of the committee in charge of prisoners, in an attempt to shift responsibility, stated, 'most of them were received here without any statement of what charge was against them. This was the fault of the Officers at the front who made them prisoners. The Commission did its best to communicate on the subject with the Officers at the front.'[20]

A few further examples illustrate the Boer treatment of, and attitude towards colonials. The Wesleyan Reverend Goodwin gave this description of the plight of the civilians in the prisoner-of-war camps.

These prisoners were treated quite differently and with much more severity than the military. They were enclosed in a sort of cattle kraal, and complained bitterly to me both of the fact of their being kept as prisoners without trial, and the way in which they were treated. These men were never tried at all. They were mostly shopkeepers and farmers, and had not taken up arms at all. These men had to sleep on the bare ground with nothing but an overhead shelter, and were very poorly fed and clothed.[21]

C.V. de V. van der Spey left this account of his experiences.

I was an accountant of the National Bank at Zeerust, and am a British subject. When war broke out the bank manager obtained permits for the bank staff who were British subjects to remain at our posts. Notwithstanding my having this permit, on the 11th December, 1899, I, in the company of six others, was arrested and placed in gaol at Zeerust, without being informed of any charge against me. I made successive applications to General Snyman, the State Attorney, and the American Consul to know the cause of our being imprisoned, but received no reply.

About the middle of January 1900, we were informed that we could either stay in gaol at Zeerust or be deported across the border, and choosing the latter I was sent to Pretoria. Here I was again lodged in gaol. I wrote again to the State Attorney requesting to be placed across the border as stipulated, and was told in reply that he was unable to comply with our request, and that I must remain in gaol. There were six of us imprisoned at Pretoria. Two were afterwards sent back to Zeerust gaol. One, a land surveyor named Crews, was taken ill with typhoid fever, and put in the prison hospital where there were some ten or fifteen patients. When we asked the chief of the prison, Mr du Plessis, to have Mr Crews removed to a proper hospital, he told us that the Transvaal hospitals were for the sick and wounded burghers, not for us. Eventually Mr Crews was removed, very ill, to the Bourke (Red Cross) hospital, and there he died. Another of us was placed across the border, but Mr van Niekirk and myself were left in gaol until the British arrived. There were as fellow prisoners of ours in Pretoria gaol,

Captain Kirkwood, South African Light Horse, and Captain Bates, Cape Police.

While in Zeerust prison six of us were confined in one cell which was kept locked all day, except for a quarter of an hour twice a day. Mr van Niekirk and myself were told in Zeerust that if we would take the oath of allegiance to the Transvaal we could be liberated at once.[22]

The gaoler Du Plessis was no doubt the same man who went out of his way to make life unpleasant for Karri and Sambo when they were imprisoned in Pretoria. One particularly unpleasant aspect of life in a Transvaal gaol was the sanitary arrangements. The latrine was a bucket in a corner of the cell regardless of the number of inmates and the hours the cell was kept locked.

After his capture on 27 January 1900, Inspector Landsburg of the Cape Mounted Police was taken to the colonial section of the camp at Waterval. On 7 April, he appealed to the authorities to release him and his fellow inmates into the general compound of the Prisoner of War camp.

He based his request on the following:

1. The place was full of vermin
2. For over 3 months they had been allowed no exercise (at one time they had been allowed to exercise once a week for an hour very early in the morning when it was bitterly cold)
3. There were no bathing or washing facilities.
4. The place was too small for the number of prisoners kept in it.
5. The den was so enclosed that they never had a breath of fresh air. At times the heat was so intense that they could hardly breathe, while at night it was so cold that they were prevented from sleeping.
6. Since being captured they had received far worse treatment than convicts.

Inspector Landsburg received no response to his request.[23]

Alex Russell was a clerk employed by the Natal Railways near Glencoe. On 2 November 1899, he was one of the group of approximately 150 Dundee residents who were put in closed trucks and taken to Pretoria. They arrived on Sunday 5 November and were taken to the Racecourse, where they were fed and put into tents. The next day they were told to get ready to go back to Natal. The prisoners' goods were searched and a telegramme, referring to a military letter, was found in Russell's baggage. He was immediately removed from the group and taken to the gaol where he was placed in a cell and told not to communicate with the other prisoners. He was fed at 6 p.m. and then locked up for the night. At 6 a.m. breakfast was served. This was mealie meal porridge without salt, and a little bread. For their midday meal he and the others would receive bread, and twice a week some boiled meat. The water in which the meat was boiled would later be served to them as soup. In the evening they would again receive unsalted mealie meal porridge. Most people would regard unsalted mealie meal as unpalatable. Pretoria was not short of food and to salt the porridge would have required little effort or expense. The inadequacy of this diet is obvious and many more would have died, had Leigh Wood not arranged for daily meals to be sent to them during the latter stages of their imprisonment.

On 24 April 1900, Russell and four other prisoners were taken to the prison office, and, without ever having been told why they had been held in gaol for so long, were told that they were to be sent across the border. They were taken under guard to the station where they boarded a train which took them and some wounded soldiers to the Portuguese colony's border. From there they made their way to Delagoa Bay where they boarded a ship, arriving in Durban on 3 May 1900.[24]

The group of Dundee residents who travelled with Russell to Pretoria in November 1899 did return to Natal – but not to Dundee. Instead they went to Ladysmith, which was already under siege. By taking them to Ladysmith, the Boers not only ensured that they continued to be incarcerated, but absolved themselves from the responsibility of feeding and accommodating them, while at the same time providing another drain on the town's medical and food resources. Furthermore, while these unfortunate people were in Ladysmith, the Boers were able to pillage, loot and destroy their farms, businesses and homes without hindrance, an opportunity they exploited to the full.

After the Boers overran the Dundee district in October 1899, they tried to persuade some of the local Dutch to join their invading army. Mr B. Liebenberg refused to take up arms against his fellow countrymen with the result that on 18 December 1899, he was arrested and taken to gaol in Pretoria. On 24 April 1900, his wife wrote to the Natal Government begging for help:

> Sir, herewith I bring to your notice that my husband B. Liebenberg, of Dundee, has been taken prisoner by the Boers on the 18th December, and sent to Pretoria gaol, where he is still kept and treated most shamefully, the food being very bad, so I was informed by some prisoners since being liberated. My husband was taken prisoner for the simple reason of being loyal to the Queen and Country; he was commandeered to go and fight, which he refused; he said he was a loyal British subject and would not fight, but wished for a passport to go to Durban with his family, which they would not grant him. I myself have been subjected to harsh treatment and rash insults. When they took my husband prisoner, he asked what they intended to do with his wife and family. Then they told him they would give us a passport to go over the border with my wagon and oxen down to Greytown, via Pomeroy. When I got as far as Helpmekaar, by the Boer laager, I was stopped and kept prisoner for three days with guards round my wagon night and day

and was threatened to be shot if any of us dared to leave the wagons. On the third day, I was sent back to Dundee, where my eldest boy, a mere lad, was taken and put in gaol and treated as a criminal, having nothing to eat, but the common mealie porridge and dry bread. After 9 days, however, I went to see the Magistrate, and asked him to let my boy off. I asked him, what they got him in gaol for and they told me it was because he said he was a British subject. On the 2nd January, I was sent to Pretoria with my family, and from there to Delagoa Bay, and from there to Durban. I earnestly beg your honourable, Sir, to take notice of this and try to do something towards getting my husband liberated: What they keep him for is quite a mystery, for there is no charge against him; I have spoken myself to the officials in Dundee and they told me that there is no charge against him and that they will soon send him to Delagoa Bay, but it is going on for five months, it is a cruel long time I should think, I am etc. Mrs D. Liebenberg.[25]

When the British army finally reached Pretoria on 5 June 1900, they were shocked by the appearance of the prisoners and appalled by the conditions in which they had been living. A Court of Inquiry was immediately set up to investigate the treatment of Prisoners of War by the Transvaal Government. On 24 June 1900, it released its findings. The Court found,

1. That the treatment of the officers of the Imperial Army, who were prisoners of war, appears on the whole to have been fairly good.
2. That the treatment of some of the Colonial prisoners was severe and unjustifiable, inasmuch as they were thrown into a common gaol and not treated as ordinary prisoners of war.
3. That non-commissioned officers and men were very badly fed, and the scale of diet, which was not strictly adhered to, was, in the matter of meat, a starvation ration.
4. That religious ministration was sparingly granted.
5. That the general treatment of sick prisoners was very bad, and has not been exaggerated, and that there is no doubt the prevalence of sickness and many deaths, which occurred amongst the prisoners, were attributable to the gross neglect of most ordinary sanitary precautions.[26]

Although the evidence and findings of the Court of Inquiry held at Pretoria concerned matters of deep and lasting significance to the people of Natal, the writer has been unable to find any reference to this matter in the Natal Archives, which perhaps is not surprising given the British decision to withhold information from Colonials. (*See* Chapter 3).

24

Invaders Chased out of Natal

While General Buller was winkling the Boers out of their positions on the Tugela, Lord Roberts was making a spectacular advance from the Cape, through the Orange Free State, towards Pretoria. On 15 February 1900, the siege of Kimberley was raised. On the 27 February, Boer General Cronje surrendered with more than 4,000 men at Paardeberg, and on 13 March, Roberts captured Bloemfontein, the capital of the Orange Free State.

In Natal, much had still to be done before any advance could begin. After the Relief, the rail link between Ladysmith and Durban had to be restored. The retreating Boers had wrought considerable damage to the line and many bridges and culverts had been destroyed. In repairing the line one of the unnecessary difficulties that was faced was the repair gangs were frequently attacked by the British Army. One group of Natal men repairing the line was attacked three times by the British. These mistakes would seem to have had their origin in the erroneous belief that Natal was inhabited by Boers, and therefore any white man not in British uniform must be a Boer.

Despite the difficulties, the line between Ladysmith and Durban had been repaired by 9 March. On the first train to leave Ladysmith for Durban was General Sir George White. On his arrival at the station he found his old regiment, the Gordons, formed up outside. He addressed them and then walked onto the platform where he took leave of General Buller, senior officers, the mayor Mr Farquhar, and other prominent residents. All noticed how tired and ill he looked. The train pulled out of the station to the swirl of bagpipes and the hurrahs and cheers of all who were privileged to be present. The Australian Donald Macdonald wrote that all who were there 'will ever have a kind wish for the General, and an affectionate remembrance of the tall soldier who in plain Khaki moved so quietly amongst us'.[1]

On that train with White was one of his staff officers, Col Sir Henry Rawlinson, who during the siege had been critical of Buller's efforts to penetrate the Boer line along the Tugela. From the train he now had a good view of the Boer entrenchments, and wondered how it was Buller had ever broken through to Ladysmith.

One of the issues the British Army could no longer shy away from was the arrest and cashiering of Captain C.G. Willson of the Natal Carbineers. It will be recalled that Willson and the Dundee Squadron of the Carbineers had ridden into Ladysmith on 22 October 1899, several days before the retreating column from Dundee staggered into the town. Not only had the Carbineers arrived safely without any assistance from the Regulars, but they also brought along some Boer prisoners. Given the attitude of some British officers towards colonials it is not surprising that they concluded the Carbineers must have ignored orders and run away from the battlefield. Charlie Willson was promptly arrested and word was put about that he was guilty of cowardice and had failed to obey orders. On the following day, a troop of the 18th Hussars arrived in Ladysmith. Unable to make contact with the British headquarters in Dundee, they too had decided to make their own way to Ladysmith, which for all practical purposes was precisely what Willson had done. Yet the commander of the troop of Hussars was not arrested, neither did he have to suffer the indignity of a Court Martial.

When the bedraggled Dundee column reached Ladysmith on 26 October 1899, it should have been obvious to all that the chain of command had broken down and Willson's decision to retire to Ladysmith was reasonable. However, if the Army withdrew the charges it would have resulted in a loss of face, which for some would have been a fate too horrible to contemplate.

On 24 March 1900, Captain Willson appeared before a Court Martial in Pietermaritzburg. An irregularity in the proceedings caused the verdict to be quashed. A fresh Court Martial was convened and on 7 May 1900, he was found guilty of some offence and sentenced to a fine of ten pounds. Charlie Willson said that as he had done nothing wrong, he would not pay the fine. He never paid the fine and no attempt was ever made to compel payment.

The record of the Court Martial seems to have disappeared. It should have been sent to the Castle in Cape Town, but no trace of it can be found there; neither is it at the University of Cape Town, where some documents of that period are now housed. In Britain, records of Courts Martial prior to 1914 were destroyed in the Blitz, and no mention of it can be found in War Office or Colonial Office papers in the Public Records Office at Kew, London, or in the Natal Archives.

We will probably never know what offence he was found to have committed. If it was a failure to obey orders, no conviction should have been possible without Colonel Yule giving evidence, as he was the person responsible for issuing the orders. As we have seen, Yule appears to have suffered some sort of breakdown and left South Africa in November 1899, never to return.

To add a twist to this tale, Willson was awarded the Volunteer Long Service Medal on 16 January 1900, and later a Queen's South Africa Medal with a bar for the Siege of Ladysmith. Subsequently the Governor appointed him a Justice of the Peace in consideration of 'his Loyalty, Integrity and Ability'.

Was Charlie Willson used by certain elements in the army as a scapegoat to cover up Yule's apparent breakdown and the incompetent handling of the situation in Dundee? The idea of using colonials as scapegoats was to occur a few years later in the notorious 'Breaker' Morant case, in which Australians were apparently sacrificed to promote a British political cause. (This interpretation of events has been challenged – See *Breaker Morant*, by Roger Roper and Joe West.)

For six weeks Colonel W. Royston, Commandant of the Natal Volunteers, was able to fight off a threatening attack of enteric, but a few weeks after the Relief the fever took a stronger hold. He was taken to hospital in Pietermaritzburg, but died on 6 April 1900. His death was a great loss to Natal. Aware of the threat posed by Boer expansionism, he had ensured that the Volunteers were trained to meet this danger, rather than following standard British military practice. The result was all his corps were to be more than a match for the Boers throughout the Natal Campaign. He had over the years won the respect of all people in Natal and he was to be much missed in the years to come. John Dartnell, now a brigadier general, replaced Royston as commandant of the Natal Volunteers.

On 12 May 1900, Buller began his advance to liberate northern Natal. The Boers had concentrated their forces in the Biggarsberg hills, thereby blocking the main road and rail links to the north, and were now well ensconced in their trenches. General Hildyard, who had replaced Warren as commander of the 5th Brigade, was sent forward with his infantry along the railway towards the Biggarsberg and Dundee, apparently to drive the Boers out of their fortified positions. Not much attention was paid to Dundonald's brigade, Dartnell's Volunteers and some artillery and infantry moving south east on a course roughly parallel to the Biggarsberg Range. From time to time, they were harassed by long-range enemy fire, which the artillery were able to contain. The column made excellent progress; by nightfall were nearing the southern limit of the Biggarsberg, beyond which lay the Pomeroy/Dundee road.

The following day the Mounted Brigade continued its advance until it reached Uithoek Mountain, the southern bastion of the Biggarsberg Range. Uithoek appeared to be unclimbable, however, Thorneycroft's MI dismounted and doing as they had done at Spion Kop, scrambled up the precipitous slope towards the summit – but the mistakes of Spion Kop were not going to be repeated. To support Thorneycroft on the left, Buller ordered three battalions of Lyttelton's infantry to assault the summit from the south west, while at the same time other units attacked from the south east. Afraid their retreat might be cut off, the Boers withdrew from Uithoek. The Biggarsberg line had been turned.[2]

With two squadrons of the Carbineers, McKenzie found himself operating on the flank with units from Dundonald's brigade. With Dundonald's consent, he attached his squadrons to Dundonald's command for the next stage of the advance.[3] This move brought McKenzie into a position where he would be able to exercise greater influence over military decisions.

The column continued to the Pomeroy/Dundee road where they were joined by the Umvoti Mounted Rifles and Bethune's Mounted Infantry who had come up from the Greytown area. Buller now turned north towards Helpmekaar and Dundee. Several times the Boers attempted to check the advance but each time Dundonald's men would threaten their flanks causing the Boers to retreat. By mid-afternoon, Buller decided to call a halt a couple of miles short of Helpmekaar. His force had covered a considerable distance that day, had turned the Boers' defensive position on the Biggarsburg and had received the welcome addition of the two colonial mounted regiments. Added to this, the Boers still did not know whether the main thrust of the British advance would come via Helpmekaar, or follow the railway line through the Biggarsberg towards Dundee.

Before dawn the next day (14 May) the mounted troops had left their bivouacs and formed up ready to advance. Dundonald's brigade and the Natal Volunteers immediately set off in pursuit of the Boers. Preceded by scouts, the mounted men swept through Helpmekaar and, deploying across a broad front, chased after the enemy. The Boers attempted to check the advance on various rocky outcrops but as soon as they were spotted, the colonials would gallop round their flanks causing the Boers to hastily make off. At one kopie the Boers showed more resolution and tarried a little longer, so the artillery was summoned. The sight of the 7th Battery of the RFA coming up at a gallop was enough to change Boer minds and away they rode with the colonials after them. In desperation the Boers set fire to the veld, hoping the flames and smoke would check their pursuers. It didn't.

Lt Dr Blake Knox, who was following the mounted column that day, recorded his impressions,

> From high ground here and there could be seen masses of horsemen, with our men hot on their heels; then the Boers tried to stem the torrent once more, but in vain, for their flanks were soon turned. Our horsemen strained every nerve, for the word was passed from General to Colonels, and Colonels to officers and men, 'Get on, fire away, don't rest or stop, but ride on, on, on!' ... On again swept the cavalry through flame and smoke, the charred veldt grass blowing into men's faces, filling their eyes, mouths and nostrils, singeing the legs of the horses and the hair of the men, and giving the brigade the appearance of an army of demons. Six miles from Dundee the enemy took up a position on the further side of a deep ravine, from the other side of which their artillery came into action with wild fire, which became wilder still when they saw the Irregulars and Natal Volunteers creeping round their flanks.[4]

As it was getting late, Dundonald received orders to halt. In a dispatch to England Buller reported that 'Dundonald's Cavalry pursued the enemy through fire and smoke for 40 miles in a waterless country, I consider his pursuit a very fine performance.'[5]

In the night the Boers slipped away from their position before Dundee and early the next morning, the mounted column rode into town. On the 14th

Gerard Bailey had heard the sound of the approaching gunfire. He cut down a small tree for a flagstaff and dug a hole for it just behind General Penn Symons' grave. It was nearly seven months since that Union Jack had been used as a shroud for the General. Gerard had hidden the flag, which he now took out of its hiding place. He was up early on 15 May, and was out and about by 5.30 a.m. It was a misty morning and all was quiet. At 7.30 a.m. he saw a 'spider' pulled by two horses coming along towards the church. The vehicle pulled up and Gerard recognised the Boer telegraph clerk. Gerard bade him goodbye and wished him luck. An hour later, a coloured man came to Gerard with the exciting news that some soldiers had been seen in town. The two men tied the flag to the crude flagstaff, which was placed in the prepared hole and raised. It was a still day so there wasn't a flutter from the Union flag, but it was aloft, a symbol of the end of their waiting. A short while later he met the first men to enter Dundee, Major Henderson and two of his guides, Dundee boys Appleby and Cooper. He gave them breakfast and by the time they had finished, the South African Light Horse were in town. During the day Gerard met and chatted with some of the leaders, General Buller, Lord Dundonald and Colonel Greene of the Carbineers and many other Natal friends, 'and there was Brigadier-General Dartnell, we Natalians are so proud of. I told him we in Dundee had not got much news of the war, but we had heard of his promotion.'[6] Bailey was once considered an Englishman and Dartnell a Canadian, but now it was 'we Natalians'.

On the 16th the troops rested, which gave Hildyard's infantry a chance to come up from the Biggarsburg. Initially they had met with determined resistance from the Boers and could make little headway but once the Boer flank was turned, they melted away leaving Hildyard free to advance to Glencoe, Dundee and beyond.

On 17 May, Buller's force continued its advance towards Newcastle, and the Transvaal border. Employing the same tactics they had used on the road to Dundee and riding hard, they covered the 37 miles to Newcastle that day, and by the 19th they were near Laing's Nek, a further 25 miles closer to the Transvaal border. To their left was Majuba Hill (6,500 feet) and on their right Pogweni Hill (5,400 feet). Between these two hills lay Laing's Nek, heavily fortified with trenches and artillery. Buller decided to halt the advance and the mounted troops were ordered to withdraw a couple of miles to the northern bank of the Ingogo River. When Dundonald's guns began their retirement, large numbers of Boers galloped forward to cut them off. This had been foreseen. McKenzie's men had concealed themselves on one flank while the South African Light Horse were similarly concealed on the other. The advancing Boers rode into the crossfire and quickly abandoned the attack.[7]

Buller decided to wait at the Ingogo River while the railway line was repaired and supplies brought up. In nine days his column had covered 138 miles and suffered few casualties. The only serious loss had been inflicted on Bethune's MI who had been sent across the Transvaal border in the direction of Vryheid so as to protect the left of the column. They were ambushed and suffered sixty-eight casualties, almost half of whom were killed.[8]

In Newcastle the advancing troops found the same destruction and looting of premises by the Boers that had occurred in other towns they had occupied. The Boers had been particularly vicious in their attack on the Newcastle Catholic Convent, tearing up Bibles and other books, smashing pictures and the Sacristy with all its contents, before setting alight to the Chapel. As in Dundee, such furniture as remained in residents' houses after the first wave of looters had had their fill, had been taken to the Town Hall for latecomers to choose whatever they wanted.

Always keen to bring the war to an end, Buller, without being authorised to do so, on 30 May, offered peace terms to the Boers.[9] An armistice was agreed until 5 June. In due course the peace terms were rejected, the Boers using the intervening period to strengthen their line.

Buller too had not been idle – Hildyard's division was sent eastwards across the Buffalo River to the little Transvaal town of Utrecht, which was taken without any opposition. Lyttelton's division was sent north eastwards towards Dornkop, which lay just to the east of Laing's Nek and Pogweni Hill. To the Boers it appeared the British would either attempt a frontal attack on the Nek, or attempt to by-pass it by an eastern route.

When darkness fell on 5 June, Hildyard, without being observed, marched rapidly back to the Newcastle/Laing's Nek road. On 8 June, Buller launched his attack, not on Laing's Nek or via some route to the east of it, but westwards via Botha's Pass over the Drakensburg and into the Free State. Hildyard's infantry, with considerable artillery support, led the way, while Dundonald's brigade and Brocklehurst's Regular cavalry covered the flanks. The attack had not been expected, with the result that the defenders, out-numbered and out-gunned, were forced to give way. By nightfall the British had reached the top of the pass. The following day was spent getting supplies up to their camp.

On 10 June, the column set off northwards towards Alleman's Pass, which provided a route down the Drakensberg and onto the plain north of Laing's Nek. The South African Light Horse led the way and at times had to fight hard to overcome pockets of resistance; in one skirmish they lost six killed and eight wounded. On the morning of 12 June, they were at the head of Alleman's Pass. The Boers had taken up strong defensive positions on the Pass but were now facing a far wiser enemy. Without cover to conceal their advance, the infantry took note of the wind direction and set fire to the veld. The smoke from the fire not only hid their advance, but the flames drove the Boers out of their concealed positions. With superb support from the artillery and Dundonald's brigade on the right flank, the infantry broke through the Boer line. Laing's Nek had been out flanked, and the road into the Transvaal was now clear.

On 14 June 1900, Buller's army crossed into the Transvaal. Ahead lay the little town of Volksrust. Corporal --leby of the Colonial Guides was sent ahead with two of his men to find out if the town was defended.

From a distance no sign of activity could be seen. Though he had no orders to enter Volksrust, Umpleby decided to ride into town to find out precisely what was happening.

Cautiously they entered the town and rode up the main street. In the distance a Swiss ambulance could be seen making its way out of town, but otherwise there was no sign of life. All the houses and businesses appeared to be closed or locked and no sign of man or beast was to be seen. Except for the sound of their horses on the road, the silence was all pervasive.

Suddenly horsemen were among them shouting, 'Hande Op' (Hands Up). A man tried to wrest Umpleby's rifle from him, but he was not going to give it up without a struggle. As he and the assailant wrestled for it, both fell from their horses, the Boer shouting as he fell, 'Skiet hom' (Shoot him). Two shots rang out and Umpleby felt the attacker's grip on his rifle slacken. Scrambling up, he saw a group of Boers galloping away. At his feet lay the wounded leader of the posse, Veldt Cornet Opperman, and a few paces further away lay another wounded Boer. Turning round he saw his two companions sitting quietly on their horses, with revolvers drawn, watching the fleeing Boers.[10]

Postscript

When Buller's army marched out of Natal they left a country devastated by war. The Boers while rampaging through Northern Natal and the Midlands, had wantonly destroyed towns, villages, businesses and farms, while at the same time they had carried off livestock, farm equipment, wagons, furniture and anything else they fancied. One of Natal's greatest assets – the railway system, with its locomotives, rolling stock, workshops, stations and other equipment – had been severely damaged and it would take many years to restore it to its pre-war condition.

The outbreak of war resulted in almost every man of military age in the colony enlisting in one of the units fighting the invaders. With their owners and staff away on military service, many businesses closed. For the Natal Government, which relied on trade for its income, this resulted in a drastic decline in revenue while the expense of keeping the Volunteers and their supporting units in the field had to be met and as well as providing for the tens of thousands of penniless refugees crowding into the colony. As early as December 1899, the colony was bankrupt and was forced to borrow £500,000 at four per cent from the Imperial Government to keep its administration running.[1]

After the invaders were driven out of Natal, almost two years were to elapse before the Boer leaders were prepared to negotiate a peace treaty. As the war dragged on, some British commanders applied the lessons learnt in Natal – but for others, it was business as usual. Commenting on the repeated failures of the British to capture the elusive Boer General Christiaan De Wet, a Cape colonial volunteer, Major C.G. Dennison wrote,

Why did De Wet escape so often? Because of jealousy and incapacity. Why were the colonials never given a chance to capture De Wet independently? Because the military authorities knew too well that the colonials might catch De Wet, and the imperial regular troops would get no kudos. Had a few columns of combined colonial forces, Australians,

New Zealanders, Canadians, and South Africans, under their own officers, been given the work to do, De Wet would have been caught, I am confident, without much trouble.[2]

Despite the ruling by Sir William Butler that blacks should not serve against the Boers, they were to play a decisive role in bringing the Boers to the negotiating table. In April, 1902, black scouts under Aubrey Woolls Sampson laid the foundation for the comprehensive defeat of the Boers at Roodevaal in the Western Transvaal. On the other side of the country, in that part of Zululand that had been annexed by the Transvaal in 1884, Boer kommandos were living off the land, a process that involved helping themselves to food, cattle and livestock belonging to the Zulus. This aggravated the ill-feeling between the Boers and the Zulus and several Boers were killed. Louis Botha, believing members of the Qulusi clan under Chief Sikobobo were responsible, instructed his kommandos to destroy their settlements and confiscate their livestock.

Acting on Botha's instructions on 3 May 1902 a Boer kommando under Jan Potgieter arrived at Chief Sikobobo's kraal only to find he was not there. Potgieter laid waste to the kraal and drove off three hundred and eighty cattle. He followed up this action by sending a message to the Chief in which he stated that Sikobobo and his people were no better than fowl-lice, and defiantly suggested they come to his laager at Holkrantz to retrieve their cattle.

The Chief accepted the challenge and on the night of the 6 May 1902, his impis fell on the kommando at Holkrantz, killing Potgieter and 55 of his men. Only a few Boers escaped, just enough to tell the Boer leadership what had happened. The Qulusi recovered all their cattle and a few more by way of interest, plus all the Boer horses.

This defeat in the east, following the defeat at Roodeval in the west, convinced the Boer leadership that the war had been lost, and they were prepared to enter into peace negotiations.

Churchill was one of the first to sense that there had been a change in the wind blowing through British politics. In 1899 he had been full of praise for the people of Natal, writing that they were entitled to the general respect and sympathy of all good Englishmen and 'a full indemnity to all individual colonists who have suffered loss, must stand as an Imperial debt of honour'. No sooner had Ladysmith been relieved than he was warning Natal against taking a hard line towards the Boers. By 1902 he had adopted a positively pro-Boer stance. He expressed contempt for those who had opposed the Transvaal's human rights abuses and expansionist aims, and was particularly derisive of the Uitlanders who, after all, had sought no more than the rights to which it is generally accepted all men are entitled. He now said the Boers were 'the Rock' on which the new South Africa was to be founded.

Churchill's friend Ian Hamilton, now a general and Lord Kitchener's Chief of Staff, was even more contemptuous of Britain's colonial allies. In his opinion the Boers were 'the best men in South Africa' and in February 1902, he told Churchill,

> Do let us profit by our experience when we smashed the Zulus for the Boers, and not repeat the mistake by annihilating the Boers for the Jewburghers. You have no idea what arrogant insolent devils you will discover as soon as Mr Boer has lost his Mauser.[3]

In making this vicious anti-Semitic statement Hamilton appears to have forgotten, or perhaps remembered too well, that two years previously the 'arrogant insolent devils' had saved both his and the British Army's reputation at Elandslaagte and Wagon Hill.

Churchill and Hamilton had judged the British political mood correctly. Only British and Boer leaders would attend the peace conference. Natal, the Cape, the Uitlander minority in the Transvaal, and all the other peoples of South Africa were denied any say in the proceedings. Predictably, the conference produced an agreement that would ensure that the Boers, now calling themselves Afrikaners, would exercise exclusive power over all the peoples of South Africa for almost a century. The road to Apartheid had been paved.

Churchill was correct about another issue. After the war, Britain did not nationalise or in any other way attempt to control the gold mines, which continued to be owned by shareholders from all over the world regardless of race, colour, or creed. In an astonishing display of the power of modern propaganda, many people in Britain still believe their country went to war against the Boer Republics because their government sought control of the Transvaal goldfields.

When peace came, Robert Samuelson enquired whether his scouts would receive their medals, and the then Natal Prime Minister, Albert Hime, assured him that they would. When Joseph Chamberlain came to South Africa in December 1902, he saw the leaders of the scouts and assured them they would get their medals. The Natal Volunteers requested Samuelson to compile a list of the scouts who had served. Assisted by Simeon Kambule and Jabers Molife the list was prepared, and subsequently checked and passed by Colonel Wales of the Volunteers, who strongly recommended that they be granted.

The issue of the medals was vetoed because it was thought that the award might 'offend the Boers.'[4]

Before, during and after the Boer War, many myths were created to serve political ends.

Kodwa thina sizonihalalisa
Koze kuwe ilanga.
(We will forever recount your deeds until the falling of the sun.)
From a praise song in Zulu to honour Natal pioneer Dick King

Biographical Notes

Walter Karri Davies

After the Relief of Mafeking, the role played by Karri in the life of the Imperial Light Horse changed. He continued to serve with the regiment until the end of the war, being primarily concerned with administrative matters such as recruiting, and the welfare of disabled veterans and the widows and families of those who had been killed. However, he was also involved with other matters. Both Lord Roberts and Lord Kitchener recognised his considerable organisational and engineering skills and co-opted him to carry out various important tasks, from ensuring railways were functioning to designing and building bridges. Such was the confidence they had in his ability and integrity that they both gave him a power of attorney, stating, 'All officers of HM Forces, Government Officials and others with whom he may come in contact will do anything he wishes to facilitate his work'. Lord Kitchener appointed him to act as his representative on several commissions.

Karri was instrumental in arranging for the future King George V to become Honorary Colonel of the Imperial Light Horse, a position that was retained by succeeding monarchs until South Africa became a republic in 1961. In August, 1901, the Prince of Wales visited Natal while returning from a visit to Australia and sent a message to Karri expressing his disappointment that they had been unable to meet.[5]

At the end of the war, Karri was offered a knighthood in recognition of the services he had rendered during the conflict. Characteristically he asked to be allowed to decline the honour because he had undertaken to serve king and country without honour or reward.[6]

On the cessation of hostilities, Karri went to Britain where he fell in love with and married an Irish girl, Annie Cochrane, from County Limerick. On his return to South Africa, he set up in practice as a consulting engineer. Over the following years he was to make a contribution to the future welfare of South Africa, which cannot be overestimated. Commissioned to advise on the possibility of establishing irrigation dams in the Orange River Colony, his recommendations were not only carried out but were to form a basis of the great irrigation schemes that were to provide food and water for the expanding mining and industrial conurbations of the Witwatersrand and the Vaal Triangle.

He encouraged the importation by farmers of quality breeding stock by persuading the government to insert in their mail contracts with shipping lines, a provision that pedigree stock should be carried free. All stock farming benefited though perhaps none more so than the wool industry, where the importation of Merino breeding stock enabled the country to substantially boost its wool production. Thereafter the export of wool was, for many years, one of the mainstays of the South African economy.

The South African Government also commissioned him to make a report on the Land Banks and Closer Settlement Systems in Tasmania and

New Zealand. This gave him a knowledge of the various methods, both private and government, of financing farmers. Out of his report came the establishment of the Land Bank of South Africa. Over the years, few successful farmers in the country would have succeeded without some help from the Land Bank, which was to play a vital role in the modernisation and development of South African agriculture.

His tact and wisdom enabled him to reconcile parties who had previously been at loggerheads and to persuade parties who appeared to have irreconcilable differences to come to agreement. As an example, shortly after the war, a dispute arose between the Transvaal authorities, the Netherlands Railway Company and the Portuguese at Delagoa Bay. As a result of intervention by Karri, an agreement was reached between the parties that enabled the railways and the harbour to work on amicable terms. During this post-war period, Karri worked tirelessly to effect reconciliation between the peoples of South Africa, only to have his illusions shattered in 1914 when several leading Boers rose in armed rebellion against the South African Government.

When his father died in 1913 he returned to Australia, where he remained until the outbreak of war in 1914. Too old to enlist in Australia, he travelled to Britain where he was appointed British Agent on the west coast of the United States. Based in San Francisco, he soon established a good rapport with the Americans – which helped the British and, perhaps more importantly, would have raised the awareness of the Americans to the strategic importance of Australia.

In 1922 he decided that the breach block, which had been taken from the Boer gun at Gun Hill, Ladysmith, on 7 December 1899, and given to Karri by General Hunter, should be returned to South Africa. It is now housed in the Ladysmith Museum.

Karri died suddenly on 29 November 1926, at Broadstairs in Kent, survived by his wife and daughter. Had he been willing to compromise his personal integrity, a knighthood and Victoria Cross might have been his. No wonder he gained the complete trust of all who knew him.

In an obituary published in the *London Times*, an old comrade from his Imperial Light Horse days, Major Percy Greathead, wrote,

> He was the kindest-hearted thing that ever happened. I doubt whether he ever said or thought an evil thing about anybody on earth. He had a fine even temper and a wonderfully stable character. With all that he was a man of iron determination, and altogether a magnificent personality.[6]

Aubrey Woolls Sampson

While the ILH were engaged in the Relief of Mafeking, Aubrey Woolls Samson underwent the operation to his thigh. It was successful in the sense that he was able to get about and ride a horse, but he lost his previous agility and would suffer pain for the rest of his life. At the beginning of July 1900, he replaced Col Edwards as commander of the ILH and joined the regiment at their bivouac near Pretoria. The period during which he commanded the regiment was not a happy time for Aubrey. Of all the people in South Africa, he probably knew more about the country and its peoples than anyone else. He had lived life from the elegant colonial society of the Cape to the rip-roaring goldfields of Barberton, from the dry high veld plains in the west to the rolling green hills of Pondoland and Zululand in the east, he had mingled with wealthy financiers, backveld Dutch farmers and the many different black peoples, learning and absorbing their languages and cultures. In contrast, Kruger and his coterie were only familiar with a small part of southern Africa – the people, languages and cultures of the rest being but dimly known to them. Yet the Boers and the British branded Aubrey an Uitlander, an outsider, an attitude that caused deep hurt. With a few exceptions, he had acquired a distrust and dislike of Imperial officers and resented any interference by them in the affairs of the regiment. He became uncommunicative and almost fanatical in his desire to finish the war as soon as possible.

On 5 January 1901, near Cyferfontein in the Western Transvaal, he received orders to 'lose no time' and occupy a hill, which had that morning been scouted by the 18th Hussars and found to be clear of the enemy. Relying on the information provided by the Hussars, Aubrey ordered two squadrons of Light Horsemen, in all about 180 men, to occupy the hill. Unknown to him, the Boers had cleverly concealed their movements and had themselves occupied the hill with 700 to 800 men. With little cover the ILH were allowed to approach to within 50 to 100 yards before the enemy opened fire. They were able to retrieve the situation, but not before they had lost eighteen killed and thirty-two wounded. Eighty horses were killed and twenty were destroyed later. The British blamed Aubrey for the debacle, resulting in his relinquishing command of the regiment and being transferred to the Intelligence Department.

As an Intelligence Officer, Aubrey was at last able to exercise to the full his vast knowledge of the country. General Sir Ian Hamilton said of him, 'In one leap he became the second figure in the war, second only to Lord Kitchener himself'.[7] Hamilton, who at the best of times was no lover of Uitlanders, would not have exaggerated.

In September 1901, the Boers appeared to be gaining the initiative. Everywhere the British were on the defensive. Louis Botha with 2,000 men appeared to be poised to again invade Natal. To meet this threat, the British had assembled 16,000 men with forty guns under General Lyttelton. On 17 September this column suffered a serious and humiliating set back at Blood River Poort where a battalion led by Hubert Gough was smashed up.

However, things were about to change. Early in September, Aubrey was posted as Intelligence Officer to a small column commanded by Colonel Benson, stationed at Carolina in the Eastern Transvaal. Although in the heart of enemy territory, and having only 800 men at his disposal, Benson was persuaded to launch a series of night attacks based on information provided by Aubrey. These raids were successfully carried out on the 10th, 15th, 16th, and 18th September. Laagers were captured complete with prisoners, wagons, horses and cattle. With his heartland threatened, Louis Botha abandoned his proposed invasion of Zululand and Natal. Although Colonel Benson was killed in an engagement at Bakenlaagte on 30 October 1901, the initiative had passed from the Boers to the British.

After Benson's death, Aubrey joined a column operating in the Eastern Transvaal, commanded by General Bruce Hamilton (no relation of Ian Hamilton) who continued the use of the tactics developed by Benson and Woolls Sampson. Black scouts would go out in the evening to check the position of any Boers within a 25-mile radius. They would return the next morning and report what they had discovered. After dark the column would leave camp, and riding through the night would attack the Boers at dawn. In eight weeks Hamilton's column had accounted for some 900 Boers and recovered one of Benson's guns, without any loss to themselves. Boer resistance in the Eastern Transvaal had been broken.

Bruce Hamilton was later to write of Aubrey, 'He had an extraordinary sense of what the Boers were likely to do, and over and over again, after marching all night, we would find them at dawn almost exactly where he expected.'[8]

Though Aubrey was on good terms with Bruce Hamilton, his antipathy towards Imperial officers caused him to shun their company, and most of his time was spent with the scouts. Fully aware of the fact that the Boers would shoot any black scouts they captured, he was unceasing in his efforts ensure their safety and win their confidence while they in turn gave him their absolute loyalty. When the scouts returned from their night-time sorties, Aubrey would spend hours talking to them, encouraging, cross-questioning, and checking all they had told him. He gave great attention to detail and his information was wonderfully accurate.

In December 1901, Aubrey moved to the north eastern Free State to assist General Sir Henry Rawlinson. Here the same pattern of intensive scouting followed by a dawn attack was repeated with success.

Kitchener, meanwhile, had been relying on an extensive and expensive system of blockhouses and wire fences to defeat the Boers. This system had some limited success in containing the Boers, as did a decision to stop bringing woman and children into the concentration camps he had established. In England, do-gooders applauded the latter decision, thinking it was an act of kindness whereas in fact it was a considered military decision. (The creation of concentration camps was a decision that stained the reputation of the British forever.)

Far more successful than the blockhouses were Aubrey and his scouts. Unable to intimidate the wily General de la Rey in the western Transvaal, Kitchener sent his Chief of Staff, Ian Hamilton, after him. Ian Hamilton took

Aubrey as his Intelligence Officer and the intelligence garnered by Aubrey and his scouts set up the defeat of the Boers at Roodeval.

To ensure they were effective, the scouts were of necessity drawn from the local community. Near Natal, they would have been Zulus; in the eastern Free State, Sotho; and in the west, Tswana. These people had different languages and customs and Woolls Sampson was one of very few men in the country who were able to converse with all in their own language. Furthermore, it was not only the words he understood. He also knew their culture and the way they used words. For example if a scout referred to an Englishman, he would not assume that the person came from England. It was this understanding of the way they used language that enabled him to obtain such precise knowledge from his scouts of the whereabouts of the Boers and the physical features of the land where they were encamped. Despite their courage and effectiveness, none of Aubrey's black scouts received a war medal.

After the war Aubrey received a knighthood in recognition of his outstanding service as an Intelligence Officer. Now Sir Aubrey Woolls Sampson, he practised as an estate agent and subsequently decided to enter politics. He had no trouble getting elected but apart from this initial success, his foray into politics was a disaster. For him things were either right or wrong, and there was no capacity in his character for the horsetrading that is part and parcel of a politician's lot. He found the debates in Parliament intolerably tedious, except on one occasion when a member challenged his integrity. Grabbing a horsewhip, he chased the offending member out of the parliamentary chamber and down Adderley Street, Cape Town's main thoroughfare. When Sir Percy Fitzpatrick pointed out that this was not the way in which parliamentary debates should be conducted, an unrepentant Aubrey retorted that this was a great pity.

When the First World War broke out, Aubrey offered his services to the country, now headed by Louis Botha and Jan Smuts. The two Boer generals were not prepared to grant any position to the man who had once played such a large part in defeating the Boer kommandos. His offer was ignored. In constant pain, Aubrey went into retirement in Johannesburg.

In 1922 General Sir Henry Rawlinson, (one time Commander of the British IV army in France, now Commander-in-Chief, India) wrote to Aubrey,

My dear Woolls Sampson,

> After a lapse of more than 20 years I was overjoyed to hear from Walter Bagot that you are still going strong at Johannesburg – and I write this short letter of greeting and good cheer to let you know that my memory of your great self in the trying times of Ladysmith, before, during and after the siege, is as fresh as ever. Much water has flown under the bridge since those days and I have seen something of the wars of nations and the battles of the giants – I look back on them as having taught me

that the thing of all others that makes victory certain in the end is that great determination and faith in the cause, of which you were so marked an exponent in Ladysmith. You may not have known it, but as a young staff officer in those days, I have treasured ever since the picture of your lying wounded in a dugout by the Klip River swearing that you would not lose your leg and that you would ride into Pretoria at the head of your Regiment – and you did it – more power and long life to you. In 1914-15 in France when things looked equally black, your example came back many times to my memory and helped much to carry me through the dark days to the sunshine and triumph beyond. Problems of a different character face me to-day but the road which leads to eventual solution is the one you originally indicated to me – unswerving determination to prevail.

Yours ever,
Rawlinson.[9]

Aubrey died in Johannesburg in 1924, survived by his wife and daughter.

Duncan McKenzie

As the Volunteers had been established solely to defend Natal, once the invaders had been driven out of the colony, they did not accompany the British troops into the Transvaal and the Free State. Instead, they were deployed along the Natal borders. Buller had wanted Duncan McKenzie with other officers from the Volunteers to join him in the Transvaal, but this move was blocked by Col Greene of the Carbineers obliging them to endure a few frustrating months of inaction doing guard duties at Dundee. At the end of September 1900, a Composite Regiment was formed from those men from the Natal regiments who volunteered for further service. They received no pay and had to provide their own boots, horses and clothing.[10] Lt Col Robert Evans of the Natal Mounted Rifles was appointed to command this regiment with McKenzie as his second in command. As colonel, Evans had to spend much of his time in Dundee; McKenzie commanded the troops in the field, their principal duty being to escort military convoys in south Eastern Transvaal.

On 4 December 1900, Lord Kitchener was travelling by train through Natal on his way to Durban. Stationed at De Jager's Drift, McKenzie received an order to proceed at once to Glencoe as the Commander-in-Chief wished to see him. Riding as hard as he could, Duncan was able to cover the 30 miles to Glencoe just in time to meet the train. He was taken into the C-in-C's saloon carriage, and after the usual polite introductory conversation, Kitchener told McKenzie that a 2nd Regiment of the Imperial Light Horse was to be formed and he would like McKenzie to command it. To encourage acceptance, McKenzie was to be promoted to Lieutenant-Colonel and could choose his own officers.[11]

Duncan immediately set about organising his new command. From the Composite Regiment he took Captains John (Galloping Jack) Royston and David Mackay, who were both promoted to the rank of Major. He also gave commissions to several men from the ranks, notably B. Nicholson whom he promoted to Lieutenant in charge of the regiment's special scouts, sixteen of whom came from the Composite Regiment and were known to be reliable. Col Robert Evans protested that McKenzie was taking all his best men, so McKenzie took no more. With the core of the regiment established, he moved to Volksrust to meet the men who had been recruited elsewhere.

Unknown to McKenzie, the 1st ILH and the 2nd ILH had the same recruiting officer. Major Karri Davies ensured the 1st ILH acquired the best recruits, while the rest were sent on to McKenzie. On their arrival at Volksrust it was found that many of the men could not ride or shoot. This provided the officers with a few problems and the other ranks a great deal of amusement. An intensive training programme began immediately, which was far from complete when they were ordered to Pretoria on 19 January 1901 where they were met by Brigadier-General Birdwood, now on Kitchener's Staff, who invited McKenzie to dine at their mess. How times had changed! After the meal Birdwood took McKenzie to see Kitchener, who wanted to know all about the regiment. McKenzie told him that the men needed more training. However, Kitchener replied the shortage of troops was such that he was not able to grant them any further time for training, they were to go to the Eastern Transvaal immediately, where some of the best Boer kommandos were operating. To comfort McKenzie, Kitchener offered a little advice. He said the Boers had developed a new tactic. On seeing a troop of dismounted men, they would gallop straight at them resulting in the surprised troop mounting and galloping off. Kitchener suggested they lie quiet and shoot the Boers, as this would teach them a salutary lesson. McKenzie replied that if the 2nd ILH dismounted they would have no choice but to lie quiet and shoot, because most were unable to mount their horses.[12] Kitchener laughed. The next day he inspected the regiment and afterwards it entrained for Wonderfontein, on the Pretoria-Delagoa Bay line, where the intensive training continued and the regiment was soon up to standard.

The 2nd ILH was to form part of General Smith-Dorien's column operating in the Eastern Transvaal. McKenzie developed an excellent relationship with his new commander, who gave him a free hand when conducting operations. Duncan applied the same principles that had been so successful in Natal, namely keeping one's whereabouts and intentions hidden from the enemy, careful scouting, avoiding frontal attacks and instead using enveloping flank movements to deliver surprise attacks. As in Natal, he was extraordinarily successful. For example, between 9 February and 11 March 1901, the regiment captured:

644 Horses
50 Mules
9,500 Cattle
31,139 Sheep
192 Wagons

57 Carts
  20,200 lbs Mealies(Maize)
  8,500 lbs Oat Hay
  170 Firearms
  15,050 lbs. Ammunition
In addition
  39 Enemy were killed
  113 Wounded
  129 Captured
  30 Surrendered
  (Total Boer losses 311men)

In contrast, the regiment suffered two men killed by lightning, two drowned, and one man shot himself in the foot.[13]

During this period Duncan received a silver medal from the Royal Humane Society for plunging into a flooded Assegai River to save a drowning British soldier.

Sometimes assisted by Regular units and sometimes on their own, the regiment continued its successful operations in the Eastern Transvaal and Swaziland through the winter of 1901. General Smith-Dorrien was transferred to India at the beginning of May and the 2nd ILH now fell under Duncan's old friend General Walter Kitchener who continued the policy of giving Duncan a wide discretion in carrying out his orders, thereby enabling the 2nd ILH to inflict setback after setback on the Boers. For example, at Coalbank they captured fourteen Boers and with them more than 6,000 cattle, innumerable sheep and about 200 good horses.[14] All captured animals were handed over to the British Army who sold them, and kept the proceeds.

The men in the regiment had signed on for six months, which had expired, so it was agreed that they should all have leave. On returning from leave in November 1901, they were ordered to Harrismith in the Free State where they were to be brigaded with the 1st ILH under General Dartnell. After a few engagements in which the regiment continued to distinguish itself, the brigade was ordered to Zululand to counter possible action by Louis Botha. On arrival, they were ordered to return to Harrismith. After the long ride back to the Free State, McKenzie went down with enteric and very nearly died. By the time he had been nursed back to health, the war was over.

Starting with a group of men, many of whom could not ride or shoot, McKenzie had welded them into a regiment that was probably the most efficient unit fighting against the Boers. In nineteen months of active service, they had not suffered a single reverse of any kind and Lord Kitchener noted that they had taken more prisoners than any other regiment. McKenzie attributed this success to the fact that he had been able to choose his own officers. They all came from Natal.

With the coming of peace in 1902, Duncan McKenzie returned to farming, though he continued his association with the Carbineers. On the retirement of Colonel Greene in 1903, he became commander of the regiment. Throughout his life he took no interest in politics and played no part in the negotiations and debates in the country that were to lead to the formation of the Union of South Africa. In 1906 a combination of the difficult economic times, the poor recognition they had received for their contribution during the war, and the lack of hope resulting from the peace terms, resulted in unrest in certain districts of Natal and Zululand. Britain decided not to intervene, leaving Natal to deal with the difficulty while at the same time any proposed action was to be cleared by a General Stephenson, who held a watching brief on behalf of the Imperial Government. Duncan McKenzie was given the task of quelling the nascent rebellion. As required, he submitted his campaign plan to General Stephenson who expressed his approval. Duncan quickly and efficiently brought the rebellion to an end, thereby saving much suffering and loss of life that would have occurred with an extended campaign. The rebels, like the British a few years before, failed to pay due regard to the killing power of the modern rifle and, as a result, suffered a disproportionately high number of casualties. After the campaign, Duncan received a long overdue knighthood.

In 1914 Louis Botha, as Prime Minister, took South Africa into the First World War alongside Britain. Many former Boer leaders opposed this move and went into armed rebellion. Among the rebels was General Beyers, Commandant General of South Africa's Defence Force. Botha's first task was therefore to crush the rebellion. Relying principally on loyal Afrikaners, but also with some aid from the Anglo South Africans, Botha inflicted a series of defeats on the rebels and by the end of February 1915, all had surrendered.

With the rebellion over, the next priority was to neutralise the threat posed by German South West Africa, which lay to the north west of the Cape Province. This vast German colony was bounded in the west by the Atlantic, in the north by the Portuguese colony of Angola, in the east by Bechuanaland, and in the south by South Africa. Apart from a strip of savannah in the north, most of the country is sparsely populated semi-desert. Along the Atlantic coast is the Namib, one of the driest places on earth. There were only two harbours of consequence on this treacherous coastline – about 160 miles north of the South African border, Luderitz, and another 350 miles further north, Walvis Bay, a small South African enclave on the German Colony's coast. A railway line ran inland from Walvis Bay to the German colony's capital, Windhoek. Running south from Windhoek the line went down the centre of the country to Seeheim, where it was joined by a branch line from Luderitz. From Seeheim it continued southwards to the border where it joined the South African rail network.

It was decided that the South Africans would make a three-pronged attack on the Germans. General Botha, in overall command, would land at Walvis Bay and follow the railway to Windhoek. A second column under McKenzie, now a brigadier general, would land at Luderitz, proceed east along the railway, and then turn north towards Windhoek. A third column would advance up the railway from the south.

The Germans did not oppose the landings at Luderitz, having decided to rely on the inhospitable terrain for their defence. The railway was blown up, wells poisoned and mines laid. In February 1915, McKenzie's column began its advance east along the railway line. It was a slow process as the railway had to be repaired as they advanced, while enemy patrols were constantly setting traps. Mines and shortage of water added to their problems. On 31 March they occupied Aus, 82 miles from Luderitz. Instead of following the railway from Aus to Seeheim, as was generally expected, McKenzie turned north across the desert so as to cut off the main German force retreating along the railway towards Windhoek.

On 26 April 1915, McKenzie caught the retreating Germans at Gibeon. Col Jack Royston was ordered to take his brigade in a wide outflanking movement round Gibeon and take up a position to the north of the town, astride the road and railway to Windhoek. McKenzie planned to launch his attack from the south at dawn on the 27th while Royston was to cut off the German retreat. Unfortunately, Royston's men took up a position too close to the Germans, whose patrols discovered them. The Germans immediately attacked and in the ensuing engagement, Royston lost twenty-three men killed, sixty-four wounded and about 200 taken prisoner before the South Africans were able to retreat.

Undeterred, McKenzie launched his attack as planned and comprehensively defeated the Germans, who lost eleven killed, thirty wounded, while 188 were taken prisoner with their guns. Included in the booty was a train with a large quantity of ammunition. Also recovered were the men previously captured by the Germans. McKenzie lost two men killed and nine wounded.

McKenzie had taken his men over 200 miles of waterless desert and then fought and won a battle. After Gibeon, German resistance in the south of the country came to an end. Louis Botha soon overcame resistance in the north thereby giving the Allies their first real victory in the war. After the capitulation of the Germans in 'South West', McKenzie returned to Natal.

In East Africa a German column operating out of Tanganyika (Tanzania) provided a constant threat to Uganda and Kenya, the British colonies in the region. To remedy what appeared to be a worsening situation, the British appointed General Smith-Dorien as commander in East Africa. He cabled an invitation to McKenzie to join him. Before Duncan could accept, Smith-Dorien fell ill so the invitation lapsed.[15] To replace Smith-Dorien, the British appointed General Jan Smuts commander in East Africa. Smuts was not prepared to share the limelight with a man who had so consistently out-smarted the Boers a few years before. In his selection of senior officers, Smuts ignored Duncan, whose campaigning days were now over.

Towards the end of 1915, Duncan was persuaded to become a non-executive director of a company known as the Smithfield Cold Storage & Exploration Company. Unfortunately, the company expanded too quickly and after a few years was in serious financial difficulty. Most of the other directors cut and ran, but not McKenzie. He believed many people had been persuaded to invest in the company because he was a director and, therefore, he felt morally bound to ensure that all who had invested in it should have their investment refunded. He was told there was no legal liability on him to reimburse them, but he was adamant. He sold assets, mortgaged his property and was finally able to pay out all investors and creditors of the company. The effort brought him close to financial ruin.[16] Today, many would regard the decision to ignore his legal rights and do what he thought correct, foolish; others might regard it as a most outstanding example of honesty and integrity.

The stress brought into his life by the Cold Storage Company probably contributed to him suffering a stroke, from which he never fully recovered. He died on 19 April 1932, and many were the tributes paid to him from people in all walks of life. General Sir Hubert Gough had his faults but he never wavered in his admiration for Duncan McKenzie. In a letter written to Sir Duncan's widow, Katherine, he said,

> I am sure you know how really fond I was of your great husband – We had not met often of late years, our paths in life prevented it, but I never forget my admiration for his character – He was a sincere true friend, kind and generous of heart – as a soldier no one had so quick an eye or appreciation of a situation and of the country, a more courageous and resolute will, but he was most balanced and prudent – Many a time has he checked and wisely guided my youthful ardour in those days around Ladysmith. Please accept these very sincere and deep tributes to him and to you and your family in your bereavement – from an old friend, Yours ever, Hubert Gough.[7]

The Reverend Gerard Bailey

A few months after the British re-occupied Dundee, Gerard contracted enteric fever and died on 1 December 1900. His recently published diary of his experiences during the Boer occupation of Dundee should be read by all people interested in those times. It is a wonderful memorial to a kind and perceptive man who was so sadly cut down in his prime of life.

Louis Botha

After the Boer War he was pre-eminent among Afrikaner politicians and became the first Prime Minister of the Union of South Africa in 1910. He expressed a desire to reconcile the English and Afrikaans sectors of the population, an attitude that resulted in his losing the support of many Afrikaners. He died in 1919.

General Sir Redvers Buller

Sir Redvers might have received a hero's welcome on his return to England but the knives of the military establishment were out. Subjected to criticism of the manner in which he had conducted the Natal campaign, he attacked his critics in public and, on 23 October 1901, he was relieved of his command at Aldershot.

He retired to his family home at Downes in Devon, where he devoted the rest of his life to good works in the local community and was loved by all. He died in 1908 and bore his final illness with his usual fortitude, his last words being, 'I am dying. Well, I think it is about time to go to bed now'.

Despite the criticism levelled at him, the men who had served under him never wavered in their loyalty and affection for their former commander.

Dr Robert Buntine

At the end of the Natal Campaign, Robert Buntine returned to private practice in Pietermaritzburg. During the southern hemisphere summer of 1901/02 he and his wife visited Melbourne to see family and friends. After their return to Natal, his wife tragically died during the birth of their second daughter, Noelle, on Christmas Day 1902. Robert felt he would not be able to bring up two young girls on his own, and arranged for them to be cared for in England.

His pleasing personality enabled him to build up an extensive practice in Pietermaritzburg and such was his nature that he would treat the indigent without remuneration.

In 1915 he was persuaded to stand for election to Parliament as representative for Pietermaritzburg South. He stood as a supporter of Louis Botha's South African Party, as did his opponent. In colonial Natal they never quite got the hang of party politics. Members always tended to vote on an issue according to their inclination rather than in accordance with party policy. This had its frustrations but it did have one advantage it worked. With both candidates nominally supporting the South African Party, the election was a test of popularity, a contest Robert easily won. He had grave doubts about many of Louis Botha's policies, but felt that in those troubled times it would be in the nation's interest to support him. In Parliament he successfully introduced a Bill requiring government support for the development of industry in South Africa. This far-reaching measure was to transform South Africa over the next seventy-five years into the industrial powerhouse of the continent with its axis on the Durban/Johannesburg corridor.

In 1918 Robert felt he should bring his daughters back to Natal, so travelled to England to collect them. He combined this visit with a parliamentary mission, which involved meetings with leading British personalities from Prime Minister Lloyd George downwards. It is not known precisely what was discussed but the probability would have been the post-war investment by British industry in South Africa.

Early in September 1918, Robert Buntine and his two daughters, aged twenty and fifteen, embarked on the *Galway Castle* for South Africa. While making its way through heavy seas in the Bay of Biscay on 12 September, the ship was struck by a German torpedo. Women and children were ordered into lifeboats. Robert watched as the lifeboat with his daughters was lowered into the water. Before it could get clear a large swell dashed it against the ship's bulwarks, tipping its passengers into the ocean. Robert plunged into the sea and managed to save his younger daughter, Noelle. He went back to save his older daughter but both she and Robert disappeared. The *Galway Castle* was to remain afloat for another two days during which time the surviving passengers were taken on board ships that answered her distress calls. Noelle eventually made her way to Pietermaritzburg, where her two sons still live.[18]

Dr Tommy Crean, VC 1901, DSO 1915

The wound suffered by Tommy at Elandslaagte healed rapidly and he took part in the Battle at Wagon Hill and in other engagements in which the ILH were involved. As the siege dragged on and additional medical help was required, he joined the medical staff at Intombi where his medical skill and cheerful personality did much to bring new life to the starved, wounded, and fever-stricken patients.

After the siege was raised, he went back to combat duty. He was given command of a troop and by 1901, he commanded a squadron. In the middle of that year he gave up combat duties and became Medical Officer to the regiment. On 18 December 1901, at Tyger Kloof in the Free State, they were heavily engaged by a Boer kommando. Exposed to close range enemy fire, Tommy continued to tend the wounded and dress their wounds despite being wounded himself. Only after he had been hit a second time did he desist. Initially it was thought that this second wound would be fatal, the bullet having passed through his stomach, but his youth and strength carried him through. In recognition of his bravery at Tyger Kloof, he was awarded the Victoria Cross.

To his disgust he was, on recovery, invalided out of the army. He went to London, where he set up in private practice.

When war broke out in 1914, he went to France as Medical Officer with the 1st Cavalry Brigade commanded by General Briggs, who had commanded the ILH in the later stages of the Boer War. Accounts of Tommy's exploits recur in many books and private letters. All tell of his incredible bravery and humane work. On one occasion a general and his staff were sheltering from a heavy bombardment when they saw Tommy walking by as if on a Sunday morning stroll. The general, a well-known martinet, told him to take cover which Tommy declined to do, saying all his stretcher bearers had been killed or wounded and he must attend to his men. Unaccustomed to having his orders queried, the General ordered him to take cover immediately. The staff looked on in horror as Tommy smiled and, putting his arm around the general's shoulders, said, 'General darling, 'Tis written that I'm to die in my bed. The boys need me. Go I must.' So saying he left to look for the wounded. Those too badly wounded to be moved had their wounds dressed and their position marked. Others he put across his broad back and carried to safety. For long hours he carried on, paying no regard to the ghastly inferno raging about him, until nightfall and exhaustion finally forced him to rest.

He survived the war, but his health had been ruined and he died in his bed, as prophesied, in 1925.[19]

How could Lord Salisbury, Ian Hamilton or anyone else, despise such people?

Nurse Kate Driver

After the siege Kate married Dr J. Boyd whom she had met before the war at Grey's Hospital. In pre-war days the nurses, including Kate, loved to watch the doctor's attempts to mount and ride a horse. After the siege she came to love him dearly and theirs was to be a long and happy marriage.

While in Ladysmith, Kate made notes of her experiences. Three years later, her husband encouraged her to write her story, drawn from those contemporaneous notes. If some facts seem a little strange and fudged it can be attributed to her desire to be tactful while at the same time leaving a memorial to the young Light Horseman who had meant so much to her. Sixty years and two World Wars later, Kate was to write that the 120 days of the siege were still 'drawn out long and very taut' and that time had not 'dulled the high strung feel of them. The sharp anxiety of those who wait for news is the same individual experience always, and the loss of snapped-off lives is bitter, bitter loss whether in the hearts of a few thousand or of world-wide millions'. And after all those years she treasured a photograph of a simple cross on a grave at Intombi and the poignant memory of one particular cup of tea. She died at the Cape in September 1960.

Lt Col Robert Evans and his son Trooper A.W. Evans, both of the NMR

On 20 February 1902, Col Evans, in command of the Composite Regiment, was killed when he approached a farmhouse to accept its surrender.

It will be recalled that his son, while serving in General White's bodyguard, had been awarded a DCM for the rescue of a comrade in a skirmish on 23 October 1899. At the end of the war he was awarded a scholarship to Columbia University. After graduating he moved with his young bride to New Zealand to take up a post as Resident Engineer of a mining company.

On the outbreak of war in 1914, he raised the 3rd Battalion of the New Zealand Rifle Brigade, which he commanded with the rank of Lieutenant Colonel in France. He received a DSO the citation stating, 'he showed the greatest coolness and energy inspiring all ranks by his magnificent personal example and never sparing himself to make the operation of his battalion the success which it was'.

He was wounded and died at Passchendaele on 13 October 1917.[20]

M.K. Gandhi

Mohandas Gandhi was to achieve many things in his life, however, through no fault on his part, his contribution to the Boer War was very small. To exaggerate his achievements in the war does his reputation no favour and would have caused him considerable embarrassment. He was to play a greater part with the Natal forces in the disturbances in Natal in 1906.[21]

Major Hubert Gough (later General Sir Hubert Gough)

An enigmatic character, he held Duncan McKenzie in awe, and was one of the first to recognise the outstanding quality of the Natal regiments. An ambitious man, he carried the burden of having a father, an uncle and a brother who had won the Victoria Cross. The impossibility of matching their achievements might account for a certain meanness of character. After Dundonald left South Africa in 1900, the SA Light Horse suffered a setback. Gough sent a description of the engagement to Dundonald, which concluded with the statement that 'The only laughable thing about it was that the Natal Volunteers were in charge of the line and of the country – whose prudence, slimness and invariable watchfulness have so aggressively been held up as patterns to the Regular soldiers in all the papers'.[21]

Whether or not the Colonials thought the disaster suffered by Gough's column at Blood River Poort in September 1901, was 'laughable,' is unknown; however, they might have thought it served him right. On that occasion colonial scouts warned him the Boers were present in considerable numbers. Like Penn Symons, Gough dismissed the information as colonial exaggeration, and his men paid the penalty. During the engagement Gough became detached from his unit, and had a humiliating time hiding from the Boers, who eventually caught him, stripped of him of clothes, and let him loose.

Towards Lord Dundonald he was polite and corresponded with him, however, it seems he resented the success achieved by the one-time commander of the locally recruited mounted brigade. Writing many years after the Boer War, when Dundonald and his contemporaries were long dead, Gough described Dundonald as, 'another of Buller's weak subordinates. Known among us as Dundoodle, he was hesitating, vacillating and vain. Mistakenly over-praised by a not well-informed Press, he was known to the people at home as "the stormy petrel". The fact behind this soubriquet was that he had men under him of independent character and initiative, whose every act was credited to Dundonald. Such men were Thornycroft, Bethune, Byng, and perhaps pre-eminently Duncan McKenzie of the Natal Carbineers.'

This attack on a man he had once courted as a friend shows a remarkable lack of loyalty. It also shows that he did not know what happened to men who lived in glass houses. He became known in the ranks as 'Bumface', apparently because of a cleft down the middle of his nose.

Gough's name will forever be linked to the slaughter in the bloody battle of Passchendaele in 1917. Total losses on the British side were in the region of 250,000, killed, wounded, and missing, a substantial portion of whom were colonials. Subsequently Gough was blamed, perhaps unfairly, for the German breakthrough in the spring of 1918 and dismissed from his command.

General Sir Ian Hamilton

He was in command at Gallipoli, one the most disastrous and bloody campaigns of the First World War. He died in 1947 and was a prolific writer on military matters.

Dr Leander Starr Jameson

Once Dr Jameson had recovered from the enteric he had contracted in Ladysmith he entered Cape politics and was elected to the Cape Legislative Assembly as member for Kimberley. In his maiden speech to the Legislature in August 1902, he asked that the Raid might be forgotten. He was elected leader of the new Progressive Party, which he led to victory in the 1904 general election, and was duly appointed Prime Minister, retaining for himself the position of Minister of Native Affairs. He showed especial interest in the recommendations of the South African Native Affairs Commission 1903–1905. He firmly believed that higher education should be available to all and he was the initial driving force behind the formation of the University of Fort Hare, which was to open in 1916. Situated at Alice in the Eastern Cape, it was the first university in sub-Saharan Africa to attend to the needs of black students.[23]

These well documented facts should dispel forever the modern theory that the Boer War was fermented by Milner, Jameson, Rhodes and the Uitlanders to oppress black people.

Jameson lost the premiership in 1908 and subsequently served as leader of the Unionist Party (South Africa). He returned to England in 1912 and died in 1917.

J.S. Marwick

Early in December 1899, Sydney Marwick enlisted, and was posted to the Intelligence Corps. Because of his knowledge of Zulu, he was assigned to the Natal Labour Corps, which served in a non-combatant role digging trenches, transporting goods and other fatigue duties. Its members received a reasonable wage, which provided some compensation for the loss of income from the mines.

At the end of the war, Marwick was appointed Native Commissioner in Johannesburg. A few years later he was elected Member of Parliament for Illovo in Natal and when that constituency was abolished, he was elected as MP for Pinetown near Durban.

When he died in 1958, Zulus came from far and wide to pay their last respects to him.

Sir Alfred Milner

After the war Milner was to prove a diligent Governor whose principal legacy to South Africa was the establishment of an efficient and incorruptible civil service. His arrogance ensured that he would never be popular and in 1906 the British parliament passed a motion of censure on him, resulting in his resignation. By December 1916 he was once more back in favour.

Aware of his organisational skills, Prime Minister Lloyd George brought Milner into the War Cabinet.

He died in 1924 after contracting malaria while on a visit to South Africa.

Charles Herbert Mullins, VC, CMG

We left Charlie Mullins lying wounded at Wright's Farm on the road to Mafeking. His body was riddled with bullets and no one thought he would survive, but survive he did. His most serious wound was an injury to his spine, which left him crippled for life and only able to get around with crutches. Added to this he had to endure constant pain and bouts of illness.

He resumed practice as a lawyer in Johannesburg, a difficult task given his disabilities. A devout Anglican, he was indefatigable in the support he gave to the Church as it revived after the war. He also maintained a constant interest in the ILH, which he had helped to found and make famous.

He died on 24 May 1916, aged 46, and was buried in Grahamstown, Eastern Cape, in the town's old cemetery. He was survived by his wife and two sons.

Teise Ndlovu

Despite his Zulu surname, Teise was a Sotho and when the British army moved into the Free State, which bordered Lesotho, he joined them. So excellent was his service that the army used him to check the reports of other scouts. In due course he was sent out to check a report that the Boers had set an ambush on a particular ridge. While reconnoitering the position, Teise must have been seen by the Boers who opened fire on him, hitting him in several places. Realising that the element of surprise had been lost, the Boers abandoned their proposed ambush and galloped off.

Teise died the next day. Robert Samuelson applied to the Natal Government for an allowance for his widow and free schooling for his children. From Natal, his widow received a gratuity of £10, quite a large sum in those days. For example a widow of a Volunteer killed on duty received a gratuity of £5. As Teise was killed while serving with the Imperial Army and he came from the Free State, any other benefits due to him should have come from the Free State or Britain.

Deneys Reitz

In his much quoted book *Commando,* relating his youthful experiences with a Boer kommando, Reitz makes no mention of the colonials in Natal except for his admission that he enjoyed looting Dundee. Perhaps he realised that whatever quarrels the Boers had with Britain, there was no excuse for the invasion of Natal or the manner in which it was smashed up by the Boers, and any mention of this topic could be embarrassing for the Boers.

Returning to South Africa in 1906 after four years of self-imposed exile, he was prominent among those Afrikaners who sought harmony between

English and Afrikaans South Africans. He took part in the campaigns in South West Africa and in East Africa. During the later stages of the First World War, he served in France as commander of the Royal Scots Fusiliers and was wounded in 1918.

In defiance of a campaign to demonise the Imperial Light Horse, he became a colonel of that regiment and was a staunch opponent of the Broederbond and Ossewa Brandwag, organisations which sought exclusive control by Afrikaners of all aspects of South African life. He entered politics and became a Member of Parliament, supporting Smuts. When Smuts became Prime Minister in 1939, Deneys was appointed Deputy Prime Minister until he was appointed South African High Commissioner to London in 1944. He died later that year.

J.R. 'Galloping Jack' Royston, DSO

In April 1901, Jack Royston was promoted to Lieutenant Colonel and left the 2nd ILH to take command of the 5th and 6th West Australian Mounted Infantry contingents, which had recently arrived in the country. Initially serving under General F.W. Kitchener, and later under General Bruce Hamilton, they took part in many of the successful operations in the Eastern Transvaal, which eventually led to the military defeat of the Boers. During this period Royston was awarded the DSO.

He raised a mounted regiment known as 'Royston's Horse' for service in the 1906 unrest and in 1914, raised the Natal Light Horse, which served first under Louis Botha in putting down the Afrikaner Rebellion, and later under McKenzie in German South West.

In 1916 Royston was able to obtain a posting to the Australian Light Horse, then engaged in keeping the Turks away from the Suez Canal. Now a brigadier general, he commanded their 3rd Brigade.

Banjo Paterson, the Australian poet and journalist, was a major serving with the Australian Remount Depot in Egypt, where he met Royston, and left this description of him,

> a square-built energetic man always doing something, a sort of prototype of Teddy Roosevelt when the latter was the colonel of the rough-riders. It is said that there were sixty generals at one time quartered in Shepheard's Hotel in Cairo. But Royston was not the Shepheard's Hotel brand of general – far from it. He had been given command of a brigade of Australian Light Horse. While it is altogether an admirable thing for a general to set his troops a good example by showing a contempt for danger, it must be admitted that Royston rather over did it; and his troops alternately admired and cursed him. It was not that he wanted to show off – he was not that sort of man – but when he got anywhere near a fight, a sort of exaltation seemed to seize him, and he took no more account of bullets than of so many house flies.

'When I'm running a show, Paterson,' he said to me. 'I stick my lance in the ground; leave Dangar (his brigade major) in charge, and I go off to see how the boys are getting on.'

The Remount Depot received batches of horses, often numbering more than a thousand, which would be broken in by rough riders, before being issued to the various units. It was a strict rule that nobody could choose the horse to be issued to him. When the first batch of horses arrived who should pitch up but General Royston. He was told of the rule that no one could select mounts, but said, 'Well at any rate I'll pick out a horse for myself. You must do the best you can to keep him for me.' He then selected what Paterson described as, 'a magnificent black horse, one of the best-looking officers' charges that ever came out of Australia.

When the day came for breaking these horses General Royston arrived and explained, 'There's no harm in looking at 'em. I'm always up early so I thought I'd ride round to have a look.' (It was four o'clock in the morning.) Royston watched quietly as the rough-riders matched their skill against the horses' determination to dislodge them – a contest which not infrequently was won by the horse. Royston asked where the black horse was and was told it had been saved for last, and in due course the horse was led forward and walked around quietly. The rough-rider mounted. Paterson described what happened next.

Away he went arching himself almost into a circle like a watchspring with his head right in under his girths. Straight ahead, sideways, round and round, backwards, he went in great bounds roaring with rage all the time and shaking and wrenching his rider at every prop and spring. He wound up landing, rider and all, in an irrigation canal with a splash like the launching of a battleship.

The Sergeant-Major said. 'He'll never make a general's charger. Best thing we can do with him is to sell him to the Turks.' Paterson gives Royston's response,

'I can ride him,' he said. 'I can ride anything. I'll be very hurt, Paterson, if you don't keep him for me.' It seemed a good chance to say that he would be very hurt if we did keep him: but one doesn't say these things to a general and off he went followed by admiring comments from the rough-riders: 'That's Hell-fire Jack. He'd ha' been shot fifty times, only he won't keep still long enough for the Turks to hit him.'

The gallant general's inability to keep out of a fight might have landed him in the equivalent of Stellenbosch (in a remount depot), or might have earned him the command of a light horse division. On one occasion he arrived at a fight in the desert, I think it was Romani, and found our forces enclosing the Turks on three sides, and apparently awaiting orders to attack. Riding up to one regiment that was waiting for its colonel to return from a conference, Royston called out: 'Come on boys.' The regiment, with howls of exultation, at once followed him. The other regiments, seeing the others go in, thought that orders had arrived for an attack, and in half a minute they were all over the Turks. The Victory went down to the credit of the man in charge of operations. But Royston had, at any rate, hurried things up. He was in line for a high command when his optimism proved his downfall.

Poison gas had been used by the Germans and experiments were being made with it on the Palestine front. Nothing would do for Royston, but that he must have a sniff of it. He was one of those men who would try anything once. He was warned against it, but no, he must have just one sniff of it so that he might be able to recognise it if it should ever be used against his troops. The result was that I found him in a hospital, a badly shaken man, passing green urine, and ordered away for long leave. But nothing would daunt him and he spoke most cheerfully of the day he would come back.[25]

He never did get back. By the time he had recovered, the war was over and he had returned to his farm at Umtentweni on the Natal South Coast, where his neighbour was his old friend, Lieutenant Colonel J.F. Rethman.

In 1934 Jack Royston visited Australia and was feted wherever he went. In five weeks he attended no fewer than fifty dinners, balls and official functions as a guest of governments and public bodies. He regretted that his schedule did not enable him to visit his friends in Queensland, Tasmania and New Zealand.

Two incidents might explain why, in contrast to the British, he was so successful with Australian units. At Deir el Belah a young trooper was found guilty of sleeping on duty, a serious offence which in many armies would have resulted in the offender being shot. He was found guilty by a Court Martial. The brigade was drawn up in a hollow square to hear the sentence imposed on the prisoner, who stood between two escorts. When the sentence, ninety days in the Cairo citadel, was passed, the young man went pale but otherwise did not flinch. Royston then addressed the brigade: 'Our young comrade here is going to pay the penalty for sleeping at his post. In future we will guard against this by doubling the men at each outpost. Until now our comrade has been a good soldier. When he comes out of the citadel I shall be proud to have him back under my command.' Turning to the prisoner, he said: 'When you are in the citadel son keep your head up.'

From time to time, concerts were arranged to entertain the men. One such concert was held on the beach at El Arish, where the stage consisted of planks laid across bales of hay. Among the entertainers was the double act of the Australian, General Granville Ryrie, and Jack Royston, whose combined weight at the time would have been about 225 kilograms. To roars of delight they entertained the troops with an exhibition of tap-dancing.[24]

When the Italian dictator Mussolini invaded Ethiopia in 1935, Royston was so outraged that he wrote to the Emperor Hailie Selassie offering his assistance. He was 75 at the time. He died at Durban in 1942.

Freda Schlosberg

The young girl who left such a vivid description of life behind the Boer lines, drowned with her husband near Pretoria in 1922 when their car was swept away in a flash flood.

Peter Smith

After the retreat of the Boers from Dundee, Peter and Ann Smith returned to their farm on Talana Hill. They had spent nine wretched months living in the outhouses of the Oaks Hotel in Pietermaritzburg where there were 'no conveniences'. On arrival, they found their home had been shattered by shellfire, the thatched roof had fallen in and was rotting on the floor, which had been stained by blood of the dead and wounded. Under the eucalyptus trees near their home were the graves of British soldiers who had died there nine months before. Apart from the hardships endured and financial loss suffered, they had the grief of losing their grandson, who had been killed by the shell that struck the Carbineers' camp in Ladysmith on 18 December 1899. Across the valley, the town of Dundee, which had once supplied the community with its needs, was devastated and its inhabitants were only just beginning to dribble back to their wrecked homes. Now in their late seventies, the old couple set about rebuilding their lives. Their cottage was refurbished with a new iron roof and veranda, the trees in the orchard were pruned and fertilised, the vegetable garden re-established and the ducks and geese, which had been stolen, were replaced. Visitors once again called at the farm where they were welcomed with the kindly hospitality that had always been shown to one and all. On leaving, visitors would receive a jar of Ann's special crab apple jelly.

Peter and Ann lie buried next to each other in the family graveyard near the farmhouse that they had made their home so many years before. It is sad that a Boer, Piet Smit, is now being put forward as the owner of Talana on the day of the famous battle.[26]

Field Marshal Jan Christiaan Smuts

The peace negotiations in 1902 were the start of a love affair between Smuts and the British who were so love-struck that they failed to compel Smuts to account for atrocities his kommando had committed against black people.

After the defeat of the Germans in South West Africa, attention now turned to German East Africa where the British colonies were struggling to contain the Germans under their astute commander Colonel von Lettow-Vorbeck who had under his command 3,500 Germans and about 12,000 black Askaris. Smuts was asked to take command of the campaign and arrived in Kenya in February 1916. By the beginning of April he had reorganised the force into three divisions with a total complement 130,000 men. The 1st Division, commanded by Major-General Hoskins, comprised a mixed bag of Rhodesians, Punjabis, Baluchis, Pathans, Kashmiris, Royal Fusiliers, King's African Rifles, the Cape Corps (Coloured South Africans) and the 5th Battery of the South African Field Artillery. The 2nd and 3rd Divisions were commanded by Major-General van Deventer and Major-General Brits respectively, both were Afrikaners, as were most of their senior officers, while the rank and file were almost exclusively Anglo South Africans. Backed by his army of 130,000 men, Smuts attacked the Germans. Victories were gained here and there, though there were little slip-ups from time to time, these could be explained away. The British were thrilled. On 20 January 1917, Smuts left Dar-es-Salaam to attend an Imperial War Conference in London, after which he became a member of the British War Cabinet. In Africa, Colonel Paul von Lettow-Vorbeck with his now reduced force held at bay the Allied Army and when peace came on 11 November 1918 the German column was still in the field. Smuts was awarded a Field Marshall's baton by the grateful British.

When Louis Botha died in 1919, Smuts took over as Prime Minister. Though defeated in an election in 1924, he was returned to power in 1939 when he took South Africa into Second World War on the Allied side.

He never had any empathy with any of the peoples in Natal. He never understood the symbolic role of the monarchy, which to the colonials of Natal represented the culture from which they had sprung. Being so far from England and under threat, they clung to those values, which they believed were their inheritance, while at the same time they developed their own colonial culture. They declined to follow Boer ways but at the same time, queried British decisions and attitudes. To Smuts this was stubborn perversity. Their passion for ball games and in particular the ritual of cricket, he found mystifying. And yet they voted for him. To understand why one must look at the other option available to voters. In 1940, when South African airmen flying with the RAF were fighting the Battle of Britain, the leader of the opposition National Party, Dr D F. Malan, told the South African Parliament that he anticipated a German victory, after which a generous Hitler would grant the Boers their Republic.

Smuts died in 1950 having been succeeded as Prime Minister by Dr Malan in 1948.

Natal Carbineer Lt William Tanner

This friend of the Driver family was promoted regularly over the years and in 1916 was in command of the 2nd Infantry Regiment (Natal) of the SA Brigade in France. With the Somme offensive underway on 15 July 1916, orders were received to capture and hold Delville Wood. Tanner, now a Lieutenant Colonel, was in command in the wood, which was captured and held. When his regiment was relieved six days and five nights later, of the 3,155 men who entered the wood only 143 staggered out for the roll call.

Other groups which had become isolated were subsequently found, the final tally of casualties being 2,435 and this was only the beginning.[27] Tanner was wounded, recovered, and was promoted to brigadier general, serving with distinction until the Armistice.

William Watson

He died in 1906. He was never able to re-establish his beloved grove of trees and bird sanctuary. His quotation from Byron is as relevant today as it was in 1900.

Charles Willson

Once his Court Martial had been finalised, he returned to Dundee where he was elected Chairman of the Town Board and Commander of the Town Guard. He organised the Guard into an efficient unit and the Boers never dared to launch another attack on the town. Perhaps to avoid British interference, he made no attempt to be restored to his former position in the Carbineers.

He died in 1912. Two years later, his son was killed in action while serving with the British Expeditionary Force in France.

Appendices

Appendix One
The Purchase of the Port of Natal

I, Inguos (Inkosi) Chaka, King of the Zulus, and the country of Natal, as well as the whole of the land from Natal to Delagoa Bay, which I have inherited from my father, for myself and heirs, do hereby, on the seventh day of August, in the year of our Lord eighteen hundred and twenty-four, in the presence of my Chiefs, and of my own free will, and in consideration of diverse goods received, grant, make over, and sell unto,

F.G. Farewell and Company,

The entire and full possession in perpetuity to themselves, heirs, and executors, of the Port or Harbour of Natal, known by the native name "Bubolongo," together with the Islands therein and the surrounding country, as herein described, viz. The whole of the neck of land or peninsula in the south-west entrance, and all the country ten miles to the southern side of Port Natal, as pointed out, and extending along the sea-coast to the northward and eastward as far as the river known by the native name, 'Gumgelote', and now called 'Farewell's River', being about twenty-five miles of sea coast to the north-east of Port Natal, together with all the country inland as far as the nation called by the Zulus 'Gowagnewkos', extending about one hundred miles backward from the sea-shore, with all the rights to the rivers, woods, mines and articles of all denominations contained therein, the said land and appurtenances to be from this date for the sole use of the said Farewell and Company, their heirs and executors, and to be by them disposed of in any manner they think best calculated for their interests, free from any molestation or hindrance from myself or subjects. In witness whereof, I have placed my hand, being fully aware that the so doing is intended to bind me to all the articles and conditions that I, of my own free will and consent, do hereby, in the presence of the undermentioned witnesses, acknowledge to have fully consented and agreed to on behalf of F.G. Farewell as aforesaid, and perfectly understand all the purport of this document, the same having been carefully explained to me by my interpreter, Clambamarnze, and in the presence of two interpreters, Coliat and Frederick, before the said F.G. Farewell, whom I hereby acknowledge as the Chief of the said country, with full power and authority over such natives that like to remain there after this public grant, promising to supply him with cattle and corn, when required, sufficient for his consumption, as a reward for his kind attention to me in my illness from a wound.

Chaka signified his acceptance by making a mark. Four witnesses, Umbequarn (Chaka's uncle), Umsega, Euntclope, and Chaka's Interpreter Clambermarnze added their marks to the grant, 7 August, 1824

Appendix 2

'Mission to His Britannic Majesty'

I, Chaka, King of the Zulus, do in the presence of my principal chiefs now assembled, hereby appoint and direct my friend, James Saunders King, to take under his charge Sotobi, one of my principal chiefs, whom I now create of the 'Tugusa' kraal, Kati, my body-servant, Jacob, my interpreter, and suite. I desire him to convey them to H.M. George's dominions, to represent that I send them on a friendly mission to King George the Fourth; and after offering him assurances of my friendship and esteem, to negotiate with His Britannic Majesty on my behalf, with my chief Sotobi, a treaty of friendly alliance between the two nations, having given the said J.S. King and Sotobi full instructions and invested with full power to act for me in every way as circumstances may seem to them most beneficial and expedient. I require my friend King to pay every attention to the comforts of my people entrusted to his care, and solemnly enjoin him to return with them to safety to me, and to report to me faithfully such accounts as they may receive from King George.

I hereby grant him, my said friend J.S. King, in consideration of the confidence I repose in him, of various services he has already rendered me, presents he has made, and above all the obligations I am under to him for his attention to my mother in her last illness, as well as having saved the lives of several of my principal people, the free and full possession of my country near the sea-coast and Port Natal, from Natal head to the Stinkein River including the extensive grazing flats and forests, with the islands in the Natal harbour, and the Matabana nations, together with the free and exclusive trade of all my dominions; I hereby also confirm all my former grants to him.

Shaka scribbled all over the paper saying that as he was a great king he should make a great show. Two witnesses made the more simple conventional mark. N.J. Issacs signed as a witness. February, 1828.

Appendix 3

Parliamentary Report, published 1837

Port Natal
At a greater distance from the eastern frontier another body of British subjects have, it appears, settled themselves at Port Natal, influenced by the wish to diffuse religious knowledge and principles amongst the natives. It is impossible to contemplate without serious distrust the attempt to combine European colonisation with plans for the conversion of natives to Christianity. The allurements to deviate to the pursuit of secular and selfish ends are many and powerful, and although they may be counteracted at first by the principles and character of the settlers, yet no permanent and effective restraint on their cupidity appears to have been devised. It will be the duty of the Government at the Cape of Good Hope to maintain, as opportunity offers, a vigilant superintendence over the growing settlement of Port Natal, so that any injuries done to the tribes may be arrested and punished before they assume the form of actual hostility.

Appendix 4

Petition for a Colony

TO THE HONOURABLE THE COMMONS OF THE UNITED KINGDOM OF GREAT BRITAIN AND IRELAND, IN PARLIAMENT ASSEMBLED.

The Petition of the undersigned Merchants, and others, interested in the Prosperity and Civilization of Southern Africa,

Humbly Sheweth, – That many of your petitioners have had much experience in the colonisation of Southern Africa, and that all of them take a warm interest in the various settlements, and in the happiness and civilization of the native tribes.

And petitioners, while they lament the difficulties and misfortunes which have too often impeded the progress of the settlements already established, especially the frequent sanguinary conflicts with the natives, submit, that such are attributable to the want of a proper system of Colonial Government, and not an impossibility of conciliating the interests of the white and coloured races.

And petitioners therefore submit to your honourable House, that it is advisable to found, in Southern Africa, a new Colony, by which not only the interests of settlers, and of Great Britain, will be honourably promoted, but also those of the natives secured, and their civilization advanced: and your petitioners show, that the country in which such a Colony can be established is Port Natal in South Eastern Africa, containing more than 15,000,000 acres of land, nearly depopulated by native conquerors, almost unoccupied, and well known to be healthy and fertile, both in the interior and coastwise. It lies between the latitudes of 29 degrees and 31,30 south and longitude 27,30 and 30,31 east beginning at the Umzimvoobo (Ivory), or St John's River, and extending about 300 miles along the coast to the Tugela, about 70 miles to the north east of Port Natal, and running inland between 60 and 100 miles to the Quathlamba Mountains.

Your petitioners possess the means of proving, by witnesses, who have visited the country in question, all the allegations contained in this petition: showing that among the advantages which may be secured by founding a Colony of Natal, are the following:- Advancing the security of the Cape of Good Hope, by promoting the civilization of the native tribes; affording a powerful aid towards abolishing the East African slave trade, by the introduction of legitimate commerce in its place; extension of religious missions; and protection for the interior trade.

Your petitioners are also able to prove, to the satisfaction of your honourable House, that the few natives dispersed within, and the populous tribes beyond the borders of the proposed Colony, have long evinced themselves anxious to have a British Colony established at Natal, and to hold friendly intercourse with white people; that large grants of the above mentioned territory have been already made by native chiefs to British subjects in the course of the last fourteen years; that during that period a number of English settlers have resided there, generally in safety, until the late unhappy events, which, from the great respect always manifested by the present Zoola chief and his predecessor to legitimate British authority, could not have occurred had a British Colony been established on a sound system.

Your petitioners also submit that, as a considerable number of other British subjects, Cape Dutch farmers, with their families and property, have lately emigrated to Natal, by the adoption of wise measures they will become valuable members of the new Colony, and greatly promote its interests.

It will not be unknown to many members of your honourable house, that, during the last fourteen years, various applications have been made to the Crown to found a Colony at Natal, and that the several governors at the Cape of Good Hope have either warmly supported the said applications, or have not disapproved of them; particularly in 1834, when a large number of the merchants, and other inhabitants of the Cape of Good Hope, represented to the Government that such a Colony was highly desirable; and your petitioners submit, that the objections then made on the score of expense, which at that period led the Government to refuse acquiescence in such applications, no longer exist, inasmuch as the self-supporting principle of selling the freehold of soil having been tested by experience, is now more fully understood; and is so available at Natal that the British Treasury will not be called upon to advance one shilling towards the establishment of the Colony.

Your petitioners submit, that it is impossible to procure the funds necessary for carrying into effect the proposed important objects if land-selling principle be not adopted; they, therefore humbly suggest, that the South Australian plan as respects the sale of land, may be employed at Natal, but with this variation, that a portion only of the money obtained by such sales shall be applied to defray the expense of the emigration of labourers – mechanics being chiefly wanted, in as much as free* native labour may be easily obtained when the Colony is established – the remaining portion of the money so raised to be applied to the purposes of surveys, the formation of roads, bridges, and the general expenses of Government, including the protection of the natives, their proper restraint by a good police, and their moral and religious improvement.

Your petitioners further submit, that a colony based upon sound principles of political and social liberty, guaranteed to all denominations of men, and properly guarded against abuse and license, will secure the confidence of capitalists, lead to a profitable investment of money, and obtain for free laborers of all classes and colors ample remuneration, with the prospect of steadily bettering their conditions; and that such a system, if established at the same time with the principle of selling the Crown lands, and applying the proceeds to public colonial objects alone, will lay a firm foundation for great improvements in the condition of large masses of men in Southern Africa.

Your petitioners likewise submit to your honourable House that the establishment of a just and well-matured system of colonial government and administration under the crown, with constitutional guarantees, is beyond all comparison preferable to the plan recently proposed for substituting the political agency of missionaries, in place of the power and influence of regular British government, wherever the fair interests and just activity of British subjects may in future carry them; your petitioners, on the contrary, submit that, whilst missionaries ought to be supported and multiplied to the utmost need by all possible means, actual experience proves that their efficiency becomes deteriorated by unnecessary political agency.

Your petitioners therefore humbly pray that the foregoing allegations may be inquired into by your honourable House, and that your honourable House, will address her Majesty not only to adopt the acquisitions already made by British subjects at Natal, but also to cause the remaining portions of the depopulated country to be acquired by treaty with the chiefs who own it. Your Petitioners likewise pray, that a colony may be established there on a new and just system with regard to the natives, and upon the principle of selling Crown lands according to a plan to be settled by Act of Parliament, so as to furnish competent means for carrying such a good system into effect for the equal benefit of all classes of men.

And your petitioners pray that the Act of Parliament may vest the government of the proposed colony in the crown, and independently, of the Cape of Good Hope, and appoint commissioners in London to sell the lands. That provision be made in the Act of Parliament to guarantee all existing rights; and that all details be also introduced into the said Act for the establishment of a steady system of just and safe intercourse with the neighbouring tribes; and for the equal protection of the coloured as well as white people within the colony; likewise that a loan of sufficient amount, according to an estimate of all the public wants of the colony, for a certain number of years may be authorized to be raised under the Act upon the security of a competent portion of the land to be sold, – And petitioners, as in duty bound, shall ever pray.

22.3. 1839

*By free labour it is meant that free men, as distinct from slaves, should provide labour.

Notes

Abbreviations

UKNA – National Archives, Kew, London.
LHS – Ladysmith Historical Society.
UKNA – National Army Museum

Chapter 1

1. UKNA, CO 179/207 and Marwick Papers, Killie Campbell Museum, Durban

Chapter 2

1. Extract from the much quoted Manifesto of Voortrekker leader Piet Retief.

Chapter 3

1. Sampson, V. and Hamilton I., 96/97.
2. Julius, Anthony, 269-276.

Chapter 4

1. Mackeurton, G., 63.
2. Ibid, 66.
3. Ibid, 67.
4. Ibid, 72/73.
5. Ibid, 69.
6. Ibid, 65.
7. Diary of H.F. Fynn, 130
8. Ibid, 234
9. Mackeurton, G., 154.
10. Gardiner, Capt the Rev A.F., 11.
11. Ibid, 183/184.
12. Mackeurton, G., 189/190.
13. Ibid, 188.
14. Chase, J.C., Part 1, 132.
15. Ibid, Part, 1 131/132, and Part 2, 71/72.
16. Ibid, Part 2, 8/9.
17. Mackuerton, G., 225/226.

18. Ibid, 228/229.
19. Goetzche, E., *Father of a City*, 30/31.
20. Lugg, H.C., 45.
21. Mackuerton, G. 239.
22. Ibid, 240/241.
23. Ibid, 241/142.
24. Ibid, 252.
25. Chase, Part 2, 119.
26. Mackuerton, G., 256/257, and Chase, Part 2, 122/123.
27. Chase, Part 2, 127/128.
28. Ibid, 129.
29. Ibid, 118.
30. Ibid, 59/160.
31. Ibid, 190.
32. Ibid. 209.
33. Ibid, 209.
34. Ibid, 214.
35. Ibid, 215/216.
36. Goetzche, E., *Father of a City*, 42.
37. Chase, Part 2, 217/218.
38. Lugg, H.C. 51.
39. Mackueton, 278/280.
40. Ibid, 281.
41. Ibid, 281/282.
42. Ibid, 282.
43. Goetzche, *Father of a City,* 47/48.
44. Chase, Part 2, 224.
45. Ibid, 237/239.
46. Bazley, D., 16.
47. McKenzie, Col A.G., 153.
48. Inter alia, The Curling Letters of the Zulu War, 50.
49. Mark Coglan, 7.
50. Samuelson, R.C.A., 218.
51. Ibid, 228.
52. Williams, A.W. 136.

Chapter 5

1. May, H.J., 30/31.
2. Amery, L.S., Vol. II, 68–70.
3. Samuelson, R.C.A., 160/161.
4. Bazley, D., 63–69.
5. Statement made by Mehlokazulu after capture in the Zulu War. Various Sources.
6. David, S., 146/147.
7. Goetsche, E., *History of the NMR*, 122.
8. LHS Diary (Lt Col B.W. Martin).
9. Lugg, H.C., 38/39.
10. Reminiscences Lt Col J.F. Rethman.
11. Amery, L.S., Vol. II, 32–37
12. Evidence of General Hunter. Commission on the War in South Africa.
13. Amery, L.S., Vol. II, 75.
14. Gibson, G.F., 18, 68

15. Ibid, 19.
16. ILH papers, African Studies Library, Johannesburg.
17. Ibid.
18. Ibid.
19. Gibson, G.F., 23.
20. Ibid, 22.
21. Evidence of General Hunter. Commission on the War in South Africa.
21. McKenzie, Col A.G., 156.
22. Dennison, C.J., 204.

Chapter 6

1. Amery, L.S. Vol. II, 141.
2. Doyle, A.C., 70.
3. Reitz, D., 15.
4. Samuelson, R.C., 142.
5. May, H.J., 17.
6. Reitz, D., 23.
7. Brink, E., 62
8. Lugg, H.C., 92.
9. Brink, E., 88.
10. Marwick Papers, Killie Campbell Museum.
11. McFadden, Pam, *Khaki Cameos*.
12. *Natal Mercury*, 10 July, 1900.

Chapter 7

1. Samuelson, R.C., 138-141.
2. Ibid, 141
3. Gordon, Dr R., 258/259.
4. Reminiscences, Lt Col J. F. Rethman.
5. Hattersley, 36/37 and others.
6. Diary of Lt. D. Howard Gill RFA., Unisa Archives.

Chapter 8

1. May, H.J., 19.
2. Reitz, D., Commando, 26.
3. Ibid, 27.
4. Amery, L.S.,Vol. II, 152.
5. Bailey, G.C., 52.
6. Amery, L.S., Vol II, 160.
7. Bailey, G.C., 26.
8. Ibid, 29.
9. Ibid, 47 quoting Lt Crum.
10. Ibid, 64.

Chapter 9

1. Letter dated 27 Sept. 1899, ILH papers, African Studies Library, Jhb.
2. Gibson, G. F., 39.
3. Schiel, Col A., *Twenty-three years of Storm and Sunshine in South Africa*. Translation.

4. Ibid.
5. Ibid.
6. Ibid.
7. Stirling, J., 30.
8. Schiel, Col A.,
9. ILH papers, African Studies Library.
10. Information from Douglas Campbell, grandson of Lt Douglas Campbell ILH.
11. Sampson, V. and Hamilton, 113.
12. Schiel, Col A.
13. Ibid.
14. Ibid.
15. Ibid
16. Gibson, G.F., 35.
17. ILH papers, African Studies Library.
18. Ibid.
19. Sampson, V. and Hamilton, I., 116.
20. Pakenham, T. 1979 Edition, 140, Illustrated Edition 1993, 78.
21. Schiel, Col A.,
22. Ibid.
23. ILH papers, African Studies Library.
24. Diary J.C. Burton.
25. Schiel, Col A.

Chapter 10

1. LHS, (Nurse Kate Driver), 3/4.
2. Ibid, 4.
3. Ibid, 5.
4. Gibson, G.F., 39, also Bridgland, A., 45.
5. Goetsche, E., *History of the NMR*, 55, also Stirling, J., 30.
6. Gibson, G. F., 39/40.
7. ILH papers African Studies Library.
8. Gibson, G. F., 321.

Chapter 11

1. Brooking, Lt Hugh, Diary. African Studies Library.
2. Ibid.
3. Goetsche, E., *History of the NMR*, 57/58.
4. Samuelson, R.C., 158
5. Steevens, W.G., 89, and others
6. Slirling, John, 31.
7. Macdonald, D., 17.
8. Watkins-Pitchford, H., 14/15.
9. Reitz, D., 32/33.
10. Bailey, G.C., 69–71.
11. Steevens, W.G., 66–68.

Chapter 12

1. Nevinson, H.W., 6.
2. Ibid, 17.
3. Ibid, 8.

4. Ibid, 18.
5. Sampson, V. and Hamilton, I., 116.
6. Nevinson, H.W., 9.
7. LHS. (Letters), 2/3.
8. Ibid, (Watson), 7.
9. Bridgland, Tony, 6.
10. Ibid, 20.
11. Ibid, 20
12. Samuelson, R.C., 151.
13. Brooking, Lt Hugh, African Studies Library.
14. Stirling, John, 32.

Chapter 13

1. Reminiscences Lt Col J.F. Rethman.
2. King's College. Diary Gen Ian Hamilton.
3. LHS, (Nurse K. Driver), 6.
4. Ibid, 7.
5. Ibid, 9.
6. Pearse, H.H.S., 20.
7. LHS, No.1 (G. Tatham), 1.
8. LHS, No.7 (W. Watson), 2.
9. Gordon, Dr R., 261.
10. Commission of Enquiry into the War in South Africa.
11. Ibid.
12. Ibid.
13. Watkins-Pitchford, H, 20.
14. Gibson, G. F., 50.
15. Ibid, 53. Quoting G.W. Steevens of the *London Daily Mail*.
16. Ibid, 54.
17. Goetsche, History of the NMR, 79.
18. Macdonald, D., 147.
19. Gibson, G. F., 56.

Chapter 14

1. McKenzie, Col A.G., 154.
2. Ibid, 154.
3. Stirling, J., 46.
4. Churchill, W.S., 20.
5. Ibid, 20.
6. Ibid, 21.
7. Ibid, 21.
8. Ibid, 21.
9. South African Military History Society Journal, Vol.2, No. 2.
10. Churchill, W.S., 28/29.
11. Ibid, 30/31.
12. Creswicke, L., 40/41.
13. Chisholme, R., 82.
14. UKNA. CO179. Affidavit received by Colonial Office 26.12. 1899.
15. McKenzie, Col A.G., 154/155.
16. Amery, L., Vol. II, 305/308.
17. Griffith, K., 130.

18. Amery, L., 305/308.
19. Pakenham, T., 172.
20. McKenzie, Col A, G., 155/156 also Stirling, J., 38/39 and Amery, L. Vol II, 305/308
21. Riall, N., 25
22. Mc Kenzie, Col A. G., 157.
23. Ibid, 159.
24. E. H. Carrick, papers in possession of his grand-daughter.
25. McKenzie, Col A.G., 157.
26. Ibid, 157–161.
27. Stirling,J., 10.
28. McKenzie, Col A.G., 161–162.
29. Dundonald, 99.
30. Ibid, 81.
31. Ibid, 97. See also Treves, 13.
32. Gough, 66/67.
33. Stirling, J., 41 and Amery, Vol II, 319.

Chapter 15

1. Churchill, W. S., 52–54.
2. Ibid, 60.
3. LHS, (Kate Driver), 11.
4. Ibid, 14/15.
5. Ibid, 16/17.
6. LHS, (Reverend Mother Marie), 22/23.
7. Ibid, 23.
8. Nevinson, H.W., 33.
9. Pearse, H.S.S., 38.
10. LHS, (Reverend Mother Marie), 23/24.
11. Ibid, 23.
12. Gibson, G.F., 52.
13. Macdonald, D., 253/254.
14. Nevinson, H.W., 42.
15. Pearse, H.S.S., 49/50.

Chapter 16

1. McKenzie, Col A. G., 162/163.
2. Dundonald, Lt Gen, 98.
3. McKenzie, Col A.G., 164.
4. Ibid, 164.
5. Ibid, 145.
6. Ibid, 166.
7. Wasserman and Kearney, 212-214.
8. McFadden, P., Khaki Cameos. No page numbers.
9. Stanford, Sir Walter, 208-210.
10. UKNA, CO, 179/209.

Chapter 17

1. Pearse, H.H.S., 28.
2. Ibid, 69.

3. Macdonald, D., 129.
4. Gibson, G.F., 117/118.
5. Pearse, H.H.S., 82.
6. LHS, (Kate Driver), 23.
7. Gibson, G. F., 81/82.
8. Ibid, 83.
9. Ibid, 85.
10. Ibid, 87.
11. Ibid, 87.
12. Ibid, 88/89.
13. Ibid, 104.
14. Ibid, 90.
15. Ibid, 91.
16. Pearse, H.H.S., 96.
17. Gibson, G.F., 92/93.
18. LHS, (Lt Col B.N. Martin.), 36
19. Macdonald, D., 165.
20. Ibid, 184.
21. LHS, (Maj. Gen. C.W. Park), 22/23.
22. Gibson, G.F., 111.
23. Macdonald, D., 167.
24. Gibson, G.F., 106.

Chapter 18

1. Sampson, V. and Hamilton, I., 122.
2. Nevinson, H. W., 68.
3. Ibid, 73.
4. Ibid, 73.
5. LHS, (Kate Driver), 18.
6. Samuelson, R. C., 163.
7. Ibid, 165.
8. Ibid, 141.
9. Ibid, 152.
10. Ibid, 154.
11. Bailey, Rev G.C., 72–73.
12. Ibid, 74. See also the Irish writer T. Pakenham, *The Boer War* 1979 ed., 210.
13. Ibid, 82.
14. Ibid, 84.
15. Ibid, 88.
16. Ibid, 96.
17. UKNA, CO 179/209.

Chapter 19

1. Dundonald, Maj. Gen., 112. also McKenzie, Col A. G., 167.
2. Gibson, G. F. 154/155.
3. Churchill, W.S. often quoted dispatch to the *Morning Post*.
4. Blake Knox, Lt Dr E., 6.
5. Dundonald, Maj. Gen., 116/117.
6. Ibid, 118/119.

7. Mc Kenzie, Col A.G. 166-167, and Natal Carbineers Record 17.1.1900.
8. Dundonald, Maj. Gen., 123/124.
9. McKenzie, Col A.G., 167.
10. Ibid, 167/169.
11. Greening Diary quoted by M. Coglan in *Defending the Home Front*.
12. Written statement by General Sir Charles Warren to supplement his evidence given to the Commission on the War in South Africa.
13. Dundonald, Maj. Gen., 128.
14. Much quoted evidence by Gen Buller to the Royal Commission on the War in South Africa.

Chapter 20

1. Churchill, W.S., 142/143.
2. Ibid, 143,
3. Ibid, 143/146.
4. Symons, J., 201, and UKNA, Spion Kop Dispatches.
5. Blake Knox, Lt Dr E., 30/31.
6. Churchill, W.S., 143/144.
7. UKNA, Spion Kop Dispatches.
8. Symons, J., 210/211.
9. Gibson, G.F., 151/152.
10. Symons, J., 213.
11. Ibid, 216.
12. UKNA, Spion Kop Dispatches.
13. Ibid.
14. Griffith, K., 267.
15. UKNA, Spion Kop Dispatches.
16. Ibid.
17. Blake Knox, Lt Dr. E., 52.
18. Stirling, J., 83–86.
19. Ibid, 85.
20. Ibid, 85/86.
21. Blake Knox, Lt Dr. E., 50.
22. Ibid, 50.
23. Griffith, K., 275.
24. Dundonald, Maj. Gen., 133.
25. Wasserman and Kearney eds., 214/218.
27 Treves, F., 77.
27. LHS, (Nurse K. Driver) 30.
28. Incident related to the writer by Major Keith Archibald NC.

Chapter 21

1. Macdonald, D., 220.
2. Pearse, H.H.S., 107.
3. LHS, (William Watson)16-19.
4. Ibid, 30
5. Macdonald, D., 235.
6. Ibid, 205.
7. Ibid, 232.

8. Ibid, 227.
9. LHS, (Bella Craw), 41.
10. Ibid, 47/48.
11. UKNA, CO179/212.
12. Ibid
13. Coulson, C., 105.
14. UKNA, CO179/212.

Chapter 22

1. Dundonald, Maj. Gen.140.
2. McKenzie, Col A.G., *Delayed Action*, 171.
3. Coetzer, Owen, 220.
4. Ibid.
5. Blake Knox, Lt Dr E, 152.
6. McKenzie, Col A.G. 171.
7. Dundonald, Maj. Gen. 141.
8. Ibid,141
9. Churchill, W.S., 174/175.
10. Dundonald, Maj. Gen., 144.
11. Ibid, 143.
12. Blake Knox, Lt Dr,148.
13. Ibid, 152.
14. McKenzie, Col A.G., 172.
15. Blake Knox, Lt Dr.,163.
16. Ibid, 174.
17. Stirling, J., 87–89.
18. Blake Knox, Lt Dr, 102.
19. Ibid,104.
20. Symons, J., 268.
21. Dundonald, Maj. Gen., 149.
22. Ibid, 147.
23. Ibid, 149.
24. McKenzie, Col A. G., 173.
25. Ibid, 174.
26. Ibid, 174.
27. Watkins-Pitchford, H., 120–122.
28. Mckenzie, Col A.G., 176–178.
29. Macdonald, D., 262.
30. Ibid, 264.
31. McKenzie, Col A.G., 174.
32. Macdonald, D., 266.
33. Gough, Lt Gen Sir Hubert, 79.
34. Dundonald, Maj. Gen., 151.
35. Churchill, W.S., 210.
36. Ibid, 209/210.
37. McKenzie, Col A.G., 189/190.
38. Gough, Lt Gen Sir Hubert, 78.
39. Blake Knox, Lt Dr, 237.
40. LHS, (Nurse Kate Driver), 35/36.
41. Bailey, the Rev G.C., 107.

Chapter 23

1. McKenzie, Col A.G., 185
2. Tucker, Private F., 82/83.
3. Samuelson, R.C., 147.
4. Gibson, F., 164.
5. Ibid, 164.
6. Ibid, 171/172.
7. Ibid, 173/174.
8. Ibid, 175-177.
9. Bailey, Rev G.C., 109.
10. UKNA, WO 108, Letter from Lt Col H.V. Hunt, RFA.
11. Ibid.
12. UKNA, WO 108, Court of Inquiry into the treatment of British prisoners, pages 3/4.
13. Ibid, 4.
14. Ibid, 5/6.
15. Ibid, 4/5.
16. Ibid, 2 and Appendix 1.
17. Ibid, Appendix VI.
18. Ibid, Appendix II,
19. Ibid, Appendix II.
20. Ibid, 9.
21. Ibid, 7.
22. Ibid, 11/12
23. Ibid, Appendix IV.
24. UKNA, CO 179/212.
25. UKNA, CO !79/211
26. UKNA, WO, Court of Inquiry, 12. Also H. J. Batts.

Chapter 24

1. Macdonald, D., 268.
2. See Chapter 8.
3. Dundonald, Maj. Gen., 157.
4. McKenzie, Col A. G., 194.
5. Blake Knox, Lt Dr E., 138
6. Stirling, J., 55
7. Bailey, The Rev. G.C.,111-112.
8. Dundonald, Maj. Gen., 160.
9. Stirling, J., 64/65.
10. Dundonald, Maj. Gen., 160.
11. Blake Knox, Lt Dr E., 267, and newspaper reports in Brenthurst Museum.

Postscript

1. Child, Daphne, 183.
2. Dennison, Maj C.G., 204.
3. Hamilton, I. Papers, King's College, London
4. Samuelson, R.C., 148.
5. Letter dated 23.8.01 from Alexander George of Tech. African Studies Library. Jhb.

6. Obituary published in the *London Times*. Copy in the Johannesburg *Star*, 30.11.26.
7. Sampson, V. and Hamilton, I., 120.
8. Ibid, 152
9. Gibson, G.F., 265.
10. Hattersley, A.F., 45
11. McKenzie, Col A.G., 200.
12. Ibid, 201.
13. Ibid, 206–220.
14. Ibid, 227–229.
15. Ibid, 330–333.
17. Ibid, 358/359.
18. Information about the drowning of Dr Buntine's from his grandson R. Lewis.
19. Gibson, G.F., 320–325.
20. Goetzche, E., *History of the NMR*, 59
21. Indian Opinion 9. 9. 05.
22. Dundonald Papers, Talana Museum.
23. Stanford Sir Walter, 242
24. Paterson, A.B., 119–127.
25. Devitt, N., 107.
26. Pakenham, T., *The Boer War*, (1979) Edition 126, Illustrated Edition (1993), 70.
27. Digby, P. K. A. 121–148.

Select Bibliography

Amery, L. S. (ed.), *The Times History of the War in South Africa 7 volumes*, (London: Sampson, Low & Co, 1907)

Atwood, Rodney, *Roberts and Kitchener in South Africa 1900–1902,* (Barnsley: Penn & Sword Military, 2011)

Bailey, Gerard C., *Seven Months Under Boer Rule*, (Dundee: R. A. Burns & Co., 1999)

Baker, A., *Battle Honours of the British and Commonwealth Armies*, (London: Ian Allen, 1986)

Barthorpe, Michael, *The Zulu War*, (Poole: Blandford Press Limited, 1980)

Batts, H.J., *Pretoria from Within during the War*, (London: F. Shaw & Co, 1901)

Bazley, D., *Nil Desperandum*, (Kloof: The Royale Trust, 2000)

Beckett, Dr Ian, *The Judgment of History, Sir Horace Smith Dorien, Lord French and 1914,* (London: Tom Donovan, 1993)

Binns, C.T., *The Last Zulu King*, (London: Longmans, 1963)

Brigland, Tony, *Field Gun Jack v The Boers*, (Barnsley: Leo Cooper, 1998)

Brink, Elsabe. *1899 The Long Walk Home*, (Cape Town: Kwela Books, 1999)

Carver, Field Marshall Lord, *The Boer War*, (London: Sidgwick & Jackson, 1999)

Cassidy, M. ed. *The Inniskilling Diaries 1899–1903*, (Barnsley: Leo Cooper, 2001)

Castle, I, *Zulu War – Volunteers, Irregulars & Auxiliaries*, (London: Osprey, 2003)

Chase, John Centlivres. *The Natal Papers*. (Facsimile reprint Cape Town: C. Struick, 1968)

Child, D. *Charles Smythe*, (Cape Town: C. Struick, 1973)

Child, D. *Portrait of a Pioneer,* (Johannesburg: Macmillan, 1980)

Childs, Lewis, *Ladysmith*, (Barnsley: Leo Cooper, 1998)

Chisholme, R., *Ladysmith,* (London: Osprey, 1979)

Churchill, Winston S., *London to Ladysmith*, (London: Longmans, 1900}

Coetzer, O., *The Anglo-Boer War, The Road to Infamy*, (Rivonia: Waterman, 1996)

Coglan Mark, *Pro Patria*, (Pietermaritzburg: Natal Carbineer Trust, 2000)

Coglan, Mark. *Defending the Home Front – The Natal Volunteers*. Privately printed.

Coulson, Charmian. *Richmond Natal, Its People and History*, (Pietermaritzburg, 1986)

Craw, Bella. *Diary 27.10.1899 to 23.3.1900*, (Ladysmith Historical Society 1970)

Creswicke, L., *South African and Transvaal War 1900–1902 7 vols.,*(London: Caxton Publishing Co, 1902)

Crisp, Robert, *The Outlanders*, (London: Peter Davies Ltd., 1964]

Crosby, A.J., *Extract from notes 1899–1900* (Ladysmith Historical Society, 1976)

Crowe, Brig. Gen., *J.H. Gen Smuts' Campaign in East Africa.* (Uckfield: Naval and Military Press, Reprint)

Cullinan, Patrick. *Robert Jacob Gordon,* (Cape Town: Struick 1992)

David, Saul, *Zulu Heroism & Tragedy in the Zulu War*, (London: Viking) 2004.

Davis, R.H., *With both Armies in South Africa,* (New York: Charles Scribners & Son, 1903)

Dennison, Maj C.J. *A Fight to the Finish*, (London: Longmans Green & Co. London 1904)

des Anges, Rev. Mother Marie, *Letters*, (Ladysmith Historical Society, 1970)

Devitt, Napier, *Galloping Jack, Reminiscences Brig. Gen. J.R. Royston,* (London: H. F. & G. Witherby, 1937)

Digby, P.K.A., *Pyramids and Poppies*, (Rivonia: Ashanti Publishing, 1993)

Dixon, Capt C.M., *The Leaguer of Ladysmith*, (London: Eyre & Spottiswoode, 1900)

Driver, Nurse Kate, *A Nurse Looks Back,* (Ladysmith Historical Society, 1994)

Doyle, A. Conan. *The Great Boer War*, (London: Smith Elder & Co., 1900)

Dundonald, Lt Gen. the Earl of. *My Army Life,* (London: Edw. Arnold & Co., 1926)

Featherstone, D., *Victorian Colonial Warfare, Africa*, (London: Blandford & Cassel, 1993)

Gardiner, The Reverend Capt, A.F., *Narrative of a Journey to the Zoolu Country in South Africa*, (London: William Crofts, 1836)

Gibson, G.F., *The Story of the Imperial Light Horse*, (London: G. D. & Co., 1937)

Goetsche, Eric, *Father of a City*, (Pietermaritzburg, Shuter & Shooter, 1966)

Goetsche, Eric, *History of the Natal Mounted Rifles*, (Durban, NMR Association 1971)

Gordon, Dr. Ruth, Ed. *Honour Without Riches.* (Durban: T. W. Griggs & Co., 1978)

Gough, Gen. Sir Hubert. *Soldiering On,* (London: Arthur Baker Ltd., 1954)

Greaves & Best, eds. *The Curling Letters of the Zulu War*, (Barnsley: Pen& Sword Books, 2001)

Griffith, K. *Thank God We Kept the Flag Flying*, (New York: Viking Press, 1974)

Hackett, R.G. *South African War Books*, (London: Privately Printed, 1994)

Hattersley, A.F., *More Annals of Natal*, (Pietermaritzburg: Shuter & Shooter, 1936)

Hattersley, A.F., *History of the Royal Natal Carbineers*, (Aldershot: Gale & Plodden Ltd., 1950)

Hurst, Col G.T. *History of the Natal Mounted Rifles,* (Durban: Privately printed 1935)

Jackson, Stanley, *The Great Barnato*, (London: Heineman, 1970)

Jackson, Tabitha. *The Boer War.* (London: Channel 4 Books, 1999)

Jameson Raid. A Centennial Retrospective, Brenthurst Press, 1966.

Julius, Anthony. *Trials of the Diaspora.* (Oxford University Press, 2010)

Klein, H., *Light Horse Cavalcade 1899–1961*, (Cape Town: H Timmins, 1969)

Knight, Ian, *Boer Commando 1876–1902*, (London: Osprey)

Knox, Dr. E. Blake, *Buller's Campaign with the Natal Field Force*, (London: Brimley Johnson, 1902)

Kruger, Rayne. *Goodbye Dolly Grey*, (London: Cassel, 1959)

Le Vaillant, Francois. *Travels into the Interior Parts of Africa. 3 vols* (London: A. G. Robinson, 1796)

Lines, G.W., *The Ladysmith Siege*, (Uckfield: Naval and Military Press, Reprint, 1900)

Lugg, H.C., *A Natal Family Looks Back,* (Durban: T. W. Griggs, 1970)

Macdonald, Donald, *How We Kept the Flag Flying* (Melbourne, Ward, Lock & Co, 1900)

Mackeurtan, Graham, *The Cradle Days of Natal (1497–1845)*, (London: Longman's Green & Co, 1930)

Martin, Col A.C., *The Concentration Camps 1900–1902, Facts Figures and Fables*, (Cape Town: Howard Timmins 1957)

Martin, Lt Col B. W. *Memoirs of the Siege of Ladysmith*, (Ladysmith Historical Society, 1970)

Marling, Col. Sir Percival, *Rifleman and Hussar*, (London: John Murray, 1931)

Maurice, Sir Frederick, Editor, *Official History of the War in South Africa 1899–1902, Vol. 1 and 2*, (London: Hurst & Blackett Ltd. 1906–1910)

May, H. J., *Music of the Guns*, (Johannesburg: Hutchinson, 1970)

Men of the Times. (London: Eyre & Spottiswood, 1905)

Mills, G. and Williams, D., *Seven Battles that shaped South Africa.* (Cape Town: Tafelberg Publishers, Cape Town, 2006)

Morris, Donald, *The Washing of Spears.* (London: Pimlico, 1965)

McFadden, Pam. *Khaki Cameos* (KZN Battlefield Promotions, 1999)

McFadden, Pam. *Elandslaagte.* (Randburg: Raven Press, 1999)

McKenzie, Col A.G., *Delayed Action*, (a biography of the life of Brig. Gen. Sir Duncan McKenzie K.C.M.G., C.B., D.S.O., V.D., Legion d'Honeur, Privately printed, 1964)

Nevinson, H.W., *Ladysmith, Diary of a Siege*, (London: Methuen & Co. 1900)

O'Mahony, C. J., *A Peep over the Barleycorn*, (1911. Republished by Naval and Military Press, Uckfield: 2010)

Pakenham, T., *The Boer War*, (London: Weidenfield & Nicholson Ltd., 1979)

Pakenham, T., *The Boer War, Abridged Illustrated Ed.*, (London: Weidenfield & Nicholson Ltd., 1993)

Park, Maj. Gen. C.W. *Correspondence.* (Ladysmith Historical Society, 1972)

Paterson, A.B. (Banjo), *Happy Dispatches.* (Sydney: Angus & Robertson, 1934)

Pearse, H.S.S., *Four Months Besieged*, (London: Macmillan, 1900)

Pollock J., *Kitchener: The Road to Omdurman* (London: Constable & Co Ltd., 1998)

Portsmouth, H., *The Story of Wyford.* (Osborne Literary Services. Westville, 2010)

Reitz, Deneys. *Commando.* (London: Faber & Faber, 1929)

Riall, N. Ed. *Letters and Photographs of Malcolm Riall*, (London: Brassey's, 2000)

Ritter, E.A., *Shaka Zulu.*, (London: Longmans, 1955)

Russell, George. *A History of Old Durban*, (Durban: P. Davis & Sons, 1899)

Sampson, V. and Hamilton, I., *Anti-Commando*, 1931.

Samuelson, R.C.A., *Long, Long Ago.* (Durban: Knox Printing and Publishing, 1929)

Sandys, Celia, *Churchill, Wanted Dead or Alive*, (London: Harper Collins, 1999)

Schiel, Col Adolf, *Twenty-three years of Storm and Sunshine in South Africa*, (Leipzig: 1902,Translation from the German in Talana Museum)

Smail, G.S. *Historical Monuments and Battlefields in Natal and Zululand* (Cape Town: Howard Timmins, 1965)

Spiers, E.M. Ed., *Letters from Ladysmith.* (Jeppestown, Jonathon Ball, 2010)

Stafford and Franklin, *Principles of Native Law*, (Pietermaritzburg: Shuter & Shooter, 1950)

Stanford, Sir Walter, *Reminiscences*, (Cape Town: Van Riebeeck Society, 1962)

Stalker, J., *The Natal Carbineers 1855–1911.* (Pietermaritzburg: P. Davies & Son,1912)

Steevens, G.W. *From Cape Town to Ladysmith*, (London: William Blackwood & Sons, 1900)

Stirling, J., *The Colonials in South Africa*, (London: Wm. Blackwood & Sons, London, 1902)

Stott, Clement H., *The Boer Invasion of Natal*, (London: S.W. Partridge & Co, 1900)

Stuart, J. and D. McK. Malcolm, Eds. *Diary of H. Fynn*, (Pietermaritzburg: Shuter and Shooter, 1950)

Strydom, Hans. *For Volk and Fuhrer*, (Jeppestown: Jonathon Ball, 1982)

Symons, Julian, *Buller's Campaign*, (London: The Cresset Press, 1963)

Tatham, George F., *Diary* (Ladysmith Historical Society, 1970)

The Stationery Office, The Siege Collection, (Norwich: 1999)

Treves, Dr Frederick, *The Tale of a Field Hospital*, (London: Cassell & Co. 1900)

Tucker, Private Frederick. *Diary* (London: Elmtree Books, 1980)

Union of South Africa. *Official History of the Great War 19141918* (Imperial War Museum and Naval and Military Press, Uckfield:)

War Services of Military Officers 1899–1902 (London: Savannah Publications, 1998)

Wasserman and Kearney (Eds.), *A Warrior's Gateway*, (Pretoria: Protea Book House, 2002)

Watkins-Pitchford, H. *Besieged in Ladysmith* (Shuter & Shooter: Pietermaritzburg, 1964)

Watson, William, *Diary* (Ladysmith Historical Society, 1989)

Wells, Walter H. ed., *Anglo African Who's Who*, (London: L. Upcott Gill, 1907)

Whitton, Lt George, *Scapegoats of the Empire*, (Bath: Adlib Books 1989, First published in Australia 1907, subsequently by Angus & Robertson in Britain in 1982)

Williams, W.A., *Commandant of the Transvaal*, (Wrexham: Bridge Books, 2001)

Willis, G.W. *Letter* (Ladysmith Historical Society, 1970)

Wilson, H.W., *With the Flag to Pretoria, Vols. 1 and 2* (London: Harmsworth, 1901)

In addition information was obtained from the following sources:-

The British Archives at Kew, London. Colonial Office Papers CO179/206 to 214. War Office Papers WO105 to 137. Evidence given to the Royal Commission on the War in South Africa. Report of and Evidence given to the House of Commons Aborigines Committee, 1836.

Brenthurst Museum Johannesburg, papers of A.A. Kelsey (secretary Reform Committee), and newspaper clippings and other data relevant to the war.

Ladysmith Siege Museum, Diaries and Photographs.

African Studies Library, Johannesburg. 8 boxes and 5 scrapbooks relevant to ILH.

Talana Museum. Dundonald Papers and various documents relating to local history.

Killie Campbell Museum, Durban re: Marwick Papers, diary of Dr Sam Campbell, and documents relating to the abuse by Boers of black refugees.

Natal Archives, Pietermaritzburg, Correspondence between the Natal Government, the Governor and the British Military, Sept. 1899 to May 1902.

The South African Museum of Military History, Johannesburg.

Reminiscences of Lt Col J. F. Rethman (unpublished).

King's College, London – papers Ian Hamilton.

Natal Carbineers Museum Pmb., Diaries of Carbineers during Boer War.

Old Fort Museum, Durban. Exhibits covering Durban's Military History.

Natal Society Library, Pmb., Newspaper reports and correspondence during the Boer War.

Natal Mounted Rifles Museum, Durban.

Diaries and photographs in private possession.

Glossary

Unless the context suggests otherwise, the words **Boer, Afrikaner,** and **Dutchman** are interchangeable, all meaning a white South African descended from Dutch or French Huguenot settlers. In the early years of the twentieth century an attempt was made to introduce the word 'Afrikander' to describe a white person born in South Africa, however, the idea failed to gain acceptance and today Afrikander refers to a breed of cattle.

Colonial is used in this work to describe those people domiciled outside the British Isles whose forebears came from there.

English has a slightly different meaning when compared with its usage in Britain. In South Africa, the word is generally used to describe a person whose home language is English, regardless of whether his forebears came from England, Ireland, Scotland or Wales; or even some other European country. Failure to take note of this linguistic quirk can result in embarrassing mistakes.

Hollander describes a person from the Netherlands, who emigrated to the Transvaal towards the end of the nineteenth century to provide the skills not readily available among the agrarian Boers.

Rooinek literally means 'red neck' is used to describe an English-speaking South African. The word does not have the class connotations 'redneck' has in the USA but it was not a term of endearment either.

Uitlander, literally an 'outlander' or foreigner, means a British immigrant living in the Transvaal who was denied citizenship by the Boers for cultural and economic reasons.

Burgher means a citizen but is only applied to Afrikaans people.
Afrikaans is a language of southern Africa, derived from the form of Dutch brought to the Cape by Protestant settlers in the 17ᵗʰ century. It is an official language of South Africa, spoken by around six million pople as their first language.

Some words with which the reader might not be familiar.

amakholwa	believers, Christians
berg	mountain
biltong	dried meat

boereperd	breed of horse, originally from Arab stock, bred for export and use by farmers
burg	town
donga	a ditch caused by erosion during flooding
Dopper	a member of the Dutch Reformed Church, a strictly orthodox Calvinistic denomination
dorp	village
drift	river crossing
inspan	to harness draught animals
impi	a body of Zulu warriors
indaba	a discussion or conference
kloof	ravine or gorge
knobkerrie, kerrie	A stick with a knob at the end, used for herding animals or fighting, like an Irish shillelagh
kommando	A group of men fighting for the Boers, recruited in a particular district
kop	hill
kopie	hillock
kraal	A village, a home, or a cattle enclosure, depending on context
krantz	cliff
Krygsraad	Council of War
laager	an encampment, often made by drawing ox wagons into a circle.
laagte	a plain
Landrost	the senior government official in a district, also a magistrate
lobolo	the dowry that forms part of a marriage settlement, usually paid in cattle
mealie(s)	maize
nek	the saddle or dip between two hills
outspan	to unharness
pont	a ferry over a river
poort	a pass between two hills
Rand	A ridge of high ground. The most famous is the Witwatersrand, literally White Waters Ridge. Johannesburg was founded on it but it extends for kilometres on either side of the city. As a reef of gold-bearing ore followed the entire line of the Witwatersrand, the whole area became known as the Rand. Later, the word was chosen as the name for the South African unit of currency.
sangar	stone breastwork erected from loose stones
schantz	a rampart, often combined with a trench
sjambok	a long stiff leather whip, originally made from hippopotamus hide
spruit	stream
stad	town
stoep	veranda
trek	go on a long arduous journey, typically on foot; migrate with one's belongings by ox wagon; (of oxen) to draw a vehicle or pull a load; to travel constantly from place to place, lead a nomadic life.

Uitlander Korps	Foreign volunteer regiments who fought for the Boers
veld(t)	African countryside
vlei	a shallow natural pool of water, swamp.
Volksraad	Afrikaner Parliament
Voortrekker	A member of one of the groups of Dutch-speaking people who migrated by wagon from the Cape Colony into the interior from 1836 onwards, in order to live beyond the borders of British rule. They settled north of the Orange River, establishing the Free State and Transvaal republics.
Vredergter	District administrator

About the Author

Hugh Rethman was born in Natal. His father's family were farmers and traders who were among Natal's early settlers. His great-grandfather was a member of the Natal Parliament and commanded the Border Mounted Rifles during initial engagements, at the siege of Ladysmith, and the subsequent pursuit of the Boers during their retreat from Natal. Another relative owned the farm, Talana, where the first battle of the campaign was fought. The Reverend Gerard Bailey, the vicar of Dundee whose diary describes what happened in the town during the Boer occupation, married the author's grandparents in Newcastle in 1897.

His maternal grandfather was an engineer from Aberdeen, who arrived in South Africa with the British forces. He never took part in any military action, being mainly concerned with the construction and repair of railway bridges. His wife was a Botha, part of an Afrikaans family. One of the author's great-uncles died in the concentration camp at Brandfort in the Free State. So Hugh Rethman grew up with the three influences – Colonial, British and Boer.

Hugh was educated at St Andrew's College in Grahamstown before reading English Literature, Economic History, and Political Philosophy at the University of Natal. After graduating, he moved to England where he read law at the University of Leeds and qualified as a barrister.

In 1970 he returned to South Africa, where he practised as an attorney in Richmond, Natal. His family has a long association with the Mandela family, going back into the nineteenth century. Nelson Mandela's father-in-law, Columbus Madikizela, leased business premises from the author's father. During school holidays, Hugh would see him on an almost daily basis. In 1993, Mandela visited Richmond and asked Hugh to move to Johannesburg to assist in the formulation of a policy to combat rural poverty. However, at the time, Hugh did not want to get involved in politics as he believed ANC cadres would not have welcomed an interloper into their ranks.

In researching this work, the author came across the minutes of the inaugural meeting of the Natal Native Congress held in 1900. The descendants of two of the prominent members of that body, Chief Patrick Majozi and Chief Goba, were friends and clients of his. The Natal Native Congress subsequently evolved into the African National Congress.

Hugh Rethman is a keen horseman and throughout his life has participated in many sports. He has written articles for the journals of the Victorian Military Society, The Military History Society of South Africa and the Military History Society of Australia. He lives in Suffolk, England.

Index

Index